INTERNATIONAL
FILM, RADIO,
AND
TELEVISION
JOURNALS

Recent Titles of
Historical Guides to the World's Periodicals and Newspapers

This series provides historically focused narrative and analytical profiles of periodicals and newspapers with accompanying bibliographical data.

Black Journals of the United States
Walter C. Daniel

Mystery, Detective, and Espionage Magazines
Michael L. Cook

American Indian and Alaska Native Newspapers and Periodicals, 1826–1924
Daniel F. Littlefield, Jr., and James W. Parins

British Literary Magazines: The Augustan Age and the Age of Johnson, 1698–1788
Alvin Sullivan, editor

British Literary Magazines: The Romantic Age, 1789–1836
Alvin Sullivan, editor

British Literary Magazines: The Victorian and Edwardian Age, 1837–1913
Alvin Sullivan, editor

Children's Periodicals of the United States
R. Gordon Kelly, editor

INTERNATIONAL FILM, RADIO, AND TELEVISION JOURNALS

Edited by
Anthony Slide

Historical Guides to the World's Periodicals and Newspapers

Greenwood Press
Westport, Connecticut • London, England

Library of Congress Cataloging in Publication Data

Main entry under title:

International film, radio, and television journals.

(Historical guides to the world's periodicals and
newspapers, ISSN 0742-5538)
   Includes index.
   1. Moving-pictures—Periodicals—Bibliography.
2. Broadcasting—Periodicals—Bibliography.   3. Moving-
pictures—Periodicals—History.   4. Broadcasting—
Periodicals—History.   I. Slide, Anthony.   II. Series.
Z5784.M9I485   1985   [PN1993]   016.79143′05   84-8929
ISBN: 0-313-23759-X (lib. bdg.)

Library of Congress Catalog Card Number: 84-8929
ISBN: 0-313-23759-X
ISSN: 0742-5538

First published in 1985

Greenwood Press
A division of Congressional Information Service, Inc.
88 Post Road West, Westport, Connecticut 06881

Printed in the United States of America

10 9 8 7 6 5 4 3 2 1

Contents

Preface

International Film, Radio, and Television Journals provides entries consisting of a critical/historical overview together with supplemental sections on "Information Sources" and "Publication History" for more than two hundred periodicals. There are further references to more than one hundred additional periodicals to be found in the appendixes, "Fan Club Journals," "Fan Magazines," "In-House Journals," and "National Film Journals."

In view of the number of film, radio, and television journals published during the last eighty years, it has obviously not been possible to include all periodicals. However, all major journals can be found here, along with a considerable assortment of minor ones. Researchers might argue that there is no such thing as a minor periodical—all journals are of some importance to someone. There is certainly some validity to such an observation, but in selecting periodicals to be included I have been careful to stress all those that have research value, no matter the area of their expertise and regardless of whether they are trade papers, fan magazines, academic journals, or popular reading matter. What have been explicitly excluded from this volume are theatre journals from the early years of this century, which gave token coverage to the motion picture industry in the early years of this century, but which remained basically theatre publications. Thus *Variety* is included because it changed from a vaudeville and theatrical journal to a primarily film publication, whereas *The Billboard*, *The New York Clipper*, and *The New York Dramatic Mirror* will not be found here because they remained basically theatre-oriented (or, in the case of *The Billboard*, switched from a theatrical journal to a music periodical). Researchers into early film history should, of course, not ignore such periodicals, just as film researchers should familiarize themselves with more recent theatrical journals, such as *Theatre Arts*, which provide considerable film coverage.

The general essay with which each entry opens provides a general evaluation of the periodical, offering insights into the journal's critical stance and historical background. To a large extent, the length of the essay indicates the importance of the journal in the eyes of the editor; thus considerable space is given to major periodicals such as *American Cinematographer*, *The Moving Picture World*, and *Variety*, while only minimal attention is paid to *AFAA Bulletin*, *The Magazine*, or *Dialogue on Film*.

With one or two exceptions, most American fan magazines are discussed only in Appendix 2, the general essay on the subject of fan magazines. However, there are entries on a considerable number of British fan magazines, largely because I feel such periodicals deserve to be better known in this country and because detailed information on them is totally nonexistent in both the United States and the United Kingdom.

The appearance of an asterisk* in an essay is an indication to the reader that the periodical so marked is the subject of an entry in its own right.

Where appropriate, the "Information Sources" sections begin with a bibliography. (There is an additional general bibliography included after the appendixes.) For film, radio, and television periodicals, "Index Sources" are generally limited to volumes published in fairly recent years. It will also become very apparent that the same periodicals tend to be indexed, over and over again, in different indexing works. There is considerable duplication in the indexing undertaken by *Film Literature Index* and the *FIAF International Index to Film Periodicals*, which began publication in 1973 and 1972 respectively. Similarly there is considerable duplication in the retrospective indexing undertaken in *The New Film Index* (E. P. Dutton, 1975) and *Retrospective Index to Film Periodicals 1930–1971* (R. R. Bowker, 1975). Some libraries have indexed various periodicals through the years—for example, the Margaret Herrick Library of the Academy of Motion Picture Arts and Sciences has a card index to *Photoplay* from 1914 to its demise—but generally most major journals of the teens, twenties, and thirties are not indexed. The earliest film indexing project was *The Film Index* (Museum of Modern Art Film Library and the H. W. Wilson Company, 1941), but unfortunately its publishers neglected to indicate which journals have been indexed. It is fairly obvious that *The Film Index* does include both *Photoplay* and *The Moving Picture World*, but it is also very obvious that the indexing is highly selective, limited not only to specific articles but also to specific years.

"Reprint Editions" refers to both hard-copy reprints and microfilm editions, and here the situation is a little better, with most major periodicals available at least on microfilm. However, even a casual reading of this volume indicates a suprising number of defunct journals which have not been microfilmed.

Up to ten libraries holding complete (or almost complete) runs of any journal may be found under "Location Sources." For more recent journals, the publishers were asked to provide these listings. Use was also made of the serial listings of the Margaret Herrick Library of the Academy of Motion Picture Arts and Sciences, the Museum of Modern Art, the University of Illinois, and the University of Southern California. Much of the information contained under this heading, however, was taken from the various volumes of the Library of Congress

Union List of Serials, and, as any researcher knows only too well, what the Library of Congress indicates as a library's holdings and what the library actually has (thanks to the ravages of time, thieves, and zealous librarians anxious to make room on the shelves) can vary considerably.

The "Publication History" section of each entry is straightforward, providing the journal's title (with any changes indicated by date), the volume and issue data, along with publisher, place of publication, and editor (with any changes indicated by volume and issue number or by date). In one or two isolated cases, lack of a complete run of a given periodical prevented the presentation of a complete publication history.

International Film, Radio, and Television Journals concludes with appendix breakdowns of periodicals by type and subject matter and by country of publication.

I am grateful to all of the contributors for what has proved at times both an exhausting as well as a mammoth project. I would particularly like to thank Nancy Allen, Alan Gevinson, Pat Hanson, Steve Hanson, Tom Johnson, Audree Malkin, Hari Rorlich, Dorothy Swerdlove, and the staffs of the Margaret Herrick Library of the Academy of Motion Picture Arts and Sciences and the Doheny Memorial Library of the University of Southern California.

Historical Introduction

Throughout this century, film, radio, and television journals have come and gone with unceasing regularity. Magazines exploiting every aspect of all three media have been around almost as long as those forms of popular communication have existed. Film periodicals date back to the early years of the twentieth century; television and radio journals to the 1920s. Some film and television periodicals have survived to become institutions known and respected throughout the world, while others have quickly (and quietly) faded from view. There is no accurate count as to the number of film, television, and radio journals published during the last eighty years; their number is certainly over one thousand, and the Library of the British Film Institute alone boasts more than eight hundred titles.

There are basically six categories into which film, radio, and television journals fall: fan magazines, in-house journals, national film periodicals, technical journals, trade papers, and popular/academic journals. The least interesting, to both the casual reader and the scholar, are the national film periodicals (dealt with here in a separate essay) published to promote the interests of a specific country's film industry.

Fan magazines (also dealt with here in a separate essay) date back to 1911, when *Photoplay** and *The Motion Picture Story Magazine* came into existence in the United States. Now widely denigrated and despised, fan magazines were once quality publications, offering intelligent articles and reviews. They had their own special writers—the best known of which is Adela Rogers St. Johns—and also offered a training ground for serious writers. (Katherine Anne Porter once wrote for the fan magazines and contributed an interview with Charles Ray to the October 1920 issue of *Motion Picture Magazine*.) The tradition of the early fan magazines is continued in little-known popular journals such as *American Classic Screen,** *Hollywood Studio Magazine*, and *Classic Film/Video Images.**

In 1927 *Close Up** demonstrated that there was a small, yet enthusiastic, audience for a magazine which took the cinema a little more seriously than the fan magazines had so far done. Other publications followed, notably *Film Art,** *Cinema Quarterly,** and *World Film News.** With the creation of the British Film Institute and the establishment of its journals, *Sight and Sound** and *The Monthly Film Bulletin,** the acceptance of the motion picture as both an art form and an educational tool became widely established.

Through the years hundreds of small film magazines have sprung up, but only a few—such as *Sequence,** *Film Quarterly,** *Films and Filming,** *Films in Review,** *Film Culture,** and *Film Comment**—have had a lasting impact, growing in stature and popularity. In recent years only one popular journal, *American Film,** has been able to compete with the likes of *Film Comment* and *Films in Review,* and that thanks to its sponsor, the American Film Institute, and to heavy government subsidy through the National Endowment for the Arts.

Aside from the "popular" film and television journals, there are the academic periodicals, many of which would appear to exist solely to publish the writings of college professors unable to find any other outlet for their work. *Quarterly Review of Film Studies,** *Literature/Film Quarterly,** *Wide Angle,** and *The Journal of Popular Film and Television** are some of the best-known academic journals. Less "stodgy," and often better written and providing examples of more intelligent research, are student-sponsored journals, the best known of which is *The Velvet Light Trap.**

America dominates the field of popular film and television journals—a field which was once a strictly European domain—but, in recent years, there have been one or two major non-American contributions. The Canadian *Take One** is sadly missed for its bright, sometimes intelligent, often infuriating articles. The French *Cahiers du Cinéma** is no longer the controversial journal it once was. From Australia *Cinema Papers** has proven to be an international journal, blending both trade news and popular articles.

The field of technical journals is dominated by *SMPTE Journal,** which has been around in various forms since the teens, and by its English opposite number, *British Kinematography.* Cinematography was well covered by *The International Photographer** and continues so to be by *American Cinematographer,** which carries on the tradition of the first cinematography-oriented periodical, *Static Flashes* (first published in 1915 by the Static Club of America). In the days when motion picture projection was something of an art form there were *International Projectionist** and *The Motion Picture Projectionist.**

Of all types of journals, it is the trade papers which prove the most valuable to the researcher, and, of course, they are the ones which are the least indexed and the most inaccessible in hard copy. Through the decades, trade papers have taken on mythological proportions to the layman and to the members of the industry. Max Miller explained it in *For the Sake of Shadows* (E. P. Dutton, 1936):

> We have no need here of reading the cosmopolitan papers. We have
> our own dailies, four or five or six or maybe seven of them, and each

morning they are placed in a row for sale on the cement bulkhead opposite the commissary entrance.

These trade papers supply us with all we need to know for existence in our world. They supply us with what pictures are going to be made, with what pictures are being finished, with who has been seen with whom lately, and with who has been hired for what, and if such made money in the box-office where, and what was said to whom in conference yesterday, and how who walked out of his contract when.

Outside somewhere is another world, but it is very tiny, and its news is of no concern to us. But if we are foolish enough to be interested, the gateman will let us step outside on the street long enough to snatch a regular newspaper off the sidewalk beside a telephone-pole there. It is reasonable that these cosmopolitan newspapers should not be sold inside the lot. They may confuse us, they may interfere with the importance of our work, they may incite in us the possibility that the world outside is larger than our own.

There is a popular misconception that *Variety** was the first show business trade paper, but this is not so. Sime Silverman did not found *Variety* until December 16, 1905, long after such important trade papers as *The New York Morning Telegraph*, *The New York Dramatic Mirror*, *The New York Clipper*, and *The Billboard* had been well established. These early show business papers paid scant attention to films, other than taking advertisements from various producers and equipment manufacturers. *Variety* first began to review films (in its vaudeville section) in January 1907, but it was Frank E. Woods, in *The New York Dramatic Mirror*, who introduced serious film reviewing to trade papers.

The earliest trade paper exclusively devoted to motion pictures was the weekly *Views and Film Index* (later to become *The Film Index**), which commenced publication in April 1906, announcing, "We intend to make a specialty of the trade and not to mix it up with a thousand theatrical details which have nothing to do with our business." As early as June 16, 1906, *Views and Film Index* began reviewing films, and as early as December 1, 1906, it published an editorial on the need for film preservation.

Without question, the most important of the early trade papers was *The Moving Picture World*,* which was followed by *Motography*,* *Motion Picture News*,* *Exhibitor's Trade Review*,* and *Exhibitor's Herald*. In Great Britain, two trade papers vied for attention: *Kinematograph Weekly** and *The Bioscope.** *The Film Daily** was the first daily trade paper, but it was published out of New York. The first Los Angeles-based daily trade paper was Billy Wilkerson's *The Hollywood Reporter*,* founded in 1930. So successful was *The Hollywood Reporter* that Wilkerson even tried a British edition (*The London Reporter*, edited by veteran British trade journalist Frank Tilley, but which lasted only from March to July 1936). *The Hollywood Reporter*'s success did, however, lead to the creation of a daily edition of *Variety*, which continues through the present to be the most influential of all Los Angeles film trade papers.

The 1930s might well be considered the "golden age" of the trade paper with the weekly *Motion Picture Herald** dominating a pack which also included *Box Office*, *Greater Amusements*, and *Motion Picture Daily*.

*Broadcasting** was the leading trade paper for the radio industry, a position which it continues to hold for the television industry, although challenged by such recent glossy publications as *Channels** and *Emmy,** just as it was challenged in the thirties by *Radio Daily*. Perhaps the best of all radio trade papers is not a daily, a weekly, or a monthly, but the annual *Variety Radio Directory,** which is far more than its title suggests and is, in fact, a gold mine of information from radio's golden era.

Allied directly to the trade papers are the in-house journals (discussed separately), which once provided both the exhibitors and the trade papers with information and now provide that information directly to the researcher. If the educational medium can be compared to the commercial film industry, then its trade papers include *Film News,** *Sightlines,** *Business Screen*, and *AV Guide*.

Radio and television are well covered, yet despite the obvious dominance of the latter over the present entertainment industry, it is the film periodicals which dominate this book and continue to dominate the publishing field. What is instantly apparent from this volume is the amazing diversity of film periodicals, decade after decade. There would seem to be no area of cinema that has not been covered, from adult films (*Continental Film Review*) to music (*Film Music Notebook**), from amateur filmmaking (*Super-8 Filmmaker**) to screenwriting (*The Photo Playwright**). Film periodicals are as diversified as the cinema itself. And perhaps they dominate because television has yet to become as innovative and as daring as the cinema has been for decades. With new areas of television (particularly with the cable and video revolution) will come new areas for television periodicals. However, as new film periodicals continue to appear with astonishing regularity while new television publications are few and far between (has the general public even heard of any television periodical other than *TV Guide**?) that time is obviously quite a distance away.

PROFILES OF INTERNATIONAL FILM, RADIO, AND TELEVISION JOURNALS

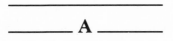

A

ABC FILM REVIEW. See Appendix 2

ACADEMY LEADER

Since its inception in 1927, the Academy of Motion Picture Arts and Sciences has produced a variety of newsletter-type publications for the enlightenment of its members. The first issue of *Academy Bulletin* appeared on June 1, 1927. Four issues of an educational newsletter were published between August 1979 and July 1980. In May 1939, the Academy published the prototype of a magazine, obviously based on *Life*, edited by its executive secretary Donald Gledhill, and titled *Montage*. It featured articles such as "Freedom of the Screen," "Is Television the Next Hurdle?" and "What Was the First Talking Picture?" However, as far as can be ascertained, only a few issues of *Montage* were ever printed and it never received a wide distribution.

In 1972, the Academy again tried to publish a film magazine; titled *Academy Leader*, it appeared for a mere three issues. Pleasantly designed and printed, *Academy Leader* featured a number of useful articles, including "Preserving the Past" by DeWitt Bodeen (April 1972), "The Dark Is Light Enough" by Kevin Brownlow (July 1972), and "Off with Their Heads" by Gavin Lambert (November 1972). Of particular value is an extract from an unpublished autobiography by Charles Chaplin's publicist, Harry Crocker, published in the April 1972 issue.

Information Sources

INDEX SOURCES: None.
REPRINT EDITIONS: None.
LOCATION SOURCES: Academy of Motion Picture Arts and Sciences.

Publication History

MAGAZINE TITLE AND TITLE CHANGES: *Academy Leader*.
VOLUME AND ISSUE DATA: No. 1 (April 1972); No. 2 (July 1972); No. 3 (November 1972).
PUBLISHER AND PLACE OF PUBLICATION: Academy of Motion Picture Arts and Sciences, 9038 Melrose Avenue, Hollywood, Calif. 90069.
EDITOR: Richard Whitehall.

Anthony Slide

ACTION

Action came into being in the fall of 1966 as a publication of the Directors Guild of America (DGA) "to represent all the membership, to address itself to all of the membership, to keep each member informed of what his fellow members are doing."[1] David Zeitlin, a *Life* magazine writer, was appointed the first editor, and until he resigned to become a producer with Universal in the spring of 1968, he turned out a bland, somewhat disappointing periodical which offered an uneasy mix between a newsletter for DGA members and a popular magazine.

With Bob Thomas's appointment as editorial consultant with the May/June 1968 issue (Thomas, a writer and critic on film matters for Associated Press, was not given the title of editor until the May/June 1972 issue) *Action* became a popular, entertaining periodical devoted to the art and craft of direction. It featured interviews with major directorial figures such as Don Siegel (Vol. 6, No. 4), Jean Renoir on *La Grande Illusion* (Vol. 7, No. 3), Lewis Milestone on *All Quiet on the Western Front* (Vol. 7, No. 4), and H. C. Potter (Vol. 8, No. 1). Mel Brooks wrote "Confessions of an Auteur" (Vol. 6, No. 6); William Friedkin wrote on the making of the chase sequence in *The French Connection* (Vol. 7, No. 2); Alan Pakula wrote "Directing *All the President's Men*" (Vol. 11, No. 2); and Fred Zinnemann penned a remembrance of Robert Flaherty (Vol. 11, No. 3). Perhaps the most extraordinary piece ever published in *Action* was Josef von Sternberg's review of Joel Finler's book *Stroheim* (Vol. 3, No. 4).

The last issue of *Action* under Bob Thomas's editorship was published in May/June 1976. There was then almost a two-year gap before *Action* reappeared under the editorship of Dick Adler. The format was totally changed, with the then DGA president Robert Aldrich offering the explanation that "we thought that the Directors Guild and the rest of the entertainment industry could use a magazine which confronted some of the more serious problems facing our business."[2]

The number of pages per issue was doubled, but *Action* now showed a markedly dull and limited interest outlook, with articles devoted to such topics as the roles of directors, assistant directors, and production managers (Vol. 11, No. 4); the new DGA contract (Vol. 11, No. 5); and "The Director: Symbol or Figurehead" (Vol. 11, No. 6). Not surprisingly, the new *Action* was short-lived, with the last issue featuring the first part of an announced two-part "tough look" at teaching film and television skills. Another publishing activity of the Directors Guild has been the production of a newsletter titled *Directors Guild of America News*.

Notes

1. "A Message from the President," Vol. 1, No. 1, September-October 1966, pp. 2–3.
2. Vol. XI, No. 4, January-February 1978, p. 5.

Information Sources

INDEX SOURCES: Film Literature Index; FIAF International Index to Film Periodicals; The New Film Index.
REPRINT EDITIONS: University Microfilms.
LOCATION SOURCES: Academy of Motion Picture Arts and Sciences; Harvard University; Iowa State University; Library of Congress.

Publication History

MAGAZINE TITLE AND TITLE CHANGES: *Action*.
VOLUME AND ISSUE DATA: Vol. I, No. 1–Vol. XI, No. 3 (September-October 1966–May-June 1976); Vol. XI, No. 4–Vol. XI, No. 9 (January-February 1978–November-December 1978), bimonthly.
PUBLISHER AND PLACE OF PUBLICATION: Directors Guild of America, Inc., 7950 Sunset Boulevard, Hollywood, Calif. 90046.
EDITOR: David I. Zeitlin (Vol. I, No. 1–Vol. III, No. 2); no editor listed (Vol. III, No. 3–Vol. VII, No. 2); Bob Thomas (Vol. VII, No. 3–Vol. XI, No. 3); Dick Adler (Vol. XI, No. 4–Vol. XI, No. 9).

Anthony Slide

ACTION (20th Century-Fox). See Appendix 3

ADULT FILM ASSOCIATION OF AMERICA BULLETIN. See AFAA Bulletin

AFAA BULLETIN

Published by and for members of the Adult Film Association of America, *AFAA Bulletin* is the only source for documentation on the adult film industry in the United States. Founded in 1971, it features news items, reprints of newspaper articles, plus (since 1977) reports, with information on nominees and winners, on the Annual Erotic Film Awards. The number of issues in any given year varies, but *AFAA Bulletin* currently appears ten times per yearly volume.

Information Sources

INDEX SOURCES: None.
REPRINT EDITIONS: None.
LOCATION SOURCES: Academy of Motion Picture Arts and Sciences (lacks some early
    issues).

Publication History

MAGAZINE TITLE AND TITLE CHANGES: *AFAA Bulletin.*
VOLUME AND ISSUE DATA: Vol. I, No. 1 (February 1971 to present), irregular.
PUBLISHER AND PLACE OF PUBLICATION: Adult Film Association of America,
    1654 Cordova Street, Los Angeles, Calif. 90007 (Vol. I, No. 1–Vol. XIII, No.
    6); Adult Film Association of America, 5445 Sunset Boulevard, Hollywood, Calif.
    90027 (Vol. XIII, No. 7, to present).
EDITOR: David F. Friedman.

Anthony Slide

AFTERIMAGE

Afterimage—for the first issue (April 1970) the editors used a small *a* and a
capital for all subsequent issues—was a British periodical which mixed serious
analytical film criticism with semiological study. The magazine was curiously
eclectic in the choice of subjects, although the approach was usually heavy-
handed and, at times, unreadable. The first issue was devoted to film and politics
and included interviews with Brazilian director Glauber Rocha and British filmmaker Tony Garnett. No. 2 was concerned with avant-garde cinema; No. 3 with
Third-World cinema. "For a New Cinema" was the theme of No. 5. No. 6 was
devoted to "Perspectives on English Independent Cinema," and No. 7 continued
the same thematic approach but applied it to non-English films and filmmakers.
The final issue of *Afterimage*, No. 8/9, tried to provide a new approach to early
film history but seemed more interested in confusing the subject than in documenting the pioneering era of filmmaking.

This British periodical should not be confused with *afterimage* [sic], a newspaper-style newsletter, published ten times a year by the Visual Studies Workshop
of Rochester, New York, since January 1973, selectively indexed in *Film Literature Index* and available from University Microfilms.

Information Sources

INDEX SOURCES: The New Film Index.
REPRINT EDITIONS: None.
LOCATION SOURCES: Academy of Motion Picture Arts and Sciences; Rice University;
    Southern Illinois University; University of California at Los Angeles; University
    of Pennsylvania; University of Southern California.

Publication History

MAGAZINE TITLE AND TITLE CHANGES: *Afterimage*.
VOLUME AND ISSUE DATA: No. 1 (April 1970); No. 2 (Autumn 1970); No. 3 (Summer 1971); No. 4 (Autumn 1972); No. 5 (Spring 1974); No. 6 (Summer 1976); No. 7 (Summer 1978); No. 8/9 (Spring 1981).
PUBLISHER AND PLACE OF PUBLICATION: Narcis Publishing Limited, 18 Carlisle Street, London W.1, England (No. 1); Narcis Publishing Limited, 12-13 Little Newport Street, London WC2H 7JJ, England (Nos. 2–3); Afterimage Publishing Ltd., 12–13 Little Newport Street, London WC2H 7JJ, England (Nos. 4–7); Afterimage Publishing Ltd., 1 Birnam Road, London N.4, England (No. 8/9).
EDITOR: Simon Field and Peter Sainsbury (Nos. 1–4); Noël Burch (Guest Editor No. 5); Simon Field (No. 6); Simon Field and Guy L'Eclair (Nos. 7–8/9).

Anthony Slide

AMERICAN CINEMATOGRAPHER

As the journal of the American Society of Cinematographers (ASC), *American Cinematographer*, has been the authoritative journal on professional and amateur photographic film concerns for over six decades. It regularly reports on the work of its members, the invention and uses of new technologies and techniques in the field of cinematography, and developments in related areas of film and video. Usually written in nontechnical language capable of being understood by those with only a basic knowledge of the technical aspects of film, the articles in the journal have been a source of countless insights for the professional and amateur wishing to keep abreast of developments in the field, for students of cinematography, and for the production-oriented film scholar. The journal concentrates on *how* things get to the screen, usually leaving *why* for others to worry about. The director, producer, and writer generally step to the back in its pages, as the technical personnel, especially the cinematographers, gain the limelight.

The ASC was incorporated on January 8, 1919, in Los Angeles, from a precursor organization formed secretly during the patents fight to gain needed recognition for the cinematographer and to secure better equipment, particularly lighting equipment, from the manufacturers. With its motto, "Loyalty! Progress! Art!" the ASC, an invitation-only membership organization, dedicated itself "to advance the art and science of cinematography and to encourage, foster, and strive for preeminence, excellence, artistic perfection, and scientific knowledge in all matters pertaining to cinematography."[1]

The ASC began its journal in November 1920 at a time when the director was the superstar and the cameraman an unsung hero. Like the Society, the journal attempted to promote the interest of its members (early on the issue of screen credit for the cinematographer was successfully dealt with), serve as a forum for the exchange of ideas and experiences with new techniques and equipment, conduct debates concerning new technologies, educate the layman and student about film production, promote the motion picture as an art form, and honor achievements of ASC members.

In over sixty years, *American Cinematographer* changed very little while covering the important changes within the industry. Abundant coverage was given for the new technologies of the "talkies" ("How First Vitaphone Film Was Photographed," Vol. 7, No. 6; "The Talking Picture" by Lee De Forest, Vol. 8, No. 11; "Talkie Technie" by William de Mille, Vol. 9, No. 12; "Stage Technique in the Talkies" by Carl Dreher, director of RKO's sound department, Vol. 10, No. 9); Technicolor ("The Advent of Color Photography" by J. A. Ball, director of photography for Technicolor, Vol. 4, No. 5; "Make-Up for the New Technicolor Process" by Max Factor, Vol. 17, No. 8; "Reaction on Making His First Color Picture" by James Wong Howe, Vol. 18, No. 10; "Controlling Color for Dramatic Effect" by Rouben Mamoulian, Vol. 22, No. 6); 3-D ("Russia's Third-Dimensional Movies" by inventor S. Ivanov, Vol. 22, No. 5; "Third-Dimensional Films in the Soviet Union" by director Michael Kalatozov, Vol. 24, No. 10; "Hollywood Launches 3-D Film Production" by Joseph Biroc, director of photography for 3-D *Bwana Devil*, Vol. 33, No. 8; and special issues Vol. 34, No. 3, and Vol. 55, No. 4); widescreen ("Wide Film Cinematography" by Arthur Edeson, Vol. 11, No. 5; "Filming the Big Dimension" by Leon Shamroy, director of photography on the CinemaScope production *The Robe*, Vol. 34, No. 5; "The Big Changeover," on the exclusive change to CinemaScope at Fox Studios, Vol. 34, No. 10); Cinerama ("And Now...Cinerama" by John W. Boyle, Vol. 33, No. 11; "The Cinerama Technique" by Joseph Brun, Vol. 35, No. 6); television ("Television in Color," Vol. 12, No. 2; "Television and the Motion Picture Industry," Vol. 29, No. 6; "Technique for Television Commercials," Vol. 33, No. 12; "Editing Techniques for Television Films," Vol. 37, No. 7; and production articles on techniques used to film "I Love Lucy," Vol. 33, No. 1, "You Bet Your Life," Vol. 33, No. 3, "The Honeymooners," Vol. 36, No. 10, and Vol. 37, No. 3, "Naked City," Vol. 40, No. 8, "The Wild Kingdom Series," Vol. 46, No. 1, "I Spy," Vol. 47, No. 3, "Cosmos," Vol. 61, No. 10, and "Smiley's People," Vol. 64, No. 11); Super-8 (special issues Vol. 50, No. 12, and Vol. 56, No. 11); and Super 16 (special issue Vol. 51, No. 6). The journal also featured accounts of technologies that were less successful: Cinemiracle (Vol. 38, No. 2), Smell-o-vision (Vol. 41, No. 2), and Sensurround (whole issue Vol. 55, No. 11, is devoted to *Earthquake*).

Articles about the production of specific films began in the early 1920s ("Film Psychology and *The Ten Commandments*" by director of photography Bert Glennon, Vol. 5, No. 5; "Preparing to Film *The Iron Horse*" by director of photography George Schneiderman, Vol. 5, No. 12; "Filming *Ben-Hur* Chariot Race Scenes" by George Mecher, Vol. 6, No. 10), but it wasn't until the late forties that production articles became a regular feature of every issue. Some of the important production articles were: "Realism for *Citizen Kane*" by Gregg Toland (Vol. 22, No. 2); "Bert Glennon Introducing New Method of Interior

Photography,'' on the filming of *Stagecoach* (Vol. 20, No. 2); ''Not an Interior in the Picture!'' on Burnett Guffey's shooting of *They Came to Cordura* (Vol. 40, No. 3); ''M-G-M Pioneers with Subjective Feature,'' on *Lady in the Lake* (Vol. 27, No. 11); ''A Year With *The Yearling*'' by Charles Rosher (Vol. 28, No. 5); ''Dramatic Pictorialism With Infrared Film'' by Archie Stout on his filming of *Fort Apache* (Vol. 29, No. 8); ''Sub-Zero Camera Operation'' by Winton Hoch on filming *The Searchers* (Vol. 37, No. 7); ''Filming *Twelve Angry Men* on a Single Set'' by director of photography Boris Kaufman (Vol. 37, No. 12); ''Filming *Anatomy of a Murder* in the Story's Actual Locale'' by director of photography Sam Leavitt (Vol. 40, No. 7); ''Filming the Chariot Race for *Ben-Hur*'' by director Andrew Morton (Vol. 41, No. 2); ''Why Renoir Favors Multiple Camera, Long Sustained Take Technique,'' on filming of *Le Dejeuner Sur L'Herbe* (Vol. 41, No. 3); ''A Method of Pre-Exposing Color Negative for Subtle Effect'' by Freddie Young, director of photography for *The Deadly Affair* (Vol. 47, No. 8); ''Creative Post-Flashing Technique for *The Long Goodbye*'' (Vol. 54, No. 3); ''Behind the Cameras on *Heaven's Gate*'' by Vilmos Zsigmond (Vol. 60, No. 11); and ''Making Film With Video for *One From the Heart*'' (Vol. 63, No. 1). The 1970s saw whole issues of the journal devoted to the production details of one film of interest to cinematographers, if sometimes not to others, such as *Tora, Tora, Tora* (Vol. 52, No. 2), *Jonathan Livingston Seagull* (Vol. 54, No. 12), and *The Muppet Movie* (Vol. 60, No. 7).

Special effects production articles included ''The 'Mad, Mad' World of Special Effects'' by Linwood G. Dunn (Vol. 46, No. 3); ''Creating the 'Psychedelic' Visual Effects for *The Trip*'' by Bob Beck, electronic and optical engineer (Vol. 49, No. 3); ''Creating Special Effects for *2001: A Space Odyssey*'' by Douglas Trumbull, and other articles on the film in a special issue (Vol. 49, No. 6); and an interview with Ray Harryhausen about *Clash of the Titans* (Vol. 62, No. 6). Whole issues in the seventies and eighties covered such effects-oriented films as *Close Encounters of the Third Kind* (Vol. 59, No. 1), *Superman* (Vol. 60, No. 1), *Star Trek* (Vol. 61, No. 2), *The Empire Strikes Back* (Vol. 61, No. 6), and *For Your Eyes Only* (Vol. 62, No. 8).

Articles on the making of documentaries were occasionally featured, especially during the Second World War: ''Documentary Films in Wartime'' by John Grierson (Vol. 23, No. 3), ''Making Documentary Films to Meet Today's Needs'' by Joris Ivens (Vol. 23, No. 7), and three articles by Russian newsreel cameraman Roman Karmen (Vol. 24, Nos. 6 and 7; Vol. 25, No. 3). The filming of the Vietnam War by Hollywood (''The Vietnam War as Filmed for *The Green Berets*'') and the Air Force (''The Vietnam War as Filmed by U.S. Air Force Cameramen'') was compared in one issue (Vol. 49, No. 9). Whole issues devoted to the filming of the Olympics were a regular occurrence beginning in 1968. Concert documentaries were reported in ''The 'Take One' Challenge of Filming *Woodstock*'' by Michael Wadleigh (Vol. 51, No. 10) and *''The Concert for Bangladesh''* (Vol. 53, No. 5). A special issue was devoted to the coverage of the walk on the moon (Vol. 50, No. 10).

Throughout the years, *American Cinematographer* detailed each change in lenses, labs, filters, film stocks, cameras, meters, lighting equipment, dollies, recording equipment, and devices to make the camera mobile. Articles dealt with the diverse conditions and strategies for filming conventions, bullfights, snake dances, night auto races, eclipses, whales, wars, disasters, subways, experimental cars, T.V. news, the behavior of hookworms, the Tournament of Roses parade, pro football, Shirley Temple, and the family dog.

Essays on technical matters were contributed by the great cinematographers such as Karl Freund (Vol. 15, No. 5; Vol. 23, No. 4; Vol. 24, No. 8; Vol. 34, No. 6), Karl Struss (Vol. 15, No. 7), Gregg Toland (Vol. 22, No. 12), James Wong Howe (Vol. 23, No. 6; Vol. 25, No. 1), Rudolph Maté (Vol. 24, No. 6), Stanley Cortez (Vol. 36, No. 1), and Sven Nykvist (Vol. 43, No. 10). From 1941 through 1947, a regular feature was "Aces of the Camera," highlighting the careers of over sixty cinematographers. In 1983 Karl Brown offered an homage to his mentor, "Billy Bitzer: A Reminiscence" (Vol. 64, No. 11), sixty-one years after he first contributed a textbook series of essays on the characteristics and uses of lenses, "Modern Lenses" (Vol. 3, Nos. 2–6).

In addition to covering cinematographers, the journal published articles by or about art directors ("Wilfred Buckland Expounds Theories," Vol. 3, No. 5; "The Set as an Actor" by Cedric Gibbons, Vol. 12, No. 10; "Imagination in Set Design" by Gordon Wiles, Fox art director, Vol. 13, No. 3; "Why Overlook the Set-Miniature" by Vincent Korda, Vol. 22, No. 12; "More Realism from 'Rationed' Sets" by Perry Ferguson of RKO, Vol. 23, No. 9; and "Production Designing," about the work of William Cameron Menzies, Vol. 26, No. 3); writers ("Scenarist and Cinematographer" by June Mathis, Vol. 3, No. 6; and "Putting the Picture on Paper" by Charles Brackett, Vol. 32, No. 12); sound crew ("Recording the Sound for *Battle of Britain*," Vol. 50, No. 9; and "Taking Sound for Low-Budget Features," Vol. 64, No. 4); lab technicians (numerous articles on new developments from the Eastman Research Laboratories); special effects crew ("Special Photographic Effects in Motion Pictures" by Ray Kellogg and L. B. Abbott, Vol. 38, No. 10); animators ("Mickey Mouse and 16mm" by Walt Disney, Vol. 12, No. 11; "Animated Cartoon Production Today" by Carl Fallberg, Vol. 23, Nos. 4–8; and "Animation Mechanisms" by John Whitney, Vol. 52, No. 1); inventors ("100,000 Pictures Per Minute" by C. Francis Jenkins, Vol. 3, No. 2; and "The History and Origin of 16mm" by Alexander F. Victor, Vol. 26, No. 11); and critics and theorists (Harry Alan Potamkin's "Tendencies in the Cinema," Vol. 11, No. 2, and "The Woman as Film Director," Vol. 12, No. 9; and Slavko Vorkapich's "Motion and the Art of Cinematography," Vol. 7, Nos. 8 and 9, "A Fresh Look at the Dynamics of Film-Making," Vol. 53, No. 2, and "Toward True Cinema," Vol. 54, No. 7).

Directors who have contributed articles to the pages of *American Cinematographer* have included Ernst Lubitsch ("American Cinematographers are Superior Artists," Vol. 4, No. 9, and "Concerning Cinematography," Vol. 10, No. 8); Lewis Milestone ("An Interview with Lewis Milestone," Vol. 11, No. 9); Frank

Capra ("An Interview with Frank Capra," Vol. 11, No. 10); Rouben Mamoulian ("Common Sense and Camera Angles," Vol. 12, No. 10); Cecil B. DeMille ("A Director Looks at Process Shots," Vol. 17, No. 11); René Clair ("Cut with Script and Camera Says Director René Clair," Vol. 22, No. 2); John Huston ("Picture Partners," Vol. 22, No. 12); Gillo Pontecorvo (*"The Battle of Algiers*: An Adventure in Filming," Vol. 48, No. 4); and Alfred Hitchcock ("Production Methods Compared," Vol. 30, No. 5, and "Hitchcock Talks About Lights, Camera, Action," Vol. 48, No. 5). Perhaps more than any other director's work, *American Cinematographer* reported on Hitchcock's films for their use of actual locales ("Using an Actual Town instead of Movie Sets" by director of photography Joseph A. Valentine on the filming of *Shadow of a Doubt*, Vol. 23, No. 10; "The Photography Is Important to Hitchcock," on *I Confess*, Vol. 33, No. 12; "'Hitch' Didn't Want It Arty," on *The Wrong Man*, Vol. 38, No. 2) or innovative techniques (*"Rope* Sets a Precedent," Vol. 29, No. 7; "The Problems of Lighting and Photographing *Under Capricorn*" by Jack Cardiff, director of photography, Vol. 30, No. 10; *"Rear Window,"* Vol. 35, No. 2; and "Filming *Torn Curtain* by Reflected Light," Vol. 47, No. 10).

American Cinematographer has been the foremost production-oriented publication from its beginning in 1920 until the present day. It has consistently proven that the contributions of the cinematographer to creative filmmaking are of the utmost importance. The journal has constantly attempted to realize the goal that theorist Slavko Vorkapich spoke of to ASC members in December 1926:

> Figuratively speaking, the camera should be able to look within a man's soul. When we achieve the mastery of our tools and find a way to express our joys and sorrows, our dreams and visions in an eloquent, cinematic manner, then only the cinema will have the right to claim its place among other arts. The attainment of this goal depends mainly on you, my friends, because cinematography is primarily *the art of the cinematographer*.[2]

Notes

1. From the constitution of the American Society of Cinematographers, as quoted in "Six Decades of 'Loyalty, Progress, Artistry,' " *American Cinematographer*, Vol. 60, No. 6, June 1979, p. 596.

2. Slavko Vorkapich, *"Motion* and the *Art* of *Cinematography,"* *American Cinematographer*, Vol. 7, No. 9, December 1926, p. 17.

Information Sources

BIBLIOGRAPHY:
"Six Decades of 'Loyalty, Progress, Artistry.' " *American Cinematographer*, Vol. 60, No. 6, June 1979.
INDEX SOURCES: Critical Index (1946–1973); FIAF International Index to Film Pe-

riodicals (1972 to present); Film Literature Index (1975 to present); Index to Critical Film Reviews in British and American Film Periodicals (1950–1971).
REPRINT EDITIONS: University Microfilms.
LOCATION SOURCES: Academy of Motion Picture Arts and Sciences (incomplete); Eastman Kodak (Rochester, N.Y., Vol. 3 to present); Harvard University (incomplete); Library of Congress (incomplete); New York Public Library (incomplete); Smithsonian Institution (Vol. 3 to present); University of Southern California (incomplete).

Publication History

MAGAZINE TITLE AND TITLE CHANGES: *American Cinematographer*.
VOLUME AND ISSUE DATA: Vol. I, No. 1–Vol. II, No. 28 (November 1, 1920–March 1, 1922), semimonthly; Vol. III, No. 1 (April 1, 1922) to present, monthly, except there is no issue for November 1958.
PUBLISHER AND PLACE OF PUBLICATION: The American Society of Cinematographers, Inc., Suite 325-331, Markham Building, 6372 Hollywood Boulevard, Los Angeles, Calif. (Vol. I, No. 1–Vol. IV, No. 10); The American Society of Cinematographers, Inc., 1103 North El Centro Street, Los Angeles, Calif. (Vol. IV, No. 11–Vol. V, No. 6); The American Society of Cinematographers, Inc., 1219-20-21 Guaranty Building, Hollywood, Calif. (Vol. V, No. 7); The American Society of Cinematographers, Inc., 1219-20-21-22 Guaranty Building, Hollywood, Calif. (Vol. V, No. 8–Vol. X, No. 1); The American Society of Cinematographers, Inc., Suite 1222, Guaranty Building, Hollywood, Calif. (Vol. X, No. 2–Vol. XIV, No. 8); The American Society of Cinematographers, Inc., 6331 Hollywood Boulevard, Hollywood, Calif. (Vol. XIV, No. 9–Vol. XVII, No. 11); The American Society of Cinematographers, Inc., 1782 North Orange Drive, Hollywood, Calif. 90028 (Vol. XVII, No. 12 to present).
EDITOR: "Captain Jack" Poland (November 1, 1920–sometime in 1921); Silas Edgar Snyder (sometime in 1921–June 1, 1922); no editor listed (July 1, 1922); Foster Goss (August 1922–August 1927); Silas Edgar Snyder (September 1927–April 1929); Hal Hall (May 1929–September 1932); Charles J. VerHalen (October 1932–February 1937); George Blaisdell (March 1937–December 1940); William Stull (January 1941–September 1942); George Blaisdell and William Stull (October 1942); William Stull (November 1942–July 1943); Hal Hall (August 1943–November 1945); Walter R. Greene (December 1945–June 1948); Arthur E. Gavin (July 1948–January 1965); Herb A. Lightman (February 1965); Will Lane (March 1965); Don C. Hoefler (April 1965–January 1966); Herb A. Lightman (February 1966–June 1982); Richard Patterson (July 1982 to present).

Alan Gevinson

AMERICAN CLASSIC SCREEN

American Classic Screen was founded in 1976 by Kansas City entrepreneur Randy L. Neil as the house organ of the Bijou Society, which eventually became the National Film Society. The main purpose of the Bijou Society originally was to stage an annual convention in or near Hollywood, an event called "Movie

Expo,'' ostensibly to allow dues-paying members to see the celebrities up close, so as to daze and dazzle the starstruck. Society promotion at the time stated that the purpose was somehow to preserve "our nation's film heritage," but the main purpose was apparently to flatter retired movie stars.

Published bimonthly, *American Classic Screen* was initially designed after *Hollywood Studio Magazine*; it was, therefore, a fanzine directed toward an audience of fans and collectors. The emphasis was on Hollywood glamour, and early issues were inclined to feature photographs of older stars hugging and kissing each other, prominently placed in order to promote Movie Expo and its Artistry in Cinema Awards. Though it was later to move in other directions, the magazine continued to serve the Society and its functions.

During his first year, Neil was fortunate to meet a multitalented cinema studies student from the University of Kansas, John C. Tibbetts,[1] who not only knew film history and was able to write but was also sufficiently skilled as an illustrator to draw and design the cover illustrations for the magazine. Tibbetts did cover illustrations of Alice Faye, Mervyn LeRoy, and Charlie Chaplin for issues of Vol. 1, then went on to do Judy Garland, Marilyn Monroe, and many others. In fact, Tibbetts designed almost every cover during the magazine's first six years and was almost entirely responsible for the magazine's distinctive visual style.

John Tibbetts also contributed a two-part career survey of Mary Pickford (published in Vol. 1, Nos. 1 and 2) and became a member of the magazine's board of editors, though Neil retained control as executive editor. By Vol. 2, No. 2 (November/December 1977), Tibbetts was promoted to managing editor and was instrumental thereafter in shaping the magazine's editorial direction. Since Tibbetts was himself one of the best informed film buffs in the country, his knowledge, intelligence, and advice were also crucial in making Movie Expo a successful, crowd-pleasing event. Without John Tibbetts, *American Classic Screen* would have become nothing more than another silly fanzine; even so, concessions to the presumed interests of the typical fan have always influenced editorial policy. Membership in the Society eventually grew to over four thousand, never quite enough during the first few years to cover staff and production costs for the magazine. Artwork and layout improved, meanwhile, and highly touted ''rare'' photographs were tastefully mounted.

In November of 1977, Neil took his operation east and staged a convention at the Shoreham-Americana Hotel in Washington, D.C. But this ''event'' was not so successful as the West Coast annual conventions, and the experiment was never again repeated, though in later years the Society staged smaller conferences in Washington, Los Angeles, Chicago, Colonial Williamsburg, and Salisbury, Maryland (the latter in conjunction with *Literature/Film Quarterly** and *Film & History**).

As managing editor of the magazine, Tibbetts wanted *American Classic Screen* to become a serious vehicle for solid scholarship dealing with film history and popular culture. But he always had to keep in mind the interest of his primary audience of buffs and collectors, which meant a constant need to compromise editorial copy in order to keep the focus primarily upon stars and celebrities, the "special people" who provided the justification and rationale for Movie Expo, the one operation of the Society that almost always managed to cover its expenses.

In 1979 with the first issue of Vol. 4, *American Classic Screen* went to quarterly publication (increasing the number of pages per issue from forty-six to fifty-four) as a means of economizing, but many National Film Society members, by then accustomed to getting their magazines every other month, expressed their displeasure by not renewing their memberships.[2] Whether this decline was due to the change in format (as it was called) and the decreasing frequency of publication, or the concurrent shift toward more serious writing, or, simply, to problems of management, it is difficult to say, but it certainly brought about a crisis that was only to be resolved by a change in management and ownership of the Society.

The new publisher was William L. Miller, whose wife Bobbi had worked with Neil from the beginning, helping to organize the conventions and helping to operate both the Society and the magazine. Under the new ownership John Tibbetts became the executive editor and continued to oversee editorial content as the magazine cut pages and returned to bimonthly publication. Moreover, under the new ownership an effort was made to pay more attention to films produced after 1958, since Miller had no strong feelings about staying with purely nostalgic movies. In addition, by that time John Tibbetts had also begun covering films for a Kansas City television station, and so he was easily able to interview contemporary talents such as Woody Allen, Dyan Cannon, Debra Winger, and others. A new feature called "Camera Ready" was designed to pay at least minimal attention to current releases, but these write-ups tended to stay at the blurb level, since Tibbetts apparently did not want to challenge the contemporary review format that had long since been established by *Films in Review*.*

From the beginning, *American Classic Screen* had tried to be all things to all people, appearing to be a glossy grass-roots imitation of *American Film** (though one that lacked the funding and resources of the American Film Institute), sponsored by an organization that was in direct competition with the Cinephiles, a grouping of collectors who had their own "Cinecon" convention and their own tabloid publication, *Classic Film/Video Images*.* Career surveys and detailed filmographies tended to be more thoroughly researched and presented by *Films in Review*, and *American Classic Screen*, lacking the industry connections of the American Film Institute, found itself also competing with *Focus on Film** for that limited audience of fans and buffs.

A subscription drive in 1982 yielded successful results, however, increasing membership in the Society to new record levels (over fourteen thousand for the year) and promising to provide the basis for a better and more substantial magazine, one geared, as always, to an audience of fans and buffs, a magazine that may be potentially "serious" but not one likely to take its place among serious academic journals. The quality of the writing, overall, is better than *Classic Film/Video Images*, but it cannot compete strongly enough with the journalistic work commissioned by either *American Film* or *Film Comment*.* *American Classic Screen* shares with *Films in Review* an interest in the stars of yesteryear, but *Films in Review* had already staked out that territory long before *American Classic Screen* was thought of. Because it serves a general audience of fans, *American Classic Screen* has avoided the wretched diction and pretentious jargon that came to dominate many of the academic film journals during the 1970s, but there is a danger also of going to the opposite extreme of breezy journalism. Tibbetts has attempted to strike a balance in style as well as in content (always involving a compromise, since Tibbetts himself would probably prefer to pay more attention to silent cinema). If Tibbetts has successfully avoided the academic ponderousness of, say, the *Quarterly Review of Film Studies*,* he has at the same time fallen short of the seriousness of *Film Quarterly*.*

After six years, then, *American Classic Screen* has experimented editorially, but its base of support, despite changes in ownership, has remained the same. Movie Expo is still the showcase event of the year. In trying to retain the interests of the fans and writing to their level, *American Classic Screen* has not yet managed to capture a large audience of specialists in cinema studies, who are not likely to be impressed by movie nostalgia. *American Classic Screen* has published a number of fine features, but it has not yet managed to realize its eclectic goal. It is still, after six years, in a period of growth and transition.

Because of its interest in stars, *American Classic Screen* has always been keenly interested in celebrity interviews and has featured, for example, Bing Crosby ("A Last Interview," Vol. 3, No. 2), Anne Baxter (Vol. 2, No. 2), Olivia de Havilland (Vol. 3, No. 3), Fred MacMurray and June Haver (Vol. 3, No. 4), Esther Ralston (Vol. 5, No. 4), Jane Withers (Vol. 3, No. 5), and Charles "Buddy" Rogers (Vol. 3, No. 3), among others. The magazine has also published interviews with cameramen (Glen MacWilliams in Vol. 3, No. 3, for example), directors (Henry King in Vol. 5, No. 5), and historians (Kevin Brownlow in Vol. 5, No. 2). Continuing features and columns have ranged from the enduring, such as Frank Edwards's "Hollywood Newsletter" and "Hollywood Hotline," Chuck Berg's "Tracking the Score," John Crawley's "World of Animation," and "Periodically Yours" (a survey of other film periodicals), to the ephemeral, such as "Reel Talk" (Vol. 2, No. 3), "Home Video News" (Vol. 5, No. 1), "Sidelong Glances" (Vol. 5, No. 2), and "Freeze Frame" (Vol. 3, No. 6).

The magazine has undergone several changes, some of them awkward, as when the table of contents was replaced with a page entitled "What's Ahead," effective with the brief change to quarterly publication in 1979. By Vol. 6 a more conventional contents page had been reestablished. Otherwise, however, the magazine achieved its best look in 1979 when it attempted to go quarterly. The full-color covers on heavy stock at that time have not been matched since, and the increased number of pages helped to give the magazine substance. One hopes that in the future, on better financial footing, the Society will return to that level of quality production.

Notes

1. John Tibbetts is coauthor of *His Majesty the American: The Cinema of Douglas Fairbanks, Sr.* (A. S. Barnes, 1977) and editor of *Introduction to the Photoplay, 1929: A Contemporary Account of the Transition to Sound in Film*, a collection of lectures given by industry figures at the University of Southern California during the spring term of 1929 for a class entitled "Appreciation of the Photoplay," published by the National Film Society in 1977.

2. After publishing three "quarterly" issues, the magazine quickly returned to bimonthly publication in 1980.

Information Sources

INDEX SOURCES: None.
REPRINT EDITIONS: None.
LOCATION SOURCES: Academy of Motion Picture Arts and Sciences; American Film Institute (Los Angeles); American Film Institute (Washington, D.C.); Central Michigan University; Library of Congress; University of Iowa; University of Kansas; Wake Forest University.

Publication History

MAGAZINE TITLE AND TITLE CHANGES: *American Classic Screen*.
VOLUME AND ISSUE DATA: Vol. I, No. 1 (September-October 1976 to present), bimonthly except quarterly in 1979.
PUBLISHER AND PLACE OF PUBLICATION: National Film Society, 8340 Mission Road, Suite 106, Prairie Village, Kans. 66206.
EDITOR: Randy L. Neil (1976); John C. Tibbetts (1977 to present).

James M. Welsh

AMERICAN FILM

American Film: Magazine of the Film and Television Arts, despite its relatively short history, has become the most widely read film and television magazine in the world. Its circulation rose from an initial subscription list of 8,000 in 1975 to more than 140,000 in just eight years. It is the official magazine of the American Film Institute, an independent, nonprofit organization established in 1967 to advance the art of film and video. Since 93 percent of its circulation derives from member subscriptions, this spectacular growth in readership is clearly due to the rapidly expanding membership of the American Film Institute.

In an early issue, editor Hollis Alpert, former film critic for *Saturday Review*, pointed out the broad range of *American Film*: "The underlying purposes of the American Film Institute, which sponsors this magazine, are largely the magazine's purposes. The heritage, the whole repository of American filmmaking, is a large subject that will be continuously explored."[1]

The American Film Institute (AFI) is funded by the film industry, the National Endowment for the Arts, and member dues. Its board of trustees is dominated by executives of the major studios and networks and others connected with the Hollywood establishment. AFI has been criticized at times for emphasizing commercial Hollywood releases at the expense of experimental or independent productions. *American Film* also emphasizes mainstream commercial cinema and for a time seemed to function as a publicity mill for the major studio releases, but this has been corrected in recent years.

The name *American Film* is something of a misnomer, since the magazine has never limited itself to coverage of films produced in this country. In its efforts to capture a large, general readership, the editors have steered away from any identifiable critical or theoretical bias. *American Film* strives to be serious but not scholarly. In fact, the subtitle *Journal of the Film and Television Arts* was changed in 1979 to *Magazine of the Film and Television Arts* precisely to avoid any association with academic periodicals.

Each issue runs approximately eighty pages and contains several feature articles (90 percent freelance) of three thousand to four thousand words. Among the several regular departments are the "Letters" page; "Newsreel," a column of brief items about film; and reviews of recent books. "AFI News," which carried announcements to members, was replaced in March 1981 by "From the Director," a column written by the current AFI director, Jean Firstenberg. Each issue still carries a calendar listing the Institute's exhibition film series and other special events.

One of *American Film*'s considerable strengths has been its ability to attract an impressive list of contributors. Distinguished foreign directors Akira Kurosawa, Luis Buñuel, and Marcel Ophuls have written for the magazine, as have film critics and scholars such as Andrew Sarris, Stanley Kauffmann, Robert Sklar, Marjorie Rosen, and Erik Barnouw. One of the highlights of the early issues was novelist-screenwriter (*The Last Picture Show*) Larry McMurtry's column "McMurtry on the Movies," which began with the first issue and ran for two years. Screenwriter Ernest Lehman (*North by Northwest*) took over and for the next three and a half years shared his insight on the Hollywood community in "Lehman at Large."

Perhaps the most helpful and enduring feature has been "Dialogue on Film," edited transcripts of interview-seminars held weekly with the fellows of AFI's Center for Advanced Film Studies in California. With directors from Frank Capra and Steven Spielberg to Ingmar Bergman and François Truffaut, actors such as Dustin Hoffman and Sidney Poitier, writers Neil Simon and Robert Towne, and television producers Norman Lear and Grant Tinker, the list of those interviewed reads like a who's who of the entertainment industry.

These dialogues were originally organized by James Powers, who served as *American Film*'s West Coast editor, and his death in 1980 has left the magazine without an immediate link to Hollywood. One of the weaknesses of *American Film* is that its editorial base is so far removed from the center of either the film or television industry, which prompted Peter Biskind, when he became editor, to observe that "putting out a magazine on American film from Washington is somewhat akin to putting out a magazine on deep-sea fishing from Kansas."[2]

Biskind, a former associate editor of *Cineaste* and *Jump Cut* and film editor of *Seven Days*, made several changes upon assuming editorial control in September 1981. The regular columns were dropped to make room for one or two more articles per issue, and two new departments were added: "Flashback," dealing with topics of film history, and "Trailers," offering short blurbs which publicize forthcoming releases from Hollywood.

Though *American Film* has always emphasized film over T.V., attention to the latter has increased in clearly visible steps. Martin Mayer's column "About Television" ran regularly from February 1978 to July/August 1981. In April 1979 a new department called "Video Spectrum" was established, and by October it had evolved into a special section of the magazine and had a new name, "The Video Scene: Developments in Programming and Technology Affecting the Home Viewer." Articles by media critics such as Gary Arlen explored trends of the cable industry, video artists, and recent advances in videocassette recorders and videodiscs.

By the summer of 1982 the section had been renamed "Videofile" and had assumed a standard form: one or two feature articles; a department called "Scanlines," offering short news items about video; "Collector's Choice," in which guest columnists pick ten favorite videocassettes, usually shaped around a specific theme; and "Videography," listing all motion pictures mentioned in the issue available on videocassette or videodisc.

With solidly written, interesting articles, slick four-color photography, and innovations such as the publication of a short story, Julio Cortazar's "We Love Glenda So Much" in April 1983, *American Film* has succeeded in attracting a huge readership of industry professionals, film teachers, students, and fans.

Notes

1. "Editorial," Vol. 3, No. 6, April 1978, p. 2.
2. "Editorial," Vol. 6, No. 10, September 1981, p. 9.

Information Sources

INDEX SOURCES: Humanities Index; The Magazine Index; FIAF International Index to Film Periodicals; Film Literature Index; Media Review Digest.
REPRINT EDITIONS: University Microfilms.
LOCATION SOURCES: Academy of Motion Picture Arts and Sciences; American Film Institute; Harvard University; Museum of Modern Art; Northwestern University; University of California at Los Angeles; University of California at San Diego; University of Illinois; University of Southern California.

Publication History

MAGAZINE TITLE AND TITLE CHANGES: *American Film: Journal of the Film and Television Arts* (October 1975– December-January 1979); *American Film: Magazine of the Film and Television Arts* (February 1979 to present).

VOLUME AND ISSUE DATA: Vol. I, No. 1–Vol. IV, No. 10 (October 1975–September 1979), monthly except combined issues for December/January and July/August; Vol. V, No. 1 (October 1979 to present), monthly except combined issues for January/February and July/August.

PUBLISHER AND PLACE OF PUBLICATION: American Film Institute, Kennedy Center, Washington, D.C. 20566.

EDITOR: Hollis Alpert (October 1975–October 1980); Antonio Chemasi (Executive Editor serving as Acting Editor, November 1980–July/August 1981); Peter Biskind (September 1981 to present).

Rick Shale

AMERICAN PREMIERE

Premiere (later *American Premiere*) evolved into a glossy publication dedicated specifically to addressing "the business equation of Hollywood," namely those aspects of filmmaking which make up the "workable elements" of the creative process.

The first year of this publication (1979) dealt with a various array of subjects within the industry and usually included an interview with a well-known personality. In addition, there would be brief profiles of individuals who worked both in front of and behind the camera. This "close-up" column ran until the publication ceased in 1983, as did other regular columns on exhibition, finance, distribution, and the Academy of Motion Picture Arts and Sciences.

Beginning with the December 1980 issue and the addition of Susan Royal as publisher, the periodical began to take on a different theme with each issue. The first of these was "The Changing Face of Hollywood" (Vol. 2, No. 3) in which articles on film preservation, genres, labor strikes, video, and market research appeared. Each succeeding issue would continue this policy by incorporating interviews and in-depth reports about the current month's topic. Themes discussed throughout the duration of the periodical included sound and music, women and film, financing and the independent producer, fantasy film and special effects, film festivals and markets, cable T.V. and video, location filming, and the first American Film Market.

Information Sources

INDEX SOURCES: None.

REPRINT EDITIONS: None.

LOCATION SOURCES: Academy of Motion Picture Arts and Sciences; American Film Institute (Los Angeles); Library of Congress; University of Southern California (all incomplete).

Publication History

MAGAZINE TITLE AND TITLE CHANGES: *Premiere: The Magazine of the Film Industry* (1979–March 1981); *American Premiere: The Magazine of the Film Industry* (May 1981–April 30, 1983).

VOLUME AND ISSUE DATA: Vol. I, No. 1–Vol. IV, No. 3 (?, 1979–April 30, 1983), monthly with some irregularity. [The dates are sometimes missing from the journal's covers and when included often do not coincide with the dates on the title pages; also, the dates of first and last issues are unconfirmed.]

PUBLISHER AND PLACE OF PUBLICATION: Brilliant Film Company, Inc., 6671 Sunset Boulevard, Suite 1581, Hollywood, Calif. 90028 (Vol. I, No. 1–Vol. II, No. 1); Premiere Publications, Inc., 6671 Sunset Boulevard, Suite 1581, Hollywood, Calif. 90028 (Vol. II, No. 2–Vol. II, No. 3); Premiere Publications, Inc., 2906 Griffith Park Boulevard, Los Angeles, Calif. 90027 (Vol. II, No. 4–Vol. II, No. 5); American Premiere Publications, Inc., 183 North Martel, Suite 1, Los Angeles, Calif. 90036 (Vol. II, No. 6–Vol. IV, No. 1); American Premiere Ltd., 8421 Wilshire Boulevard, Suite 205, Beverly Hills, Calif. 90211 (Vol. IV, No. 2–Vol. IV, No. 3).

EDITOR: Noel Huntley (1979–March 1980); Spanky Taylor (May 1980–October 10, 1980); Michael J. Firmature (December 5, 1980–March 20, 1982); Judith McGuinn (May 12, 1982–April 30, 1983).

Lisa Mosher

ANTHOLOGIE DU CINÉMA

Anthologie du Cinéma began as a pamphlet-size supplement to *L'Avant-Scène du Cinéma** in October 1976. The purpose of this supplement, which many libraries treat as a separate publication inasmuch as it has its own issue numbering and pagination, is to present and evaluate the career of a single outstanding film figure. No living people are the subjects of these biographical/critical profiles. Although compiled by a variety of writers, the format is always the same. Early biographical details are given, and the person's career is traced with a discussion of important films and an overall evaluation of the individual's contribution to the art of the film. Each piece concludes with a filmography and a bibliography of secondary sources. Interspersed in the text are numerous illustrations.

An examination of the first one hundred issues shows that directors are favored—sixty-eight issues featured a director (nineteen of which were American, eighteen were French, seven German, seven Russian, five British, and twelve from other countries). Actors and actresses were the subjects of twenty-four issues, and eight issues profiled a miscellaneous group of people important in the history of the cinema.

In addition to biographical information, the authors tend to draw attention to themes that have engaged a director's attention. Many times there are comments on those cinematic techniques which in the writer's opinion have been most effective in developing the various themes. Sometimes there are comments as to how a person's work is characteristic of the American, French, or German cinemas at that time.

The pamphlets tend to run from forty-eight to fifty-six pages, and since incorporating into the main body of *L'Avant-Scène du Cinéma*, thirty-two pages. The text comprises ten thousand to twelve thousand words and is illustrated with thirty to forty stills. The series is written mostly by French writers, and some who have undertaken four or more numbers are Jean Mitry, Claude Beylie, Charles Ford, and Pierre Leprohon. Most of the other writers already have articles or books to their credit.

The subjects have been drawn from throughout film history, from Lumière and Méliès down to the recently deceased. Alfred Hitchcock and Terence Fisher, both of whom died in 1980, were featured during 1982.

The bibliography section slights non-French publications. If sources published outside of France are mentioned, it is on a very selective basis. Published scripts or autobiographies by the subject are always noted.

These biographical sketches are more critical and lengthier than one would expect in a handbook or encyclopedia, even a specialized one. Also, the gathering of so many illustrations about a single individual is a unique feature, something seldom found in book-length biographies and not expected in magazines.

Information Sources

INDEX SOURCES: FIAF International Index to Film Periodicals.
REPRINT EDITIONS: None.
LOCATION SOURCES: University of Oregon.

Publication History

MAGAZINE TITLE AND TITLE CHANGES: *Anthologie du Cinéma*.
VOLUME AND ISSUE DATA: Issued as a supplement to *L'Avant-Scène du Cinéma*; Nos. 1–60 (1965–1970), monthly except for combined July/September issues; No. 86 (January 1976); No. 87 (March 1976); No. 88 (May 1976); No. 89 (July/September 1976); No. 90 (October 1976); Bound with *L'Avant-Scène du Cinéma* from No. 91 (November 1976); Nos. 92–95 (1977); Nos. 96–99 (1978); Nos. 100–103 (1979); Nos. 104–106 (1980); Nos. 107–108 (1981); Nos. 109–110 (1982), irregular.
PUBLISHER AND PLACE OF PUBLICATION: L'Avant-Scène, 27 Rue Saint-André-des-Arts, Paris 75006, France.
EDITOR: Jacques Charrière (1965–1970); Jacques Charrière and Robert Chandeau, General Editors, with Claude Beylie, *Anthologie* Editor (1970–1976); no editor listed after incorporation into *L'Avant-Scène du Cinéma*.

Richard Heinzkill

ART ET ESSAI

Intended primarily for French exhibitors, *Art et Essai* offered short (heavily illustrated) interviews and articles. There was a regular historical section by Jean Mitry (which included a series of articles on Hollywood studios) and schedules of Paris theatre screenings. From No. 13, *Art et Essai* featured "Nos Dossiers Filmographiques," devoted to individual films, with credits, synopses, critical comment, and biographies of personalities involved.

Information Sources

INDEX SOURCES: None.
REPRINT EDITIONS: None.
LOCATION SOURCES: University of Illinois; University of Iowa; University of Southern
    California.

Publication History

MAGAZINE TITLE AND TITLE CHANGES: *Art et Essai.*
VOLUME AND ISSUE DATA: No. 1–No. 12 (April 1965–July 1966), monthly; No.
    13 (October 1966); No. 14–No. 51 (November 16, 1966–February 17, 1969),
    twice a month; No. 52 (March 1969); No. 53 (May 1969).
PUBLISHER AND PLACE OF PUBLICATION: Dossiers Art et Essaai, 174 Quai de
    Jemmapes, Paris 10, France (Nos. 1–20); Dossiers Art et Essai, 47 Quai des
    Grands Augustins, Paris 6, France (Nos. 21–53).
EDITOR: Jeander.

Anthony Slide

THE AUSTRALIAN JOURNAL OF SCREEN THEORY

Beginning in 1976 as a periodical subsidized by the Film, Radio, and Television Board of the Australia Council, *The Australian Journal of Screen Theory* originally was dedicated to the goal of disseminating new ideas and approaches to film criticism and theory that no other Australian journal was covering. The editors wanted to establish an interdisciplinary dialogue for film teachers in several fields (such as sociology, history, drama, media and communication studies, comparative literature, semiology, psychology, and linguistics) in order to help close the "gap between the needs of their students and the hermeticism of existing journals of film theory" through articles that would be "readable by people who are not necessarily specialists in the specific theory under consideration."

By 1977, however, after the first two issues of the journal had appeared, budget cuts made by the Fraser government discontinued the original subsidy, and financial support to help cover publication costs was not forthcoming from the Australian Film Commission. Publication of issue No. 3 (1977) was assisted by a grant from the Humanities Faculty at Griffith University. Issue No. 5/6 (a double issue printing papers from the First Australian Film Conference, held in 1978 and published in 1979) had grant support from the Faculty of the Arts of the University of New South Wales and Mitchell College of Advanced Education in Bathurst, New South Wales. Double issue 9/10 (1981) was produced by the

Department of Media Services, Nedlands College of Advanced Education, in Perth.

The trend has been to link the journal to academic film conferences held in Australia, and the editors have managed to obtain academic funding to support both the conferences and the periodical. The "most significant outcome" of this activity, announced in the editoral for issue 9/10, was "the foundation of the Australian Screen Studies Association," initially to be controlled by a screening committee located in Victoria.

This shifting base of operations has produced some interesting variations in format: double issue 11/12 (1982, exploring television) resembles issue No. 3 (1977); intermediate issues display a variety of shapes, sizes, bindings, and covers, but all of them are well designed and readable. The movement toward founding the Australian Screen Studies Association may eventually bring about an Australian equivalent to the Society for Education in Film and Television (SEFT) in the United Kingdom.

One early announced purpose of *The Australian Journal of Screen Theory* (*AJST*) was to import ideas from abroad to the Australian continent. Issue No. 3 (1977), for example, reviews Garth Jowett's *Film: The Democratic Art*, Bill Nichols's *Movies and Methods*, and Dudley Andrew's *The Major Film Theories*, and includes essays by Geoffrey Nowell-Smith and Laura Mulvey and an essay by Sylvia Lawson, "The Peirce/Wollen Code Signs." In issue No. 4 (1978) Sam Rohdie discusses semiotic constraints in *Now Voyager*, Geoff Mayer examines formula and genre (paying particular attention to Will Wright and John Cawelti), and William D. Routt counters "vulgar auteurism" in his consideration, "The Hollywood Screenwriter." This issue also includes a transcript of engaging comments made by Hollywood screenwriter Casey Robinson concerning his work at the Warner Bros. Studio made at the Conference of the Tertiary Screen Education Association of Victoria in 1977. Since Casey Robinson died on December 6, 1979, his comments concerning *Dark Victory* in issue 4 have historical importance, and American scholars should be grateful to *AJST* for publishing them. Double issue 9/10 (1981) includes papers by Stephen Heath, Edward Buscombe, and Brian Henderson.

The conference orientation of issues over the years has tended to establish a number of dominant topics, therefore, for the issues of *AJST*: television (issue 11/12), Hollywood screenwriting (issue No. 4), and film and theatre (issue No. 7), for example. The film and theatre issue, though not typical of the magazine's general editorial focus, as was made clear in an editorial that appeared in issue No. 8, was remarkable in what it accomplished. The editors stated, however, that issue 7 "largely consisted of contributions from specialists in drama attempting (sometimes within a traditional literary-critical framework) to establish connections between the study of the stage and of the screen. While film study has clearly moved away from such approaches, as it is still the case that the academic study of film is frequently tied to departments of 'English' or 'Drama' (especially in Australian universities as distinct from Colleges of Advanced

Education), the drama-film relationship inevitably demands student attention."
The editors therefore seemed needlessly embarrassed that their "Film and Theatre" issue was not in line with SEFT-sanctioned approaches. However, regular
AJST editor Peter R. Gerdes himself made extraordinarily clear distinctions
between film and theatre in that issue, which also included an interview with
Australian playwright and screenwriter David Williamson, and the issue was
later advertised a "the ideal textbook!" That an "ideal" collection should at
the same time be considered something of an anomaly speaks for the confused
eclectic state of film criticism and theory, but that confusion is not indigenous
to Australia.

Regardless, *AJST* has established itself as perhaps the most important serious
periodical in cinema studies in Australia. Its theoretical concentration makes it
distinctive from *Cinema Papers*,* and its interdisciplinary and international orientation sets it apart from other Australian publications such as *Federation News*
(the "Quarterly Journal of the Federation of Victorian Film Societies") or its
later incarnation, *Filmviews* (the "Film Users' Quarterly"), which provide little
more than a descriptive-review function and convey information about local film
societies and collections. *AJST* will no doubt eventually command an international readership as film scholars outside of Australia eventually discover what
it has to offer.

Information Sources

INDEX SOURCES: None.
REPRINT EDITIONS: None.
LOCATION SOURCES: Academy of Motion Picture Arts and Sciences; Cornell Uni-
    versity; Harvard University; Library of Congress; Stanford University; University
    of Southern California.

Publication History

MAGAZINE TITLE AND TITLE CHANGES: *The Australian Journal of Screen Theory*.
VOLUME AND ISSUE DATA: Vol. I, No. 1 (1976 to present), biannual.
PUBLISHER AND PLACE OF PUBLICATION: School of Drama, University of New
    South Wales, P.O. Box 1, Kensington N.S.W. 2033, Australia.
EDITOR: Philip Bell, Stephen Crofts, Peter R. Gerdes, Neil McDonald, John Tulloch.

James M. Welsh

THE AUTOGRAPH NEWSREEL. See NEWSREEL

L'AVANT-SCÈNE DU CINÉMA

In its first twenty years, *L'Avant-Scène du Cinéma* (founded in 1961) featured
approximately 450 film scripts, presented in the format used for armchair reading
of plays. The scene is laid and the dialogue summarized. No attention is paid

to camera angles, close-ups, and so forth, except what can be deduced from the dialogue and the descriptions given. Not all visual effects are ignored, however, because there are numerous still photographs—between fifteen and twenty-five per film—and each one is numbered and keyed to the script. In a medium whose "text" is not readily available for leisurely study, it would seem that *L'Avant-Scène du Cinéma* should play an important role. However, the magazine's world-wide influence is diminished by its being entirely in French. Thus *The 39 Steps* becomes *Les 39 Marches* and opens with, "Mesdames et Messieurs, je demande votre aimable attention."

Accompanying each script is a short biographical sketch of the director along with a filmography. Also very often there is a short article or two on some aspect of the film, and sometimes an additional page or so devoted to quoting paragraphs from contemporary reviews.

The approximately twenty films presented each year are a varied lot. There is no pattern, but usually less than half are current releases and the remainder vary in age. One issue may feature a "classic" from the thirties, the next issue a notable film released within the past ten years, and even an occasional silent film (such as Buster Keaton's *The General/Le Mecano de la General*). The coverage is international with a slight preference for French films. Occasionally there are special issues, which in the past have been devoted to Georges Franju, "Fantomas", Joris Ivens, or Sergei Eisenstein, among others.

In 1976 two additional features were added—*Anthologie du Cinéma** and "Cinematheque"—both of which continue to appear at irregular intervals. The latter provides an opportunity to discuss various matters of interest, such as films and a novelist, some aspect of a director's work, or a theme such as space travel in films.

During 1980 and 1981, parts of the 1930 film periodical, *Cinemagazine*, were reprinted. *Cinemagazine* was similar in style to an American fan magazine but included some interesting material, such as a three-page article by Charlie Chaplin, a two-page piece on King Vidor by Marcel Carné, and "Souvenirs de Ma Vie" by Harold Lloyd. For a time, subscribers received "Cine-Posters," consisting of a single still photograph, usually in color, on a loose sheet of about twelve by twenty inches.

Information Sources

BIBLIOGRAPHY:
Beylie, Claude. "Dans les coulisses de *L'Avant-Scène*." *L'Avant-Scène du Cinéma*, No. 262 (February 15, 1981), p. 71.
INDEX SOURCES: Current Contents; FIAF International Index to Film Periodicals.
REPRINT EDITIONS: None.
LOCATION SOURCES: University of Oregon (incomplete).

Publication History

MAGAZINE TITLE AND TITLE CHANGES: *L'Avant-Scène du Cinéma*.
VOLUME AND ISSUE DATA: No. 1 (February 15, 1961 to present), bimonthly but no issues in August and September.

PUBLISHER AND PLACE OF PUBLICATION: L'Avant-Scène, 27 Rue Saint-André-des-Arts, Paris 75006, France.

EDITOR: Robert Chandeau (General Editor, 1961–1970); Robert Chandeau and Jacques Charrière (General Editors, 1970–1977); Jacques Charrière (General Editor, 1977–1979); Christian Dupeyron (General Editor, 1979 to present); position of Cinéma Editor first held by Jacques Perret (1975–1977); then Claude Beylie (1977 to present).

Richard Heinzkill

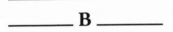

B

BANTHA TRACKS. See Appendix 1

BARBRA. See Appendix 1

BEULAH BONDI BULLETIN. See Appendix 1.

BIANCO E NERO

In 1937, *Bianco e Nero* began publication in Rome as a journal tied to the "Centro sperimentale di cinematografia" (the experimental cinema center). Though devoted primarily to Italian cinema, the journal also had a heavy European leaning, with some articles on American films and filmmakers as well. Originally issued twelve times a year, the journal contained interviews, film reviews, long reviews of film books, technical articles, and lengthy analyses of the works of a particular performer or director. The European films and filmmakers discussed had a fairly broad base, but American topics tended to be few and unimportant by modern standards. In the late thirties, for example, *In Old Chicago* (1938) was reviewed, but *Stagecoach* (1939) was not.

The journal ceased publication during the latter part of the Second World War and did not commence again until October 1947. At this time it became a quarterly. In the fifties and onward more articles were devoted to American and British films than before the war, no doubt a reflection of the changed attitudes toward those countries by the former Axis power. In recent years many of the journal's issues have been special issues devoted to one particular topic or filmmaker and often with a designated guest editor for that issue. For example, in 1980 there was an important special issue on Italian silent films (*cinema muto*).

The journal is well indexed within each volume, with authors, titles, and film titles cited. Although still published quarterly, the journal is very far behind in publication yet still retains its continuous dating and numbering system.

Information Sources

INDEX SOURCES: FIAF International Index to Film Periodicals; Film Literature Index.
REPRINT EDITIONS: None.
LOCATION SOURCES: University of Southern California.

Publication History

MAGAZINE TITLE AND TITLE CHANGES: *Bianco e Nero: Quaderni mensili del centro sperimentale di cinematografia* (1937–1969); *BN: mensile di studi sul cinema e lo spettacolo* (1970 to present).
VOLUME AND ISSUE DATA: Vol. I, No. 1–Vol. VIII (January 1937–September 1943), monthly; ceased publication October 1943–October 1947; Vol. IX, No. 1 (October 1947 to present), quarterly.
PUBLISHER AND PLACE OF PUBLICATION: Centro sperimentale di cinematografia, Via Foligno, 40, Rome, Italy (1937–1939); Centro sperimentale di cinematografia, Via Tuscolana, Rome, Italy (1939–1943); Centro sperimentale di cinematografia, Via dei Gracchi, 128, Rome, Italy (1947–1953); Centro sperimentale di cinematografia, Via Tuscolana, 832, Rome, Italy (1953–1961); Centro sperimentale di cinematografia, Via Antonio Musa, 15, Rome, Italy (1962–1969); Centro sperimentale di cinematografia, Via Tuscolana, 1524, Rome, Italy (1970 to present).
EDITOR: No editor listed (1937–1938); Luigi Chiarini (1939–1957); Michele Lacalamita (1957–1959); Floris L. Ammannati (1960–1975); Ernesto G. Laura (1976 to present).

Patricia King Hanson

BIJOU. See Appendix 2

THE BIOGRAPH. See Appendix 3

BIOGRAPH BULLETIN. See Appendix 3

THE BIOSCOPE

Among the early British trade papers, one of the most respected was *The Bioscope*. This trade paper was essentially the reflection of the character of its editor—one John Cabourn, a genteel, courteous man whose high principles and integrity were never in doubt. Forsaking the profession for which he had trained—

the law—he took to the stage, making his debut in 1896. Then in 1908, when *The Bioscope* was founded, Cabourn became associated with it, first as secretary and business manager; then, very shortly afterward, he took over the editorship. Later he acquired the controlling interest in the paper, which he retained until his death on January 16, 1929. After his death the paper continued for several years until it came into conflict with some members of the Kinematograph Renters' Society (KRS) who wanted to promote a merger of the three existing film trade journals, of which *The Bioscope* was one. The single resultant journal would receive guaranteed advertising from the renter-members of the KRS. Fearing the effect on control of editorial policy and its loss of independence, *The Bioscope* indicated to the KRS that it could not be bought or merged. This resulted in a decline in new advertising contracts, and *The Bioscope* ran into financial difficulties. There was also some criticism of a change of form in the film review service adopted in October 1931, which started to give a "percentage analysis" of the film's story, direction, acting, recording and dialogue, and photography. The paper was put into voluntary liquidation in May 1932, then merged by Odhams Press into their *Kinematograph Weekly*,* the leading British trade paper of the time.

Whatever difficulties and controversies confronted the film industry, *The Bioscope* endeavored to take an independent and honest view. From the day Cabourn became proprietor, he refused to invest money or hold any sort of interest in any film enterprise. He believed that a trade paper could be impartial only if it was absolutely independent, and he was quite willing to sacrifice opportunities of making money in order to preserve this independence.

The Bioscope was the first British trade paper to give a review service. It supported the formation of the Cinematograph Defence League, which protected the interests of exhibitors, and was first among the trade papers to fight for Sunday Opening. It championed the Films Act of 1927, an act which was subsequently acknowledged as the safeguard of British films and British theatres. The Cinematograph Exhibitors' Association was particularly indebted to *The Bioscope* for the publicity and support it received. Its technical comments were highly regarded at the time, and there was comprehensive coverage of activities in the regions. It foretold the eclipse of the silent film and urged exhibitors to prepare for sound without delay.

Perhaps the demise of *The Bioscope* would have been inevitable. In the ever-increasing hurly-burly of the film trade world of the 1930s, its gentility would have been its downfall and not its strength.

Information Sources

INDEX SOURCES: None. [Film review references are contained in the British Film Institute Film Title Index 1908–1978, available on microfilm from World Microfilms.]

REPRINT EDITIONS: World Microfilms.

LOCATION SOURCES: Academy of Motion Picture Arts and Sciences (1909–1914 only); New York Public Library (incomplete). [British Film Institute has a complete run.]

Publication History

MAGAZINE TITLE AND TITLE CHANGES: *The Bioscope.*
VOLUME AND ISSUE DATA: Vol. I, No. 1–Vol. LXXXXI, No. 1335 (September 18, 1908–May 4, 1932), weekly. [The first issue is numbered 101.]
PUBLISHER AND PLACE OF PUBLICATION: Bioscope Publishing Co. Ltd., 170 Fleet Street, London E.C., England (September 18, 1908–November 6, 1908); Bioscope Publishing Co. Ltd., 8 Cecil Court, Charing Cross Road, London W.C., England (November 13, 1908–June 3, 1909); Bioscope Publishing Co. Ltd., 31 Litchfield Street, Charing Cross Road, London, W.C., England (June 10, 1909–July 28, 1910); Bioscope Publishing Co. Ltd., 85 Shaftesbury Avenue, London W.C., England (August 4, 1910–September 21, 1922); Bioscope Publishing Co. Ltd., Faraday House 8-10 Charing Cross Road, London W.C.2 (September 18, 1922–May 4, 1932).
EDITOR: John Cabourn (1908–1929); William H. Mooring and Frank Fowell (1929–1932).

Pat Coward

THE BISON MAGAZINE. See Appendix 3

BN. See BIANCO E NERO

BOYS CINEMA

Intended for young male readers, and a companion to *Girls Cinema,* * *Boys Cinema* looked at the film industry from a decidedly stereotypical masculine viewpoint. It featured articles on sports, westerns, and adventure dramas. There were articles on how to make a home telephone and alarm, and actor William Duncan wrote "How To Be Strong." By 1922 the periodical had become more of a boys' adventure paper and less of a film magazine. The quality of the paper stock and reproductions was always exceedingly poor.

Screen Stories, which began publication on February 8, 1930, merged with *Boys Cinema* on August 17, 1938.

Information Sources

INDEX SOURCES: None.
REPRINT EDITIONS: None.
LOCATION SOURCES: No information.

Publication History

MAGAZINE TITLE AND TITLE CHANGES: *Boys Cinema.*
VOLUME AND ISSUE DATA: Nos. 1–1063 (December 13, 1919–May 18, 1940),
    weekly.
PUBLISHER AND PLACE OF PUBLICATION: Amalgamated Press, Fleetway House,
    Farringdon Street, London, England.
EDITOR: No editor listed.

Thomas A. Johnson

BRIGHT LIGHTS

Bright Lights, subtitled "The Magazine of American Film," displayed all the exuberance of a student-oriented and produced periodical, offering a mixture of heavy analysis and light film history. Despite its subtitle, however, not all of the articles were devoted to American cinema, and there were, for example, occasional pieces on Jean Renoir (Vol. 2, No. 1) and the German film (Vol. 1, No. 3).

Joan Crawford graced the cover of the first issue (Fall 1974), an issue which did not even carry the magazine's name, and set the style for *Bright Lights'* critical, yet friendly, view of Hollywood's glamor years. That first issue featured an article on George Cukor's *A Star Is Born* (1954), as well as an interview with the director. The films of Frank Borzage were considered in Nos. 2 and 3. John Belton wrote lengthy analyses of Samuel Fuller's *Shark!* (Vol. 1, No. 2) and Howard Hawks's *Scarface* (Vol. 1, No. 4). Jerry Lewis's career was considered in Vol. 1, No. 3, and director Anthony Mann was profiled in Vol. 2, No. 1. Vol. 1, No.4 was a special bicentennial issue devoted—with a curious sense of humor and irony—to American violence, while Vol. 2, No. 2, was given over to the cinema of Douglas Sirk.

Vol. 2, No. 3, brought *Bright Lights* a little more up to date with articles on *Love and Death, Marathon Man,* and *In a Lonely Place,* but the next issue took the magazine back to a period in which it seemed more at ease. Devoted to Hollywood classics, Vol. 2, No. 4, included articles on Joan Crawford and Gregory La Cava, as well as interviews with Allan Dwan and George Stevens. The last published issue (Vol. 3, No. 1) featured articles on Bette Davis, animator Tex Avery, and two musicals—*Show Boat* and *Kiss Me Kate*—by George Sidney.

Bright Lights was a curiosity, a popular film magazine aimed at a semi-intellectual audience, a publication devoid of advertising, in which a letter from Joan Crawford (No. 4) seemed at once both appropriate and out of place. (There is some validity to the actress' description of the magazine as "clean, precise and beautiful.") If *Bright Lights* had an antecedent it was probably *The Velvet Light Trap,** but while the latter was a less physically attractive periodical, its articles contained more substance and generally indicated more background research than those in *Bright Lights.*

Information Sources

INDEX SOURCES: None.
REPRINT EDITIONS: None.
LOCATION SOURCES: Academy of Motion Picture Arts and Sciences; Iowa State
    University; Museum of Modern Art; University of Iowa; University of Tennessee;
    University of Utah; Wesleyan University.

Publication History

MAGAZINE TITLE AND TITLE CHANGES: *Bright Lights*.
VOLUME AND ISSUE DATA: Vol. I, No. 1 (Fall 1974); Vol. I, No. 2 (Winter 1974);
    Vol. I, No. 3 (Summer 1975); Vol. I, No. 4 (Summer 1976); Vol. II, No. 1
    (Summer 1977); Vol. II, No. 2 (Winter 1977–1978); Vol. II, No. 3 (1978); Vol.
    II, No. 4 (1979); Vol. III, No. 1 (1980).
PUBLISHER AND PLACE OF PUBLICATION: Gary Morris, 4234 Greenlee Avenue,
    St. Bernard, Ohio 45217 (Vol. I, Nos. 1–2); Gary Morris, 1705 1/2 Morton
    Avenue, Los Angeles, Calif. 90026 (Vol. I, No. 3); Gary Morris, P.O. Box
    26081, Los Angeles, Calif. 90026 (Vol. I, No. 4–Vol. III, No. 1).
EDITOR: Gary Morris.

Anthony Slide

BRIGHTON FILM REVIEW. See MONOGRAM

BROADCASTING

Broadcasting began publication on October 15, 1931, as a semimonthly trade
paper devoted to radio. It was founded and edited by Sol Taishoff, a radio
newswriter, who remained its editor until his death in 1982.

In its first issue, the magazine cited Edmund Burke's designation of print
journalism as the "Fourth Estate" (this citation has been disputed over the years)
and editorialized that radio must, therefore, be considered the "Fifth Estate."
Broadcasting has described itself, since that first issue, as the "news magazine
of the Fifth Estate." However, as new technologies have developed, the realm
of the Fifth Estate has expanded to include television, cable, and satellite transmission. (Weekly publication began in 1941.)

As a trade journal, *Broadcasting* places special emphasis on news items of
particular interest to the broadcasting industry. The "Cablecastings" and "Tel-
ecastings" sections, for example, contain brief news notes regarding programming, acquisitions, and production on cable and commercial television stations;
"Riding Gain" is devoted to news about radio and independent radio producers.
"Business Briefly" summarizes news related to radio and television advertising
campaigns. "Changing Hands" lists radio and television station sales (including
the names of the buyers and sellers, and sale prices); while "For the Record"

is a compilation of applications for new radio and television stations filed with the Federal Communications Commission (each entry includes the names of the principals and their other broadcast interests, if any). "Fates and Fortunes" lists promotion and other career moves of people in the field. Along with these departments, which are essentially brief summaries gleaned from press releases and other sources, are lengthier, in-depth articles.

Longer articles in *Broadcasting* serve to examine subjects which affect the broadcasting industry as a whole or large segments of the industry. Issues such as syndication rules, federal deregulation of the industry, sex discrimination suits and other media-related legal matters, technological advances, and major trends are given extensive coverage. Also examined closely are the actions of the Federal Communications Commission (FCC) and other governmental agencies. In this way, *Broadcasting* serves two functions: by reporting on agencies such as the FCC, the magazine is keeping its readers informed and up to date on key issues that often have far-reaching ramifications, and it is also providing the industry with a Washington presence which is important in terms of media-related legislation. (*Broadcasting*'s main office and editorial staff are based in Washington, D.C., with bureaus in New York and Hollywood.)

Broadcasting also maintains close links with the members of the industry it represents by highlighting the activities of trade organizations such as the National Association of Broadcasters and the Radio and Television News Directors Association. For example, the magazine devotes whole issues to the annual conventions held by these groups, covering panel discussion and other presentations. Regular features of the magazine also include "Monday Memo," which provides space for commentary by a member of the industry; and "Fifth Estater," which profiles a prominent broadcasting industry executive.

Information Sources

BIBLIOGRAPHY:
Broadcasting Magazine. *The First 50 Years of Broadcasting*. Washington, D.C.: Broadcasting Publications, 1982.
INDEX SOURCES: None.
REPRINT EDITIONS: Bell & Howell Micro Photo Division; University Microfilms.
LOCATION SOURCES: Library of Congress; New York Public Library; University of Illinois; University of Southern California (lacks issues prior to 1934).

Publication History

MAGAZINE TITLE AND TITLE CHANGES: *Broadcasting* (October 15, 1931–August 18, 1934); *Broadcasting/Broadcast Advertising* (September 1, 1934–November 19, 1945); *Broadcasting/Telecasting* (November 26, 1945–October 7, 1957); *Broadcasting* (October 14, 1957, to present).
VOLUME AND ISSUE DATA: Vols. I–XIX (October 15, 1931–January 1941), semimonthly; Vol. XX, No. 1 (January 13, 1941, to present), weekly.

PUBLISHER AND PLACE OF PUBLICATION: Broadcasting Publications, 1735 DeSales Street, N.W., Washington, D.C. 20036.
EDITOR: Sol Taishoff (1931–1982); Lawrence Taishoff (1982 to present).

Kay Salz

BROADCASTING BIBLIOPHILE'S BOOKNOTES. See COMMUNICATION BOOKNOTES

BULGARIAN FILM NEWS. See Appendix 4

BULGARIAN FILMS. See Appendix 4

BULLETIN OF HUNGARIAN CINEMATOGRAPHY. See Appendix 4

BULLETIN OF THE CZECHOSLOVAK NATIONALIZED FILM. See Appendix 4

THE BUSINESS OF FILM

A glossy trade paper devoted to the serious business of financing and marketing motion pictures and television, *The Business of Film* began publication in England in the winter of 1982. Each issue features brief news items and reports from various countries, as well as articles on subjects such as "Pay-TV Makes the Running" (No. 3) and "The Independent Producer" (No.8). From No. 4 onward, *The Business of Film* has included "The Business Information Service" section, with guides to films in production and released around the world, as well as one-time guides to reputable video buyers, courier and freight services, and so forth.

Information Sources

INDEX SOURCES: None.
REPRINT EDITIONS: None.
LOCATION SOURCES: Academy of Motion Picture Arts and Sciences.

Publication History

MAGAZINE TITLE AND TITLE CHANGES: *The Business of Film.*
VOLUME AND ISSUE DATA: Vol. I, No. 1 (November 1982 to present), monthly.

PUBLISHER AND PLACE OF PUBLICATION: Brook Press Limited, 56 Grosvenor Street, London W.1, England.
EDITOR: Elspeth Tavares.

Anthony Slide

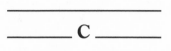

C

CAHIERS DU CINÉMA

Cahiers du Cinéma was founded in 1951 by André Bazin, perhaps France's most influential post–Second World War film critic, and Jacques Doniol-Valcroze. Both men had been editors of an earlier journal, the glossy and prestigious *La Revue du Cinéma*, which had a brief flowering between 1947 and 1950. Its successor, *Cahiers du Cinéma*, maintained the earlier journal's overall appearance, including its yellow cover in the initial issues, and carried over a number of its writers, including Lotte Eisner, Henri Langlois, and Bazin himself. Soon, however, the increasing prestige of the journal attracted a new breed of writer. Jacques Rivette, Eric Rohmer, and Jean-Luc Godard came over from the short-lived tabloid *Gazette du Cinéma* and were joined by others such as Claude Chabrol from the publicity department of the Paris bureau of Twentieth Century-Fox, and Bazin's own protege, François Truffaut.

In January 1954, these younger writers led by Truffaut, who was rapidly gaining a reputation as the most caustic of the new critics, succeeded in giving the journal a distinct identity and editorial position. In an article entitled *"Une certaine tendence du cinéma français,"* Truffaut attacked the traditional orientation of the French cinema and advocated *"cinéma d'auteur"* which would view film as a work of art and as a reflection of the personality of its creator. Adhering to this auteur theory, subsequent criticism in *Cahiers du Cinéma* treated individual films regardless of their own merit as integral parts of a director's larger body of work and thus of certain significance. In the years between 1954 and 1968, the journal was heavily biased toward the work of about thirty-five directors who could conceivably qualify as auteurs. Although the list was primarily oriented toward the French cinema and the giants of other countries, a few surprising entries such as Jerry Lewis and Sam Fuller were treated with greater respect than by critics in their own country.

Inevitably, the critiques became more and more prescriptive and were less reflective of actual films than of potential films. Truffaut, Godard, Rivette, and Rohmer began to experiment with their own films and in 1959 ushered in the movement known as the *"Nouvelle Vague"* (New Wave) with such films as Godard's *A Bout de souffle* (*Breathless*) and Truffaut's *Les quatre cents coups* (*The 400 Blows*). This placed the film journal in the position of first defining the aesthetic on a theoretical basis and then demonstrating it on the screen. Bazin died in 1958, but his successor continued to define the aesthetic of cinema according to auteurist theories.

Yet, by 1968, the aesthetic became less important than content. Such politically based journals as *Positif* and *Cinéthèque* began to evaluate films according to the degree in which they reflected a dialectical viewpoint and dismissed the more esoteric criticism of *Cahiers du Cinéma* as essentially bourgeois. Much of this was, of course, related to the student-worker uprising of that year which left virtually no middle ground in the arts. Consequently, the new staff of *Cahiers du Cinéma* began to reexamine the Russian film theorists of the twenties for their merging of form and content.

In the seventies the magazine merged the Russian approach with other aesthetic theories, notably the linguistic ideas of Christian Metz, and with other political theories reflective of the emerging French artistic environment. By 1973, *Cahiers du Cinéma* defined itself as Marxist-Leninist but did not really take a rigid position other than tentatively reaching out to other revolutionary elements in French culture. Today it continues its concentration on French and American films but has broadened its coverage of Third-World cinema. It still attempts to be a prescriptive force guiding the work of filmmakers, but its thrust is revolutionary and ideological rather than aesthetic, which has reduced its appeal for the general readership once envisioned by Bazin. It published a short-lived English-language edition from 1966 to 1967.

Information Sources

BIBLIOGRAPHY:

Browne, Nick. *"Cahiers du Cinéma*'s Re-reading of Hollywood Cinema: An Analysis of Method." *Quarterly Review of Film Studies,* Summer 1978, pp. 405–416.

"Cahiers buff bible, marks 30th; gave birth to auteur theory." *Variety,* July 1, 1981, p. 33.

Daney, S., and Taubiana, S. "Editorial." *Cahiers du Cinéma,* February 1978, pp. 4–5.

Guynn, W. "The Political Program of *Cahiers du Cinéma,* 1969–1977." *Jump Cut,* April 1978, pp. 32–35.

Spellerberg, I. "Technology and Ideology in the Cinema." *Quarterly Review of Film Studies,* August 1977, pp. 288–301.

Taubiana, S. "Special Event: *Cahiers du Cinéma*." *Thousand Eyes,* 1978, p. 5.

Turin, Maureen. "The Aesthetic Becomes Political: A History of Film Criticism in *Cahiers du Cinéma*." *Velvet Light Trap,* No. 9 (Summer 1973), pp. 13–17.

INDEX SOURCES: Current Contents; FIAF International Index to Film Periodicals; Film
    Literature Index.
REPRINT EDITIONS: AMS.
LOCATION SOURCES: Art Institute of Chicago; Columbia University; Dartmouth Col-
    lege; Indiana University; New York Public Library; Smithsonian Institution; Uni-
    versity of California at Los Angeles; University of Colorado; University of Southern
    California.

Publication History

MAGAZINE TITLE AND TITLE CHANGES: *Cahiers du Cinéma.*
VOLUME AND ISSUE DATA: Vol. I, No. 1 (April 1951 to present), monthly.
PUBLISHER AND PLACE OF PUBLICATION: Edition de L'Etoile, 9 Passage de la
    Boulevard Blanche, 75012 Paris, France.
EDITOR: André Bazin (1951–1958); Jacques Doniol-Valcroze and Eric Rohmer (1959–
    1964); Jean Louis Ginibre (1967–1972); Jacques Aumont (1973–1977); Serge
    Daney and Serge Taubiana (1978 to present).

Stephen L. Hanson

CAHIERS DU CINÉMA IN ENGLISH

Here was a noble, if futile, attempt to publish an English-language edition
of the popular French critical journal, *Cahiers du Cinéma.** The first issue
(January 1966) featured what editor Andrew Sarris considered some of the best
articles from back issues of *Cahiers du Cinéma*: "On the Politique des Auteurs"
by André Bazin; an interview with Michelangelo Antonioni by Jean-Luc Godard;
"My Experience" by Max Ophuls, and so forth. Later issues reprinted pieces
from the French jounal but also included some new articles, all of which tended
to demonstrate the somewhat conservative attitude of the English edition's editor.
Happily, Sarris proved himself a competent editor who had the good sense always
to indicate the number of *Cahiers du Cinéma* in which the article originally
appeared and generally to include articles and filmographies which had no English-language counterpart. The journal ceased publication in December 1967.

Information Sources

INDEX SOURCES: The New Film Index.
REPRINT EDITIONS: None.
LOCATION SOURCES: Academy of Motion Picture Arts and Sciences; Art Institute of
    Chicago; Cornell University; Ohio University; Princeton University; University
    of Arkansas; University of Iowa; University of Oregon; University of Southern
    California; University of Virginia.

Publication History

MAGAZINE TITLE AND TITLE CHANGES: *Cahiers du Cinéma in English.*
VOLUME AND ISSUE DATA: Nos. 1–6 (January 1966–December 1966), bimonthly;
    Nos. 7–9 (January 1967–March 1967), monthly; No. 10 (May 1967); No. 11
    (September 1967); No. 12 (December 1967).

PUBLISHER AND PLACE OF PUBLICATION: Joseph Weill, 635 Madison Avenue,
    New York, N.Y. 10022.
EDITOR: Andrew Sarris.

Anthony Slide

THE CALL BOARD. See Appendix 1

CAMERA OBSCURA

Each issue of *Camera Obscura*, which began publication in the autumn of
1976, has the look of a quality paperback book of between 150 and 250 pages.
The subject matter is feminism and film theory, with many of the essays purely
analytical in content, such as "The Avant-Garde and Its Imaginary" by Constance Penley (No. 2), "Feminine Discourse in *Christopher Strong*" by Jacquelyn
Suter (Nos. 3–4), and "*Now Voyager*: Some Problems of Enunciation and Sexual
Difference" by Lea Jacobs (No. 7). However, *Camera Obscura* has also published some major reference articles, notably "Women Filmmakers in West
Germany: A Catalog" by Marc Silberman (No. 6).

Information Sources

INDEX SOURCES: Arts and Humanities Citation Index; Current Contents/Arts and
    Humanities; FIAF International Index to Film Periodicals; Film Literature Index.
REPRINT EDITIONS: None.
LOCATION SOURCES: Academy of Motion Picture Arts and Sciences; Northwestern
    University; Stanford University Libraries; University of California at Los Angeles;
    University of Iowa; University of Southern California.

Publication History

MAGAZINE TITLE AND TITLE CHANGES: *Camera Obscura*.
VOLUME AND ISSUE DATA: No. 1 (Fall 1976); No. 2 (Fall 1977); No. 3-4 (Summer
    1979); No. 5 (Spring 1980); No. 6 (Fall 1980); No. 7 (Spring 1981); No. 8-9-10
    (Fall 1982).
PUBLISHER AND PLACE OF PUBLICATION: Camera Obscura Collective, P.O. Box
    4517, Berkeley, Calif. 94704 (Nos. 1–7); Camera Obscura Collective, P.O. Box
    25899, Los Angeles, Calif. 90025 (No. 8-9-10 to present).
EDITOR: Camera Obscura Collective.

Anthony Slide

CANTRILLS FILMNOTES

A unique Australian periodical devoted to independent and experimental cinema, *Cantrills Filmnotes* is edited and published by filmmakers Arthur and
Corinne Cantrill,[1] quite obviously as a labor of love. Despite its title, the mag-

azine does not heavily feature the work of the Cantrills, and the couple generally only interject themselves into the journal with notes on film festivals they have visited or with interviews (for which they seldom take credit).

Founded in 1971 and printed in mimeograph form during its first year, *Cantrills Filmnotes* offers articles, interviews and reviews on films and filmmakers about which information is almost nonexistent elsewhere. Among the filmmakers included have been John Phillips (No. 7), Mike Kuchar (No. 10), Peter Kingston (No. 11), Woody and Steina Vasulka (No. 13), Robert Wyatt (Nos. 14 and 15), Paul Winkler (No. 19), Byron Black (No. 20), James Clayden (Nos. 23 and 24), Michael Glasheen (Nos. 27 and 28), and Pat and Dick Laster (Nos. 37 and 38). In addition, there are articles by more established figures in the independent filmmaking field, including Lenny Lipton, Gregory Markopoulos, and Stan Brakhage; book reviews; and even an occasional historical piece (usually limited to Australian cinema).

With its unique contents, unusual shape (10 1/2" wide by 8 1/4" high), its heavy reliance on frame enlargements rather than posed still photographs, and its irregular, indefinable schedule (six issues in 1971 and only one in 1977), *Cantrills Filmnotes* is a small-circulation, specialist publication deserving of greater fame.

Notes

1. For more information on Arthur and Corinne Cantrill see an interview with them in *Cinema Papers*,* May-June 1979, pp. 359–361,400, 403.

Information Sources

INDEX SOURCES: None.
REPRINT EDITIONS: None.
LOCATION SOURCES: Academy of Motion Picture Arts and Sciences; Anthology Film Archives; International Museum of Photography at George Eastman House; Library of Congress; Museum of Modern Art; Pennsylvania State University; Sarah Lawrence College; University of California at Los Angeles; University of Oklahoma; University of Texas; University of Wisconsin at Madison; Wright State University; Yale University.

Publication History

MAGAZINE TITLE AND TITLE CHANGES: *Cantrills Filmnotes*.
VOLUME AND ISSUE DATA: No. 1 (March 1971 to present), irregular but presently biannual.
PUBLISHER AND PLACE OF PUBLICATION: Arthur and Corinne Cantrill, Box 1295L, G.P.O., Melbourne, Victoria 3001, Australia.

EDITOR: Arthur and Corinne Cantrill.

Anthony Slide

CHAD'S QUARTERLY. See Appendix 1

CHANNELS

The start of the eighties ushered in a new era in the history of television. The rise of new technologies, modes of transmission, government and private interest group pressure have all brought about massive changes in the nature of telecasting and the ways in which society relates to its most pervasive and powerful medium of communications.

Channels magazine, which first appeared in April/May 1981 and has been published bimonthly ever since, is the brainchild of the Media Commentary Council, Inc., a not-for-profit corporation created by the Markle Foundation for the purpose of helping us to understand and deal with this revolution in communications.

The editors of *Channels* have long recognized that television is one of the most important forces in our social, political, and cultural world. *Channels* was designed to inquire into the ways in which television affects our lives and how it is changing our political system, the ways in which we are bought and sold, and what it is doing to our children. It is directed at those people more interested in what television does to our society than in what it shows on the screen. It is "devoted to ideas, thoughtful analysis and investigative reporting" and is concerned not with T.V.'s past but rather with the medium's future and how it will shape our world in the coming years.

Channels' premiere issue featured the first of editor Les Brown's regular "Public Eye" columns. Brown, the former T.V. correspondent of *The New York Times*, T.V. editor of *Variety*,* and author of *The Business Behind the Box* and the *New York Times Encyclopedia of Television*, is one of America's foremost television analysts and critics. His challenging and liberal political stance has become the focus of *Channels'* editorial slant and has made the magazine a leader in the analysis of the medium.

Foremost in the listing of *Channels'* accomplishments is its annual "Field Guide to the Electronic Media," special issues that educate readers to the newest developments in the video environment. These field guides are designed to demystify and dispel fears of the new technologies by analyzing all aspects of the recent video boom. Thus each guide deals with such areas as cable, satellites, pay T.V., videotex, home video, and computers, and the latest advances in high-definition T.V., stereo T.V., fiber optics, cellular radio, and low-power T.V. In addition, space is devoted to the new powers-that-be in pay and cable T.V.;

a glossary of terms that familiarizes readers with new and often confusing jargon; and a complete comparison of the many and varied pay and cable channels.

Many issues are devoted to examining specialized areas of concern. Vol. 3, No. 1, offers a special report on T.V. talk shows; Vol. 3, No. 2, analyzes "Cable at the Crossroads"; while Vol. 3, No. 3's "At the Threshold of 1984" provides two views on the coming of that watershed year by Peter C. T. Ellsworth and Peter Mareth. One of *Channels'* most insightful pieces appeared in Vol. 1, No. 6. "The Second American Revolution" by Benjamin Barber discussed at length how the "wired republic" may prove hazardous to democracy. The same issue offered "The New World," a description of how the new technologies are affecting many diverse areas of our society.

Channels does not limit its investigations to television in America but increases our awareness of T.V. around the world. *Channels* has provided articles on T.V. in Poland (Vol. 1, No. 4), the Arab world (Vol. 2, No. 5), Nicaragua (Vol. 3, No. 3), and Mexico (Vol. 3, No. 2). Also, *Channels* has delved into nonbroadcast areas, typified by Steven Levy's "Fantastic Worlds: Inside the Computer Game" (Vol. 3, No. 4).

Information Sources

INDEX SOURCES: FIAF International Index to Television Periodicals.
REPRINT EDITIONS: None.
LOCATION SOURCES: Library of Congress; University of California at Los Angeles (incomplete).

Publication History

MAGAZINE TITLE AND TITLE CHANGES: *Channels*.
VOLUME AND ISSUE DATA: Vol. I, No. 1 (April/May 1981 to present), bimonthly.
PUBLISHER AND PLACE OF PUBLICATION: The Media Commentary Council, Inc.,
    1515 Broadway, New York, N.Y. 10036
EDITOR: Les Brown.

Daniel Einstein

CHAPLIN

The Swedish publication *Chaplin* is the largest film magazine in northern Europe, with a reported circulation of over nine thousand. It was founded in 1959 by Bengt Forslund as an independent film magazine and remained so until its takeover in 1965 by the Swedish Film Institute.

The expressed aims of *Chaplin* are to discuss the role of film in society; to spread information about film; to analyze and discuss the function of film and its specific means of expression.[1] Although each issue usually contains material on world cinema, the preponderance of articles in *Chaplin* are concerned with filmmaking in Scandinavia. The magazine regularly features film reviews, and there is also the occasional book review.

Notes

1. Marieanne Broddesson Utku in a letter to the editor, dated December 15, 1983.

Information Sources

INDEX SOURCES: FIAF International Index to Film Periodicals; Film Literature Index. REPRINT EDITIONS: None.
LOCATION SOURCES: New York Public Library (incomplete); University of California at Los Angeles (incomplete); University of Iowa (incomplete); University of Southern California (incomplete).

Publication History

MAGAZINE TITLE AND TITLE CHANGES: *Chaplin*.
VOLUME AND ISSUE DATA: April 1959–December 1959, six issues a year; 1960–1974, nine issues a year; 1975 to present, six issues a year.
PUBLISHER AND PLACE OF PUBLICATION: Svenska Filminstitutet, Filmhuset Borgvägen, Box 27126, 10252 Stockholm 27, Sweden (1965 to present).
EDITOR: Lars Åhlander (current).

Anthony Slide

CHARLES RAY'S HOLLYWOOD DIGEST. See Appendix 1

CHARM. See Appendix 2

CHINA'S SCREEN. See Appendix 4

CINEASTE

The first issue of *Cineaste* appeared in the summer of 1967 when founding editor Gary Crowdus, then a film student at New York University, mimeographed and stapled the magazine's first print run of five hundred copies. This issue was circulated to filmmakers and film students throughout the country, soliciting a small number of paid subscriptions and establishing contact with writers who would contribute to subsequent issues.

For its first two years, *Cineaste* was subtitled "A Magazine for the Film Student," and it reflected the concerns of film students and educators as well as independent filmmakers. Articles covered new film equipment and technical matters as well as film criticism, and these were largely student-written. But as the early anti–Vietnam War protest years galvanized many students, Crowdus's own political radicalization began to be reflected in the magazine. The decision was made to reorient *Cineaste*'s editorial position, and in the Fall 1969 issue, *Cineaste* became a political magazine.

This was the first, tentative effort in the United States at this time to determine what a political film magazine might be. Foreign film publications like *Cahiers du Cinéma** in France were experiencing a similar transformation. *Cineaste*'s premiere "political" issue featured the first U.S. interview with Fernando Solanas and Octavio Getino, codirectors of the now-classic four-and-a-half-hour Argentine agit-prop epic, *The Hour of the Furnaces*. It also included an *Easy Rider* cover along with an upbeat report on the youth "revolution" underway in Hollywood.

Editorially, the major difficulty at the time was finding writers who could not only write well but who also possessed a working knowledge of film, sharp, critical faculties, and a leftist political viewpoint. In 1970 Crowdus invited Dan Georgakas and Lenny Rubenstein to join a newly formed editorial board. Today, these three continue to guide the magazine's editorial direction. In addition, contributing editors and international editors have lent special expertise and geographical range to the magazine's scope.

Cineaste has specialized in publishing film criticism, interviews, and essays which consider the cinema's social, political, and economic context. Initially the editors set out to provide an alternative to the then-predominant textual or self-enclosed, purely aesthetic criticism of film by offering a broader, contextual social analysis of the cinema. The magazine's viewpoint was distinctly Marxist but nonsectarian to avoid the obscurity which support of any one polemical tendency might confer. The trick was to keep the writing free of rhetoric and Marxist jargon, always stressing good writing. The editors avoided articles overly academic, esoterically theoretical, or excessively film-buff oriented. They strove to be sensitive to the aesthetics and craft of filmmaking, concerns which many Marxists neglected in an overemphasis on ideology defined by plot lines and character analysis. They eschewed blanket approval for left-wing films, refusing to lower their critical standards "simply because we are on the same side of the barricades."

To reach a broader, non-Marxist audience, *Cineaste* resolved not to publish polemical editorials, manifestos or position papers on political issues or debate with other leftist organization and cultural publications. Rather, the magazine concentrated on broadening support for a leftist analysis of film and culture, providing a Marxist perspective on the cinema in popular, readable format.

Cineaste is well known for its insightful interviews with filmmakers. The aim has been to give a voice to the artists themselves, to give the creators equal space with the critics, to allow the reader to understand what the artist's intentions are with a work and how artistic problems are dealt with. *Cineaste* interviews also serve almost as a data bank from which critics and other writers can draw for subsequent analysis. Some of the foremost international filmmakers on the left have been featured, including Costa-Gavras, Gillo Pontecorvo, Bernardo Bertolucci, Joris Ivens, Lina Wertmüller, Francesco Rosi, and R. W. Fassbinder, among others. In addition, interviews with leading film production collectives such as Cine Manifest, Kartemquin, and the Mariposa Film Group have appeared.

All the editorial and business work of *Cineaste* is done on a part-time basis. The magazine is self-supporting, deriving its income from subscriptions, newsstand sales, and advertising. However, timely grants from the New York State Council on the Arts through the Coordinating Council of Literary Magazines have helped pay production costs. Contributing editors and freelance writers receive token payments. The present circulation is six thousand.

In 1982 a new format appeared, beginning with Vol. 11, No. 4. Then, in 1983, the editors expanded coverage of independent films, in particular establishing a regular feature on 16mm titles. Since the mid-seventies *Cineaste* has published a variety of pamphlets. The magazine's first book appeared in 1983, *The Cineaste Interviews*, a collection of some of the best interviews published by *Cineaste*.

Information Sources

BIBLIOGRAPHY:
"Editorial: A Little History," *Cineaste*, Vol. IX, No. 1 (Fall 1978), p. 2–3.
Georgakas, Dan, and Rubenstein, Lenny. *The Cineaste Interviews* (Lake View Press, 1983).
INDEX SOURCES: Alternative Press Index; The Critical Index; FIAF International Index to Film Periodicals; Film Literature Index; The New Film Index; Retrospective Index to Film Periodicals.
REPRINT EDITIONS: University Microfilms.
LOCATION SOURCES: Academy of Motion Picture Arts and Sciences (lacks some early issues); Library of Congress; Museum of Modern Art; University of Illinois; University of Southern California; University of Washington.

Publication History

MAGAZINE TITLE AND TITLE CHANGES: *Cineaste*.
VOLUME AND ISSUE DATA: Vol. I, No. 1 (Summer 1967 to present), quarterly.
PUBLISHER AND PLACE OF PUBLICATION: Cineaste, Inc., 27 West Eleventh Street, New York, N.Y. 10011 (Vol. I, No. 1–Vol. III, No. 2); Cineaste, Inc., 144 Bleecker Street, New York, N.Y. 10012 (Vol. III, No. 3–Vol. V, No. 2); Cineaste, Inc., 244 West Twenty-seventh Street, New York, N.Y. 10001 (Vol. V, No. 3–Vol. VI, No. 2); Cineaste, Inc., 333 Sixth Avenue, New York, N.Y. 10014 (Vol. VI, No. 3–Vol. IX, No. 4); Cineaste, Inc., 419 Park Avenue South, New York, N.Y. 10016 (Vol. X, No. 1–Vol. XII, No. 4); Cineaste, Inc., 200 Park Avenue South, New York, N.Y. 10003 (Vol. XIII, No. 1 to present).

EDITOR: Gary Crowdus (1967–1970); Editorial Board of Gary Crowdus, Dan Georgakas, and Lenny Rubenstein (1970 to present).

Deirdre Boyle

CINEFANTASTIQUE

Cinefantastique started out as a biweekly mimeographed newsletter in 1967 when its editor, Frederick S. Clarke, was a college freshman. It ceased after five publications. The magazine, in its present format, was first published in November 1970 with Clarke as its publisher and editor. This magazine is intelligently written and glossy, with approximately twenty thousand subscribers, the majority of whom are between the ages of twenty-five and thirty-four and, according to the magazine's demographic survey, are made up of middle- and upper-middle-class readers. *Cinefantastique* can boast that 33 percent of its subscribers have had four years of college, 21 percent are students, 14 percent are professionals, and 12 percent are in the writing and/or publishing business. The magazine also has a group of correspondents who assist Clarke and who are located in the major film capitals: New York, California (Los Angeles), the United Kingdom (London), and France (Paris), and the magazine has even sent writers to places like Madrid (to cover the filming of *Conan the Barbarian* [Vol. 12, Nos. 2 and 3]).

There is no other magazine within the genre (including *Starlog* and *Famous Monsters*) that can match *Cinefantastique*'s in-depth reportage and sophisticated stance on films dealing with horror, fantasy, and science fiction (S.F.). In the first issue, Clarke described the philosophy of the magazine in an article entitled "How's Your Sense of Wonder?" The style was disarmingly unpretentious and openly antagonistic to "art" critics (the "intellectual eunuchs" as Clarke described them) who didn't consider the genre "art." In the second issue (Winter 1971) Clarke agreed that the area covered by the magazine was quite broad so that although readers seemed to find a problem in what constituted S.F., fantasy, and horror, Clarke had no problem including in that issue such diverse films as *Brewster McCloud*, *Scrooge*, and *On a Clear Day You Can See Forever*, as well as *Taste the Blood of Dracula*.

Clarke has managed to retain this sense of wonder in all subsequent issues in a style that has moved from more idiosyncratic writing to homogenized and slick by combining well-documented reportage with intellectually provoking articles that are more evaluative rather than simply descriptive.

The breakdown of the contents of any given issue falls into three general categories: (1) feature articles (three or four per issue) dealing with film aesthetics (present films as well as those in retrospect), directors (contemporary as well as pioneers), special effect technique, and in-depth interviews; (2) reviews of current films in the field (the emphasis is again on evaluating the film rather than a plot summary with a few comments); and (3) departments (for example, an editorial by Clarke, letters, capsule reviews of films, and previews of films not yet in release). Some of the magazine's reporting on films still in production has gotten *Cinefantastique* in trouble as well as free publicity when, for instance, the plot of *Return of the Jedi* was revealed before the film was in official release (June/July 1983, Vol. 13, No. 5).

Along with the magazine's abundant use of photos, it has increased its use of color plates and color graphics since the spring of 1972. Frequently, major portions of the magazine since its inception have been devoted to directors like Terence Fisher (Vol. 4, No. 3), mass-audience-appeal films like *Planet of the Apes* (Summer 1972), special effects as in *Star Wars* (Vol. 6, No. 4, and Vol. 7, No. 1), an actor in the field such as Christopher Lee (Vol. 3, No. 1), retrospect films such as *The Day the Earth Stood Still* (Vol. 4, No. 4) and *War of the Worlds* (Vol. 5, No. 4), as well major contributors to the art of the film like Ray Harryhausen (Vol. 11, No. 4).

Information Sources

INDEX SOURCES: Film Literature Index.
REPRINT EDITIONS: None.
LOCATION SOURCES: Academy of Motion Picture Arts and Sciences; Library of Congress; University of Oregon.

Publication History

MAGAZINE TITLE AND TITLE CHANGES: *Cinefantastique*.
VOLUME AND ISSUE DATA: Vol. I, No. 1–Vol. XI, No. 4 (Fall 1970–December 1981), quarterly; Vol. XII, No. 1 (February 1982 to present), bimonthly.
PUBLISHER AND PLACE OF PUBLICATION: Frederick S. Clarke, P.O. Box 270, Oak Park, Ill. 60303.
EDITOR: Frederick S. Clarke.

Michael Sevastakis

CINEFEX

A sumptuously illustrated (the majority of the photographs are in color) journal begun in 1980 and devoted to special effects, *Cinefex* provides a unique blend of "fan" worship with technical know-how. Each issue is concerned with one or two current motion pictures, such as *Blade Runner* (No. 9) and *Return of the Jedi* (No. 13), with the issues discussing both the films and those involved in the creation of their special effects. *Cinefex* has shown only minimal interest in the history of special effects, although it did interview Ray Harryhausen in No. 5, and the entire contents of No. 7 were devoted to Willis O'Brien. The latter's seventy pages possibly provided more information on the subject than any book could offer, which is one of the joys of *Cinefex*—each number is practically a book in itself and priced at under five dollars per copy.

Information Sources

INDEX SOURCES: FIAF International Index to Film Periodicals (1983 to present); Film Literature Index; Science Fiction Research Index.
REPRINT EDITIONS: None.
LOCATION SOURCES: Academy of Motion Picture Arts and Sciences; Brooklyn Center for the Performing Arts; Burbank Public Library; Library of Congress; Rauh Memorial Library, Indianapolis; Texas A&M University; University of California at Los Angeles.

Publication History

MAGAZINE TITLE AND TITLE CHANGES: *Cinefex.*
VOLUME AND ISSUE DATA: No. 1 (March 1980); No. 2 (August 1980 to present), quarterly.
PUBLISHER AND PLACE OF PUBLICATION: Don Shay, P.O. Box 20027, Riverside, Calif. 92516.
EDITOR: Don Shay.

Anthony Slide

THE CINEGOER

A short-lived weekly of 1916, printed on glossy paper, *The Cinegoer* appears to have been published as a promotional vehicle for the films and stars of the Pathé Company. Its pages were replete with pieces on Pearl White, Ruth Roland, and Baby Marie Osborne.

Information Sources

INDEX SOURCES: None.
REPRINT EDITIONS: None.
LOCATION SOURCES: No information.

Publication History

MAGAZINE TITLE AND TITLE CHANGES: *The Cinegoer.*
VOLUME AND ISSUE DATA: Nos. 1–11 (February 26, 1916–May 6, 1916), weekly. [Date of last issue unconfirmed.]
PUBLISHER AND PLACE OF PUBLICATION: The Cinegoer, Imperial House, Kingsway, London, England.
EDITOR: Charles Frederick Higham.

Thomas A. Johnson

THE CINEMA (1913–1957). See SCREEN INTERNATIONAL

CINEMA

Subtitled "The Magazine of the Photoplay," *Cinema* was a quality "fan" journal featuring occasional covers by Alberto Vargas; superior film reviews by editor James Shelley Hamilton; and major, virtually uncited articles. Among the last were "The Rise and Fall of the German Cinema" by Harry Alan Potamkin (Vol. 1, No. 3), "A Plea for Pies" by Pare Lorentz (Vol. 1, No. 4), "The Cinema in Great Britain" by Harry Alan Potamkin (Vol. 1, No. 4), "Miracles and Dreams" by E. E. Cummings (Vol. 1, No. 5), "Good, Bad and Corporate Taste" by Pare Lorentz (Vol. 1, No. 5), and "Cinema Iberia" by Harry Alan Potamkin (Vol. 1, No. 8). In addition, *Cinema* during its one year of existence published a series of articles by Merritt Crawford, "Men in the Movie Vanguard," dealing with such film pioneers as Eugene Lauste and Louis Aimé Augustin Le Prince.

Information Sources

INDEX SOURCES: The Film Index.
REPRINT EDITIONS: None.
LOCATION SOURCES: Academy of Motion Picture Arts and Sciences (incomplete); New York Public Library.

Publication History

MAGAZINE TITLE AND TITLE CHANGES: *Cinema*.
VOLUME AND ISSUE DATA: Vol. 1, No. 1–Vol. 1, No. 8 (January–December 1930), monthly.
PUBLISHER AND PLACE OF PUBLICATION: Cinema Magazine Publishing Company, Inc., 11 West Forty-second Street, New York, N.Y.
EDITOR: James Shelley Hamilton.

Anthony Slide

CINEMA (1947)

Subtitled "The Magazine for Discriminating Movie-Goers," *Cinema* appeared for three issues—June, July, and August—in 1947. Lewis Jacobs remembers the history of the publication:

The editor and publisher, Eli Willis (Wilentz), is my brother-in-law. In late '46 or early '47, Eli came to live with us. He had just been discharged from the army in California and we were living at that time in Hollywood. I had been a screenwriter at M-G-M and assistant story editor at Columbia as well as a producer in charge of training young novelists and playwrights in screenwriting. Eli, reluctant to take a job in the work he had been trained for—architectural draftsman—and because of his intense interest in photography, began to write on photography and photographers on a free lance basis. A number of photo journals accepted his articles and prompted him to consider the idea of publishing a photomagazine. In discussing the matter with me, I believe I persuaded him to try a film journal instead, promising him all the help I could provide.

The magazine *Cinema* was born and published from my back yard, where I had erected a pre-fab building as a sort of photoworkshop and lab. Most of the editorial board and correspondents were people I asked him to contact. One of the editorial assistants was my wife. I helped with the editorial chores and layout at night after my own work at the studio and on weekends. As I recall, Dana Kingsley was one of my then pseudonyms. Eli paid for the printing and distribution of the magazine. 2,500 copies of each issue were printed. Subscriptions were few; most of the copies were sent on consignment to bookstores around the country. Very few shops ever paid for copies sold; none returned unsold copies. With little money coming in from the venture, Eli decided to abandon the project after six or seven months, and went to New York.[1]

The list of contributors to *Cinema* is impressive, including Terry Ramsaye, Jean Cocteau, Richard Griffith, and Hortense Powdermaker. Roger Manvell wrote from London on British films, while Herman G. Weinberg reviewed the latest foreign-language releases.

Notes
1. Lewis Jacobs in a letter to the editor, dated September 15, 1983.

Information Sources
INDEX SOURCES: None.
REPRINT EDITIONS: None.
LOCATION SOURCES: Academy of Motion Picture Arts and Sciences; New York Public Library; Princeton University; University of Washington.

Publication History
MAGAZINE TITLE AND TITLE CHANGES: *Cinema*.
VOLUME AND ISSUE DATA: Vol. I, No. 1 (June 1947); Vol. I, No. 2 (July 1947); Vol. I, No. 3 (August 1947).
PUBLISHER AND PLACE OF PUBLICATION: Avant Film Publications, 8066 Beverly Boulevard, Hollywood 36, Calif.
EDITOR: Eli Willis and Dana Kingsley.

Anthony Slide

CINEMA (1962–1976)

While it may seem strange that very few film magazines have been published in Los Angeles, one need only to remember that L.A. is as much a company town as Detroit or Pittsburgh to understand the reason. Any journal which publishes in Los Angeles has to acknowledge the existence and temptations of the film industry in a way in which other film magazines do not. It is this fact which accounts for the direction, or lack of it, which *Cinema* initially exhibited upon its founding in 1962.

It was immediately apparent that *Cinema* was not interested in academic criticism or, in fact, criticism of any kind. What did concern the editor was the graphic look of the magazine. That and young actresses. The former tendency was summed up by James Silke, the initial editor, in the first issue. *Cinema* was to be "a graphic magazine of information on the diverse world of film entertainment . . . the types of film selected for review will be based on no single artistic standard, have no basic geographical origin, nor be aimed at any one audience."[1] As befitted a "graphic" magazine, the first few issues were characterized by a large number of stills with very little text, and what text was offered usually had no writer's name attached. As for the second characteristic, photo essays on actresses (Yvette Mimieux and Brigitte Bardot in Vol. 1, No. 2; Carol Lynley in Vol. 1, No. 5; and so on) fit in well with a policy in which the *look* of the magazine was most important.

However, while the magazine may have appeared only to be serving up publicity for the Hollywood industry, other tendencies were apparent within the journal, such as regular reviews of foreign films (*The Bad Sleep Well* and *Last Year at Marienbad* in the first issue). Some notice was also paid to independent films, such as *The Connection* and *Night Tide* in the second issue. Basically, though, *Cinema* had no clear focus (except to feature at least one young actress in each issue) until it discovered auteurism. As an editorial declared, "*Cinema* regards the principle of individualism as the source of creativity. Having applied that principle to the movies and singled out the director as the principal individual in motion picture creation, we have extended the pages of this magazine to the director as a platform for their [*sic*] own opinions."[2]

It was, though, a curious type of auteurism practiced by the magazine. Having decided that the director was the main creative force, no attempt was made to defend the statement or to prove it through career articles. Instead, *Cinema* concentrated on interviews with directors such as Hitchcock and Kurosawa (Vol. 1, No. 5), Howard Hawks (Vol. 1, No. 6), and Fred Zinnemann (Vol. 2, No. 3) without any attempt to assess the importance of their films. This orientation changed somewhat when Curtis Lee Hanson became editor with Vol. 2, No. 6, but in the direction of closer ties to the film industry and farther away from any critical inquiry. His approach was exemplified by the topic of the first issue he edited, which was devoted to the upcoming films of Martin Ransahoff and his career as a producer, as discovered through interviews.

Under Hanson the magazine became standardized, with each issue consisting of interviews, previews of new films, and a photo essay devoted either to a young actress (such as Samantha Eggar in Vol. 3, No. 2) or to a specific group of actresses (for example, "the vamp" in Vol. 3, No. 3). While there was the odd critical or historical article which was published during this period (on Andy Warhol in Vol. 3, No. 6; the script to *The Gold Rush* in Vol. 4, No. 2; the shutdown of the Cannes Film Festival in Vol. 4, No. 3), and while the interviews were often informative, for the most part *Cinema* had become little more than a high-grade fan magazine.

After Hanson left the editorship in 1968, the magazine began to change direction again, with more and more critical and historical articles appearing among the interviews and photo essays. For a while the editors permitted an uneasy mixture of articles, such as that on the "pin-up" throughout movie history and the one on the Motion Picture Association of America (MPAA) Ratings Board (Vol. 5, No. 2); or an interview with Marlo Thomas, an article on comic strip heroes in film, and an article on Karl Freund (all in Vol. 5, No. 4). This type of mixture changed when Paul Schrader became editor in 1970 and abruptly made *Cinema* a journal of critical inquiry.

Where the magazine had been an instrument of passive acquiescence to Hollywood throughout most of its history, Schrader published analytic and historical articles that were not bound by a reverence for American film. This attitude was plain in the first issue that he edited (Vol. 6, No. 1), which was devoted to a major exploration of Yasujiro Ozu, a special report on the rise of videotape and cartridges, and a Marxist analysis of several films dealing with politics. Where one might, with justification, have called the earlier issues of *Cinema* bland, under Schrader the magazine exhibited an excitement and partisanship which made each issue special. Whether it was an article on black American film (Vol. 6, No. 2), D. W. Griffith and Carol Dempster (Vol. 7, No. 1), Christian Metz and semiotics (Vol. 7, No. 3), or Lindsay Anderson on John Ford (Vol. 6, No. 3), there was a palpable sense that the articles were important and were written with passion. Whether you agreed or not, the magazine was interesting.

This bright period ended when Schrader resigned from the editorship to work in the film industry. Only one more issue of *Cinema* was published, and, perhaps fittingly, it reverted to the format of the earliest issues, with most of the articles consisting of little text and many photographs.

In retrospect, it becomes clear that *Cinema* paid a price for being located in Hollywood. For most of its history the magazine had no direction, as the editors reported what the industry willingly fed them (hence the preponderance of interviews). It was only during Schrader's editorship that the magazine flowered and incidentally proved that proximity to the industry does not have to intimidate analysis and criticism.

Notes

1. Vol. 1, No. 1, p. 2.
2. Vol. 1, No. 5, p. 3.

Information Sources

INDEX SOURCES: FIAF International Index to Film Periodicals; Film Literature Index; Retrospective Index to Film Periodicals 1930–1971.
REPRINT EDITIONS: University Microfilms.

LOCATION SOURCES: Academy of Motion Picture Arts and Sciences (incomplete); Harvard University; Tulane University; University of Oregon; University of Southern California.

Publication History

MAGAZINE TITLE AND TITLE CHANGES: *Cinema*.
VOLUME AND ISSUE DATA: Vol. I, No. 1–Vol. III, No. 4 (1962–December 1966), bimonthly; Vol. III, No. 5–Vol. V, No. 4 (Summer 1967–1969), quarterly; Vol. VI, No. 1–Vol, VIII, No. 2, (1970–1974), triannually; No. 35 (1976).
PUBLISHER AND PLACE OF PUBLICATION: Spectator International, Box 1309, Hollywood 28, Calif. (Vol. I, No. 1–Vol. II, No. 2); Jack Martin Hanson/Spectator International, 9641 Santa Monica Boulevard, Beverly Hills, Calif. 90211 (Vol. II, No. 3–Vol. III, No. 3); Jack Martin Hanson/Spectator International, 9667 Wilshire Boulevard, Beverly Hills, Calif. 90212 (Vol. III, No. 4–Vol. IV, No. 3); Jack Martin Hanson/Spectator International, 9641 Santa Monica Boulevard, Beverly Hills, Calif. 90211 (Vol. IV, No. 4); Jack Martin Hanson/Spectator International, 9667 Wilshire Boulevard, Beverly Hills, Calif. 90212 (Vol. V, No. 1–Vol. VIII, No. 2); Jack Martin Hanson/Spectator International, 307 North Rodeo Drive, Beverly Hills, Calif. 90212 (No. 35).
EDITOR: James R. Silke (1962–1965); Curtis Lee Hanson (1965–1968); Grace Nagata (1968); Michael Lindsay (1968–1969); Paul Schrader (1970–1972); Stephen Mamber (1972–1973); Paul Schrader (1973–1974); Arlene Friedman and Sandy Brown Wyeth (1976).

Val Almendarez

CINEMA (Romania)

Romania's *Cinema*, in publication since 1964, has a rather stable content: each issue contains an unsigned editorial which discusses various matters of movie making and reflects the official Romanian Communist Party viewpoint, as in "Tinereţea unei arte mature" (The youthfulness of a mature art; Vol. 19, No. 7) and "Munca artistului in dialog cu o ţară a muncii" (The actor's work in direct dialog with a working country; Vol. 21, No. 4). In the column "Filme noi" (New movies) new Romanian productions are analyzed. Valerian Sava wrote "Filmul Românesc" (Romanian film; Vol. 14, No. 12), and M. Pîrîianu wrote "Cinemateca română la cinemateca Franceză" (Romanian cinematheque at the French cinematheque; Vol. 17, No. 3). Very often an entire issue is dedicated to the national cinema. A decade of making feature films, documentaries, and shorts is reviewed in a sequence of interviews with established Romanian film directors and critics (Vol. 19, No. 12).

The permanent column "Opinii" (Opinions) provides an open forum for the discussion of the interrelation between film and literary aesthetics, as in Gelu Ionescu's "Film şi literatura" (Film and literature; Vol. 11, No. 8) and "Estetica fără etică?" (Aesthetics without ethics?; Vol. 11, No. 10) by Dan Comşa.

National and international film festivals are covered in "Festivalul filmului"

(Film festivals), with articles such as "Cannes" by Ecaterina Oproiu (Vol. 21, Nos. 8 and 10) and M. Mihăilescu's "Acei oameni minunaţi şi aparatele lor de filmat" (Those wonderful men and their cameras; Vol. 17, No. 5) on the Karlovy Vary film festival.

Well-known literary critics and philosophers often write articles on philosophy and film, such as "Filmul şi filosofia" (The film and philosophy), a collective interview with philosophers Ion Ianoşi, Henri Wald, and Al. Paleologu (Vol. 19, No. 11). The effect of films on the audience's social and political attitudes is given special attention, as in "Filmul artă colectivă" (The film as collective art; Vol. 18, No. 8) and in a sequence of articles and interviews with prominent Romanian writers entitled "Scriitorii români şi filmul" (Romanian writers and the film; Vol. 2, Nos. 1–2, 7–8, 10, 12, and Vol. 3, Nos. 1–2).

Cinema regularly boasts about Romanian movies shown in the West. In Vol. 21, No. 4, is found an article by Adina Darvan—"11 filme româneşti şi o retrospectivă comentate de critica italiană" (Eleven Romanian movies and a retrospective discussed by Italian critics). The journal shows a surprising permissiveness and variety in its coverage of Western and American films. It even has a foreign correspondent, Ray Arco, who periodically reports on various cinematic events as well as on the U.S.-based Oscars and Golden Globe awards, as in "Globul de aur şi primii laureaţi" (The Golden Globe and its first winners; Vol. 21, No. 3). "Cinerama," a permanent column, informs its readers on the latest French, West German, Italian, South American, and U.S. movies.

In addition, there is coverage of film books, films for television, documentaries, and brief news items on Soviet actors, films, and film directors, as well as their counterparts in other Eastern European countries.

Information Sources

INDEX SOURCES: FIAF International Index to Film Periodicals.
REPRINT EDITIONS: None.
LOCATION SOURCES: Harvard (incomplete); Library of Congress (incomplete); University of Southern California (incomplete).

Publication History

MAGAZINE TITLE AND TITLE CHANGES: *Cinema*.
VOLUME AND ISSUE DATA: Vol. I, No. 1 (1964 to present), monthly.
PUBLISHER AND PLACE OF PUBLICATION: Consiliul Culturii şi Educaţiei Socialiste, Piaţa Scînteii no. 1, Bucureşti, România.
EDITOR: Ecaterina Oproiu.

Hari S. Rorlich

CINEMA (United Kingdom)

The British *Cinema* was a short-lived magazine whose rise coincided with a new impetus in British film theory in the late sixties. Initially published in late 1968 in Cambridge, with financial assistance from the Cambridge Film Society, its concerns reflected the intellectual currents at the university.

In its first issue, *Cinema* announced its interest in "direct confrontation and contact with contemporary movements in acting, directing and aesthetics" while its articles tackled subjects as diverse as an interview with literary commentator Raymond Williams and with Peter Wollen writing "Notes Towards a Structural Analysis of the Films of Sam Fuller," Raymond Durgnat "Symbols and Modesty Blaise," and Tony Rayns "The Underground Film."

Unlike Britain's other theoretical journal of the period, *Screen,* * *Cinema* both wrote in a more accessible language and addressed film and filmmaking more directly. Articles appeared on a variety of subjects and from a diversity of viewpoints so that Clive James, Bruce Beresford, and Colin McArthur could easily write alongside one another. While part of its initial brief was to provide a "boost for new directors in British film," its articles were solidly Hollywood-oriented, with occasional pieces on European directors such as Bernardo Bertolucci and Roberto Rossellini.

The first few issues carried more general analysis like Durgnat's article "Brain Drains," but despite a brief flirtation with current film reviews (No. 8), by No. 9 (the final issue) *Cinema* had lost its eclectic approach and lapsed into auteurism, with articles on Howard Hawks, Dziga Vertov, Roberto Rossellini, and Dusan Makaveyev. Many of its writers continued to contribute to the more successful *Screen*.

Information Sources

INDEX SOURCES: The New Film Index.
REPRINT EDITIONS: World Microfilms ("Little Magazines" series).
LOCATION SOURCES: No information.

Publication History

MAGAZINE TITLE AND TITLE CHANGES: *Cinema*.
VOLUME AND ISSUE DATA: Nos. 1–9 (December 1968–February 1971), quarterly.
PUBLISHER AND PLACE OF PUBLICATION: CALL, Cambridge, England (Nos. 1–4); Halesworth Press, Halesworth, Suffolk, England (Nos. 5–7); Cinema Rising, 10-13 Little Newport Street, London W.C.2, England (Nos. 8–10).
EDITOR: Stephen Crofts and Noel Purdon (Nos. 1–3); Robert Mundy, Mike Wallington, and Tony Rayns (Nos. 4–5); Noel Purdon (Nos. 6–7); Michael Armitage and Angela Kirtland (Nos. 8–9).

Sally Hibbin

CINEMA ARTS

Perhaps the most sumptuous film magazine ever published, *Cinema Arts* first appeared in September 1936 in an oversize, spiral-bound edition. It was followed, a year later, by three additional issues, all oversize and with hard covers featuring caricatures of film personalities by Jaro Fabry. The first issue contained some pieces which had also appeared in the preview issue. On a par with the quality of artwork was the quality of the articles, written by the likes of Homer Croy, Mordaunt Hall, Kenneth Macgowan, Archibald MacLeish, Rouben Mamoulian, Frank Nugent, Helena Rubinstein, Bella and Samuel Spewack, Richard Watts, Jr., and Archer Winsten.

Information Sources

INDEX SOURCES: None.
REPRINT EDITIONS: None.
LOCATION SOURCES: Academy of Motion Picture Arts and Sciences; Columbia University; Library of Congress; New York Public Library.

Publication History

MAGAZINE TITLE AND TITLE CHANGES: *Cinema Arts*.
VOLUME AND ISSUE DATA: No. 1 (1936, preview issue "for private circulation and not for public sale"); Vol. I, No. 1 (June 1937); Vol. I, No. 2 (July 1937); Vol. I, No. 3 (September 1937).
PUBLISHER AND PLACE OF PUBLICATION: Cinema Magazine, Inc., 250 Park Avenue, New York, N.Y.
EDITOR: No editor listed (No. 1 preview issue); Paul F. Husserl (Vol. I, Nos. 1–3).

Anthony Slide

CINEMA CANADA

The declared intention of *Cinema Canada*, which was founded in 1972 by the Canadian Society of Cinematographers, was that the periodical "should serve as a forum in which issues of common concern can be debated and common policies derived or differences resolved."[1] It began life as a journal obviously aimed at the struggling independent Canadian filmmaker, but within a couple of years *Cinema Canada* had become the country's leading periodical for all interested in local film production. It features news items, interviews, book and film reviews, and festival reports (all heavily nationalistic).

There are regular reports on the Directors Guild of Canada, the Canadian Society of Cinematographers, and the Canadian Film Editors Guild. No. 9 featured a major piece on the career of Norman McLaren; No. 14 boasted a detailed study of the making of *Apprenticeship of Duddy Kravitz*; No. 51 included a section on "Women and Film" from a Canadian perspective; No. 60-61 featured a special section on Canadian film music.

With No. 73 (April 1981), *Cinema Canada* expanded in size and took on the newspaper cum magazine appearance of the Australian *Cinema Papers*.* It joined with another Canadian magazine, *CineMag*, and an editorial explained, "By combining *CineMag* with *Cinema Canada*, we are improving on what are already the best film magazines in Canada. The new format will allow us to get the news out quickly, while providing us with space to add interviews, comments, reviews and the rest."[2]

Notes

1. No. 2, May-June 1972, p. 3.
2. No. 73, April 1981, p. 4.

Information Sources

INDEX SOURCES: FIAF International Index to Film Periodicals; Film Literature Index.
REPRINT EDITIONS: None.
LOCATION SOURCES: Academy of Motion Picture Arts and Sciences (lacks early
    issues); Dartmouth College; Duke University; University of Southern California.

Publication History

MAGAZINE TITLE AND TITLE CHANGES: *Cinema Canada*.
VOLUME AND ISSUE DATA: No. 1–No. 20 (March 1972–July/August 1975), bi-
    monthly; No. 21–No. 72 (September 1975–March 1981), ten times a year; No.
    73 (April 1981 to present), monthly.
PUBLISHER AND PLACE OF PUBLICATION: Canadian Society of Cinematographers,
    22 Front Street, Toronto, Canada (No. 1); Canadian Society of Cinematographers,
    72 Isabella, No. 8, Toronto 5, Canada (Nos. 2–3); George Csaba Koller, 6
    Washington Avenue, No. 3, Toronto, Canada M5S 1L2 (Nos. 4–17); Cinema
    Canada Magazine Foundation, 406 Jarvis Street, Toronto, Canada M4Y 2G6 (Nos.
    18–39); Cinema Canada Magazine Foundation, 67 Portland Street, Toronto, On-
    tario, Canada M5V 2M9 (No. 40 to present).
EDITOR: George Csaba Koller and Philip S. McPhedran (March 1972–July/August 1972);
    George Csaba Koller (October/November 1972–December/January 1975); A.
    Ibranyi-Kiss (March/April 1975–July/August 1975); Jean-Pierre Tadros and Con-
    nie Tadros (September 1975 to present).

Anthony Slide

CINEMA CHAT

A small, pocket-size weekly published from 1919 to 1920, *Cinema Chat*
featured a ''chat'' with a leading film personality, stories adapted from current
film releases, short biographical sketches, and even shorter reviews. It is noteworthy for the splendid series of photogravure postcards of the leading film
players of the day presented free with each issue. With issue No. 68 (September
6, 1920), it combined with *Home News*, and film items were relegated to a few
pages. With issue No. 74 (October 18, 1920), it became simply *Home News*,
and by issue No. 91, it was *Dainty Novels & Home News*, a typical woman's
magazine of the period.

Information Sources

INDEX SOURCES: None.
REPRINT EDITIONS: None.
LOCATION SOURCES: No information.

Publication History

MAGAZINE TITLE AND TITLE CHANGES: *Cinema Chat*.
VOLUME AND ISSUE DATA: No. 1–No. 67 (May 26, 1919–August 30, 1920), weekly.
PUBLISHER AND PLACE OF PUBLICATION: Shurey's Publications, 17 Tudor Street,
　　London, England.
EDITOR: No editor listed.

Thomas A. Johnson

CINEMA DIGEST

Subtitled "A Symposium of Motion Picture Opinions," *Cinema Digest* provided a cold, harsh look at the film industry in the early thirties. Its contents chiefly consisted of interesting, often cynical, quotes on the industry from the likes of Sergei Eisenstein, D. W. Griffith, and Theodore Dreiser. It also reprinted editorial comments on the film industry along with reviews of current motion pictures, taken from newspapers around the country.

During *Cinema Digest*'s first year, the journal included many editorials by Tamar Lane on the problems and future of the film business. Later, editor Howard R. Hall would commence each issue with comments which were often so outspoken that in October 1932 the Hays Office refused accreditation to *Cinema Digest*, meaning it no longer had access to studio publicity outlets. Hall was equally blunt in discussing the industry's past. He did not sentimentalize, describing D. W. Griffith in the issue of May 1, 1933, as "an old-timer who has been outmoded for years.... The Griffiths should retire from the picture—and the picture business—gracefully!"

On February 27, 1933, Kansas City *Star* film critic John C. Moffitt[1] became associate editor, writing a one-page editorial initially titled "Cinema Cynicisms" and later called "Critic on the Hearth."

As far as can be ascertained, *Cinema Digest* ceased publication with the issue of June 12, 1933, and was immediately superseded by *Cinema Hall-Marks*.* The digest should not be confused with a magazine of the same title published in the late thirties and early forties by IATSE Cameramen's Local 666.

Notes

1. John C. (Jack) Moffitt (1901–1969) was the film critic in the twenties and thirties for the Kansas City *Star*, well known for his biting wit. He wrote a number of plays and was also a Hollywood screenwriter from the thirties onward. His film credits include *St. Louis Blues* (1939), *Night and Day* (1946), *Ramrod* (1947), and *The Story of Will Rogers* (1952).

Information Sources

INDEX SOURCES: None.
REPRINT EDITIONS: None.
LOCATION SOURCES: Academy of Motion Picture Arts and Sciences; New York Public
　　Library.

Publication History

MAGAZINE TITLE AND TITLE CHANGES: *Cinema Digest.*
VOLUME AND ISSUE DATA: Vol. I, No. 1–Vol. II, No. 4 (May 16, 1932–December
26, 1932), biweekly; Vol. II, No. 5–Vol. IV, No. 5 (January 9, 1933–June 12,
1933), weekly. [Date of last issue unconfirmed.]
PUBLISHER AND PLACE OF PUBLICATION: Cinema Digest Publishing Co., P.O.
Box 1911, Hollywood, Calif.
EDITOR: Howard R. Hall.

Anthony Slide

CINÉMA FRANÇAIS. See Appendix 4.

CINEMAGES

Published for only a few years in the mid-fifties, this mimeographed journal
contained writing by some very prominent authors and filmmakers. The editor
defines the publication in this way:

> *Cinemages* is a collection of periodical publications devoted to a mean-
> ingful exploration of the cinema, its history, and its trends. It is a publi-
> cation of record, and a publication of opinion. *Cinemages'* main purpose
> is to impart a sense of the cinema's significance as a major art form and
> social expression; to provide a background of historical and critical facts;
> to assist the film viewer in establishing his own criteria for judging a
> motion picture by exploring its history and the motivation of its creators,
> to create, eventually, a discriminating audience for a mature screen product.[1]

It comprises two "collections," each published over several years. The first,
containing six issues, appeared in 1955 and 1956 and included writing by Henry
Miller, Salvador Dali, Jean Cocteau, Abel Gance, William Everson, and the
editor, Gideon Bachmann, among others. One issue was on Jean Epstein, one
was composed of interviews on G. W. Pabst (with an index to his creative work),
and one special issue was a republication of the *Index on Birth of a Nation* by
Seymour Stern. The second collection appeared through 1958 and contained
three issues, although four more were planned. The three issues were a reprint
compilation and update of the first collection, a list of 1,151 film periodicals,
and unproduced scripts and treatments by Henry Miller, Maxim Gorky, Salvador
Dali, Romain Rolland, Dylan Thomas, and James Agee.

Notes

1. No. 1, 1955, p. 2.

Information Sources

INDEX SOURCES: The Critical Index.
REPRINT EDITIONS: None.
LOCATION SOURCES: Dartmouth College; Duke University; Library of Congress; New York Public Library; University of California at Los Angeles; University of Illinois.

Publication History

MAGAZINE TITLE AND TITLE CHANGES: *Cinemages*.
VOLUME AND ISSUE DATA: Nos. 1–6 plus one special issue (1955–1956) called "First Collection"; C-55, special issue 2 and No. 9 (1956–1958) called "Second Collection." [Nos. 6, 7, 8, and 10 were listed but apparently not published.]
PUBLISHER AND PLACE OF PUBLICATION: Group for Film Study, Inc., 3951 Gouverneur Avenue, New York 63, N.Y. ("First Collection"); Gideon Bachmann, 3951 Gouverneur Avenue, New York 63, N.Y. ("Second Collection").
EDITOR: Gideon Bachmann.

Nancy Allen

CINEMA HALL-MARKS

Editor Howard Hall continued the biting and cynical criticism of the film industry which he had commenced with *Cinema Digest** in *Cinema Hall-Marks*, a four-page periodical published from 1933 through 1936. Each issue contained one-paragraph film reviews, together with commentary by Hall, with headlines such as "Fox Publicity Explains Why Their Pictures Are So Lousy!" (September 10, 1934) or "What Is Nick Schenck Going to Do about Mayer?" (November 26, 1934). In addition, John C. Moffitt[1] continued the column which he had established in *Cinema Digest*. Moffitt's column disappeared in 1935, replaced with a "Post-Views" column written by Harold W. Cohen, cinema critic of the Pittsburgh *Post-Gazette*.

Notes

1. For more information on Moffitt, see the entry on *Cinema Digest*.

Information Sources

INDEX SOURCES: None.
REPRINT EDITIONS: None.
LOCATION SOURCES: Academy of Motion Picture Arts and Sciences (lacks Vol. I).

Publication History

MAGAZINE TITLE AND TITLE CHANGES: *Cinema Hall-Marks*.
VOLUME AND ISSUE DATA: Vol. I, No. 1–Vol. III, No. 28 (July 10, 1933–January 13, 1936), weekly. [Date of first and last issue unconfirmed.]

PUBLISHER AND PLACE OF PUBLICATION: Cinema Hall-Marks, P.O. Box 1911,
    Hollywood, Calif.
EDITOR: Howard R. Hall.

Anthony Slide

CINEMA JOURNAL

The historical development of *Cinema Journal* provides a complex, interesting
compass which includes some two decades of pronounced transformations. Today
it is the main publication of the Society for Cinema Studies, and throughout its
history it has always been connected with that organization's evolution.

In 1957, Professor Robert Gessner of New York University helped found the
small organization which was initially called the Society of Cinematologists
(SOC). The growth of this society over the next several years included the
institution of an annual publication, *Journal of the Society of Cinematologists*,
which would automatically print public papers presented at the Society's annual
meetings. Typewritten, double-spaced, multilithed copies were sent to the membership. Vols. 1 and 2 were edited by Gerald Noxon of Boston University; Vol.
3 was edited by Norman Holland, literary and film critic for *Hudson Review*;
and Vols. 4–6 were edited by William Sloan, then audio-visual director of the
New York Public Library.

In 1966, the Society's secretary—Richard Dyer MacCann—proposed a "more
substantial publication" at SOC's annual meeting. MacCann's experience as a
reporter for the *Christian Science Monitor* (1951–1957) and as author of three
film books (*Hollywood in Transition, Film and Society*, and *Film: A Montage
of Theories*) led to his eventual appointment as editor of the revised journal.
First under Sloan and then under MacCann, the title *Cinema Journal* was employed, the work became a true periodical with biannual publication, and *Cinema
Journal* incorporated the resource of associate editors which would allow the
valuable scholarly status that is predicated upon juried/refereed submissions. In
response to the increased scholarly posture of the journal, the organization changed
its name to the Society for Cinema Studies in 1969.

MacCann began his editorship with Vol. 7 at the University of Kansas at
Lawrence. In the fall of 1970 the journal moved with him to the University of
Iowa, where he continued editorship through Vol. 15, No. 2. Subsequently,
Jack C. Ellis became the new editor, and *Cinema Journal* moved to Northwestern
University where it continued for the next six years. Finally in 1982 (with Vol.
22), Virginia Wright Wexman became the editor and increased publication to
three issues per year. She instituted quarterly publication with Vol. 22, No. 4
(Summer 1983).

Cinema Journal's scope has always been somewhat selective. Its explicit
commitment is to avoid "the temptation to publish topical articles on current

films.'' However, significant scholarly work in film studies—history, theory, or criticism—is accepted for review regardless of ''context and methodology.'' The journal no longer publishes reviews of books and now limits submitted manuscripts to seventy-five hundred words (which must conform to the University of Chicago Press *Manual of Style*). Pertinent illustrations, especially frame enlargements, may be accepted.

The main strength of *Cinema Journal* has always been film history, though it has provided a forum for some film criticism and some film theory. (Indeed, Wexman has recently sought submissions in theory and semiotics.) Rarely has it directed its publication to matters of film production. Largely, its address is the fictional feature, followed by documentary work; least attention has been given to experimental film. Finally, most, if not all, of its published essays are marked by quality research and logical exposition. The recent publication of *Cinema Examined* (Dutton, 1982) by past editors, MacCann and Ellis, provides an excellent overview of the journal's scope and sophistication, through the years 1965–1981. The book's four categories are instructive: auteur studies, national cinema, profiles of films, and theory and criticism.

Information Sources

INDEX SOURCES: Art Index; Arts and Humanities Citation Index; FIAF International Index to Film Periodicals; Film Literature Index.
REPRINT EDITIONS: None.
LOCATION SOURCES: Library of Congress; Museum of Modern Art; University of Illinois.

Publication History

MAGAZINE TITLE AND TITLE CHANGES: *Journal of the Society of Cinematologists* (1961–1965); *Cinema Journal* (1966 to present).
VOLUME AND ISSUE DATA: Vol. I (1961); Vol. II (1962); Vol. III (1963); Vols. IV and V (1964/1965); Vol. VI (1966–1967); Vol. VII (Winter 1967–1968); Vol. VIII, No. 1–Vol. XIII, No. 2 (Fall 1968–Spring 1974), biannual; Vol. XIV, No. 1 (Fall 1974); Vol. XIV, No. 2 (Winter 1974/1975); Vol. XIV, No. 3 (Spring 1975); Vol. XV, No. 1–Vol. XXI, No. 2 (Fall 1975–Spring 1982), biannual; Vol. XXII, No. 1 (Fall 1982 to present), quarterly.
PUBLISHER AND PLACE OF PUBLICATION: Society of Cinematologists, no address listed (Vol. I–Vols. IV and V); Society of Cinematologists, Donnell Library Center, 20 West Fifty-third Street, New York, N.Y. 10019 (Vol. VI); Society of Cinematologists, University of Kansas, Lawrence, Kansas 66044 (Vol. VII–Vol. VIII); Society for Cinema Studies, University of Kansas, Lawrence, Kansas 66044 (Vol. IX); Society for Cinema Studies, Broadcasting and Film Division, University of Iowa, Iowa City, Iowa 52240 (Vol. X–Vol. XV); Society for Cinema Studies, Film Division, Northwestern University, Evanston, Ill. 60201 (Vol. XVI–Vol. XXI); Society for Cinema Studies, Department of English, University of Illinois at Chicago, Box 4348, Chicago, Ill. 60680 (Vol. XXII to present).

EDITOR: Gerald Noxon (1961–1962); Norman N. Holland (1963); William J. Sloan
    (1964–1967); Richard Dyer MacCann (1967–1976); Jack C. Ellis (1976–1982);
    Virginia Wright Wexman (1982 to present).

Edward S. Small

CINEMA PAPERS

The appearance of *Cinema Papers* in 1974 coincided with the beginnings of
the dramatic reemergence of Australia on the international filmmaking scene.
Although it had once boasted a thriving silent film industry, the development of
what has been termed the Australian "New Wave" marked the rise of a national
cinema that is uniquely Australian in tone and theme; and *Cinema Papers*, until
it suspended publication in June 1983, served as a chronicle of its growth. From
its inception, the publication provided detailed information concerning the Australian film industry, presenting a behind-the-scenes look at a vital filmmaking
community that has been represented internationally by a relatively small number
of films. A regular feature entitled "The Quarter" offered a summary of recent
events in the industry, and the majority of the issues contained a comprehensive
list of all Australian films then in production.

Although *Cinema Papers* published its share of articles on such acclaimed
directors as Peter Weir and Bruce Beresford, the journal did not restrict its
coverage to those filmmakers who have gained recognition outside their own
country. In a series of reports on individuals within the industry, *Cinema Papers*
interviewed cinematographers, editors, and assistant directors, often accompanying these articles with a complete filmography. In addition, the magazine
spotlighted such little-known figures as Ken G. Hall (January 1974), whose films
of the twenties and thirties made him the most financially successful director in
Australia's history, and Richard Prowse (April 1974), Australia's Chief Film
Censor. The journal also proved remarkably adept at singling out talented young
filmmakers early in their careers. An interview with Gillian Armstrong (January
1974), who would later direct *My Brilliant Career*, appeared in *Cinema Papers*
while Armstrong was still a student at the Australian Film School.

Yet the magazine did not limit its scope to Australian filmmaking. Its editors—
Peter Bielby, Scott Murray, and, until 1979, documentary filmmaker Philippe
Mora—chose instead to include articles on a broad range of films and subjects,
giving *Cinema Papers* an international flavor in spite of its primary concentration
on the Australian film industry. Thus the journal's first issue contained not only
the interview with Gillian Armstrong and a profile of Peter Weir but reviews of
Jean-Pierre Melville's *La Samourai* and Andrei Tarkovsky's *Solaris* as well.
The magazine maintained this balance in recent years, offering such diverse
articles as "Film Under Allende" (April 1974), a two-part study of Australian
women directors (June/July and September/October 1976); an interview with
Swiss filmmaker Alain Tanner (October/November 1978); a special supplement

on filmmaking in New Zealand (June/July 1980); and an interview with Judy Davis (May/June 1981).

First and foremost, however, *Cinema Papers* has been a journal of contemporary Australian cinema, and its blend of interviews, production updates, and reviews has provided an invaluable record of a rapidly growing film industry. If its publication suspension is a permanent one, it will mark the disappearance of an informative companion piece to Australia's exciting new national cinema.

Information Sources

INDEX SOURCES: FIAF International Index to Film Periodicals; Film Literature Index.
REPRINT EDITIONS: None.
LOCATION SOURCES: Academy of Motion Picture Arts and Sciences; University of Southern California.

Publication History

MAGAZINE TITLE AND TITLE CHANGES: *Cinema Papers*. [With the December/January 1979/1980 issue, the subtitle "Incorporating Television" was added.]
VOLUME AND ISSUE DATA: January 1974–December 1974, quarterly; March/April 1975–November/December 1975, three times a year; March/April 1976–December/January 1980/1981, quarterly; March/April 1981–December 1982, bimonthly; March 1983; May/June 1983.
PUBLISHER AND PLACE OF PUBLICATION: Cinema Papers Pty Ltd., 644 Victoria Street, North Melbourne, Victoria, Australia 3051.
EDITOR: Peter Bielby, Philippe Mora, Scott Murray (January 1974–March/April 1979); Peter Bielby and Scott Murray (May/June 1979–May/June 1983).

Janet Lorenz

CINEMA PROGRESS

In the summer of 1935, the American Institute of Cinematography, Inc., an organization based at the University of Southern California (USC), created the National Cinema Workshop and Appreciation League. The League organized annual conventions, presented awards of excellence in filmmaking, and also published a magazine which began life in December 1935 as the *National Cinema Workshop and Appreciation League Bulletin*.

Edited by Dr. Boris V. Morkovin, chairman of the Department of Cinematography at USC, the *Bulletin* became a magazine titled *Cinema Progress* with its double issue, No. 2-3, published in July 1936. The magazine was concerned with film from an educational viewpoint but not specifically concerned with film education, although many of its articles were written by educators and obviously were aimed at cinema appreciation classes in high schools and colleges. Among the many interesting articles to be found in *Cinema Progress* during its five years of existence are "Thoughts about Directing" by William Dieterle (Vol. 2, No.

5), "The Theme's the Thing" by Robert Riskin (Vol. 3, No. 1), "A Motion Picture World's Fair" by Rudolph Arnheim (Vol. 3, No. 3-4), and "Director's Notebook" by King Vidor (Vol. 4, No. 1-2).

Information Sources

INDEX SOURCES: None.
REPRINT EDITIONS: None.
LOCATION SOURCES: Academy of Motion Picture Arts and Sciences (incomplete); University of California at Los Angeles; University of Southern California.

Publication History

MAGAZINE TITLE AND TITLE CHANGES: *National Cinema Workshop and Appreciation League Bulletin* (December 1935); *Cinema Progress* (July 1936–June-July 1939).
VOLUME AND ISSUE DATA: Vol. 1, No. 1 (December 1935); Vol. 1, No. 2-3 (July 1936); Vol. I, No. 4-5 (November 1936); Vol. II, No. 1 (March 1937); Vol. II, No. 2 (June 1937); Vol. II, No. 3 (August 1937); Vol. II, No. 4 (October 1937); Vol. II, No. 5 (December-January 1937-1938); Vol. III, No. 1 (February-March 1938); Vol. III, No. 2 (May-June 1938); Vol. III, No. 3-4 (January 1939); Vol. IV, No. 1-2 (June-July 1939).
PUBLISHER AND PLACE OF PUBLICATION: The American Institute of Cinematography, Inc., University of Southern California, 3551 University Avenue, Box 74, Los Angeles, Calif.
EDITOR: Dr. Boris V. Morkovin.

Anthony Slide

CINEMA QUARTERLY

Cinema Quarterly was a small, intellectual film magazine, very much in the tradition of *Close Up**; and just as the latter was published in the unlikely location of Switzerland, so *Cinema Quarterly* was steadfastly a Scottish periodical. The magazine even boasted on its masthead of a London correspondent, a position initially held by Basil Wright and later taken over by Paul Rotha.

Like its writers—who included Paul Rotha, Rudolph Arnheim, and Herman Weinberg—*Cinema Quarterly* was seeking to establish a new, aesthetic approach to the cinema. In the first issue (Autumn 1932), Rotha wrote "Approach to a New Cinema" and Herbert Read "Towards a Film Aesthetic." The magazine's reviews were often limited to such obvious art house fare as Fedor Ozep's *The Murder of Dimitri Karamazov* and G. W. Pabst's *Atlantide*, although *Cinema Quarterly* did have the insight to review Laurel and Hardy's *The Music Box* (Vol. 1, No. 1), which Basil Wright hailed as "a modern version of the legend of Sisyphus." In an editorial in the first issue, Norman Wilson wrote, "Whatever else *Cinema Quarterly* stands for, it stands for sincerity. With all the vigor it can muster, it will attack the empty masquerade of sham sentiments and false emotions that is the stock-in-trade of most commercial movies.''[1]

The quality of writing in *Cinema Quarterly* was of a high standard, and the magazine boasted many fine, and little-known, articles, including "Flaherty" by John Grierson (Vol. 1, No. 1); "*Que Viva Mexico!*" by Seymour Stern (Vol. 1, No. 2); "Leontine Sagan," interviewed by Forsyth Hardy (Vol. 1, No. 1); "Joris Ivens," interviewed by J. Hulsker (Vol. 1, No. 3); "Alexander Korda and the International Film" by Stephen Watts (Vol, 2, No. 1); "Alfred Hitchcock on Music in Films" by Stephen Watts (Vol. 2, No. 2); "Filming in Ceylon" by Basil Wright (Vol. 2, No. 4); "The Function of the Art Director" by Alberto Cavalcanti (Vol. 3, No. 2); and "New Trends in Soviet Cinema" by Marie Seton (Vol. 3, No. 3–Vol. 3, No. 4). In addition, there was coverage of film societies, amateur filmmaking, and film books. The approach was carefully geared toward European filmmaking, and only sparse attention was given to the American cinema scene, or any other cinema scene for that matter, although in Vol. 2, No. 2, would be found an article by H. R. van der Poel, "The Film in South Africa." It says much for *Cinema Quarterly*'s bias that probably as much space was given to South African cinema in the three years of the magazine's existence as was given to filmmaking in the United States.

The first issue of *World Film News and Television Progress** indicated that it incorporated *Cinema Quarterly* in early 1936.

Notes

1. "The Spectator," Vol. 1, No. 1, Autumn 1932, pp. 3–6.

Information Sources

INDEX SOURCES: The Film Index.
REPRINT EDITIONS: World Microfilms ("Little Magazines" series).
LOCATION SOURCES: Academy of Motion Picture Arts and Sciences; Columbia University; Harvard University; Library of Congress; New York Public Library.

Publication History

MAGAZINE TITLE AND TITLE CHANGES: *Cinema Quarterly*.
VOLUME AND ISSUE DATA: Vol. 1, No. 1–Vol. III, No. 4 (Autumn 1932–Summer 1935), quarterly.
PUBLISHER AND PLACE OF PUBLICATION: Cinema Contact, Ltd., 24 N.W. Thistle Street Lane, Edinburgh 2, Scotland.
EDITOR: Norman Wilson.

Anthony Slide

CINEMA STUDIES

The British-based Society for Film History Research was founded in January 1959 at the initiative of Ernest Lindgren, the late curator of the British National Film Archive. It was formed "with the object of encouraging historical research into all aspects of the cinematograph, both in the British Isles and abroad."[1] A little over a year after the organization came into being, it commenced publication of a small, spartan-looking journal, *Cinema Studies*, under the editorship of Neville March Hunnings, a barrister with a special interest in film censorship and related matters.

Cinema Studies contained no photographs and set itself apart from anything that smacked of a popular approach to film history. One would look in vain for material on the history of the film musical or the work of D. W. Griffith; instead readers would find Sidney, the son of the British film pioneer Birt Acres, writing "The First Command Film Performance" (No. 3, August 1961) or "Kinematography and the Kiel Canal" (No. 6, December 1962). A pioneering British filmmaker, Dave Aylott, contributed "Reminiscences of a Showman" (Vol. 2, No. 1, June 1965), while the distinguished Irish film historian Liam O'Leary wrote on the life and career of the Spanish chanteuse and occasional film actress Raquel Meller (Vol. 2, No. 5, June 1967).

In the only editorial published by *Cinema Studies*, in its first issue (March 1960), Hunnings wrote: "It is the purpose of this journal, and of this Society, to encourage the basic research necessary to enable the history of the cinema, especially in Britain, to be adequately written." This avowed intent was evident from the esoteric nature of the bulk of the short essays that *Cinema Studies* offered: enthusiastic, obscurantist articles such as "Early Film Criticism in Leicester" (No. 4, December 1961), "William Morton and the Hull Cinemas" (No. 8, December 1963), and "The Cinema Comes to Birmingham" (Vol. 2, No. 5, September 1967).

Despite its ties to the Society for Film History Research, *Cinema Studies* plotted a course determined exclusively by its editor, Neville March Hunnings. His overwhelming interest in film censorship was continually in evidence with articles such as "The Origins of Film Censorship in India" (No. 2, December 1960), and *Cinema Studies* was obviously influential in creating an atmosphere sympathetic enough for a major British publisher, Allen and Unwin, to bring out Hunning's *Film Censors and the Law* (1967). Hunnings must also be credited for his early concern with documenting important periodical articles on the motion picture appearing in nonfilm publications. In an effort to bring these writings to the attention of the film historian, he inaugurated "Digest of Periodical Articles," beginning with issue No. 3 (August 1961).

However independent Hunnings's role, *Cinema Studies* was still dependent upon the Society for Film History Research for funding; and, as a small, nonprofit organization, totally reliant upon members' contributions for its survival, the Society was increasingly unable to finance its journal. Between March 1960 and June 1964, the Society did publish nine issues of *Cinema Studies* (comprising Vol. 1), appearing biannually. Between June 1965 and September 1967, five issues of *Cinema Studies* were produced. However, because of financial problems, there was a gap of one year between publication of Vol. 2, No. 1, and Vol. 2, No. 2.

The Society for Film History Research disbanded in 1968, without publication of a final issue of the journal to explain its demise. To a large extent, the Society was a victim of the growth of serious interest in film history, particularly in the United States, where the academic-based Society of Cinematologists was gaining in strength, eventually changing its name to the Society for Cinema Studies and expanding its publication, *Cinema Journal.** The late sixties saw the publication of an increasing number of "small" film journals, better equipped to harness the growing audience for serious film study, including *The Brighton Film Review* (British; See *Monogram**) and *The Silent Picture** (British/U.S.). The latter was cofounded by Anthony Slide, who had served at one time as honorary secretary of the Society for Film History Research[2] and who then utilized his own magazine to disseminate his individualistic approach to film history, which had been somewhat stifled by Hunning's editorial control of *Cinema Studies*.

Cinema Studies' approach to film research was very much that of an English gentleman. There could be no vituperative disagreement over a fellow writer's approach to any particular subject, and what little correspondence the journal published is remarkably similar to the types of letters to be found in *The Times*. *Cinema Studies* was a quiet publication, unwilling to blow its own trumpet or to promote itself too blatantly. The Society for Film History Research made no effort to sell the magazine through bookshops or newsstands, and what little advertising it accepted was very discreet. *Cinema Studies* was determinedly sober, and in an age when film study was bursting on the scene, when Kevin Brownlow, with *The Parade's Gone By* (1968), was proving that film history could be entertaining, the journal stood no chance for survival. It died of its own stuffiness.

Notes

1. From a prospectus issued by the Society for Film History Research and which also appeared inside the front cover of each issue of *Cinema Studies*.

2. Rosemary Heaword was the first honorary secretary of the Society for Film History Research. She was succeeded by Anthony Slide, and he, in turn, was succeeded by David Francis, who later became curator of the British National Film Archive.

Information Sources

INDEX SOURCES: The New Film Index.
REPRINT EDITIONS: World Microfilms ("Little Magazines" series).
LOCATION SOURCES: Academy of Motion Picture Arts and Sciences; Harvard University; Stanford University; University of Chicago; University of Colorado; University of Illinois; University of Iowa; University of Southern California.

Publication History

MAGAZINE TITLE AND TITLE CHANGES: *Cinema Studies*.
VOLUME AND ISSUE DATA: Vol. 1, Nos. 1–9 (March 1960–June 1964); Vol, II, Nos. 1–5 (June 1965–September 1967), irregular.

PUBLISHER AND PLACE OF PUBLICATION: The Society for Film History Research,
    1 Dane Street, High Holborn, London, W.C.1, England.
EDITOR: Neville March Hunnings.

Anthony Slide

CINEMA-T.V.-DIGEST. See CTVD

CINEMA T.V. TODAY. See SCREEN INTERNATIONAL

CINEMA WORLD ILLUSTRATED

A short-lived British fan magazine founded in 1927, *Cinema World Illustrated*
chiefly featured condensed stories adapted from current film releases, as many
as twenty to an issue.

Information Sources

INDEX SOURCES: None.
REPRINT EDITIONS: None.
LOCATION SOURCES: No information.

Publication History

MAGAZINE TITLE AND TITLE CHANGES: *Cinema World Illustrated.*
VOLUME AND ISSUE DATA: Vol. I, No. 1–Vol. II, No. 10 (May 1927–February
    1929), monthly.
PUBLISHER AND PLACE OF PUBLICATION: W. Southern, 3 Bolt Court, Fleet Street,
    London, England.
EDITOR: No editor listed.

Thomas A. Johnson

CLASSIC. See Appendix 2

CLASSIC FILM COLLECTOR. See CLASSIC FILM/VIDEO IMAGES

CLASSIC FILM/VIDEO IMAGES

Classic Film/Video Images was founded in the summer of 1962 as *8mm
Collector* by a Pennsylvania film collector and furniture dealer named Sam Rubin.
The purpose of the paper, the first issue of which was a mere six mimeographed

pages, was to aid 8mm film collectors in securing the best possible prints and to help them complain when they did not. With issue No. 3 (December 31, 1962), the paper improved in terms of both printing and the amount of text and with No. 5 (August 15, 1963) adopted a newspaper-size format with which it was to continue to the present. The title of the publication was changed to *Classic Film Collector* with issue No. 15 (Summer 1966), by which time the contents of the periodical had become fairly established: news items relating to all aspects of film collecting, reprints of articles of historical interest from other newspapers and magazines, articles of a historical nature by enthusiastic fans, a column on 9.5mm, reprints of obituaries, book reviews, and reviews of films newly offered to film collectors.

In the fall of 1978, Sam Rubin sold the paper to Blackhawk Films of Davenport, Iowa, which published it through the Muscatine Journal, a subsidiary of Lee Enterprises, which, at that time, also owned Blackhawk. With the first issue under the new ownership, the periodical became bimonthly and changed its name to *Classic Film/Video Images*, reflecting the new interest in films on video tape and disc. *Classic Film/Video Images* became a monthly publication with No. 79 (January 1982) and presently (1983) has a circulation of three thousand. In addition to *Classic Film/Video Images*, the paper's new publisher also produced a ''giveaway'' quarterly sampler of items from the periodical, under the title of *Classic Images Review*.

Sam Rubin's enthusiasm and joy in what he does is apparent on every one of the periodical's fifty to sixty pages. It was he who, in 1965, founded the Society for Cinephiles, which holds an annual Cinecon convention over the Labor Day weekend, attended by film enthusiasts from across the country, and the activities of the Society are given much space in Rubin's publication.

Despite its somewhat amateurish and often cluttered look, there is much valuable information to be found in the journal's pages. One of the most notable series of articles was by Sam Gill on various silent comedians: Larry Semon (No. 10), Charlie Chase (Nos. 11 and 12), Mack Swain (No. 13), and Lloyd Hamilton (No. 14).

Information Sources

INDEX SOURCES: Film Literature Index.
REPRINT EDITIONS: University Microfilms.
LOCATION SOURCES: Academy of Motion Picture Arts and Sciences.

Publication History

MAGAZINE TITLE AND TITLE CHANGES: *8mm Collector* (No. 1, June 7, 1962–No. 14, Spring 1966); *Classic Film Collector* (No. 15, Summer 1966–No. 60, Fall 1978); *Classic Film/Video Images* (No. 61, Winter 1978 to present).
VOLUME AND ISSUE DATA: Nos. 1–60 (June 7, 1962–Fall 1978), quarterly; Nos. 61–78 (Winter 1978–December 1981), bimonthly; No. 79 (January 1982 to present), monthly.

PUBLISHER AND PLACE OF PUBLICATION: Samuel K. Rubin, 734 Philadelphia
    Street, Indiana, Pa. 15701 (Nos. 1–60); Muscatine Journal, P.O. Box 4079,
    Davenport, Iowa 52808 (No. 61 to present).
EDITOR: Samuel K. Rubin.

Anthony Slide

CLOSE UP

According to her memoirs, Bryher and her husband Kenneth Macpherson were
walking by a lake near their home in Territet, Switzerland, when he noted that
ripples on the water would make a good film effect. Bryher says she asked him,
"If you are so interested, why don't you start a magazine?"[1]

So in 1927 *Close Up* was begun, with Macpherson as editor and Bryher, who
had experience in the magazine business, as assistant editor. From their office
in Switzerland, they had the unique opportunity to study films from France,
America, Germany, England, and Russia without censorship.

As a monthly international film journal, *Close Up* was designed to establish
rapport among film devotees and producers, and to address the problems of
cinema as a developing art form. In its politics, *"Close Up* was determined to
be quite liberal, and to be a sort of battle ground."[2]

The journal had its moments of intellectual snobbery, especially in its youth;
writers denigrated films with mass appeal and the masses to whom these films
appealed, called "the lump" in an early article by poet H.D. (appropriately, the
intellectuals were called "the leaven").[3] The journal's aesthetic tastes were with
Russian and German films and the avant-garde; writers came down hard on most
Hollywood fare, except Chaplin, and they were totally unimpressed by England's
efforts, except for John Grierson's documentaries.

In spite of its biases, *Close Up* published an extensive range of articles in its
six-and-a-half years, including information on the film industries in Japan, Argentina, and Belgium; essays on avant-garde films; animation, especially by
Disney; and over the years indicated a growing interest in the documentary.
When frequent negative criticisms in *Close Up* prompted reader responses, these
were duly printed in the journal's "Comment and Review" section.

Many well-known writers contributed to *Close Up*, including Gertrude Stein,
H.D., and Marianne Moore. Sergei Eisenstein contributed exclusive articles on
film theory and on the Russian film industry. Novelist Dorothy M. Richardson
wrote a regular column, "Continuous Performance," which often dealt with the
sociology of cinema attendance. An example is her insightful study of the after-
noon matinee as a "sanctuary," offering escapism and involvement for "tired
women."[4] Humorous observations on the film industry and technical know-how
were offered in regular contributions from English cameraman Oswell Blakeston.
His comment on the then-trendy "iris" effect was, "People do not think in
elastic circles."[5]

Other regular features were "As Is," Macpherson's editorial which usually began each issue, and "Comment and Review," which included news, opinions, and notes from around the world. Over the years, the journal added to its staff correspondents from Paris, London, Hollywood, Berlin, Geneva, New York, and Moscow.

Though it claimed to be "independent of bias,"[6] *Close Up* was outspoken in its protests against film censorship, especially in England, where it reported that "women fighting with knives" and "animals gnawing on men and children" were included on a long list of forbidden images.[7] Most Russian films were censored there, as was Germaine Dulac's *The Seashell and the Clergyman*, on the grounds that if it *were* understood, its message undoubtedly would be offensive.[8] A righteously indignant *Close Up* circulated petition forms and, with Dorothy Richardson's assistance, mounted a campaign to change England's stringent censorship code; the campaign was not successful. The journal also supported a related issue, an international copyright for directors, to prevent the reediting of films to accommodate each country's censorship regulations.

Close Up advocated the use of films in education and, in a time when many thought cinema to be ruining the eyesight and morals of youth, regular film viewing by children. "Instead of forbidding the cinema, we should insist the children see a film each week," commented the editor.[9] Bryher, who had a particular interest in education, suggested films like Vsevolod Pudovkin's *Mother* and documentaries like *Moana* for youthful viewing. She also offered a radical suggestion for her time: "There is no reason why children should not write, direct, photograph and make their own films with very little instruction."[10]

The journal offered support and praise for women in film, including attention to Dorothy Arzner's directorial efforts in Hollywood, to feature films by Russia's Olga Preobrashenskaga and Germany's Lotte Reiniger. The fact that many women wrote for *Close Up* certainly had its effect, but praise for female filmmakers came from both sexes.

In 1928, *Close Up* began to devote certain issues to special topics, such as one on the Russian film industry in September 1928 and the "talkie" issue in September 1929. There was an issue on the censorship question in February 1929, on the British film industry in March 1929, and an issue on blacks in films in August 1929 which suggests that "universal cinema...is strictly racist cinema" and that blacks should make films of themselves.[11]

By far the biggest aesthetic issue in *Close Up*'s history was the advent of the sound film, noted first in Macpherson's November 1927 editorial: "Noises with films have long been...hanging over us like an incipient cold in the head, or some other vague threat."[12] In the same issue, H.D. remarks, "do we want a lot of new toys, mechanical and utterly proficient?"[13]

Early sound efforts were criticized severely. "This monstrosity is descending fullspeed upon us," said Macpherson in July 1928, and Dorothy Richardson made sound a feminist issue in her March 1932 article, "The Film Gone Male."

In time, however, *Close Up* began to appreciate the possibilities of sound, especially after Eisenstein's October 1928 article on the sound film appeared, pointing out that sound might be used more subtly and that the sound-image counterpoint offered new aesthetic possibilities worth developing. In *Close Up*'s later issues, the sound problem seemed mostly settled, and writers began grappling with other new technological issues, such as color, widescreen cinema, "olfactory cinema" experiments, and television, which would be more, promised Oswell Blakeston, than "talkies by the fireside."[14]

Close Up offered unique practical self-help for film societies, ranging from projection techniques to acquiring nonbutchered prints and, perhaps because its staff included independent filmmakers, information for those producing their own films, such as camera and lighting techniques and information about filmstocks. The journal advocated free experimentation for amateurs and eschewed their trying to copy Hollywood. To this end, Blakeston and Roger Burford printed several suggested scenarios which amateurs might try developing into films. (The journal was just as quick to criticize poor efforts by amateurs as by professionals, however.)

Close Up regularly printed articles on film theory, such as "From Abstract to Epic," a wide-ranging essay by Roger Burford in which he creates a diagrammed basis for criticism to accommodate all film forms. Several writers applied Freud's dream theories to the cinema.

The most interesting theoretical writing came after the introduction of sound, including ideas on "The Compound Cinema" by Harry Potamkin; how the "flat silent film" could incorporate sound, color, and more; and, of course, Eisenstein's contributions on film form.

Each issue of *Close Up* printed stills from current films of all types and by 1932 printed captions for these in three languages. The photographs were of exceptional quality and often of exclusive origin.

Throughout its history, the writing in *Close Up* was excellent; an article was often artistry in itself. A favorite piece is Macpherson's very impressionistic essay, "Matinee," which recreates the experience of attending a movie with phrases like "girls with torches and fuchsia carpets and a slope to the floor" and "Greta Garbo in a frame with glass and light flung across my eyes."[15] Another is E. L. Black's "Animals on the Films," in which the writer presents a reasonable argument that opportunities for trained animals in the cinema might increase: "Nearly always their best qualitites are entirely ignored." Of camels, he says, "many of their habits would commend them both for comic and serious films, but one only sees them occasionally carrying Arabs."[16] There is much pleasure in discovering that the writer is only 15 years old! Finally, there is H.D.'s beautifully serious article on "restraint" in the cinema, a voicing of her poetic sensibilities: "To present the 'classics' it is not necessary to build up pasteboard palaces, the whole of Troy, the entire overwhelming of a battle fleet."[17]

In 1931 *Close Up* became a quarterly and was printed in a larger format. By 1932 the journal had lost a lot of its intellectual and aesthetic savvy, evidenced by more articles on movie stars and conventional cinema and less on theory and technique, although the final volume includes Eisenstein's excellent three-part series on training filmmakers in the Soviet Union and on his experiences in Hollywood.

Bryher's memoirs blame the sound film, perhaps too harshly, for the end of *Close Up*, although the language restrictions imposed by sound films did limit the international appeal of the journal. References to political unrest in Europe and Nazism on the rise in Germany no doubt also contributed to *Close Up*'s demise at the end of 1933.

Notes

1. Bryher, *The Heart to Artemis* (New York: Harcourt, Brace and World, 1962), pp. 245–247. Bryher (born Winifred Ellerman) is known as a historical novelist; she and poet H.D. (Hilda Doolittle) were long-time companions. Bryher's second husband, Kenneth Macpherson, produced his own experimental films, including a feature, *Borderline*, starring Paul Robeson and H.D. When *Close Up* began, Bryher, H.D., and Macpherson all lived in Territet, Switzerland.

2. Vol. 3, No. 1, July 1928, p. 7.
3. No. 1, July 1927, p. 23.
4. p. 35.
5. Vol. 2, No. 4, April 1928, p. 42.
6. Vol. 2, No. 6, June 1928, p. 4.
7. Vol. 4, No. 2, February 1929, pp. 13–15.
8. Vol. 6, No. 3, May 1930, p. 233.
9. Vol. 2, No. 2, February 1928, p. 72.
10. No. 2, August 1927, p. 54.
11. Vol. 5, No. 2, August 1929, p. 85.
12. No. 5, November 1927, p. 5.
13. p. 21.
14. Vol. 7, No. 1, July 1930, p. 38.
15. No. 5, November 1927, pp. 59–60.
16. No. 1, July 1927, pp. 41–43.
17. No. 2, August 1927, p. 30.

Information Sources

BIBLIOGRAPHY:
Bryher. *The Heart to Artemis*. New York: Harcourt, Brace and World, 1962.
INDEX SOURCES: The Film Index; "Index to *Close Up*" compiled by Melinda Ward, published in *Bulletin of the New York Public Library*, Vol. 73, No. 8, October 1969, pp. 491–524; The New Film Index.
REPRINT EDITIONS: Arno Press; Kraus-Thomson; Nendeln/Liechtenstein (Vol. 9 and 10 only); World Microfilms.
LOCATION SOURCES: Academy of Motion Picture Arts and Sciences (lacks later volumes); Library of Congress; University of South Carolina.

Publication History

MAGAZINE TITLE AND TITLE CHANGES: *Close Up*.
VOLUME AND ISSUE DATA: Vol. I, No. 1–Vol. VII, No. 6 (July 1927–December
    1930), monthly; Vol. VIII, No. 1–Vol. X, No. 4 (March 1931–December 1933),
    quarterly. [Issues originally published as Nos. 1–6 are now designated Vol. I.]
PUBLISHER AND PLACE OF PUBLICATION: Pool, Territet, Switzerland (1927–
    1930); Pool, 26 Litchfield Street, Charing Cross Road, London W.C.2, England
    (1931–1933).
EDITOR: Kenneth Macpherson.

Jan Millsapps

CLOSE-UP (Selznick Studios). See Appendix 3

COLUMBIA MIRROR. See Appendix 3

COMMENTATOR

In 1910 Edward Small[1] formed an agency to handle various vaudeville and
stage personalities. That organization became the Small-Landau Agency in September 1933 when Arthur M. Landau became Small's partner, and on May 24,
1935, Small-Landau began publication of a magazine titled *Commentator* to
promote its clients through news items, articles, and interviews. Beginning with
a four-page issue, later expanded to six pages, *Commentator* provided a vast
amount of useful information and would often publish articles and news items
of a more general interest. Of great value are the interviews, which always
appeared on the second page, in which many Hollywood personalities expressed
their views on a variety of subjects. Among those interviewed during the magazine's one-year life were: Jesse L. Lasky (Vol. 1, No. 1), Norman Taurog
(Vol. 1, No. 2), Kenneth Macgowan (Vol. 1, No. 7), Cecil B. DeMille (Vol.
1, No. 11), Pandro S. Berman (Vol. 1, No. 13), Walter Wanger (Vol. 1, No.
14), Frances Marion (Vol. 1, No. 15), Robert Edmond Jones (Vol. 1, No. 23),
Lucien Hubbard (Vol. 1, No. 27), B. P. Schulberg (Vol. 1, No. 28), Hal Wallis
(Vol. 1, No. 35), William K. Howard (Vol. 1, Nos. 36 and 37), Victor Schertz-
inger (Vol. 1, No. 39), Dudley Nichols (Vol. 1, No. 43), Merian C. Cooper
(Vol. 1, No. 46), Hunt Stromberg (Vol. 1, No. 48), and Hal Roach (Vol. 2,
No. 1).

Notes

1. Edward Small (1891–1977) was also a leading independent Hollywood producer
from the mid-twenties onward. Among his better-known films are *I Cover the Waterfront*
(1933), *The Man in the Iron Mask* (1939), *Valentino* (1951), *Monkey on My Back* (1957),
and *Witness for the Prosecution* (1958).

Information Sources

INDEX SOURCES: None.
REPRINT EDITIONS: None.
LOCATION SOURCES: Academy of Motion Picture Arts and Sciences; New York Public Library.

Publication History

MAGAZINE TITLE AND TITLE CHANGES: *Commentator*.
VOLUME AND ISSUE DATA: Vol. I, No. 1–Vol. II, No. 6 (May 24, 1935–June 27, 1936), weekly.
PUBLISHER AND PLACE OF PUBLICATION: Small-Landau Publishing Co., Suite 414, Guaranty Building, 6331 Hollywood Boulevard, Hollywood, Calif.
EDITOR: Isadora Bennett.

Anthony Slide

COMMUNICATION BOOKNOTES

From its three page debut as *Broadcasting Bibliophile's Booknotes* of September 1969 (it was *Mass Media Booknotes* from September 1973 to January 1982), *Communication Booknotes* (from February 1982) has been edited and guided by its founder, Christopher H. Sterling, director of the Center for Telecommunications Studies at George Washington University. His lucid and accurate-as-possible sharing of printed matter about nonprint media, caring about subscribers as payers and readers, and crediting contributors and staff have remained clear, strong, and constant editorial and personal policy.

During its fourteen years of monthly "descriptive comment" via "Recent Titles in Telecommunications, Information and Media," the newsletter has seen slight changes in format, an increase in number of pages and price, a new publisher, and on the masthead the addition of names of foreign and American regional specialists for an ever-expanding list of titles in such categories as broadcasting, production and performance, German media books, popular culture, media regulation, motion pictures, journalism, international communications, and others. The range of subtopics, as reflected in the books, magazines, documents, and pamphlets listed in any given month is large, including, for example, studies of comic books, telephone communications, and media in Poland, Sweden, Africa, and Arab countries. Titles, described in the newsletter in about one hundred to two hundred words, are listed each month on a page one index, alphabetized according to author or name of magazine. Categories and the number of them may change from month to month; for each there may be from two to thirteen (sometimes more) books listed.

Sterling and contributors describe each book's content, usually appending author's credentials and affiliations, occasionally welcoming the book as a needed contribution. Criticism is almost nonexistent, although a dated bibliography may be (gently) chastised. Tone and emphases are often indicated, comparisons with past editions and a book's place in a series mentioned, or lines from an introduction to explain the book's purpose quoted. There is complete bibliographical information with price and format. Media personalities' biographies that sound like public relations promotions are not included; there is no hyperbole but often enthusiasm expressed for material that Sterling feels sure will be helpful to various readers.

Constantly aiming to improve his service, Sterling incorporated special features early in *Communication Booknotes'* history. November 1971 saw the first "Book of the Month" section. Featured books have included Don R. Le Duc's *Cable Television and the FCC: A Crisis in Media Control* (November 1973), *Report of the Committee on the Future of Broadcasting, UK* (June 1977), James Monaco's *American Film Now: The People, the Power, the Money, the Movies* (June 1979), and Kathleen Conkey's *The Postal Precipice: Can the U.S. Postal Service Be Saved?* (April 1983).

Other special features are the regular annual issues devoted to United States Government Communications Publications and to film and/or photography books. Among other documents described in *Mass Media Booknotes* of August 1980 are the Commerce Department's *1980 World's Telephone Cable System* and the Federal Communication Commission's *An Analysis of the Network Affiliate Relationship in Television*. Another special was the *Thirteenth Annual Review of Film Books* (December 1982), filling one complete issue, written by specialist Douglas Gomery of the University of Maryland. David McClintick's *Indecent Exposure: A True Story of Hollywood and Wall Street*, Gomery's "Book of the Month," headed descriptions of sixty-three books in the categories of general motion picture, motion picture reference works, film and society, and film history and theory.

In addition, the newsletter has offered supplemental publications at low or no cost, among them a publishers address list, Arno Press brochures, and more recently such titles as *Telecommunications Policy: A Survey Bibliography*. There have been brief articles by Sterling or readers about shops for used and inexpensive books, occasional reader letters—for example, a publisher justifying his prices, a binder describing his strong binding—and regular appearance of "Short Takes," a repository of mini book reports.

While the type of information in each "descriptive comment" has remained about the same, writing style has changed. For years, Christopher Sterling performed the remarkable feat of providing serious, condensed information in a personal, lively style—as sole writer, to say nothing of typist. He actually talked to the readers, at times interjecting feisty comments, linking reports through apt and graceful sentences, explaining a publishing decision, praising contributors and staff, relating the magazine's history, making sure everyone was keeping up with volume and number, and asking readers to request information. In the May 1983 issue, the most impersonal thus far, there is still a little note urging readers to offer suggestions for improving the publication.

While some Sterling style still seeps in, and correspondent/specialists like Douglas Gomery and Frank Oglesbee (popular culture, Southern Illinois University, Carbondale) carry on the tradition of personal style (they even include adverse criticism), the publication is now more formal. The editor's extensive knowledge, his organizing ability, his wish to provide excellent, reliable service, all continue in evidence.

Information Sources

INDEX SOURCES: None.
REPRINT EDITIONS: None.
LOCATION SOURCES: Temple University.

Publication History

MAGAZINE TITLE AND TITLE CHANGES: *Broadcasting Bibliophile's Booknotes* (September 1969–August 1973); *Mass Media Booknotes* (September 1973–January 1982); *Communication Booknotes* (February 1982 to present).
VOLUME AND ISSUE DATA: Vol. I, No. 1 (September 1969 to present), monthly.
PUBLISHER AND PLACE OF PUBLICATION: The Center for Telecommunications Studies, George Washington University, 2000 G Street N.W., Washington, D.C. 20052.
EDITOR: Christopher H. Sterling.

Lillian Schiff

CONTINENTAL FILM AND VIDEO REVIEW. See
Appendix 2

CONTINENTAL FILM REVIEW. See Appendix 2

CTVD

Hampton Books, operated by Ben Hamilton and Muriel Hamilton is one of the better resources for rare film books and periodicals in the United States. In addition, it publishes a uniquely valuable periodical titled *CTVD* (or *Cinema-T.V.-Digest*), advertised as "a quarterly review of the serious, foreign-language cinema-TV press."

An editorial in the first issue (Winter 1961) read, "*CTVD* reports what the film critics say—*CTVD* does not criticize. . . . We give the news of what is going on in the highest intellectual reaches of cinema: we do not make that news."[1] Each issue of the somewhat unattractively printed journal contains translated resumés of articles and film reviews in foreign-language periodicals, as well as a small number of special articles (appearing at the front of each issue), contributed by *CTVD*'s worldwide correspondents. Such articles have included "Chrysanthemums & Corn: Recent Japanese Films" by Tats Yoshivama (No. 7, Winter 1963-1964), "Films in Hungary" by Tibor Hirsch (No. 10, Winter 1964-1965), "Berthold Bartosch" by Alexandre Alexeieff (No. 22, Winter 1968-1969), and "The Screens of Paris" by Nelly Kaplan (No. 27, Fall 1970). Of *CTVD*'s various correspondents—a number of whom do not appear to have an adequate grasp of the English language—Paris-based filmmaker and journalist Nelly Kaplan is undoubtedly the best known.

Among the dozens of foreign-language journals from which *CTVD* has synopsized reviews and essays are *Cahiers du Cinéma** (France), *Chaplin** (Sweden), *Cinema Nuovo* (Italy), *Filmkritik** (Germany), *Iskusstvo Kino** (USSR), *Kosmorama** (Denmark), and *Tiempo de Cine* (Argentina). *CTVD* also includes information as to the addresses, prices in U.S. dollars, and frequency of issue of each of the journals featured in a particular number.

Despite its apparent noncontroversial approach to the cinema, *CTVD* has always featured an outspoken editorial page, headed "News: What's Happening—or Shouldn't Have," and this section has not been above criticizing filmmakers or film events. The most severe of *CTVD*'s attacks came in the Winter 1967 (No. 19) issue, when the magazine found serious fault with the New York Film Festival, noting "the festival was not primarily consecrated to film art, nor to any art, but primarily to objectives to which any art is incidental."[2]

For the first twelve years of its existence, *CTVD* stuck to its avowed publishing schedule as a quarterly (with issues numbered both sequentially and four to a volume), but problems came about after No. 35, dated Spring 1973, and published July 1974. From that point on, *CTVD* became, to all extents and purposes, an annual, although there was a two-year gap between the Summer 1980 publication of No. 40 and the Summer 1982 publication of No. 41. Such a worthwhile and unusual periodical as *CTVD* deserves continued publication, and one trusts that the quarterly publishing schedule will be readopted in the not-too-distant future.

Notes

1. No. 1, Winter 1961-1962, p. 3.
2. No. 19, Winter 1967, p. 1.

Information Sources

INDEX SOURCES: None.
REPRINT EDITIONS: None.
LOCATION SOURCES: Academy of Motion Picture Arts and Sciences; Buffalo-Erie Public Library; Chicago Public Library; Illinois State University; New York Public Library; San Antonio Public Library; University of California at Los Angeles; University of Florida; University of Houston.

Publication History

MAGAZINE TITLE AND TITLE CHANGES: *CTVD*.
VOLUME AND ISSUE DATA: Vol. 1, No. 1 (Winter 1961) to present, irregular.

PUBLISHER AND PLACE OF PUBLICATION: Hampton Books, Hampton Bays, N.Y.
    11946 (Vol. 1, No. 1–Vol. VII, No. 1/No. 25); Hampton Books, Box 738,
    Newberry, S.C. 29108 (Vol. VII, No. 2/No. 26 to present).
EDITOR: Ben Hamilton.

Anthony Slide

THE CZECHOSLOVAK FILM. See Appendix 4

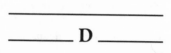

D

THE DAILY CINEMA. See SCREEN INTERNATIONAL

DAILY FILM RENTER. See SCREEN INTERNATIONAL

DAILY VARIETY

Three years after *The Hollywood Reporter** had begun publication as a daily film trade paper for the Los Angeles community, *Daily Variety* was launched on Wednesday, September 6, 1933. It was edited by Arthur Ungar, who had served for ten years as Hollywood representative for the weekly edition of *Variety** and was to remain *Daily Variety*'s editor until his death on July 24, 1950. At the time of his passing, *Variety* wrote of its long-time editor:

> Ungar combined two rare qualities—honesty and fearlessness. He printed the truth as he found it, and he usually found it, regardless of how much digging was necessary. He respected his profession of newspaperman, and he further respected the dignity of showbusiness. More, he fought for showbusiness. He unmasked the phoneys, he plumbed always for the straight-shooters. He was a pivotal point in the heart of the swirl of showbusiness, and he championed it. His courage constantly was shown, particularly when defending the film industry which he particularly loved.

Arthur Ungar established a format for *Daily Variety* which has changed little through the years. The paper provided news items which were not based solely on press releases but actually sought out by the paper's reporters. *Daily Variety* began to review films as they were first shown in Los Angeles, often at previews, and indeed for many years the paper billed these reviews as "previews." Reviews, often taking a different critical stance, would appear later in weekly *Variety*. The gaps between the daily's and weekly's reviews of the same films could vary substantially, but it was generally a couple of weeks; for example, *Footlight Parade* was "previewed" in *Daily Variety* on September 30, 1933, and reviewed in weekly *Variety* on October 10, 1933.

Just as today *Daily Variety* contains a considerable amount of advertising in its center pages, particularly around the time of the voting for Academy Awards, so did the paper at its beginning contain several pages of advertising for forthcoming film releases. Particularly in the thirties, these advertising "spreads" were lavish in style and layout. For example, on March 9, 1936, *Daily Variety* contained a twenty-four-page full-color centerfold promoting forthcoming United Artists releases.

Occasionally *Daily Variety* would print a document of major importance to the film industry in its entirety, as with the text of the Motion Picture Industry Code, which appeared in the December 1, 1933, issue. Front page headlines in early issues of *Daily Variety* announce such important events as the formation of the Screen Directors Guild (January 17, 1936). On October 23, 1935, *Daily Variety* printed a two-page letter from William Randolph Hearst, explaining that he was leaving California because of the rise in the state's income tax. Here the paper obviously utilized Hearst's letter to put across its own editorial viewpoint. But generally, under Arthur Ungar, *Daily Variety* could be both hard-hitting and blunt in its editorials. On June 6, 1940, Ungar came out strongly against Communism in the film industry. On December 8, 1941, he editorialized in "The Nation's at War." Perhaps the best known of Ungar's editorials are those in the fall of 1941, in which he attacked the Chicago mob-supported efforts of Willie Bioff and George Browne to take over the film industry through the then-discredited International Alliance of Theatrical Stage Employees and Moving Picture Machine Operators (IATSE) union syndicate.

As early as 1934, *Daily Variety* began publishing a "Pictures in Production Today" column, which was replaced that same year by two columns, "Productions Starting Today" and "Productions Finishing." In 1937 each Monday's edition of the newspaper contained the charts "Features Started Last Week," "Pictures Ready to Roll This Week," and "Films Skedded to Start Within Month." These charts had moved to the Friday editions by 1940. In 1942 *Daily Variety* commenced publication of a production chart, studio by studio, which appeared every Friday and was later expanded to include television.

From its first issue, *Daily Variety* published an unsigned gossip column titled "Hollywood Inside." But it was not until the forties that the paper began publishing a variety of columns: Jack Hellman's "Light and Airy," which dealt with broadcasting; Radie Harris's "Broadway Runaround," which covered the New York scene; and—most importantly—"Just for Variety," first written by Florabel Muir, later taken over by Alta Durant, Viola Swisher, and Sheilah Graham, and written since April 27, 1953, by Army Archerd.

After Ungar's death, the new editor, Joe Schoenfeld, made few changes. He did publish editorials under the heading "Time and Place," but he insisted that *Daily Variety* take a middle-of-the road policy, particularly with regard to the issue of Communism in Hollywood. Schoenfeld was succeeded by Thomas Pryor, a former *New York Times* writer, who has brought a great deal of sophistication and intelligence to *Daily Variety*. Pryor hired young, intellectual writers such as Joseph McBride and Todd McCarthy, who were equally at ease writing for *Film Comment** as for *Daily Variety*. A. D. Murphy provided the paper with the best commentary possible on the business aspects of the industry, while Bill Edwards continues to offer the best theatre coverage of any Los Angeles publication (as well as compiling *Daily Variety*'s renowned crossword puzzles). Under Pryor's editorship, *Daily Variety* also made the only change in the paper's size, expanding it from a 9-by-12-inch to an 11 1/2-by-15-inch format. A new typeface was introduced in 1983. The number of pages seems to depend on the amount of news or advertising and can run as few as eight and as many as thirty-six. The present circulation (1983) is approximately nineteen thousand.

Unlike its weekly counterpart, *Daily Variety* pays scant attention to entertainment outside of the sphere of film, broadcasting, and Los Angeles theatre. Articles and news items which appear in *Daily Variety* may not always be published in the weekly *Variety* and vice versa.

Since October 1, 1934, *Daily Variety* has published an annual anniversary issue which contains articles usually of only immediate interest and a vast amount of advertising. The anniversary issue also reprints all of *Daily Variety*'s film reviews from the previous year in alphabetical order, provides a necrology with brief biographies on each individual, and a day-by-day news summary for the period. The date of the anniversary issue varies from year to year, but in the last twenty-three years it has appeared between October 24 and October 31. Also, between 1949 and 1951, *Daily Variety* published a useful production schedule booklet with lists of current and planned features, top grossing films, and general information on an individual studio's product.

Daily Variety's green title against a white background has become as familiar a part of the Hollywood scene as M-G-M's lion and Columbia's lady with a torch—and will probably prove to be more enduring.

Information Sources

BIBLIOGRAPHY:
"Arthur Ungar Dies," *Daily Variety*, Vol. LXVIII, No. 34, July 25, 1950, pp. 1–2.
Oldfield, Col. Barney. "Daily Variety, Vol. I, No. 1, Has Been to War, through Fire, and around the World," *Daily Variety*, Vol. CLXXXI, No. 41, October 31, 1978, pp. 211, 216–217.
INDEX SOURCES: None.
REPRINT EDITIONS: None.
LOCATION SOURCES: Academy of Motion Picture Arts and Sciences.

Publication History

MAGAZINE TITLE AND TITLE CHANGES: *Daily Variety.*

VOLUME AND ISSUE DATA: Vol. I, No. 1–Vol. XXVIII, No. 15 (September 6, 1933–June 22, 1940), daily except Sundays and holidays; Vol. XXVIII, No. 16 (June 24, 1940 to present), daily except Saturdays, Sundays, and holidays.

PUBLISHER AND PLACE OF PUBLICATION: Daily Variety Ltd., 6282 Hollywood Boulevard, Hollywood, Calif. (Vol. I, No. 1–Vol. III, No. 64); Daily Variety Ltd., 1708-1710 Vine Street, Hollywood, Calif. (Vol. III, No. 65–Vol. LIII, No. 40); Daily Variety Ltd., 6311 Yucca Street, Hollywood 28, Calif. (Vol. LIII, No. 41–Vol. XCIII, No. 61); Daily Variety Ltd., 6404 Sunset Boulevard, Hollywood, Calif. (Vol. XCIII, No. 62–Vol. CLVI, No. 14); Daily Variety Ltd., 1400 North Cahuenga Boulevard, Hollywood, Calif. 90028 (Vol. CLVI, No. 15, to present).

EDITOR: Arthur Ungar (September 6, 1933–July 24, 1950); no editor listed (July 25, 1950–September 15, 1950); Joe Schoenfeld (September 18, 1950–January 30, 1959); no editor listed (February 2, 1959–March 23, 1959); Thomas M. Pryor (March 24, 1959, to present).

Anthony Slide

DEANNA'S DIARY. See Appendix 1.

DIALOGUE ON FILM

One of the more important early aspects of the work of the American Film Institute was its oral history program, and an extension of that program was the series of seminars with prominent filmmakers held at the Institute's Center for Advanced Film Studies in Beverly Hills, California. In an effort to disseminate the proceedings of those seminars to a wider audience, the Institute began publication of *Dialogue on Film* in March of 1972. *Dialogue on Film* consisted of nothing more than edited transcripts of those seminars and replaced an earlier Institute publication, *Discussion*, which was suspended with issue No. 3 devoted to Frank Capra.[1]

The first seven issues of *Dialogue on Film*, all published during 1972, were produced in mimeograph form and came with a loose-leaf binder. Vol. 2 of the publication offered a new format, which included photographs and a glossy cover. The first two issues of Vol. 2 were published during 1972, and Vol. 2, No. 3, of *Dialogue on Film* was dated January 1973. The magazine subsequently appeared on a monthly basis, except that there were no issues published during September of each year and the May and June issues were merged during 1974 and 1975. The final number of *Dialogue on Film* (Vol. 4, No. 8), with the publication date of May-June 1975, was devoted to George Stevens. Thereafter *Dialogue on Film* appeared as part of the American Film Institute's new publication, *American Film.**

Among the personalities featured in *Dialogue on Film* were Charlton Heston and Jack Nicholson (No. 1), Alfred Hitchcock (No. 5), Liv Ullman (Vol. 2, No. 5), Stanley Kramer (Vol. 2, No. 9), Henry Fonda (Vol. 3, No. 2), Lucille Ball (Vol. 3, No. 6), Olivia de Havilland (Vol. 4, No. 3), Robert Altman (Vol. 4, No. 5), and Martin Scorsese (Vol. 4, No. 7).

Notes

1. Aside from *American Film*, other American Film Institute publications are *AFI Report* (1970–1974), *AFI News* (1972–1975), and *AFI Education Newsletter* (1978 to present).

Information Sources

INDEX SOURCES: None.
REPRINT EDITIONS: None.
LOCATION SOURCES: Academy of Motion Picture Arts and Sciences; Harvard University; Louisiana State University in New Orleans; Museum of Modern Art; Stanford University; University of Illinois; University of Iowa; University of New Hampshire; University of Oregon; University of Texas at Austin; University of Vermont.

Publication History

MAGAZINE TITLE AND TITLE CHANGES: *Dialogue on Film*.
VOLUME AND ISSUE DATA: Vols. I–IV (March 1972–May-June 1975), monthly except September.
PUBLISHER AND PLACE OF PUBLICATION: American Film Institute, Center for Advanced Film Studies, 501 Doheny Road, Beverly Hills, Calif. 90210.
EDITOR: Bruce Henstell (1972); Rochelle Reed (1972–1975).

Anthony Slide

THE DIRECTOR. See THE MOTION PICTURE DIRECTOR

THE DIRECTORS' ANNUAL AND PRODUCTION GUIDE. See THE FILM DAILY

DIRECTORS GUILD OF AMERICA NEWS. See ACTION

DISCUSSION. See DIALOGUE ON FILM

THE DISNEYANA COLLECTOR. See Appendix 1

DISNEY TIMES. See Appendix 3

THE DISTRIBUTOR. See Appendix 3

DOSSIERS ART ET ESSAI. See ART ET ESSAI

THE DOTTED LINE. See Appendix 3

DOVE TAILS. See Appendix 1

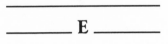

E

THE ECLAIR BULLETIN. See Appendix 3

THE EDISON KINETOGRAM. See Appendix 3

8mm COLLECTOR. See CLASSIC FILM/VIDEO IMAGES

EKRAN

Among the Eastern European countries, Yugoslavia occupies a somewhat privileged position. With its Communism being resolutely national, Yugoslavia was capable of maintaining its independence since 1948 in spite of all the pressure from the Soviet Union and its Eastern satellites. This peculiar political position is reflected in the country's various publications, and *Ekran*, founded in 1962, is no exception. The official liberalization in many areas of the country's cultural life makes *Ekran* an open forum for personal expression of the new methods and cinematic techniques, often in direct defiance of former conventions of the encasing rules of Socialist Realism. In one of the early issues, Boris Babackin wrote "V čem je posebnost filma?" (What are the distinctive features of film? No. 22, 1965), and Boris Grabnov wrote "Dramatika za industriju komunikacij" (The dramatism of the communication industry; No. 55-56, 1968).

In its quest to establish the journal's solid theoretical reputation, *Ekran*'s editorial staff assured the collaboration of well-known Yugoslav and foreign film critics. Its writers included Paddy Chayefsky, who wrote "Televizijski pisatelj" (Writers for television films; No. 9-10, 1963); Jean Cocteau, "Verujem v prevzetost" (We believe in subjective opinion; No. 13-14, 1964); Jean Béranger, "Tri metamorfoze Ingmara Bergmana" (Ingmar Bergman's three metamorphoses; No. 4, 1963); Elie Faure, "Ples in film" (Dance in film; No. 6, 1963); Alfred Hitchcock, "O igralcu" (About the actor; No. 5, 1963); and Jean-Luc Godard, "Manifest" (No. 67-68, 1969).

Seeking to provide its readers with a wide perspective on the foreign film scene, *Ekran* regularly publishes articles on the most interesting and important international cinematic events. In one of the early issues, Dr. Gertrude Behringer wrote "Razvoj filmske vzgoje v Austriji" (The development of film culture in Austria; No. 43-44, 1967). John Belton wrote "Japonski film" (the Japanese films; No. 115-116, 1974), Lorenzo Codelli contributed "Festival ameriškega filma v Deauville" (American Film Festival in Deauville; No. 9-10, 1978), and Mircea Alexandrescu wrote "Romanska kinematografija" (Romanian cinematography; No. 5-6, 1980).

Ekran gives an equal importance to problems of film ethics and aesthetics. Examples of this include Mirijana Borcic's "Človek v našem času" (Man in our times; No. 8-9, 1981), Stanko Godnic's "Iskanje novih prostorov" (In search of new horizons; No. 1-2, 1977), and Manca Košir's "Za nove sveze oci" (For new, fresh eyes; No. 3-4, 1977). On cinematic expression, the language of film, Marjan Ciglić wrote "Film-jezik, film-komunikacija" (Film as language, film as a means of communication; No. 94-95, 1972), and Nuša Dragan wrote "Prostor komunikacije" (The open space of communication; No. 77-78, 1970).

Another feature of the journal is interviews with prominent national and international film directors, such as Toni Tršar's "Razgorov s Polonskim" (A conversation with Polonski; No. 6, 1963) and "Razgorov s Aleksandrom Petrovićem" (A conversation with Aleksandr Petrović; No. 51-52, 1968).

All the major national and international film festivals are given coverage, as in Neva Mužić's "Locarno '73" (No. 108-109, 1973), Tom Frelih's "Berlin '73" and Vasko Pregelj's "Moskva '73" (both in No. 108-109, 1973), and Z. Verdlovec's "Festivali, Cannes '79" (No. 5-6, 1979). Television in general and movies made for television in particular are covered in such permanent columns as "Televizija" and "Teleobjektiv" and in Boris Grabnar's articles "Novi žurnalizem pri T.V." (New journalism on T.V.; No. 4, 1963), and "Televizija v Sloveniji" (Television in Slovenia; No. 3-4, 1976).

In addition, in each issue *Ekran* features film reviews, descriptions of film books, short news items on domestic and foreign films, and profiles of Yugoslav and international actors, film directors, and cinema personalities.

Information Sources

INDEX SOURCES: FIAF International Index to Film Periodicals.
REPRINT EDITIONS: None.
LOCATION SOURCES: University of Southern California (incomplete).

Publication History

MAGAZINE TITLE AND TITLE CHANGES: *Ekran, Revija za film i televizijo.*
VOLUME AND ISSUE DATA: No. 1 (1962) to present, published as double to quadruple
  issues.
PUBLISHER AND PLACE OF PUBLICATION: Ekran, Dalmatinova 4/11, Soba 9, 6100
  Ljubljana, Yugoslavia.
EDITOR: Denis Poniz (1962–December 1975); Viktor Konjar (January 1976–December
  1978); Saša Schrott (January 1979 to present).

Hari S. Rorlich

ELECTRONIC ENGINEERING. See TELEVISION

**ELECTRONICS AND TELEVISION AND SHORT-WAVE
WORLD.** See TELEVISION

ELVISHLY YOURS MAGAZINE. See Appendix 1

EMMY

Emmy, the official publication of the Academy of Television Arts & Sciences,
was founded in 1979 by that organization's board of governors shortly after the
settlement of a bitter and protracted dispute which had resulted in the splitting
of the thirty-year-old National Academy into two separate bodies and which had
created the new Academy of Television Arts & Sciences out of the national
group's Hollywood chapter.

As outlined in its first issue, *Emmy* was created to fill a "necessary and long
overdue" need of the Hollywood television community to have its own high-
quality, general-interest magazine "designed to serve both the television industry
and the intelligent television viewer." Its purpose was to bring coverage of the
television medium commensurate with its importance in our society and to inform
and entertain those people involved in T.V. production with the information they
would require to keep abreast of what was taking place within their industry.

Emmy was founded at a critical juncture in T.V. history. By the end of the
seventies, new technologies and new modes of presentation were beginning to
alter radically the structure of the industry; special interest groups were applying
constant and direct pressure to producers and networks; and new federal regulations and legislation were threatening to change dramatically the course of the
business of television. All of these issues were to be, and are still, addressed
by *Emmy*.

The first issue, published in Winter 1979, featured a variety of articles and features. Highlighting Vol. 1, No. 1, were pieces on T.V. censorship; the perils of writing for network T.V.; a conversation among producers David Gerber, Lee Rich, Grant Tinker, and Norman Lear focusing on the problems involved in creating network programming; profiles of three up-and-coming young actresses; and two features dealing with T.V.'s past: a look into the booming market in antique T.V. sets and the first of *Emmy*'s profiles, "The Great Shows."

These "Great Shows" articles are a continuing series of pieces on landmark programs and series of the past. The first issue outlined the history of "Gunsmoke." Subsequent issues have profiled such beloved shows as "Playhouse 90," "Omnibus," "The Dick Van Dyke Show," "You Are There," "Naked City," "The Twilight Zone," and "The Fugitive," just to name a few.

Emmy is a magazine conscious of the medium's history, and it has devoted space to a number of fine articles dealing with T.V.'s past. Pieces have ranged from a look into Alfred Hitchcock's television career to the Hollywood blacklist to delightful interviews with actors Charlton Heston and Jack Lemmon focusing on their personal experiences in T.V.'s "Golden Age."

The magazine also takes great pains to cover the present status of and significant issues facing today's commercial broadcast industry. It examines current trends, profiles top personalities both in front of and behind the camera, and attempts to provide its industry-oriented audience with updated information on T.V.'s constantly changing landscape. Selected articles of note are "T.V. Sex" by Isobel Silden (Vol. 4, No. 6) and pieces by Richard Mahler on T.V. in the courtroom ("T.V. on Trial," Vol. 5, No. 6) and the depiction of the aged on T.V. ("Through a Glass Darkly," Vol. 4, No. 4).

The third area *Emmy* studies is television's future. Each issue usually features a look at new technologies and equipment; the rise and future of pay, cable, and low-power telecasting; or some other aspect new to the medium. A fine example is "Disney and Ma Bell" by Gersh Morningstar (Vol. 5, No. 3), which discussed how the newly opened EPCOT Center revealed the marriage of Bell technology and Disney marketing skills to be a force that might alter all of our lives.

Occasionally, *Emmy* features special sections devoted to reporting on industry symposiums sponsored in part by the Television Academy. One such gathering was Vol. 1, No. 3's docudrama symposium which discussed in detail the nature and standards of this unique T.V. form. Other symposiums held and chronicled were "Cable T.V. in the Eighties" (Vol. 2, No. 4) and "The Proliferation of Pressure Groups in Prime Time" (Vol. 3, No. 3).

Emmy is geared toward commercial network television in the United States, although Vol. 5, No. 6, does contain an article on Canadian television. It is an industry-oriented publication which focuses quite effectively on the concerns, special problems, and issues faced by American television personnel as they go about the business of creating the programs we watch.

Information Sources

INDEX SOURCES: Access; FIAF International Index to Television Periodicals.
REPRINT EDITIONS: University Microfilms.
LOCATION SOURCES: American Film Institute (Los Angeles); Iowa State University; Library of Congress; Oregon State University; University of California at Los Angeles; University of Iowa; University of Oregon; University of Southern California.

Publication History

MAGAZINE TITLE AND TITLE CHANGES: *Emmy*.
VOLUME AND ISSUE DATA: Vol. I, No. 1–Vol. III, No. 4 (Winter 1979–Fall 1981), quarterly; Vol. IV. No. 1 (January/February 1982 to present), bimonthly.
PUBLISHER AND PLACE OF PUBLICATION: Academy of Television Arts & Sciences, 6363 Sunset Boulevard, Hollywood, Calif. 90028 (Vol. I, No. 1); Academy of Television Arts & Sciences, 4605 Lankershim Boulevard, North Hollywood, Calif. 91602 (Vol. I, No. 2, to present).
EDITOR: Stephen Zito (Winter 1979–Summer 1979); Pamela E. Gates (Fall 1979–Winter 1981); Richard Krafsur (January/February 1982 to present).

Daniel Einstein

ENTERTAINER. See Appendix 3

ENTERTAINMENT LAW REPORTER

A unique, eight-page newsletter, *Entertainment Law Reporter* provides succinct summaries of court decisions affecting all aspects of the entertainment industry: motion pictures, television, radio, music, theatre, publishing, and sports. Each entry is notated with the name of the case, the docket number, and the date of the judicial decision. There is no editorializing, simply a statement of the facts in the case.

Following a special preview issue, the first number of *Entertainment Law Reporter* was published on June 1, 1979, and it set the formula and look (basically austere) for all future issues of this twice-monthly publication. An impressive editorial board is listed to serve, in an advisory capacity, editor Lionel S. Sobel, who is currently visiting professor at Loyola Law School, Los Angeles. A typical issue, January 15, 1983 (Vol. 4, No. 16), included the following film- and television-related decisions: "Producers of *Boulevard Nights* are not liable for injuries inflicted on movie-goer by assailant in vicinity of theater," "Bystander's brief appearance in an ABC television documentary on sex-related business was capable of a defamatory meaning, Federal Court of Appeals rules in overturning lower court decision granting judgment to ABC," and "Bruce Jenner television commercial for Tropicana orange juice is ruled to be false and further broadcasts are enjoined by Federal Court of Appeals.'' In addition to the legal summaries, recent issues of *Entertainment Law Reporter* have included information on articles of interest in journals such as *Comm/Ent, A Journal of Communications and Entertainment Law; Communications and the Law; Journal of Law and Economics*; and *Journal of the Patent Office Society*, together with details of educational programs and conferences of interest to readers.

Information Sources

INDEX SOURCES: None.
REPRINT EDITIONS: None.
LOCATION SOURCES: Academy of Motion Picture Arts and Sciences; Fordham University; Los Angeles County Law Library; New York University; Southwestern University; University of California at Los Angeles; University of Denver; University of Southern California; University of Texas; University of Utah.

Publication History

MAGAZINE TITLE AND TITLE CHANGES: *Entertainment Law Reporter*.
VOLUME AND ISSUE DATA: Vol. I, No. 1 (June 1, 1979, to present), twice a month.
PUBLISHER AND PLACE OF PUBLICATION: Entertainment Law Reporter Publishing Company, 9440 Santa Monica Boulevard, Suite 600, Beverly Hills, Calif. 90210 (Vol. I, No. 1–Vol. IV, No. 18); Entertainment Law Reporter Publishing Company, 2210 Wilshire Boulevard, Suite 311, Santa Monica, Calif. 90403 (Vol. IV, No. 19, to present).
EDITOR: Lionel S. Sobel.

Anthony Slide

ENTERTAINMENT WORLD

During its eight months of existence spanning 1969 and 1970, *Entertainment World* was promoted as a "vitally dynamic" trade paper covering film, television, theatre, night life, business and finance, and the recording industry. It included film and television reviews as well as production and casting charts. All of the articles dealt with contemporary cinema, except for the following: "Hollywood, Movies, and the Novelist," a 1936 unpublished piece by James Hilton (Vol. 1, No. 1); "Retrospect: Director Josef von Sternberg" by Fred W. Fox (Vol. 2, No. 1); and "A Nice Little Dinner Party: Academy Awards, 1927/ 1928" by Margaret Redfield (Vol. 2, No. 7). In 1970 *Entertainment World* merged with its sister publication, *Show*.*

Information Sources

INDEX SOURCES: None.
REPRINT EDITIONS: None.
LOCATION SOURCES: Academy of Motion Picture Arts and Sciences; Library of Congress.

Publication History

MAGAZINE TITLE AND TITLE CHANGES: *Entertainment World.*
VOLUME AND ISSUE DATA: Vol. I, No. 1–Vol. II, No. 21 (October 3, 1969–May
    29, 1970), weekly except no issue for November 28, 1969.
PUBLISHER AND PLACE OF PUBLICATION: Entertainment World Publications, Inc.,
    6548 Sunset Boulevard, Hollywood, Calif. 90029.
EDITOR: Howard A. Coffin II (October 3, 1969–February 6, 1970); Lewis Segal (Feb-
    ruary 13, 1970–May 29, 1970).

Anthony Slide

THE ESSANAY GUIDE. See Appendix 3

ESSANAY NEWS. See Appendix 3

E. T. COMMUNICATOR. See Appendix 1

EXCEPTIONAL PHOTOPLAYS. See FILMS IN REVIEW

EXHIBITORS' BULLETIN. See Appendix 3

EXHIBITORS DAILY REVIEW. See EXHIBITOR'S TRADE
REVIEW

EXHIBITORS REVIEW. See EXHIBITOR'S TRADE REVIEW

EXHIBITOR'S TRADE REVIEW

On December 9, 1916, *Exhibitor's Trade Review* entered the field of motion
picture trade publications as an advocate for the exhibitor. Amid lawsuits, an
investigation of its founder, and vituperative accusations by the other trade
papers, *Exhibitor's Trade Review* established itself legitimately in its role as
advisor to and fighter for the independent exhibitor.

Founder Lee A. Ochs (then president of the Motion Picture Exhibitors League
of America) by the second issue had his review declared the official organ of
the League. He had attempted to purchase *Motography** to this end, but when

the stockholders of that publication blocked the sale, Ochs went to *The Moving Picture World** and acquired the services of editorial staff member W. Stephen Bush, veteran reviewer and writer, to be his editor. After weathering an attack on its founder (that Ochs had once used his office for personal gain) and an attack on its foundation (that it was supported by an interested production company) the review settled in to a respectable, yet always quite vocal, existence as the exhibitors' representative.

Through its reviews, news, special features, services, advertising, and advocacy, *Exhibitor's Trade Review* guided the exhibitor through his various struggles. The exhibitor's role during the silent era was of far greater involvement than in the later sound days. D. W. Griffith, quoted in *Exhibitor's Trade Review*, said, "a picture needs an artist to properly present it."[1] In addition to booking and advertising the features, the exhibitor was responsible for the musical accompaniment, selection of short subjects, and organization of stage presentations to go with the feature. The theatres themselves were in some cases large palaces needing decoration and upkeep unheard of today.

In weekly sections, *Exhibitor's Trade Review* provided the exhibitor with reviews giving cast, credits, synopsis, points of appeal and general critical appraisal, advertising and promotional advice and materials for each feature, indications on how leading theatres arranged their programs, complete music cue sheets for major films of the week, and synopses from the studios of coming attractions. Technical advice on equipment and theatre operation was given in sections titled "The Projection Booth," "From Studio to Laboratory," "The Cameraman's Department," and "Theatre Construction and Equipment."

The reviews were geared to the exhibitor rather than to the general public or the intelligentsia. Thus the observations, praise, or damnation all revolved around projected box office fare. For major films, especially those of D. W. Griffith, full-page reviews appeared. Often multipage advertising guides attempted to help the exhibitor exploit the picture. Some of the stunts suggested may today seem offensive (for *Poor Boob*, since a fat girl figured prominently in the plot, exhibitors were encouraged to obtain a scale for their lobbies and admit free of charge any woman weighing 190 pounds or more).[2] Other tactics would today seem saccharine (for *Please Get Married*, a Zanesville, Ohio, exhibitor was applauded for offering twenty-five dollars to a couple who would get married on stage at the end of the picture—this did occur without audience catcalls, so the exhibitor wrote).[3] But at the time such strategies were quite popular.

In its editorials, *Exhibitor's Trade Review* championed the exhibitors' interests. Issues such as censorship, the uniform contract, the music tax, the war revenue tax, booking systems (whether syndicated, selective, open, collective, or percentage based), the deposit system, influenza epidemics, the length of the "superpictures," admission prices, the "double-feature evil," reformers, the Hays Office, the "expensive prologue menace," and the threat of radio (and motion pictures transmitted by radio into homes) all were addressed openly and with the exhibitors' interests in mind. Although the exhibitors' practice of "operating" (that is, cutting out offensive or long parts) was condoned, "sniping" (or adding advertisements in the middle of the picture) was harshly rebuked. The most serious issues of the period for the exhibitor—the "Wall Street invasion" and the acquisition of theatres and theatre chains by the production companies—were confronted through collaboration with the exhibitor organizations and direct negotiations with the interested parties.

In its nearly ten years of weekly publication, *Exhibitor's Trade Review* offered some outstanding articles and features that deserve to be remembered. The career of D. W. Griffith was followed in detail. (He in turn called *Exhibitor's Trade Review* "the exhibitor's bible.")[4] Griffith's speeches across the country denouncing censorship were reproduced in full. In 1920, a special section of seventy-two pages on Griffith included his biography.[5] Griffith, however, was not the only director given acclaim. In 1918, *Exhibitor's Trade Review* published a special section devoted to the Motion Picture Directors Association giving photographs and brief histories of its sixty-four members.[6]

Editor W. Stephen Bush toured the country in 1917 and contributed essays on the history of film exhibition in the various regions. In 1920, editor Leslie Mason's trip to Europe resulted in similar lengthy essays on conditions over there and to the inclusion of foreign film reviews. Perhaps the most intellectual piece the *Review* published was an essay on stage presentations accompanying pictures written by Rouben Mamoulian, then of the Eastman Theatre in Rochester, New York.[7] Mamoulian's theory of "dramatic movement," while not being of much practical use to the average theatre owner, does give written documentation to some of his ideas that the world would soon experience in his Broadway and Hollywood work.

Although *Exhibitor's Trade Review*'s affiliation with the various exhibitor organizations changed through its existence and charges against its biases were occasionally invoked, it can be fairly said that except for one short period (in 1923 it seemed to be more concerned with producers and distributors than exhibitors), *Exhibitor's Trade Review* was an able and important journal for the exhibitor and for the industry as a whole. Its length dwindled near the end as *Exhibitors Daily Review* came into being. In April 1926 the weekly disappeared as the daily ventured toward the sound era. (*Exhibitors Daily Review* continued publication until December 20, 1930, when it became *Motion Picture Daily*.)

Notes

1. Vol. 6, No. 20, October 18, 1919, p. 1721.
2. Vol. 5, No. 15, March 15, 1919, p. 1127.
3. Vol. 7, No. 15, March 13, 1920, p. 1543.
4. Vol. 6, No. 20, October 18, 1919, p. 1721.
5. Vol. 7, No. 17, March 27, 1920.
6. Vol. 3, No. 26, June 1, 1918.
7. Vol. 19, No. 9, January 16, 1926, "Exciting the Imagination of the Picture Audience" by Rouben Mamoulian.

Information Sources

INDEX SOURCES: None.
REPRINT EDITIONS: Library of Congress Photoduplication Service.
LOCATION SOURCES: Library of Congress (all but last seven issues); New York Public
  Library.

Publication History

MAGAZINE TITLE AND TITLE CHANGES: *Exhibitor's Trade Review* (December 9,
  1916–February 5, 1921); *Exhibitors Trade Review* (February 12, 1921–January
  30, 1926); *Exhibitors Review* (February 6, 1926–April 17, 1926).
VOLUME AND ISSUE DATA: Vol. I, No. 1–Vol. XIX, No. 22 (December 9, 1916–
  April 17, 1926), weekly.
PUBLISHER AND PLACE OF PUBLICATION: Exhibitor's Trade Review, Inc., 1587
  Broadway, New York, N.Y. (Vol. I, No. 1–Vol. IX, No. 10); Exhibitors Trade
  Review, Inc., 1587 Broadway, New York, N.Y. (Vol. IX, No. 11–Vol. X, No.
  19); Exhibitors Trade Review, Inc., Knickerbocker Building, Broadway and Forty-
  second Street, New York, N.Y. (Vol. X, No. 20–Vol. XIV, No. 14); Exhibitors
  Review Publishing Corporation, Knickerbocker Building, Broadway and Forty-
  second Street, New York, N.Y. (Vol. XIV, No. 15–Vol. XV, No. 22); Exhibitors
  Review Publishing Corporation, Hearn Building, 45 West Forty-fifth Street, New
  York, N.Y. (Vol. XV, No. 23–Vol. XIX, No. 22).
EDITOR: Merritt Crawford (December 9, 1916); W. Stephen Bush (December 16, 1916–
  March 9, 1918); Leslie Mason (March 16, 1918–January 8, 1921); Monte W.
  Sohn (January 15, 1921–December 24, 1921); L. W. Boynton (December 31,
  1921–April 28, 1923); Howard McLellan and George Blaisdell (May 5, 1923–
  July 21, 1923); George Blaisdell (July 28, 1923–August 9, 1924); Willard C.
  Howe (August 30, 1924–February 20, 1926); Fred J. McConnell (February 27,
  1926–April 17, 1926).

Alan Gevinson

EXPERIMENTAL CINEMA

Experimental Cinema was a small Marxist film journal that appeared five times
between 1930 and 1934. Its editorial staff, which grew and changed from issue
to issue, included Lewis Jacobs, Seymour Stern, David Platt, Barnet Braver-
Mann (a.k.a. Braverman), H. A. Potamkin, and many contributing editors including Bela Balazs. Just as its editorial board was never constant, neither was
its place of publication. *Experimental Cinema* was published wherever its various
editors happened to be living at the time: Philadelphia, New York, Hollywood.

From its first appearance, *Experimental Cinema* revealed its single and rather
narrow approach to the film. Almost all the articles printed in the five issues
dealt in one way or another with the greatness and superiority of the Soviet
cinema and with the Soviet Union as a true revolutionary workers' society. The

"Hollywood cinema," on the other hand, was regarded with an almost frantic fear and loathing as a tool of the bourgeoisie and capitalism. An editorial statement in No. 3 stated that *Experimental Cinema* desired to establish

> the ideological and organizational foundations of an American working-class cinema. This is particularly desirable at a time when the current Hollywood movie boasts a banality and a stupidity that seems to wax greater in proportion to the growth in the unsettlement and distress of American life.... Hollywood, while it is an almost inexhaustible source of stupifying "entertainment", is also at the same time the tool of American imperialist political policy, which serves so faithfully and so supinely through the medium of war films, anti-USSR films, news reels, etc.

Experimental Cinema saw as its purpose the bringing of Soviet films to the American public and the use of Soviet film methods in creating a true workers' cinema. In these endeavours a number of the journal's editors were actively involved—making their own documentary films and participating in the Film and Photo League. These activities were described in Nos. 4 and 5.

In spreading the gospel of Soviet film technique, *Experimental Cinema* was particularly important in that it was one of the first English-language journals to publish essays by Sergei Eisenstein and Vsevolod Pudovkin: "The Cinematographic Principle and Japanese Culture" (No. 3), "The Principles of Film Form" (No. 4), and "Que Viva Mexico" (No. 5) by Eisenstein and "Film Direction and Film Manuscript I & II" (Nos. 1 and 2) and "Scenario and Direction" (No. 3) by Pudovkin. Other Soviet directors who wrote about their methods in the pages of *Experimental Cinema* included Leonid Trauberg (No. 4), Mikhail Kaufman (No. 4), and Alexander Dovzhenko (No. 5). Non-Soviet filmmakers whose articles appeared in the journal included Alberto Cavalcanti ("Evolution of Cinematography in France," No. 1) and René Clair ("The Kingdom of Cinema," No. 5).

The writing in *Experimental Cinema* was rather uneven, ranging from the anti-Hollywood ravings of Seymour Stern ("Hollywood and Montage: The Basic Fallacies of the American Film Technique," No. 4; and "Hollywood Bulletin," Nos. 2–5) to the more thoughtful and theoretical examinations of Lewis Jacobs ("The New Cinema: A Preface to Film Form," No. 1; and "Decomposition," No. 2). Nevertheless, the general tone of the journal was extremely proscriptive. Any filmmaker, American or European, was to be condemned if he/she did not use Soviet montage or a dialectical approach to filmmaking or if he/she did not fully explore social problems and social structures: "Vidor and Evasion" (No. 3) and "Josef von Sternberg" (No. 5), both by B. G. Braver-Mann.

By issues No. 4 and 5, *Experimental Cinema* had doubled in size and included many more photographs than had previous issues. Editorial statements indicated continuing financial difficulties in publishing the journal regularly, although subscribers were promised twelve issues. In No. 4 Theodore Dreiser provided a statement of his belief in the policies of *Experimental Cinema*.

Nos. 4 and 5 are particularly interesting because of their coverage of Eisenstein's controversial production of *Que Viva Mexico*. No. 4 contained many stills from the film, which was still in production as that issue went to press. Articles included "Eisenstein's Film on Mexico" by Agustin Aragon Leiva, a special assistant to Eisenstein, and "*Que Viva Mexico*, Eisenstein in Mexico" by Morris Helprin. By the time No. 5 appeared, one year later, production of *Que Viva Mexico* had been discontinued and the unedited footage had been taken away from Eisenstein by his sponsor, Upton Sinclair, who had it edited and released as *Thunder over Mexico*. *Experimental Cinema* appears to have been in the center of a campaign to return the original footage to Eisenstein. "Notes on Activities of *Experimental Cinema* during 1933" and "Manifesto on 'Que Viva Mexico' " indicated the journal's position: "The editors of *Experimental Cinema* decided that although the Sinclairs might be legally empowered to dispose of the film as they saw fit, they should not be permitted to commit this act of treachery and vandalism." The editors stated that they attempted to raise money to buy the film material back for Eisenstein and were now campaigning to save at least the negative. In their desire to discredit *Thunder over Mexico*, *Experimental Cinema* printed the scenario of *Que Viva Mexico* written by Eisenstein and V. G. Alexandroff. Accompanying the scenario was an "Introduction to Synopsis for 'Que Viva Mexico' " by Seymour Stern explaining the controversy surrounding the film (as *Experimental Cinema* saw it) and describing Eisenstein's original intentions for the film.

After the appearance of No. 5, Lewis Jacobs resigned as editor, and although No. 6 was promised, no further issues appeared.

Information Sources

INDEX SOURCES: None.
REPRINT EDITIONS: Arno Press.
LOCATION SOURCES: Library of Congress; Museum of Modern Art; New York Public Library; University of California at Los Angeles.

Publication History

MAGAZINE TITLE AND TITLE CHANGES: *Experimental Cinema*.
VOLUME AND ISSUE DATA: No. 1 (February 1930); No. 2 (June 1930); No. 3 (January 1931); No. 4 (1932); No. 5 (1934).
PUBLISHER AND PLACE OF PUBLICATION: Experimental Cinema, 919 Locust Street, Philadelphia, Pa. (No. 1); Experimental Cinema, 1629 Chestnut Street, Philadelphia, Pa. (No. 2); Experimental Cinema, 302 East Fifty-ninth Street, New York, N.Y. (No. 3); Experimental Cinema, 407 East Pico, Los Angeles, Calif. (No. 4); Experimental Cinema, 51 West Forty-seventh Street, New York, N.Y. (No. 5).

EDITOR: Lewis Jacobs, David Platt, Seymour Stern, and B. G. Braver-Mann.

Aniko Bodroghkozy

EYEPIECE

An enthusiastic if not always literate journal devoted to the art and craft of the cinematographer, *Eyepiece* has been sponsored by the Guild of British Camera Technicians since the journal's founding in 1978. Despite its sponsorship, the magazine is not exclusively devoted to British cameramen, although it is mainly concerned with current cinema. Exceptions have been articles on the 1925 *She* (Vol. 2, No. 7) and an interview with Geoffrey Faithfull (Vol. 2, No. 5). *Eyepiece* has featured a number of special issues, including those on video (Vol. 2, No. 9), special effects (Vol. 3, No. 3), processing (Vol. 3, No. 7), and the inevitable "The Making of *Gandhi*" (Vol. 3, No. 10).

Information Sources

INDEX SOURCES: None.
REPRINT EDITIONS: None.
LOCATION SOURCES: Academy of Motion Picture Arts and Sciences (lacks early issues).

Publication History

MAGAZINE TITLE AND TITLE CHANGES: *Eyepiece*.
VOLUME AND ISSUE DATA: Vol. I, No. 1 (May 1978 to present), bimonthly.
PUBLISHER AND PLACE OF PUBLICATION: The Guild of British Camera Technicians, 303-315 Cricklewood Broadway, London N.W.2, England.
EDITOR: Kevin Kavanagh (May 1978–July/August 1982); John Gainsborough (September/October 1982 to present).

Anthony Slide

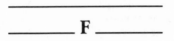

_____ **F** _____

FACTS ABOUT FILM IN FINLAND. See Appendix 4

FACTS ABOUT FINLAND. See Appendix 4

FALLING FOR STARS. See Appendix 1

FAMOUS MONSTERS OF FILMLAND. See Appendix 2

FANGORIA. See Appendix 2

FANTASCENE

One of the better periodicals devoted to fantasy, horror, and science-fiction films, *Fantascene* was written by and for film buffs (although its editor, Robert F. Skotak, was to become a special effects technician). Among the more useful items to be found in the magazine's four-issue run spanning the years 1975 to 1978 are an article on Ib Melchior (No. 1), an interview with Jim Danforth (No. 2), and a career profile on William Cameron Menzies with an excellent in-depth study of Menzies's *Invaders from Mars* (No. 4). *Fantascene* was profusely illustrated and also included book and film reviews.

Information Sources

INDEX SOURCES: None.
REPRINT EDITIONS: None.
LOCATION SOURCES: Academy of Motion Picture Arts and Sciences (lacks No. 1).

Publication History

MAGAZINE TITLE AND TITLE CHANGES: *Fantascene*.
VOLUME AND ISSUE DATA: No. 1 (Fall 1975); No. 2 (Summer 1976); No. 3 (1977);
    No. 4 (1978).
PUBLISHER AND PLACE OF PUBLICATION: Cinema Vista Productions, 1707 Broad-
    view Lane, Suite 114, Ann Arbor, Mich. 48105 (No. 1); Fantascene Productions,
    1701 Broadview Lane, Suite 103, Ann Arbor, Mich. 48105 (No. 2); Fantascene
    Productions, P.O. Box 1859, Hollywood, Calif. 90028 (No. 3); Fantascene Pro-
    ductions, 8564 Cardwell Street, Westland, Mich. 48185 (No. 4).
EDITOR: Robert F. Skotak and Robert Scott (No. 1); Robert F. Skotak (Nos. 2–4).

Anthony Slide

FAR EAST FILM NEWS. See MOVIE/T.V. MARKETING

FIGHTING STARS. See Appendix 2

FILM

Film, a periodical "devoted to the interests of the film society movement,"[1]
was first published by the British Federation of Film Societies (BFFS) in October
1954. Promising to search for a balance "between opinion and information;
between the entertainment film and the documentary; between the discussion of
films and news of the film society movement; between types of review; between
text and illustration,"[2] the fledgling publication was enthusiastically welcomed
by the British film community.

Over the next nineteen years, *Film*, a quarterly magazine,[3] offered articles
and features on a wide variety of popular topics designed to appeal to film society
members and movie enthusiasts alike. Regular columns included film society
news, transcripts of lectures and speeches, analyses of technical innovations,
festival reports from around the world, and reviews of new as well as classic
motion pictures, with an eye on their potential as film society fare.

Of course, along with the columns which appeared in each issue, *Film* also
included feature articles on a variety of well-known themes, with an emphasis
on the American as well as the European cinema. Ranging from genre studies
to profiles of directors and evaluations of popular film theories, the commonplace
topics were brought to life by consistently strong writing from a roster of con-

tributors including Paul Rotha, Lotte Eisner, Peter Armitage, Kevin Brownlow, and many others. Of special note were Rotha's views on the documentary in the fifties, and Brownlow's series of in-depth articles on legendary filmmakers like Charles Chaplin, William Wyler, and Josef von Sternberg, which appeared in issues throughout the early sixties.

In addition, readers were encouraged to contribute their views about the various articles in each issue. The editors evidently wanted *Film* to be a cooperative effort, to the point where one very negative piece, entitled "The Curious Cult of John Ford" (No. 2), was accompanied by an inset asking: "Do you agree with this estimate of Ford? If not let us have your views." Although this kind of active recruitment of reactions didn't last long, the editors continued to be concerned with making their publication one which reflected the readers' interests and opinions.

In late 1972, editor Peter Cargin announced that *Film* would be undergoing a format change in order to incorporate several other BFFS publications, including *FilmNews*, *Featureguide*, and the *Newsletter*. Called a move of "economics and rationalisation," the decision transformed *Film* into a monthly journal which contained shorter articles and more information pertinent to the running of film societies. Highlighted items included articles on where to obtain certain films, a guide to projectors (Series 2, No. 18), and, in each issue, an increased number of brief movie reviews. There was still coverage of festivals and BFFS news, but features started to become infrequent. An exception was the series of interviews with Hollywood luminaries (Howard Hawks, Series 2, No. 14; Robert Redford, Series 2, No. 26) conducted by John Kobal, who also contributed several other articles in the early seventies. For the most part, however, the focus of *Film* had undergone a fundamental change.

Since 1976, *Film* has been devoted almost completely to the organization of the BFFS, providing tips on the rental and projection of films and featuring columns like "Dates for Your Diary" and "Critical Opinion," a compilation of critics' reactions to current films. Occasional special issues concentrate on specific subjects (CinemaScope issue, Series 2, No. 100; Polish issue, Series 2, No. 101), but for the most part, the approach has become extremely practical and of interest only to film society enthusiasts.

Notes

1. No. 1, October 1954, p. 5.
2. No. 2, December 1954, p. 5.
3. From 1964 through 1969, *Film* was published triannually, not quarterly.

Information Sources

INDEX SOURCES: The New Film Index.
REPRINT EDITIONS: World Microfilms.
LOCATION SOURCES: New York Public Library; University of Southern California.

Publication History

MAGAZINE TITLE AND TITLE CHANGES: *Film*.

VOLUME AND ISSUE DATA: Nos. 1–67 (October 1954–Autumn 1972), quarterly (Nos. 1–38), triannually (Nos. 39–56), quarterly (Nos. 57–67); Series 2, No. 1 (April 1973 to present), monthly.

PUBLISHER AND PLACE OF PUBLICATION: British Federation of Film Societies, 35 Priory Road, Sheffield 7, England (Nos. 1–28); British Federation of Film Societies, Elm Cottage, Upton Pyne, Exeter, England (Nos. 29–32); British Federation of Film Societies, 198 Bridgewater Road, Wembley, Middlesex, England (Nos. 33–34); British Federation of Film Societies, 42 Bloomsbury Street, London W.C.1, England (Nos. 35–39); British Federation of Film Societies, 55A Welbeck Street, London W.1, England (Nos. 40–42); British Federation of Film Societies, 21 Larchwood Road, St. John's, Woking, Surrey, England (Nos. 43–45); British Federation of Film Societies, 81 Dean Street, London W1V 6AA, England (Nos. 46–67; Series 2, No. 1, to present).

EDITOR: Alan Borshell and Jon Evans (Nos. 1–11); Jon Evans (Nos. 12–16); Peter Armitage (Nos. 17–54); Peter Cargin (Nos. 55–67; Series 2, No. 1, to present).

Barbara Hall

FILM (John Stuart Fan Club). See Appendix 1

FILM A DOBA

Founded in 1954, *Film a Doba* is the official film periodical of the Czech Ministry of Culture. The journal features articles, essays, and brief commentaries as well as extensive editorials dealing with various ideological aspects of movie making, all following a rather rigid political line. Restrictions on what could be dealt with, and how, are a characteristic feature of articles discussing Western and American cinematic culture. Such a visibly enforced approach is obvious in Jan Dvořák's article, "Tradice v poválečné Americké kinematografii" (American cinematography after the war; Vol. 11, No. 10); in the editorial entitled "Politický film v světě" (Political film in the world; Vol. 18, No. 7); as well as in Jiři Levý's "Rozpory současného světa" (Today's world contradictions reflected in film; Vol. 18, No. 10).

The journal's firm Marxist orientation leads to a wide coverage of various, very often minor, aspects of movie making in the Soviet Union as well as in other Eastern European countries. L. Poupětova wrote "Sovětské filmy v Dušanbe" (Soviet films at the Dushanbe Film Festival; Vol. 26, No. 9), and V. Zhdan (editor of the Soviet film journal *Iskusstvo kino**) wrote "Pravdivost metody" (The truthfulness of the method; Vol. 26, No. 11), an article discussing Socialist Realism as applied to filmmaking. The officially prescribed treatment of the world of cinema is also evident in Jiři Hrbas's monthly column on Soviet and East European film directors and actors.

Film a Doba often publishes interviews with leading Czech film directors, such as Galina Kopaněvová's "Dvě hodiny s Milošem Formanem" (Two hours with Milos Forman; Vol. 14, No. 8) and Kopaněvová's interview with the Soviet actor Jurii Ozerov, "Žít dokořán a hodně pracovat" (To live fully and to work hard; Vol. 28, No. 10). Technical aspects of filmmaking are discussed by M. R. Novotny in "Audiovizuální syntéza ve filmu" (The audiovisual synthesis in film; Vol. 26, No. 2).

The journal's coverage of national and international film festivals is rather limited to Soviet, Czech, and other Eastern European countries' events—J. Levy periodically writes on this topic as in his coverage of the Karlovy Vary Film Festival Anniversary, "Ve znamení jubilea" (Under the flag of jubilee; Vol. 26, No. 6).

In keeping with its commitment to Marxist ideology, the journal often features extended articles on the "ill effects" of the bourgeois aesthetics on cinema culture as seen in Vladimir Baskakov's "Likvidátoři realismu" (The enemies of realism; Vol. 26, No. 9).

In the column "Objektiveně kritiki" (Through the lenses of criticism), critical reviews are regularly published on controversial Czech films. Lothar Warenke wrote "Náš krátký život" (Our short life; Vol. 29, No. 2), Antonin Kachlik wrote "Kouzelné dobrodužstvi" (A magic adventure; Vol. 29, No. 6), and S. Uher wrote on the movie "Pásla koně na betóně" (She fed horses on concrete; Vol. 29, No. 7).

Only sparse attention is given to the Western and American film scene. In "Portrety světových hercú (Portraits of world actors), each issue publishes photographs of Western and American cinema figures, accompanied by brief biographical notes. Czech, Soviet, and Eastern European filmmakers and actors are profiled in "Tvurci, Filmy, Názory" (Authors, films, opinions).

In addition, *Film a Doba* regularly covers amateur filmmaking, documentaries, and movies made for television, as well as reviewing film books. An annual analytical index accompanies each December issue.

Information Sources

INDEX SOURCES: FIAF International Index to Film Periodicals.
REPRINT EDITIONS: None.
LOCATION SOURCES: University of Southern California.

Publication History

MAGAZINE TITLE AND TITLE CHANGES: *Film a Doba: Měsíčník pro filmovu kulturu.*
VOLUME AND ISSUE DATA: Vol. I, No. 1 (1954 to present), monthly.
PUBLISHER AND PLACE OF PUBLICATION: Orbis, Václavské náměstí 43, Praha 1, Czechoslovakia.

EDITOR: Dr. Antonin Novak (1954–June 1964); Galina Kopaněvová (July 1964–August 1964); Jiři Hrbas (September 1964–November 1980); Dr. Vladimir Kolár (December 1980 to present).

Hari S. Rorlich

FILM & HISTORY

Founded in 1971 by John E. O'Connor and Martin A. Jackson, *Film & History* is the quarterly publication of the Historians Film Committee, a 450-member organization affiliated with the American Historical Association. The Committee was formed in 1970 by historians seeking to encourage the use of film for research and teaching by historians and social scientists. Though *Film & History* is edited by both Professors O'Connor and Jackson, production of the magazine appears to be mainly the responsibility of John O'Connor, the driving force behind this publication that has carved out its distinctive niche of specialization.

Film & History demonstrates a recent trend whereby specialists with training in disciplines other than cinema studies (which is still in gestation as an academic "discipline") have moved to establish and develop a particular orientation for film study. John O'Connor's own training is in early American history (Ph.D., CUNY Graduate Center, 1974), and foremost among his publications is a widely respected biography, *William Paterson: Lawyer and Statesman*, published in 1979 by the Rutgers University Press. His interest in local and regional history is further demonstrated by his coauthored monograph, *Newark: An American City*, published by the Newark, New Jersey, Bicentennial Commission in 1979.

At the same time, however, O'Connor has also extended his research to cinema-related topics. One of his most recent books is the beautifully illustrated *The Hollywood Indian: Stereotypes of Native Americans in Films*, published by the New Jersey State Museum in 1980. He has also edited the screenplay of *I Am a Fugitive from a Chain Gang*, published in the Wisconsin/Warner Bros. Screenplay Series in 1981, and wrote the critical introduction that traced that film's production history. In 1977 he edited a monograph entitled *Film & the Humanities* that was published by the Rockefeller Foundation. With Martin Jackson he wrote another monograph entitled *Teaching History With Film*, published by the American Historical Association in 1974. But without question Jackson and O'Connor are best known in cinema circles for their coedited book, *American History/American Film: Interpreting the Hollywood Image* (Frederick Ungar Publishers, 1979), which has been so successful that the editors are now working on a companion volume, *American History/American Television*.

Such productivity, along with teaching and administrative duties, cannot leave much time for magazine production, yet John O'Connor continues to bring out *Film & History* on schedule. The format is modest and serviceable. Typical issues run to about twenty-four pages, averaging two longer features per issue, followed by a mix of shorter reviews (books, mainly) and "Film & History News."

Film & History has featured essays and interviews (with Sydney Pollack in Vol. 4, No. 2, for example, and with Basil Wright in Vol. 10, No. 4) but mainly the former, which have been useful in directing attention to obscure and forgotten films like David Miller's *Seeds of Destiny*, written by Art Arthur for the United Nations Relief and Rehabilitation Administration, produced in 1945 to draw attention to children who had been victims of the war, and the winner of the Academy Award for best documentary in 1947. (This essay, by Irene Kahn Atkins, who personally interviewed the writer and director, appeared in May 1981, Vol. 11, No. 2). *Film & History* has also covered more conventional feature films, such as Elia Kazan's *Splendor in the Grass* (Kenneth Hey, Vol. 11, No. 1), Hitchcock's *Foreign Correspondent* (John Rossi, Vol. 12, No. 2), *The China Syndrome* (Robert F. Willson, Jr., Vol. 9, No. 3), and *On the Waterfront* (Kenneth Hey, Vol. 9, No. 4). In addition, there are typically essays that stress historical applications of film study, such as "Recent Cinematic Images of Nazism" (Ralph Berets, Vol. 9, No. 4), "A Lost Legacy of Labor Films" (Leslie Fishbein, Vol. 9, No. 2), "British Newsreels and the Spanish Civil War" (Anthony Aldgate, Vol. 3, No. 1), or "Hollywood and...Russian-American Relations" (Melvin Small, Vol. 10, No. 1). On occasion *Film & History* has produced "special" issues, such as Vol. 11, No. 3 (1981), "Film Study and the History of Technology." The writers are almost exclusively academics, centered mainly in departments of history nationwide but occasionally also in departments of American studies or English.

The editors of *Film & History* value solid scholarship and prefer essays that are carefully researched. The focus is obviously scholarly rather than popular, though popular films have been increasingly treated in this journal. *Film & History* is the only specialized journal of its kind in the United States. It predates its nearest competitor, *The Historical Journal of Film, Radio & Television** by a decade. Though of some general interest, *Film & History* is mainly intended for the historian-specialist and comes with membership in the Historians Film Committee.

Information Sources

INDEX SOURCES: America: History and Life; Historical Abstracts.
REPRINT EDITIONS: None.
LOCATION SOURCES: Columbia University; Library of Congress; Princeton University; Rutgers University; University of California at Los Angeles; University of Illinois; University of Iowa; University of South Carolina; University of Tulsa; University of Wisconsin at Madison.

Publication History

MAGAZINE TITLE AND TITLE CHANGES: *Historians Film Committee Newsletter* (Vol. I); *Film & History* (Vol. II to present).
VOLUME AND ISSUE DATA: Vol. I, No. 1 (1971 to present), quarterly.

PUBLISHER AND PLACE OF PUBLICATION: The Historians Film Committee, New
    Jersey Institute of Technology, Newark, N.J. 07102.
EDITOR: John E. O'Connor and Martin A. Jackson.

James M. Welsh

FILM AND TELEVISION DAILY. See THE FILM DAILY

FILM AND T.V. CAREERS. See Appendix 2

FILM AND T.V. MUSIC

Film and T.V. Music (earlier *Film Music Notes*, then *Film Music*) throughout
its existence (1941–1957) sought to illustrate the uses of film in music education.
In doing so, the magazine carried many informative articles by film composers
and presented a perspective that combined film, music, and education.

The publisher of *Film and T.V. Music* was the National Film Music Council,
which was founded and probably funded by the National Federation of Music
Clubs. The Council's purpose, according to its prospectus, was "to foster interest
in music in the films; to encourage musicians who are developing this new art
form; to awaken teachers and students to the educational, artistic and practical
possibilities of this new medium of expression."

While production quality and substance of the magazine improved throughout
its run, its format remained consistent. Each issue reviewed and analyzed the
music of one or two films in detail and several other films briefly. Feature articles
focused on the film industry and music of countries other than the United States,
performing musicians, and various production technicians, such as the music
mixer, studio librarian, and engineer. Regularly, brief reviews and articles were
devoted to 16mm films, cartoons, documentaries, newsreels, television, and
"lighter films."

Film and T.V. Music was most interested, however, in the relationship between
films and music education, in particular how films could encourage appreciation
of "good" music. Film reviews critiqued the success of a film's music in relation
to the dramatic function of the music, as pure music, and as a potential tool in
the classroom.

From Vol. 3 on, excerpts of film scores were included in each issue. In early
issues only themes were reproduced; later, substantial score excerpts and analyses
were presented, often with commentary by the composers. Virtually every major
Hollywood film composer is represented in the run of the magazine by score
excerpts, analyses, and frequent interviews. Composers often outlined the par-

ticular problems a film presented and their solution. Special issues of *Film and T.V. Music* were devoted to *Cyrano de Bergerac* (music, Dimitri Tiomkin), *The Red Pony* (Aaron Copland), and *Carnegie Hall* (various classical composers).

Information Sources

INDEX SOURCES: The Music Index (post-1949 only); Vol. XI contains an index to Vols. VI–XI.

REPRINT EDITIONS: Several articles are reprinted in *Film Music: From Violins to Video*, edited by James L. Limbacher (Scarecrow Press, 1974).

LOCATION SOURCES: Academy of Motion Picture Arts and Sciences (incomplete); New York Public Library; University of California at Los Angeles; University of Colorado at Boulder.

Publication History

MAGAZINE TITLE AND TITLE CHANGES: *Film Music Notes* (Vols. I–XI); *Film Music* (Vols. XII–XV); *Film and T.V. Music* (Vols. XVI–XVII).

VOLUME AND ISSUE DATA: Vol. I (October 1941–May/June 1942), eight issues; Vols. II–V (October 1942–June 1946), monthly except for July, August, and September; Vols. VI–XVI (September/October 1946–May/June 1957), five issues per volume; Vol. XVII (Fall and Winter 1957–1958), one issue.

PUBLISHER AND PLACE OF PUBLICATION: No publisher listed, 6162 Hollywood Boulevard, Hollywood 28, Calif. (Vols. I–III); National Film Music Council, 6162 Hollywood Boulevard, Hollywood 28, Calif. (Vols. IV–V); National Film Music Council, Old Greenwich, Conn. (Vol. VI); National Film Music Council, 250 East Forty-third Street, New York 17, N.Y. (Vol. VII); National Film Music Council, 31 West Union Square, New York, N.Y. (Vols. VIII–X); National Film Music Council, Old Greenwich, Conn. (Vol. XI); National Film Music Council, 26 East Eighty-third Street, New York, N.Y. (Vol. XII, No. 1–Vol. XIV, No. 3); National Film Music Council, 11 East Eighty-seventh Street, New York, N.Y. (Vol. XIV, No. 4–Vol. XVI, No. 4); National Film Music Council, 845 West End Avenue, New York, N.Y. (Vol. XVI, No. 5–Vol. XVII).

EDITOR: Grace Widney Mabee (Vol. I); Grace Widney Mabee and Constance Purdy (Vols. II–IV); Constance Purdy (Vol. V); Frederick W. Sternfield and other guest editors (Vols. VI–IX); Marie L. Hamilton (Vols. X–XVII).

Samuel S. Brylawski

FILM ART

Obviously influenced by *Close Up*,* *Film Art* was typical of the small film magazines which appeared in the thirties and which were very much concerned with raising cinema from a mere vehicle of entertainment to an art form. Rather naive in its approach and containing a number of simplistic articles, *Film Art* declared in its first issue (Summer 1933):

Film Art has not been published merely to high-hat and condemn the commercial film. Our desire is to promote a better understanding of those things which constitute a perfect work of one of the foremost arts—cinema. Also to encourage the making and showing of really intelligent films. Rather than attempt to destroy a sensation-seeking public, we wish to create a new one. This second public should exist as a definite group of persons whose desire is to see artistic films. And who may have a chance of doing so.

Film Art did boast a number of familiar names among its contributors, notably Seymour Stern, Lewis Jacobs, Herman Weinberg, and Thorold Dickinson. Some of the journal's more interesting pieces are "Where Does Art Begin?" by Rudolf Arnheim (No. 2), "Imitation and Creativeness in the Balkan Cinema" by Marie Seton (No. 2), "Open Letter to Dr. Goebbels" by S. M. Eisenstein (No. 5), "Whither Films?" by Michael Balcon (No. 5), "I Believe in the Sound Film" by Fritz Arno Wagner (No. 8), "Moving Silhouettes" by Lotte Reiniger (No. 8), and "The Future of Documentary" by Basil Wright (No. 8). A photographic section was added with issue No. 5. The first issue was apparently published in a smaller form under the title of *Film* before appearing in a new first issue as *Film Art*.

Information Sources

INDEX SOURCES: None.
REPRINT EDITIONS: None.
LOCATION SOURCES: New York Public Library; University of Southern California.

Publication History

MAGAZINE TITLE AND TITLE CHANGES: *Film Art*.
VOLUME AND ISSUE DATA: No. 1 (Summer 1933); No. 2 (Winter 1933); No. 3
    (Spring 1934); No. 4 (Summer 1934); No. 5 (1934–1935); No. 6 (Autumn 1935);
    No. 7 (First Quarter 1936); No. 8 (Second Quarter 1936).
PUBLISHER AND PLACE OF PUBLICATION: Film Art, 5 Joubert Studios, Jubilee
    Place, London S.W.3, England.
EDITOR: B. Vivian Braun (Nos. 1–6); Irene Nicholson and John C. Moore (Nos. 7–8).
                                                                    Anthony Slide

FILM/A.V. NEWS. See FILM NEWS

FILM COMMENT

While all film magazines are generally eclectic in what they publish, the best ones do have a rationale (if not the overt project which guided *Screen** in the seventies) which imbues the magazine with a specific tone and viewpoint. If

Film Comment now seems to be the *Vogue* of film magazines, it was not that long ago when things were quite different.

Film Comment began publication in 1962 under the title *Vision* and changed to the present title beginning with the third issue. From the beginning the magazine, under the editorship of Gordon Hitchens, presented a mixture of articles about experimental films and filmmakers (such as "A Report on the Films of Rudy Burckhardt" in No. 1 and an interview with Ron Rice in No. 3), sociological/political articles ("Anti Negro Propaganda in Film" in No. 1 and an interview with a lawyer fighting censorship in No. 4), and articles about commercial films and filmmakers (such as "Prospects of *Cleopatra*" in No. 1).

By the publication of the second volume, it became clear that Hitchens was trying to make the magazine a forum for asking political questions about films and (to a lesser extent) provide information about, as well as support to, independent filmmakers. In line with this policy, Hitchens published articles on and an interview with Leni Riefenstahl (Vol. 3, No. 1), articles on the Hollywood Ten and the blacklist of the fifties (Vol. 3, No. 4), and devoted most of one issue (Vol. 4, No. 4) to a history of the Legion of Decency.

While this editorial policy made for unusual reading, it did not attract enough of an audience, and the magazine suffered numerous financial problems during its early years of publication. The worst time may have been between 1965 and 1967 when only one issue (Vol. 4, No. 1) appeared. These financial problems undoubtedly took a toll of Hitchens and the staff, and there was some attempt to make the magazine more palatable to a general audience. Several innovations were tried, beginning with a new graphic style for the Summer 1968 (Vol. 4, No. 4) issue and then devoting the bulk of each issue to a single theme (such as "U.S. Film History," Vol. 5, No. 3; and "Chaplin," Vol. 5, No. 4).

Yet even these changes did not sway Hitchens from emphasizing political and social questions. For example, in the special issue on Chaplin, while articles analyzed the individual films, there were also major articles detailing Chaplin's political problems in the fifties and the facts behind his leaving the United States. Unfortunately, this new direction did not prove popular enough, and Hitchens sold the magazine in June 1969, ending his editorship with the Summer 1970 issue (Vol. 6, No. 2).[1]

Richard Corliss became the new editor with the following issue, and he immediately signalled his difference from Hitchens by using Andrew Sarris's article on the auteur theory in 1970 as the selling point for the issue. The emphasis of the magazine shifted from political and social questions to auterism and the American/Hollywood cinema. Corliss, however, was no simple auterist, as he proved with a special issue devoted to the Hollywood screenwriter (Vol. 6, No. 4). If the format of the issue was a trifle slavish in aping Sarris and *The American Cinema* (with Corliss substituting an Acropolis for the Parthenon), the emphasis on the screenwriter offered a necessary corrective to the director studies which dominated most film magazines of the period.

It was this willingness to question the auterism disseminated by Sarris which made *Film Comment* so interesting in the early seventies. For example, in the Fall 1971 (Vol. 7, No. 3) issue, Robin Wood reconsiders John Ford's late films and attacks the excesses of Ford's admirers. This in turn led to Joseph McBride and Michael Wilmington's trying to answer Wood's criticisms by closely analyzing individual films and demonstrating what they felt Wood had overlooked.[2] Corliss attempted to spark the same type of discussion by establishing new departments in the magazine: "Journals," which mitigated the provincialism of New York by looking at the film culture of other cities and countries; "Film Favorites," which allowed in-depth looks at older and little-known films; "Critics," which attempted an overview of the strengths and weaknesses of well-known critics; "Midsection," which gives ten to twenty pages of each issue for exploring a single subject.

Yet the revisionist stance the magazine was assuming had one major flaw, which was that it staked everything on the continuing importance of auterism. As the seventies waned, though, auterism became less and less important for many writers and readers. Where other magazines (for good or ill) were challenged by the theories coming out of France and England (*Screen, Movie,** and *Film Quarterly,** to name a few), *Film Comment* continued on its course of being a moderating voice on auterist excesses. However, when all the other voices changed and altered their policies, *Film Comment* found itself one of the last bastions of auterism, with almost every issue dominated by interviews with, and articles on, directors.

This in itself might not be so bad, except there is nothing new being said in most of the articles. Auterism is now accepted as given and hardly questioned at all. Having won the battle for taking seriously those people who worked in the American/Hollywood cinema, *Film Comment* now seems trapped by its success. There is no sense of challenge in the articles it now publishes. Too often, instead, the magazine exhibits a trendiness and lack of depth which substitutes style for substance. (The *reductio ad absurdum* of this policy may be seen in the January-February 1983 issue, where the "Midsection" is devoted to video games.)

Editorial policies do change, though, and it is to be hoped that this is only a fallow period and that *Film Comment* will once again become an organ of comment which says something.

Notes

1. Vol. 6, No. 2, Summer 1970, p. 2
2. The articles are "The Civil War," Vol. VII, No. 3, Fall 1971, pp. 21–23; and "Seven Women," Vol. VIII, No. 1, Spring 1972, pp. 56–60.

Information Sources

INDEX SOURCES: The Critical Index; FIAF International Index to Film Periodicals; Film Literature Index; The Magazine Index; The New Film Index; Readers Guide to Periodical Literature; Retrospective Index to Film Periodicals, 1930–1971.

REPRINT SOURCES: Johnson Reprint (Vols. I–III); University Microfilms.
LOCATION SOURCES: Academy of Motion Picture Arts and Sciences; Boston University; Museum of Modern Art; Temple University; University of Chicago; University of Idaho; University of Illinois; University of Louisville.

Publication History

MAGAZINE TITLE AND TITLE CHANGES: *Vision* (Vol. I, Nos. 1–2); *Film Comment* (Vol. I, No. 3, to present).
VOLUME AND ISSUE DATA: Vol. I, No. 1–Vol. VIII, No. 2 (Spring 1962–Summer 1972), quarterly; Vol. VIII, No. 3 (September-October 1972 to present), bimonthly.
PUBLISHER AND PLACE OF PUBLICATION: Joseph Blanco, 8 West 102 Street, New York, N.Y. (Vol. I, Nos. 1–2); Lorien Publications, 11 St. Luke's Place, New York, N.Y. (Vol. 1, No. 3–Vol. III, No. 3); William Duffy, 838 West End Avenue, New York, N.Y. (Vol. III, No. 4); Film Comment Publishing Corporation, 42 Dustin Street, Boston, Mass. (Vol. IV, No. 1–Vol. X, No. 2); The Film Society of Lincoln Center, 140 West Sixty-fifth Street, New York, N.Y. 10023 (Vol. X, No. 3, to present).
EDITOR: Gordon Hitchens (1962–1970); Richard Corliss (1970 to present).

Val Almendarez

FILM CRITIC

The 1963 pilot issue of *Film Society*—originated as a quarterly devoted to cinema as both a fine art and a dynamic, influential medium of communication—featured articles by *Village Voice* film critic Andrew Sarris ("Ripples From A Wave"), *Esquire* film critic Dwight MacDonald ("Our Elizabethan Movies"), and writer Mark Sufrin ("The Silent World of Slapstick [1912–1916]").

The choice of the publication's original title sprang from a recognition of the importance of cine-clubs and film societies to serious filmmakers, film goers, and film lovers during the early decades of this young art form's existence.

Five years later, *Film Society* became *Film Society Review*, a monthly (September through May) aspiring to bring a broader film perspective to its expanding readership, a group the publication's editors saw as the leaders in the movement to explore the full potential of the cinema and bring it to bear in improving the culture of which it was an increasingly more significant, interesting, and impactful part.

Still published by the American Federation of Film Societies (as was its predecessor), *Film Society Review* would hold its title from 1968 until 1972, featuring such writers as Raymond Durgnat, Michael Sragow, Ronald Holloway, Gary Crowdus, Lita Paniagua, Leonard Rubenstein, and Foster Hirsch.

Regular columns included "Magazines," "Books," "Critics," "International," and "News." Feature articles often considered individual films (*Alice's Restaurant, Z, 2001: A Space Odyssey, Midnight Cowboy, Zabriskie Point, I Vitelloni, The Confession, Five Easy Pieces*). Other feature articles reported on film festivals (New York, Cannes, Chicago, San Francisco), addressed subjects ("Social Documentary in Yugoslavia," "The Political Theatre of John Wayne," "Frank Capra and the Cinema of Populism," "Cinema and Man at War," "The Mafia on Film"), and offered interviews with artists (Abraham Polonsky, Costa-Gavras and Jorge Semprun, Peter Watkins, Dalton Trumbo).

The range and depth of columns and articles in *Film Society Review* mirrored the publication's editorial thrust, which challenged the assumption that the purpose of the movies was to provide lowest-common-denominator divertissement and distraction for the mass audience. Rather, the approach was toward an examination of not only the techniques, approaches, and intricacies of filmmaking, but also the purpose of cinema: to inform, enlighten, and inspire even as it entertains.

In 1971, *Film Society Review* expanded its media coverage, adding a column entitled "Television" to the regular lineup, its aim being to provide a more critical perspective on the most voracious and influential of the mass media.

In September of 1972, *Film Society Review* became *Film Critic* (the third and final title), a bimonthly which was to succeed and incorporate its precursor. The explanation offered for the title change was that the critical film magazine would henceforth have an intensified sociopolitical critical orientation but with essentially the same format and blend of columns.

Film Critic's mandate was to broaden the publication's frame of reference: to deal with not only national but international cinema in a larger social, political, and cultural context. "Functional criticism" was the byword.

Among the offerings in *Film Critic*'s only two issues were reports from the Cannes Film Festival and the New York Film Festival, "Bogged Down: A Twitch in the Auteur Niche" by Pete Rainer, an interview with Marcel Ophuls, "Vichy Cinema: The 'Official Myths' of the Nazi Occupation Years" by Jean Pierre Jeancolas, and consideration/critiques of *The Sorry and the Pity* and *A Sense of Loss*.

With the November-December 1972 issue, *Film Critic*, a.k.a. *Film Society Review*, a.k.a. *Film Society*, ceased publication.

Information Sources

INDEX SOURCES: Index to Critical Film Reviews; Retrospective Index to Film Periodicals, 1930–1971.
REPRINT EDITIONS: None.
LOCATION SOURCES: Academy of Motion Picture Arts and Sciences; Grinnell College; New York Public Library; Smith College; Stanford University; University of Arizona; University of Oregon; University of Pennsylvania; University of Wisconsin at Madison.

Publication History

MAGAZINE TITLE AND TITLE CHANGES: *Film Society* (1963–1971); *Film Society Review* (1971–1972); *Film Critic* (1972).
VOLUME AND ISSUE DATA: Vol. I, No. 1–Vol. VII, No. 7-9 (September 1963–May

1972), monthly September–May; with title change to *Film Critic*, recommenced with Vol. I, No. 1–Vol. I, No. 2 (September/October 1972–November/December 1972), bimonthly.

PUBLISHER AND PLACE OF PUBLICATION: American Federation of Film Societies, 144 Bleecker Street, New York, N.Y. 10012.

EDITOR: William A. Starr.

Bill Wine

FILM CRITICISM

During its first year *Film Criticism* was a magazine in search of an identity. Issue No. 1 appeared in the spring of 1976 under the editorship of James Goldsworthy, the premiere editorial booming forth its manifesto: "True friends of the cinema, ARISE!" Goldsworthy claimed that "true creativity" was "being crushed in the iron fist of the Establishment," and the first issue appeared to be a heavy-handed smaller format imitation of *Cineaste*,* protesting, on the one hand, the political imprisonment of Sergei Paradjanov in the Soviet Union, and, on the other, the murder of Pier Paolo Pasolini in Italy, which one supposes was a personal tragedy and not a political assassination. The Marxist market in cinema studies had already been cornered by *Jump Cut** and *Cineaste*, however, and cooler heads were later to prevail at *Film Criticism*. Out of the energy, enthusiasm, and rather jumbled polemics of the first issue, a substantial little magazine was eventually to emerge, as James Goldsworthy's initial concept was modified by Luciana Bohne and Lloyd I. Michaels, who replaced Goldsworthy as chief editor effective with Vol. 1, No. 3, the winter issue of 1976-1977. Lloyd Michaels proved influential in turning the magazine in academic and more scholarly directions, stressing in particular close "readings" of individual films. This sort of work had been typical of *Film Heritage*,* a periodical that had ceased publication about the time *Film Criticism* was started.

During the magazine's first year, *Film Criticism* published essays by several established film critics—particularly Gerald Mast, Leland Poague, and Louis Giannetti. The editorial offices moved from Edinboro, in northwestern Pennsylvania, to Meadville, some twenty-five miles distant, since Lloyd Michaels taught at Allegheny College, located in Meadville. Associate Editor Luciana Bohne and Managing Editor Chris Dubbs both eventually landed part-time teaching positions at Allegheny College, the new editorial center. Under the editorship of Lloyd Michaels, *Film Criticism* turned to another established model, *Literature/Film Quarterly*,* which *Film Criticism* closely resembles in format and the editorial mix of essays, interviews, and reviews it offers. As the editorial focus became less political and more academic, the editorial board added academics like Joseph A. Gomez, Louis D. Giannetti, and J. P. Telotte, all of whom also served as contributing editors for *Literature/Film Quarterly*.

Lloyd Michaels participated in the first National Endowment for the Humanities Summer Seminar in Film Theory, organized by Dudley Andrew (who is the author of the 1976 Oxford University Press book, *The Major Film Theories*) at the University of Iowa, and Andrew later served as guest editor for a special double issue of *Film Criticism* (Vol. 2, Nos. 2-3) that appeared in 1978. In 1979 David Bordwell likewise assembled a special issue (Vol. 4, No. 1) on film theory. In 1982 J. P. Telotte served as guest editor for a special issue (Vol. 7, No. 1) dealing with horror and fantasy films. In 1979 Luciana Bohne edited an Italian neorealism issue (Vol. 3, No. 2). The previous year *Film Criticism* published an interview special issue (Vol. 2, No. 1) covering directors Peter Watkins, Marcel Ophuls, and John Frankenheimer, as well as cameraman Odd Geir Saether. German director Volker Schlondörff was interviewed in Vol. 1, No. 3; cultist horror director George A. Romero was interviewed in Vol. 7, No. 1; and Richard Corliss, the editor of *Film Comment*,* was interviewed in Vol. 6, No. 3, on the politics of editing.

Like *Literature/Film Quarterly*, *Film Criticism* is one of a dwindling number of cinema journals that publishes essays treating individual films rather than career surveys. Both periodicals serve a similar readership. *Film Criticism* is published three times a year, and going into its seventh year it seems to be firmly established. It is intelligently designed and well edited, and the physical appearance of the magazine has improved demonstrably over the years. In some instances the copy appears academic to the point of being intimidating for the general reader (see, for example, Mary Palmer's "Temporal Disjunction and Alternating Syntagma in *Petulia*," in Vol. 4, No. 1), but, in fact, the essays are generally lively and readable. *Film Criticism* deserves a wider general readership that its present (1984) estimated circulation of four hundred has captured.

Information Sources

INDEX SOURCES: FIAF International Index to Film Periodicals; Film Literature Index; Media Review Digest; Humanities Citation Index.

REPRINT EDITIONS: None.

LOCATION SOURCES: Dartmouth College; Harvard University; Iowa University; Library of Congress; New York Public Library; Stanford University; University of Illinois.

Publication History

MAGAZINE TITLE AND TITLE CHANGES: *Film Criticism*.

VOLUME AND ISSUE DATA: Vol. 1, No. 1 (Spring 1976 to present), three times a year.

PUBLISHER AND PLACE OF PUBLICATION: Film Criticism, Allegheny College, Box D, Meadville, Pa. 16335.

EDITOR: James Goldsworthy (Nos. 1–2); Lloyd I. Michaels (No. 3 to present).

James M. Welsh

FILM CULTURE

Film Culture first appeared in January 1955 as a somewhat more intellectual and loftier version of *Films and Filming*.* With *Films in Review*,* it is the only major American film magazine of the fifties to survive to the present. In the first issue, Jonas Mekas, who always carried the title of editor-in-chief, explained:

> It is then the chief objective of this magazine to help impart depth and vigour to cinematic culture in our country by becoming a meeting ground for outspoken discussion and constructive analysis of ideas, achievements and problems in the domain of the film. Also, in order to present to the American reader a complete image of the attainments and function of film in our civilization, the magazine will give ample scope to the exposition of the current trends and events in cinematic production abroad.[1]

In its early years, *Film Culture* was a typical film magazine, featuring book reviews, film reviews, reports on film festivals, and interviews. Many of the articles were historically oriented, and among the many illustrious names who contributed to the journal were Hans Richter, William K. Everson, Lewis Jacobs, Siegfried Kracauer, Arlene Croce, Rudolf Arnheim, Thorold Dickinson, Richard Griffith, James Card, Andrew Sarris (who served at one time as associate editor), Lotte H. Eisner, Jay Leyda, Joris Ivens, John Grierson, and Parker Tyler. Gordon Hendricks contributed an early column on film music, titled "The Sound Track." Herman G. Weinberg's column, "Coffee, Brandy and Cigars," appeared for the first time in issue No. 2 and was a regular feature for more than a decade.

A number of celebrities submitted pieces to *Film Culture*. Josef von Sternberg wrote "Acting in Film and Theatre" (No. 5-6); Carl Th. Dreyer wrote "Metaphysic in Ordet" (No. 7); Tony Richardson contributed a "London Letter" (No. 8); and Louise Brooks wrote "Charlie Chaplin Remembered" (No. 40), "On Location with Billy Wellman" (No. 53-54-55), and "Marion Davies' Niece" (No. 58-59-60).

Film Culture was subtitled "America's Independent Picture Magazine," and through the years it has provided considerable coverage on independent and avant-garde filmmakers, notably Gregory Markopoulos, Jack Smith, and Stan Brakhage. No. 30 (1963) was a special issue, "Metaphors on Vision," devoted to Stan Brakhage's writings "on the film as seen and made by Stan Brakhage." No. 61 was devoted to the work of James Broughton. No. 62 was a guide to independent film and video, edited by Hollis Melton.

Through the years *Film Culture* has published a number of special issues, notably Nos. 28 and 29, featuring Andrew Sarris on American directors, which was later published in book form as *The American Cinema* (E. P. Dutton, 1968). Sarris, generally considered the creator of the auteur theory, published "Notes on the Auteur Theory in 1962" in No. 27. Of major scholarly interest is issue No. 36, devoted to Seymour Stern's rambling study of D. W. Griffith's *The Birth of a Nation*. No. 50-51 was a special double issue on blacklisting, edited by Gordon Hitchens.

From No. 19 onward, *Film Culture* changed from a typical-looking film magazine to more a paperback book. Around the same time (1962), publication became considerably irregular, and in later years issues have appeared at the rate of one a year or less. *Film Culture* has always pointed out that it has no regular financial backing and that each new issue is published after sufficient money has been collected to pay the printer for the previous issue. However, as it also notes, "Our dedication and persistence remain unfailing." Also noteworthy is *Film Culture*'s continual physical change. It is a librarian's nightmare, with issues of varying shapes and sizes; one (No. 43), devoted to the avant-garde arts, was published in newspaper format!

Notes

1. Editorial, No. 1, January 1955, p. 1.

Information Sources

INDEX SOURCES: Art Index; The Critical Index; FIAF International Index to Film Periodicals; Film Literature Index; The New Film Index; Retrospective Index to Film Periodicals, 1930–1971.
REPRINT EDITIONS: University Microfilms.
LOCATION SOURCES: Academy of Motion Picture Arts and Sciences; Columbia University; Dartmouth College; Duke University; Library of Congress; New York Public Library; University of California at Berkeley; University of California at Los Angeles; Yale University.

Publication History

MAGAZINE TITLE AND TITLE CHANGES: *Film Culture*.
VOLUME AND ISSUE DATA: No. 1 (January 1955); No. 2 (March-April 1955); No. 3 (May-June 1955); No. 4 (Summer 1955); No. 5-6 (Winter 1955); No. 7 (1956); No. 8 (1956); No. 9 (1956); No. 10 (1956); No. 11 (1957); No. 12 (1957); No. 13 (October 1957); No. 14 (November 1957); No. 15 (December 1957); No. 16 (January 1958); No. 17 (February 1958); No. 18 (April 1958); No. 19 (1959); No. 20 (1959); No. 21 (1960); No. 22-23 (Summer 1961); No. 24 (Spring 1962); No. 25 (Summer 1962); No. 26 (Fall 1962); No. 27 (Winter 1962); No. 28 (Spring 1963); No. 29 (Summer 1963); No. 30 (1963); No. 31 (Winter 1963-1964); No. 32 (Spring 1964); No. 33 (Summer 1964); No. 34 (Fall 1964); No. 35 (Winter 1964-1965); No. 36 (Spring-Summer 1965); No. 37 (Summer 1965); No. 38 (Fall 1965); No. 39 (Winter 1965); No. 40 (Spring 1966); No. 41 (Summer 1966); No. 42 (Fall 1966); No. 43 (Winter 1966); No. 44 (Spring 1967); No. 45 (1968); No. 46 (Autumn 1967, published October 1968); No. 47 (Summer 1969); No. 48-49

(Winter & Spring 1970); No. 50-51 (Fall & Winter 1970); No. 52 (Spring 1971); No. 53-54-55 (Spring 1972); No. 56-57 (Spring 1973); No. 58-59-60 (1974); No. 61 (1975-1976); No. 62 (1976); No. 63-64 (1977); No. 65-66 (1978); No. 67-68-69 (1979); No. 70-71 (1983).

PUBLISHER AND PLACE OF PUBLICATION: Film Culture, 215 West Ninety-eighth Street, New York 25, N.Y. (Nos. 1–18); Film Culture, G.P.O. Box 1499, New York, N.Y. 10001 (No. 19 to present).

EDITOR: Jonas Mekas.

Anthony Slide

THE FILM DAILY

One of the major trade journals, *The Film Daily* ran from 1915 through half of 1970. Its companion piece, *The Film Daily Year Book of Motion Pictures*, a one-volume key to the contents of the daily, began publication in 1918 and continued through its fifty-second edition. During that long run, New York City remained the trade's place of publication, although *The Film Daily* acquired correspondents and opened offices in cities as diverse as London, Hawaii, Paris, the Philippines, and Mexico City.

Wid Gunning started *The Film Daily* under the title *Wid's Films and Film Folks*, shaping it as an independent voice for movie fans as well as members of the film industry. He soon found a fan magazine too costly to produce and decided to structure his journal solely for exhibitors and other film industry personnel. Upon acquisition of a staff of "real news people" headed by the former editor of the *New York Dramatic Mirror*, the trade featured world and industry news and relegated film reviews to the Sunday issue. News events were presented through the varied perspectives of producer, distributor, exhibitor, and star. A chronological listing of the year's events in headlines is an indispensable section of *The Year Book*.

A demand for more information on films caused reviews to be integrated again into the daily paper, and the Sunday issue was dropped. Not long after, the Saturday issue also was suspended. The last dramatic change in emphasis for *The Film Daily* arrived with the inclusion of television reviews as early as 1949, although the paper's title was not changed to reflect such coverage until March 1968 when *Film and Television Daily* was adopted.

Although appearing sporadically, reviews of film and television were a large part of *The Film Daily* and were essential tools for exhibitors. In the early issues of the trade, a section entitled "Feature Films As Wid Sees Them" includes major stars, production company, story synopsis, cameraman, comments on the film, and the film's length. Reviewers soon presented "The Box Office Angle," suggesting new advertising tactics. In 1916, Wid Gunning offered a special carbon-sheet advance service for first-run feature reviews, promising to review films, if possible, before their commercial run. The quality of writing in reviews varies, as does the choice of titles and the number of films that were reviewed daily. Reviews of interest include: *Intolerance* in the September 7, 1916, issue; *Remodelling Her Husband*, directed by Lillian Gish, starring Dorothy Gish, in the June 13, 1920, issue; Ernst Lubitsch's *Passion* in the October 10, 1920, issue; and *The March of Time*'s "Inside Nazi Germany" in the February 2, 1938, issue.

Coverage of short subjects in *The Film Daily* is fairly extensive. A section of brief informational paragraphs mirroring feature film reviews appears in the Sunday issue of the daily in the early issues. Later the section evolved into the *Short Subject Quarterly* featuring a complete review of the year's offerings in the short feature field. The *Short Subject Quarterly*, Vol. 65, No. 81, reveals several articles on the state of the art of short subjects, questions on censorship, and lists of producers and stars in the short feature field. *The Film Daily* also contains short synopses of newsreels, including *Kinograms*, *Pathé News*, and *Selznick News*. Reviews of feature films can be located in *The Year Book* under a section entitled "Features Released since 1915" and short subjects under their producer, director, or production company.

In addition to getting reviews to exhibitors as quickly as possible, *The Film Daily* also immediately delivered the news, and its articles demonstrate the connections between the film industry and the political/economic state of the world. In film-related news, a pervasive issue for viewers has always centered on the moral implications of what they see. The question for people in the industry has been whether censorship should be externally or internally imposed. These issues are most frighteningly evident on the pages of *The Film Daily* in the late forties and early fifties. An article, "Alleged Communist Penetration of Hollywood," is followed by one whose headline reads "Fear of Film Censorship Hanging over Hollywood." Regarding censorship but differently stated is the editorial summing up the preceding year, "1953: A Review, Censorship and Industry—Self Regulation," in Vol. 104, No. 125. An index to editorials is another key section of *The Year Book of Motion Pictures*.

The Film Daily strove to be "Intimate in Character, International in Scope, Independent in Thought" (its banner headline) in its reporting on foreign markets. Several articles investigate different national cinemas. The September 11, 1936, issue contains a "Survey of the British Film Industry," and the November 5, 1926, issue begins a series of articles on film in Russia by Ernest W. Fredman, the editor of London-based *The Film Renter*. Foreign film reviews were included with the weekly film reviews. A major section of *The Year Book* is devoted to "Surveys of Foreign Markets: A Compendium of Statistical Data Covering the Industry in Every Country throughout the World."

The pages of *The Film Daily* are lined with special unique features. The "Equipment News" section, which appeared regularly, contains articles on theatre equipment and is supplemented by "Business Boosters," a section on concessions. Another useful feature is *The Directors' Annual and Production Guide*, a self-contained volume published mid-year, which presents a comprehensive review of directorial activity. In the 1923 edition there are articles by motion picture luminaries such as June Mathis on "Harmony in Picture Making," Hal Roach on "The Making of Comedies," Allan Dwan on how "Pictures Appeal to [the] Dream Mind," and a comparison between European and American methods of filmmaking by Ernst Lubitsch and Victor Seastrom. That year the section "Biographies of Important Directors" includes the names of only three women—Alice Guy Blache, Frances Marion, and Lois Weber. In 1929 an article by Alan Crosland, "Color, A Problem," and in 1932 "Some Timely Subjects Entertainingly Discussed by Alert Directors" including Tay Garnett, Mark Sandrich, and Roy Del Ruth, are just a few examples of the many interesting pieces.

The Film Daily Year Book Of Motion Pictures continued during the many years of *The Film Daily*'s run, growing as it grew, embodying all of its numerous changes and reflecting the altering events of the preceding year. *The 1943 Year Book* documents the film industry's activities during World War II most vividly through articles like Walter Wanger's "The Academy in War Time" and Colonel Darryl F. Zanuck's "The Research Council's War Activities." In 1947 *The Year Book* features editorials on the "Special Purpose Film" by Chester B. Bahn and Ralph Wilk. Technological innovations are spotlighted in *The 1953 Year Book* with articles like that of Sol Lesser on 3-D and CinemaScope called "More Than A Novelty," and "CinemaScope: Industry Boon" by Spyros P. Skouras.

The Film Daily and *The Year Book of Motion Pictures* discontinued publication in 1970.

Information Sources

INDEX SOURCES: None.
REPRINT EDITIONS: Brookhaven Press; International Microfilm Press; New York Public Library Photoduplication Division; *The Film Daily Director's Annual and Production Guide* (1929–1932, 1934–1937), Gordon Press, 1976; *The Film Daily Year Book*, 52d edition, Arno Press, 1970; *The Film Daily Year Books*, 1918–1922, Arno Press, 1973; *The Film Daily Year Books*, 1918–1941, Gordon Press, 1971; *The Film Daily Year Books*, 1918–1969, Arno Press, 1972; *The Film Daily Year Books*, 1918–1969, Microfilming Corporation of America, 1972.
LOCATION SOURCES: Academy of Motion Picture Arts and Sciences; Library of Congress; New York Public Library.

Publication History

MAGAZINE TITLE AND TITLE CHANGES: *Wid's Films and Film Folks* (October 1915–July 1918); *Wid's Daily* (July 1918–December 1921); *The Film Daily* (January 1922–March 1968); *Film and Television Daily* (March 1968–November 1969); *Film T.V. Daily* (November 1969–June 1970).
VOLUME AND ISSUE DATA: Vol. 1, No. 1–Vol. LIX, No. 55 (October 1915–June 1932), 7 days a week (except holidays); Vol. LIX, No. 56–Vol. LXXIV, No. 49 (June 1932–August 1938), 6 days a week (except Sundays and holidays); Vol.

LXXIV, No. 50–Vol. CXXXVI, No. 131 (August 1938–June 1970), 5 days a week (except Saturdays, Sundays, and holidays).
PUBLISHER AND PLACE OF PUBLICATION: Wid's Films and Film Folk, Inc., New York City. (Vol. 1, No. 1–Vol. XIX, No. 1); *The Film Daily*, New York City. (Vol. XIX, No. 1–Vol. CXXXVI); DFI Communications, Inc., Co., New York City. (Vol. CXXXVI–Vol. CXXXVI, No. 131).
EDITOR: Lynde Denig (1918–1921); Chester B. Bahn (1937–1962); Al Finestone (1962–1965); Gene Arneel (1965–1969); Edward Lipton (1969–1970).

Cecile B. Horowitz

THE FILM DAILY YEAR BOOK OF MOTION PICTURES. See THE FILM DAILY

FILM DIRECTIONS

Having begun publication in 1977, *Film Directions* is not the first Irish film periodical, but it is certainly the best and it deserves praise for appearing at a time when most newspapers would have one believe that Northern Ireland could produce little more than terrorist bombings. As an editorial in the first issue stated:

The launching of an all-Ireland film magazine is an important event, by any standards. That it takes place at this particular moment is a reflection in no small way of the important developments in film which are now taking place in this country. In film-making, the showing of films and film study, Ireland's film consciousness is growing enormously. . . . The brief for *Film Directions* is to expand the collective film awareness and by so doing encourage greater participation in film activities of all kind.[1]

To a certain extent, *Film Directions* is a typical semiserious film journal, offering book and film reviews, reports on film festivals, and the types of interviews and articles which might appear, say, in *Film Comment,** such as "Interview with Brian de Palma" by Ian Christie, Chris Petit, and Phil Hardy (Vol. I, No. 1); "Interview with Jerzy Skolimowski" by Michael Open (Vol. II, No. 2); or "A Language of Vision: The Films of John Boorman" by Aidan Dunne (Vol. II, No. 3). But *Film Directions* also provides some unique coverage of contemporary Irish film productions, such as *Wheels* and *Down the Corner* (Vol. I, No. 2) and *Poitín* (Vol. I, No. 3). It has also published articles on various aspects of Irish filmmaking, including "Prospects for an Irish Film Industry" by Cyril Farrell (Vol. I, No. 2) and "A National Film Archive" by

Michael Dolan (Vol. I, No. 3). Vol. II, No. 1, was a special Irish filmmaking issue, while Vol. III, No. 1, was devoted to censorship, with particular emphasis on film censorship as it affected Ireland.

Notes

1. Vol. I, No. 1, p. 3.

Information Sources

INDEX SOURCES: None.
REPRINT EDITIONS: None.
LOCATION SOURCES: No information.

Publication History

MAGAZINE TITLE AND TITLE CHANGES: *Film Directions.*
VOLUME AND ISSUE DATA: Vol. I, No. 1 (1977 to present), quarterly.
PUBLISHER AND PLACE OF PUBLICATION: Arts Council of Northern Ireland, 181a
     Stranmillis Road, Belfast 9, Northern Ireland, and the Arts Council, 70 Merrion
     Square, Dublin 2, Eire.
EDITOR: Michael Open.

Anthony Slide

FILM DOPE

Produced in a mimeographed and typewritten format, *Film Dope* is not so much a magazine as an encyclopedia. Each issue since the first (December 1972) provides an average of twenty-five biographies, with complete filmographies, on personalities from both behind and in front of the camera. A photograph usually accompanies each of the entries, which are well researched and critical in tone. Many issues open with interviews of subjects as varied as Sir Arthur Bliss (No. 5), Thorold Dickinson (No. 11), and Paul Grimault (No. 22).

Entries are arranged in strict alphabetical order, and issue No. 24 (March 1982) ended with entry No. 727, on cinematographer Winton C. Hoch. Additions and corrections appear from time to time, but, unfortunately and obviously, there is no way, in looking up a particular individual, to know that additional information on that person is to be found in an issue some two years later. *Film Dope*'s publication schedule is highly erratic; No. 1 appeared in December 1972, Nos. 2 and 3 in 1973, Nos. 4, 5, and 6 in 1974, Nos. 7 and 8 in 1975, Nos. 9 and 10 in 1976, and so on. A bumper year for *Film Dope* subscribers was 1979 with four issues, Nos. 16–19, published, but the following year the magazine returned to its average of two per year.

There are, of course, many encyclopedias which cover much the same territory as *Film Dope*, but none provides quite as detailed information and seems quite as reliable or as enthusiastic in their search for accuracy.

Information Sources

INDEX SOURCES: None.
REPRINT EDITIONS: None.
LOCATION SOURCES: Academy of Motion Picture Arts and Sciences; California Institute of the Arts; New York Public Library; Stanford University; Syracuse University; University of California at Los Angeles.

Publication History

MAGAZINE TITLE AND TITLE CHANGES: *Film Dope*.
VOLUME AND ISSUE DATA: No. 1 (December 1972) to present, irregular.
PUBLISHER AND PLACE OF PUBLICATION: *Film Dope*, 5 Norman Court, Little Heath, Potter's Bar, Hertfordshire, EN6 1HY, England (Nos. 1–14); *Film Dope*, 40 Willifield Way, London NW11 7XT, England (No. 15 to present).
EDITOR: David Badder, Bob Baker, Derek Owen, and Markku Salmi (No. 1); David Badder, Bob Baker, and Markku Salmi (Nos. 2–7); David Badder and Bob Baker (No. 8 to present).

Anthony Slide

FILMEX FLASH. See Appendix 2

FILMFACTS

When editor Ernest Parmentier established the journal *Filmfacts* in 1958, he did so to provide anyone interested in films a central source of information. According to Parmentier, a former actor, he once searched in vain for good reference sources on movie research, and when he found none, he decided to start one himself.[1] The first issue of *Filmfacts* appeared on February 5, 1958. Originally published once a week, the first issue included information on eight films, the initial offering being Douglas Sirk's *The Tarnished Angels*. From that time on, the format of *Filmfacts* varied only slightly. Each issue covered about ten films (although later biweekly installments doubled the amount), and for each film Parmentier provided extensive credits, a plot synopsis of about one hundred words, and excerpts of reviews. The number of excerpts varied from two to six in the early years and later expanded to as many as ten. The number of journals to which Parmentier made reference also varied; the first issue included only *Variety*,* *Time*, *The New York Times*, *Saturday Review*, and *The New York World Journal and Tribune*, while the last had expanded the number of periodicals to sixteen.

Unlike many cinema reference works, *Filmfacts* made no attempt to be critical or qualitative. Instead, Parmentier and his small staff attempted to include every film, American or foreign, released in the United States in any given year. The excerpts themselves were also more reflective of the overall opinion of the review rather than the standard selections seen in promotions.

Other features which became a part of the standard format were the index of titles and names included each year; a listing of the major film awards from the Oscars to various "ten best" lists; the "Film Praise" name and title index to awards; and a compendium of thumbnail sketches of foreign and American films released in the United States which were not extensively reviewed.

Although the issues of *Filmfacts* were often published late, especially in the later years, it does offer a historically accurate record of the films of each year which has not been duplicated to such an extent either before or since its publication.

Beginning in January 1969, *Filmfacts*, still under the editorship of Parmentier, was published under the auspices of the American Film Institute in Washington, D.C. This association lasted until 1972 when Parmentier was given a grant by the Center for Understanding Media and began to publish *Filmfacts* under that body. The final change in the journal took place in 1976 when Parmentier moved the journal to Los Angeles and became affiliated with the University of Southern California's School of Cinema. The relationship was not a happy one, and the publication stopped in 1977, after which time Parmentier took legal action against the university for failure to live up to their agreement with him. The last film included in *Filmfacts* was Ron Howard's *Grand Theft Auto* released in June 1977.

Notes

1. Gregg Kilday, "Who's Afraid of the Big Bad Critic?" *The Los Angeles Times*, March 8, 1975.

Information Sources

INDEX SOURCES: None.
REPRINT EDITIONS: None.
LOCATION SOURCES: Although many libraries have various years of *Filmfacts*, the only known location holding a complete set is the University of Southern California.

Publication History

MAGAZINE TITLE AND TITLE CHANGES: *Filmfacts*.
VOLUME AND ISSUE DATA: Vols. I–XI (February 5, 1958–December 1968), weekly; Vol. XII, No. 1–Vol. XX. No. 13 (January 1969–June 1977), twice a month.
PUBLISHER AND PLACE OF PUBLICATION: Filmfacts, P.O. Box 53, Village Station, 150 Christopher Street, New York, N.Y. 11014 (Vol. I, No. 1–Vol. VII, No. 28); Filmfacts, 29-14 Northern Boulevard, Long Island City, N.Y. 11101 (Vol. VII, No. 29–Vol. VII, No. 41); Filmfacts, P.O. Box 53, Village Station, 150 Christopher Street, New York, N.Y. 11014 (Vol. VII, No. 42); Filmfacts, 29-14 Northern Boulevard, Long Island City, N.Y. 11101 (Vol. VII, No. 43); Filmfacts: A Publication of the American Film Institute, Box 213, Village Station, New York, N.Y. 10014 (Vol. XII, No. 1–Vol. XIV, No. 24); Film facts: A Publication Associated with the American Film Institute, Box 213, Village Station,

New York, N.Y. 10014 (Vol. XV, No. 1–Vol. XV, No. 12); Filmfacts: In Associaton with the Center for Understanding Media, Box 213, Village Station, New York, N.Y. 10014 (Vol. XV, No. 13–Vol. XVIII, No. 24); Filmfacts: A Publication of the Division of Cinema of the University of Southern California, P.O. Box 69610, West Station, Los Angeles, Calif. 90069 (Vol. XIX, No. 1– Vol. XX, No. 13).

EDITOR: Ernest Parmentier.

Patricia King Hanson

FILM FANCIES. See Appendix 3

FILM FAN MONTHLY

In 1961 *Film Fan Monthly* began as a news publication for 8mm and 16mm film collectors. Its founder, Daryl A. Davy, was then sixteen years old. Early issues were printed with a ditto stencil, but Davy gradually transferred most of the publication to a more professional-looking offset format.

After publishing the chatty, informal magazine for five years, Davy found himself unable to keep up the pace and offered ownership to Leonard Maltin, who had been contributing an 8mm movie review column for the past two years. Maltin accepted. He was fifteen years old at the time but had been publishing his own mimeographed journal, called *Profile*, for several years. So officially, in May of 1966, the magazine transferred editorial reins—and format—and for a short time was known as *Film Fan Monthly including Profile*.

Maltin made an effort to continue the home-movie news aspect of the publication but was much more interested in printing feature stories on the "golden age of Hollywood." His first issue, No. 59, featured Robert Benchley on the cover, with a short summary of his film career inside and an accompanying filmography.

After writing most of the contents himself for some time, Maltin began to attract a number of steady contributors, most of whom have since written or contributed to various books on film: Doug McClelland, David Chierichetti, Arthur McClure, John Cocchi, Gregory Mank, Anthony Slide, James Limbacher, Stuart Oderman, and Don Stanke. Daryl Davy contributed a column of notes and observations to the magazine for several years.

Film Fan Monthly's specialty was the obscure and the unsung. A number of issues were devoted to character and supporting actors: Billy Gilbert (Nos. 67 and 88), Anne Revere (No. 96), Grady Sutton (No. 100), Sara Allgood (No. 108), Lionel Atwill (No. 139), to name a few.

FFM, as it was known, also sought interviews, not only with these character players but with little-documented directors (Elliott Nugent, No. 94; Mitchell

Leisen, No. 103), fan-magazine editors (Ruth Waterbury of *Photoplay*, No. 141), and others (British musical star Jessie Matthews, No. 139; silent film veteran and cowboy star George O'Brien, No. 131; actor and long-time associate to Cecil B. DeMille, Henry Wilcoxon, No. 104).

Regular features included extensive book review coverage, an annual survey of veteran on-screen actors called "Old Faces in New Films," and two long-running series, "MGM Revisited" and "RKO Revisited," which presented capsule comments based on fresh screenings of obscure films from those studios. Earlier in its history, *FFM* published a series of articles by James Stringham on the independently produced serials of the thirties.

FFM remained an eclectic magazine throughout Maltin's nine-year tenure as editor and publisher. Its appearance improved during that time, with clearer and larger still photos illustrating most articles, but the format and goals remained essentially the same. *FFM* strove to be less stuffy than Henry Hart's *Films in Review** and more regular in its publication schedule than Alan Barbour's similar *Screen Facts.**

In June of 1975 Maltin announced that he was discontinuing the magazine, owing to time pressures, and wound up with a scrapbook issue (No. 168) looking back at some favorite subjects of the previous nine years.

Articles from *Film Fan Monthly* have been collected in a number of paperback books edited by Maltin for Curtis Books and Popular Library: *The Real Stars* (three volumes on character actors) and *Hollywood: The Movie Factory*.

Film Fan Monthly still makes back issues available and has a supply of most issues from 1966 through 1975, but neither Maltin nor any of the libraries with runs of *FFM* has a complete set from the magazine's first five years, when it was published in Canada by Daryl A. Davy.

Information Sources

INDEX SOURCES: Film Literature Index.
REPRINT EDITIONS: None. [Back issues are still available directly from Leonard Maltin, 200 West Seventy-ninth Street, New York, N.Y. 10024.]
LOCATION SOURCES: Academy of Motion Picture Arts and Sciences; American Film Institute (Los Angeles); Chicago Public Library; Detroit Public Library; Minneapolis Public Library; Museum of Modern Art; New York Public Library; University of Pennsylvania; University of Texas at Austin (all incomplete).

Publication History

MAGAZINE TITLE AND TITLE CHANGES: *Film Fan Monthly* (July 1961–April 1966); *Film Fan Monthly including Profile* (May 1966–December 1970); *Film Fan Monthly* (January 1971–June 1975).
VOLUME AND ISSUE DATA: Nos. 1–168 (July 1961–June 1975), monthly except combined July-August issues.

PUBLISHER AND PLACE OF PUBLICATION: Daryl A. Davy, 210 Durham Street West, Vancouver, B.C., Canada (Nos. 1–58); Leonard Maltin, 77 Grayson Place, Teaneck, N.J. 07666 (Nos. 59–168).
EDITOR: Daryl A. Davy (1961–1966); Leonard Maltin (1966–1975).

Lawrence Haverhill

FILMFAUST: ZEITSCHRIFT FÜR DEN INTERNATIONALEN FILM

Filmfaust belongs to the clutch of film journals with a difference that came onto the market in West Germany in the seventies (two notably innovative contemporaries that have also stood the test of time are the feminist quarterly *Frauen und Film* and the consistently intelligent monthly *Medium*, in which film is placed democratically alongside the other mass media). When first published in December 1976, *Filmfaust* announced that it would be appearing every second month. However, the first issue was a double number, and the journal did not make its next appearance until April 1977. There have since been further double issues. *Filmfaust* began life under the (short-lived) collective editorship of Bion Steinborn, Alexandra Kluge, Gert Delp, and Peter Krieg. Kluge had already made a name for herself with performances in two of her brother Alexander's films (*Yesterday Girl*, 1965/1966; *Occasional Work of a Female Slave*, 1973), while Krieg was actively involved in documentary work. It was with some justification, therefore, that the first editorial claimed *Filmfaust* was "made by filmmakers."

From the outset, *Filmfaust* looked upon itself as a journal with a mission, brought into being as it was by a feeling of profound dissatisfaction with the status quo in West Germany's system of film funding. Issue No. 1/2 considered this funding to be oriented toward the established names of the "New German Cinema"—an "institution" devoid of ideas and bent on self-preservation—at the expense of the new generation of aspiring filmmakers. It was equally scathing in its remarks about West Germany's film critics, who it claimed had allowed themselves to be inhibited by a climate of fear accompanying measures taken to combat extreme (left-wing) radicalism. The journal's objectives in the face of this apparent ossification of the national film scene were summed up by the first of its characteristic agitprop-style slogans: "*Filmfaust* intends to stir things up"; or "*Filmfaust*: the organ of the new generation of filmmakers in the Federal Republic." At the heart of its strategy was the cinema goer, who was—and still is—encouraged to submit film reviews for publication ("There is no such thing as a schooled film critic—and nobody should forget it!") To underline the needs of the viewer, condemnatory reviews of Scorsese's *Taxi Driver* and Schlöndorff's *Coup de Grâce* in the first issue took into account audience displeasure as noted personally by each reviewer. A further role for the movie goer was touched upon in an in-depth interview with documentary filmmakers Joris Ivens and Marceline

Loridan. Concerned above all with the possibilities for making "critical, i.e., socialist films" in Europe, the conversation turned (in the second half, published in No. 4) to the idea of audience participation in film planning at all levels. This was to become another of the journal's preoccupations.

Although *Filmfaust* has consistently given prominence to the politics and economics of film (and occasionally also of television) in the Federal Republic, it has also maintained a wide-ranging coverage of films and filming, and regularly includes extensive essays on film history and theory (the latter having become a major feature since No. 31). Informed and informative interviews, however, continue to prove one of *Filmfaust*'s most stimulating attractions, those with West German filmmakers being indispensable to the serious student of the New German Cinema. On the other hand, the journal's attempt at attracting publishable reviews from its readers has not been the success that it is fond of claiming. The pages devoted to "cinemagoer criticism" are not infrequently bolstered by contributions from staff writers, and repeatedly there are appeals to the readership for reviews.

Filmfaust is still the most loyal and the most outspoken ally that film tiros have in West Germany. But in other respects—namely in the journal's outlook and appearance—changes are evident. The declamatory assertiveness of the earlier numbers has been gradually tempered by pragmatism, particularly as far as the circumstances of domestic film production are concerned. As if to embody this, the title page since No. 23 (July/August 1981) has shown the "Faust" (fist) in the name *Filmfaust* confined within the large dot over the i in "Film." Similarly, the abandonment with No. 7 (March 1978) of the original, small format and rather austere bookish exterior for something approaching conventional magazine size with an eye-catching, glossy look had marked a mellowing of editorial policy, in this instance specifically with regard to the big names of the New German Cinema. In the last of the small-format numbers (December 6, 1977), an interview with Alexanger Kluge demonstrated that there was common ground between himself and *Filmfaust* on the importance of a productive interrelationship between filmmakers and cinema goers, and the first of the new-style issues (the title page included) was dominated by an interview with the makers of *Germany in Autumn*, a collective film project bringing together household names and relative newcomers. Like Kluge's film *Strong-Man Ferdinand* (1975ff), which had given rise to the interview in No. 6, *Germany in Autumn* was considered by *Filmfaust* to be an example of responsiveness to the views of the cinema audience, for each was revised in the light of moviegoers' reactions to pilot showings. In Kluge's case, it was noted that the subsequent improvements were "in form as well as in content," an observation which was symptomatic of a departure from the journal's tendency hitherto to judge a film by whether or not it had its heart in the right place. Progressively thereafter, the established figures of the New German Cinema were given the kind of attention that they merited, and they have even been used in issues featuring their work to promote subscriptions. From No. 24 (October/November 1981) to No. 30 (October/November 1982), *Filmfaust* provided the Federal Association of German Film with space for a "working journal" in order to help improve communication among the Association's wide-ranging membership. Since No. 32 (February/March 1983) the journal has published a top-ten list of films. Inevitably, this takes into account the opinions of the readership.

Information Sources

BIBLIOGRAPHY:
Kötz, Michael. "Es spricht statt deiner. Vom Kino und seinen Zeitschriften." *Frankfurter Rundschau*, July 24, 1982.
INDEX SOURCES: FIAF International Index to Film Periodicals; Film Literature Index.
REPRINT EDITIONS: None.
LOCATION SOURCES: Goethe Institute (all U.S. locations); Howard University (Washington, D.C.); University of California at Santa Barbara; University of Southern California; University of Texas.

Publication History

MAGAZINE TITLE AND TITLE CHANGES: *Filmfaust: Zeitschrift für den internationalen Film.*
VOLUME AND ISSUE DATA: No. 1-2 (December 1976); Nos. 3–23 (April 1977–August 1981), irregular; No. 24 (October 1981 to present), bimonthly.
PUBLISHER AND PLACE OF PUBLICATION: *Filmfaust*, Verlag und Redaktion, Fürstenberger Strasse 175, 6000 Frankfurt 1, Federal Republic of Germany.
EDITOR: Bion Steinborn, Alexandra Kluge, Gert Delp, and Peter Krieg (December 1976); Bion Steinborn, Alexandra Kluge, and Peter Krieg (April 1977); Bion Steinborn and Alexandra Kluge (June/July 1977–December 1979); Bion Steinborn (February 1980 to present).

David Head

FILM FLASHES

Film Flashes appeared at a bad time for periodicals in general, at the height of the First World War when the cost of paper was high and staff was depleted. It was a fan magazine sold on newsstands and in theatres, but it was also intended as a trade paper for exhibitors. It contained the usual features, a page for boys and girls, competitions, short reviews, biographical articles, gossip, and even a glossary of film terms. From the amount of space devoted to the TransAtlantic Film Company (the British distributor for Universal), it would appear to have been sponsored by that company.

Information Sources

INDEX SOURCES: None.
REPRINT EDITIONS: None.
LOCATION SOURCES: No information.

Publication History

MAGAZINE TITLE AND TITLE CHANGES: *Film Flashes*.
VOLUME AND ISSUE DATA: No. 1–No. 31 (November 13, 1915–June 10, 1916),
    weekly.
PUBLISHER AND PLACE OF PUBLICATION: Film Flashes, 125 Strand, London,
    England.
EDITOR: Fred K. Adams.

Thomas A. Johnson

FILM FOLLIES. See Appendix 3

FILMFRONT

Filmfront was the official 1934 to 1935 publication of the National Film and
Photo League, whose national secretary was David Platt.[1] Providing a left-wing
view of the industry, through articles and reviews, *Filmfront* appeared in mimeographed form (except for the last issue, which was printed).

It might be argued that *Filmfront* was somewhat removed from the original
aims of the League, which—from a distance—appeared more concerned with
film production, but David Platt points out:

> There was never a time when *Filmfront* and the Photo League were not
> deeply concerned with both production and criticism. The League had
> among its members many people who were not necessarily interested or
> involved in film production; one of our original aims was to organize
> opposition to German fascist and other racist, anti-labor and pro-war films
> of which there were quite a few in the early 1930s, made in Hollywood
> as well as abroad. Some League members and *Filmfront* contributors manned
> picket lines or wrote articles in the left press against films like *S. A. Mann
> Brand*, *Red Salute*, *Call to Arms*, *No Greater Glory*, and in support of
> the newsreels and documentaries produced by the League.[2]

When *Filmfront* ceased publication in 1935, many of its writers joined *New
Theatre* (later *New Theatre and Film**), which greatly expanded its film coverage.

Notes

1. For more information on the National Film and Photo League, see ''Radical Cinema
in the 30's'' by Russell Campbell in *Jump Cut*, No. 14, March 30, 1977, pp. 23–25,
and David Platt's response in *Jump Cut*, No. 16, November 1977, p. 37.
2. David Platt in a letter to the editor, dated November 6, 1983.

Information Sources

INDEX SOURCES: None.
REPRINT EDITIONS: Scarecrow Press.
LOCATION SOURCES: Academy of Motion Picture Arts and Sciences; New York Public
    Library.

Publication History

MAGAZINE TITLE AND TITLE CHANGES: *Filmfront.*
VOLUME AND ISSUE DATA: No. 1 (December 15, 1934); No. 2 (January 7, 1935);
    No. 3 (January 28, 1935); No. 4 (February 15, 1935); No. 5 (March 15, 1935).
    [No. 5 is erroneously numbered 6.]
PUBLISHER AND PLACE OF PUBLICATION: National Film and Photo League, 31
    East Twenty-first Street, New York, N.Y.
EDITOR: David Platt (Nos. 1–4); Victor Kandel, M. Levy, David Platt, Julian Roffman,
    and Phillip Russell (No. 5).

Anthony Slide

FILM HERITAGE

   With principal founder F. Anthony Macklin acting also as its editor, *Film
Heritage* began as an independent journal in the fall of 1965. Professor Macklin
received early assistance from the Student-Faculty Film Society of Notre Dame
University and from several individuals, including Ann Franklin, William Hoben,
and Mary Ann Macklin. In the nearly twelve years of its run, the journal also
endured a variety of economic problems, receiving financial support in different
amounts from a number of subscribers and institutional assistance from the
University of Dayton (twice) and from Wright State University. Funds eventually
ran out, and *Film Heritage* ceased with the Summer 1977 issue.
   The forty-seven issues of *Film Heritage* carried a wide range of scholarly
articles, stills, film festival reports, as well as film and book reviews. There
were also critical articles that addressed past and present film topics. Each issue
usually featured three to five articles, an editorial, and criticism of new books
dealing with the cinema. As the journal progressed, however, certain patterns
began to develop. The early numbers of *Film Heritage* strove for a balance,
including articles not only on contemporary films, but also on older ones. A
brief sample of the names and subjects will illustrate this diversity. Among the
films discussed were *The Pawnbroker*, *The Virgin Spring*, *Metropolis*, and *2001:
A Space Odyssey*. There were pieces on such people and groups as the Beatles,
King Vidor, James M. Cain, Luis Buñuel, and D.W. Griffith. Film festival
reports as well as technical and educational subjects were treated. The relationship
between film and foreign-language learning was explored in several early issues.
On a more technical note, the journal also covered the history of the moving

camera. There was a small series called "The Writer in Hollywood." Interviews with Norman Mailer and Lawrence Durrell were a part of this series.

The editor blended other interviews into issues of the journal, a trend that was to increase as *Film Heritage* came closer to its end. The individuals ranged from critics and performers to directors and technical people. Important names in these categories were Dwight McDonald, John Simon, Stanley Kauffmann, Andrew Sarris, and Molly Haskell. There were also interviews with John Wayne and Charlton Heston. The list of directors and technical people included Michelangelo Antonioni, Josef von Sternberg, Martin Scorsese, Raoul Walsh, Alfred Hitchcock, Sam Peckinpah, Robert Altman, Robert Sylbert, Oswald Morris, and Vilmos Zsigmond.

Special numbers, centering on a specific person or topic, were also a feature of *Film Heritage*. Among the people to whom an entire issue was devoted were Michelangelo Antonioni, Sam Peckinpah, John Wayne, and Robert Altman. The topics of women in film and technical aspects of cinematography were likewise approached in this manner.

The later numbers of the journal saw other changes. While continuing to emphasize more contemporary films and directors in interviews and extended articles, Macklin became interested in reviews from other cities. He began to reprint film reviews that had appeared in newspapers in Houston, Denver, and Cincinnati, starting in Spring 1974. The critics who wrote these reviews were David Elliott, William Gallo, Joel Siegel, Jerry Stein, and Jeff Millar.

Another early feature of *Film Heritage* was the inclusion of editorials, a practice which was to continue into Vol. 3. Macklin wrote on such topics as James Agee, the Academy Awards, and the National Catholic Office for Motion Pictures. He also explored the question of the nature of film criticism in general in several editorals, taking on Pauline Kael in the process.

The success of any academic journal is predicated on a number of factors. Although Macklin attributed the success of *Film Heritage* to luck, persistence, and personal commitment, he also suggested the important factor of obtaining a national distributor.[1] In this case, it was B. Deboer of Nutley, New Jersey. Further success can be assured through the contributions of able writers. One of Macklin's concerns was that the journal not be considered provincial. For that reason, he recruited associate editors, including Bob Haller, a Notre Dame student; the late Bob Steele, who taught at Boston University; the well-known writer and critic, David Madden; and Joel Siegel, mentioned above, who taught at Georgetown University. In addition to an outstanding group of associate editors, however, Macklin was interested in providing a forum for writers, especially unpublished ones. Among the most notable was Joseph McBride, whose article on Orson Welles appeared in *Film Heritage*. McBride is today recognized as a prominent scholar in film. Another contributor, Richard Corliss, is known now for his film reviews in *Time*.

The cessation of *Film Heritage* was unfortunate. During its existence, however, the journal presented a well-edited and scholarly body of criticism with emphasis on contemporary films and individuals. It remains an important film journal of the sixties and seventies and should be consulted by those interested in the films of that period.

Notes

1. Letter received from F. Anthony Macklin, June 9, 1983; this and other information in this paragraph has been provided from this source.

Information Sources

INDEX SOURCES: America: History and Life; The Critical Index; FIAF International Index to Film Periodicals; Film Literature Index; Historical Abstracts; The New Film Index.
REPRINT EDITIONS: University Microfilms.
LOCATION SOURCES: Columbia University; Harvard University; Library of Congress; New York Public Library; Ohio University; Swarthmore College; University of Alabama; University of California at Los Angeles; University of Iowa; University of Vermont.

Publication History

MAGAZINE TITLE AND TITLE CHANGES: *Film Heritage*.
VOLUME AND ISSUE DATA: Vol. I, No. 1–Vol. XII, No. 3 (Fall 1965–Spring 1977), quarterly.
PUBLISHER AND PLACE OF PUBLICATION: Film Heritage, Box 652, University of Dayton, Dayton, Ohio 45409 (Vols. I–VII); Film Heritage, College of Liberal Arts, Wright State University, Dayton, Ohio 45431 (Vols. VIII–X); Film Heritage, Department of Information Services, University of Dayton, Dayton, Ohio 45409 (Vols. XI–XII).
EDITOR: F. Anthony Macklin.

Kim Fisher

THE FILM INDEX

The earliest of film trade papers, *The Film Index* (which was founded as *Views and Film Index* on April 25, 1906) announced itself as "a trade paper for the exhibitor and showman." It was concerned strictly with exhibition rather than production or distribution, and the paper's first issues featured news items, along with lists of suppliers of everything from calcium lights to theatrical trunks. Pathé was the first company to advertise in the journal, taking the back page in No. 1, quickly followed by Vitagraph, which utilized the back page in No. 2 to promote its films of the San Franciso earthquake. (A story on these San Francisco films appeared in No. 6.) Both Pathé and Vitagraph were to remain the paper's leading advertisers.

Interviews began to be featured in the paper with issue No. 4, which included a visit with J. A. Berst, manager of the New York office of Pathé. With No.

8, *Views and Film Index* began to include "reviews" of new releases, which were, in reality, nothing more than lengthy plot synopses. New song slides were listed beginning with No. 15. Soon the paper started to include editorials, such as "Do Moving Pictures Breed Immorality?: An Unfair Attack" (No. 22). By 1908 there was a considerable increase in the number of pages and many more feature articles, such as Frederick J. Haskin's "Nickelodeon History" (Vol. 3, No. 4).

Although it is generally considered to have been the mouthpiece for the Motion Picture Patents Group of Companies, this was certainly not always the case. One of its first editors was Leon J. Rubinstein, who went on to edit the Independent Producers' journal, *Film Reports*.* As late as Vol. 3, No. 30, *The Film Index* featured an article on William Fox and carried advertising by Carl Laemmle, two of the most prominent members of the anti-Motion Picture Patents Group. Even in January 1910 there were references to P. A. Powers and the independents.[1]

By the end of 1910, however, *The Film Index* was billing itself as the "Leading American Exponent of the Photoplay," and the photoplays which it was exploiting were those of the Patents Group. It published only licensed release schedules and reviewed only licensed releases. These later reviews were still nothing more than synopses, although by 1911 many of them also included brief cast listings.

Eventually, *The Film Index* was acquired by *The Moving Picture World*,* which also acquired the journal's last editor, James L. Hoff, as well as its Chicago correspondent, James S. McQuade.

Notes

1. However, James L. Hoff, writing in *The Moving Picture World*, March 10, 1917, p. 1482, states that the journal was owned jointly by Vitagraph and Pathé, and that "the owners paid its deficits and charged up the loss to advertising."

Information Sources

INDEX SOURCES: None.
REPRINT EDITIONS: None.
LOCATION SOURCES: Academy of Motion Picture Arts and Sciences (incomplete); New York Public Library (incomplete).

Publication History

MAGAZINE TITLE AND TITLE CHANGES: *Views and Film Index* (April 25, 1906– September 19, 1908); *The Film Index* (September 26, 1908–July 1, 1911).
VOLUME AND ISSUE DATA: Vol. I, No. 1–Vol. VII, No. 26 (April 25, 1906–July 1, 1911), weekly.
PUBLISHER AND PLACE OF PUBLICATION: Films Publishing Company, 114 East Twenty-eighth Street, New York, N.Y. (April 25, 1906–May 4, 1907); Films Publishing Company, 36 East Twenty-third Street, New York, N.Y. (May 11, 1907–May 1, 1909); Films Publishing Company, 1 Madison Avenue, New York, N.Y. (May 8, 1909–July 1, 1911).

EDITOR: E. Mitchell (listed as Manager, April 25, 1906–May 12, 1906); no editor listed
(May 19, 1906–August 18, 1906); Ellis Cohen (August 25, 1906–November 10,
1906); Alfred H. Saunders (November 17, 1906–?, 1907); no editor listed (?,
1907–May 16, 1908); Leon J. Rubinstein (May 23, 1908–?, 1909); James L. Hoff
(?, 1909–July 1, 1911).

Anthony Slide

FILM IN FINLAND. See Appendix 4

FILM IN SWEDEN. See Appendix 4

THE FILM JOURNAL

The Film Journal was one of the best small, independent film periodicals to
emerge in the seventies. It was well designed, profusely illustrated, printed on
good quality paper, and offered serious articles on both contemporary and historical cinema. Editor Thomas R. Atkins set down in the first issue the criteria
by which *The Film Journal* would operate when he noted that the journal "will
contain new source material about film—not the kind of topical essays or current
movie reviews that are available in abundance today but original documents and
critical evaluations that will be useful to scholars, teachers, students or anyone
seriously interested in film." [1]

The first issue (Spring 1971) concentrated on Swedish film director Vilgot
Sjöman, with an interview, biography, and filmography. No. 3-4 featured a
major article on *Broken Blossoms* by Arthur Lennig and also offered an essay
by Steven P. Hill, "Classic Period of Soviet Cinema," along with a biography,
filmography, and bibliography on Japanese director Yasujiro Ozu. Later issues
were generally devoted to single themes. Vol. 2, No. 1, was concerned with
sexuality and included major essays on eroticism and sex in the cinema (a subject
which, one suspects, the editor selected in an effort to boost circulation). Vol.
2, No. 2, took as its theme "The Art of the Horror Film" and included an
interview with Rouben Mamoulian (to whom the issue was dedicated), Arthur
Lennig on *The Raven*, and Paul Jensen on *The Mummy*. "The Science Fiction
Film Image" was the subject of Vol. 2, No. 3, and screen violence the subject
of Vol. 2, No. 4. In addition to well-researched articles, most issues included
book reviews.

Notes

1. Vol. I, No. 1, inside front cover.

Information Sources

INDEX SOURCES: The Critical Index; FIAF International Index to Film Periodicals; Film Literature Index; Humanities Index.
REPRINT EDITIONS: None.
LOCATION SOURCES: Auburn University; Harvard University; Library of Congress; Massachusetts Institute of Technology; Swarthmore College; University of Georgia; University of Illinois; University of Iowa; University of Oregon; University of Southern California.

Publication History

MAGAZINE TITLE AND TITLE CHANGES: *The Film Journal*.
VOLUME AND ISSUE DATA: Vol. I, No. 1 (Spring 1971); Vol. I, No. 2 (Summer 1971); Vol. I, No. 3-4 (Fall-Winter 1972); Vol. II, No. 1 (September 1972); Vol. II, No. 2 (January-March 1973); Vol. II, No. 3 (1974); Vol. II, No. 4 (1975).
PUBLISHER AND PLACE OF PUBLICATION: The Film Journal, Box 9602, Hollins College, Va. 24020.
EDITOR: Thomas R. Atkins.

Anthony Slide

FILMKRITIK

The monthly *Filmkritik* is the oldest of West Germany's independent journals of film criticism. It first appeared in January 1957, roundly condemning the subjectivity and superficiality which it found to be endemic among the nation's leading film reviewers and declaring its affinity with Walter Benjamin's conviction that the critic best serves the public by never being deferential toward it. Accordingly, *Filmkritik*'s own view of the role of film criticism was, from the outset, both didactic and partisan. Its avowed aim was to improve the responsive cinema goer's perception of ''aesthetic structures'' and ''social and political images'': ''Criticism should illuminate the social mechanisms at work in the production and impact of films; identify the positive examples, in which films contribute to social self-awareness; and denounce the negative cases, in which political narrow-mindedness is promoted and perpetuated'' (No. 1, 1957).

Initially, *Filmkritik*—which appeared without stills until issue No. 1, 1958—contained a mixture of long, titled reviews and brief notices, some of which were followed by more expansive commentaries in subsequent numbers. Most of the films discussed had either been newly released or were about to be released in the Federal Republic, but rereleased early films were also included. The journal's movie coverage was comprehensive, and it included films appearing on television. Also to be found in the earlier numbers of *Filmkritik* were book reviews, festival reports, a news section, and essays on specific topics or broader issues relating to the cinema. Each film review, whether long or short, was accompanied by a coded indication of the reviewer's recommendation in the form of dots. From No. 1, 1958, these dots were tabulated in such a way as to give a comparative impression of the staff writers' opinions. In 1969 they became the expression of a major shift in editorial policy.

Inspired by the decision of *Cahiers du Cinéma** to replace its ratings tables covering all premiered films with selective lists of recommended films only, *Filmkritik* announced in No. 1, 1969, that it shared the French journal's objective in wanting to free itself from the limited range of films on offer from distributors and at film festivals. Its own tabulated ratings would continue to appear, but in a modified form and would henceforth serve instead to concentrate the reader's attention on "essential viewing." However, there would be no further coverage of televised films. Restriction of the scope of *Filmkritik* at the end of the sixties was the culmination of a process of self-appraisal begun in No. 3, 1961, when editor Enno Patalas[1] and critic Wilfried Berghahn asked the question, "Is there such a thing as left-wing criticism?" Throughout the decade, the journal acted as a friction surface for argument on the functions of film criticism. It emerged (in No. 1, 1969) confident that it had established itself as "the German film establishment's most loyal opposition," but determined not to allow this status to turn it into an extension of the establishment. Consequently, the journal felt it must cease to be the "preserve" of its staff writers and open its columns to potential "allies" outside who were now speaking "the language of resistance" in films and in "other forms of public activity." In this way, it would be reaffirming its belief in the virtue of being "decidedly partisan."

In No. 3, 1969, under the modish heading "Readers' Co-determination," letters from the readership were published which suggested an indignant response to the recent changes in policy, particularly to the impression given that *Filmkritik* was telling its readers what was best for them. Such complaints met only with a rebuke from editor Patalas, who looked upon them as symptoms of undiscerning consumerism. At the same time, he felt compelled to make a "shameless appeal" for new subscriptions and to give voice to a Utopian vision of local film pressure groups growing up around readers of *Filmkritik* and thereby creating a wider readership. A lengthy critique of the journal, which also appeared in No. 3, 1969, and which faulted among other things *Filmkritik*'s growing tendency to monologize was answered with a riposte that bordered on the contemptuous.

That same year, *Filmkritik* published (in No. 12, 1969) a constitution for the journal that heralded its "democratization"; from No. 1, 1970, editorial control would be in the hands of a cooperative. Among the cosignatories of the document were the founding editor, Patalas, and one of the more recent acquisitions from the ranks of the filmmakers, Wim Wenders. The constitution guaranteed publication of all contributions submitted by members of the cooperative, which on the face of it did not seem to be in keeping with the desire expressed in No. 1, 1969, to break away from the concept of a narrow circle of collaborators. *Filmkritik* continues to be edited by the cooperative and under its guidance has tended to appear in the form of special issues concentrating on particular themes (though it still manages now and then to include some film and book reviews).

For example, No. 6 (1978), No. 8 (1978), No. 3 (1979), and No. 8 (1980) all dealt exclusively with the films of John Ford. Some of the more recent numbers—No. 1 (1982), No. 7 (1982), and No. 10 (1982)—have only the most tenuous relationship to film and lay *Filmkritik* open to the charge of self-indulgence. In No. 1, 1982, an editorial justified steep price increases by documenting the journal's parlous financial record in the years since the inception of the cooperative and the ascendancy of the "authorial principle," but there is no clear acknowledgment of a causal connection between the two. The accompanying formulation of editorial policy can best be described as arcane.

Notwithstanding the erratic course steered by *Filmkritik* in recent years, the lasting achievements of the journal remain considerable. In its early issues it did much to overcome the "cultural provincialism" (No. 1, 1960) of the Federal Republic by broadening awareness of films that might not otherwise have come to the attention of West German cinéphiles. Furthermore, *Filmkritik* was watchful, informative, and helpfully provocative concerning all aspects of the emerging "New German Cinema," including proposals for legislation to revive the domestic film industry.

Notes

1. Since his editorial control of *Filmkritik* ended, Enno Patalas has been best known for his work as head of the film section of the Munich City Museum (Münchner Stadtmuseum—Abteilung Film, Sankt-Jakobs-Platz 1, 8000 Munich 2).

Information Sources

BIBLIOGRAPHY:
Kötz, Michael. "Es spricht statt deiner. Vom Kino und seinen Zeitschriften." *Frankfurter Rundschau*, July 24, 1982.
Kreimeier, Klaus. "Filmkritik und Klassenkampf." *Film* (Velber), No. 4, 1969.
"Lebensläufe" (biographical notes on the staff of *Filmkritik*). *Filmkritik*, No. 4, 1965.
Schöler, Franz. *17 x 24 Materialien zum Verständnis der Zeitschrift Filmkritik*. Hamburg, 1969.
Schütte, Wolfram, and Vöbel, F. W. "Abschied von gestern. Enno P." *Filmstudio*, No. 51, October 1966.
Vogel, Wolfgang. "Zur Position der linken Filmkritik." *Filmstudio*, No. 38, February 1963.
"Was die 'Filmkritik' ist. Eine Kollektivantwort der Zeitschrift auf drei Fragen." *Frankfurter Rundschau*, June 28, 1975.
W. K. (Werner Kliess). "Blinde Seher. Zur Krise der Zeitschrift 'Filmkritik.'" *Film* (Velber), No. 7, 1969.
INDEX SOURCES: FIAF International Index to Film Periodicals.
REPRINT EDITIONS: Filmkritiker-Kooperative (1964–1965); Zweitausendeins (1957–1963).
LOCATION SOURCES: New York Public Library (incomplete); University of California at Los Angeles (incomplete); University of Southern California (incomplete).

Publication History

MAGAZINE TITLE AND TITLE CHANGES: *Filmkritik: Aktuelle Informationen für Filmfreunde* (No. 1, 1957–No. 12, 1960); *Filmkritik* (No. 1, 1961, to present).

VOLUME AND ISSUE DATA: No. 1, 1957 (January 1957 to present), monthly.

PUBLISHER AND PLACE OF PUBLICATION: Filmkritiker-Kooperative, Kreittmayr-strasse 3, 8000 Munich 2, Federal Republic of Germany.

EDITOR: Enno Patalas (No. 1, 1957–No. 5, 1961); Enno Patalas and Wilfried Berghahn (No. 6, 1961–No. 10, 1964); Enno Patalas (No. 11, 1964–No. 5, 1966); Helmut Färber (No. 6, 1966); Enno Patalas (No. 7, 1966–No. 12, 1969); Filmkritiker Kooperative (No. 1, 1970, to present).

David Head

FILM LIBRARY QUARTERLY

With support from the recently created Film Library Information Council, *Film Library Quarterly* began publication in 1967. The Council, comprised of public library film librarians and people interested in promoting community use of films, saw several reasons for the development of a nationwide journal of this kind. The level of audio-visual services in public libraries had grown dramatically in the decade before the Council's conception. Similar growth occurred in the number of films created and audio-visual materials being sold during that time. The increasingly large body of material made media selection by the film librarian an even more challenging task. The *Film Library Quarterly* was to serve in part as a medium for the criticism of films, audio tapes, and later video materials which might be chosen for a public library. In addition to its utility as a media selection tool, it also became a forum for the discussion of other issues and problems faced by film librarians.[1]

The evaluation of audio-visual materials and books continues to be a major focus of the *Quarterly*. Each issue features columns devoted to film and book reviews written by individuals in the field. Coverage of video began in 1978. It should be noted that popular film is generally not covered in these columns; rather, shorter features, such as *The Atomic Cafe* and *Rosie the Riveter* are reviewed. Full-length feature films are occasionally discussed but most often in the context of larger articles which discuss a particular theme, such as labor-related films. In this case, a film like *Norma Rae* would be discussed.

While providing film and book reviews, the *Quarterly* has also printed technical and bibliographic articles of interest to the film librarian. Specific subjects covered have included film and the public library, the "ideal film library," a library stereo tape collection, a film library's book collection, a core film collection, video cassettes, a core Afro-American film collection, and the cataloging of video art. Closely related to these technical questions was the practical issue of programming. The questions in this area concern not only what should be in a program, but also to or for whom a program would be most appropriate.

Articles on programming independent and feature films have been printed along with those concerning the programming of a single filmmaker's works. The topic of specialized audiences, such as minorities, the handicapped, and hearing impaired, has also been addressed.

It would be a mistake to consider *Film Library Quarterly* a journal only for film librarians. Despite its emphasis on film and book reviews, as well as programming and technical matters, *Film Library Quarterly* also offers a variety of other features. Interviews and articles about people in filmmaking have been a popular attraction and have included people such as documentary filmmaker Frederick Wiseman, Andy Warhol, Paul Strand, and Ernst Lubitsch. An entire issue was also devoted to Louis Malle and the documentary film.

Over the years *Film Library Quarterly* has also examined contemporary media-related issues, some of which have been controversial. Censorship, always an explosive issue, was discussed in an article about "the Los Angeles 19." There have also been pieces on special issue films, such as those on Vietnam or labor unions. Even television programs, such as the documentary "The Selling of the Pentagon," have been scrutinized. Some topics were also considered important enough to have entire issues devoted to them. These have included films related to labor issues, as well as women and film. The latter subject has been so popular that it has been covered twice. The *Quarterly* has also occasionally featured reports from international film festivals.

While there has been greater emphasis on current topics and problems, *Film Library Quarterly* has at times published articles on historical matters. German cinema in the Nazi period, for example, was one topic discussed in this category. There have also been articles on Charlie Chaplin and the avant-garde, as well as on the avant-garde movement in France. The relationship between modern history and modern films proved to be another thought-provoking article.

Other topics published have been more miscellaneous in nature. They have included articles on topics as diverse as the state of animation and the role of the Library of Congress in the creation of a national film gallery. Minority filmmakers have been covered as well.

While the major concern of the journal is the twin questions of media review and programming for certain audiences, *Film Library Quarterly* has developed into a publication doing much more. Its indexing in a variety of sources also speaks well for its broadened coverage. The essays are well written and intelligently presented by informed individuals, scholars, and librarians. With Vol. 14 the *Quarterly* began receiving partial support in the form of a grant from the Coordinating Council of Literary Magazines, and the *Quarterly* continues to make an important and serious contribution to the body of media scholarship.

Notes

1. William Sloan, "Projections, 1967/68," *Film Library Quarterly*, Vol. I, No. 1, 1967, p. 3.

Information Sources

BIBLIOGRAPHY:
Sloan, William, "Projections, 1967/68," *Film Library Quarterly* Vol. I, No. 1, 1967,
   pp. 3–4.
INDEX SOURCES: The Critical Index; FIAF International Index to Film Periodicals;
   Film Literature Index; Humanities Index; The New Film Index.
REPRINT EDITIONS: University Microfilms.
LOCATION SOURCES: Academy of Motion Picture Arts and Sciences; Library of
   Congress; New York Public Library; Ohio State University; University of Cali-
   fornia at Los Angeles; University of Cincinnati; University of Iowa; University
   of Southern California; University of Utah; University of Wisconsin at Madison.

Publication History

MAGAZINE TITLE AND TITLE CHANGES: *Film Library Quarterly.*
VOLUME AND ISSUE DATA: Vol. I, No. 1 (Winter 1967/1968 to present), quarterly.
PUBLISHER AND PLACE OF PUBLICATION: Film Library Information Council, P.O.
   Box 348, Radio City Station, New York, N.Y. 10019.
EDITOR: William Sloan.

Kim Fisher

FILMMAKERS FILM & VIDEO MONTHLY

Filmmakers Film & Video Monthly began as a simple, inexpensive newsletter
called *Filmmakers Newsletter* in 1967. Designed by editor Suni Mallow as "a
clearing house for all and any information pertaining to filmmakers and filmmaking," subscription rates began at a modest three dollars a year.

Never a refereed, scholarly journal, *Filmmakers Newsletter* was the well-read,
well-known delight of the growing number of film students in graduate and
undergraduate programs throughout the United States. Its early offerings were
at once an amalgam of almost underground observations and very aboveground
concerns for established cinema institutions. Vol. 1, No. 12, for example, contains such an admixture as a homely, personal plea for a missing friend followed
by a Jonas Mekas apology for the temporary closing of his Cinematheque—both
in the famous (and open) "Bulletin Board" section—as well as Society of Motion
Picture and Television Engineers (SMPTE), University Film Association (UFA),
and American Film Institute (AFI) concerns, in the larger body of the twenty-
five page issue.

By 1969, under the same editor and from the same office, *Filmmakers Newsletter* had grown a bit larger, a bit longer, and a bit more expensive (fifty cents
per issue) to cover better-quality printing and illustrations. It was during this
period that it also began to devote its attentions to experimental production and
artists, such as Scott Bartlett and Kenneth Anger, as well as workshops, festivals,
and cooperatives. This period also marks *Filmmakers Newsletter*'s particular

concern for reviewing new technology, especially the then-innovative Super 8mm format.

In the early seventies there was less concern with experimental film and increased attention to new equipment and technology. Mainstays like "Bulletin Board" and festival reviews remained, though they suffered increased competition with full-page advertisements by such corporations as Arriflex. It was also during this period (with Vol. 4) that the *Newsletter* took on its "mature" look—glossy cover, sixty-some pages, quality illustrations—and sophisticated coverage. Vol. 4, No. 3, for example, showcased the Worth and Adair research on participatory ethnographic filming among Navajos. At the same time L. Bruce Holman's hand-illustrated and very practical "Building Cine Stuff" article (a regular for many years) instructed the reader in the use and construction of a homemade tripod "spider."

By Vol. 11, *Filmmakers Newsletter* came to advertise itself as "a magazine for professionals and semi-professionals working in film and videotape," a change in emphasis that was soon to transform the publication into *Filmmakers Film & Video Monthly*. During its last years of existence, the journal was far more devoted to Hollywood feature releases and to broadcast/narrowcast video gear than in earlier issues. Still, the independent artist was not forgotten. For example, Vol. 13, No. 9, deals with a PBS documentary (*The Land Where Blues Began*) and a Holman-like article (by Rusty Kearns) on construcing an inexpensive special effects device. Super 8mm also found attention, and there were reviews of a number of international festivals. Indeed the article on *All That Jazz* took up a little more space than the classic—if no longer free and open—"Bulletin Board." In fact, the magazine still had a "used equipment" section, which suggests it had not forgotten its roots.

Information Sources

INDEX SOURCES: The Critical Index; FIAF International Index to Film Periodicals; Film Literature Index.
REPRINT EDITIONS: University Microfilms.
LOCATION SOURCES: Colorado State University; New York Public Library.

Publication History

MAGAZINE TITLE AND TITLE CHANGES: *Filmmakers Newsletter* (November 1967–September 1978); *Filmmakers Film & Video Monthly* (October 1978–January-February 1982).
VOLUME AND ISSUE DATA: Vol. I, No. 1–Vol. VII, No. 12 (November 1967–October 1974), monthly except for combined July-August issue; Vol. VIII, No. 1–Vol. XV, No. 2 (November 1974–December 1981), monthly; Vol. XV, No. 3 (January-February 1982).
PUBLISHER AND PLACE OF PUBLICATION: Filmmakers Newsletter Co., 80 Wooster Street, New York, N.Y. 10012 (Vol. I, No. 1–Vol. IV, No. 5); Filmmakers Newsletter Co., 41 Union Square West, New York, N.Y. 10003 (Vol. IV, No. 6–Vol. VI, No. 7); Suncraft International, Inc., 41 Union Square West, New

York, N.Y. 10003 (Vol. VI, No. 8–Vol. XII, No. 6); Suncraft International, Inc.,
P.O. Box 115, Ward Hill, Mass. 01830 (Vol. XII, No. 7–Vol. XII, No. 10);
Suncraft International, Inc., P.O. Box 607, Andover, Mass. (Vol. XII, No. 11–
Vol. XV, No. 3).

EDITOR: Suni Mallow (November 1967–November 1970); Suni Mallow and H. Whitney
Bailey (December 1970–April 1979); H. Whitney Bailey (May 1979–January-
February 1982).

Edward S. Small

FILMMAKERS NEWSLETTER. See FILMMAKERS FILM &
VIDEO MONTHLY

THE FILM MERCURY

Like *Hollywood Spectator*, *The Film Mercury* was typical of a number of
small, serious, trade-oriented magazines which appeared in the twenties. Also
like the *Spectator* it had a longer life than most of its contemporaries. Thanks
to the high quality of the paper used, *The Film Mercury* looked solid and reliable,
and to all extents and purposes it was.

It was founded in 1924 by Tamar Lane,[1] who wrote most of the reviews (which
seem basically honest and sincere), aided by Fred W. Fox and Lane's sister
Annabel (who initially contributed a "Gotham Gossip" column). As well as
film reviews, *The Film Mercury* featured news items and lengthy editorials. It
campaigned for better working conditions and pay for performers but opposed
the Equity closed shop. On October 23, 1925, it defended "Fatty" Arbuckle,
demanding to know why he was still victimized despite his acquittal.

From October 29, 1926, to November 19, 1926, Slavko Vorkapich contributed
a series of articles on "The Motion Picture as an Art." A special section,
"Prominent Writers and Their Work," first appeared in the summer of 1927,
and the October 5, 1928, issue was a special writers number, including articles
by George Jean Nathan and Iris Barry. On July 6, 1928, Richard Watts, Jr.,
contributed "George Bernard Shaw and the 'Talkies,' " and in that same issue
began a regular column of criticism, titled "The Film Parade."

Notes

1. Tamar Lane was the author of a number of books, including *What's Wrong with
the Movies?* (Los Angeles: The Wavery Company, 1923), *Hollywood and the Movies*
(Hollywood, Calif.: Mercury Publishing Company, 1930) and *The New Technique of
Screen Writing* (New York: Whittlesey House, 1936).

Information Sources

INDEX SOURCES: None.
REPRINT EDITIONS: None.
LOCATION SOURCES: Academy of Motion Picture Arts and Sciences (incomplete); New York Public Library (incomplete).

Publication History

MAGAZINE TITLE AND TITLE CHANGES: *The Film Mercury*.
VOLUME AND ISSUE DATA: Vol. I, No. 1–Vol. XIV, No. 2 (1924–November 23, 1933), weekly. [Date of last issue unconfirmed; no issues published October 23, 1931–November 8, 1933].
PUBLISHER AND PLACE OF PUBLICATION: Mercury Publishing Company, Taft Building, Hollywood Boulevard at Vine Street, Hollywood, Calif. (Vol. I, No. 1–Vol. IV, No. 20); Mercury Publishing Company, 1524 1/2 Cahuenga Avenue, Hollywood, Calif. (Vol. IV, No. 21–Vol. VIII, No. 13); Mercury Publishing Company, 7556 Melrose Avenue, Hollywood, Calif. (Vol. VIII, No. 14–?).
EDITOR: Tamar Lane and Fred W. Fox (1924–March 27, 1925); Tamar Lane (April 3, 1925–November 23, 1933).

Anthony Slide

FILM MUSIC. See FILM AND T.V. MUSIC

FILMMUSIC NOTEBOOK

Published beginning in 1974 for the members of Elmer Bernstein's Film Music Collection (which produced albums of film music), *Filmmusic Notebook* offered much valuable documentation in its field, including interviews, articles, and filmographies. Elmer Bernstein's own far from unimpressive career was covered in Vol. 1, No. 2 (Winter 1974/1975). Other composers featured included Max Steiner and Hugo Friedhofer (Vol. 1, No. 1), Miklos Rozsa and Richard Rodney Bennett (Vol. 2, No. 1), Alfred Newman (Vol. 2, No. 2), David Raksin (Vol. 2, No. 3), John Green (Vol. 2, No. 4), Alex North (Vol. 3, No. 1), Jerry Fielding (Vol. 3, No. 3), and Bronislau Kaper and Dimitri Tiomkin (Vol. 4, No. 2). *Filmmusic Notebook* "temporarily suspended" publication in 1978.

Information Sources

INDEX SOURCES: Film Literature Index.
REPRINT EDITIONS: None.
LOCATION SOURCES: Academy of Motion Picture Arts and Sciences; Library of Congress; New York Public Library; University of California at Los Angeles; University of Southern California.

Publication History

MAGAZINE TITLE AND TITLE CHANGES: *Filmmusic Notebook.*
VOLUME AND ISSUE DATA: Vol. I, No. 1–Vol. IV, No. 2 (Autumn 1974–Fall 1978),
    quarterly.
PUBLISHER AND PLACE OF PUBLICATION: Elmer Bernstein's Film Music Collec-
    tion, P.O. Box 261, Calabasas, Calif. 91302 (Vol. I, No. 1–Vol. III, No. 1);
    Elmer Bernstein's Film Music Collection, P.O. Box 25198, West Los Angeles,
    Calif. 90025 (Vol. III, No. 2–Vol. IV, No. 2).
EDITOR: Eve Adamson.

Anthony Slide

FILM MUSIC NOTES. See FILM AND T.V. MUSIC

FILM NEWS

Commencing in December 1939 and initially supported by a grant from the
General Education Board of the Rockefeller Foundation, *Film News* for four
decades reported and influenced the development of film as a primary communication medium and fostered the growth of the medium into a viable industry.
It was described in a Twentieth Century/Columbia University report as "a combination reporting-critical journal, containing probably the best all-round news
and analysis of nontheatrical adult film production and use here and abroad."
For thirty-four years of its life, *Film News* was owned, edited, and published
by Rohama Lee.

The magazine began as the typewritten and mimeographed news organ of the
now-defunct American Film Center, a Rockefeller Foundation activity housed
at 45 Rockefeller Plaza. At this time, the publication's title was *News from the
American Film Center, Inc.* (a title retained for only the first five months of the
magazine's life). Set up on the basis of a ten-year grant, the Center served as
focus for the burgeoning movement toward film (both 35mm and 16mm) as a
medium not simply of entertainment but of information, communication, orientation, and education. In June 1940, after five issues, *Film News* became a
printed journal with a subscription price of one dollar per year. It moved from
a semiprivate newsletter to a public journal serving the educational field.

The history of the nontheatrical film in its many aspects is chronicled in the
pages of *Film News* from December 1939 to Summer 1981. In its American
Film Center days, it played an enormously important role in the allied Second
World War effort, serving as a liaison medium between the U.S. government
film production agencies and the public and also as a reporter of news of wartime
film production and use, particularly with respect to Canada, the United Kingdom, and the Netherlands—which gave the magazine, from the start, a cosmopolitan character that was maintained by its purchaser (Rohama Lee) when

the Rockefeller grant was finished and the American Film Center disbanded. In 1946 *Film News* was moribund for a year, and whatever of its effects could be found literally had to be dug out of haphazard storage in the basement of 45 Rockefeller Plaza.

Together with Cecil Morgan Jones, a British engineer and journalist who worked with Rohama Lee on the magazine for several years, what could be rescued was moved over to "The Penthouse," a protuberance on the roof of 15 West Thirty-eighth Street in New York City, a building devoted to millinery. There, *Film News* carried on with respect to its commitment except for one deviation; it dropped 35mm and went increasingly in the direction of the non-theatrical (16mm) format, which more and more was becoming the vehicle for conveying "information, communication, orientation and education" to the public via schools, public libraries, health and welfare agencies, religious and other community organizations and associations. Entertainment features, reduced from 35mm and available in 16mm, were regularly included, beginning with *The Blue Angel* in 1950. Ruth Goldstein of the New York City school system and writer of the classic Brandon catalogs, conducted this department. *Film News* also introduced the first full-scale reviews of the filmstrip in another regular department, conducted by Dr. Irene Cypher of New York University. Educational television was variously discussed when it became a concern. "What's New in Equipment" was a steady feature, as was "What They Are Showing" (program suggestions) and book and periodical reviews.

Inasmuch as the early media journals (then called audio-visual publications) were school-oriented (for example, *Educational Screen*), with *Film World* in Los Angeles and *Business Screen* in Chicago trade-oriented, *Film News* gradually, within its first decade, moved into wider fields, extending its horizons with an esoteric collection of between twenty-five and thirty film reviews to each issue, establishing a reputation for reliability on the part of both user and producer. Coverage of films on dance and art commenced in 1948, and *Film News* was unique in its reporting on festivals in this country and abroad. An important series in *Film News'* early years was "We Use Films in Our Programs," a survey of community organizations by Lillian Wachtel, and, in later issues, "A-V in Public Libraries," reports by librarians on their organizations from around the country.

The accent of *Film News* was on the domestic scene, but its approach was from a world viewpoint, as evidenced from the contents of the revived magazine's "pilot" issue, dated March 15, 1947, and designated Vol. 8, No. 1, for continuity with the original American Film Center publication. That issue, priced at twenty cents, carried an article by John Grierson titled "Far Horizons" and, prophetically, "Sound Recorded on Paper Tape" by John Flory of the Society of Motion Picture Engineers. Also included were an on-the-scene report titled "Walt Disney, M.D., Shows Ecuador the Road to Health," along with "News of the Trade," "A Letter from London," and reviews of a newly available series from Young America (later absorbed by McGraw-Hill), *The New France* from the

"March of Time" and *Peoples of the Soviet Union* by Julien Bryan. In subsequent issues there were letters from Latin America, Mexico, Germany, Japan, Canada, and other parts of the world.

Several special issues were devoted to Canada, notably a 1979 number celebrating the fortieth anniversary of the National Film Board of Canada. Many issues were built around specific themes, such as the twenty-fifth anniversary of 16mm; the Army Pictorial Service; forty years of mental health films; the United Nations; the U.S. Information Service; and film activities in Alaska, Israel, Yugoslavia, Expo 67, and the Festival of Britain. One special issue was about blacks, and another was concerned with American Indians.

Initially most of the writing and reporting was done by the editor, but as *Film News* developed it acquired a coterie of accomplished, loyal writers and reviewers without whom the magazine could not have continued as long as it did. There were contributions also, without renumeration, by special people such as Pearl Buck, Dr. Gerald Wendt, Richard Griffith, and Arthur L. Mayer. *Film News* is also replete with interviews, through the years, with industry leaders and educators, beginning with a rare conversation with Willard Cook, "father of the nontheatrical film in the United States." *Film News* also featured interviews with and articles by John Grierson, Stuart Legg, and Stanley Hawes, as well as prominent church people. It initiated the first regular "Religious and Interfaith" department.

Among other prominent contributors have been Helen Van Dongen, Joris Ivens, Mary Field, Hans Richter, Arthur Knight, Robert Flaherty, and Frances Hubbard Flaherty.

From a twenty-page, black-and-white tabloid, *Film News* had progressed, by 1981, to a forty-eight and sometimes fifty-two page journal, with an abundance of illustrations and a color cover. Greater concern for editorial excellence together with rising costs impelled the publisher to seek outside financial backing. In 1968 a trial arrangement with IDD, Inc., publishers of a financial periodical, was made, but after finding the magazine did not jibe with its interests IDD returned *Film News* to Rohama Lee. *Film News* was subsequently sold to Open Court Publishing, but publication was suspended after four issues. In October 1983 *Film News* was again sold, to John Grandits, who anticipates the revival of *Film News* some time 1984, with himself as editor/publisher.

Information Sources

INDEX SOURCES: Film Literature Index.

REPRINT EDITIONS: University Microfilms.

LOCATION SOURCES: Academy of Motion Picture Arts and Sciences (incomplete); American Archives of the Factual Film (Iowa State University); Educational Film Library Association; Library of Congress; New York Public Library; University of Denver; University of Illinois; University of Pennsylvania; University of Southern California (incomplete).

Publication History

MAGAZINE TITLE AND TITLE CHANGES: *News from the American Film Center, Inc.* (December 1939–April 1940); *Film News* (except April 1958 and May-June 1958 issues titled *Film/A.V. News*).

VOLUME AND ISSUE DATA: Vol. I, No. 1–Vol. I, No. 5 (December 1939–April 1940), monthly; Vol. I, No. 6–Vol. II, No. 6 (June 1940–June 1941), monthly; Vol. II, No. 7–Vol. III, No. 4 (October 1941–April 1942), monthly; Vol. III, No. 5 (Early Summer 1942); Vol. III, No. 6 (Late Summer 1942); Vol. III, No. 7–Vol. III, No. 9 (September 24, 1942–November 26, 1942), monthly; Vol. IV, No. 1 (Summer 1943); Vol. IV, No. 2–Vol. IV, No. 3 (November 1943–December 1943), monthly; Vol. V, No. 1–Vol. VII, No. 4 (January 1944–January 1946), monthly except no issues published for July and August 1944 and July, August, and September 1945; Vol. VII, No. 5 (February-March 1946); Vol. VII, No. 6 (April 1946); Vol. VIII, No. 1–Vol. VIII, No. 3 (March 15, 1947–May 21, 1947), monthly; Vol. VIII, No. 4-5 (September-October 1947); Vol. VIII, No. 5-6 [*sic*] (November-December 1947); Vol. VIII, No. 8 (January 1948); Vol. VIII, No. 9 (February 1948); Vol. VIII, No. 10 (March-April 1948); Vol. VIII, No. 11 (May 1948); Vol. VIII, No. 12 (June-July 1948); Vol. IX, No. 1–Vol. IX, No. 12 (September 1948–August 1949), monthly except double issues for April-May 1949 and June-July 1949; Vol. X, No. 1–Vol. XI, No. 10 (September 1948–November-December 1951), irregular; Vol. XII, No. 1 (January 1952); Vol. XII, No. 2 (March 1952); Vol. XII, No. 3 (April 1952); Vol. XII, No. 4 (Summer 1952); Vol. XII, No. 5–Vol. XII, No. 8 (September 1952–December 1952), monthly; Vol. XIII, No. 1 (January 1953); Vol. XIII, No. 2 (1953); Vol. XIII, No. 3 (1953); Vol. XIII, No. 4 (1953); Vol. XIII, No. 5 (Summer 1953); Vol. XIII, No. 6 (September 1953); Vol. XIII, No. 7 (October 1953); Vol. XIII, No. 8 (1953); Vol. XIII, No. 9 (1953); Vol. XIV, Nos. 1–9 (1954); Vol. XV, No. 1– Vol. XVII, No. 4 (Spring 1955–Winter 1957-1958), quarterly; Vol. XVII, No. 5 (April 1958); Vol. XVII, No. 6 (May-June 1958); Vol. XVIII, Nos. 1–6 (October 1960–October 1961), six times a year; Vol. XIX, Nos. 1–5 (January-February 1962–November-December 1962), five times a year; Vol. XX, Nos. 1–4 (1963), quarterly; Vol. XXI, No. 1–Vol. XXX, No. 6 (1964–1973), bimonthly; Vol. XXXI, No. 1–Vol. XXXVI, No. 5 (1974–1979), five times a year; Vol. XXXVII, Nos. 1–4 (1980), quarterly; Vol. XXXVIII, No. 1 (Spring 1981); Vol. XXXVIII, No. 2 (Summer 1981); Vol. XXXVIII, No. 3 (Fall 1981).

PUBLISHER AND PLACE OF PUBLICATION: American Film Center, Inc., 45 Rockefeller Plaza, New York 20, N.Y. (Vol. I, No. 1–Vol. VII, No. 6); Film News Company, "The Penthouse," 15 West Thirty-eighth Street, New York 18, N.Y. (Vol. VIII, No. 1–Vol. VIII, No. 12); Film News Company, 13 East Thirty-seventh Street, New York 16, N.Y. (Vol. XI, No. 1–Vol. X, No. 6); Film News Company, 112 West Forty-eight Street, New York 19, N.Y. (Vol. X, No. 7– Vol. XI, No. 7); Film News Company, 444 Central Park West, New York, N.Y. 10025 (Vol. XI, No. 8–Vol. XVII, No. 4); Keegan Publishing Co. Inc., 1775 Broadway, New York, N.Y. 10019 (Vol. XVII, Nos. 5–6); Sairlee Enterprises, Inc., World Press Center, 54 West Forty-first Street, New York, N.Y. 10018 (Vol. XVIII, No. 1–Vol. XX, No. 1); Sairlee Enterprises, Inc., 250 West Fifty-seventh Street, New York, N.Y. 10019 (Vol. XX, No. 2–Vol. XXIV, No. 4);

FN/International Inc., 250 West Fifty-seventh Street, New York, N.Y. 10019 (Vol. XXIV, No. 5–Vol. XXV, No. 4); Film News Company, 250 West Fifty-seventh Street, New York, N.Y. 10019 (Vol. XXV, No. 5–Vol. XXXVII, No. 3); Open Court Publishing Company, 1500 Eighth Street, La Salle, Ill. 61301 (Vol. XXXVII, No. 4–Vol. XXXVIII, No. 3).

EDITOR: Donald Slesinger and John McDonald (December 1939–October 1940); John McDonald (November 1940–May 1945); no editor listed (June 1945); Thomas Baird (Editor-in-Chief, October 1945–December 1945); Donald Slesinger (January 1946–April 1946); Rohama Lee (March 15, 1947–Winter 1957-1958); Stephen F. Keegan (April 1958–May-June 1958); Rohama Lee (October 1960–Winter 1980); J. Paul Carrico (Spring 1981–Fall 1981).

Rohama Lee

FILMOGRAPH

Filmograph, which was published from 1970 to 1975, was very much in the mold of *Films in Review*,* if perhaps a little more esoteric and film buff-oriented. *Filmograph* featured a number of interviews and career articles (often written by the editor), along with reviews of books and periodicals and considerable material on the western genre of movies. Among the more unlikely pieces to be found in *Filmograph* are "The Story of a 'Smash-Up,' " a piece on the Susan Hayward vehicle of the same name (Vol. 3, No. 1); "Meet Cal Culver," an interview with the gay porno star (Vol. 3, No. 2); and "Ridin' and Singin' with Smith Ballew," a career article on the radio personality turned singing cowboy star (Vol. 4, No. 4).

Information Sources

INDEX SOURCES: Film Literature Index.

REPRINT EDITIONS: University Microfilms.

LOCATION SOURCES: Library of Congress; University of Southern California (incomplete).

Publication History

MAGAZINE TITLE AND TITLE CHANGES: *Filmograph*.

VOLUME AND ISSUE DATA: Vol. I, No. 1–Vol. IV, No. 4 (First Quarter 1970–Second Quarter 1975), quarterly.

PUBLISHER AND PLACE OF PUBLICATION: Murray Summers, 7926 Ashboro Drive, Alexandria, Va. 22309 (Vol. I, No. 1–Vol. III, No. 1); Murray Summers, Orlean, Va. 22128 (Vol. III, No. 2–Vol. IV, No. 4).

EDITOR: Murray Summers.

Anthony Slide

FILM PICTORIAL

Film Pictorial was a weekly photogravure magazine of 1932–1939 which billed itself (with its first issue) as "The Newest and Brightest of Weekly Periodicals." The contents were similar to other British fan magazines of the period, with articles on films and personalities, as well as film reviews with detailed cast listings. Interestingly, in the first issues Edgar Wallace wrote "Hollywood in Focus."

In common with other British film periodicals of the period, *Film Pictorial* also published a set of six hardcover annuals from 1935 through 1940, as well as summer and Christmas "extra" editions from 1933 through 1939.

Information Sources

BIBLIOGRAPHY:
Gifford, Denis. "Hollywood in Your Hands: The Film Pictorial Story." Supplement to 1972 reprint of September 30, 1933, issue of *Film Pictorial*.
INDEX SOURCES: None.
REPRINT EDITIONS: The September 30, 1933, issue was reprinted in 1972 by Peter Way Ltd. (London) as part of the "Great Newspapers Reprinted" series.
LOCATION SOURCES: No information.

Publication History

MAGAZINE TITLE AND TITLE CHANGES: *Film Pictorial*.
VOLUME AND ISSUE DATA: Vol. I, No. 1–Vol. XVI, No. 397 (February 17, 1932–September 30, 1939), weekly.
PUBLISHER AND PLACE OF PUBLICATION: Amalgamated Press, Ltd., The Fleetway House, London E.C.4, England.
EDITOR: Clarence Winchester.

Thomas A. Johnson

FILMPLAY JOURNAL. See Appendix 2

FILM POLSKI. See Appendix 4

FILM PROGRESS. See FILMS IN REVIEW

FILM QUARTERLY

Film Quarterly, like its predecessors *Hollywood Quarterly* and *Quarterly of Film, Radio and Television*, is published by the University of California Press. Four times a year it presents articles giving an academic appraisal of the current state of filmmaking, criticism, theory, and history. It regularly contains interviews with directors of note and investigations into areas of filmmaking largely ignored in the more popular-oriented film periodicals. While serving admirably as an organ of both film intelligentsia and cultists, the journal has, in later years, bypassed a constituency it had originally wished to represent—that of the concerned and creative worker in the industry.

Hollywood Quarterly began in October 1945 under the joint sponsorship of the Hollywood Writers Mobilization and the University of California, continuing a wartime collaboration between educators and workers in media to respond to social needs growing out of the war that could be helped, they felt, by a better use of Hollywood resources and talent. Led by writer John Howard Lawson, the five coeditors (two from the industry, three from the university) hoped their complementary perspectives would produce a journal to discuss the problems of the industry, investigate the societal effects of media, and thus work toward a more creative use of media in America.

The early issues of *Hollywood Quarterly* experimented with these concerns. Articles relating to the war and its aftermath were in abundance. "Warriors Return: Normal or Neurotic," (Vol. 1, No. 1) by coeditor Franklin Fearing, dealt in essay form with the psychological readjustment of the veteran, while Abraham Polonsky's "The Case of David Smith" (Vol. 1, No. 2), a radio script, treated the same material dramatically. "The Documentary and Hollywood" (Vol. 1, No. 2) by Philip Dunne described the experiences of "a typical Hollywood 'picturemaker' " called into the field of wartime documentary production, while "A Film at War" (Vol. 1, No. 4) by Harold Salemson related the extraordinary effect a particular film, Jean Renoir's *La Marseillaise*, had in occupied Tunisia when it played for a week in the summer of 1943.

People from different phases of production contributed articles on their work in general, on particular productions, and their views on improving the industry. Writers Lester Cole and John Paxton, directors Irving Pichel and Curtis Harrington, actor Alexander Knox, composers Adolph Deutsch and Franz Waxman, production designer Harry Horner, costume designer Edith Head, dialogue directer Hugh MacMillan, technical advisors Louis Van Den Ecker and Cyril Hughes Hartmann, story analyst Frances Kroll Ring, sound mixer David Forrest, and subtitler Herman G. Weinberg collectively contributed a body of writing on filmmaking practice that was unparalleled in the film literature of the time.

Early issues presented short scripts on social concerns ("Brotherhood of Man," Vol. 1, No. 4; "To Secure These Rights," Vol. 3, No. 3; "The Empty Noose," Vol. 2, No. 2), descriptions of film production schools and research institutions around the world, advice on legal matters in media, research studies on radio audiences, and scholarly insights into film history. All kinds of media were covered, from Hollywood movies and radio to experimental cinema and television.

The first sign of a change in policy came in late 1946 as ripples of Red-baiting approached the Hollywood community. Coeditor Lawson (who was later jailed as one of the Hollywood Ten) left the journal after the provost of the University of California told him the journal would have to fold or disassociate itself from the university if Lawson continued his position. Abraham Polonsky (himself later blacklisted) as coeditor and contributor continued Lawson's concerns (his review of *Odd Man Out* and *Monsieur Verdoux*, Vol. 2, No. 4, is an excellent example of socially oriented film criticism). The journal, however, eventually lost its critical bite and turned academic, emphasizing studies, albeit excellent ones in many cases, of foreign and past filmmakers (Jean Vigo, Roberto Rossellini, Vittorio De Sica, Robert Flaherty, Carl Theodor Dreyer), Shakespearean adaptations, and television programming. *Hollywood Quarterly* was condemned in a House Committee on Un-American Activities hearing as being a Communist organ, and in 1951, it changed its name to *Quarterly of Film, Radio and Television*, stating that the journal no longer spoke for the Hollywood community.

Under the new name the *Quarterly* published, through the mid-fifties, high-quality but politically safe pieces on a variety of subjects. Some articles of note included Curtis Harrington's history of the horror film, "Ghoulies and Ghosties" (Vol. 7, No. 2); Norman McLaren's "Notes on Animated Sound" (Vol. 7, No. 3), detailing his method of creating soundtracks directly on film; and T. W. Adorno's "How to Look at Television" (Vol. 8, No. 3), which with the aid of categories of depth-psychology attempted to arrive at concepts by which the impact of television on the various layers of personality could be studied.

The journal stopped publication in 1957. After a year's inactivity, the University of California decided to revive their film journal. Under its new name, *Film Quarterly*, and new editor, Ernest Callenbach, the journal strove to establish itself at the center of American film criticism. Declaring that "a body of serious critical thought about films is possible, and...would be both useful and enjoyable,"[1] Callenbach specified his journal would be an "arena" rather than a "line" journal, publishing views from the whole spectrum of critical thought without committing itself to any one point of view.

Callenbach's "arena" was the scene of perhaps the most bitter controversy staged in print over the theory of film criticism. Pauline Kael in "Circles and Squares" (Vol. 16, No. 3) attacked the neo-auteurists Andrew Sarris in this country and the staff of *Movie** in England. Sarris and *Movie* rebutted just as vituperatively in a subsequent issue only to have Kael respond with further abuse. The discussion at times centered more on making insinuations about the other's supposed sexual predilections than on detailing ways of interpreting films.

The Kael-Sarris-*Movie* interchange set a precedent that characterized a great many articles published in the journal's pages: articles ostensibly about particular films or filmmakers would instead comment at length about other critics' opinions and reactions to these films and filmmakers, or invoke an "authorized" critic or theorist to justify the writer's own point of view. Perhaps the worst case came when one reviewer justified his own low opinion of Michael Curtiz by quoting Andrew Sarris—"If many of the early Curtiz films are hardly worth remembering, none of the later ones are worth seeing"[2]—as if Sarris's words were written in tablet.

A number of *Film Quarterly*'s contributors have been adherents of Claude Levi-Strauss, Jacques Lacan, Louis Althusser, Christian Metz, A. J. Greimas, Vladimir Propp, Gerard Genette, and/or Ernest Jones. All too often toeing a particular ideological line seemed to be more important to the writer than good, clear writing and thinking. Sentences such as "A powerful *Angst* penetrates this scene, for which the physical metaphors are Mary's battered face and listless voice"[3] and "Roemer's film is in that dialect of the culture which I denominate as 'liberal/sensitive' "[4] were not uncommon.

With the increase in film courses in the universities across the country, and complex films, particularly foreign, which demanded explication, *Film Quarterly* in the seventies filled a role as a journal for, by, and of the university film instructor and student. It has not succumbed to the temptation to go slick and superficial in order to compete with more popular film magazines. It covered important developments in Polish, Hungarian, Czech, African, Arabic, Latin-American, Japanese, and experimental film. The left-wing politicized film of the seventies was explained in cogent articles by James Roy MacBean. Marsha Kinder and Beverle Houston contributed feminist points of view to analyze contemporary trends. William F. Van Wert reported on films by Chris Marker and Marguerite Duras unseen in America. Jay Leyda's intermittent reports from the world of film history were fresh antidotes to the more pretentious theory-ridden articles.

Particular articles of interest for their unique subject matter or insightful treatment of more commonly written on subjects included: Paul Schrader's interview and essay on Charles Eames (Vol. 23, No. 3); Umberto Eco's attempt to understand the violently negative Chinese reaction to Michelangelo Antonioni's film about them ("De Interpretatione, or the Difficulty of Being Marco Polo," Vol. 30, No. 4); "Robert J. Flaherty, 1884–1951" by his editor Helen Van Dongen (Vol. 18, No. 3); "From Book to Film—via John Huston" by Hans Koningsberger, on the adaptation of his novel *A Walk With Love and Death* (Vol. 22, No. 3); Paul Sharits on Jean Luc Godard's use of color in "Red, Blue, Godard," (Vol. 19, No. 4); Gavin Lambert on working with Nicholas Ray in Hollywood after having been a critic in England in "Good-bye to Some of All That" (Vol. 12, No. 1); Stephen Farber interviewing and writing about "The Writer in American Films" (Vol. 21, No. 4); "Dissolves by Gaslight: Antecedents to the Motion Picture in 19th-Century Melodrama" by John C. Fell (Vol. 23, No. 3); and "The Comic Strip and Film Language" by Francis Lacassin (Vol. 26, No. 1).

In the twenty-five years since becoming *Film Quarterly*, the journal printed over sixty interviews covering the major directors and also some figures not as often interviewed, such as George de Beauregard (Vol. 20, No. 3), Conrad Hall (Vol. 24, No. 3), Stepin Fetchit (Vol. 24, No. 4), Tom Brandon (Vol. 26, No. 5), Helen Van Dongen (Vol. 30, No. 2), cinema vérité editor Ellen Hovde (Vol. 32, No. 2), Jean-Claude Carriere (Vol. 34, No. 3), and Vittorio Storaro (Vol. 35, No. 3). Occasionally the journal conducted multiple interviews with people connected with particular films, such as the writer, producer, cinematographer, editor, composer, and director of *Outrage* (Vol. 18, No. 3); the director, cinematographer, and editor of *A Married Couple* (Vol. 23, No. 4); and the director, writer, and composer of *Nashville* (Vol. 29, No. 2).

Each summer the special book review issue attempts a survey of all the film books published the previous year. The film reviews, generally long and involved, tend to be more interpretive than informational (names of cast and crew are often omitted).

With all its limitations, *Film Quarterly* remains one of the most important film journals. In encouraging serious articles on rarely discussed aspects of film, providing a forum for current critical debate, and allowing unknown writers an opportunity of expression, the journal speaks to the film student and enthusiast of the present day and possibly the filmmaker of the future influenced and provoked by its critical stances and insights.

Notes

1. Ernest Callenbach, "Editor's Notebook," *Film Quarterly*, Vol. 12, No. 3, Spring 1959, p. 2.
2. R. C. Dale reviewing "Hollywood In The...", *Film Quarterly*, Vol. 23, No. 1, Fall 1969, p. 60.
3. Charles W. Eckert, "The Anatomy of a Proletarian Film: Warner's *Marked Woman*," Vol. 27, No. 2, Winter 1973/1974, p. 15.
4. Stefan Fleischer, "Dying to Be on Television," *Film Quarterly*, Vol. 31, No. 4, p. 31.

Information Sources

BIBLIOGRAPHY:
Davis, Dave, and Goldberg, Neal. "Organizing the Screen Writers Guild: An Interview with John Howard Lawson." *Cineaste*, Vol. 8, No. 2.
Hollywood Quarterly, press release, 1946, on file in the Margaret Herrich Library of the Academy of Motion Picture Arts and Sciences.
Shaw, Robert. "New Horizons in Hollywood." *The Public Opinion Quarterly*, Vol. 10, No. 1, Spring 1946, pp. 71–77.
INDEX SOURCES: Access (1978 to present); Art Index (1959 to present); Critical Index (1946–1973); FIAF International Index to Film Periodicals; Film Literature Index; Humanities Index (1974 to present); Index to Critical Reviews in British and American Film Periodicals (1946–1971); Index to Literature on the American Indian (1971–1973); Index to Popular Periodicals (1978 to present); Magazine Index (1978 to present); Music Index (1951–1953); The New Film Index; Readers Guide to Periodical Literature (1968–1977); Retrospective Index to Film Periodicals 1930–1971; Social Sciences and Humanities Index (1955–1965).

REPRINT EDITIONS: AMS Press; University Microfilms.

LOCATION SOURCES: Academy of Motion Picture Arts and Sciences; Chicago Public
Library; Columbia University; Dartmouth College; Library of Congress; New York
Public Library; Stanford University; University of California at Berkeley; Uni-
versity of Illinois; University of Texas at Austin; University of Wisconsin at
Madison.

Publication History

MAGAZINE TITLE AND TITLE CHANGES: *Hollywood Quarterly* (October 1945–
Summer 1951); *The Quarterly of Film, Radio and Television* (Fall 1951–Summer
1957); *Film Quarterly* (Fall 1958 to present).

VOLUME AND ISSUE DATA: Vol. I, No. 1 (October 1945 to present), quarterly. Vol.
3, No. 4, has no date and comes between Vol. 3, No. 3 (Spring 1948) and Vol.
4, No. 1 (Fall 1949); there were no issues between Vol. 11, No. 4 (Summer
1957) and Vol. 12, No. 1 (Fall 1958); a number of issues are misnumbered on
the title page.

PUBLISHER AND PLACE OF PUBLICATION: University of California Press, Berkeley, Calif. 94720.

EDITOR: Samuel T. Farquhar, Franklin Fearing, John Howard Lawson, Kenneth Mac-
gowan, and Franklin P. Rolfe (October 1945–October 1946); John Collier, Samuel
T. Farquhar, Franklin Fearing, James Hilton, Kenneth Macgowan, Irving Pichel,
Abraham Polonsky, and Franklin P. Rolfe (January 1947–Vol. 3, No. 4, undated);
Franklin Fearing, Kenneth Macgowan, Irving Pichel, Abraham Polonsky, and
Franklin P. Rolfe (Fall 1949); Franklin Fearing, Walter K. Kingston, Kenneth
Macgowan, Irving Pichel, Abraham Polonsky, and Franklin P. Rolfe (Winter
1949–Summer 1954); Franklin Fearing, Walter K. Kingston, Kenneth Macgowan,
Irving Pichel, and Abraham Polonsky (Fall 1954–Summer 1955); Kenneth Mac-
gowan (Fall 1955–Summer 1957); Ernest Callenbach (Fall 1958 to present).

Alan Gevinson

FILM READER

The appearance of *Film Reader* coincided with the proliferation of film studies
programs throughout American universities and colleges. As academia sought
to validate the film medium as an object worthy of serious, intellectual inquiry,
a group of graduate students and faculty of Northwestern University's Radio-
Television-Film Department established *Film Reader* in 1975 as an annual "dedicated to the application of current theories in film scholarship."[1] The Film
Division of the Radio-Television-Film Department had early in the decade taken
a strong interest in European and British attempts to unite contemporary linguistic
and literary theories, particularly structuralism and semiotics, with the study of
film. In 1974 and 1975, with the encouragement and guidance of two visiting
faculty members, Peter Wollen (author of *Signs and Meaning in the Cinema*)
and Geoffrey Nowell-Smith, a group of graduate film students secured funding

from Northwestern's School of Speech and other university sources to launch an annual publication devoted to publishing the students' scholarly attempts at practical application of contemporary film theory. The first number, *Film Reader 1*, set the editorial policy and format for the next three issues: each number would include heavily theoretical articles dealing with one or two general themes. With an introduction by Wollen, the first section of *Film Reader 1* consisted of a detailed semiotic analysis of *Citizen Kane*, applying Christian Metz's syntagmatic models from *Film Language*; this section, a collaborative effort on the part of Film Division graduate students, grew out of a Wollen seminar on semiology. The second section dealt with the concept of authorship, long an important aspect of the Northwestern film curriculum, as applied to new "auteurs," directors of Hollywood in the seventies. This dual-topic format, for the first four issues, provided both a relatively new area of theoretical speculation, such as semiotics, with a more established or general area, such as authorship. For example, *Film Reader 2*, appearing in 1977, concerned itself with the relatively straightforward application of narrative theories to film, while the other topic dealt with the current French Marxist critique of film technology's ideological complicity. *Film Reader 2* marked a new direction for the annual, with its contributors drawn from the national academic community in addition to Northwestern students and the inclusion of pertinent foreign writing in translation, including work by Gerard Genette, Tzvetan Todorov, and Jean-Louis Comolli.

Film Reader 3, dealing with film genres and the relation between film and other arts, appeared in 1978, while *Film Reader 4*, published in 1979, concerned itself with the historiography of film and the concept of point of view in the cinema. The first four numbers of *Film Reader* were financed and staffed in similar manners: the Northwestern School of Speech provided a substantial loan, supplemented by contributions from elsewhere, particularly from the campus film society, to print each issue, while Radio-Television-Film faculty members appointed a board of editors for each issue, composed generally of doctoral film students. Since revenue was realized only through the sales of each press run of an issue, and since the loan agreement stipulated that the bulk of a previous loan must be repaid to the school before funding would be granted for a subsequent issue, it proved occasionally difficult for *Film Reader* to adhere to a yearly publication schedule, although so far it has succeeded in appearing almost annually.

Film Reader 5 represented a different editorial approach. Although still segmented into two distinct themes, one section was devoted to a selection of papers delivered at a feminist film criticism conference held at Northwestern in 1980 and edited collectively by the Feminist Film Seminar of the Radio-Television-Film Department; the second section concerned the relation between film and cultural studies. *Film Reader 5* also reflected new political interests within the Northwestern Radio-Television-Film Department, particularly feminism and Marxism as applied to communication studies. *Film Reader 6*, in press as of

Summer 1983, also represents a deviation in format, with the entire issue devoted to new historical research in both film and television: it is believed that future issues of *Film Reader* will also incorporate writing on video topics.

As *Screen** endeavored to import French theoretical issues into British film culture during the early 1970s, so did *Film Reader*, heavily influenced by *Screen*, seek to introduce current continental theory into American film studies, leading it to become, in the words of Ron Magliozzi, "The most substantial U.S. film periodical dedicated almost exclusively to the application of current theories of film to the study of the medium."[2] Its 1983 circulation is one thousand.

Notes

1. *Film Reader 1*, 1975, p. 3.
2. Ron Magliozzi, "Film Periodicals," in Leonard Maltin, ed., *The Whole Film Source Book* (New York: New American Library, 1983), p. 363.

Information Sources

INDEX SOURCES: FIAF International Index to Film Periodicals; Film Literature Index.
REPRINT EDITIONS: None.
LOCATION SOURCES: Emory University; Illinois State University; Library of Congress; Swarthmore College; University of Arizona; University of California at Los Angeles; University of Illinois.

Publication History

MAGAZINE TITLE AND TITLE CHANGES: *Film Reader*.
VOLUME AND ISSUE DATA: No. 1 (1975 to present), annual.
PUBLISHER AND PLACE OF PUBLICATION: Film Division, Radio-Television-Film Department, School of Speech, Northwestern University, Evanston, Ill. 60201.
EDITOR: Patricia Erens, Steve Fagin, Joseph Hill, and William Horrigan (1975); Patricia Erens and Bill Horrigan (1977); Valentin Almendarez, Bruce Jenkins, and Karl Stange (1978); Blaine Allan, Valentin Almendarez, and William Lafferty (1979); Jae Alexander, Blaine Allan, Gretchen Bisplinghoff, Jane Gaines, Charlotte Herzog, Lisa Lewis, Gina Marchetti, Maryann Oshana, Ellen Seiter, and Carol Slingo (1980); Greg Faller and William Lafferty (1983).

William Lafferty

FILM REPORTS

In its first issue (1910) *Film Reports* made its viewpoint perfectly plain: "*Film Reports* recognizes no factional influences. It is a paper that's going to help the Independents fight the Patents Company."[1] It billed itself as "The Trust Buster" and "The only paper that covers the independent field" and, as such, was the most outspoken of early trade periodicals.

A small, pocket-size magazine, *Film Reports* featured plot summaries of current independent releases; advertising by American, IMP, Thanhouser, Solax, and other independent producers; and, from the fall of 1910, a column titled "The Pall Bearer," which featured highly critical reviews of releases from the Motion Picture Patents Group of companies. Of Biograph's *White Roses*, *Film Reports* (December 31, 1910) reported, *"White Rose [sic] is enough to bring red noses—drive us to drink."*

After slightly less than one year of existence, *Film Reports* ceased publication.

Notes

1. "Hello," Vol. I, No. 1, June 25, 1910, p. 8.

Information Sources

INDEX SOURCES: None.
REPRINT EDITIONS: None.
LOCATION SOURCES: Academy of Motion Picture Arts and Sciences (lacks some later issues); University of Southern California.

Publication History

MAGAZINE TITLE AND TITLE CHANGES: *Film Reports*.
VOLUME AND ISSUE DATA: Vol. I, No. 1–Vol. II, No. 24 (June 25, 1910–June 3, 1911), weekly.
PUBLISHER AND PLACE OF PUBLICATION: Film Reports, 19 Union Square, New York, N.Y. (Vol. I, No. 1–Vol. I, No. 10); Film Reports, 10 East Fifteenth Street, New York, N.Y. (Vol. I, No. 11–Vol. I, No. 25); Film Reports, 147 Fourth Avenue, New York, N.Y. (Vol. I, No. 26–Vol. II, No. 24).
EDITOR: Leon J. Rubinstein.

Anthony Slide

FILM REVIEW DIGEST

As its title suggests, *Film Review Digest* published edited versions of film reviews from two dozen American, British, and Canadian periodicals as varied as *Cineaste*,* *Films in Review*,* *The Los Angeles Times*, *Ms*, *The Nation*, and *Rolling Stone*. Also included were basic credits, which were indexed in each issue, along with the names of the reviewers. All reviews were cumulated in an annual hardcover edition.

Film Review Digest, which existed from 1975 through mid-1977, was similar in format to two earlier periodicals, H. W. Wilson's *Motion Picture Review Digest* (December 16, 1935–January 22, 1941) and *New York Motion Picture Critics' Reviews* (published weekly from March 20, 1944 to April 26, 1946). The former, like *Film Review Digest*, published only heavily edited reviews, whereas the latter reprinted reviews in their entirety.

Information Sources

INDEX SOURCES: None.
REPRINT EDITIONS: None.
LOCATION SOURCES: Academy of Motion Picture Arts and Sciences; Columbia University; Library of Congress; Milwaukee Public Library; University of Alabama; University of Florida; University of Georgia; University of Illinois; University of Pennsylvania; University of Tennessee.

Publication History

MAGAZINE TITLE AND TITLE CHANGES: *Film Review Digest*.
VOLUME AND ISSUE DATA: Vol. I, No. 1–Vol. II, No. 4 (Fall 1975–Summer 1977), quarterly.
PUBLISHER AND PLACE OF PUBLICATION: Kraus-Thompson Organization Limited, Millwood, N.Y. 10546.
EDITOR: David M. Brownstone and Irene M. Franck.

Anthony Slide

FILMS

The philosophical approach of *Films* toward the cinema is best descibed in the opening sentences of an article titled "Towards a New Ethical Base," which appeared in issue 1 of the magazine: "Film at its best is an art-form—and a social manifestation. It can be of little consequence merely as a casual entertainment despite the insistence of some trade papers to the contrary." Published on a quarterly basis between November 1939 and the winter of 1940, *Films* boasted a number of prominent film commentators among its writers, including Jay Leyda, Harry Alan Potamkin, James Agee, Richard Griffith, and Otis Ferguson. Kurt London wrote on film music, and book reviewers included Joris Ivens and Budd Schulberg (who contributed an interesting piece in No. 2 on novels with a Hollywood theme).

Among the important essays to be found in *Films* are "Sound in Film" by Alberto Cavalcanti (No. 1), "A Bibliography of the Film Writings of Harry Alan Potamkin (1900–1933)" (No. 1), and "Music in Films," a composers' symposium including comments by Marc Blitzstein, Benjamin Britten, Aaron Copland, Dmitri Shostakovich, and Virgil Thomson (No. 4).

Films had a solid, academic appearance, with no illustrations. Its reviews of films were published under the heading of "Film Problems of the Quarter." It is sad to note that the last published issue, No. 4, contained a listing of articles planned for publication, including "Films in the Spanish Civil War" by Luis Buñuel, "The Fan Magazine" by Norbert Lusk, "The Film Ballet" by George Balanchine, and "El Greco y El Cinema" by Sergei Eisenstein.

Information Sources

INDEX SOURCES: The New Film Index.
REPRINT EDITIONS: Arno Press.
LOCATION SOURCES: Academy of Motion Picture Arts and Sciences; Art Institute of
Chicago; Buffalo and Erie Public Library; Columbia University; Detroit Public
Library; Harvard University; Library of Congress; New York Public Library; New
York University; University of Illinois.

Publication History

MAGAZINE TITLE AND TITLE CHANGES: *Films*.
VOLUME AND ISSUE DATA: Vol. I, No. 1–Vol. I, No. 4 (November 1939–Winter
1940), quarterly.
PUBLISHER AND PLACE OF PUBLICATION: Kamin Publishers, 15 West Fifty-sixth
Street, New York, N.Y.
EDITOR: Lincoln Kirstein, Jay Leyda, Mary Losey, Robert Stebbins, and Lee Strasberg.

Anthony Slide

FILMS (1980 to present). See FILMS AND FILMING

FILMS AND FILMING

Films and Filming was one of the first film magazines of recent vintage to
combine successfully both a popular and serious view of the cinema. It began
publication in October 1954 as one of a series of magazines—the others being
Dance and Dancers, *Music and Musicians*, *Plays and Players*, and (later) *Books
and Bookmen*—produced by Hanson Books. The first editor was Peter Brinson,
an Oxford graduate who had written extensively on film and ballet for *Time and
Tide*, *The New Statesman*, and *The Nation*. He was succeeded after a year by
Peter G. Baker, who had been chief reporter and senior feature editor for *Kinematograph Weekly*** and who was to remain with the magazine for some thirteen
years and build it into one of the world's leading popular film magazines.

From the first issue, *Films and Filming* contained no contents page—an an-
noying omission—but instead always featured on page three a column titled
"Personality of the Month," which remained an integral part of the journal
through February 1963. Other early regular features included "In Camera," a
series of one-paragraph news items, and "People of Promise." Films reviews
were, of course, a major part of *Films and Filming*, and from March to June
1961, C. A. Lejeune served as the lead film critic (following her retirement from
The Observer).

From the beginning, *Films and Filming* included well-written articles by such
major figures as John Grierson, Roger Manvell, Derek Hill, William K. Everson
(who wrote a regular column in the early years titled "....... and in New

York''), Catherine de la Roche, Ivor Montagu, and Paul Rotha (who was the magazine's lead critic in the late fifties). Ken Gay began writing on documentary films from March 1956. Raymond Durgnat was a regular contributor from 1960 onward.

In the fifties *Films and Filming* included some extraordinary articles and contributors, including ''Performing Sartre for the Screen'' by Arletty (October 1955), ''Ealing's Way of Life'' by Kenneth Tynan (December 1955), ''Dreams and Shadows'' by Ingmar Bergman (September and October 1956), ''Nothing Is More Artifical Than Neo-Realism'' by René Clair (June 1957), ''My Life as a Monster'' by Boris Karloff (November 1957), ''Silence Was Our Virtue'' by Lillian Gish (December 1957), and ''There Must Be a Reason for Every Film'' by Michelangelo Antonioni (April 1959). There were a number of special issues: ''25 Years of Musicals'' (January 1956), including articles by Michael Kidd, Arthur Freed, and Louis Levy; ''British Films'' (September 1957), including an essay by Andrew Sarris on Carol Reed; ''French Cinema'' (October 1960), with articles by François Truffaut, Fernandel, and Bouvril; ''Italian Cinema'' (January 1961), with articles by Antonioni, Pasolini, and Visconti. A series of ''Critical Self-Portraits'' began in June 1959 with a piece by C. A. Lejeune, and the valuable ''Great Films of the Century'' series began in 1960.

Robin Bean, who had been Peter Baker's assistant, became editor in October 1968, and around the same time there was a considerable increase in the number of pages but also a decrease in the quality of many of the articles. There was also a definite homosexual slant to the photographic essays from the sixties onward. Every issue seemed to feature endless shots of seminude male stars, and this trend reached its zenith when a reader, P. M. Eavis, wrote a letter of complaint (in the July 1971 issue) concerning a full frontal male nude featured in a photo spread on Pasolini's *Decameron*. Eavis was soundly derided by the editor, but his comments were to the point.

Films and Filming ceased publication with the June 1980 issue. In December 1980 Robin Bean began editing a new magazine with a format and look very similar to *Films and Filming* but titled simply *Films*. *Films and Filming* was resurrected in October 1981 when Allen Eyles became editor and the magazine was combined with Eyles's *Focus on Film*.* John Russell Taylor, the former film critic of *The* (London) *Times* and a well-known writer and lecturer, took over the editorship in February 1983. Eyles had produced a magazine which was somewhat staid, even a little dull. Taylor sought to brighten its image somewhat, but neither has succeeded in editing a popular magazine of the quality of *Films and Filming* in its heyday under the editorship of Peter Baker.

Information Sources

INDEX SOURCES: The Critical Index; FIAF International Index to Film Periodicals; Film Literature Index; The New Film Index; Retrospective Index to Film Periodicals 1930–1971.
REPRINT EDITIONS: None.

LOCATION SOURCES: Academy of Motion Picture Arts and Sciences; Cleveland Public Library; Library of Congress; Purdue University; University of Colorado; University of Florida; University of Southern California.

Publication History

MAGAZINE TITLE AND TITLE CHANGES: *Films and Filming.*
VOLUME AND ISSUE DATA: Vol. I, No. 1–Vol. XXVI, No. 9 (October 1954–June 1980), monthly; No. 325 (October 1981 to present), monthly.
PUBLISHER AND PLACE OF PUBLICATION: Hanson Books, 21 Lower Belgrave Street, Buckingham Palace Road, London S.W.1, England (Vol. I, No. 1–Vol. VIII, No. 2); Hanson Books, 7 & 8 Hobart Place, London S.W.1, England (Vol. VIII, No. 3–Vol. IX, No. 4); Hanson Books, 16 Buckingham Palace Road, London S.W.1, England (Vol. IX, No. 5–Vol. XV, No. 4); Hanson Books, Artillery Mansions, 75 Victoria Street, London S.W.1, England (Vol. XV, No. 5–Vol. XXIII, No. 10); Hanson Books, 2-4 Old Pye Street, Victoria Street, London SW1P 2LE, England (Vol. XXIII, No. 11–Vol. XXVI, No. 9); Brevet Publishing Limited, P.O. Box 252, London SW1P 2LD, England (No. 325 to present).
EDITOR: Peter Brinson (October 1954–October 1955); Peter G. Baker (November 1955–September 1968); Robin Bean (October 1968–June 1980); Allen Eyles (October 1981–January 1983); John Russell Taylor (February 1983 to present).

Anthony Slide

THE FILM SEASON. See KOSMORAMA

FILMS IN REVIEW

Films in Review has been the publication of the National Board of Review of Motion Pictures, Inc., since 1950. As such, it has served the Board's stated aims of representing the public's interest in motion pictures by reviewing films, classifying and disseminating information about them, organizing audience support for them, and providing media for the expression of the public's opinions about films and their cultural and social effects.

Although *Films in Review*, particularly in its first decade, has published articles on film esthetics, the general emphasis of the publication has been on film facts and film history rather than criticism and interpretation. Even such a potentially charged topic as cross-dressing in film which would be mined for all its psychological, political, and social significance in most other film publications in the eighties is dealt with in a simple, descriptive fashion in *Films in Review* ("Film in Drag" by Edward Connor in Vol. 32, No. 7).

Films in Review's early years saw regular contributions by film historians such as William K. Everson, Lewis Jacobs, Arthur Knight, Roger Manvell, Richard Griffith, and Lotte Eisner. Even then, such articles far outnumbered the contributions by estheticians such as Herman Weinberg and Jean Debrix or psychological critics such as Siegfried Kracauer. A broad spectrum of filmmakers supplied the magazine with written reflections on their artistic views and their techniques—for example, "How I Cartooned *Alice*" by Walt Disney (Vol. 2, No. 5), "Film Style" (Vol. 3, No. 1) and "Color and Color Films" (Vol. 6, No. 4) by Carl Dreyer, "An Artist Makes a Movie" by Ian Hugo (Vol. 1, No. 6), "New Faces in New Places" by Ida Lupino (Vol. 1, No. 9), "I Know Where I'm Going" by Jean Renoir (Vol. 3, No. 3), and "On Filming *Julius Caesar*" by John Houseman (Vol. 4, No. 4). Many more filmmakers (producers, directors, actors, composers, and so forth) were (and continue to be) represented by interviews.

Films in Review also endeavored to expose its readers to lesser-known foreign film industries and, for example, printed the first articles in an American film magazine on the cinema of India ("World's Second Largest Film Maker" by William D. Allen in Vol. 1, No. 1) and of New Zealand ("New Zealand's Film Production" by Russell Reid in Vol. 2, No. 8).

After the first decade of publication, film history (usually in the form of career review articles with filmographies), simple essays on the technical aspects of film production, and interviews predominated; the article actually written by a filmmaker became relatively rare.

Films reviewed have tended to be American or British releases and art house films, with the foreign titles being reviewed as they open in New York City. Foreign titles have not always fared well, however. In a brief critique of the magazine, Andrew Sarris noted, "In the prayerful pages of *Films in Review*, such art-house deities as Resnais, Bergman, and Fellini are defiled as incompetent perverts with subversive intentions."[1] This evaluation is borne out by a review of Bergman's *The Silence* which had appeared earlier the same year (1964) in which the reviewer H. H. (editor Henry Hart) characterized the film as "one of Bergman's sexploiters—a quickly and inexpensively made black-&-whiter depending on notoriety from scenes of coition (clothed) and masturbation (also clothed)."[2] Reviews in later years are cast in less extreme terms.

Career articles and interviews also include foreign filmmakers, but the great majority of such articles deal with American or British artists, including those whose careers are relatively forgotten today (for example, a career article on actress Leatrice Joy by J. E. A. Bawden in Vol. 28, No. 4). Surveys of foreign cinema continue to appear ("Australian Cinema Renaissance: From *Sentimental Bloke* to *Breaker Morant*" by Rob Edelman in Vol. 32, No. 3; and "The Great Film Bazaar of India" by Richard Greenbaum in Vol. 32, No. 8), though at typical lengths of four to six pages, these are at best cursory.

Films in Review occasionally displays a tendency toward the obscure or quirky in some of its articles. Thus one can find a career review of South American actress Eva Duarte, better known subsequently as Evita Peron ("Evita" by Daniel Lopez in Vol. 31, No. 6), and a series of pieces by Roi A. Uselton on stars who died in automobiles (Vol. 11, No. 10), in airplanes (Vol. 7, No. 5), and by their own hands (Vol. 8, No. 4).

Reports on festivals, both foreign and domestic, are regular features of the magazine. Columns deal with film music and soundtrack albums, films available on 8mm and 16mm for collectors, and television. Typically, six to a dozen films are reviewed in each issue, as well as four to six books on film.

Films in Review superseded the National Board of Review's *New Movies* (1942–1949) which was originally published as *National Board of Review Magazine* (until 1942) and which itself had been formed by the union of the Board's earlier publications, *Exceptional Photoplays* (1920–1925), *Film Progress* (1917–1926), and *Photoplay Guide to Better Movies* (1924–1926). The National Board of Review of Motion Pictures, Inc., was originally established as The National Board of Censorship of Motion Pictures in 1909, with a large part of its funding coming from the Motion Picture Patents Company.

Notes

1. Andrew Sarris, "The Farthest-Out Movie Goers," *The Saturday Review*, Vol. 47, No. 52, December 26, 1964, pp. 14–15.
2. *Films in Review*, Vol. 15, No. 3, March 1964, p. 176.

Information Sources

INDEX SOURCES: *An Index to Films in Review: 1950–1959*, compiled by Marion Fawcett (The National Board, 1961); *An Index to Films in Review: 1960–1964*, compiled by Marion Fawcett (The National Board, 1966); *An Index to Films in Review: 1965–1969*, compiled by Sandra Lester (The National Board, 1972); Art Index; FIAF International Index to Film Periodicals; Film Literature Index; Index to Critical Reviews; The New Film Index; Retrospective Index to Film Periodicals 1930–1971.

REPRINT EDITIONS: Arno Press (1950–1953); University Microfilms.

LOCATION SOURCES: Academy of Motion Picture Arts and Sciences; Columbia University; Dartmouth College; Library of Congress; New York Public Library; University of California at Los Angeles; University of Illinois; University of Southern California; University of Wisconsin at Madison; Yale University.

Publication History

MAGAZINE TITLE AND TITLE CHANGES: *Films in Review*.

VOLUME AND ISSUE DATA: Vol. I, No. 1 (February 1950 to present), monthly except for combined June-July and August-September issues. [In 1950 and 1951 each issue was page numbered individually; since 1952 each volume is page numbered consecutively.]

PUBLISHER AND PLACE OF PUBLICATION: National Board of Review of Motion Pictures, Inc., 31 Union Square West, New York, N.Y. 10003 (Vol. I, No. 1–Vol. XXI, No. 6); National Board of Review of Motion Pictures, Inc., 210 East Sixty-eighth Street, New York, N.Y. 10021 (Vol. XXI, No. 7–Vol. XXIV, No. 6); National Board of Review of Motion Pictures, Inc., P.O. Box 589, New York, N.Y. 10021 (Vol. XXIV, No. 7, to present).

EDITOR: John B. Turner (1950); Henry Hart (1950–1972); Charles Phillips Reilly (1972–
    1979); Ronald Bowers (1979–1981); Charles Phillips Reilly (1981); Brendan Ward
    (1981–1983); Robin Little (1983 to present).

                                                                    Richard J. Leskosky

FILM SOCIETY. See FILM CRITIC

FILM SOCIETY REVIEW. See FILM CRITIC

FILM STAR WEEKLY. See GIRLS CINEMA

THE FILM TEACHER. See SCREEN EDUCATION

FILM T.V. DAILY. See THE FILM DAILY

FILM WEEKLY

Beginning publication in 1928, *Film Weekly* was the first serious film periodical
to be produced in the United Kingdom. It was unique among British film magazines in that it did not have to rely on gimmicks, such as free photographs or
supplements, in order to boost sales; instead it concentrated entirely on offering
film news for the serious enthusiast. In that it was concerned with the film
industry as a whole and with the medium's development from a silent to a sound
art form, *Film Weekly* appealed rather less to the man in the street than did its
competitors, such as *Picture Show** and *The Picturegoer.**
    In its first issue, the editor commented:

> It will be a newspaper for all those interested in the improvement of films,
> in the better exhibition of films, in the personalities of the films. News
> about films, fearless criticism of films and filmmakers, constructive sug-
> gestions for the still further extension of the immense community of film
> lovers, service in the interest of the public for which it will speak—these
> will be the keynote of our policy.

Film reviews in *Film Weekly* were always extensive and informative, and the
magazine would provide detailed cast and credit listings as well as the storyline.
In 1931, *Film Weekly* began giving the running time for each film and urged,

"If you find any difference between running time given in *Film Weekly* and the actual time occupied by the showing of the film at your local cinema you will be justified in taking the matter up with the manager." A year later, the magazine announced the addition of a complete guide to all current pictures, edited by John Gammie, covering approximately 150 features a month.

In 1930, Harry Lauder offered 150 pounds and fifty presents to readers for choosing twelve songs they would like him to sing on screen. The following year a Complaints Bureau appeared, to which readers were urged to send any complaint they had with regard to their treatment in theatres; one correspondent complained about the lack of ash trays! As early as 1929, *Film Weekly* had offered a 500-pound acting scholarship (for free training at England's largest studio) in which theatres throughout the country cooperated.

Many major figures from both sides of the camera contributed to *Film Weekly*. Paul Rotha wrote on "The Art of the Film." Nerina Smith, and later Freda Bruce Lockhart, contributed "News from the British Studios." In 1929, William S. Hart wrote on the making of westerns. In 1931, Alfred Hitchcock paid tribute to D. W. Griffith. A year later, Sinclair Lewis wrote on thirty years of filmmaking and Ivor Novello interviewed Garbo. In 1933, Ruth Roland reminisced about Rudolph Valentino; Irving Thalberg wrote about his wife, Norma Shearer; and J. B. Priestley contributed a piece, "Writing for the Screen."

Film Weekly was unique among fan magazines in that it offered for sale photographs of film personalities at one shilling each. From 1931 onward, it was noted for its special winter issues and its "British Film Numbers," which contained between eighty and one hundred pages and sold for the regular price of threepence a copy. In company with *Picture Show* and *Film Pictorial*,* *Film Weekly* also published special summer and Christmas extras from 1936 to 1939.

Television was a frequent topic of interest to *Film Weekly* writers. In 1934, Hubert Harris asked, "Can T.V. Kill the Cinema?" That same year Sam Goldwyn prophesied that television would soon be a reality. Leonard Wallace, a regular contributor, wrote, in 1936, "T.V. and the Cinema," and two years later Dr. Lee De Forest announced that the film industry was safe from the dangers of television for at least another ten years.

On *Film Weekly*'s tenth birthday, October 22, 1938, editor Herbert Thompson wrote on the aims and achievements of his magazine:

The time has come to make an effort to lift film journalism beyond the tittle-tattle about stars clothes, private lives and fabulously foolish scandal mongering. The screen was important enough, and filmgoers intelligent enough, to deserve a paper that would reveal to them the reality of the back screen world.... We have not ceased our campaign against stale films—we drew attention of the heads of all the great companies as long ago as 1929 to the complaints of our readers against irresponsible cutting of films. We inspired the practice of publishing running time of every film with our release review so that filmgoers might check up and report any positive discrepancy. We have protested against idiotic censorship and the morbid sensationalism of certain newsreels and of horror films, convinced that the sane filmgoer's natural good taste demands moderation. We have also been consistently determined to tell the truth as we see it without fear or favour. *Film Weekly* has furthered the interests of British films today, and is liked as well as respected in Wardour Street as much as by filmgoers. I like to think that the far more dignified status of the modern cinema, in the eyes of both press and public, is due in some way to our pioneering efforts. The opinions of Bernard Shaw, Ethel Mannin, George Birmingham, Sir Philip Gibbs, A. J. Cronin, H. G. Wells, Warwick Deeping and others were published in our magazine, and even Edith Sitwell wrote about film people she would like to massacre.

Certainly *Film Weekly* was true to its ideals. Indeed, its Hollywood correspondent, Cedric Belfrage, was so outspoken in his column that he was barred from the majority of American studios. Sadly, *Film Weekly* lost its identity when the Second World War forced its amalgamation with *Picturegoer*, on September 23, 1939.

Information Sources

INDEX SOURCES: None.
REPRINT EDITIONS: None.
LOCATION SOURCES: Library of Congress. [The British Film Institute Library has a complete run.]

Publication History

MAGAZINE TITLE AND TITLE CHANGES: *Film Weekly*.
VOLUME AND ISSUE DATA: Vol. I, No. 1–Vol. XXII, No. 570 (October 22, 1928–September 16, 1939).
PUBLISHER AND PLACE OF PUBLICATION: English Newspapers, Ltd., 112 Strand, London, England (October 1928–October 1935); Odhams Press, Ltd., London W.C.2, England (November 1935–February 1936); Odhams Press. Ltd., Martlett House, Bow Street, London, England (February 1936–September 1939).
EDITOR: Herbert Thompson.

Thomas A. Johnson

FILMWISE

"Founded as a forum for the discussion of the works of the aesthetic cinema," *Filmwise* was a mimeographed periodical of 1961 to 1967, devoting each issue to a specific independent, experimental filmmaker. No. 1 featured Stan Brakhage; No. 2 Maya Deren; No. 3 & 4 Gregory Markopoulos; No. 5 & 6 Marie Menken and Willard Maas. A unique publication, *Filmwise* boasted an impressive list of contributors, including Parker Tyler, Stan Brakhage, Gregory J. Markopoulos, P. Adams Sitney, Richard Griffith, Rudolf Arnheim, Anais Nin, and Gordon Hitchens. As well as featuring articles on and tributes to the various filmmakers, each issue also included a filmography on the individual featured in that issue.

Information Sources

INDEX SOURCES: None.
REPRINT EDITIONS: None.
LOCATION SOURCES: Anthology Film Archives; New York Public Library; University of Oregon.

Publication History

MAGAZINE TITLE AND TITLE CHANGES: *Filmwise*.
VOLUME AND ISSUE DATA: No. 1 (1961); No. 2 (1962); No. 3 & 4 (1963); No. 5 & 6 (1967).
PUBLISHER AND PLACE OF PUBLICATION: New Haven Film Society, 416 Edgewood Avenue, New Haven, Conn.
EDITOR: P. Adams Sitney.

Anthony Slide

THE FINISHING TOUCH. See Appendix 1

FINLAND FILMLAND. See Appendix 4

THE FLASH. See Appendix 3

FOCUS!

Focus!, subtitled "Chicago's Movie or Film Journal," was a typical student film periodical from the period when many similar enterprises—notably *The Velvet Light Trap**—appeared briefly on the publishing scene. There was no publication schedule, editors changed almost from issue to issue, and the magazine vanished as abruptly as it had appeared.

In the first issue of *Focus!* (February 1967), the magazine's unidentified editor(s) explained, "*Focus!* is a magazine for people interested in the movies: people who don't dismiss an Anthony Mann film because it's just a cowboy movie, or an Edgar G. Ulmer pic because it was shot in five days." The magazine was almost exclusively concerned with the American film industry, and its chief interest today lies in occasional articles by critics such as Robin Wood ("Who the Hell Is Howard Hawks?" in Nos. 1 and 2) and interviews with the likes of

Arch Oboler (No. 1), Otto Preminger (No. 3/4), John Ford (No. 5), Jerry Lewis (No. 7), and Robert Mulligan (No. 8). Articles by John Belton and Fred Kamper create some value for the special feature on Frank Borzage in the last issue of *Focus!* (No. 9), which is otherwise best forgotten in view of the poor quality of the writing.

Information Sources

INDEX SOURCES: Film Literature Index.
REPRINT EDITIONS: None.
LOCATION SOURCES: Academy of Motion Picture Arts and Sciences; Library of Congress.

Publication History

MAGAZINE TITLE AND TITLE CHANGES: *Focus!*
VOLUME AND ISSUE DATA: No. 1 (February 1967); No. 2 (no date); Nos. 3/4 (no date); No. 5 (October 1969); No. 6 (Spring 1970); No. 7 (Spring 1972); No. 8 (Autumn 1972); No. 9 (Spring-Summer 1973).
PUBLISHER AND PLACE OF PUBLICATION: The Documentary Film Group, c/o Doc Films, University of Chicago, Faculty Exchange, Chicago, Ill. 60637 (Nos. 1–4); The Documentary Film Group, c/o Doc Films, University of Chicago, 5811 South Ellis Avenue, Chicago, Ill. 60637 (Nos. 5–9).
EDITOR: None listed (Nos. 1 and 2); Stephen Manes (No. 3/4); Charles Flynn (Nos. 5 and 6); Myron Meisel (Nos. 7 and 8); Donald M. Drucker (No. 9).

Anthony Slide

FOCUS ON FILM

Focus on Film, a publication of the British Tantivy Press (a wholly owned subsidiary of the U.S.-based A. S. Barnes and Company), commenced publication in January 1970. Modeled on the American *Films in Review** in its featuring of career articles with detailed filmographies as well as reviews, *Focus on Film* went to the opposite extreme in design. In contrast to its pocket-sized competitor, it appeared in a rectangular shape totally unsuitable for shelving in libraries and bookshops but which its publisher noted was proportionally of similar dimension to a CinemaScope screen.

Focus on Film was superior to *Films in Review* in two areas. The latter published short, often poorly written, reviews of contemporary films, while *Focus on Film* included lengthy essays on recent film releases, many written by critics of the caliber of Tom Milne, with each review concluding with one-paragraph biographies and complete filmographies of the film's leading participants: actors, actresses, director, cinematographer, writer, and composer. It was a totally unique approach to film reviewing, a happy blend of critical, highly personal opinion and good, solid, factual research. The career articles in *Focus on Film* differed from those in *Films in Review* by virtue of their length, attention to detail, and more complete credit listings in the filmographies.

The career articles in *Focus on Film* included major, popular figures such as Bob Hope (No. 1), Lon Chaney (No. 3), and Clint Eastwood (No. 9), and also lesser-known and cult personalities such as Tuesday Weld (No. 1), Sidney A. Franklin (No. 10), Conrad Veidt (No. 21), and Lowell Sherman (No. 23). Its writers included some—particularly DeWitt Bodeen—who had been regulars in *Films in Review*, but *Focus on Film* was also able to develop its own stable of contributors. Notable among them was Jeffrey Richards, who contributed a considerable number of pieces contemplating films and players and their relationship to Britain and to right-wing British history. Typical of Richards's essays are "Ronald Colman and the Cinema of Empire" (No. 4), "A Star without Armour: Robert Donat" (No. 8), and "Gracie Fields" (Nos. 33, 34). Another unique contributor was Louise Brooks, who had written previously for *Sight and Sound** and *Film Culture*,* but here she developed her very personal views on film history and became even more of a "cult" figure with "Actors and the Pabst Spirit" (No. 8), "On Location with Billy Wellman" (No. 12), and "Why I Will Never Write My Memoirs" (No. 29).

Focus on Film was created by a young British writer on motion pictures, Allen Eyles, who, prior to assuming the editorship, had been an editorial assistant with the Tantivy Press.[1] In one of his few—always brief—editorial comments in *Focus on Film*, Eyles wrote in the first issue:

> Though a rather superfluous undertaking, it seems almost obligatory to make out a case for the appearance of a new magazine and describe its aims. Suffice to say that there are more than enough unexplored areas of film research to keep a dozen magazines on the lines of this one busy (though rather too many magazines, if one really surveys the field, dispensing mere *opinion*, almost entirely on new films).[2]

That first issue established the general content of the magazine as far as the career articles and reviews were concerned. Because that issue was devoted primarily to American comedy—with career articles on Bob Hope, Edward Everett Horton, and Tuesday Weld—Allen Eyles also included a checklist of books on American comedy (compiled, authoritatively, by Gillian Hartnoll, the librarian of the British Film Institute) and a survey of American comedies available for rental in 16mm. The checklists of books continued for a short while—No. 2 featured Russian reading and No. 3 British cinema—as did the 16mm surveys, but eventually both sections were replaced by the more ordinary capsule reviews of new books and a "Discovery" section, consisting of a lengthy review of an "old" film recently brought back into 16mm circulation.

In another of his rare editorials, Eyles noted, "To me, the cinema has always meant more than the films themselves; it has also meant the buildings in which they played, which were at least interesting when not comfortable, and my front room with the T.V. set in the corner is sometimes a necessary, but regretted and inadequate substitute."[3] This editorial attitude led to the addition, beginning with issue No. 4, of a section devoted to various aspects of the cinema as a building, usually an overview of a theater chain or perhaps an essay on a specific, notable British movie house. It was an unusual and worthwhile feature of *Focus on Film*, perhaps of little interest to many of its readers (particularly those in the United States), but it defined the magazine as a somewhat homely journal which recognized that its readers had spent many of their film viewing hours in suburban cinemas—Odeons or Granadas—not in the art house atmosphere from which many of the American periodicals seem to observe the cinema. Even the idea of an editor sitting in his front room looking at T.V. (not television, but T.V.) has a down-home, honest-to-goodness ring to it.

Certain issues of *Focus on Film* would be devoted to specific subjects. No. 6 was a special John Ford issue, including important articles "Forgotten Ford" by William K. Everson and "Ford's Lost World" by Jeffrey Richards. No. 36 was devoted to cinema in the seventies and included Pat McGilligan's "Actors Directing," Scott Eyman's "Against Altman," Martyn Auty's "French Cinema in the Seventies," and William K. Everson's "Discoveries of the Seventies." The most unusual special issue to be published by *Focus on Film* was No. 13, an eighty-four-page edition devoted to great cameramen, which listed all the Academy Award winners for best cinematography from 1928 through 1971, followed by brief biographies and full filmographies of 150 cameramen, based on research by Erique J. Rebel.

The publisher of *Focus on Film*, the Tantivy Press, must be held responsible for the one major negative aspect of the magazine, the totally out-of-place "Focus on Sponsored Cinema," which began in No. 7 and which obviously served to give editorial space to producers and distributors of industrial and noncommercial films willing to advertise in the periodical. Also on the negative side were the lack of a table of contents at the front of the early issues and the magazine's insistence on running still photographs to the tops and bottoms of pages, thus interfering with their numbering and making it difficult to find a specific article.

Beginning with No. 18, *Focus on Film* featured interviews, often at the expense of career articles. Here again the interviewees included the famous, people like Fritz Lang (No. 20), Joel McCrea (No. 30), John Schlesinger (No. 31), and Otto Preminger (No. 33), as well as the lesser known, such as Walter Lang (No. 18), Joseph Ruttenberg (No. 24), Margaret Booth (No. 25), and John Carradine (No. 33). All in all, *Focus on Film* provided a well-rounded approach to the cinema. Historical pieces predominated but never to the exclusion of an analysis of contemporary cinema. The magazine was a pleasing blend of past and present.

In October 1981, *Films and Filming** reappeared on the scene in a new and revised format with a new editor, Allen Eyles. In another of his short editorials, Eyles announced: "*Films and Filming* has taken over a historically oriented rival, *Focus on Film*, and also its editor."[4] *Focus on Film* was no more, and although the new *Films and Filming* promised to continue some of the traditions of its former rival, the approach was different. For one thing, *Films and Filming* was a different shape. The Tantivy Press might have continued *Focus on Film* under a new editorship, but obviously—as the sometimes curious publishing schedule indicated[5]—it was hard-pressed to find an adequate, paying audience for its magazine. No doubt the publisher was more than happy to use the excuse of losing its editor to cease publication.

Notes

1. Eyles's books include *The Marx Brothers: Their World of Comedy* (London: Zwemmer/Cranbury, N.J.: A. S. Barnes, 1966), *Hollywood Today*, with Pat Billings (London: Zwemmer/Cranbury, N.J.: A. S. Barnes, 1971), *Bogart* (New York: Doubleday, 1975), and *The Western* (Cranbury, N.J.:A. S. Barnes, 1975).

2. No. 1, January-February 1970, n.p.

3. No. 4, September-October 1970, p. 13.

4. *Films and Filming*, No. 325, October 1981, p. 11.

5. *Focus on Films* was first published every other month; it then announced a publishing schedule of five issues a year and eventually became, more or less, a quarterly.

Information Sources

INDEX SOURCES: FIAF International Index to Film Periodicals; Film Literature Index.
REPRINT EDITIONS: University Microfilms.
LOCATION SOURCES: Academy of Motion Picture Arts and Sciences; Emory University; Iowa State University; Museum of Modern Art; Purdue University; Smith College; University of California at Berkeley; University of Illinois; University of Southern California.

Publication History

MAGAZINE TITLE AND TITLE CHANGES: *Focus on Film*.
VOLUME AND ISSUE DATA: Nos. 1–37 (January-February 1970–March 1981), irregular.
PUBLISHER AND PLACE OF PUBLICATION: The Tantivy Press, 108 New Bond Street, London WIY OQX, England (Nos. 1–24); The Tantivy Press, Magdalen House, 136-148 Tooley Street, London SE1 2TT, England (Nos. 25–37).
EDITOR: Allen Eyles.

Anthony Slide

FOCUS ON FOX. See Appendix 3

FRAMEWORK

Born in the summer of 1975, *Framework* originated from "a desire to bring together several different and uncoordinated approaches towards film and film criticism, and from the view that there is an urgent need for a serious and independent film magazine in Britain that is not totally dominated by a specific approach to film, be that literary, semiological, or any other."[1] The original editorial committee consisting of Donald Ranvaud, Elizabeth Aherne, Marion Doyen, Jenny Norman, Steve Rutt, and Paul Nightingale aimed to "render this diversity more coherent by creating a framework through which a given theme or subject [could] be explored and analysed in a more disciplined and constructive way."

Attempting to "ensure that only rigorous and pertinent methods [were] employed in the examination of any given theme or subject," the editors chose interviews with Alain Resnais and Robin Wood, and articles on Shakespearean films, Polish cinema, film theory, Gianfranco Bettetini, François Truffaut, and Sam Peckinpah for the first issue. Issue No. 2 contained articles such as "The Ambiguous Forms of Narrative Rituality," "Neorealism," "Bertolucci: The Narrow Road to a Forked Path," "Before the Revolution: Immediacy and Mediation in the Narrative Structure," "Liliana Cavani: The Dawn of a Tormented Coherence," "Lina Werthmuller & Entertainment," "The International Convention of Women in the Cinema," "Why Custer at the 'Halles' in Paris 1973?," and "Marco Ferreri: Cinema as the Internal Overthrow of the System."

Interviews with Bernardo Bertolucci, Marco Bellocchio, Krzysztof Zanussi, and Sohrab Shahid Saless along with an essay on Jean Luc Godard and a theoretical article by Pier Paolo Pasolini appeared in issue No. 3. Issue No. 4 contained part one of a piece on Hollywood, articles on psychoanalysis and *Jaws*, and an editorial reading of *Reckless Moment*. Hollywood, part two, was completed in No. 5, accompanied by analyses of *River of No Return*, *To Be or Not to Be*, *One Flew over the Cuckoo's Nest*, Douglas Sirk, Billy Wilder, and Michael Ritchie. No. 6 began a two-part work on ideology and contained articles on Hans Syberberg, sexuality and power, Japanese independents, Jean-Louis Comolli, and Godard.

Issue No. 13 boasted a new editorial committee and statement of purpose. The committee consisted of Martyn Auty, Jane Clarke, Sylvia Harvey, Tony Kirkhope, Laura Mulvey, Chris Rodrigues, Rod Stoneman, Archie Tait, Paul Taylor, Sheila Whitaker, Paul Willemen, and Peter Wollen led by Donald Ranvaud as editor-in-chief. Together they took the following oath:

> We intend to operate a policy of 'limited pluralism,' where the limits of the pluralism are decided by the Editorial Committee according to agreed procedures aimed at ensuring the avoidance of factionalism. The broadly defined limits of the non-sectarian policy initially adopted could be formulated in the following terms: Framework will favour work bearing on its four key terms (discourse, institution, representation, conjuncture) produced from positions opposed to bourgeois idealism, (individualism, anti-intellectualism, mysticism, consumerism, aestheticism) and advocating the transformation of capitalist and feudal-social relations. All these terms are fairly vague, but that very vagueness is intended as a positive alternative to tendencies towards the production of 'absolute' and fixed definitions crystallizing in the the 'pure' and thus dogmatic positions.[2]

The variety of critical approaches continues to be reflected in articles that cover a broad spectrum of film subjects from Godard, Alfred Hitchcock, and the U.S. independents to television, Australian cinema, and the archeology of film theory. Included in the magazine's format are film, periodical and book reviews, interviews with filmmakers and film critics, film festivals, and editorials. In addition, there are sections devoted to archeology, news, and footnotes. With issue No. 13 a new section emerged which "considers the status of film studies in Education from the point of view of students engaged in research work."

This quarterly cinema journal continues to be published by the Warwick University Arts Federation with financial assistance from the British Film Institute's education department.

Notes

1. Editorial, No. 1, Summer 1975, p. 2.
2. Editorial, No. 13, Autumn 1980, p. 1.

Information Sources

INDEX SOURCES: Film Literature Index; Media Review Digest.
REPRINT EDITIONS: None.
LOCATION SOURCES: Emory University; University of Kansas; University of Southern California.

Publication History

MAGAZINE TITLE AND TITLE CHANGES: *Framework*.
VOLUME AND ISSUE DATA: No. 1 (Summer 1975 to present), quarterly.
PUBLISHER AND PLACE OF PUBLICATION: Warwick University Arts Federation, 64 Spencer Avenue, Earlsdon, Coventry, Warwickshire, England (Nos. 1–10); English & American Studies, University of East Anglia, Norwich NR4, 7TJ, England (No. 11 to present).
EDITOR: Donald Ranvaud.

Michele McCauley

THE FREEDONIA GAZETTE. See Appendix 1

FUNNYWORLD

The origins of *Funnyworld: The World of Animated Films and Comic Art* are linked to the rising interest in comic book collecting which occurred in the sixties. A small club called Comics Amateur Press Association (CAPA) was established by comic book collectors and devotees from around the country, and among the members was Mike Barrier, who would soon establish his own magazine. Each member of CAPA was asked to contribute to *CAPA-alpha*, the organization's newsletter, and Barrier's contributions led to the first issue of *Funnyworld*, published in October 1966.

His fledgling journal took its name from a defunct forties comic book. Each monthly issue, mimeographed and circulated mainly to club members, was written entirely by Barrier and averaged about a dozen pages.

Most early issues emphasized comics with special attention given to Carl Barks, a former Disney Studio story director who became best known for his Donald Duck comic book work and for the creation of Uncle Scrooge. Issue No. 6 (June 1967) which signaled a shift to less frequent publication and an increase in pages per issue, contains Barrier's long article on Barks, "The Lord of Quackly Hall." Over the next ten issues, which span eight years, Barrier continued to document Barks's career by publishing an exhaustive bibliography of his comic book output. This material was published in book form in 1982 under the title *Carl Barks and the Art of the Comic Book*.

Publication of *Funnyworld* remained erratic due to minimal staff and a lack of advertising or outside funding. Issue No. 9 (May 1968) was the first to be sold. With issue No. 12 (Summer 1970) *Funnyworld* switched from mimeograph reproduction to offset printing and left its fanzine origins behind. The move to a more professional format and slick cover caused circulation to jump from a few hundred to a few thousand.

Funnyworld, now averaging about fifty pages per issue, became in the seventies the preeminent source of information on animation. Each issue typically contained an editorial by Barrier in which he called attention to recent developments in the field, new films and books of interest, errata from past issues, and plans for future articles. Letters to the editor often contained helpful information, for they were frequently written by industry people such as Disney artists Ward Kimball and Wilfred Jackson, Canadian-born animator Richard Williams, and the veteran Shamus Culhane.

Four to six feature stories and a review of animated films or books, usually written by the editor, rounded out each issue. The sporadic publication schedule robbed many reviews of their timeliness, but the detail and depth of criticism generally made up for this. Articles in *Funnyworld* were profusely illustrated, often with previously unpublished sketches and photographs from private collections. The length of the articles was flexible; most averaged two thousand words, but some ran much longer, such as a lengthy account of the Disney Studio during the Second World War in issue No. 17 (Fall 1977) and a major piece on the personalities who provide the voices for cartoons in No. 18 (Summer 1978).

One of the highlights of *Funnyworld* was the publication of a series of long, detailed interviews with significant figures in animation and cartooning, some of which Barrier collected over a period of years for a forthcoming history of animation. Among the subjects Barrier taped were: Bob Clampett and Chuck Jones, whose work formed the golden age of Warner Bros. cartoons; composer Carl Stalling, who worked for Disney on the first Silly Symphony and went to

Warner Bros. where he scored over six hundred cartoon shorts; Will Eisner, the comic book artist who created The Spirit; Canadian animator Richard Williams; and the Fleischer and Disney veteran Dick Huemer. After the publication of his two-part interview, Huemer began to write a column, "Huemeresque," which appeared in the last five issues of *Funnyworld*.

Barrier was able to get other veteran animators to contribute articles. I. Klein, for example, describes in issue No. 14 (Spring 1972) his first job with the Hearst Studio, and in issue No. 21 (Fall 1979) Disney director Jack Kinney reminisces about working on *Bambi* and the Goofy cartoons.

Other contributors of note include Disney Studio archivist David R. Smith on Ub Iwerks and Walt Disney's Kansas City days, Joe Adamson on Tex Avery, and John Canemaker (himself a gifted animator) on contemporary independent artists Suzan Pitt and George Griffin.

The lack of proper staff and funding continued to plague the magazine, and in 1977 Mark Lilien became the publisher and assumed control of advertising and circulation. Issue No. 17 (Fall 1977) became the first to carry advertisements, though these were always kept to a minimum. Unfortunately, the goal of regular, quarterly issues was never realized, and *Funnyworld* ceased publication with issue No. 22 (April 1981).

Despite the explosion of film books and periodicals in the 1970s and 1980s and the rising interest in popular culture, *Funnyworld* remained the only magazine devoted to serious writing about animation and the comics. In its pages one can find clearly written articles, solid criticism which sets standards against which animation should be judged, and a variety of historically important primary and secondary materials which add immeasurably to the understanding of animation and comic art.

Information Sources

INDEX SOURCES: Film Literature Index.
REPRINT EDITIONS: University Microfilms.
LOCATION SOURCES: Academy of Motion Picture Arts and Sciences; Library of Congress (No. 11 onward).

Publication History

MAGAZINE TITLE AND TITLE CHANGES: *Funnyworld: The World of Animated Films and Comic Art*.
VOLUME AND ISSUE DATA: No. 1 (October 1966); No. 2 (November 1966); No. 3 (December 1966); No. 4 (January 1967); No. 5 (April 1967); No. 6 (June 1967); No. 7 (September 1967); No. 8 (December 1967); No. 9 (May 1968); No. 10 (November 1968); No. 11 (May 1969); No. 12 (Summer 1970); No. 13 (Spring 1971); No. 14 (Spring 1972); No. 15 (Fall 1973); No. 16 (Winter 1974); No. 17 (Fall 1977); No. 18 (Summer 1978); No. 19 (Fall 1978); No. 20 (Summer 1979); No. 21 (Fall 1979); No. 22 (April 1981).
PUBLISHER AND PLACE OF PUBLICATION: Mike Barrier, Box 5229, Brady Station, Little Rock, Ark. 72205 (Nos. 1–15); Mike Barrier, 1716 Barkston Court, Atlanta,

Ga. 30341 (No. 16); Mark Lilien, P.O. Box 1633, New York, N.Y. 10001 (Nos. 17–21); Pam Clement, P. O. Box 1635, New York, N.Y. 10001 (No. 22).

EDITOR: Mike Barrier (Nos. 1–21); No. 22 is made up mostly of material edited by Barrier, and the publisher, Pam Clement, is also listed as Editorial Consultant.

Rick Shale

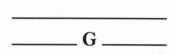

G

GERMAN FILM EXPORT. See Appendix 4

GIRLS CINEMA

A companion to *Boys Cinema** but intended for a female audience, *Girls Cinema* featured romantic stories adapted from current film releases, articles on fashion, beauty, and film star love affairs. The popularity of *Boys Cinema* led to the creation of this magazine in 1920, but it failed to have the following of the former and ceased publication some eight years earlier than *Boys Cinema*.

Girls Cinema merged with a new publication, *Film Star Weekly*, first published November 26, 1932, and which carried on the tradition of the former. *Film Star Weekly* ceased publication on October 5, 1935, when it merged with *Picture Show*.*

Information Sources

INDEX SOURCES: None.
REPRINT EDITIONS: None.
LOCATION SOURCES: No information.

Publication History

MAGAZINE TITLE AND TITLE CHANGES: *Girls Cinema*.
VOLUME AND ISSUE DATA: Vol. I, No. 1–Vol. XXV, No. 631 (October 16, 1920–December 19, 1932), weekly.

PUBLISHER AND PLACE OF PUBLICATION: Amalgamated Press, Fleetway House,
    Farringdon Street, London, England.
EDITOR: No editor listed.

Thomas A. Johnson

GLOBAL MOVIE MARKETING. See MOVIE/T.V.
MARKETING

THE GOLDEN COMET. See Appendix 1

GRACELAND NEWS. See Appendix 1

GRAND ILLUSIONS

Grand Illusions is a small, academic film journal published by the film society
of Boston's Emerson College. The staff is comprised of undergraduate students
and changes from year to year, along with the quality and direction of the
magazine. The concentration, however, has been in oral histories with filmmakers.

Grand Illusions was founded in 1977 by a group of Emerson film students,
including John Gallagher, John Hanc, Sam Sarowitz, and Marino Amoruso.
They were responsible for the journal's ambitious start, with three issues in its
first year. Since then, *Grand Illusions* has appeared once a year.

The first number (February 1977) included interviews with Elia Kazan, Sam
Spiegel, and Herbert Ross, with critical pieces on Frank Capra by Amoruso,
William Wellman by Gallagher, and Arthur Penn's *Bonnie and Clyde*, and was
cited in *American Film** (March 1977). The second issue (Summer 1977) con-
tinued the emphasis on American cinema with articles on John Ford, Charlie
Chaplin, and Sidney Lumet.

With the third issue of *Grand Illusions* (Winter 1977), the publication changed
from a newspaper format to book form and highlighted Gallagher's interviews
with François Truffaut, Tay Garnett, Steven Spielberg, Robert Wise, Joan Mick-
lin Silver, and Win Sharples, Jr. The Truffaut interview was later excerpted in
Joseph McBride's *Hawks on Hawks* (University of California Press, 1982), with
the Garnett interview forming the basis of Gallagher's *Tay Garnett* (Scarecrow
Press, 1985).

With the graduation of the founding editors, *Grand Illusions* was continued
by a new series of film students, and the 1978–1979 issue offered dialogues with
Robert Altman, Eric Rohmer, Philip Kaufman, and James Toback. The quality
of writing, however, was not up to that of the previous issues, and the 1979–
1980 issue was also disappointing. It featured interviews with Sydney Pollack

and Robert Gale, with critical articles on Erich von Stroheim, David Cronenberg, Roger Corman's Poe films, and the Monty Python features.

The 1981–1982 incarnation of *Grand Illusions*, under the editorial guidance of Mark Kelsey, returned to the standards of the earlier numbers and changed the format to a large magazine. The issue was dedicated to an excellent survey of independent cinema and gave considerable space to "outlaw" filmmakers such as Andy Warhol and John Waters. In the tradition of the first *Grand Illusions*, the magazine included interviews with John Sayles, George Roy Hill, Barbara Kopple, and Ray Harryhausen. In addition, the magazine provided a supplementary article, "Fund-Raising for the Non-Fiction Film," by David Smith.

Information Sources

INDEX SOURCES: None.
REPRINT EDITIONS: None.
LOCATION SOURCES: Emerson College; Library of Congress; Museum of Modern Art.

Publication History

MAGAZINE TITLE AND TITLE CHANGES: *Grand Illusions*.
VOLUME AND ISSUE DATA: Vol. I, No. 1 (February 1977); Vol. I, No. 2 (Summer 1977); Vol. II, No. 1 (Winter 1977); Vol. III, No. 1 (1978–1979); Vol. IV, No. 1 (1979–1980); Vol. V & VI (1981–1982).
PUBLISHER AND PLACE OF PUBLICATION: Emerson College Film Society, 100 Beacon Street, Boston, Mass. 02116.
EDITOR: John A. Gallagher and John G. Hanc (Vol. I, No. 1–Vol. I, No. 2); John A Gallagher (Vol. II, No. 1); Nora Linda Cassar (Vol. III, No. 1); Richard Denzer (Vol. IV, No. 1); Mark Kelsey (Vol. V & VI).

John A. Gallagher

GUTH NA SCANNÁN. See SCANNÁN

G.W.T.W. COLLECTORS CLUB NEWSLETTER. See
Appendix 1

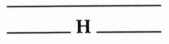

H

HI NEWS. See Appendix 2

HISTORIANS FILM COMMITTEE NEWSLETTER. See
FILM & HISTORY

THE HISTORICAL JOURNAL OF FILM, RADIO & TELEVISION

One of the newest and most promising directions for professional historical scholarship is the research and writing of the history of the mass media. The trend can be explained in part by the general desire of the public to learn more about what goes on behind the scenes in movies and television, a factor which often gives the work of the media historian more appeal to the general public than to his colleagues in traditional political or diplomatic history. Another factor, of perhaps even greater importance, is that in the past decade significant collections of archival manuscript materials—the types of evidence with which historians are usually most comfortable—have begun to become available for study. Founded in 1981, at a point when more and more historians were coming to recognize these new opportunities opening to them, *The Historical Journal of Film, Radio & Television* has become respected and relied upon as a resource in this growing and dynamic field. It is the official journal of the International Association for Audio Visual Media in Historical Research and Education.

From its inception, the publication has given clear evidence of the scope of interest and high standards of scholarship to which editor K. R. M. Short has devoted the new enterprise. While the subject of media history does tend to expand the readership for the work of some academic historians, there should be no question that this journal is directed to the serious scholar rather than the "film buff." Unlike the primarily descriptive/narrative approach to nostalgic chapters on the lore of the media which sometimes passes for "media history," here the focus is on analysis and archival documentation for the conclusions put forth. Most of the articles published here address one or another analytical question of the kind common to historical scholarship: How did the British Board of Film Censors operate in trying to control the image of Britain put forth on the screen there? How can we better understand the sociopsychological signif- icance of the French cinema during the period of Nazi occupation? How was the production of *Wilson* (Twentieth Century-Fox, 1944) influenced by the prop- aganda demands of the Second World War?

The most important readership of this journal is made up of scholars who are themselves doing research in the history of the mass media. This sets it apart from *Film & History*,* the older quarterly (somewhat more modest in number of pages) which also focuses attention on subjects of interest to historian-film- makers and to history teachers who relate to film and television as a vehicle for the classroom rather than as a subject for research. One feature which serves to emphasize this special commitment of *The Historical Journal of Film, Radio & Television* to the application of traditional historical documentation (and one which should provide a valuable introduction to those interested in what types of archival materials are available) is the regular publication of archival docu- ments in their unedited form. For example, Vol. I, No. 2 included a series of letters and interoffice memos between radio newscaster Arthur Hale, the president of Transradio Press Service (his employer), and the sponsor of Hale's regular newscasts (the Richfield Oil Company) dealing with the sponsor's concern about Hale's personal interpretation of the news as broadcast. With the exception of a two-page introductory note putting the documents in context (in this case identifying the personalities and the issues involved in the interpretation of international news in 1941–1942) the letters and memos are published in their entirety and are allowed to speak for themselves. Another such document section dealt with manuscript and oral history evidence on broadcasting in the Pacific during the Second World War.

The journal also publishes news, notices, and comments of special interest to media historians as well as critical reviews of books. Of particular interest for those concerned to "keep up" with the growing literature are the inclusion of current lists of recent dissertations in the history of cinema and the electronic media and titles of recent articles in the field drawn from a remarkably wide range of other publications.

Information Sources

INDEX SOURCES: America: History and Life; Current Contents; FIAF International
    Index to Film Periodicals; FIAF International Index to Television Periodicals; Film
    Literature Index; Historical Abstracts; History & Life; The Journal of American

History; Media Review Digest; Recently Published Articles (American Historical Association).
REPRINT EDITIONS: None.
LOCATION SOURCES: Academy of Motion Picture Arts and Sciences; Library of Congress; University of Southern California.

Publication History

MAGAZINE TITLE AND TITLE CHANGES: *The Historical Journal of Film, Radio & Television.*
VOLUME AND ISSUE DATA: Vol. I, No. 1 (March 1981 to present), twice a year in March and October.
PUBLISHER AND PLACE OF PUBLICATION: Carfax Publishing Company, P.O. Box 25, Abingdon, Oxfordshire, OX14 1RW, England.
EDITOR: K. R. M. Short.

John E. O'Connor

HOLLYWOOD QUARTERLY. See FILM QUARTERLY

THE HOLLYWOOD REPORTER

In 1930 *The Hollywood Reporter* was founded as a trade paper for the film industry. In many respects, it was intended by its creator, W. R. "Billy" Wilkerson, to be a daily motion picture counterpart of *Variety,** which had begun as a theatrical trade journal and later broadened its scope to include other aspects of the entertainment industry. *The Hollywood Reporter* became a daily compendium of film industry information including such things as statistics on movie grosses, production expenses, attendance, film reviews, and industry news. Its motto and guiding inspiration was "Today's Film News Today." Over the years, the paper's advertising sections, which have achieved a certain reputation for raising the personal message to the status of an art form, have also established a unique reference valve covering all major film-related services from publicity representatives to animal trainers.

Most of the features and columns with which the journal began have remained constant from the publication's beginning. One notable exception was editor and publisher W. R. Wilkerson's "Trade Views," which ceased with his death. The "Rambling Reporter" feature was unsigned for the first two decades and then featured a succession of columnists culminating in Hank Grant's long-running byline until 1983, when the "Rambling Reporter" became Robert Osborne and Grant became an occasional contributor with his newly established column, "Off the Cuff." Other columns, while maintaining the same content, change names with each columnist. However, as new mediums have evolved—such as television, cable television, video cassettes, and video discs—features such as "Televisions" and "Cable Column" have been added. The legitimate stage and New

York gossip has been reported for a number of years in the "Broadway Ballyhoo" column of Radie Harris. Now special sections of *The Hollywood Reporter* address significant space to such topics according to the day of the week. For example, the international news appears to a greater extent on a Wednesday, and film and television production charts appear regularly every Friday.

Special editions are now frequently published for film festivals, conventions, film markets, and the beginning of the television season. These editions include news items and advertisements which promote shows, companies, films, and individuals which take up a far greater percentage of space in the paper than its usual daily editions.

Information Sources

BIBLIOGRAPHY:
Roberts, Glenys. "The Unlikely Boss of the 'Reporter,' " *Los Angeles*, Vol. 12, No. 8, August 1967, pp. 32, 54–56.
INDEX SOURCES: None.
REPRINT EDITIONS: Kraus-Thomson (1935–1941).
LOCATION SOURCES: The only complete run of *The Hollywood Reporter* in hard copy known to exist is owned by the journal.

Publication History

MAGAZINE TITLE AND TITLE CHANGES: *The Hollywood Reporter*.
VOLUME AND ISSUE DATA: Vol. I, No. 1–Vol. LVIII, No. 30 (September 3, 1930–June 25, 1940), daily except Sundays and holidays; Vol. LVIII, No. 31 (June 26, 1940, to present), daily except Saturdays, Sundays, and holidays.
PUBLISHER AND PLACE OF PUBLICATION: The Hollywood Reporter, Inc., 6715 Sunset Boulevard, Hollywood, Calif. 90028.
EDITOR: W. R. Wilkerson (September 3, 1930–February 10, 1950); Don Carle Gillette (February 13, 1950–November 18, 1955); McCullah St. Johns (November 21, 1955–June 22, 1956); Don Carle Gillette (June 25, 1956–June 12, 1964); Mac St. Johns (June 15, 1964–March 12, 1965); Don Carle Gillette (March 15, 1965–July 8, 1966); Frank Barron (July 11, 1966–February 12, 1968); James Powers (February 13, 1968–August 2, 1971); Paul Sargent Clark (August 3, 1971–July 11, 1972); no editor listed (July 12, 1972–August 10, 1972); Hal Bates (August 11, 1972–June 18, 1973); no editor listed (June 19, 1973–September 14, 1973); Ralph Kaminsky (September 17, 1973–January 31, 1975); no editor listed (February 3, 1975–February 18, 1975); Mike Kizziah (February 19, 1975–November 17, 1975); no editor listed (November 18, 1975–November 24, 1975); Barbara Jane Franklin (November 25, 1975–November 19, 1976); no editor listed (November 22, 1976–August 17, 1981); Martin Kent (August 18, 1981–June 10, 1982); no editor listed (June 11, 1982–July 23, 1982); Bruce Binkow (July 26, 1983, to present). (In recent years Tichi Wilkerson Miles has always been listed as Editor-in-Chief).

Stephen L. Hanson

HOLLYWOOD STUDIO MAGAZINE. See Appendix 2

HOLLYWOOD VAGABOND

From its look and feel, *Hollywood Vagabond* was right to advertise itself as "The Quality Filmpaper." First published on February 10, 1927, its average of eight pages featured an eclectic selection of articles and news items, such as a poem, "Long Pants," by Harry Langdon (Vol. 1, No. 3) and articles such as "Farina: Negro Child Genius of the Photoplay" (Vol. 1, No. 8) and "The Passing of June Mathis" (Vol. 1, No. 24). Vol. 1, No. 15 (May 19, 1927) was a special edition devoted to Cecil B. DeMille's *King of Kings*. Because no complete run of the paper appears to exist in any library, it is difficult to determine the date of *Hollywood Vagabond*'s demise and the exact dates of the changes in editors or publication addresses.

Information Sources

INDEX SOURCES: None.
REPRINT EDITIONS: None.
LOCATION SOURCES: Academy of Motion Picture Arts and Sciences (incomplete).

Publication History

MAGAZINE TITLE AND TITLE CHANGES: *Hollywood Vagabond*.
VOLUME AND ISSUE DATA: Vol. I, No. 1–Vol. I, No. 21 (February 10, 1927–June 30, 1927), weekly; Vol. I, No. 22–Vol. II, No. 20 (July 14, 1927–June 2, 1928), bimonthly. [Date of last issue unconfirmed.]
PUBLISHER AND PLACE OF PUBLICATION: Billy Joy, 620 Taft Building, Hollywood, Calif. (Vol. I, No. I–Vol. II, No. ?); Billy Joy, 1605 Cahuenga Avenue, Hollywood, Calif. (Vol. II, No.?–Vol. II, No. 20).
EDITOR: Fred W. Fox (February 10, 1927–September 5, 1927); Billy Joy (September 19, 1927–?); Clark Richardson (?–June 2, 1928).

Anthony Slide

HUNGAROFILM BULLETIN. See Appendix 4

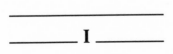

I

ILLUSTRATED FILMS MONTHLY. See PICTURE STORIES
MONTHLY

IMAGE

Image has been published by the International Museum of Photography at George Eastman House since January 1952. Although the journal focuses on the history of photography, it has consistently included articles on film. Through the long tenures of James Card, the director of the film department, and his associate, George C. Pratt, *Image* has concentrated on the development of cinema and the history of silent film. As an in-house publication, both the quality of the writing and the areas of film history under consideration are dependent largely on the staff of the museum, yet articles in *Image* very often rise above the anecdotal and descriptive.

Most of the important pieces on film published in the first twenty-five years of *Image* have been collected into a book, *"Image" on the Art and Evolution of the Film*, edited by Marshall Deutelbaum. The book includes the best work by Card, "The Films of Mary Pickford" (Vol. 8, No. 4), and George C. Pratt's series of interviews with Alice Terry (Vol. 16, No. 1), Ramon Novarro (Vol. 16, No. 4), Buster Keaton (Vol. 17, No. 4), Harold Lloyd (Vol. 19, No. 3), Hal Mohr (Vol. 19, No. 1), and James Wong Howe (Vol. 20, No. 1). Several articles were written by people directly involved in early film history, including "Reminiscences of an Early Motion Picture Operator" (Vol. 5, No. 6) by Lumière cameraman Francis Doublier; "Reminiscences of the Early Days of Movie Comedies" (Vol. 6, No. 5) by Clarence C. Badger, a director for Keystone; and the original appearance of Louise Brooks's "Mr. Pabst" (Vol. 5, No. 7). Other important articles in the book are: "The Pre-Hollywood Lubitsch"

(Vol. 18, No. 4) by Jan-Christopher Horak; Pratt's two articles on the early western, "The Posse Is Riding Like Mad" (Vol. 7, No. 5) and "The Posse Is Still Riding Like Mad" (Vol. 7, No. 7); and "Silent-Film Speed" (Vol. 4, No. 7) by James Card. Two essays not included in the book but indicative of *Image* at its best are Marshall Deutelbaum's "Rediscovering *The Yellow Girl*" (Vol. 21, No. 3) and George Pratt's "The Oneness of All Ages" (Vol. 15, No. 4), which centers on *Intolerance* but also mentions Ezra Pound, James Joyce, and the modernist movement. *Image* occasionally publishes indexes organized by actors, directors, or film companies, and the journal includes notices of exhibitions and film series at the Eastman House.

Image is one of the few publications which chart the history and problems of film archives. A valuable introduction to the collection and preservation of films in America is Herbert Reynolds's penetrating interview with James Card, " 'What Can You Do for Us, Barney?' Four Decades of Film Collecting: An Interview with James Card" (Vol. 20, No. 2). Card has written several pieces of interest: "Collecting Old Films" (Vol. 1, No. 7) and "Film Archives" (Vol. 7, No. 6). John Kuiper contributed "The Preservation of America's Film Heritage" (Vol. 21, No. 2).

The most attractive feature of *Image* is the reproduction of still photographs from the museum's vast collection. In addition to well-presented photographs in articles such as Marshall Deutelbaum's "King Vidor's *The Crowd*" (Vol. 17, No. 3) and James Card's "Movies: The Mirror of the Spirit of Our Times" (Vol. 3, No. 2), *Image* provides rarely seen production stills and reproductions of advertisements in "Recent Acquisitions: Film Stills of the Twenties (1 and 2)" (Vol. 22, Nos. 3 and 4) and examples of still photographs as art in "Coming Attractions: American Movie Stills as Photography" (Vol. 18, No. 2) by Marshall Deutelbaum and George C. Pratt.

In recent years, the publication of *Image* has been somewhat sporadic.

Information Sources

BIBLIOGRAPHY:
Deutelbaum, Marshall, ed. *"Image" on the Art and Evolution of the Film* (New York: Dover Publications and the International Museum of Photography, 1979).
INDEX SOURCES: The New Film Index.
LOCATION SOURCES: Columbia University (incomplete); Dartmouth College; Library of Congress; Museum of Modern Art (incomplete); New York Public Library (incomplete); Smithsonian Institution; University of California at Los Angeles; University of Iowa; University of Miami.

Publication History

MAGAZINE TITLE AND TITLE CHANGES: *Image*.
VOLUME AND ISSUE DATA: Vol. I, No. 1–Vol. VII, No. 10 (January 1952–December 1958), monthly except summers; Vol. VIII, No. 1–Vol. IX, No. 4 (March 1959–December 1960), quarterly; Vol. X, Nos. 1–6 (1961); Vol. XI, Nos. 1–6 (1962); Vol. XII, Nos. 1–3 (1963); Vol. XII, Nos. 4–6 (1964); Vol. XIII, No. 1 (1965);

no issues published 1966–1970; Vol. XIV, Nos. 1–6 (1971); Vol. XV, No. 1–
Vol. XXII, No. 4 (1972–1979), quarterly; Vol. 23, No. 1 (1980 to present),
irregular.
PUBLISHER AND PLACE OF PUBLICATION: The International Museum of Photog-
raphy at George Eastman House, 900 East Avenue, Rochester, N.Y. 14607.
EDITOR: Oscar N. Solbert, Beaumont Newhall, and James G. Card (1952–1956); Minor
White (1956–September 1957); Beaumont Newhall (October 1957–December 1960);
no editor listed (1961–1965); F. Van Deren Coke (1971); F. Van Deren Coke
and Thomas F. Barrow (1972, Nos. 1–2); James Card (1972, No. 3); Robert
Doherty and George C. Pratt (1972, No. 4–1975); Robert Doherty and George
C. Pratt, with W. Paul Rayner as Guest Editor (1976); George C. Pratt and W.
Paul Rayner (1977); George C. Pratt (1978); George C. Pratt and Dan Meinwald
(1979); George C. Pratt (1980); no editor listed (1981 to present).

Gregory Martino

THE IMPLET. See Appendix 3

INTERNATIONAL FILM REVIEW

International Film Review was a unique publication providing news items and
brief articles on "foreign" personalities at work in the Hollywood studios. It
also included sections on film matters worldwide, a survey of critical reaction
to American films abroad, and reviews of non-American film books. Unfortunately, it appears to have survived for only three issues in early 1933.

Information Sources

INDEX SOURCES: None.
REPRINT EDITIONS: None.
LOCATION SOURCES: Academy of Motion Picture Arts and Sciences.

Publication History

MAGAZINE TITLE AND TITLE CHANGES: *International Film Review*.
VOLUME AND ISSUE DATA: Nos. 1–3 (January 1, 1933–February 1, 1933), bimonthly.
PUBLISHER AND PLACE OF PUBLICATION: Joseph B. Polonsky, 6724 Hollywood
Boulevard, Hollywood, Calif.
EDITOR: Joseph B. Polonsky.

Anthony Slide

THE INTERNATIONAL PHOTOGRAPHER

The official bulletin of the International Photographers of the Motion Picture
Industries, Local No. 659, *The International Photographer* was first published
in February 1929 and has appeared on a monthly basis through the present. It

proves an invaluable research tool for the study of the history of Hollywood cinematography, not only through contemporary articles but also in its reports on labor matters affecting the local and news items on cinematography and cinematographers.

When Silas Edgar Snyder (who had previously been with *American Cinematographer**) took over the editorship in May 1929, *The International Photographer* expanded its number of pages to more than thirty and, at times, up to one hundred. At the same time, it commenced publication of articles which were of contemporary interest then and are now of historical importance. Such articles include "Wide Film" by Arthur Reeves (June 1929), "Shooting *Hell's Angels*" by Harry Perry (July 1929), "Knights of the Camera" by Harry Alan Potamkin (September 1930), "From Pigs to Pictures: Life Story of David Horsley" by William Horsley (March 1934 and April 1934), and "*Intolerance*— 'The Sun Play of the Ages' " by Billy Bitzer (October 1934).

George Blaisdell became editor in November 1930, and he began reviewing films in the journal through February 1933.[1] Blaisdell also concentrated on publishing articles on technical innovations and the filming of current productions.

By 1937, *The International Photographer* had lost much of its research value, concentrating on specific departments such as "Camera," "Sound," "Lighting," "Sets," "New Patents," and "Projection." Herbert Aller took over as editor in December 1939—a position he was to hold for the next thirty years. Aller introduced a 16mm department and a column titled "Television Topics." Also, during the Second World War, *The International Photographer* published seminude pin-up photographs by William Mortensen, which were replaced after the duration by photographs of landscapes. (From its earliest days, *The International Photographer* had included "still" photographs, often by major cinematographers such as Karl Struss.)

Major articles began to appear once again in the journal. Lee Garmes contributed a piece on his career for the May 1940 issue titled "Peoria Boy Makes Good" and subtitled "Eliminating the 'Bags' under Adolphe Menjou's Eyes." Other interesting pieces include "What Is a Soundie?" (October 1940), an interview with George Hurrell (September 1941), "Making Puppetoons" (August 1942), "I Remember" by Billy Bitzer (March 1944), "What the Camera Means to Advertising Photography" by George Hurrell (October 1947), "Lighting for Technicolor as Compared with Black and White Photography" by Joseph Valentine (January 1948), and "Shooting Live T.V. with Motion Picture Cameras" by Karl Freund (November 1952).

However, by the late fifties, *The International Photographer* had reduced its size to under twenty pages and seemed to rely on a mixture of articles of technical complexity, slight and trivial pieces on new films, and occasional reprints from other periodicals. In recent years, the magazine has come to have only negligible research value, with each issue consisting of a several-page production report, short articles on and interviews with cinematographers, and reports on new equipment and technical innovations.

Notes

1. George Blaisdell was one of the industry's first film reviewers, being associated with *The Moving Picture World** almost from its inception.

Information Sources

INDEX SOURCES: None.
REPRINT EDITIONS: None.
LOCATION SOURCES: Academy of Motion Picture Arts and Sciences; Harvard University; Library of Congress; University of Southern California.

Publication History

MAGAZINE TITLE AND TITLE CHANGES: *The International Photographer*.
VOLUME AND ISSUE DATA: Vol. I, No. 1 (February 1929 to present), monthly.
PUBLISHER AND PLACE OF PUBLICATION: Local 659, 428 Markham Building, 6372 Hollywood Boulevard, Hollywood, Calif. (Vol. I, No. 1–Vol. 1, No. 9); Local 659, 1605 North Cahuenga Avenue, Hollywood, Calif. (Vol. I, No. 10–Vol. VIII, No. 8); Local 659, 506 Taft Building, Hollywood, Calif. (Vol. VIII, No. 9–Vol. XI, No. 6); Local 659, 6461 Sunset Boulevard, Hollywood, Calif. (Vol. XI, No. 7–Vol. XVII, No. 2); Local 659, 7614 Sunset Boulevard, Hollywood, Calif. 90046 (Vol. XVII, No. 3–Vol. XXXII, No. 8); Local 659, 7715 Sunset Boulevard, Hollywood, Calif. 90046 (Vol. XXXII, No. 9, to present).
EDITOR: Ira B. Hoke (February 1929–April 1929); Silas Edgar Snyder (May 1929–October 1930); George Blaisdell (November 1930–February 1933); Silas Edgar Snyder (March 1933–April 1937); no editor listed (May 1937–October 1937); Ed Gibbons (November 1937–November 1939); Herbert Aller (December 1939–June 1971); no editor listed except George J. Toscas as Managing Editor (July 1971–June 1975); Gerald K. Smith (July 1975–February 1981); George J. Toscas (March 1981 to present).

Anthony Slide

INTERNATIONAL PROJECTIONIST

Coincident with the new responsibilities placed upon the theatre projectionists during the late twenties and early thirties accompanying increasingly sophisticated projection techniques and the arrival of sound films was the appearance of several magazines devoted exclusively to the concerns of the projectionists. *International Projectionist*, launched in October 1931, endured as the longest of these publications, lasting over thirty years. James J. Finn, former managing editor of *The Motion Picture Projectionist*,* founded the magazine and immediately instilled within it an advocacy for the rights and welfare of union projectionists conspicuously missing in the other major projectionist journals, *The Motion Picture Projectionist* and *Projection Engineering*.* In a statement appearing in its first issue, Finn implicitly referred to what he felt were the limitations of his competitors, the policies of *Projection Engineering* to print only technical articles and of *The Motion Picture Projectionist* to publish craft news while assiduously avoiding discussion of union politics and controversy:

> Merely printing technical data does not justify the existence of a publication purporting to serve a craft. Technical data—yes; but also craft news, a sympathetic understanding of the craftsman's needs at work and away from work, and a constant vigilance to herald and to fight any danger to either his welfare or his work—such a service marks the true craft paper.[1]

While Finn was editor of *International Projectionist* the magazine included both editorials and a "Monthly Chat" column, providing Finn with forums from which to voice his opinions. For example, in the second issue's "Monthly Chat," Finn lambasted industry "big boys" for allowing screen image to decline while they paid inordinate attention to sound quality, and while assuring theatre projectionists that, judging from contemporary demonstrations, the film industry had "nothing to worry about" from television.[2] Meanwhile, in a feature article in that same issue, Finn exposed what he deemed a projectionist school "racket" in Pennsylvania run, as it turned out, by a frequent contributor to *Projection Engineering*; Finn was more outraged that the school's graduates might displace union projectionists than he was that the students were being bilked or provided with poor instruction.[3] Throughout its publication *International Projectionist* offered its readers in-depth technical articles encompassing all facets of projection technique and engineering, as well as regular columns covering patents, technical hints, and International Alliance of Theatrical Stage Employees and Moving Picture Machine Operators (IATSE) news. However, even technical articles were seldom exempt from editorial comment. For example, prefacing a September 1950 piece from *American Cinematographer** concerning production use of magnetic recording, the editors cautioned that such an efficient production technique presented "another grave problem to the already hard-pressed studio workers in their continuing struggle to maintain the employment level."[4]

By 1932 *The Motion Picture Projectionist* had folded, and the following year *International Projectionist* purchased *Projection Engineering*, indicating, perhaps, that James Finn's unabashed advocacy on behalf of projectionists' interests proved a better commercial policy than ignoring labor politics within the IATSE. The magazine's commitment to both engagement in labor issues involving the welfare of projectionists and providing the craft with the latest in technical news remained intact throughout the thirty-three-year life of *International Projectionist*, but by the late fifties and early sixties the declining fortunes of both the film industry and the projectionist craft were reflected by the magazine's diminishing space devoted to features and advertising. In 1964 *Greater Amusements* absorbed *International Projectionist*, bringing the end to the only national publication devoted to the projectionist craft. Today, the historical value of *International Projectionist* lies not only in the compendium of technical information it published concerning projection technology and motion picture technology in general, but also in its documentation of the politics and controversies involved within one of the more vociferous labor segments of the International Alliance, the various projectionist locals.

Notes

1. *International Projectionist*, October 1931, p. 7.
2. "Monthly Chat," *International Projectionist*, November 1931, p. 3.
3. James J. Finn, "Sound and Television School Racket," *International Projectionist*, November 1931, pp. 28–30.
4. Loren D. Ryder, "Magnetic Recording Upsurge in Studios," *International Projectionist*, September 1950, p. 21.

Information Sources

INDEX SOURCES: Engineering Index (1939–1949).
REPRINT EDITIONS: University Microfilms (1950–1959 only).
LOCATION SOURCES: Eastman Kodak Company (Rochester, N.Y.); Illinois Institute of Technology; University of California at Los Angeles.

Publication History

MAGAZINE TITLE AND TITLE CHANGES: *International Projectionist*.
VOLUME AND ISSUE DATA: Vol. I, No. 1–Vol. XXXIX, No. 12 (October 1931– December 1964), monthly.
PUBLISHER AND PLACE OF PUBLICATION: James J. Finn Publishing Corp., New York, N.Y. (October 1931–July 1942); International Projectionist Publishing Co., Inc., New York, N.Y. (August 1942–December 1959); Northern Publishing Co., Minneapolis, Minn. (January 1960–December 1964).
EDITOR: James J. Finn (October 1931–February 1942); Aaron Nadell (March 1942– February 1943); C. F. Alexander (March 1943); C. F. Alexander and W. L. Lightfoot (April 1943–December 1943); W. L. Lightfoot (January 1944–December 1945); Henry B. Sellwood (January 1946–January 1952); James J. Finn (February 1952–March 1952); Henry B. Sellwood (April 1952–July 1952); Aaron Nadell (August 1952–January 1953); James J. Finn (February 1953–July 1953); Frederick Hodgson (August 1953–December 1953); R. A. Entracht (January 1954–March 1954); James J. Finn (April 1954–August 1955); R. A. Entracht (September 1955); James Morris (October 1955–January 1957); Robert C. Macleod (February 1957– March 1958); James J. Finn (April 1958–December 1959); Frank W. Cooley, Jr. (January 1960–December 1964).

William Lafferty

INTIMATE CAROLYN JONES. See Appendix 1

THE IRISH LIMELIGHT

Ireland's only film trade journal was *The Irish Limelight*, which began in January 1917 and continued through December 1920. Its editor was John S. Warren, who remained with it for its four-year run. In the 1920 Christmas number, Warren, in a farewell message to his readers, mentions that he has transferred his interest in the paper to P. J. Flanagan, a journalist, but the periodical does not appear to have survived this date.

In the extraordinary circumstances of the 1916 Rebellion, the Film Company of Ireland, under the management of the returned Irish-American lawyer and diplomat James Mark Sullivan, was formed, and, in spite of the unsettled times, produced a sizable output of films in that year. This gave a local and national stamp to the existing Irish film trade, whose activities had hitherto been chronicled by Irish correspondents in the British *Bioscope** and *Kinematograph Weekly.**

Indeed *The Irish Limelight* devoted a great deal of space to the Film Company of Ireland and reflected the national resurgence of its time. A particular contributor was Joseph A. Power, who was through all his journalistic career an ardent propagandist for an Irish film industry and was in the late thirties a member of the advisory council of the Irish Film Society.

The first issue of the journal, which averaged twenty pages with advertising cover, had an article entitled "What the Irish Film Company Is Doing," as well as trade news and photographs of Irish players, films, and personalities of the industry.

Typical articles over the years included one on the historical inaccuracies of Walter MacNamara's *Ireland a Nation*, a controversial film banned by the British military (February 1917); an interview with Kathleen Murphy from the Irish feature film, *The Girl of Glenbeigh* (April 1917); very full coverage of the Film Company of Ireland's first 1917 release, *Rafferty's Rise*; an item on Erwin Goldwater, the Prague-trained violinist of the Carlton Cinema, Dublin; and reports on the current filming of the ambitious *Knocknagow*, the Film Company of Ireland's super production. All these items were in the May 1917 issue.

The paper continued to record film events in Ireland when production was very active. Dublin had at this time no less than three film laboratories. The newsreels of Norman Whitten, entitled *Irish Events*, recorded contemporary history on film which later became grist to the mill of film anthologists and compilers. Films from Hollywood and Europe were reviewed. Hollywood personalities of Irish origin contributed; and distributors, cinemas, and films were advertised. There did not, however, seem to be much support from the larger Hollywood and British companies. Many of the 1920 issues gave much space to the production and presentation of *Willy Reilly and His Colleen Bawn*, John McDonagh's film of the William Carleton novel, and the swan song of the Film Company of Ireland.

In the last issue, December 1920, the editorial stressed the depressing state of the Irish film trade at that time, harassed by increasing political difficulties, military restrictions, curfews, and violence. An article, "Film Men's Real Life Dramas," dealt with the trials of the trade in Ireland, many of whose members were in prison or on the run. Leon Poirier's *Narayana*, Clara Kimball Young's *The Feast of Life*, and the Eugene Sue film *Martin the Foundling* received full-page coverage. Josie Sedgwick, the Irish-American star, greeted her Irish admirers, and Harold Lloyd sent a message to the readers as well as enclosing a subscription.

In its coverage of Irish film events of the time, *The Irish Limelight* is a unique and valuable source for Irish film history.

Information Sources

INDEX SOURCES: None.
REPRINT EDITIONS: None.
LOCATION SOURCES: No information. [Incomplete runs exist at the National Library of Ireland, Dublin; the Liam O'Leary Film Archives, Dublin; The British Library, London.]

Publication History

MAGAZINE TITLE AND TITLE CHANGES: *The Irish Limelight*.
VOLUME AND ISSUE DATA: Vol. 1, No. 1–Vol. IV, No. 12 (January 1917–December 1920), monthly.
PUBLISHER AND PLACE OF PUBLICATION: The Irish Limelight, 13 Fleet Street, Dublin, Eire.
EDITOR: John S. Warren.

Liam O'Leary

ISKUSSTVO KINO

In January 1925, Narodnyi Komissariat Prosveshcheniia, or NARKOMPROS, published the first issue of a film journal entitled *Sovetskii Ekran*. The journal's main objective was to reflect the state's use of the cinema as a powerful propaganda tool for the benefit of the young Soviet film industry. The motion pictures were to keep alive the political awareness of the masses. *Sovetskii Ekran*, being faithful to its militant socialist ideology, almost completely ignored the prerevolutionary Russian film production. A significant silence was kept on Western as well as on American cinematography. Exceptions were made for Charles Chaplin, David Griffith, and Ernst Lubitsch, whose progressive social views were presented and analyzed in many articles and critical essays. In the journal's opinion, the Western cinema was highly pessimistic and deeply decadent, lacking the ability to discover and cinematically reveal the liberal tendencies of their own societies.

In January 1930, *Sovetskii Ekran* changed its name to *Proletarskoe kino*, to reflect its ideological affiliation. Published by the Assotsiatsiia Rabotnikov Revoliutsionnoi Kinematografii under the editorship of V. Pudovkin, the journal was a clear example of the manipulative function of the media and an awareness of Marxist ideology. Its editorials were forums of discussion of theoretical aspects of filmmaking from a Marxist perspective. Examples include V. Sutyrin's "O sotsialisticheskoi rekonstruktsii kinematografii" (On the socialist reconstruction of the film industry; No. 1, 1931) and V. Grigoriev's "K metodologii opredeleniia kinozhanrov'' (The methodology of determining the cinematic genres; No. 7, 1931).

The journal's commitment to reinforce the memories of the revolution and civil war led to the dedication of an entire issue (No. 8, 1931) to the First Congress of the War Correspondents. M. Roizen wrote ''Voennye fil'ma'' (The military film) and E. IAkushkin wrote ''Ispol'zovanie voennouchenoi fil'my'' (The use of the military scientific films).

In 1933, *Sovetskoe kino* replaced the proletcultist *Proletarskoe kino*. Although the journal's ideological orientation remained unchanged, the quality of writing became an important element in the new publication. Professional literary critics, as well as well-known filmmakers were among its writers. V. Popov wrote ''Rozhdenie stilia'' (The birth of style; No. 2, 1935), E. Zil'ber and I. Krinkin contributed ''Preodolenie empirizma'' (The avoidance of the empiric; No. 3, 1935), and S. IUtkevich wrote ''Nashi tvorsheskie raznoglasiia'' (Our creative differences; No. 8, 1935).

The first Soviet film festival is analyzed in the editorial entitled ''K itogam pervogo sovetskogo kinofestivalia'' (The results of the First Soviet Film Festival; No. 3, 1935). Various aspects of children's film production are discussed by N. Kal'varskaia in ''O detskom filme'' (On the children's films) and by N. Stepanov in ''O geroicheskom, fantasticheskom i komicheskom v detskom kino'' (On the heroic, fantastic and comic in movies for children).

The journal underwent another name change in January 1936 when it became *Iskusstvo kino*, published by Glavnoe Upravlenie Kinofotopromyshlenosti Vsesoiuznogo Komiteta po delam iskusstva pri SNK SSSR. The change was only cosmetic. The journal's profile, however, remained unaltered. In its opening editorial the journal reinforced its intention to explore the complexities of past and present revolutionary experiences of the Soviet cinema, revealing simultaneously the antihumanist qualities of the capitalist film industry. The cinema as a mirror of social and economic relations is discussed by V. Messer in ''Doroga, krutaia, prekrasnaia'' (The road, a steep and yet a beautiful one) and by I. Krinkin in ''Realizm i naturalizm v tvorchestve khudozhnikov kino'' (Realism and naturalism in the creation of cinema artists; No. 3, 1936).

One of its first editorials, ''Za chistotu realisticheskogo iskusstva'' (For the purity of the realistic art), dealt with the meanings and values of realism as applied to filmmaking (No. 2, 1936). Well-known Soviet film directors were among *Iskusstvo kino*'s permanent writers. S. Eisenstein wrote ''Programma prepodovaniia teorii i praktiki reshissury'' (The teaching of theory and practice of film directing; No. 4, 1936) and the article ''Pokazat' liudei nashei rodiny'' (To show the peoples of our land; No. 7, 1936), stressing the necessity of making movies about the new Soviet man and woman.

Very often, progressive foreign filmmakers were among the journal's writers. Charlie Chaplin wrote ''Budushchee nemogo kino'' (The future of the silent movies), and Harold Lloyd wrote "Amerikanskaia kinokomediia" (The American comedy; No. 8, 1937)

In 1940, *Iskusstvo kino* dedicated a double issue to the twentieth anniversary of the establishment of the Soviet film industry. S. Eisenstein wrote "Gordost' (Pride), M. Chiaureli "Pered tret'em desiatiletiem" (Before the third decade), Eduard Tisse "Nezabyvaemye gody" (The unforgettable years), and V. Pudovkin wrote "Masterskaia Kuleshova" (Kuleshov's studio; all in No. 1/2, 1940).

For the duration of the war, between January 1942 and September 1945, *Iskusstvo kino* suspended publication.

After three years, in October 1945, the journal began its postwar life, as the official organ of the Soviet Ministry of Cinematography. Its first editorial, "Nashi blizhaishie zadachi" (Our immediate objectives), reiterated and underlined the cinema's role as a political propagandist of the reconstruction. Postwar issues stress the successes of the Soviet movie industry. Film scripts of war movies are published in their entirety, such as N. Virta's "Stalingradskaia bitva" (The battle of Stalingrad; No. 5, 1947). A permanent column, "Literaturnyi stsenarii" (Literary script), is dedicated to film scripts.

Extended excerpts from autobiographical works by Soviet directors and actors were published in the journal's "Memuary" (Memoirs) section, such as Ivan Pyr'ev's "O proidenom i perezhitom" (On past events and experiences; No. 7, 1970) and L. Anninskii's "Prostota istiny" (The simplicity of the truth; No. 10, 1970).

Keeping up with its primary objective to inform, interpret, and indoctrinate, the journal also publishes articles on foreign filmmakers. Sergei IUtkevich wrote "Kinematograf Robera Bressona" (Robert Bresson's movies; No. 3, 1979), Barbara Mruklih wrote "Chelovek truda na pol'skom ekrane" (The man of labor on the Polish screen; No. 6, 1979), and Nikolai Sovitskii wrote "Ob'iatiia Kuby" (The embraces of Cuba; No. 7, 1980).

National and international film festivals are periodically covered, as in V. Baskakov's "V ritme vremeni" (In rhythm with the time; No. 1, 1980), a detailed analysis of the 1979 Moscow Film Festival, and V. Ishimov's account of the East German Film Festival, "K epitsentru borby" (Toward the center of the struggle; No. 8, 1980).

Iskusstvo kino approaches the Soviet cinema biographically, socially, historically, thematically, and most of all politically. M. Zak's essay, "Literatura i rezhisser" (The literature and the film director; No. 7, 1980), discusses literary and film characters, plots, and thematic structures. The role of the movie actor as the educator of the masses is the topic of Mark Donskoi's article "Vospityvat' kommunisticheskogo cheloveka" (To educate the communist man; No. 10, 1980). History and cinema is the topic of V. Pashuto's "Kino i otechestvennaja istoriia" (The cinema and the history of the fatherland; No. 2, 1980). The journal also covers amateur filmmaking, books on film ("Kinigi o filme"), foreign cinematic events in "Za rubezhom" (Abroad), and occasionally films made for television.

Information Sources

INDEX SOURCES: FIAF International Index to Film Periodicals.
REPRINT EDITIONS: None.
LOCATION SOURCES: Library of Congress (incomplete); New York Public Library (incomplete); University of California at Berkeley (incomplete); University of Southern California (incomplete).

Publication History

MAGAZINE TITLE AND TITLE CHANGES: *Sovetskii Ekran* (January 1925–November 15, 1929); *Proletarskoe kino* (January1930–December 1932, with the first issue published under the title of *Kino-i-zhizn'*); *Sovetskoe kino* (January 1933–December 1935); *Iskusstvo kino* (January 1936 to present).
VOLUME AND ISSUE DATA: No. 1 (January 1925 to present), monthly. [Publication suspended January 1942–September 1945.]
PUBLISHER AND PLACE OF PUBLICATION: Soiuz kinematografistov SSSR, 125319 Moscow, A-319, U1. Usievich 9, USSR.
EDITOR: V. Pudovkin (January 1931–December 1936); K. Iakov (January 1937–May 1937); N. Semenov (January 1937–November 1938); A. IA. Mitlin (December 1938–December 1940); I. A. Pyr'ev (October 1945–January 1947); N.A. Lebedev (February 1947–December 1947); D. I. Eremin (January 1948–February 1951); V. N. Zhdan (March 1951–November 1956); L. P. Pogozheva (December 1956–April 1969); E. D. Surkov (May 1969 to present).

Hari S. Rorlich

J

JOLIE. See Appendix 1

THE JOLSON JOURNAL. See Appendix 1

THE JOURNAL OF POPULAR FILM. See THE JOURNAL
OF POPULAR FILM AND TELEVISION

THE JOURNAL OF POPULAR FILM AND TELEVISION

In the early seventies few books or periodicals approached the study of film
from a sociocultural perspective. *The Journal of Popular Film*, established in
the fall of 1971, sought to fill this gap, and in the premiere issue, dated Winter
1972, the editors explained that the new quarterly magazine would not ignore
"the unalterable fact that the box-office, the American public, has determined
the developmental thrust of its films." In the following issue they added that
popular films "are, first of all, artifacts and as such demand to be studied
culturally as do all artifacts."

The journal's founders were and are affiliated with Bowling Green State
University's Popular Culture Center in Ohio. Originally published by the Bowling
Green Popular Press, *The Journal of Popular Film* was listed for several years
as an official publication of the Popular Culture Association, though this designation is no longer carried.

Articles, customarily footnoted and illustrated with black and white photographs, run from twenty-five hundred to four thousand words. In keeping with

its interest in appealing to academics who have an interest but perhaps no formal training in film, the journal avoids jargon and adheres to no particular critical or theoretical attitude. Concentration is on commercial cinema and television with emphasis, as the masthead page tells us, on "stars, directors, producers, studios, networks, genres, series, and the audience." Some recent titles reflect this broad range: "Linkage: Pudovkin's Classics Revisited," "Triple X: Erotic Movies and Their Audiences," "Hitchcock's Forgotten Films: The Twenty Teleplays," and "Every Which Way But Lucid: The Critique of Authority in Clint Eastwood's Police Movies."

The journal also carries essays categorized as "Perspectives," which are generally shorter and more opinionated than articles. Review essays and original poetry on some aspect of film or television appear regularly. Letters to the editors are not published unless they are substantive or helpful in understanding or clarifying an issue. In such cases they appear under the title "Reader's Forum."

An especially useful feature carried in most issues is a bibliography, filmography, or checklist on a wide variety of subjects. Sample bibliographies include science fiction films of the fifties, popular Asian films, the serials, cold war films, blacks and Indians in American film, and film audience research. Filmographies have ranged from Vietnam and *film noir* to R-rated sexploitation films released during the seventies.

A number of articles which first appeared in *The Journal of Popular Film* led to books which have made the sociocultural approach to film study commonplace in the late seventies and early eighties. In the fifth anniversary issue, the editors noted that portions of Julian Smith's *Looking Away: Hollywood and Vietnam*, Garth Jowett's *Film: The Democratic Art*, Frank McConnell's *The Spoken Seen*, and Daniel Leab's *From Sambo to Superspade* had been first printed in *The Journal of Popular Film*.

A growing concern about the state of television criticism led the editors in 1979 to broaden the scope of the magazine and change the title to *The Journal of Popular Film and Television*. Readers were assured that the change was not meant to "merge" these two media but simply to widen critical attention "to include not only the movie theater but also the living room."

The most visible change in the journal came in 1980 when Heldref Publications replaced the Bowling Green Popular Press as publisher. Editorial control remained at Bowling Green, but decision making on layout, printing, and distribution shifted to Washington, D.C. Beginning with Vol. 8, No. 1 (Spring 1980), the size of the journal was changed from a 6" x 9" to an 8-1/2" x 11" format. This enlarged page size as well as financial considerations caused the average pages per issue to be reduced from 120 to 45 or 50.

The editors have honored superior scholarly writing through the Gish Award, named for Dorothy and Lillian Gish and given since 1976 "to the best critical work of American film history published in the *Journal of Popular Film and Television* in the previous year." Lillian Gish, a native Ohioan whose acting debut occurred near Bowling Green, serves on the journal's advisory board and has participated in the annual judging.

Unlike other periodicals, such as *American Film** or *Film Comment,** which also cover commercial films, *The Journal of Popular Film and Television* is an academic journal, scholarly yet readable; the eclectic nature of its content makes it useful to film and video students and teachers and appealing to film buffs as well as those teaching in fields other than film and television.

Information Sources

INDEX SOURCES: Abstracts of Popular Culture; America: History and Life; The Explicator; FIAF International Index to Film Periodicals; Film Literature Index; Historical Abstracts; Media Review Digest.

REPRINT EDITIONS: University Microfilms.

LOCATION SOURCES: Academy of Motion Picture Arts and Sciences; Auburn University; Emory University; Harvard University; Museum of Modern Art; New York Public Library; University of California at Los Angeles; University of Illinois; University of Massachusetts.

Publication History

MAGAZINE TITLE AND TITLE CHANGES: *The Journal of Popular Film* (1972–1978); *The Journal of Popular Film and Television* (1979 to present).

VOLUME AND ISSUE DATA: Vol. I, No. 1 (Winter 1972 to present), quarterly.

PUBLISHER AND PLACE OF PUBLICATION: Bowling Green University Popular Press, Bowling Green, Ohio 43403 (Vol. I, No. 1–Vol. VII, No. 4); Heldref Publications, 4000 Albemarle Street, N.W., Washington, D.C. 20016 (Vol. VIII, No. 1, to present).

EDITOR: Michael T. Marsden, John G. Nachbar, and Sam L. Grogg (1972–1975); Michael T. Marsden and John G. Nachbar (1975 to present).

Rick Shale

JOURNAL OF THE PRODUCERS GUILD OF AMERICA

For many years, the working producers of the Hollywood film industry watched in frustration as directors assumed greater importance in the eyes of critics and the public as the true creative forces behind successful motion pictures.

To counteract that trend, in 1950 a group of thirty-five highly successful and publicity-wise producers banded together to form the Screen Producers Guild. Among the founders were William Perlberg, its first president, Pandro Berman, Buddy Adler, Bryan Foy, Joseph Pasternak, Sol Siegel, and Jerry Wald. The new organization was not originally intended to be a union nor to act as a collective bargaining agency like the Screen Actors Guild, the Screen Directors Guild, and the Screen Writers Guild.

As a means of communicating with its members and with the rest of the industry, in 1952 the Screen Producers Guild commenced publication every other month of a four-page house organ called the *Screen Producers Guild Journal*. The format was undistinguished, an inexpensive amalgam of the two trade press dailies, *The Hollywood Reporter** and *Daily Variety**. The content was similar to articles which press agents frequently ghost-wrote for producers for the annual editions of these trade publications.

Those pieces were self-congratulatory and self-adulatory in which the producer put forth a point of view but then coyly illustrated it with examples from his own successful career. The journal also published news items about its members, and for two years members of the Guild took turns as editor, among them Samuel Marx, Frank Rosenberg, and Harriet Parsons, daughter of the famous Hollywood columnist, Louella Parsons.

Then in August 1954, a distinguished writer-director-producer and former associate of Orson Welles, John Houseman, took over the editorial duties. Houseman, a man of great taste and discrimination, set to work to upgrade the house organ into a publication of worth. He assigned graphic artist Saul Bass to design a new format for the cover page and reduce the size from 11″ x 8-½″ to 8-½″ x 5″. To distinguish it from its nondescript predecessor, the name was changed to *The Journal of the Screen Producers Guild* and it became a quarterly. When the guild became simply the Producers Guild in 1967, the title of the journal was similarly changed.

Under the perceptive leadership of Houseman and his successor, Jud Kinberg, the publication flourished and soon gained a measure of respect from the press and industry alike. *The New York Times* started quoting from its pages as the journal devoted each issue to single themes such as the marketing of films or the career of director-producer Cecil B. DeMille, winner of the Guild's prestigious Milestone Award. Outside writers like film critics Bosley Crowther of *The New York Times* and Arthur Knight of the *Saturday Review of Literature* were invited to contribute articles, and this enhanced the image and improved the quality of the publication.

Houseman and Kinberg had been volunteers, and the Guild's board of directors realized that the journal required a full-time paid editor to continue the new level of excellence which the magazine had achieved. In June 1959, they hired a veteran of both film production and motion picture journalism, Louis Greenspan, former writer for both *The Hollywood Reporter* and *Daily Variety*, a literate and forceful writer in his own right.

Within a year, Greenspan developed the successful format which would remain with the magazine until its final issue in June 1977. Because of its smaller size, the publication ran to between thirty and forty pages an issue. There were usually five, six, or seven articles by guest writers, followed by six or seven pages of concise but erudite book reviews by Greenspan. Occasionally, Greenspan would write lead editorials to introduce the themes of particular issues, which were usually headlined, "The Journal Looks At. . . . "

Among the many issues which the journal examined between June 1959 and June 1976 were overseas production, Hollywood's star system, films and education, film censorship around the world, college films and Hollywood, industry legal aspects, and the church's look at the new code.

And under Greenspan's guidance, the journal also took into recognition the importance of the role of the producer in television, for more and more members of the Guild were coming from the rank of television. By the time the journal ceased publication in 1977, the Guild had a membership of five hundred which received copies of the journal. In addition, three thousand copies were mailed free to members of the national and international press and to libraries and university film departments throughout the world.

Greenspan followed the splendid example of Houseman and Kinberg by inviting guest writers outside of the boundaries of Hollywood. Thus in his first issue, that of June 1959, dealing with pay T.V., his guest contributors included Dr. Frank Stanton, president of the Columbia Broadcasting System; Ralph Bellamy, president of Actors Equity; Jack Gould, television critic for *The New York Times*; Senator Warren Magnussen; and Congressmen Oren Harris and Emanuel Cellers.

In his next issue, Greenspan had guest articles by writers Rod Serling and Ray Bradbury, actor Kirk Douglas, director Mark Robson, producer Hal Wallis, and journalist Joe Hyams, interviewing William Faulkner on the novelist's experience as a Hollywood screenwriter.

A typical issue under Greenspan's editorial hand was the December 1967 journal which examined violence in films. It ran forty-eight pages, with ten pages of book reviews by Greenspan as well as an opening editorial by him. His twelve guest contributors included psychiatrist Frederic Wertham, British film censor John Trevelyan, motion picture exhibitor Sherril C. Corwin, film critics Judith Crist and Charles Champlin, network executive David Levy, screenwriter Malvin Wald, university professor G. William Jones, religious editor Rev. James M. Wall, publisher Jay Emanuel, director Arthur Penn, and producer Saul David.

For the next ten years, the journal maintained its policy of seeking contributions from the best minds in and out of show business. Sometimes these would be in the form of copies of lectures these individuals had given to groups, but mostly they were especially written for the journal. Some of the better-known individuals who so contributed to the journal were Maxwell Anderson, Bernard Baruch, Michael Blankfort, Niven Busch, Norman Cousins, Joan Crawford, Jules Dassin, Robert Gessner, George Gerbner, John Huston, Bishop Gerald Kennedy, Joseph Levine, Groucho Marx, Newton Minow, Edward R. Murrow, George Jean Nathan, Louis B. Mayer, Jean Renoir, Louis Nizer, Darryl Zanuck, Harry Reasoner, and Ronald Reagan.

In 1976, Greenspan became ill and could no longer devote his full energies toward securing new articles. To compensate, he began running reprints of articles from other publications or speeches made by prominent individuals in the area of communication. With the June 1977 issue, publication was ceased, but for almost a quarter of a century, it did an outstanding job of acquainting its readers with the changing tides of production in film and television and as such will remain a valuable resource for scholars doing research in the period of 1952 to 1977.

Information Sources

INDEX SOURCES: FIAF International Index to Film Periodicals; Film Literature Index; The New Film Index.

REPRINT EDITIONS: None.

LOCATION SOURCES: Academy of Motion Picture Arts and Sciences; New York Public Library; Producers Guild of America; University of Chicago; University of Illinois; University of Kansas; University of Southern California.

Publication History

MAGAZINE TITLE AND TITLE CHANGES: *Screen Producers Guild Journal* (1952–1954); *Journal of the Screen Producers Guild* (1954–1966); *Journal of the Producers Guild of America* (1967–1977).

VOLUME AND ISSUE DATA: *Screen Producers Guild Journal*, Vol. I, No. 1–Vol. II, No. 2 (April 1952–April 1954), bimonthly; *Journal of the Screen Producers Guild*, Vol. II, No. 3–Vol. VII, No. 1 (August 1954–March 1959), quarterly; *Journal of the Screen Producers Guild*, Vol. I, No. 1 (new numbering system)–Vol. VIII, No. 4 (June 1959–December 1966), quarterly; *Journal of the Producers Guild of America*, Vol. IX, No. 1–Vol. XIX, No. 2 (March 1967–June 1977), quarterly.

PUBLISHER AND PLACE OF PUBLICATION: Screen Producers Guild, 141 El Camino Drive, Beverly Hills, Calif. (1952–1966); Producers Guild of America, 141 El Camino Drive, Beverly Hills, Calif. (1967–1971); Producers Guild of America, 8201 Beverly Boulevard, Los Angeles, Calif. 90048 (1972–1977).

EDITOR: Samuel Marx and Maxwell Shane (Vol. I, No. 1); Frank P. Rosenberg (Vol. I, Nos. 2 and 3); Maxwell Shane (Vol. I, Nos. 4–8); Harriet Parsons (Vol. II, No. 1); John Houseman (Vol. II, No. 2–Vol. III, No. 4); Jud Kinberg (Vol. IV, No. 1–Vol. VI, No. 4); Arthur Freed (Vol. VII, No. 1); Lou Greenspan (Vol. I, No. 1 [new numbering system]–Vol. XIX, No. 2).

Malvin Wald

JOURNAL OF THE SCREEN PRODUCERS GUILD. See JOURNAL OF THE PRODUCERS GUILD OF AMERICA

JOURNAL OF THE SMPTE. See SMPTE JOURNAL

JOURNAL OF THE SOCIETY FOR EDUCATION IN FILMS AND TELEVISION. See SCREEN

JOURNAL OF THE SOCIETY OF CINEMATOLOGISTS.
See CINEMA JOURNAL

JOURNAL OF THE SOCIETY OF MOTION PICTURE AND TELEVISION ENGINEERS. See SMPTE JOURNAL

JOURNAL OF THE SOCIETY OF MOTION PICTUE ENGINEERS. See SMPTE JOURNAL

THE JOURNAL OF THE UNIVERSITY FILM AND VIDEO ASSOCIATION

Beginning in 1947 as notes of the University Film Producers Council, *The Journal of the University Film and Video Association* was at first no more than a mimeographed newsletter for an association of film producers on university campuses. As the scope and membership of the Council changed, so did the journal. In 1968 the Council became the University Film Association, and in 1982 it became the University Film and Video Association. The change of name represented the changing membership of the organization, as more and more teachers of film and film scholars became members.

Along with the changes in the composition of the association it represented, the journal underwent various name alterations and itself changed from a members' newsletter to a well-produced serious film periodical. Early issues are concerned with such topics as news from film production units on university campuses, lists of equipment necessary for such productions, discussions of how to work with a film laboratory, and the future of 16mm film.

During the sixties such topics as Nazi newsreels, film in British universities, and films and film training in Korea began to appear, reflecting the interests of the members who were more interested in film education and film scholarship than in film production.

By the mid-seventies, especially under the editorship of Timothy J. Lyons, the journal began publishing scholarly, even esoteric, articles on film theory, film history, and film and society. Although film education and film teaching were not ignored, articles on those topics appeared less frequently than before.

The policy of concentrating on only one topic per issue and the frequent use of guest editors have made the quality of the publication inconsistent, but the journal has contained many articles of interest to any student of film.

Information Sources

INDEX SOURCES: Abstracts in Popular Culture; Arts and Humanities Citation Index; FIAF International Index to Film Periodicals; Film Literature Index; The New Film Index.

REPRINT EDITIONS: University Microfilms.

LOCATION SOURCES: Academy of Motion Picture Arts and Sciences (1976 to present); Library of Congress (incomplete); University of Southern California.

Publication History

MAGAZINE TITLE AND TITLE CHANGES: *University Film Producers Council (Notes)* (August 17–21, 1947); *University Film Producers Association Journal* (March 1949–January 1950); *Journal of the University Producers Association* (April 1950– August 1952); *University Film Producers Association Journal* (Fall 1952–Spring 1953); *Journal of the University Film Producers Association* (Fall 1953–1967); *Journal of the University Film Association* (1968–Fall 1981); *The Journal of the University Film and Video Association* (Winter 1982 to present). [There is a lack of conformity as to whether the definite article is used in the title.]

VOLUME AND ISSUE DATA: No volume and issue numbers (August 17–21, 1947); Vol. I, No. 1 (March 1949); Vol. I, No. 2 (June 1949); Vol. I, No. 3 (January 1950); Vol. II, No. 1 (April 1950); Vol. II, No. 2 (July 1950); Vol. III, No. 1 (October 1950); Vol. III, No. 2 (January 1951); Vol. III, No. 3 (June 1951); Vol. IV, No. 1 (November 1951); Vol. IV, No. 2 (June 1952); Vol. IV, No. 3 (August 1952); Vol. V, No. 1 (Fall 1952); Vol. V, No. 2 (Winter 1953); Vol. V, No. 3 (Spring 1953); Vol. VI, No. 1 (Fall 1953 to present), quarterly.

PUBLISHER AND PLACE OF PUBLICATION: University Film Producers Council, no address listed (1947); University Film Producers Association, 123 College Place, Syracuse University, Syracuse 10, N.Y. (March 1949); University Film Producers Association, no address listed (June 1949–August 1952); University Film Producers Association, Audio-Visual Center, Syracuse University, Collendale at Lancaster Avenue, Syracuse 10, N.Y. (Fall 1952–Spring 1953); University Film Producers Association, Radio-Television-Film Program, State University of Iowa, Iowa City, Iowa (Fall 1953–Summer 1956); University Film Producers Association, Department of Photography, Ohio State University, Columbus, Ohio 43210 (Fall 1956–1968); University Film Association, Department of Photography and Cinema, Ohio State University, Columbus, Ohio 43210 (1968–1975); University Film Association, Department of Radio-Television-Film, Temple University, Philadelphia, Pa. 19122 (1975–Fall 1978); University Film Association, School of Communication, University of Houston, Houston, Texas 77004 (Winter 1979– Summer 1980); University Film Association, Department of Cinema and Photography, Southern Illinois University, Carbondale, Ill. 62901 (Fall 1980–Fall 1981); University Film and Video Association, Department of Cinema and Photography, Southern Illinois University, Carbondale, Ill. 62901 (Winter 1982–Fall 1982); University Film and Video Association, Rosary College, 7900 West Division Street, River Forest, Ill. 60305 (Winter 1983 to present).

EDITOR: No editor listed (1947); Luella Snyder (March 1949); no editor listed (June 1949–August 1952); Sol Dworkin (Fall 1952–Spring 1953); John Mercer (Fall

1953–Summer 1956); Robert W. Wagner (Fall 1956–1975); Robert W. Wagner and Timothy J. Lyons (Fall 1975); Timothy J. Lyons (Winter 1976–Fall 1982); Patricia Erens (Winter 1983 to present).

Timothy Johnson

JOURNAL OF THE UNIVERSITY FILM ASSOCIATION. See THE JOURNAL OF THE UNIVERSITY FILM AND VIDEO ASSOCIATION

JOURNAL OF THE UNIVERSITY FILM PRODUCERS ASSOCIATION. See THE JOURNAL OF THE UNIVERSITY FILM AND VIDEO ASSOCIATION

JOURNAL, SMPTE. See SMPTE JOURNAL

JUMP CUT: A REVIEW OF CONTEMPORARY CINEMA

Jump Cut is a politically radical film journal which has its roots in the turbulent activism of the sixties. First published in 1974, with offices in both Chicago and California, the magazine has offered a consistently challenging, if sometimes didactic, alternative to the world of mainstream film criticism. Writing in *Jump Cut*'s debut issue, its founding coeditors John Hess and Chuck Kleinhaus state:

> Jump Cut is committed to presenting and developing film criticism which recognizes theories often unfamiliar to Americans, such as structuralism, semiology and Marxism.... We stand for a political film criticism because understanding film has meaning only when we are also trying to change the world.[1]

During its ten-year history, the magazine has adhered closely to this declaration of intent and editorial policy, offering a wide range of subjects and balancing its criticism of Hollywood films with discussions of Third World and alternative cinema. Its premiere issue contained reviews of films as diverse as *Sleeper* and *Reed: Insurgent Mexico*, as well as articles on the future of video and a reexamination of the auteur theory. Twenty-eight issues later, in May/June of 1983, a feminist evaluation of *Tootsie* appeared in its pages alongside an article on filmmaking in Mozambique. This broad spectrum of topics and the magazine's clearly articulated framework for film analysis reflect *Jump Cut*'s dedication to the concept of art as a force for political and social change.

Jump Cut's focal interest in film as both a reflection of, and a force within, the society around it has led the publication to devote frequent "Special Sections" to lengthy, in-depth considerations of such subjects as "Gays and Film" (No. 16), "Revolutionary Cuban Cinema" (Nos. 19, 20 and 22), and "Film and Feminism in Germany Today" (No. 27). Its discussion of more traditional Hollywood fare has included such provocative articles as Charles Eckert's "Shirley Temple and the House of Rockefeller" (No. 2) and Robert Entman and Frances Seymour's review, "Close Encounters with the Third Reich" (No. 18). The magazine has also provided coverage of feminist, independent, and minority-group film festivals and conferences, as well as chronicling the emergence of Third World cinematic movements such as the Brazilian Cinema Novo.

Jump Cut has attracted a number of well-known contributors in its relatively short history, among them Gerald Peary, Patricia Erens, James Monaco, and Joan Mellen, and its format includes an informal, frequently humorous description of each issue's writers. Once planned as a bimonthly publication, the magazine upgraded its paper quality in 1977 and has expanded to three times its original length. In recent years, however, *Jump Cut* has published somewhat sporadically, with two issues appearing in 1981 and only one in 1982.

Notes

1. "The Last Word," No. 1, May/June 1974, p. 28.

Information Sources

INDEX SOURCES: Alternative Press Index; FIAF International Index to Film Periodicals; Film Literature Index.
REPRINT EDITIONS: University Microfilms.
LOCATION SOURCES: Academy of Motion Picture Arts and Sciences; University of California at Los Angeles; University of Illinois; University of Oregon; University of Texas at Austin; Yale University.

Publication History

MAGAZINE TITLE AND TITLE CHANGES: *Jump Cut: A Review of Contemporary Cinema*.
VOLUME AND ISSUE DATA: Nos. 1–6 (May/June 1974–March/April 1975), bimonthly; Nos. 7–9 (May/July 1975–October/December 1975), quarterly; Nos. 10/11–19 (June 1976–December 1978), two or three times a year; Nos. 20–26 (May 1979–December 1981), biannual; No. 27 (July 1982 to present), annual.
PUBLISHER AND PLACE OF PUBLICATION: Jump Cut Associates, 122 Myrtle, Cotati, Calif. 94928 (Nos. 1–2); Jump Cut Associates, 2012 Channing Way, Berkeley, Calif. 94704 (Nos. 3–5); P.O. Box 865, Berkeley, Calif. 94701 (No. 6 to present).
EDITOR: John Hess and Chuck Kleinhaus (1974–1979); John Hess, Chuck Kleinhaus, and Julia Lesage (1979 to present).

Janet E. Lorenz

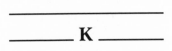

KALEIDOSCOPE

A small-format, film-buff-oriented publication, *Kaleidoscope* began publication in Autumn 1962 with an initial circulation of five hundred, rising to approximately one thousand at its demise. It has the dubious distinction of probably holding the record for delay in publication of its second issue, with a three-year gap between No. 1 and No. 2. In fact, *Kaleidoscope* parallels the life of its editor from high school senior to college student. What makes *Kaleidoscope* useful is the series of interviews which it published, with Buster Crabbe (Vol. 2, No. 2), Gregory Peck and Peter Falk (Vol. 2, No. 3), and Karl Malden (Vol. 3, No. 1).[1] The articles were always well written, and one can see that Don Shay was developing into the fine editor he was to become with the creation of *Cinefex** some years later.

Notes

1. These interviews were subsequently gathered into book form by Don Shay under the title of *Conversations* (Albuquerque, N. Mex.: Kaleidoscope Press, 1969).

Information Sources

INDEX SOURCES: None.
REPRINT EDITIONS: None.
LOCATION SOURCES: Academy of Motion Picture Arts and Sciences (incomplete).

Publication History

MAGAZINE TITLE AND TITLE CHANGES: *Kaleidoscope*.
VOLUME AND ISSUE DATA: Vol. 1, No. 1 (September 1962); Vol. II, No. 1 (1965); Vol. II, No. 2 (1966); Vol. II, No. 3 (1967); Vol. III, No. 1 (1967).
PUBLISHER AND PLACE OF PUBLICATION: Kaleidoscope, 8 Wintergreen Avenue,

MD15, Newburgh, N.Y. (Vol. I, No. 1); Kaleidoscope, 95 Dearborn Street, East Longmeadow, Mass. 01028 (Vol. II, No. 1–Vol. III, No. 1).
EDITOR: Don Shay (Vol. I, No. 1); Don Shay and Ray Cabana, Jr. (Vol. II, No. 1–Vol. III, No. 1).

Anthony Slide

KALEM KALENDAR. See Appendix 3

KINEMATOGRAPH AND LANTERN WEEKLY. See KINEMATOGRAPH WEEKLY

KINEMATOGRAPH WEEKLY

For anyone wishing to research the history of the British film industry, the pages of the *Kinematograph Weekly* are in themselves vital source material. The origins of *"Kine"* are to be found in *Optical Magic Lantern Journal and Photographic Enlarger*, which first appeared on June 15, 1889. In November 1904, the name was changed to the *Optical Lantern and Cinematograph Journal*, appearing monthly. Then, in May 1907, it became the *Kinematograph and Lantern Weekly*. The decision to publish weekly was one of great daring when it is realized that at this time there was not a single kinema theatre in London, there were no films over one thousand feet in length, and the chief users of film were fairgrounds showmen, many of whom were unable to read. However, as the industry grew, so did the *Kine*—from 16 pages in May 1907 to 218 pages by May 1917. During the twenties, by which time the magazine was entitled *Kinematograph Weekly*, it was published in competition with three other major trade papers, but, without question, *Kine* was the top one in prestige and net paid sales. When its rival, *The Bioscope*,* went into liquidation in 1932, it was merged by Odhams Press into the *Kine*.

But, unlike *The Bioscope*, which fully foresaw the significance, *Kine* made a major error of judgment on the question of sound. It reviewed *The Jazz Singer* somewhat patronizingly, completely overlooking the fact that here was a revolutionary technical development. *Kine*, however, was not caught out again, and coverage of later developments such as ratios and stereoscopy was excellent, often with special supplements.

And so until September 1971, *Kine* continued to cover all aspects of the British film industry—legislation affecting the industry, the "quota" system, news of company personnel, photographic coverage of opening nights, production reports, film reviews, box-office business, activities of film organizations, and a television column appeared.

Kine's high standards and reputation continued until the very end, when, in

1971, IPC Specialist Press received an offer from British and American Film Holdings that it was unable to refuse. Largely due to falling advertising revenue, the magazine, in commercial terms, was no longer making sufficient financial return. So despite the great affection with which it was held, the paper was merged into *Today's Cinema*, making that publication Britain's one remaining trade paper.

From 1955 to the end of publication, the editor was Bill Altria. Altria joined Odhams Press in 1928, working where required on various of their leisure magazines and joining the staff of *Kine* the following year. This came about as the result of a tragic accident. Copies of *Kine* were being flown to Yarmouth for the Cinematograph Exhibitors' Association Conference when the plane crashed and two of the *Kine* staff were killed. Altria was appointed as the replacement editorial assistant. He was to remain with *Kine* until its end. Although lacking in the charisma of some of the previous editors, Altria's strength was his enormous technical background and wide comprehension of the film industry. In his final editorial he was to write, "It has been a satisfying experience helping to write a substantial part of the history of the film industry in the U.K. And contributing in some measure to the influence that the Kine has brought to bear in shaping policies."

Information Sources

INDEX SOURCES: None. [Film-review references are contained in the British Film Institute Film Title Index 1908–1978, available on microfilm from World Microfilms.]

REPRINT EDITIONS: World Microfilms.

LOCATION SOURCES: Library of Congress (incomplete); New York Public Library (incomplete). [British Film Institute has an almost complete run up to 1929 and a complete run of 1933–1971.]

Publication History

MAGAZINE TITLE AND TITLE CHANGES: *Optical Magic Lantern Journal and Photographic Enlarger* (June 15, 1889–October 1904); *Optical Lantern and Cinematograph Journal* (November 1904–April 1907); *Kinematograph and Lantern Weekly* (May 16, 1907–November 27, 1919); *Kinematograph Weekly* (abbreviated to *Kine Weekly* on cover; December 4, 1919–September 25, 1971).

VOLUME AND ISSUE DATA: Vol. I, No. 1–Vol. DCLI, No. 3,337 (May 16, 1907– September 25, 1971), weekly.

PUBLISHER AND PLACE OF PUBLICATION: E. T. Heron & Co., 9 & 11 Tottenham Street, London W., England (May 16, 1907–May 10, 1917); Odhams Ltd., 93 Long Acre, London W.C.2, and 189 High Holborn, London W.C.1, England (May 17, 1917–March 1962); Longacre Press, 161 Fleet Street, London E.C.4, England (April 1962–April 1970); IPC Specialist Press, 161 Fleet Street, London E.C.4, England (May 1970–September 1971).

EDITOR: Theodore Brown (May 1907–June 1908); no editor listed (July 1908–1911); Low Warren (1912–May 1917); no editor listed (June 1917–1918); Frank Tilley (1918–1924); Bruce Allan (November 1925–December 16, 1926); S. G. Rayment

(December 23, 1926–February 8, 1945); Connery Chappell (Acting Editor, February 15, 1945–January 24, 1946); A. L. Carter and Connery Chappell (January 31, 1946–July 29, 1948); Bill Altria (June 30, 1955–September 25, 1971).

Pat Coward

KINE WEEKLY. See KINEMATOGRAPH WEEKLY

KINO (Bulgaria). See KINOIZKUSTVO

KINO (Poland)

Kino was founded in 1966 and is one of Poland's most prestigious publications on film and film culture. The journal's editorial board includes well-known filmmakers, critics, writers, actors, and literary critics such as Jerzy Kawalerowicz, Henryk Kluba, Jerzy Passendorfer, Andrzej Wajda, Witold Zalewski. Because of its coverage of a wide range of cinematic topics such as film theory, national and international cinema, interviews, and book and film reviews, *Kino* is popular with both the average spectator and film professionals.

As done by many of its East European counterparts, *Kino* features the mandatory editorial which aims to be a systematic discussion of the Marxist ideology as applied to filmmaking and the spokesman for the official modes of cinematic expression. Nevertheless, the Polish journal has acquired a solid reputation for being an open forum for ideological controversy missing in other similar East European publications.

The awareness of a free critical tradition makes *Kino* the most immediately accessible and attractive reading. It promotes a systematic comprehension of the aesthetic trends of the Polish cinema as seen in Andrzej Werner's "Z dalszej perspektywy" (From a distant perspective; Vol. 9, No. 1), Edward Szynal's "Forma a tworzywo filmowe" (The form and the creation of the film; Vol. 9, No. 9), and in Tadeus Lubelski's "Wędrówki realne i wyobrazone" (Real and imaginary excursions; Vol. 15, No. 1). The cinematic style of contemporary films is discussed in "Sprobujmy skreślić styl. . ." (Let's try to define the style), an ample two-part article published in two consecutive issues (Vol. 14, Nos. 7–8).

One of *Kino*'s goals is to establish and develop a systematic study of the past and present of the Polish cinema. Film and literary critics are given the opportunity to express their views on the various stages of the development of the Polish film industry. Keeping up with the journal's task, B. Michalek wrote on "Duch filmoteczny" (The spirit of the cinematique; Vol. 15, No. 6), M. Gulczyński wrote "Kino odmowy moralnej" (The cinema of a renewed morality;

Vol. 15, No. 7), and Marek Halborda wrote "Polskie filmy made of Paramount" (Polish movies made at Paramount; Vol. 17, No. 5).

The editorial staff consistently seeks to promote the "peaceful" confrontation of Eastern and Western cultures by the coverage given to various national and international film festivals, as seen in D. Stamborska's "Międzynarodowe festiwale filmów" (International film festivals; Vol. 15, No. 2) and in J. Plazewski's "Pod znakiem lwów—Wenecja '80" (Under the sign of the lions—Venice '80; Vol. 15, No. 12).

Kino has constantly encouraged the young generation of scriptwriters, filmmakers, and film critics by publishing their scripts, articles, and essays, thus asserting their place and their contribution to the contemporary Polish cinema. Examples include the round-table discussion "Mloda proza i film" (The young prose and the film; Vol. 11, No. 4), Aleksander Jackiewicz's portrait of the young actor Jerzy Stuhr in "Stuhr" (Vol. 14, No. 7), and Pawel Kędzierski's script "Na smyczy" (On leash; Vol. 16, No. 12).

The journal concerns itself with the foreign film productions by defining them biographically, socially, historically, and thematically. Zbigniew Czeczat-Gawrak wrote on "Rebelianckie początki teorii filmu w USA" (The rebellious beginnings of film theory in the USA; Vol. 11, No. 1), Bogumil Drozdowski wrote "Solaris" (Vol. 7, No. 3), and in the same issue, Alicja Helman wrote on Fellini's films "Fellini czyli film to ja" (Fellini—the film and I).

Foreign movies are also covered in "Kto? Co? Gdzie?" (Who? What? Where?), a column containing presentations of film credits as well as the date and place of their first public screenings. Under the headings "Aktorzy znani i nieznani" (Known and unknown actors) and "Ksiązki o filme" (Books on film), the journal's book review section in each issue features portraits of Polish and foreign actors as well as extensive book reviews. Reviews of Polish films are published in each issue under the generic title "Filmy, ktore widzielismy" (Movies we have seen). *Kino* has a brief summary in French and English and an annual index.

Information Sources

INDEX SOURCES: FIAF International Index to Film Periodicals.
REPRINT EDITIONS: None.
LOCATION SOURCES: Library of Congress; University of Southern California (incomplete).

Publication History

MAGAZINE TITLE AND TITLE CHANGES: *Kino—Miesięcznik Poświęcony Twórczosci i Kulturze Filmowej* (A monthly dedicated to creativity and film culture).
VOLUME AND ISSUE DATA: Vol. I, No. 1 (?, 1966 to present), monthly.
PUBLISHER AND PLACE OF PUBLICATION: Kino, 00-058, Warszawa, ul. Kredytowa 5/7, Poland.

EDITOR: Editor prior to 1973 unknown; Ryszard Koniczek (1973–April 1979); Janusz
Skwara (May 1979–May 1980); Leslaw Bajer (June 1980–February 1983); Stan-
isław Kuszewski (March 1983 to present).

Hari S. Rorlich

KINO I FOTO. See KINOIZKUSTVO

KINO-I-ZHIZN'. See ISKUSSTVO KINO

KINOIZKUSTVO

Since its beginnings in 1945 under the title of *Kino i foto*, *Kinoizkustvo* has
been a good example of the ''customary'' relation between arts in general, that
of cinema in particular, and Marxist ideology. The task of this Bulgarian journal
is to interpret films, to tell the spectator-reader what they mean, and make explicit
the existence or lack of political message of any given movie. The journal's
editorial staff shows a strong predilection for the Soviet cinematography and its
films, directors, actors, and critics.

Kinoizkustvo's readers are permanently reminded that ''socialist realism'' is
the official and only state aesthetic. In comparison with other East European
film publications, *Kinoizkustvo* still gives very little coverage to Western or
American cinematography. ''The decadent capitalistic'' film industry had and
still has very little appeal for the editorial board.

In its early years of publication, articles such as ''Frantsiia, koiato se bori''
(France, the fighting country) by Boris Milev (Vol. 5, No. 7) and H. Kirkov's
''I Veliko-britaniia pod kholivudska peta'' (Great Britain under Hollywood's
foot; Vol. 5, No. 8) were nothing but ideologically dictated attacks on the
''vagueness of messages'' and the ''morbidity of the decadent Western movies.''
Lately, however, the critical coverage was replaced by a positive permissiveness
though a bland presentation of Western films, as in G. Angelov's interview with
David Stratton, director of the Sydney Film Festival, in ''Deivid Stratton'' (Vol.
34, No. 12). Materials dedicated to the Soviet film and filmmakers prevail,
however, as seen in the ample editorial, ''30 godiny S″vetska kinematografiia''
(30 years of Soviet cinema; Vol. 10, No. 3) and Pantelej Matveev's ''Mnogon-
atsionalnata s″vetska kinematografiia'' (Multinational Soviet cinematography) in
the same issue, as well as in D. Ivanova's ''Kino leninianata tradicii, razdasti
novatorstvo'' (The Leninist traditions of the cinema lead to innovation; Vol. 35,
No. 4).

Feature articles by Soviet film critics and directors regularly appear. In one
of its first issues (Vol. 5, No. 5) Aleksandr Shein wrote ''Pisateliat i kinoto''
(The writer and the cinema), G. Eizenberg wrote ''Neizpolzuvani rezervi'' (Un-

used resources), and Nikolai Cherkasov contributed "Mir za tseliia sviiat" (Peace to the entire world). Soviet-Bulgarian cooperation is covered by Mikhail Manev in "B″lgaro-s″vetska druzhba chrez kinoto" (The cinema as the basis for the Bulgarian/Soviet friendship; Vol. 10, No. 3), by S. Ivanova in "Tashkent '80" (Vol. 35, No. 8), and by A. Tihov's "Tvorceski obmen na idei i informaciia" (Creative exchange of ideas and information; Vol. 35, No. 7).

West European film festivals are analyzed from the viewpoint of socialist ideology, as seen in I. Znepolski's "Kan '80—tendenciite v s″vremennoto kino, taka, kakto gi vizda festival" (Cannes '80—trends in the contemporary cinema as shown at the festival; Vol. 35, No. 9).

Under the permanent heading "Kinokritika" are published articles on film theory and criticism, as in St. Stanchev's "Neobkhodimi izvodi za kinokritikata" (The necessity for film criticism; Vol. 5, No. 4), Al. Zharonov's "Kinokhudozhnik″t v igralniia film" (The artist in the feature film; Vol. 5, No. 6), and K. Apostolova's "Otkravenicata na kinokritika" (The sincerity of film criticism; Vol. 35, No. 9). In addition, *Kinoizkustvo* publishes book reviews, short reviews of new Bulgarian films, editorials on national film festivals, and under the heading "Kinoinformatsiia" periodical information on film production in other East European countries.

The journal has an annual index and infrequently a table of contents in Russian, French, and English.

Information Sources

INDEX SOURCES: FIAF International Index to Film Periodicals.
REPRINT EDITIONS: None.
LOCATION SOURCES: University of Southern California (incomplete).

Publication History

MAGAZINE TITLE AND TITLE CHANGES: *Kino i foto* (1945–1952); *Kino* (1952–1954); *Kinoizkustvo* (1955 to present).
VOLUME AND ISSUE DATA: Vol. I, No. 1–Vol. V, No. 4 (Autumn 1945–Spring 1950), bimonthly; Vol. V, No. 5 (Spring 1950 to present), monthly.
PUBLISHER AND PLACE OF PUBLICATION: Kinoizkustvo, Organ na Ministerstvo na prosvetata i kulturata, na suyouza na kinodeitsite i suyouza na bulgarskite pisateli, ul. Angel K'ncev, 5 Sofia, Bulgaria.
EDITOR: Stefan Stanchev (1945–1953); Kiril Voinov (1953–1954); Iako Molkhov (1954–1963); Khristo Santov (October 1963–April 1964); Emil Petrov (May 1964 to present).

Hari S. Rorlich

KOSMORAMA

Kosmorama is published by the Danish Film Museum, and it is the oldest, largest, and most authoritative of several Danish film periodicals. Starting on a modest scale in October 1954 with a twelve-page issue, the magazine appeared nine times a year during its first five years. It was the creation of Erik Ulrichsen, who was the most enthusiastic, intelligent, and sensitive Danish film critic at that time. He was inspired by British critics such as Gavin Lambert and Lindsay Anderson and the magazine *Sequence*.* The first editorial was titled "There Is a Need for Us," and it was Ulrichsen's aim to make *Kosmorama* a serious and critical alternative to the rather poor standard of film criticism in the daily Danish newspapers. In the beginning *Kosmorama* was considered a controversial magazine, constantly accused of elitism and sectarian points of view. *Kosmorama*'s policy was and has always been to consider the cinema as an art form, and the stress has been on critical, aesthetic, and historical matters.

The first year saw a special issue on fifty years of Danish cinema. Ten writers studied individual five-year periods, and this issue stirred a lot of controversy and was heavily attacked by the older, better-established critics. But *Kosmorama* grew steadily. From issue No. 19, it adopted a color cover, and the third volume (1956–1957) contained two hundred pages. With the sixth volume (1959–1960), *Kosmorama* became a quarterly. When Erik Ulrichsen left the magazine in 1960, Ib Monty took over as editor in chief (with issue No. 50). From 1965 onward *Kosmorama* was extended to five issues per year and the number of pages was increased. Finally, in October 1967, *Kosmorama* underwent its biggest change when a new, large format was introduced. It was published six times a year, and Ib Monty was replaced as editor-in-chief by Øystein Hjort. In November 1969 Martin Drouzy took over, and from October 1972 Per Calum has been the editor-in-chief and at which time *Kosmorama* adopted its present format. Since 1975 *Kosmorama* again has been a quarterly. In 1984 Jan Kornum Larsen became editor-in-chief.

Kosmorama has always been an internationally oriented magazine, with a special affection for American cinema. Apart from articles on Carl Th. Dreyer, Benjamin Christensen, and Asta Nielsen, the Danish cinema did not play an important role in the magazine's first years. But from the sixties, when a new Danish cinema emerged, Danish films and filmmakers have been thoroughly analyzed in articles and interviews. Danish critics have comprised the main contributors to *Kosmorama*, but prominent foreign writers on film have also occasionally contributed original material; Lotte H. Eisner has written on Asta Nielsen, Colin Young on "The New American Cinema," Donald Richie on Japanese film, and Gösta Werner and Rune Waldekranz on Scandinavian films.

Each of the first eighty issues contained a complete filmography of a Danish or foreign filmmaker. From January 1975 through June 1979, *Kosmorama* published extensive credits for all films shown in Denmark, but since 1979 these credits have been published in a yearly volume titled *The Film Season*.

In its 1983 survey of the world's leading film periodicals, *The International Film Guide* describes *Kosmorama* as "perhaps the most attractive of the Nordic movie magazines, with particularly splendid emphasis on large photos."

Information Sources

INDEX SOURCES: FIAF International Index to Film Periodicals.
REPRINT EDITIONS: World Microfilms.
LOCATION SOURCES: Library of Congress; New York Public Library.

Publication History

MAGAZINE TITLE AND TITLE CHANGES: *Kosmorama*.
VOLUME AND ISSUE DATA: Vols. I–V (1954–1959), nine times a year; Vols. VI–X (1959–1964), quarterly; Vols. XI–XIII (1965–1967), five times a year; Vols. XIV–XXII (1967–1975), six times a year; Vol. XXIII (1976 to present), quarterly.
PUBLISHER AND PLACE OF PUBLICATION: Det Danske Filmmuseum, St. Søndervoldstraede, 1419 Copenhagen K, Denmark.
EDITOR: Erik Ulrichsen (1954–1960); Ib Monty (1960–1967); Øystein Hjort (1967–1969); Martin Drouzy (1969–1972); Per Calum (1972–1984); Jan Kornum Larsen (1984 to present).

Ib Monty

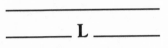

LIMELIGHT

Published from late 1959 through 1961, *Limelight* was a typical film trade paper, featuring lengthy film reviews, news items, and so on, but also including a gossip column by Florabel Muir and four biographies of film personalities as a regular feature on page three of each issue. Television reviews were also included, and eventually the paper added samplings of reviews from New York newspapers, as well as a record and Las Vegas section.

Information Sources

INDEX SOURCES: None.
REPRINT EDITIONS: None.
LOCATION SOURCES: Academy of Motion Picture Arts and Sciences.

Publication History

MAGAZINE TITLE AND TITLE CHANGES: *Limelight*.
VOLUME AND ISSUE DATA: Vol. I, No. 1–Vol. III, No. 50 (November 19, 1959–December 14, 1961), weekly. [Date of last issue unconfirmed.]
PUBLISHER AND PLACE OF PUBLICATION: Paul K. Devoe, 6331 Hollywood Boulevard, Hollywood 28, Calif.
EDITOR: Len Simpson.

Anthony Slide

LIMELIGHT ON LIZA. See Appendix 1

THE LION'S ROAR. See Appendix 3

LITERATURE/FILM QUARTERLY

In January 1973 *Literature/Film Quarterly*, supported by a small subsidy from Salisbury State College in Maryland, commenced publication. Conceived by editors Thomas L. Erskine and James M. Welsh as a forum for the scholarly discussion of film, the journal quickly established a place for itself, attaining a list of approximately five hundred subscribers by the end of its second year of existence. Despite great increases in publication costs, which caused a reduction in size from ninety-six to sixty-eight pages per issue, and competition from a number of better-funded journals appearing with film's entry into the mainstream of academic study, *Literature/Film Quarterly* has managed to maintain its readership and its place as a major voice in scholarly film criticism.

Despite its title, the journal has never limited its scope to examinations of the interrelationships of film and literature. While its first issue was devoted to the detailed examination of screen adaptations of D. H. Lawrence's fiction and subsequent issues have taken a similar focus on the work of authors like Graham Greene, Thomas Hardy, and Shakespeare, *Literature/Film Quarterly* has from its inception marked off a much broader field for its investigations. Besides analyses of literary adaptations, the journal's editors have invited contributions dealing with film style and theory, examinations of individual films, studies on the role of the screenwriter and on distinctly cinematic characteristics in an author's work, film reviews, interviews with those in the film industry, and reviews of significant film literature. A typical issue contains seven or eight articles and interviews, and two or three review pieces. A short "Notes and Queries" feature, offering current news of interest to film scholars, was replaced after Vol. 7, No. 2, with a regular editorial page, serving a similar function and also noting recent books by contributors.

While a consistent strength of the journal is its typical collection of detailed discussions of diverse films, *Literature/Film Quarterly* has regularly devoted entire numbers to in-depth treatments of specific film topics. In addition to the previously mentioned issues on D. H. Lawrence (Vol. 1, No. 1) and Graham Greene (Vol. 2, No. 4), the journal has now published three numbers dealing with Shakespeare on film (Vol. 1, No. 4; Vol. 4, No. 2; Vol. 5, No. 4), in addition to issues devoted to the "New German Cinema" (Vol. 7, No. 3), European directors (Vol. 8, No. 2) and genre and theory (Vol. 8, No. 3). The issue on *das neue Kino*, including an overview of the movement by guest editor Charles Eidsvik and analyses of the major German films and directors, has attracted special attention, with the editor of a British film journal lauding it as "the first extensive coverage of its kind on a subject that has been surrounded with a great deal of echo and rumor and little substantial research."[1] This sort of praise, however, seems applicable to most of the other special issues as well, but especially those on Lawrence and Greene which provided the first comprehensive analyses of the various ways in which these authors' works have been transposed to the screen.

In addition to its usual critical essays, *Literature/Film Quarterly* has regularly published important source material for film scholarship. This material takes the form of primary sources, such as interviews with directors, screenwriters, and others, and of reference tools, such as bibliographies. Among the many directors who have been interviewed in the journal are William Friedkin (Vol. 3, No. 4), Billy Wilder (Vol. 4, No. 1), Andre Wajda (Vol. 5, No. 1), John Schlesinger (Vol. 5, No. 2; Vol. 6, No. 2), Marcel Ophuls (Vol. 6, No. 1), Robert Wise (Vol. 6, No. 4), Louis Malle (Vol. 7, No. 2), Frank Capra (Vol. 9, No. 3), Peter Weir (Vol. 9, No. 4), and René Clair (Vol. 10, No. 2). Ulrich Wicks compiled a lengthy bibliography on the relationship between literature and film for Vol. 6, No. 2, and Richard Lindell has contributed an updated supplement to this list in a later issue (Vol. 8, No. 4). A feature of several of the special numbers has been an extensive bibliography, such as the one covering the literature about Shakespeare on film included in Vol. 5, No. 4. A valuable addition to the Graham Greene number is a listing of the author's uncollected film writings.

One note of confusion has seemed to mark *Literature/Film Quarterly* from its earliest years; as the masthead reflects, the editorial board has undergone frequent and considerable revision. Originally, Erskine served as the journal's editor, and he was assisted by Professors Welsh and Gerald R. Barrett as associates, as well as an advisory board composed of established film scholars, representatives of the Motion Picture Division of the Library of Congress, the American Film Institute, and writer-director Dalton Trumbo. With Vol. 3, No. 3, in a move designed to reflect more nearly the true distribution of labor, Erskine and Welsh began sharing the editor's position. However, by Vol. 5, No. 3, the editorial structure became muddled once more, with the creation of two associate editor positions and the formation of a group of contributing editors, working along with the advisory board. Only recently have the editorial responsibilities been clarified and the proliferation of positions ended. In an effort "to indicate more accurately those editors who are actually doing some of our work,"[2] the editors deleted the associate position and the advisory board—which had become, they admit, "increasingly cosmetic"—substituting an expanded list of contributing editors, which represents those who do much of the evaluation of manuscripts for the journal.

Even with these shifts in the editorial structure, it should be noted, *Literature/Film Quarterly* has consistently maintained a standard of thorough scholarship and high readability. In general, the journal has a decidedly academic flavor, as it usually prints the academic affiliations of its contributors in each issue's table of contents and requires proper documentation for each article. The latter standard especially, however, represents a welcomed and valuable change from the rather breezy and often frustratingly allusive approach which characterizes many popular film periodicals. James Welsh admits that his journal is "not trendy, nor...especially political",[3] and it seems clear that *Literature/Film Quarterly* subscribes to no specific or limiting critical bias, such as the structuralist policy which informs *Screen** in England or the political stance of the Canadian journal

Cine-Tracts. Rather, the articles printed in the journal demonstrate a broad spectrum of theories and methodologies, fully representing the variety of critical activity which characterizes current film study. A single issue, such as the genre and theory number, can therefore range from a discussion of phenomenology and the horror film, to a comparison of the work of Chaplin and Bertolt Brecht, to a discussion of psychology and the "filmic dream." What such articles generally share is a commendable freedom from cant and current critical jargon, coupled with an emphasis on clarity of style and presentation. This combination makes *Literature/Film Quarterly*'s articles consistently among the most accessible in contemporary film criticism.

Its unwavering standard of scholarship, openness to a variety of critical approaches, and a quality of readability continue to distinguish *Literature/Film Quarterly* from a number of journals which, often with much larger subsidies and staffs, have attempted to follow its pattern. Working from their modest resources, often even doing their own typesetting,[4] the journal's editors have managed to build up a circulation of over seven hundred, approximately half of these subscriptions going to the major academic libraries in the United States; they have achieved a distribution that reaches to over twenty-five foreign countries; and they have obtained inclusion in a number of the most important national and international indexes. As a result, they have established for *Literature/Film Quarterly* a solid and respected place in the field of film scholarship.

Notes

1. Donald Ranvaud, "Periodicals," *Framework*, No. 12, 1981, p. 48.

2. "Editorial Changes: The South Will Rise," *Literature/Film Quarterly*, Vol. X, No. 1, 1982, p. 24.

3. "Editorial: Our First Ten Years," *Literature/Film Quarterly*, Vol. X, No. 1, 1982, p. 2.

4. See James Welsh's summary of the problems involved in producing *Literature/Film Quarterly* during the first ten years of its existence in his essay, "Periodical Frustrations," *AFI Education Newsletter*, Vol. VI, No. 2, 1982, p. 2.

Information Sources

INDEX SOURCES: Abstracts of English Studies; Annual Bibliography of English Language and Literature; The Critical Index; FIAF International Index to Film Periodicals; Film Literature Index; The Humanities Index; PMLA International Bibliography.

REPRINT EDITIONS: University Microfilms.

LOCATION SOURCES: Academy of Motion Picture Arts and Sciences; Chicago Public Library; Harvard University; Los Angeles Public Library; Museum of Modern Art; New York Public Library; Purdue University; University of California at Berkeley; University of California at Los Angeles; University of Chicago; University of Illinois; University of Iowa; University of Texas; Yale University.

Publication History

MAGAZINE TITLE AND TITLE CHANGES: *Literature/Film Quarterly*.
VOLUME AND ISSUE DATA: Vol. I, No. 1 (January 1973 to present), quarterly.
PUBLISHER AND PLACE OF PUBLICATION: Salisbury State College, Salisbury, Md.
     21801.
EDITOR: Thomas L. Erskine and James M. Welsh.

J. P. Telotte

LOWBROW CINEMA. See Appendix 2

THE LUBIN BULLETIN. See Appendix 3

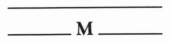

M

MAC/EDDY TODAY. See Appendix 1

MACK SENNETT WEEKLY. See Appendix 3

THE MAGAZINE

Published by the now-defunct Los Angeles Film and Television Study Center, *The Magazine*'s chief function was to report on the activities of the Center's members, notably the American Film Institute, the Academy of Motion Picture Arts and Sciences, Filmex, the University of California at Los Angeles, and the University of Southern California. Surviving for only four issues spanning 1975–1976, it included articles on the UCLA Theatre Arts Library (No. 1), the Animated Study Collection at UCLA (No. 1), the film program at the Los Angeles County Museum of Art (No. 2), the film-related holdings of the Los Angeles County Museum of Natural History (No. 2), the USC Cinema Library (No. 3), and the film-related holdings of the Huntington Library (No. 3).

Information Sources

INDEX SOURCES: Film Literature Index.
REPRINT EDITIONS: None.
LOCATION SOURCES: Academy of Motion Picture Arts and Sciences; University of
    California at Los Angeles; University of Southern California.

Publication History

MAGAZINE TITLE AND TITLE CHANGES: *The Magazine.*
VOLUME AND ISSUE DATA: Special Issue (November-December 1975); No. 1 (January-February 1976); No. 2 (March-April 1976); No. 3 (May-June 1976).
PUBLISHER AND PLACE OF PUBLICATION: Film and Television Study Center, Inc., 6233 Hollywood Boulevard, Hollywood, Calif. 90028.
EDITOR: None listed.

Anthony Slide

MAGYAR FILM

A Hungarian magazine published in the last days of that country's independence, *Magyar Film* combined the best ideals of both a fan and a trade periodical. It featured film reviews, articles, and a regular listing of Hungarian production companies, laboratories, distributors, and theatres. *Magyar Film* covered both the Hungarian cinema and world cinema as it affected Hungarian film goers.

Information Sources

INDEX SOURCES: None.
REPRINT EDITIONS: None.
LOCATION SOURCES: Academy of Motion Picture Arts and Sciences.

Publication History

MAGAZINE TITLE AND TITLE CHANGES: *Magyar Film.*
VOLUME AND ISSUE DATA: Vol. I, No. 1–Vol. II, No. 24 (February 18, 1939–June 15, 1940), weekly. [Date of last issue unconfirmed.]
PUBLISHER AND PLACE OF PUBLICATION: Magyar Film, Budapest VI, Andrássy Út 69 (Vol. I, No. 1–Vol. I, No. 24); Magyar Film, Budapest VI, Bajza-Utca 18 (Vol. I, No. 25–Vol. II, No. 24).
EDITOR: Ágotai Géza.

Anthony Slide

MARQUEE

Marquee is a unique publication, devoted to the history of cinema house architecture. Each issue since the first (February 1969) has featured articles, profusely illustrated with both photographs and architect's plans, on specific theatres as varied as the Gaumont State, London (Vol. I, No. 2); the RKO Palace, Rochester, New York (Vol. 4, No. 4); the Five Flags Theatre, Dubuque, Iowa (Vol. 8, No. 4); and the Roxy, New York (Vol. 11, No. 1). There are also articles of a general nature which in the past have included ''Modern Theatres of the West'' by John E. Miller (Vol. 4, No. 1) and ''The Atlantic City Story'' by Irwin R. Glazer (Vol. 12, Nos. 1 and 2), as well as news items and book reviews.

The magazine comes with membership in the Theatre Historical Society, and *Marquee* also publishes supplements and special annual editions, such as the 1977 brochure on the Paradise Theatre, Chicago, and the 1982 brochure on the Fox Brooklyn Theatre. The only publication similar in content to *Marquee* is the British *Cinema Theatre Association Bulletin* (published since 1977), which is, as its title suggests, less a magazine and more a mimeographed newsletter.

Information Sources

INDEX SOURCES: Film Literature Index.
REPRINT EDITIONS: University Microfilms.
LOCATION SOURCES: Academy of Motion Picture Arts and Sciences.

Publication History

MAGAZINE TITLE AND TITLE CHANGES: *Marquee*.
VOLUME AND ISSUE DATA: Vol. I, No. 1–Vol. II, No. 6 (February 1969–December 1970), bimonthly; Vol. III, No. 1 (First Quarter 1971 to present), quarterly.
PUBLISHER AND PLACE OF PUBLICATION: Theatre Historical Society, P.O. Box 4445, Washington, D.C. 20017 (Vol. I, No. 1–Vol. VI, No. 2); Theatre Historical Society, P.O. Box 101, Notre Dame, Ind. 46556 (Vol. VI, No. 3–Vol. XIV, No. 3); Theatre Historical Society, 2215 West North Avenue, Chicago, Ill. 60647 (Vol. XIV, No. 4, to present).
EDITOR: Andrew Corsini (Vol. I, No. 1–Vol. XI, No. 4); Robert K. Headley (Vol. XII, No. 1, to present).

Anthony Slide

MASS MEDIA BOOKNOTES. See COMMUNICATION BOOKNOTES

THE MAX STEINER ANNUAL. See Appendix 1

THE MAX STEINER JOURNAL. See Appendix 1

THE MAX STEINER MUSIC SOCIETY NEWSLETTER.
See Appendix 1

MCA INK. See Appendix 3

MGM STUDIO CLUB NEWS. See Appendix 3

MGM STUDIO NEWS. See Appendix 3

MGM/UA EXCLUSIVE STORY. See Appendix 3

MILLENNIUM

Millennium, founded in the winter of 1977/1978, advertises itself as a publication "dedicated to avant-garde film theory and practice which provides a forum for discussion and debate in this country and abroad." As such, it is one of the best periodicals of its type published in the United States, with each issue containing articles generally well written and researched, accompanied by adequate footnotes and documentation. The articles are also readable, something fairly uncommon in periodicals of this nature.

The established avant-garde filmmaker is, naturally, well represented in the pages of *Millennium*, be he Chick Strand (No. 2), Stan Brakhage (No. 6), or Larry Jordan (No. 12). But many of the pieces in *Millennium* are of considerable historical value, discussing the avant-garde movements of the past with articles as varied as "German Worker's Films 1919–1932: Some Thoughts about the Red Front in Film" by Mel Gordon (No. 4/5) and "Approaching Borderline" by Anne Friedberg (No. 7/8/9), a study of the 1930 Swiss film featuring Paul Robeson. There are extensive interviews, such as those with Peter Wollen and Laura Mulvey (No. 4/5) and Carolee Schneemann (No. 7/8/9), and coverage of local independent filmmaking in the United States and abroad.

Each issue generally has a specific theme—such as "Feminism, Dreams and Animation" (No. 6) or "Dance/Movement and Performance/Theater" (No. 10/11)—but these themes are sufficiently broad to allow almost any type of article and commentary. Occasionally, writers for *Millennium* display a marked lack of understanding of anything outside of their particular spheres, as with E. Ann Kaplan in No. 12 who attacks a popular song about British aviatrix Amy Johnson, commenting that "it is inconceivable that a parallel male achievement would be minimalized in this manner"[1]—a statement which ignores the many popular songs written about Charles Lindbergh or the obvious fact that a popular song is the ultimate compliment, not to mention a fairly reliable assurance for posterity. Thankfully, such misreadings are not that common, and *Millennium* (with each issue resembling a paperback book in both format and number of pages) deserves a wider readership and a more frequent publishing schedule.

Notes

1. E. Ann Kaplan, "Approaching the Heroine: An Analysis of Mulvey and Wollen's *Amy!*," No. 12, Fall-Winter 1982-1983, p. 94.

Information Sources

INDEX SOURCES: FIAF International Index to Film Periodicals.
REPRINT EDITIONS: None.
LOCATION SOURCES: Academy of Motion Picture Arts and Sciences; University of Pittsburgh; University of Southern California.

Publication History

MAGAZINE TITLE AND TITLE CHANGES: *Millennium*.
VOLUME AND ISSUE DATA: No. 1 (Winter 1977-1978); No. 2 (Spring-Summer 1978); No. 3 (Winter-Spring 1979); No. 4/5 (Summer-Fall 1979); No. 6 (Spring 1980); No. 7/8/9 (Fall-Winter 1981-1982); No. 10/11 (Fall-Winter 1981-1982); No. 12 (Fall-Winter 1982-1983).
PUBLISHER AND PLACE OF PUBLICATION: Millennium Film Workshop, Inc., 66 East Fourth Street, New York, N.Y. 10003.
EDITOR: David Shapiro, Alister Sanderson, and Vicki Z. Peterson (Nos. 1–2); Noël Carroll, Victorina Z. Peterson, and David Shapiro (No. 3 to present).

Anthony Slide

MODERN SCREEN. See Appendix 2

MONOGRAM

There have been attempts to create a serious magazine fueled by the enthusiasm of fans (*Sequence** and *Movie** come to mind), but they usually foundered on the reef of respectability once the magazine became accepted, as if it was embarrassing to be so enthusiastic for movies. Following in this tradition, *Monogram* began publication in England in 1971 as an outgrowth of, and with the same editorial staff as, *Brighton Film Review* (which was published from 1968 to 1970). *Monogram* was a serious, even theoretical, magazine which was based on a polemical enthusiasm not for actors or directors but for the classical American cinema.

This British enthusiasm for Hollywood is apparent from the title of the magazine (a reference to the B-movie studio of the forties and fifties) and in the first issue, where, under a still from *The Big Heat* of Gloria Grahame provocatively lounging on a sofa, is the statement "Why Hollywood." Instead of apologizing or being embarrassed by their affection for Hollywood, the editors present a generally reasoned, if polemical, defense of the American cinema. The critical position advocated by the magazine is succinctly expressed by David Morse in that issue:

As film critics, we ought to be committed, at the very least, to two distinct propositions: the cinema is a serious and important form of artistic expression and that any argument for its significance must take full cognizance of the practice of the American cinema.... Hollywood is the greatest fact to be reckoned with, but not solely in terms of sheer output but in terms of the cinematic creativity which it wittingly or unwittingly fostered.... Further, if anything, it is the American cinema that sets the standards against which the European art cinema is to be judged and not vice versa.[1]

Yet even at this point, the magazine's relationship to the American cinema was not uncritical, nor did the editors concentrate only on American films. In fact, in the first issue there was a review of *The Wild Child*, a long article on Sergei Eisenstein and the style of *Ivan the Terrible*, and an unfavorable review of Phil Hardy's book on Samuel Fuller. Though enthusiastic, the editors' appreciation of the American cinema always had a polemical edge to it. What they wanted to do with *Monogram* was to use the American cinema as the ground (both aesthetic and historical) against which to view modern cinema, since the editors perceived that it was the tradition of Hollywood which modern cinema amplified, reacted against, scavenged from, or sought to deny.

The scope of the questions raised by the magazine may be judged by the fact that the next two issues did not deal with the American cinema at all but with the question of narrativity and the European cinema (No. 2) and the question of the nondevelopment of the British cinema (No. 3). The second issue concentrated on all aspects of the European cinema from the practical (a long article on the meaning of the abandoning of classical narrative in the films of Jean Luc Godard, Eric Rohmer, Pier Paolo Pasolini, and Luis Buñuel; reviews of *The Spider's Strategy*, *An American Soldier*, *Andrei Rublev*) to the theoretical (an article on the place of *Cinethique* and French film theory in the abandonment of the American cinema). In No. 3, the examination of British cinema varied from an article on the lack of style in British films and the reasons for that, to interviews with Michael Powell and Barney Platt-Mills, to an article on the education department of the British Film Institute.

With the next two issues, the magazine turned to genre studies, No. 4 being devoted to melodrama and No. 5 to the cinema of irony. This was a natural evolution for the magazine since the earlier issues had been, in a real sense, genre studies—treating a national cinema as a genre and working to lay bare the shared characteristics and ideology of that cinema. The sharpening of focus led to a more political reading of the genres than had been apparent in the earlier issues (particularly in No. 4), but it was nothing to compare with what was happening at *Screen*,* say, at the same time. While other magazines abandoned aesthetics for politics in the seventies, *Monogram*'s primary emphasis was always on aesthetics, without ignoring the fact that style/aesthetics does not exist in a vacuum.

However, by the time No. 5 appeared, it was clear that the magazine was experiencing problems, financial or otherwise, since there was a gap of at least a year between the publication of No. 4 and No. 5. The difficulties obviously continued since a gap of another year ensued before No. 6 appeared (without any advertising at all in the issue). There have been no issues since No. 6. Even at the end, though, the editors continued to assess the influence of the American cinema in articles which explored the way history is staged on the screen, the type of hero in modern American cinema (by Robert Altman, Monte Hellman, Sam Peckinpah, and so forth), and, in particular, an article on *Dodge City* and its role in the development of the western.

Though *Monogram* is seemingly dead, it should be remembered for the questions it raised and the way it explored in depth those issues. Not appreciated much at the time, the same apparently holds true today as Gilbert Adair makes clear in a recent issue of *Sight and Sound** where he characterizes *Monogram* as the "looniest" offspring of *Movie** given that he sees the first issue as a manifesto for the auteur theory.[2] Such was never the case since, Gilbert Adair notwithstanding, *Monogram* was not interested in auterism but in developing a blend of stylistic/ideological genre criticism which too few magazines have attempted then or now.

Notes

1. No. 1, April 1971, p. 2.
2. "The Critical Faculty," *Sight and Sound*, Vol. LI, No. 4, Autumn 1982, p. 253.

Information Sources

INDEX SOURCES: FIAF International Index to Film Periodicals; Film Literature Index.
REPRINT EDITIONS: None.
LOCATION SOURCES: Cornell University; Southern Illinois University; University of California at Santa Barbara; University of Oregon.

Publication History

MAGAZINE TITLE AND TITLE CHANGES: *Monogram*.
VOLUME AND ISSUE DATA: No. 1 (April 1971); No. 2 (Summer 1971); No. 3 (1972); No. 4 (1972); No. 5 (1974?); No. 6 (October 1975).
PUBLISHER AND PLACE OF PUBLICATION: The Brighton Film Review, 3 Fawcett Street, London S.W.10, England (Nos. 1–2); Monogram Publications, 63 Old Compton Street, London W1V 5PN, England (Nos. 3–6).
EDITOR: Thomas Elsaesser (Nos. 1–4); Thomas Elsaesser, Mark Le Fanu, Richard Collins, and Peter Lloyd (Nos. 5–6).

Val Almendarez

MONTAGE. See ACADEMY LEADER

THE MONTHLY FILM BULLETIN

The British Film Institute was formed in October 1933, and in February 1934 it published the first number of *The Monthly Film Bulletin*. Of its sixteen pages, fourteen were concerned with documentary and educational films and only two with "entertainment" productions. From the start, *The Monthly Film Bulletin* was intended primarily as a work of reference, giving as complete a list as possible of feature films as they became available in Great Britain, but the details were necessarily sparse. This general layout continued, with minor variations such as fuller credits for "entertainment" films, until September 1949. A "Notes of the Month" section was added in 1947 with brief reports on the activities of the British Film Institute. In September 1949 the reviewing of "classroom films" was dropped, and the credit lists and synopses given to features were further enlarged. These films were divided into two categories: those which had "a purpose beyond simple entertainment" (which were reviewed at length) and "straightforward, unambitious entertainment films which made no real claims on critical faculties" (which were covered in brief, graded paragraphs). This slightly invidious and arbitrary distinction continued right up to the end in 1970. Coverage of a limited number of shorts and documentaries was retained.

The *Bulletin* survived uninterrupted during the Second World War and during the printing dispute of 1950 when it was brought out by a photographic process. In January 1951 the "Notes of the Month" section was replaced by a "Membership Newsletter," but this lasted only for a year. The price in 1952 was two shillings, and in its early years the *Bulletin* was free to full members of the British Film Institute and twopence to associates. By 1947 it was on sale at one shilling and sixpence. April 1962 saw a change in cover design and the start of a new feature when a panel of critics allotted star ratings to a selection of each month's films. This was not looked on wholly favorably by the film trade; it was later dropped, revived, then again discontinued. In 1963 a very useful occasional checklist was started, a complete record of a filmmaker's work. By the October 1982 issue, the number of these excellent lists had reached 130.

In September 1968 the price was raised to two shillings and sixpence, and the names of the principal reviewers were given; hitherto, reviews had been merely initialled. From January 1971 all were signed in full, including even those for the short films. In the same year, at a price of fifteen pence, the page size was enlarged, reviews and credit lists were lengthened, and the first illustration appeared, consisting of a relevant film still on the cover. The revived critics' star rating panel continued until March 1976, when its place was taken by a series of articles on the back page. During this period an interesting section of "Retrospective" reviews was introduced. Between 1975 and 1983 the price increased by stages from twenty-five to sixty-five pence. In July 1982 a radical alteration took place: a major change in layout, the introduction of a section on video, a number of feature articles, and stills. The feature film section was divided in two: in the first part, reviews of selected films, with supplementary information (interviews, biographies, background pieces, and so forth) were run out of alphabetical order; in the second part, other reviews followed in alphabetical sequence. Fears might have arisen that these new additions would result in less space being devoted to reference material and appraisals of current films, but assurance has been given that, as hitherto, all current productions available— good, bad, and indifferent—will be fully covered. It is interesting to compare the number of features appearing over the years: for January 1983 it was twenty-three; January 1979, thirty-two; January 1969, thirty-five; January 1959, forty-two. In the financial year 1969–1970, the *Bulletin* claimed coverage of what was until then a record number of 420 films.

Through the years *The Monthly Film Bulletin* reviews have aroused some criticism. In 1961 a number of them were described as "mannered and unfair." Ten years later was noted:

It does seem that the faceless writers of the shorter notices in particular are not easy to please. The ordinary filmgoer returning innocently happy from some less-than-masterpiece may well find himself glancing furtively into his *Bulletin* to see whether he should have had such a pleasant evening, and end up guiltily conscious of having been severely admonished for having enjoyed himself.[1]

Since then criticism has sometimes been sharper, reviews sometimes (though with honorable exceptions) seeming to reflect a personal bias rather than an impartial verdict based on the writer's experienced judgment of a particular film's quality as a *film*.

Regarded as a general reference work, however, *The Monthly Film Bulletin* is still unsurpassed, with its superb full cast and credit lists (at least since 1950), its generally excellent concise synopses, and its full index to each yearly volume. Its unbroken run from its inception makes it an invaluable asset for anyone working on or interested in the history of the cinema.

Notes

1. Ivan Butler, *To Encourage the Art of the Film* (London: Robert Hale, 1971).

Information Sources

INDEX SOURCES: FIAF International Index to Film Periodicals.
REPRINT EDITIONS: World Microfilms.
LOCATION SOURCES: Academy of Motion Picture Arts and Sciences.

Publication History

MAGAZINE TITLE AND TITLE CHANGES: *Monthly Film Bulletin.*
VOLUME AND ISSUE DATA: Vol. 1, No. 1 (February 1934 to present), monthly.
PUBLISHER AND PLACE OF PUBLICATION: The British Film Institute, 4 Great

Russell Street, London W.C.1, England (1934–1948); The British Film Institute, 164 Shaftesbury Avenue, London W.C.2, England (1948–1960); The British Film Institute, 81 Dean Street, London W1V 6AA, England (1960 to present).

EDITOR: No editor listed (1934–1968); David Wilson (1968–1971); Jan Dawson (1971–1973); Richard Combs (1973 to present).

Ivan Butler

MOOREHEAD MEMOS. See Appendix 1

MOTION PICTURE. See Appendix 2

MOTION PICTURE CLASSIC. See Appendix 2

THE MOTION PICTURE DIRECTOR

The Motion Picture Directors Association appears to have been a loose-knit group to which most film directors belonged and which met more for social purposes than for any desire to improve working conditions or contracts of employment as the Directors Guild of America was to do. The association began in the early teens and remained in existence through the early thirties, although in its last years its membership seemed comprised more of "old-timers" than major figures in the industry. In June 1924 the Motion Picture Directors Association commenced publication of a monthly magazine, *The Director*, in whose pages directors and others in the industry could write on their work.

In the first few issues, veteran film director-producer J. Stuart Blackton contributed a series of articles, "Winding Backwards with J. Stuart Blackton," in which he discussed his career. For almost the first two years of its existence, *The Director* ran a serialization of an unpublished novel, *Thundering Silence*, by H. H. Van Loan. Among the contributors were Edward Laemmle, King Vidor, Frank Lloyd, Henry King, Sam Taylor, Pete Smith, Allan Dwan, June Mathis, Jesse L. Lasky, Elinor Glyn, Irving Cummings, Robert Vignola, Al Christie, Fred Niblo, and Cecil B. DeMille—a veritable who's who of behind-the-camera talent. Even Louis B. Mayer contributed an article, "The Importance of the Director" (Vol. 1, No. 10).

With Vol. 2, No. 3 (September 1925), *The Director* changed its name to *The Motion Picture Director*, and with the name change came a change in the look of the magazine. It took on the appearance of a fan journal, even down to a front section featuring full-page photographs of screen players. (For some inexplicable reason, Kate Price seemed to be featured in each issue.) In an editorial,

George L. Sargent (the magazine's first editor) explained that "the 'new' *Director* will henceforth be conducted as a semi-technical publication of genuine interest to all studio folk, and as a semi-fan publication appealing to the host of men and women throughout the country who are seriously concerned with knowing more intimately about the making of the pictures they see." [1]

A section, "New Pictures in the Making," was added, consisting of charts showing film titles, directors, studios, stars, scenarists, and production status. Readers were invited to send in their questions to an "Ask the Director" column. News items on "studio folk" were given prominence. However, the change meant no decrease in the interesting nature of the articles. Sid Grauman wrote on staging of prologues (Vol. 2, No. 4) and discussed with director Sidney Olcott "Do Prologues Make or Mar a Picture?" (Vol. 2, No. 10). Even Pola Negri contributed a piece, "I Became Converted to the Happy Ending" (Vol. 2, No. 8).

George L. Sargent resigned as editor, for medical reasons, in October 1925 and was succeeded by J. Stuart Blackton, who was currently president of the Motion Picture Directors Association. The magazine underwent no great change under Blackton's guidance, except that perhaps there was a little more interest in film history than heretofore. Blackton resigned in January 1927, and one final issue was edited by George E. Bradley. The publication offered no explanation for nor hint of its demise.

Notes

1. Vol. 2, No. 3, September 1925, p. 5.

Information Sources

INDEX SOURCES: None.
REPRINT EDITIONS: None.
LOCATION SOURCES: Academy of Motion Picture Arts and Sciences (incomplete); New York Public Library.

Publication History

MAGAZINE TITLE AND TITLE CHANGES: *The Director* (June 1924–August 1925); *The Motion Picture Director* (September 1925–February 1927).
VOLUME AND ISSUE DATA: Vol. I, No. 1–Vol. III, No. 5 (June 1924–February 1927), monthly. [Date of last issue unconfirmed.]
PUBLISHER AND PLACE OF PUBLICATION: Motion Picture Directors Holding Corporation, 1925 North Wilcox Avenue, Hollywood, Calif. (Vol. I, No. 1–Vol. II, No. 8); Motion Picture Directors Holding Corporation, 6362 Hollywood Boulevard, Hollywood, Calif. (Vol. II, No. 9–Vol. II, No. 12); Motion Picture Directors Holding Corporation, Suite 611, Taft Building, Hollywood, Calif. (Vol. III, No. 1–Vol. III, No. 5).

EDITOR: George L. Sargent (June 1924–October 1925); J. Stuart Blackton (November 1925–January 1927); George E. Bradley (February 1927).

Anthony Slide

MOTION PICTURE HERALD

Virtually all of the early trade papers—*Exhibitors Herald, Motion Picture News,** *The Moving Picture World,** *Motography,** and *The Film Index**— eventually merged into one periodical, *Motion Picture Herald*, which proudly advertised itself, in its first issue of January 3, 1931, as "a consolidation of all the weekly trade papers" (a slight exaggeration in view of the importance of the independent *Variety**).

Motion Picture Herald was the brainchild of Martin Quigley, who had entered the field of trade periodicals in 1915 with the publication of *Exhibitors Herald*; two years later he acquired *Motography*. In addition to his film periodicals, Quigley also published *The Chicagoan* and *The Polo*, both of which he had disposed of by the early thirties. As a prominent Catholic layman—who received a number of Papal decorations—Martin Quigley was considerably interested in the moral attitude displayed by the cinema, and he is generally credited with the creation of the Motion Picture Production Code in the early thirties. In addition to *Motion Picture Herald*, Martin Quigley published *The International Motion Picture Almanac* (from 1933 to the present), *The International Television Almanac* (from 1956 to the present), *Fame* (1934–1973), and a Spanish-language film trade periodical *Teatro al Día* (first published July 1936). He died at the age of seventy-three on May 4, 1964.

To edit *Motion Picture Herald*, Quigley selected Terry Ramsaye (1885–1954), one of the most important figures in the history of film trade periodicals and the author of the first major history of the cinema, *A Million and One Nights* (1926). Ramsaye was to remain editor of *Motion Picture Herald* until June 25, 1949 (at which time he became consulting editor and continued to contribute editorials), and to him should go much of the credit for the establishment of the various departments for which *Motion Picture Herald* was so well known.

Throughout its life *Motion Picture Herald* continued to include much of the same type of information, columns, and articles. Its hard-hitting editorials (usually from the pen of Martin Quigley) appeared weekly. Regular features were reviews of shorts and feature-length films, theatre receipts, articles, and news items on production, exhibition, music, and technical matters. "Managers' Round Table" was described as "conducted by exhibitors for exhibitors" and included a section in which the local theatre managers described "what the picture did for me." Other regular features included obituaries, "In British Studios," and the release charts, which provide easy access to information as to release dates for features and shorts and also serve as an index to the magazine's reviews. (Unfortunately, *Motion Picture Herald* never published a yearly index to its contents, but knowing the year of a film's release makes it a fairly simple matter to track down the date of the film's review.)

Motion Picture Herald also published a supplement titled "Better Theatres," entirely devoted to the operation and construction of motion picture theatres, a supplement which had begun life in *Exhibitors Herald*. At the height of its importance in the thirties, *Motion Picture Herald* published *Better Theatres* as a separate periodical, but in the magazine's last days *Better Theatres* was simply included as a section in its parent publication.

With Terry Ramsaye's retirement in 1949, Martin Quigley, Jr. (who had been on the staff of *Motion Picture Herald* since 1939 and associate editor since 1945) took over as editor. He became editor-in-chief in 1956 and was succeeded by Richard Gertner and Charles S. Aaronson.

As the cinema declined in importance, so did *Motion Picture Herald*. It had commenced publication as a weekly (published first on a Friday, then a Thursday, then a Saturday, and finally a Wednesday), became a biweekly in 1962, and a monthly in 1971. In its last years, it was down from one hundred pages to a mere thirty. The last issue of *Motion Picture Herald* was dated December 1972. At that time Martin Quigley, Jr., announced publication of *QP Herald*, a new weekly, which "will be a publication designed for 1973 and the years ahead. There will be a strong emphasis on news: news of product, news of people, news that affects the business in a variety of ways." *QP Herald* also incorporated *Motion Picture Daily* and *Television/Radio Today*. An eight-page weekly, *QP Herald* ceased publication after only eighteen issues.

Information Sources

BIBLIOGRAPHY:

Aaronson, Charles S. "Martin Quigley—Quigley Publications and the Motion Picture." *Motion Picture Herald*, July 2, 1960, pp. 31, 32, 45, 48, 49, 52.

———. "Martin Quigley, Jr.: A Career—30 Years A-Growing." *Motion Picture Herald*, June 17, 1970, pp. 6, 15.

Arnold, Kenneth. "Motion Picture Herald." *Films*, Vol. 1, No. 2, Spring 1940, pp. 81–92.

Hart, Henry. "Terry Ramsaye, 1885–1954." *Films in Review*, Vol. 5, No. 8, October 1954, pp. 385–386.

Quigley, Martin, Jr. "A Remarkable Man—My Father." *Motion Picture Herald*, May 13, 1964, pp. 1, 9, 16.

Ramsaye, Terry. "The House That Movies Built." *Rockefeller Center Magazine*, September 1940, pp. 17, 32.

Weaver, William R. "Quigley as Father of the Code." *Motion Picture Herald*, June 18, 1938, pp. 14–16.

INDEX SOURCES: None.

REPRINT EDITIONS: University Microfilms (1950–1954 only).

LOCATION SOURCES: Academy of Motion Picture Arts and Sciences; Library of Congress; University of Southern California (lacks some issues).

Publication History

MAGAZINE TITLE AND TITLE CHANGES: *Motion Picture Herald* (January 3, 1931–
December 1972); *QP Herald* (January 6, 1973–May 5, 1973).

VOLUME AND ISSUE DATA: Vol. CII, No. 1–Vol. CCXXVII, No. 12 (January 3,
1931–June 27, 1962), weekly; Vol. CCXXIIX, No. 1–Vol. CCXXXXI, No. 2
(July 11, 1962–January 27, 1971), biweekly; Vol. CCXXXXI, No. 3–Vol.
CCXXXXII, No. 12 (February 24, 1971–December 1972), monthly; as *QP Herald*, No. 1–No. 18 (January 6, 1973–May 5, 1973), weekly. [Please note the first
volume of *Motion Picture Herald* is numbered Vol. CII.]

PUBLISHER AND PLACE OF PUBLICATION: Quigley Publishing Company, 729
Seventh Avenue, New York, N.Y. (Vol. CII, No. 1–Vol. CII, No. 7); Quigley
Publishing Company, 1790 Broadway, New York, N.Y. (Vol. CII, No. 8–Vol.
CXXII, No. 5); Quigley Publishing Company, Rockefeller Center, 1270 Sixth
Avenue, New York, N.Y. 10020 (Vol. CXXII, No. 6–Vol. CCXXXXII, No. 7);
as *QP Herald*, Quigley Publishing Company, Rockefeller Center, 1270 Sixth
Avenue, New York, N.Y. 10020 (No. 1–No. 18).

EDITOR: Terry Ramsaye (January 3, 1931–June 25, 1949); Martin Quigley, Jr. (July 2,
1949–December 22, 1965); Richard Gertner (July 6, 1966–January 27, 1971);
Charles S. Aaronson (February 24, 1971–July 1972); no editor listed (August
1972–December 1972); as *QP Herald*, Richard Gertner (January 6, 1973–May 5,
1973).

Anthony Slide

MOTION PICTURE MAGAZINE. See Appendix 2

MOTION PICTURE NEWS

Moving Picture News began in May 1908 as an alternate trade paper to the
then-dominant *The Moving Picture World** at a time when the industry was torn
apart with struggles for power among the major production companies. Alfred
H. Saunders left his position as editor of *The Moving Picture World* to form the
Moving Picture News "so that we might be free to express our own opinions
and work for the progress of cinematography; another reason was, we could not
act as a spy and sycophant or betray our friends."[1] Under Saunders, the *News*
attacked first the Edison company and the Film Service Association, the distribution arm of the major manufacturers, for their attempts to control the industry.
Later, when the major companies formed the Motion Picture Patents Company,
the *News* supported the excluded independents.

By the time William A. Johnston bought *Moving Picture News* in September
1913 and merged it with his *Exhibitors' Times*, the licensed versus the independents battle had ended. Johnston renamed the paper *Motion Picture News*
("the pictures as such do not move. They are pictures of motion"[2]) and concentrated on establishing it as primarily an outlet for picture advertising and

industry news and a compendium of services for the exhibitor. During Johnston's sixteen-year reign, the *News* prospered as one of the leading trade papers serving the industry as it grew from one-reel to feature production, became the world's leader, and adjusted itself to sound technology. At the end of 1930, Quigley Productions purchased the *News* and merged it with *Exhibitors Herald-World* (itself a 1928 consolidation of *Exhibitors Herald* and *The Moving Picture World*) to form *Motion Picture Herald.**

Throughout its first period of existence (1908–1913), the *News* supported the independents with editorials, advertising, listings of new releases, biographical essays about their leaders, news about developments in the court battles, and descriptions of new cameras and other inventions to help them survive. By July 1912, the independents had so solidified their position within the industry that the *News* was able to begin including ads and listings for the licensed companies and articles and interviews with their heads.

The other major fight the *News* engaged in during this time was provoking the production companies to make films of social and educational value. Margaret I. MacDonald contributed weekly essays on practical aspects of the educational film. Saunders editorialized that films could be a great positive force to deal with social problems, assist scientific progress, and promote industry. In August 1913, he left the paper to become manager of the education department of the Colonial Motion Picture Corporation.

Regular features during this period included weekly notes from correspondents in Chicago, Washington, the West, and London; descriptions and diagrams of the latest related patents, trademarks, designs, and copyrights; reports on new theatres built throughout the country; technical advice to projector operators; manufacturers' synopses of films; articles on theatres; and columns of news and gossip. Editorials addressed issues of exhibitor organization, censorship, Sunday showings, and theatre fires, while articles featured explanations of technological developments such as color, sound, and foreign cameras. Virginia West wrote prose versions of the stories of current films. Robert Grau, author of *The Theatre of Science*, an important early history of the industry, wrote articles on the evolution of the motion picture, the organ used in the theatre as a one-man orchestra, and vaudeville. C. Francis Jenkins, inventor with Thomas Armat of the motion picture projector, in "Trust vs. Independents" (Vol. 4, No. 4) gave his opinions of the conflict.

The merger with *Exhibitors' Times* in September 1913 brought an increased attempt to serve both the distribution and exhibition ends of the industry through increased advertising and exhibitor service sections. Advertisements for coming releases filled the front of the paper with colorful enticements far more extravagant than those in trade papers today. Sections for the exhibitor included reports on how particular shows were exploited around the country, reviews of current and previews of upcoming releases, articles on all aspects of theatre operation, descriptions of technological advancements in equipment, and features on the latest in theatre design and decoration. Within nine months of the merger, the size of the journal more than doubled and staff correspondents extended to sixty-seven cities in the United States and Canada.[3]

The news of the industry that these correspondents brought back and recorded for posterity is a most valuable source of information for present-day historians. As with the other trade papers of the day, the news and the current press releases were perhaps the best part of the paper, while the reviews were the worst part. In 1921, Robert E. Sherwood, then motion picture critic for *Life*, wrote a letter to editor Johnston praising the *News* for its service departments and editorials but complained that, as was the case with the other trade papers, the reviews "are more like press notices than criticisms.... Do you consider that they are taken seriously?"[4] In most cases the reviewers merely retold the plot and either waxed enthusiastically about the production or tactfully avoided any negative judgments. Credit listings were not as complete as with rival paper, *Exhibitor's Trade Review.** There was a short time in 1914–1915 as features grew in popularity that critic Peter Milne, later to become a screenwriter, did offer some decent analyses of the dramatic impact, atmosphere, acting, and plot structure of the films he reviewed, but in general the reviews merely gave the reader an idea of the kind of film it was, its storyline, and stars.

The *News* did not concern itself with in-depth articles on the art of the film, but in its twenty-two years there were some fine studies of the state of the business. In 1915, the twenty-four part series "Weak Spots in a Strong Business" (Vol. 11, No. 4–Vol. 12, No. 8) featured weekly two-page articles on an important figure's views on how to improve the industry. George Kleine, Siegmund Lubin, Charles Kessel, Carl Laemmle, Horace G. Plimpton, Sol L. Lesser, Edwin Thanhouser, J. Stuart Blackton, W. W. Hodkinson, D. W. Griffith, Adolf Zukor, Lewis J. Selznick, and Thomas H. Ince were among those who contributed their views. Statistical studies of the industry appeared in 1916 (Vol. 14, No. 17) and 1922 (Vol. 26, Nos. 21–26). The 1922 study, conducted by the Babson Statistical Organization and Columbia University, was a thorough analysis of exhibition practices and viewing preferences of the public. In 1925, William Basil Courtney of the Vitagraph scenario staff wrote a series of eleven articles on the early days of the Vitagraph Company (Vol. 31, Nos. 6–16). The most insightful series was John Grierson's six articles of advice for the industry written in 1926 for the Famous Players-Lasky Company (Vol. 34, Nos. 19–25). In analyzing Hollywood's failure to make many pictures that achieved greatness, Grierson gave his views on the qualities a great picture needed, how these qualities could be achieved, and what the obstacles were that inhibited Hollywood from producing many great films. His suggestion that a more enlightened organization was needed to create a sense of community within the industry, while not exactly catching on in Hollywood, did perhaps come to fruition when he took his ideas, filmmaking abilities, and leadership qualities to the National Film Board of Canada.

Other notable articles included two on D. W. Griffith that quote him at length at different points in his career: "A Vital Theme is Necessary for a Classic

Picture" (Vol. 14, No. 11, September 16, 1916) and "Directors Write—Cutters Make" (Vol. 35, No. 9, March 4, 1927). In 1929, the *News* persuaded nearly two hundred Hollywood personalities to contribute a paragraph each for "Hollywood Tells What It Takes to Make a Record Smasher" (for Jolson "knowing what the public likes and giving it to them" while for Louis B. Mayer "cleanliness, sincerity and humanity" made a "record smasher"; Vol. 39, No. 19). In 1926, a six-page coverage of the Vitaphone premiere gave technical details and an enthusiastic welcome to the new system (Vol. 34, No. 8). A fifty-page tribute to Carl Laemmle appeared in 1929 (Vol. 40, No. 22). Public reaction to the Arbuckle case was surveyed in "Mr., Mrs. and Miss Average-Citizen's Opinion on Arbuckle's Contemplated 'Come-Back' " (Vol. 27, No. 1, January 6, 1923).

Two regular features of use for reference purposes both then and today were the semiannual "Studio Directory," begun January 29, 1916 (Vol. 13, No. 4), and the "Trade Annual," an industry yearbook begun July 28, 1917 (Vol. 16, No. 4). An interesting feature that unfortunately lasted only from October 1919 until April 1920 was "The Fiction Mart" (later "Fiction Works Suited to the Screen") which gave plots for stories available for production.

Motion Picture News is today an invaluable source for historians concerned with the world of film in its formative stages. Because it maintained an on-going weekly record of events, personalities, ideas, and achievements in the industry from 1908 through 1930, the *News* along with the other trade papers, the business records of the various companies, and surviving correspondence can provide information and atmosphere to better interpret the films themselves and the memories and memoirs of the historical participants.

Notes

1. *Moving Picture News*, Vol. 4, No. 18, May 6, 1911, p. 5.
2. *Ibid.*, Vol. 8, No. 13, September 27, 1913, p. 17.
3. Robert Grau, *The Theatre of Science* (New York: Broadway Publishing Company, 1914), p. 248.
4. *Motion Picture News*, Vol. 23, No. 20, May 7, 1921, p. 2893.

Information Sources

BIBLIOGRAPHY:
Grau, Robert. *The Theatre of Science*. New York: Broadway Publishing Company, 1914.
INDEX SOURCES: None.
REPRINT EDITIONS: Kraus-Thomson (microfilm edition from the holdings of the New York Public Library lacks Vols. 1–3; Vol. 4, Nos. 1–3, 25–28; Vol. 8, No. 7; Vol. 21, No. 3; Vol. 35, No. 3); microfilm edition of *Motion Picture News Booking Guide*, Vols. 1–15 (December 1921–March 1930), published by the State Historical Society of Wisconsin.
LOCATION SOURCES: Academy of Motion Picture Arts and Sciences (incomplete); Library of Congress (incomplete); New York Public Library (incomplete). [No complete run is known to exist.]

Publication History

MAGAZINE TITLE AND TITLE CHANGES: *Moving Picture News* (May 1908–October 4, 1913); *Motion Picture News* (October 11, 1913–December 27, 1930).

VOLUME AND ISSUE DATA: Vol. ?, No. ?–Vol. XLII, No. 26 (May 1908–December 27, 1930), weekly. [The exact date and volume number of the first issue is not known—according to *The Moving Picture World*, Vol. 2, No. 2, May 30, 1908, p. 472, *Moving Picture News* began with a continuation of the volume number and serial number of *The Moving Picture World* but was forced to give it up.]

PUBLISHER AND PLACE OF PUBLICATION: The Cinematograph Publishing Company, 30 West Thirteenth Street, New York, N.Y. (Vol. IV, No. 1 [this is the earliest issue the author has found]–Vol. VIII, No. 12); Exhibitors' Times, Inc., 220 West Forty-second Street, New York, N.Y. (Vol. VIII, No. 13–Vol. XIII, No. 6); Exhibitors' Times, Inc., 729 Seventh Avenue, New York, N.Y. (Vol. XIII, No. 7–Vol. XIII, No. 12); Motion Picture News, Inc., 729 Seventh Avenue, New York, N.Y. (Vol. XIII, No. 13–Vol. XLII, No. 26).

EDITOR: Alfred H. Saunders (May 1908–August 2, 1913); no editor listed (August 9, 1913–September 20, 1913); William A. Johnston (September 27, 1913–September 14, 1929); Maurice D. "Red" Kann (September 21, 1929–December 20, 1930); no editor listed (December 27, 1930).

Alan Gevinson

THE MOTION PICTURE PROJECTIONIST

With the advent of more sophisticated motion picture projection technology and techniques, as well as the introduction of sound into the film industry, a number of periodicals appeared during the late twenties and early thirties intended to provide theatre projectionists with current technical information necessary for their new responsibilities. The first of these was *The Motion Picture Projectionist*, which began publication in October 1927. An editorial appearing in the first issue lamented that North America's thirty thousand projectionists had no publication addressed to the craft's particular needs and concerns but that *The Motion Picture Projectionist*, aided by such associate editors as Lester Isaac, supervisor of projection for Loew Theatres, would provide such a forum for technical developments and news in the profession. However, as with *Projection Engineering** founded in 1929, *The Motion Picture Projectionist* eschewed involvement within the often-strident politics of the projectionists' labor groups, leading its editors to issue somewhat contradictory intentions in that initial editorial:

> Wherever the Projectionist is concerned, there this publication promises to be in to the finish, fighting lustily for him, bringing to him information about projection gathered from the four corners of the earth to enable him to become more expert and to better his condition in life, entertaining him whenever possible, but always constructive, worthwhile and efficient. Let this paper become the voice of the mighty Projection craft, let Projectionists

speak through it and let it speak for them. Only one reservation the editors make: that the paper shall not engage in political or personal controversies that may engage the interest of Projectionists from time to time. It is obvious that it must hold itself aloof from all matters that may compromise its proud impartiality or lessen its usefulness in its single purpose to help the craft as a whole and each Projectionist singly to become better craftsmen.[1]

For the next five years *The Motion Picture Projectionist* published a wide variety of feature articles highlighting current technical progress in motion pictures, including comprehensive descriptions of early sound film apparati and speculations upon the impact the emerging television technology might have on film theatres and their projectionists.[2] Regular departments encompassed the latest equipment news, "how-to" articles to help projectionists make their theatres' projection operation more efficient, news of the International Alliance (I.A.) and its projectionist locals, and practical advice ranging from standardized projection cue sheets to hints on more efficacious change-over routines. With its detailed technical articles, *The Motion Picture Projectionist* provides today's film historians a comprehensive overview of advances in motion picture projection and sound technology during the change to sound.

As with *Projection Engineering*, the reluctance of *The Motion Picture Projectionist* to enter into political matters involving the I.A. and its projectionist locals may have contributed to the magazine's demise. In 1931 the editor of *The Motion Picture Projectionist*, James Finn, left the publication to form another monthly devoted to the projectionist's craft, *International Projectionist**; with its first issue in November 1931, *International Projectionist* established itself as an outspoken advocate of the projectionists' welfare within the industry and the I.A., broaching controversial political subjects within the trade which neither *Projection Engineering* nor *The Motion Picture Projectionist* would touch. After the appearance of *International Projectionist*, *The Motion Picture Projectionist* endured for little more than a year. In its final issues was published a "platform" which tacitly acknowledged the competition felt from *International Projectionist* and the two publications' divergent editorial policies:

That we be interested in neither the politics or the personalities involved in the politics of the International Alliance of Theatrical Stage Employees and Moving Picture Operators or of any other group or body of projectionists, because such interference with internal affairs of labor organizations will make this a partisan and political paper and destroy its value to the craft which lies in educational work only.

That by maintaining our policy of education we will enjoy the support of projectionists everywhere for many years to come as we have enjoyed this support for the last five years as the leading projection publication in the country.[3]

The support *The Motion Picture Projectionist* foresaw was not forthcoming from the craft; the magazine suspended publication with its December 1932 issue, succumbing to the economic rigors of the Great Depression and competition from *International Projectionist*, which would purchase *Projection Engineering* two years later and become the industry's preeminent publication for the projectionist craft.

Notes

1. "Let There Be Light!" *The Motion Picture Projectionist*, October 1927, p. 6.

2. See, for example, "Radio Movies and the Theatre," *The Motion Picture Projectionist*, January 1928, pp. 13, 31–32; and "Vitaphone: System 'B,' " *The Motion Picture Projectionist*, March 1928, pp. 7–14, 22.

3. "Our Platform," *The Motion Picture Projectionist*, December 1932, p. 9.

Information Sources

INDEX SOURCES: None.
REPRINT EDITIONS: None.
LOCATION SOURCES: University of California at Los Angeles.

Publication History

MAGAZINE TITLE AND TITLE CHANGES: *The Motion Picture Projectionist*.
VOLUME AND ISSUE DATA: Vol. I, No. 1–Vol. VI, No. 2 (October 1927–December 1932), monthly except no issue published for August 1929.
PUBLISHER AND PLACE OF PUBLICATION: Craft Publications Co., New York, N.Y. (Vol. I, No. 1–Vol. II, No. 1); Mancall Publishing Corp., New York, N.Y. (Vol. II, No. 2–Vol. VI, No. 2).
EDITOR: Lester B. Isaac and Frank R. Day, Associate Editors (October 1927–December 1927); James J. Finn, Managing Editor (January 1928–August 1931); Charles E. Brownell (September 1931–July 1932); Cecil B. Fowler, Robert J. Marcy, and Kaskel Kallman, Editorial Board (August 1932–December 1932).

William Lafferty

MOTION PICTURE REVIEW DIGEST. See FILM REVIEW DIGEST

MOTION PICTURE STORY MAGAZINE. See Appendix 2

MOTION PICTURE SUPPLEMENT. See Appendix 2

MOTION PICTURE TIMES. See Appendix 3

THE MOTION PICTURE WEEKLY. See Appendix 2

MOTOGRAPHY

"MOTO- means motion; -GRAPH means written, delineated or pictured; hence MOTOGRAPHY, the art of motion delineation, or motion in illustration."[1] So began an editorial announcing the forthcoming appearance of the new trade paper in the final issue of its predecessor, *The Nickelodeon*. Like *The Nickelodeon*, *Motography* prided itself on being a high-class trade journal, representing scientific enterprise rather than the marketplace.

Unlike its competitors *The Moving Picture World,** *Moving Picture News* (later *Motion Picture News**), *The Film Index,** and later *Exhibitor's Trade Review,** *The Nickelodeon* and *Motography* were published in Chicago rather than New York. Closer than New York to distributors and exhibitors west of Pittsburgh, Chicago also housed several studios and was the proving ground of a group of film distributors (Carl Laemmle, George Kleine, George K. Spoor, William N. Selig, S. S. Hutchinson, John R. Freuler, and others) who would later greatly influence the industry. After the production center of the industry moved to California, *Motography* justified its steadfastness in remaining in Chicago by speculating that "Chicago, within two years at the most, will be the motographic metropolis of the world."[2]

Beginning as a monthly in January 1909, *The Nickelodeon* did not at first try to compete with the established New York weeklies. Advertising was minimal, and reviews did not appear until later. Dedicating itself to the advancement of science, education, art, and industry, *The Nickelodeon* covered such issues as the patents fight ("Important Motion Picture Patents," Vol. 2, Nos. 2 and 3, is a detailed discussion of the claims of the Edison Company), new technologies ("A New Process for Coloring Films," Vol. 2, No. 2, has a drawing of the machine used), early history ("The History of Talking Pictures," Vol. 4, No. 5), social uses of film ("Moving Pictures Curing Insanity," Vol. 4, No. 9), the development of noninflammable film, ventilation in theatres, and the possibility of stereoscopic moving pictures.

In its second year (1910), *The Nickelodeon* began issuing semimonthly. At the beginning of 1911, it became a weekly in an attempt to become the top trade journal. Complaining that it didn't receive the promised support it needed to succeed as a weekly, it went back to issuing monthly when it changed its name to *Motography* in April 1911.

Motography continued *The Nickelodeon*'s concern with science, industry, art, and education but focused as well on entertainment. Maintaining its reputation as a class publication, *Motography* published some of the most valuable articles of its time. Early on there appeared feature articles by and about the great directors. D. W. Griffith was given the most abundant coverage beginning in June 1911 with a two-page report reprinted from the *Los Angeles Times* on the filming of a covered wagon spectacular ("A Great Biograph Picture," Vol. 5, No. 6). If not the first, this report was certainly one of the earliest testimonies to Griffith's directorial habits, flamboyant manner, and concern with authenticity and spectacle. The year 1914 saw two articles about Griffith (Vol. 11, No. 8; Vol. 12, No. 21). Griffith wrote "The Motion Picture—An Art" (Vol. 13, No. 1) in 1915. Orville Manhood, the conductor of the orchestra accompanying *The Birth of a Nation*, contributed an article describing his work ("Dramatic Music and the Big Picture," Vol. 15, No. 6). Carli D. Elinore, composer of the music accompanying *The Birth of a Nation* and *Hearts of the World*, told how he worked with Griffith ("Setting *Hearts of the World* to Music," Vol. 19, No. 19).

Maurice Tourneur wrote two short studies, "America's Picture Land" (Vol. 14, No. 17) and "The Photoplay Writer" (Vol. 18, No. 26). In "Effects Spoiled by Projection Speed" (Vol. 19, No. 2) and "R. A. Walsh Directs without a Script" (Vol. 19, No. 10), Raoul Walsh discussed his directing methods. Chaplin was interviewed passing through Chicago in early 1915 ("Charles Chaplin in a Serious Mood," Vol. 19, No. 10). Numerous essays by and about Thomas H. Ince and Mack Sennett described their studios and views.

Columnist Mabel Condon in "Sans Grease Paint and Wig" drew portraits of featured players. Her articles on the industry, "What Happens to the Scenario" (Vol. 9, No. 5, following a typical comedy script through all the stages it goes through at the studios), "Three Minutes Before the Camera" (Vol. 9, No. 4, describing her experience as an extra), and "The Completion of Universal City" (Vol. 13, No. 1), were of the highest quality. Alan Crosland, who began his career with the Edison Company in 1912, wrote a long essay detailing that studio's history ("How Edison's 'Black Maria' Grew," Vol. 19, No. 17). "Growing Menace of Chicago Censors" (Vol. 12, No. 14) included the censor board's daily reports detailing cut scenes. Stage actresses making their debuts in moving pictures were publicized ("Billie Burke's First Day as a Screen Star," Vol. 14, No. 14; "Billie Burke Likes Picture Acting," Vol. 14, No. 16; "Why I Went into Motion Pictures" by Geraldine Farrar, Vol. 14, No. 15) to emphasize the legitimacy of motion pictures. The technical history of the industry was provided with the serialization of John R. Rathburn's 1913 book in "Motion Picture Making and Exhibiting" (Vol. 9, No. 6–Vol. 11, No. 10).

Regular features included guides for the exhibitor, technical articles for the projectionist, news of the industry, help for the scenario writer, and recent patent descriptions. Reviews were of high quality for the time but were discontinued in August 1911 and again in April 1918 because the editors felt they served no constructive purpose. In their place feature articles described the more important films.

Like *The Nickelodeon* before it, *Motography* became a semimonthly and finally a weekly. In 1918 it merged with *Exhibitors Herald* to form *Exhibitors Herald and Motography*.

Notes

1. *Motography*, Vol. 15, No. 12, March 25, 1911, p. 321.
2. *Ibid.*, Vol. 15, No. 8, February 19, 1916, p. 389.

Information Sources

INDEX SOURCES: None.
REPRINT EDITIONS: Brookhaven Press; Kraus-Thomson.
LOCATION SOURCES: Library of Congress (incomplete); New York Public Library.

Publication History

MAGAZINE TITLE AND TITLE CHANGES: *The Nickelodeon* (January 1909–March 25, 1911); *Motography* (April 1911–July 13, 1918).
VOLUME AND ISSUE DATA: Vol. I, No. 1–Vol. II, No. 6 (January 1909–December 1909), monthly; Vol. III, No. 1–Vol. IV, No. 12 (January 1, 1910–December 15, 1910), semimonthly; Vol. V, No. 1–Vol. V, No. 12 (January 7, 1911–March 25, 1911), weekly; Vol. V, No. 4 [new numbering]–Vol. VII, No. 6 (April 1911–June 1912), monthly; Vol. VIII, No. 1–Vol. XI, No. 13 (July 6, 1912–June 27, 1914), biweekly; Vol. XII, No. 1–Vol. XX, No. 2 (July 4, 1914–July 13, 1918), weekly.
PUBLISHER AND PLACE OF PUBLICATION: The Electricity Magazine Corporation, Monadnock Building, Chicago, Ill.
EDITOR: Ed J. Mock and Paul H. Woodruff (January 1909–January 15, 1916); Paul H. Woodruff (January 22, 1916–July 13, 1918).

Alan Gevinson

MOVIE

Movie, which began publication in June 1962, initially sought "to help remedy the unhealthy lack of reasoned disagreement about films in Britain."[1] Chief target of its disagreement was the sociological criticism of *Sight and Sound,** a journal subsequently described in the pages of *Movie* as "an intellectual amoeba aimlessly engulfing all manner of critical detritus."[2]

Influenced in part by *Cahiers du Cinéma*'s* *politique des auteurs*, *Movie* declared its auteurist bias clearly in its first issue through the means of a chart ranking several hundred British and American directors under categories such as "great" (Alfred Hitchcock, Howard Hawks), "brilliant" (Joseph Losey, George Cukor, Vincente Minnelli, Otto Preminger, Nicholas Ray), "very talented" (Hugo Fregonese, Robert Aldrich, Budd Boetticher, John Ford, Samuel Fuller, Arthur Penn, Don Siegel, Frank Tashlin), "talented" (John Huston, Phil Karlson, Robert Mulligan), "competent or ambitious" (David Lean, Carol Reed, Tony Richardson, Lewis Milestone, Billy Wilder, Robert Wise), and "the rest" (Paul Czinner, Sidney Gilliat, Frank Launder, H. Bruce Humberstone, Henry Koster, Norman Taurog). *Movie* also observed *Cahiers*' policy of reviewing only those films which interested its critics, a practice which resulted in greater attention being paid to American than to British films. *Movie*'s commitment to the cinema of directors can be charted in its special issues devoted to Otto Preminger (Nos. 2 and 4), Howard Hawks (No. 5), Nicholas Ray (No. 9), Richard Brooks (No. 12), Josef von Sternberg (No. 13), Elia Kazan (No. 19), and Max Ophuls (No. 29/30).

Movie began as an offshoot of the film section of an undergraduate magazine, *Oxford Opinion*, to which Ian Cameron, V. F. Perkins, and Mark Shivas contributed articles while at Oxford. Influenced by the F. R. Leavis school of "close analysis," the articles in *Movie* were less flamboyant and more thoughtfully reasoned than those in the *Cahiers* of the late fifties but were also decidedly less academic than those of *Screen*,* its chief English-language rival in the seventies. Somewhat phenomenological in its approach to the cinema, *Movie* is characterized by a commonsensical, descriptive criticism which seeks to account for its critics' experiences of films.[3] Until the late seventies when *Movie* began to confront *Screen*, it avoided issues of film theory.[4] Its own policies were felt, by its editors, to be implicit in its critical practice.[5]

The addition of Andrew Britton, author of a twenty-six-page attack on the ideology of *Screen* in No. 26 (Winter 1978/1979), to the editorial board and that of Richard Dyer as a regular contributor illustrated a broadening of interest in theoretical as well as other issues that can be dated back to the magazine's reemergence (in a new format), after a three-year hiatus, in 1975 (No. 20). Starting with No. 20, *Movie* began to broach topics such as television, genre, and period studies; *Movie* No. 24 dealt exclusively with the musical, while No. 27/28 analyzed American cinema in the seventies, a topic treated earlier in sections devoted to that subject in Nos. 21, 22, 23, and 25.

The tone of *Movie* in the early sixties was set by editor Ian Cameron and associate editors Mark Shivas, V. F. Perkins, and Paul Mayersberg, who wrote the bulk of the magazine. American auteurists such as Andrew Sarris, Eugene Archer, and Peter Bogdanovich also wrote feature articles and "news" columns for *Movie*; and essays by Jacques Rivette, Claude Chabrol, J.-A. Fieschi and other *Cahiers* regulars were occasionally reprinted during this period. At the same time, Laurence Alloway, Charles Barr, Barry Boys, and Ray Durgnat provided *Movie* with a range of approaches to director studies and stylistic issues that made it the most eclectic of British journals. But the character of *Movie* has become inextricably identified, over the years, with the writings of Cameron, Perkins, and Robin Wood, the last of whom began contributing to the magazine in September 1962 (No. 2). Wood's work, in particular, typifies the attempts of the magazine to integrate discussions of style and theme through close readings of individual films and the collective works of individual filmmakers. And Wood's changing interests from questions of directors to those of genre (the American horror film) and period (the American cinema of the seventies) and from nontheatrical to quasi-theoretical concerns best reflect those of the magazine as a whole.

Though its publication history is somewhat erratic, the editorial policy of *Movie* has remained more or less consistent during the twenty-two years of its operation. For *Movie* today, as in 1962, enthusiasm for the cinema is "the first essential of good criticism,"[6] and its authors continue to use their own experiences of the films as starting points for their criticism.

Notes

1. *Movie*, No. 1, June 1962, n.p.
2. *Movie*, No. 26, Winter 1978/1979, p. 1.
3. John Caughie, ed., *Theories of Authorship* (London: Routledge & Kegan Paul, 1981), p. 50.
4. Caughie, pp. 49–50.
5. *Movie*, No. 26, Winter 1978/1979, p. 1.
6. *Movie*, No. 1, June 1962, n.p.

Information Sources

BIBLIOGRAPHY:
Cameron, Ian. *Movie Reader* (New York: Praeger, 1972).
Caughie, John, ed. *Theories of Authorship* (London: Routledge & Kegan Paul, 1981).
Rohdie, Sam. "Movie Reader, Film as Film." *Screen*, No. 13, Winter 1972/1973, pp. 135–145.
INDEX SOURCES: British Humanities Index; The Critical Index; FIAF International Index to Film Periodicals; Film Literature Index; The New Film Index.
REPRINT EDITIONS: University Microfilms.
LOCATION SOURCES: Columbia University; Cornell University; Library of Congress; New York Public Library; Northwestern University; University of Oregon.

Publication History

MAGAZINE TITLE AND TITLE CHANGES: *Movie*.
VOLUME AND ISSUE DATA: Nos. 1–11 (June 1962–July and August 1963), monthly; Nos. 12–14 (Spring 1965–Autumn 1965), quarterly; Nos. 15–19 (Spring 1968–Winter 1971/1972), annual; Nos. 20–29/30 (Spring 1975–Summer 1982), irregular. [Many issues of *Movie* contain no dates.]
PUBLISHER AND PLACE OF PUBLICATION: Movie Magazine Ltd., 3 Antrim Mansions, London N.W. 3, England (Nos. 1–5); Nicholas Luard, 3 Antrim Mansions, London N.W.3, England (Nos. 6–9); Nicholas Luard, 18 Greek Street, London W.1, England (Nos. 10–11); Nicholas Luard, 3 Cork Street, London W.1, England (Nos. 12–14); Nicholas Luard/Movie Magazine Ltd., 21 Ivor Place, London N.W.1, England (Nos. 15–17); Nicholas Luard/Movie Magazine Ltd., 23-29 Emerald Street, London WC1N 3QL, England (Nos. 18–19); Ian Cameron, 25 Lloyd Place, Baker Street, London WC1X 9AT, England (Nos. 20–27/28); Ian Cameron, 2a Roman Way, London N7 8XG, England (No. 29/30).
EDITOR: Ian Cameron (Nos. 1–19); Editorial Board of Charles Barr, Ian Cameron, V. F. Perkins, Mark Shivas, Michael Walker, and Robin Wood (Nos. 20–29/30),

with the addition of Joe Stefanos (Nos. 21–26), Douglas Pye (Nos. 23–29/30), Andrew Britton (Nos. 25–29/30), and Jim Hillier (Nos. 27–29/30).

John Belton

THE MOVIE

The Movie, a unique venture in film magazines, was designed week by week to build into an encyclopedia of world cinema. Beginning with the birth of the talkies, working its way through to the present, and then returning to silent cinema (including two issues on the prehistory of film), in its first 132 issues it covered a wide span of movies, trends, countries, directors, and stars.

With its two consultant editors, David Robinson of *The Times* (London) and Richard Schickel of *Time* magazine, *The Movie* aimed at a popular, but serious, readership trying to satisfy both the movie buff's thirst for information as well as a more general audience. With readable and reliable articles and an attractive, picture-oriented layout, it by and large succeeded. Each issue began with a general historical analysis followed by trend and genre articles, film spreads, and director/star profiles: all were designed to fall into the particular theme of that issue.

Within this general framework there was room for the occasional, more exploratory writing—for example, on the portrayal of women in cinema (Nos. 8, 95, and 112), psychology and film (No. 90), or immigrants in film (No. 102). Or room could be found for more idiosyncratic areas of coverage—movie memorabilia (No. 132), fan magazines (No. 12), or Hitler comedies (No. 20). But *The Movie*'s greatest strength was the range of topics and countries that the magazine covered dealing with areas of cinema history that are less familiar to Western audiences—Third World cinema (No. 70), commercial Indian films (No. 93), underground films (No. 65), or silent music hall stars (No. 106) all appeared alongside the more traditional articles on Hollywood and European cinema.

The Movie never pushed a particular line, deliberately choosing to be eclectic in its approach—a decision that could result in quite divergent views being presented in the same issue. No. 90, for instance, which dealt with the history of film criticism, had contributions from several conflicting trends of analysis.

Toward the end of its run (from Nos. 133 to 158) *The Movie* changed into an A-to-Z of personalities. It was a disappointing conclusion to the series as it finally lost its breadth to concentrate on popular British and American cinema.

Information Sources

INDEX SOURCES: Nos. 145 and 156 were an index to the magazine.
REPRINT EDITIONS: Orbis has reprinted portions of the magazine in hard cover.
LOCATION SOURCES: No information.

Publication History

MAGAZINE TITLE AND TITLE CHANGES: *The Movie: The Illustrated History of the Cinema* (Nos. 1–132); *The Movie: The Illustrated Who's Who of the Cinema* (Nos. 133–158).
VOLUME AND ISSUE DATA: Nos. 1–158 (February 1980–March 1983), weekly.
PUBLISHER AND PLACE OF PUBLICATION: Orbis Publishing, 22 Bedfordbury, London W.C.2, England.
EDITOR: Ann Lloyd.

Sally Hibbin

MOVIE ACTION MAGAZINE. See Appendix 2

MOVIE AND RADIO GUIDE. See Appendix 2

MOVIE CLASSIC. See Appendix 2

MOVIE DIGEST (1925). See Appendix 2

MOVIE DIGEST (1972). See Appendix 2

MOVIE FAN. See Appendix 2

MOVIEGOER

Moviegoer was, by admission, an attempt. Described by its editor, James Stoller, as beginning "small, loose, and hopeful" and advertised as being "without definite corporate personality," *Moviegoer* sought to establish itself as a forum for the critical discussion of the cinema where good writers could gather and be offered "an intelligent and human frame for their work" within a larger criticism "weakened by frivolity, outlandishness, a want of firmness and good sense."[1] Accepting Paul Goodman's challenge, declared in 1940, that no serious magazine on the cinema could exist where there are no serious films—a view Goodman steadfastly maintained in a piece written for the inaugural issue of *Moviegoer* (Winter 1964)—Stoller and his associate editor, Roger Greenspun, tried to prove otherwise for the cinema of the sixties, offering an impressive array of established critics and newcomers whose essays and reviews covered a wide range of films and subjects from an equally diverse range of perspectives.

Moviegoer's three issues featured some writers who at that time possessed both national and international reputations. Paul Goodman, the novelist, poet, and literary critic, was also a film critic. Articles written for *Partisan Review* in the forties are reprinted: "Film Chronicle (1940): Chaplin" (No. 1) and "Griffith and the Technical Innovations" (No. 2). And Goodman comments not only on his erstwhile occupation—film critic—but also on his present opinion of the cinema in "A Reply" (No. 1). Pauline Kael, newly arrived from California to the New York scene but already embroiled in the film versus movies controversy, contributed a review of Tony Richardson's *Loneliness of the Long Distance Runner* ("Throwing the Race," No. 1, later reprinted as "The Long Distance Runner Throws the Race" in *I Lost It at the Movies*, Boston: Little, Brown, 1965) and a selection of her "Berkeley Film Notes" (No. 1, later reprinted in "Notes on 280 Movies" in *Kiss Kiss Bang Bang*, Boston: Little, Brown, 1968). Andrew Sarris, the auteur critic, elaborated on his theory in "Pop Go the Movies!" (No. 2, later reprinted in *The Primal Screen*, New York: Simon and Schuster, 1973) and discussed Max Ophuls's style in "Memory and Max Ophuls" (No. 3). Susan Sontag, at the beginning of her career as a novelist, literary critic, philosopher, and filmmaker, explained Jean Luc Godard's *Vivre Sa Vie* (No. 2), an essay that would appear later in her important collection, *Against Interpretation* (New York: Noonday Press, 1966), while the well-known theatre critic Eric Bentley reviewed Chaplin's *Woman of Paris* and the filmmaker's auto-biography in "Charlie Chaplin and Peggy Hopkins Joyce: A Comment on a Woman of Paris" (No. 3). Finally, the French critic and semiotician, Roland Barthes, by 1966 somewhat controversial in his own country but still relatively unknown in the United States, is given one of his earliest introductions to the American critical scene. Barthes's essay, "Garbo's Face" (No. 3), offered *Moviegoer* readers not only an early glimpse of the celebrated critic but also a translation of this famous *Mythologies* essay by the eminent French translator and personal friend of Barthes, Richard Howard.

Moviegoer's major deficiency concerns the bulk of articles written by its young critics. Although at times perceptive and witty and always enthusiastic, writers like Stoller ("After the 400 Blows," No. 1), Greenspun ("Through the Looking Glass," No. 1, and "Individual Combat," No. 2), and David Phelps ("Rosselini and the Flowers of St. Francis," No. 1, and "Rosencrantz vs. Guildenstern," No. 1) penned long and elaborate essays and reviews that although insightful needed editing and intellectual restraint. After reading an essay on *Shoot the Piano Player* ("Through the Glass Darkly," No. 1), one reader felt compelled to write: "I don't pretend to understand Greenspun's article in any detail but is that what he saw on the screen? Doesn't it do Truffaut an enormous injustice to make him come on like Descartes?"[2]

Despite certain sophomoric excesses and academic-leaden profundity, how-ever, enthusiasm always won out. Love of the cinema and a serious regard for its criticism is evident throughout the miscellany of reviews and studies that complemented the major contributions. Moreover, articles written by William

S. Pechter on Alfred Hitchcock ("The Director Vanishes," No. 2) and Alain Resnais ("On Resnais," No. 1)—both of which are reprinted in the author's *24 Times a Second*, New York: Harper & Row, 1971—and Noel Burch's study of Luis Buñuel, "Two Cinemas: Diary of a Chambermaid" (No. 3), compared favorably with the criticism of Sontag, Sarris, and Kael; while reviews by Paul Brodkorb, Jr., of François Truffaut's *La Peau Douce* (No. 3) and Otto Preminger's *The Cardinal* (No. 2), and Paul Breslow's review of Francesco Rosi's *Salvatore Giuliano* (No. 3) were sensitive and concise in a style reminiscent of the review-essays of *Film Quarterly** and *Sight and Sound.**

Moviegoer, despite its faults, provided three issues of decent film criticism. In keeping with its editorial policy, subject coverage was wide; and considering the diversity of its authors, the claim of no corporate personality was justified. Viewed from the eighties, *Moviegoer*'s brief life may tempt us to file it away as just another film periodical. Still we must marvel at the ambition and praise the intent, agreeing with the editors that the early sixties was indeed a time for a serious journal of the cinema. *Moviegoer* attested to such a cinema, and the journal's swift demise was unfortunate.

Notes

1. No. 1, Winter 1964, unpaginated verso of cover.
2. No. 2, Summer/Autumn 1964, unpaginated verso of cover.

Information Sources

INDEX SOURCES: None.
REPRINT EDITIONS: None.
LOCATION SOURCES: Library of Congress; New York Public Library; University of Illinois; University of Southern California.

Publication History

MAGAZINE TITLE AND TITLE CHANGES: *Moviegoer*.
VOLUME AND ISSUE DATA: No. 1 (Winter 1964); No. 2 (Summer/Autumn 1964); No. 3 (Summer 1966).
PUBLISHER AND PLACE OF PUBLICATION: Moviegoer, Box 128, Stuyvesant Station, New York, N.Y. 10019.
EDITOR: James Stoller.

Dennis R. Brunning

MOVIELAND & T.V. TIME. See Appendix 2

MOVIE LIFE. See Appendix 2

MOVIE MARKETING. See MOVIE/T.V. MARKETING

MOVIE MIRROR. See Appendix 2

MOVIE PICTORIAL. See Appendix 2

MOVIE PLAY. See Appendix 2

MOVIES. See Appendix 2

THE MOVIES

Published for five months in 1983, *The Movies* has been described as the motion picture equivalent to *Sports Illustrated* and *Gentleman's Quarterly*. At times it was silly, at other times pretentious, and only occasionally witty or clever. Its contents were a distinctly uneasy mix of intelligent commentary and childish pseudofan material. Only *The Movies* could boast an issue (No. 1) which featured an article by Louis Malle on Sean Penn and a profile of James Stewart by President Reagan's former ballet-dancing son Ron. An expensively produced magazine, it ceased publication after only five issues when (according to *The Wall Street Journal* of October 17, 1983), "*The Movie*'s sole financial backer, Neil C. Morgan, a Houston real estate developer, declined to provide additional money."

Publication History

BIBLIOGRAPHY:
Block, Alex Ben. "Could This Become the Movie World's Sports Illustrated?" *Los Angeles Herald Examiner*, May 5, 1983, Section A, p. 8.
Colker, David. "Movies Magazine May Collapse Soon." *Los Angeles Herald Examiner*, October 11, 1983, Section B, p. 11.
London, Michael. "A Movie-Oriented Movie Magazine?" *Los Angeles Times*, August 31, 1983, Part VI, p. 1.
Searles, Jack. "The Movies Premieres at Newsstands." *Los Angeles Herald Examiner*, June 13, 1983, Section C, p. 1.
INDEX SOURCES: None.
REPRINT EDITIONS: None.
LOCATION SOURCES: Academy of Motion Picture Arts and Sciences.

Publication History

MAGAZINE TITLE AND TITLE CHANGES: *The Movies*.
VOLUME AND ISSUE DATA: Vol. I, No. 1–Vol. I, No. 5 (July 1983–November 1983), monthly.

PUBLISHER AND PLACE OF PUBLICATION: Joe Armstrong, 30 East Forty-second
    Street, New York, N.Y. 10017.
EDITOR: Charles Michener.

Anthony Slide

MOVIE SHOW. See Appendix 2

MOVIES ILLUSTRATED. See Appendix 2

MOVIES NOW. See Appendix 2

MOVIE STARS PARADE. See Appendix 2

MOVIE STORY. See Appendix 2

MOVIE STORY MAGAZINE. See Appendix 2

MOVIETONE NEWS

Movietone News began life in 1971 as the newsletter of the Seattle Film Society
with the look and contents of a typical newsletter. The first issue opened with
"Report from the Program Director," R. C. Dale (who was to contribute many
interesting pieces through the years). Early issues featured reports on and criticism of local film going in Seattle, book reviews, and film reviews, usually by
Peter Hogue and Richard Jameson. The latter also wrote as Jed Leland (and
provided an obituary on him in issue No. 14).

The periodical became a "real" magazine with issue No. 12 (March 15, 1972)
but listed no editor—only an editorial board—until Richard Jameson was officially given the title with issue No. 24. *Movietone News* featured chiefly film
criticism—of both current and past films—which was always of a high and
readable quality. Some interviews began to appear from 1977 onward.

Movietone News received national attention in the winter of 1976/1977 when
20th Century-Fox learned of its existence and its use of the registered name of
the company's newsreel library. After various requests to cease and desist and
talk of holding the Seattle Film Society "accountable in damages," 20th Century-
Fox agreed to permit the magazine to continue using the name. However, the

"fuss" seemed to have a bad effect on the magazine. During most of its life it had appeared monthly, but now *Movietone News* took on a highly irregular publication schedule, and the last issue to appear was No. 66-67 (March 13, 1981).

Information Sources

INDEX SOURCES: FIAF International Index to Film Periodicals; Film Literature Index.
REPRINT EDITIONS: None.
LOCATION SOURCES: Academy of Motion Picture Arts and Sciences.

Publication History

MAGAZINE TITLE AND TITLE CHANGES: *Movietone News*.
VOLUME AND ISSUE DATA: No. 1 (March 24, 1971); No. 2 (April 7, 1971); No. 3 (April 28, 1971); No. 4 (May 19, 1971); No. 5 (July 7, 1971); No. 6 (September 15, 1971); No. 7 (October 15, 1971); No. 8 (November 15, 1971); No. 9 (December 15, 1971); No. 10 (January 15, 1972); No. 11 (February 15, 1972); Nos. 12–46 (March 1972–December 1975), monthly with some exceptions; No. 47 (January 21, 1976); No. 48 (February 29, 1976); No. 49 (April 18, 1976); No. 50 (June 28, 1976); No. 51 (August 29, 1976); No. 52 (October 11, 1976); No. 53 (January 16, 1977); No. 54 (June 20, 1977); No. 55 (September 16, 1977); No. 56 (November 4, 1977); No. 57 (February 22, 1978); No. 58-59 (August 14, 1978); No. 60-61 (February 5, 1979); No. 62-63 (December 29, 1979); No. 64-65 (March 13, 1980); No. 66-67 (March 13, 1981).
PUBLISHER AND PLACE OF PUBLICATION: Seattle Film Society, 3937 Fifteenth Avenue N.E., Seattle, Wash. (Nos. 1–5); Seattle Film Society, P.O. Box 22110, Seattle, Wash. 98122 (Nos. 6–14); Seattle Film Society, 1213 N.E. Fifty-second Street, Seattle, Wash. 98105 (Nos. 15–16); Seattle Film Society, Eighteenth Avenue N.E., Seattle, Wash. 98105 (Nos. 17–54); Seattle Film Society, 3002 N.E. Ninety-second Street, Seattle, Wash. 98115 (Nos. 55–60-61); Seattle Film Society, P.O. Box 17477, Seattle, Wash. 98107 (Nos. 62-63–66-67).
EDITOR: No editor listed (Nos. 1–23); Richard T. Jameson (Nos. 24–66-67).

Anthony Slide

MOVIE/T.V. MARKETING

In the early fifties, Glenn F. Ireton was living in Japan as a civilian employee of the U.S. Department of Defense, specializing in motion pictures. Ireton was convinced by George Weltner and Al Daff, the then-presidents of Paramount and Universal studios respectively, that Japan would soon become a major market for American films and that there was a need for a trade paper covering the Far East. Resigning from the Department of Defense, Ireton in 1953 established *Far East Film News* with the help of his wife, Kikuko Koboyashi, the second daughter of a Bank of Japan official.[1] The paper flourished from an initial circulation of 5,000 to its present 100,000 circulation, changing its name twice in the sixties before settling on *Movie/T.V. Marketing*.

Although noted for its heavy coverage of the Asian film industry, *Movie/T.V. Marketing* provides information on all aspects of the film and television industry worldwide, with each issue containing such regular features as "Dateline Digest," "New Product," "Asian BoxOffice," "Worldwide T.V.," "Festivals and Trade Fairs," "Communications Now," and "Specialized Cinema." Perhaps the most valuable listing to be found in *Movie/T.V. Marketing* is the regular "Calendar of Film and Television Festivals and Related Events." In recent years, the paper has adopted the curious idea of printing the back half, with its non-Asian news, upside down.

In addition to the paper, which began as a weekly and is now published monthly, *Movie/T.V. Marketing* produces two useful reference volumes annually: *Global Motion Picture Yearbook*, published since 1955, offers trade listings for producers, exporters, importers, distributors, associations, and government departments; *Worldwide Television Survey*, published since 1964, provides similar listings for the television industry, along with airtime information and T.V. set count/sales situations.

Notes

1. Information provided in a letter, dated August 25, 1983, from William J. Ireton.

Information Sources

INDEX SOURCES: None.
REPRINT EDITIONS: University Microfilms.
LOCATION SOURCES: Academy of Motion Picture Arts and Sciences (lacks some early issues); Princeton University.

Publication History

MAGAZINE TITLE AND TITLE CHANGES: *Far East Film News* (June 15, 1953–May 1961); *Global Movie Marketing* (June 1961–December 1961); *Movie Marketing* (January 1962–January 1966); *Movie/T.V. Marketing* (February 1966 to present).
VOLUME AND ISSUE DATA: Vol. I, No. 1–Vol. XI, No. 1 (June 15, 1953–July 4, 1958), weekly; Vol. XI, Nos. 2 & 3–Vol. XII, Nos. 18–19 (July 11 and 18, 1958–May 1959), biweekly; Vol. XIII, No. 1 (June 1959 to present), monthly.
PUBLISHER AND PLACE OF PUBLICATION: Glenn F. Ireton, Box 30, Central Post Office, Tokyo, Japan.
EDITOR: Glenn F. Ireton (June 15, 1953–January 1978); Asia M. Ireton (February 1978 to present).

Anthony Slide

MOVIE WEEKLY. See Appendix 2

MOVING IMAGE. See SUPER-8 FILMAKER

MOVING PICTURE NEWS. See MOTION PICTURE NEWS

MOVING PICTURE STORIES. See Appendix 2

THE MOVING PICTURE WEEKLY. See Appendix 3

THE MOVING PICTURE WORLD

One of the original, independent weekly trade papers for motion picture exhibitors, *The Moving Picture World* was first published on March 9, 1907. It was founded by James P. Chalmers, Jr., former editor of *Camera and Darkroom*, and Alfred Saunders, an editor at *Views and Film Index*. According to pioneer historian and journalist Terry Ramsaye, *The Moving Picture World* was originally to be titled *The Lantern Slide View and Motion Picture Renter*. Saunders brought a mock copy of the first issue to the offices of Herbert Miles, an early New York exchangeman, who in return for purchasing advertising space prevailed upon Chalmers to illustrate the cover with a world globe and to rename the paper *The Moving Picture World.*[1]

The World Photography Publishing Company had offices at 361 Broadway in New York. The first issue cost five cents with an annual subscription rate of two dollars. Saunders took editorial charge of the weekly while Chalmers handled the business end. John A. Archer acted as circulation manager, bookkeeper, stenographer, and general office assistant.

The Moving Picture World and View Photographer, as *The Moving Picture World* was initially called, was dedicated to all interested in animated photography and its projectionists, lanternists, slide makers, vocalists and song slide lecturers, and travel storytellers. It promised to give all the latest information procurable here and abroad. Special features to be published monthly were English and French letters of motion picture doings abroad. It was open to all who had information or news to communicate. Exhibitors were encouraged to make it their guide, philosopher, and friend when they were in doubt or when they wished to buy a lantern projecting machine or any numerous accessories appertaining thereto.[2] Its declaration of purpose also was to give "only the best news concerning the film industry, describing briefly each new film as it is produced, taking note of its quality and giving an unbiased opinion of its merits or demerits."[3]

After a falling out over editorial policies, Alfred H. Saunders left *The Moving Picture World* in April 1908. Chalmers took over full editorial charge and became the guiding power behind the paper until his untimely death in an elevator accident on March 27, 1912. His father, Charles P. Chalmers, Sr., then took over publication of *The Moving Picture World* as president of the Chalmers Publishing Company.

Several staff members came to work at the paper before Chalmers's death. G. P. Von Harleman started as advertising solicitor in 1908 and later became Chicago and Los Angeles representative. In 1909, Archie MacArthur became advertising manager. Later additions to the staff included George Blaisdell who arrived in May 1912, Robert L. McElroy who also arrived in 1912, and Randall M. White who came in 1914.

Frequently, *The Moving Picture World* had "to reiterate its position that it was absolutely independent and free of control from any house, firm or member of any firm, or connected with any manufacturers of films, machines, or accessories connected with this industry."[4] Despite this, Terry Ramsaye has implied that *The Moving Picture World* prospered through hard work but also because of the support of the newly formed Motion Picture Patents Company.

The Moving Picture World's editorial and advertising point of view was geared toward the exhibition field. It possessed a slightly paternalistic, slightly condescending writing style, yet purported to be the "friend" of the exhibitor. The paper's policy, as stated in the issue for August 7, 1909, was "to watch over the interests of the industry as a whole—to provide even justice to all branches of the industry, to keep in touch with every progressive movement, and to bring home to the reader the importance of manufacturers to their interests. These are the simple duties of a trade paper."

Like the infant motion picture industry which strove for legitimacy and acceptance in the eyes of the other branches of the performing arts and the general public, *The Moving Picture World* desired a reputation for respectability. Though based in New York, it was remarkably thorough in covering news items about exhibition, exchanges, and film manufacturing both in the United States and abroad. Such columns as "Chicago News," "Among Motion Picture Theatres," "Doings in Los Angeles and Vicinity," "Observations by Our Man about Town" (originating in New York), and "On the Screen" by Lux Graphicus admirably covered domestic industry news. "Foreign Trade Notes" and the occasional "London Letter" discussed European news. Some interesting, early full-page articles dealt with the shooting of Colonel William Selig and director Francis Boggs in Los Angeles (November 11, 1911), the Kalem Company in the Orient (December 2, 1911), "The Film in France" by W. Stephen Bush (September 8, 1913), "South African Newsletter" (April 10, 1915), and white slave films doing "capacity business" in Columbus, Ohio (February 14, 1914).

The format of *The Moving Picture World* remained basically the same for the duration of its publication. The contents would generally consist of an editorial or "Facts and Comments," news from Chicago or Los Angeles, "Music for Pictures," "The Motion Picture Educator," "Advertising for Exhibitors," "Comments on Films," "Reviews of Notable Releases," "The Projection Department," "Manufacturers Advanced Notes," "Licensed and Independent Releases," "Calendar of Independent Releases," "Index of Film Stories,"

"Correspondence," "Classifieds," and profuse advertising matter at the front and back of each issue.

"Facts and Comments" dealt with current events and issues pertaining to exhibition and the motion picture community at large. Some of the topics are still of concern to the industry today, while others provide a wealth of information for the scholar. Many of the editorials were written by Louis Reeves Harrison or W. Stephen Bush, both of whom were long-time contributors to *The Moving Picture World*. Some examples of editorial topics which appeared in the paper are "Why Vaudeville Is Finished in Moving Picture Theatres" (April 23, 1910), "How the Pictures Cause Juvenile Delinquency" (November 18, 1911), "Combatting Official Censorship" (September 18, 1913), "Dramatic License v. Plausibility" (March 28, 1914), "Copyright Law: The *Ben Hur* Case" (December 9, 1911), and "Is the Nickel Show on the Wane?" (February 28, 1914).

Several features provided by *The Moving Picture World* are of exceptional value to the film scholar. "Comments on Films," "Manufacturers Advanced Notes," "Reviews of Notable Films," and "Stories of the Films" offer invaluable information on cast and production credits, plot synopses, and contemporary critical evaluation. Happily through the twenties, *The Moving Picture World* did publish an index to its reviews and synopses with each volume.

"The Projection Department," which was edited for some twenty years by F. H. Richardson, included a questions-and-answers section and featured exceptionally detailed operating instructions—with diagrams, illustrations, and photographs—for early projection machines such as the Motiograph (April 9, 1910), the Edison Model B Machine (June 1, 1912), and the Simplex Projector (November 18, 1911).

For several years, Epes Winthrop Sargent was responsible for the "Advertising for Exhibitors" column, which provided advice and tips on all aspects of exhibition and featured articles by and about pioneer exhibitors such as S. L. Rothapfel (September 28, 1909). For a time Sargent also edited "The Scenario Writer" column (later called "The Photoplaywright" in an example of upgrading the heading for the sake of legitimacy). It provided tips on how to sell your screenplays and what types of stories studios would buy.

Clarence E. Sinn was responsible for the column first titled "The Song and the Singer" (when song slides were a popular feature of the motion picture theatre program) which was later called "Music for the Picture." In 1919 George W. Benyon wrote this column.

Two new columns appeared in the twenties: "Straight from the Shoulder Reports," featuring single-paragraph reports as to the box-office prospects of individual films as mailed in by local exhibitors; and "The Pep of the Program," providing reviews of short subjects from the various studios. Stock market quotes were also included, beginning in 1925.

The Moving Picture World is equally valuable in that it provides photographs and news stories on contemporary personalities. Among those it featured in the teens are Mabel Taliafero (December 23, 1911), John Bunny (July 21, 1911),

J. Stuart Blackton and Albert E. Smith (June 1, 1912), Alice Blaché (June 15, 1912), Mignon Anderson (June 11, 1913), W. W. Hodkinson (February 14, 1914), and Albert Capellani (May 1, 1915).

With the publication of the December 31, 1927, issue, John F. Chalmers, president of the company which had published *The World* since 1914, concluded publication of the paper as a separate entity. It merged with *Exhibitor's Herald* and on January 7, 1928, became *Exhibitor's Herald and Moving Picture World* (later shortened to *Exhibitor's Herald World*).

In announcing the merger, John F. Chalmers wrote:

> J. P. Chalmers Jr., the founder and leader of *MPW*, was privileged to lay the foundation of character and high principles of independence, service, fair play, and rugged honesty from which we who have followed have never departed.... *MPW* has steadily won and held the greatest of all verified exhibitor circulation and the corresponding goodwill and confidence of the industry.[5]

While much of the above may be true, beginning about the tenure of Arthur James as editor-in-chief in 1920 and continuing under Robert E. Welsh's and William J. Reilly's editorship, the quality had declined appreciably in terms of writing style, content, and even in terms of the quality of the paper stock on which *The Moving Picture World* was published. The articles were much shorter and seemed to consist predominantly of studio advertising and planted stories concerning a studio's latest stars and productions. The articles were also extremely redundant, with a piece on a star's latest vehicle being filled with reports on past cinematic exploits and interminable lists of "bit" acting credits. The number of articles on industry leaders or business news, which were an important aspect of *The Moving Picture World* in the teens, diminished. *The World* became more sensationalist and exploitive in its post-1920 reporting; the coverage of Rudolph Valentino's funeral is especially blatant.

Notes

1. Terry Ramsaye, "A Greater Paper for a Greater Industry," *Motion Picture Herald*, Vol. 102, No. 1, January 3, 1931, p. 31.
2. *The Moving Picture World*, Vol. 1, No. 1, March 9, 1907, p. 3.
3. *Ibid.*, March 10, 1917, p. 1482.
4. *Ibid.*, Vol. 1, No. 3, April 27, 1907, p. 115.
5. *Ibid.*, Vol. 89, No. 9, December 31, 1927, p. 7.

Information Sources

BIBLIOGRAPHY:
Hoff, James L. "Story of the Beginning." *The Moving Picture World*, March 10, 1917, pp. 1481–1483.
INDEX SOURCES: An Index to Volume 1, 1907, of *The Moving Picture World and*

View Photographer compiled by Rita Horwitz (American Film Institute, 1974); The Film Index.

REPRINT EDITIONS: Datamatics; Library of Congress Photoduplication Service.

LOCATION SOURCES: Academy of Motion Picture Arts and Sciences; Library of Congress; New York Public Library; University of California at Los Angeles; University of Illinois.

Publication History

MAGAZINE TITLE AND TITLE CHANGES: *The Moving Picture World and View Photographer* (March 9, 1907–May 4, 1907); *The Moving Picture World* (May 11, 1907–December 31, 1927).

VOLUME AND ISSUE DATA: Vol. I, No. 1–Vol. LXXXIX, No. 9 (March 9, 1907–December 31, 1927), weekly.

PUBLISHER AND PLACE OF PUBLICATION: World Photographic Publishing Company, 361 Broadway, New York, N.Y. (Vol. I, No. 1–Vol. II, No. 21); World Photographic Publishing Company, 125 East Twenty-third Street, New York, N.Y. (Vol. II, No. 22–Vol. XII, No. 2); Chalmers Publishing Company, Inc., 125 East Twenty-third Street, New York, N.Y. (Vol. XII, No. 3–Vol. XIV, No. 9); Chalmers Publishing Company, Inc., 17 Madison Avenue, New York, N.Y. (Vol. XIV, No. 10–Vol. XXXIV, No. 5); Chalmers Publishing Company, 516 Fifth Avenue, New York, N.Y. (Vol. XXXIV, No. 6–Vol. LXXXIX, No. 9).

EDITOR: Alfred Saunders (March 9, 1909–April 25, 1908); J. P. Chalmers, Jr. (May 2, 1908–March 27, 1912); no editor listed (1912–1919); George Blaisdell (1919–June 26, 1920); Arthur James (Editor-in-Chief, 1920–1922); Robert E. Welsh (1922–1925); William J. Reilly (1925–1927).

Anne Kail

THE MOVING PICTURE WORLD AND VIEW PHOTOGRAPHER. See THE MOVING PICTURE WORLD

THE MUPPET MAGAZINE. See Appendix 1

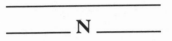

NATIONAL BOARD OF REVIEW MAGAZINE. See
FILMS IN REVIEW

**NATIONAL CINEMA WORKSHOP AND
APPRECIATION LEAGUE BULLETIN.** See CINEMA
PROGRESS

THE NEW MOVIE. See Appendix 2

NEW MOVIES. See FILMS IN REVIEW

NEW RKO RADIO FLASH. See Appendix 3

NEWS FROM THE AMERICAN FILM CENTER, INC.
See FILM NEWS

NEWSREEL

First published in June 1978, *Newsreel* is a useful publication for anyone
concerned with collecting autographs of film personalities. It features addresses
of such personalities, articles on the subject (covering topics as diverse as the

authenticity of Jean Harlow's autographs and the question of whether John Wayne used an autopen during his last years), and examples of facsimile signatures. (The July 1981 issue was exclusively devoted to facsimile autographs.) The majority of the articles on show business personalities published in *Newsreel* are valueless for research purposes, although in its early years *Newsreel* did feature a number of interesting interviews: Mary Miles Minter (Vol. 1, No. 1) Colleen Moore (Vol. 1, No. 5), Blanche Sweet (Vol. 1, No. 6), Joan Bennett (Vol. 2, No. 5), and Lois Wilson (Vol. 2, No. 6).

The numbering system used by *Newsreel* in its formative years is just about impossible to document. It began as a monthly and then became bimonthly but in some years would publish only four issues. It was published by Tom Parry but would sometimes include the names of either Motion Picture Collectibles Association, Entertainment Enterprises, or The International Association of Philographers. In May 1979 *Newsreel* combined with *The Autograph Magazine*, and from May to October 1979 it was published as *The Autograph Newsreel*. Bob Bennett took over as editor and publisher in May 1982, and since then *Newsreel* has appeared on a regular bimonthly basis.

Information Sources

INDEX SOURCES: None.
REPRINT EDITIONS: None.
LOCATION SOURCES: Academy of Motion Picture Arts and Sciences (incomplete).

Publication History

MAGAZINE TITLE AND TITLE CHANGES: *Newsreel* (June 1978–March 1979); *The Autograph Newsreel* (May 1979–October 1979); *Newsreel* (December 1979 to present).
VOLUME AND ISSUE DATA: Vol. 1, No. 1 (June 1978 to present), irregular but presently bimonthly.
PUBLISHER AND PLACE OF PUBLICATION: Thomas Parry, Box 33433, Raleigh, N.C. 27606 (Vol. I, No. 1–Vol. I, No. 8); Thomas Parry, 621 Second Street, Indian Rocks Beach, Fla. 33535 (Vol. I, No. 9/10–No. 17); Thomas Parry, Dayton, Tenn. 37321 (July 1981–November 1981); Bob Bennett, 1 Governors Lane, Shelburne, Vt. 05481 (Vol. V, No. 1, to present).
EDITOR: Thomas Parry (June 1978–November 1981); Bob Bennett (May 1982 to present).

Anthony Slide

NEW STARS. See Appendix 2

NEW THEATRE. See NEW THEATRE AND FILM

NEW THEATRE AND FILM

Reading through issues of *New Theatre* and *New Theatre and Film* (the latter name was used for only the last two issues of the journal's run) is perhaps the best way to get an insider's picture of the growth of the radical theatre movement in the United States during the mid-thirties. As chronicler, mouthpiece, organizer, and supporter for theatre groups such as the Workers Laboratory Theatre (later the Theatre of Action), the Group Theatre, the Theatre Union, Artef, and the Theatre Collective, the journal was at the heart of a decade that witnessed an increasingly successful popularization of theatre due to its commitment to approaching social problems through dramatization. While establishing itself, according to drama critic John W. Gassner, as "the most vital publication in the theatre,"[1] *New Theatre* also spoke for the more progressive elements in dance and film.

In its three years of existence (Fall 1933 to Spring 1937), the journal published articles from an impressive array of filmmakers. V. I. Pudovkin contributed essays on the use of sound (Vol. 3 [old numbering], No. 4), directing nonactors (Vol. 2, No. 9), and the new era of Soviet films (Vol. 2, No. 3). Sergei Eisenstein's classic three-part essay "Film Form: New Problems" first appeared here (Vol. 3, Nos. 4–6). Herbert Biberman, former Theatre Guild director who went to Hollywood, compared directing for the stage and the screen (Vol. 3, No. 7). Joris Ivens (Vol. 3, No. 10), King Vidor (Vol. 1, No. 8), John Ford (Vol. 3, No. 4), and Lewis Milestone (Vol. 4, No. 1) all commented on the experience of making films in Hollywood. G. W. Pabst (Vol. 2, No. 10) and Max Ophuls (Vol. 3, No. 10) analyzed and praised certain films. Robert Edmond Jones was interviewed concerning his color work on *Becky Sharp* (Vol. 2, No. 6). George Antheil wrote on composing (Vol. 2, No. 10).

As the sometime official organ of the National Film and Photo League, a group formed in 1930 to promote and produce films dealing with the country's abundant social crises, *New Theatre* reported on its conferences, events, and plans in Tom Brandon's column "The Movie Front." Editor Herbert Kline was a filmmaker and member of the League. Filmmakers Ralph Steiner and Leo T. Hurwitz, also members, set forth a program for the development of truly socially oriented productions (Vol. 2, No. 9).

Critic Bela Balasz set the tone for critical reviewing in two important essays, "The Films of the Bourgeoisie" (Vol. 1, No. 8) and "Film into Fascism: The Road to Hitler is Paved with Film Stars" (Vol. 1, No. 9). By showing how the pre-Nazi German film prepared its audience for the acceptance of the ideology that followed, Balasz hoped to encourage critics in other countries to analyze and demythologize present-day films to uncover reactionary tendencies. The *New Theatre* film reviewers strove to follow Balasz's example, but could not match his subtlety of approach, analytic powers, and knowledge of film and history.

Reviewers Irving Lerner and Robert Stebbins covered the major films of the month. In general they lauded the Soviet output, such as *Chapaev, Peasants,*

The Youth of Maxim, and *Three Songs for Lenin*, while ridiculing the Hollywood fare as mediocre, insubstantial, prowar, or reactionary. Only such outstanding films as *Modern Times*, *Mr. Deeds Goes to Town*, *Fury*, and *The Informer* were considered on a par with Soviet and other European films.

Hollywood institutions such as Will Hays, Louis B. Mayer, Louella Parsons, William Randolph Hearst, and the publishers of the major trade papers were scathingly attacked in a series of exposes. James Cagney, John Ford, and Fritz Lang were commended for their individuality and brilliance.

It was in the theatre arena, however, that the journal functioned integrally. As the official organ of the League of Workers Theatres (later the New Theatre League), *New Theatre* allowed each theatre group to address the public in its pages. Harold Clurman, Lee Strasberg, Stella Adler, and Clifford Odets of the Group Theatre contributed essays on their productions, the Soviet theatre, and the new theatre movement. Alfred Saxe and Stephen Karnot of the Theatre of Action detailed their methods of operation from selection of script to performance. Morris Watson of the Federal Theatre Project's Living Newspaper described a number of his productions. Mordecai Gorelik wrote involved essays on set design.

The Soviet theatre served as a constant source of inspiration for the movement. Important essays on Stanislavski's method (by M. I. Chekhov [Vol. 1, No. 11, and Vol. 2, No. 2]), Meyerhold's theatre (by Lee Strasberg [Vol. 1, No. 8] and H. W. L. Dana [Vol. 2, Nos. 1–2]), and the Vakhtangov Theatre (by V. Zakhava, writing from Moscow [Vol. 2, No. 8]) gave these ideas to Americans eager to assimilate them in their own fashion.

The monthly theatre reviews of John W. Gassner were outstandingly comprehensive, perceptive, and sensitive to dramatic and philosophic concerns. John Howard Lawson wrote ideological tracts for the new theatre. Archibald MacLeish warned in "Theatre against War and Fascism" (Vol. 2, No. 8) that when the choice of fascism comes, all the forces that can be bought will be enlisted on the side of fascism.

The journal functioned as a purveyor of news, an arena for debate, and a place for exhibition of new talent. Both Clifford Odets and Irwin Shaw rose from obscurity to fame when their plays *Waiting for Lefty* (Vol. 2, No. 2) and *Bury the Dead* (Vol. 3, No. 4) respectively, were printed in *New Theatre* and performed at the League's "New Theatre Nights."

The Workers Dance League (later the New Dance League) was also a sponsor. Edna Ocko, as dance editor, succeeded in demonstrating the place of the revolutionary dance company among the other arts. Blanche Evans's "From a Dancer's Notebook" (Vol. 3, Nos. 3–4) gave an intimate look at the Mary Wigman and Martha Graham dance schools.

New Theatre can accurately be called the voice of the radical theatre movement of the thirties. Its three years of existence provided needed support to a movement and to individuals within that movement at the start of their careers. The articles were seldom solemn think pieces. Like the theatre they came from, they were passionate, enthusiastic arguments concerned with discovering and implementing the most effective methods to deal dramatically with injustice, fascism, the threat of war, poverty, racism, and antilabor sentiments. Today the journal stands as a historical document testifying to the commitment of a socially oriented group of people and their attempt to change the world with art.

In January 1937, editor Herbert Kline left to collaborate in Spain on the documentary *Heart of Spain*. After the April 1937 issue, the journal folded when its commercial distributor went bankrupt.

New Theatre and Film was initially a continuation of *Workers Theatre*, which had begun publication in April 1931.

Notes

1. John W. Gassner, "The One-Act Play in the Revolutionary Theatre," in William Kozlenko, ed., *The One-Act Play Today* (New York: Harcourt, Brace and Company, 1938), p. 258.

Information Sources

BIBLIOGRAPHY:
Barnouw, Eric. *Documentary: A History of the Non-Fiction Film*. New York: Oxford University Press, 1974.
Gassner, John W. "The One-Act Play in the Revolutionary Theatre." In *The One-Act Play Today*, edited by William Kozlenko. New York: Harcourt, Brace and Company, 1938.
INDEX SOURCES: None.
REPRINT EDITIONS: New York Public Library Photoduplication Department.
LOCATION SOURCES: Academy of Motion Picture Arts and Sciences (incomplete); Buffalo and Erie County Public Library; Milwaukee Public Library; New York Public Library; University of California at Berkeley.

Publication History

MAGAZINE TITLE AND TITLE CHANGES: *New Theatre* (September/October 1933–November 1936); *New Theatre and Film* (March 1937–April 1937).
VOLUME AND ISSUE DATA: No. 1 (September/October 1933) has no volume number; No. 2 (January 1934) is Vol. III, No. 2 (taking over the numbering from *Workers Theatre*, which this magazine replaced); February 1934–May 1934 are labelled Vol. III, No. 3–Vol. III, No. 6; June 1934 and July/August 1934 have no volume numbers; September 1934 begins new numbering as Vol. I, No. 8; last issue is April 1937, Vol. IV, No. 2. The publication was monthly, but there are no issues for December 1936, January 1937, and February 1937.
PUBLISHER AND PLACE OF PUBLICATION: Workers Theatres of U.S.A. (Section of the International Union of Revolutionary Theatre) and Workers Dance League, 42 East Twelfth Street, New York, N.Y. (September/October 1933); League of Workers Theatres of the U.S.A. (Section of the International Union of the Revolutionary Theatre), Workers Dance League, and National Film and Photo League, 5 East Nineteenth Street, New York, N.Y. (January 1934–May 1934); League of Workers Theatres and National Film and Photo League, 114 West Fourteenth

Street, New York, N.Y. (June 1934–September 1934); League of Workers The-
atres, Film and Photo League, and Workers Dance League, 114 West Fourteenth
Street, New York, N.Y. (October 1934–January 1935); New Theatre League,
National Film and Photo League, and Workers Dance League, 114 West Four-
teenth Street, New York, N.Y. (February 1935); New Theatre League and New
Dance League, 114 West Fourteenth Street, New York, N.Y. (March 1935–
November 1935); New Theatre League and New Dance League, 156 West Forty-
fourth Street, New York, N.Y. (December 1935–November 1936); Social Theatre
Publications, Inc., 156 West Forty-fourth Street, New York, N.Y. (March 1937–
April 1937).

EDITOR: Ben Blake (September/October 1933–May 1934); Ben Blake, Herbert Kline,
Oscar Saul, Leo T. Hurwitz, Sam Brody, and Charles Dibner (June 1934); Herbert
Kline (July/August 1934–November 1936); George Redfield, Robert Stebbins,
Edna Ocko, and Eleanor Flexner (March 1937); George Redfield, Robert Stebbins,
Edna Ocko, Eleanor Flexner, and Mark Marvin (April 1937).

Alan Gevinson

NEW YORK MOTION PICTURE CRITICS' REVIEWS.
See FILM REVIEW DIGEST

NEW ZEALAND FILM. See Appendix 4

THE NICKELODEON. See MOTOGRAPHY

NSEC NEWS. See SCREEN EDUCATION

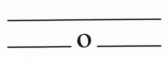

O

ONE WOMAN. See Appendix 2

ON FILM

With its "silver screen" cover, 102 pages printed on a variety of good-quality paper, and its enclosed phonograph recording of an interview with Otto Preminger, *On Film* was one of the most glamorous and expensively mounted film periodicals ever to be produced in the United States. Unfortunately, it was so expensively produced that only one issue ever appeared, a twenty-thousand-circulation test marketing number, issued in December 1970. (The first issue was officially to appear March-April 1971.) That test marketing number included Tim Hunter's interview with William Clothier, Peter Bogdanovich's interview with Otto Preminger, and Robin Wood's analysis of *Night of the Hunter*. But for all the talent involved, *On Film* proved nothing more than an unwanted luxury.

Information Sources

INDEX SOURCES: None.
REPRINT EDITIONS: None.
LOCATION SOURCES: Academy of Motion Picture Arts and Sciences.

Publication History

MAGAZINE TITLE AND TITLE CHANGES: *On Film*.
VOLUME AND ISSUE DATA: Test Marketing Number (December 1970).

PUBLISHER AND PLACE OF PUBLICATION: Cinema Ventures, Inc., 133 West
     Fourteenth Street, New York, N.Y. 10011.
EDITOR: Thomas W. Russell III.

Anthony Slide

ON LOCATION

In the premiere issue of *On Location: The Film and Videotape Magazine*,
editor Lynn Rothman dedicated the establishment of the periodical to the original
location—Hollywood—and all the memories conjured up by the silent sign which
still overlooks the "new" Hollywood that stretches far beyond its original location and today knows no boundaries.

The initial black-and-white issue of October 1977 numbered a mere forty-five
pages and included an interview with American producer David Wolper and
location features on shooting in Hawaii and Hollywood circa 1912. As do the
current issues, products and services were reviewed.

Some sixty issues later the December 1983 issue had grown to over 166 pages
with special sections for commercials, animation, production, special effects,
video, film, equipment, audio, and music video. Each of these sections profiles
cities and states with unique production facilities and location shoots of interest
to filmmakers throughout the country. As the periodical grew in size, so did the
type and quality of information included. The writers today are always careful
to include addresses and contacts for the companies and services discussed.
These details make it a useful introductory reference tool for the production
professional needing a quick and brief overview of an unknown location.

Whereas the initial issues incorporated little or no color, the magazine is now
totally characterized by high-quality photographic color reproduction and heavy
glossy paper. The articles and columns flow easily from one to the next, with
continuations clearly marked. An advertisement index concludes each issue.

The *On Location Film and Videotape Production Directory* has been published
annually since the inception of the magazine. In one volume are listed alpha-
betically by state, then city, all the contacts needed to carry out production in
a given area, from accounting services to wardrobe rentals. Each section is
introduced by a letter from the state governor and a brief description of the state
including time zones, special events, types of locations, liquor laws, taxes,
trucking laws, special regulations, and a helpful list of productions filmed within
the state to date.

Information Sources

INDEX SOURCES: None.
REPRINT EDITIONS: None.
LOCATION SOURCES: Academy of Motion Picture Arts and Sciences (lacks early
     issues); American Film Institute (Los Angeles); Brown University; Grossmont

College (California); Library of Congress; Mill Valley (California) Public Library; University of California at Berkeley; University of California at Los Angeles; University of North Carolina; University of Southern California.

Publication History

MAGAZINE TITLE AND TITLE CHANGES: *On Location.*
VOLUME AND ISSUE DATA: Vol. I, No. 1–Vol. III, No. 3 (October 1977–January/ February 1980), bimonthly; Vol. III, No. 4 (March 1980 to present), monthly.
PUBLISHER AND PLACE OF PUBLICATION: On Location Publishing, Inc., 6464 Sunset Boulevard, Suite 570, Hollywood, Calif. 90028 (Vol. I, No. 1–Vol. V, No. 8); On Location Publishing, Inc., 6777 Hollywood Boulevard, Hollywood, Calif. 90038 (Vol. V, No. 9, to present).
EDITOR: Lynn Rothman (October 1977–May/June 1978); Michael E. Clark (July/August 1978–September/October 1978); Ray Herbeck, Jr. (November/December 1978– September 1981); Jonathan Barnert (November 1981–June 1982); Fred Silverman (July 1982–January 1983); Steven Bernard (Editor-in-Chief and Publisher, September 1981 to present).

Lisa Mosher

ON THE MARK. See Appendix 1

OPTICAL LANTERN AND CINEMATOGRAPH JOURNAL. See KINEMATOGRAPH WEEKLY

OPTICAL MAGIC LANTERN JOURNAL AND PHOTOGRAPHIC ENLARGER. See KINEMATOGRAPH WEEKLY

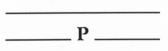

PANORAMA

Beginning publication in the summer of 1979, *Panorama*[1] was an ambitious attempt by Walter Annenberg, publisher of *T.V. Guide*,* to produce a quality periodical on contemporary television. The monthly magazine boasted more than 120 pages per issue, with glossy paper, impressive advertising, and an even more impressive list of contributors. Explaining his decision to publish *Panorama*, Annenberg wrote:

> The T.V. screen influences nearly every aspect of our society and its mores, as well as public attitudes on foreign affairs, social issues and government. We live in a time of rapid and significant changes. On network and public T.V., programming is changing; movies and miniseries are creating an opportunity to develop characters and make social statements. And there is a technological revolution going on that by greatly increasing program sources for the home screen will drastically affect the viewing habits of the public, with cable, pay-cable and subscription television, satellite transmission, and videocassettes and discs growing in importance. *Panorama* will offer its readers an authoritative perspective on programming, new and future uses of the home screen, developments in governmental regulation and changes in society that the 'television revolution' is causing.[2]

The magazine was published at a time of significant change in the television industry (as Annenberg's comments indicate), when cable and the video market were heralding a new era for the medium. *Panorama* recognized that change, and a substantial portion of each issue was given over to the growth of home video use, with lightweight critic Gene Shalit reviewing the latest video cassettes available for public sale and David Lachenbruch contributing a monthly column,

"Videocassettes and Discs." As the periodical's logo indicated, it was concerned with "Television Today and Tomorrow."

There was little interest displayed in nostalgia (unlike the other serious television journal, *Emmy**), but *Panorama* did seem to have a fascination with "star" names as contributors, among whom were William F. Buckley, Jr., John le Carré, Alex Haley, Molly Haskell, former British Prime Minister Edward Heath, Katharine Hepburn, Jessica Mitford, Edwin Newman, and William L. Shirer. Unfortunately, too many of these contributors seemed to have little of import to say, and *Panorama* must be chastised for trading so heavily on personality names rather than concentrating on serious journalists able to provide solid, in-depth articles.

Many of the articles in *Panorama* were an uneasy mix of popular television and serious critical thought. Ron Nessen interviewed Hodding Carter III (Vol. 2, No. 4). A group of mystery writers were asked to solve the puzzle of who shot J. R. Ewing on "Dallas" (No. 8). Other articles were concerned with whether Dan Rather would make it as Walter Cronkite's replacement (Vol. 2, No. 3) and with "Edith Bunker's Legacy" (Vol. 2, No. 5). However, one of the better features of *Panorama* was a succinct survey of the best television programming of the forthcoming month.

A little over a year after it had commenced publication, *Panorama* was closed down, with its last issue—May 1981—giving no indication that it was to be the magazine's final one. *Panorama* was a noble effort at a serious yet popular television periodical, and its failure, perhaps, proves that Americans are unwilling to take a serious look at television programming.

Notes

1. *Panorama* was also the title of a magazine on amateur filmmaking published by Bell and Howell in the forties and fifties.
2. No. 1, February 1980, p. 1.

Information Sources

INDEX SOURCES: None.
REPRINT EDITIONS: None.
LOCATION SOURCES: Academy of Motion Picture Arts and Sciences; Duke University; Library of Congress; New York Public Library; University of Florida; University of Illinois; University of Missouri; University of Southern California; University of Tennessee; University of Texas.

Publication History

MAGAZINE TITLE AND TITLE CHANGES: *Panorama*.
VOLUME AND ISSUE DATA: Prototype Issue (July 1979); Vol. I, Nos. 1–11 (February 1980–December 1980); Vol. II, Nos. 1–5, (January 1981–May 1981), monthly.

PUBLISHER AND PLACE OF PUBLICATION: Triangle Communications, 850 Third
    Avenue, New York, N.Y. 10022.
EDITOR: Roger Youman (1980); David Sendler (1980–1981).

Anthony Slide

PANTOMIME. See Appendix 2

PARAMOUNT AROUND THE WORLD. See Appendix 3

PARAMOUNT-ARTCRAFT PROGRESS ADVANCE. See
Appendix 3

PARAMOUNT INTERNATIONAL NEWS. See Appendix 3

PARAMOUNT MAGAZINE. See Appendix 3

PARAMOUNT PARADE. See Appendix 3

PARAMOUNT PICTURES CORPORATION NEWS. See
Appendix 3

PARAMOUNT PROGRESS. See Appendix 3

PARAMOUNT SERVICE. See Appendix 3

PARAMOUNT WORLD. See Appendix 3

PASTE-POT AND SHEARS. See Appendix 3

PATHÉ MESSENGER. See Appendix 3

PATHÉPLAYS. See Appendix 3

PENGUIN FILM REVIEW

When Roger Manvell met Sir Allan Lane, the originator of Penguin Books, in 1942, neither of them realized that their meeting would ultimately lead to the creation of the *Penguin Film Review* some four years later. Manvell, then a regional film officer in the Ministry of Information, initially discussed with Lane the possibility of producing a book on cinema. At that time there was no work on that subject in the Penguin list. From that came Manvell's famous Pelican volume, *Film*, which was first published in 1944. It was later revised and released several times in later years. The success of that volume led to Sir Allan's idea of a quarterly publication about film, to be produced in a paperback format. The result of this idea was the *Penguin Film Review*.

Manvell was selected as the executive editor and was able to enlist the aid of two competent associate editors. Nielson Baxter, a well-known documentary producer and director, served in this capacity along with H. H. Wollenberg, a German-Jewish refugee who had been well known as a film journalist in Berlin in the twenties. The first issue of the *Review* came out in August 1946.

Although he states in the preface to the reprint edition of this title that he had no "hardline editorial policy," Manvell did suggest the coverage of the *Review* in his very first issue.[1] The key aspects of his policy statement were that the publication would be a survey of the field of the cinema, with international film coverage to be included. The economic, social, and aesthetic problems of film-making would also be discussed. In addition, he wished to cover the past history and achievements of film. In rounding out the coverage, Manvell wished to consider artistic and technical aspects of filmmaking, as well as current news and statistics.

With this framework in mind, Manvell divided each issue into several sections. He began with an editorial dealing with some aspect of the cinema, from film theory, for example, to film's role in society. He also addressed such practical questions as the training of technical people in filmmaking or the problem of film pricing and distribution. This section was usually followed by about a dozen articles on a broad range of topics. There was also great diversity in the authors who wrote for the *Review* since it was the policy of the publication to include works by established as well as new writers. On occasion, even directors were given an opportunity to write for the *Review*. Some of the writers we have come to recognize today included Arthur Knight, Dilys Powell, Richard Griffith, and Jacques Brunius. David Lean, Fritz Lang, Thorold Dickinson, and Sergei Eisenstein were among the filmmakers who contributed.

In addition to the articles, there were also several standard sections included in each 120-page issue. Wollenberg had a news feature entitled "Round the World's Studios." Baxter was responsible for a column of short book reviews called "Books about Films." Each issue also carried a section of black-and-white stills from a variety of countries, time periods, and films. Coverage was international, and there were stills from older and more recent productions, including such classics as *Metropolis*, *Citizen Kane*, *Ivan the Terrible* (Part I), *Oliver Twist*, and *Monsieur Verdoux*.

The subjects written about were as varied as the writers themselves. No real pattern emerged in the nine issues that were published, but a brief review of the highlights will provide some evidence of the range of topics. Each issue, while having a number of articles about cinema in a particular country, also addressed issues related to particular aspects of filmmaking. There was, for example, coverage of kinds of films, such as documentaries, European cartoons, and scientific films. Technical questions were also covered in such articles as Eisenstein's comments on stereoscopy; also published was a technical article on color film. There were a great number of references to aesthetics and film theory, as well. Most notable were Manvell's "The Poetry of Film," Eric Ambler's "Film of the Book," and John Gassner's "Expression and Realism in Films." The relationship between the stage and the screen was also explored in such works as "Acting for Stage and Screen," "Dialogue for Stage and Screen," and "The Film of Hamlet."

The editor also selected articles on actors, directors, and particular films. Commentary on the Marx Brothers and actors in the Soviet Union were published along with scholarly pieces on Eisenstein, Frank Capra, Lang, and Lubitsch. E. Arnot Robinson also produced a timely article entitled "Women and the Film." The *Review* featured lengthy commentary on such films as *Brief Encounter*, *Paisa*, in addition to *Hamlet*, which was noted above.

The *Penguin Film Review* attempted to be as timely as possible, providing critical material on historical as well as recent issues. The editors noted, however, that there was a three-month time lag from the receipt of an article to its eventual publication.[2] This was simply an innate problem common to all quarterly publications.

A major factor in the demise of the *Review* proved to be the economics of publishing.[3] The publishers had calculated that it would require fifty thousand copies per issue to break even on their venture. Sales, however, averaged only twenty-five thousand per issue during the life of the title. Despite its departure, the *Penguin Film Review* produced a diverse, well-edited body of cinema literature. That an American and an English publisher each saw fit to reprint the nine issues is a fortunate publishing event; scholars and students of film should be quite pleased.

Notes

1. Roger Manvell, Introduction, *The Penguin Film Review, 1946–1949* (London: Rowman and Littlefield, 1978), Vol. I, p. vi.

2. "Editorial," *The Penguin Film Review*, No. 2, January 1947, p. 8.

3. Manvell, p. viii.

Information Sources

BIBLIOGRAPHY:

"Editorial." *The Penguin Film Review*, No. 2, January 1947, pp. 7–8.

Manvell, Roger. Introduction. *The Penguin Film Review, 1946–1949*. London: Rowman and Littlefield, 1978.

INDEX SOURCES: The New Film Index.

REPRINT EDITIONS: Rowman and Littlefield; The Scolar Press.

LOCATION SOURCES: Academy of Motion Picture Arts and Sciences; Auburn University; Clark University; Emory University; Illinois State University; University of California at Santa Barbara; University of Minnesota; University of Missouri; University of Utah.

Publication History

MAGAZINE TITLE AND TITLE CHANGES: *Penguin Film Review*.

VOLUME AND ISSUE DATA: Nos. 1–9 (August 1946–May 1949), quarterly.

PUBLISHER AND PLACE OF PUBLICATION: Penguin Books Limited, Hamondsworth, Middlesex, England.

EDITOR: Roger Manvell.

Kim Fisher

THE PHOTO DRAMA MAGAZINE. See Appendix 2

PHOTOPLAY

Published in Chicago instead of Brooklyn and established to do for the independent companies what *The Motion Picture Story Magazine* was doing for the "licensed" or general film companies, *Photoplay* brought out its first number in August 1911. The pattern was the same: a gallery of portraits of players to begin with, followed by illustrated stories of films, with a few articles and embryonic departments like "Answers to Inquiries." But in the beginning it was a much smaller magazine (ten cents instead of *Motion Picture*'s fifteen until November 1912) and much less handsomely printed in smaller type. There were fewer stories (only three in March 1912, for example), less lavishly illustrated than in *Motion Picture*, and supplemented by a section, "Photoplays in Tabloid," which amounted to little more than summaries of plots. The editors were obviously attempting culture, however. The leading story for May 1912 was taken from the Milano production of Homer's *Odyssey* (foreign films were not neglected), followed by Thanhouser's *The Cry of the Children* suggested by Mrs. Browning's poem, and Eclair's *The Raven*, whose story was followed by a reprint of Poe's verses. Alice Blache, president of Solax, and Robert Grau contributed articles in 1912, a section of scenario writing appeared, a popular players contest was announced, and there were interviews with Florence LaBadie, Florence Lawrence, King Baggot, and J. Warren Kerrigan.

By 1913 the trend away from fiction to articles on various phases of picture making and everything connected with it and on the personalities of the players had already begun to crowd out the stories. The August 1913 number opens with an interview with Mary Pickford as a featured independent article. By this time the tabloid stories happily vanished, but an original story was printed and a prize of one hundred dollars offered for the best scenario based upon it.

By 1915 *Photoplay* was a big magazine, still not as handsomely printed as *Motion Picture* but probably more alert to readers' tastes and interests. Picture stories were played down, but there was a serialized novel which seems to have had very little to do with the movies, and the editor, Julian Johnson, was publishing a serialized story of Mary Pickford's life and career. David Belasco, too, wrote on his contacts with Mary, Hobart Bosworth on the movie pioneers in California, and Channing Pollock on "The Discovery of Fort Lee," while Morris Gest, who persuaded Geraldine Farrar to make films for Lasky, contributed an article which one may hope is more accurate than the frontispiece, showing Miss Farrar allegedly as Salome, a role she never sang. Best of all, Johnson was now devoting generous space to a wide-ranging and free-wheeling department of photoplay review, which he would soon supplement with annual all-over reviews of the season. Though sometimes carelessly written and self-indulgent, Johnson's reviews were always stimulating and based on a thorough knowledge of the medium, and they had a very large influence upon motion picture criticism, then just getting under way.

In 1916 the magazine opened with an article on the cost of picture making, and there were articles on, among others, Charles Ray, who had just made his hit in *The Coward*, and on Maurice Tourneur (readers were now becoming conscious of directors as well as actors). There were two pages of pictures showing the walls of Babylon under construction for *Intolerance*. In November the leading article would be "The Real Story of *Intolerance*," and in January 1917 there would be a piece on Geraldine Farrar's experiences while making *Joan the Woman*. By now, too, there was an abundance of cartoons, squibs, news items, and so forth, and endless ingenuity was being shown in bringing together an array of material covering everything that could possibly be expected to interest patrons of motion pictures.

The tendencies outlined above continued to rule *Photoplay* pretty well to the end of the silent period. By all means, the most important serial was Terry Ramsaye's pioneering history of the American film, *A Million and One Nights*, commissioned in 1920 by James R. Quirk, then editor and publisher of *Photoplay*, who at first contemplated a series of twelve articles. It expanded far beyond the confines originally considered, was published in two large volumes by Simon and Schuster in 1926, and greatly stimulated research into matters cinematic. After the departure of Julian Johnson as editor, however, "The Shadow Stage" inevitably fell into other hands, first Randolph Bartlett's then Burns Mantle's, and finally Quirk's own. Both Bartlett and Mantle did good work, though Mantle, essentially a drama critic, was perhaps not always completely aware of the differences between a good play and a good film. Quirk's criticisms, however, were erratic, full of prejudices, and aroused much controversy both inside and outside the industry.

Edward Wagenknecht

Through the mid-thirties *Photoplay* continued to contain much of historical interest; as late as May 1934 it featured an article, "What Price Has Griffith Got for So Much Glory," by Mildred Mastin. "The Shadow Stage" review section continued to be intelligently written even in the mid-forties. Indeed in the late thirties, the reviews in *Photoplay* were longer than those published in the twenties.

By the forties, however, Photoplay was nothing more than a typical fan magazine, no worse and perhaps a little better than its competitors. In January 1941 it merged with *Movie Mirror* (adopting that magazine's volume and issue numbering system). The most important event to emerge from *Photoplay* in its later years was the revival of the Photoplay Awards, first presented from 1919 to 1927. The awards were revived from 1946 to 1950, and, later, from 1953 to the magazine's demise.

In 1950, *Photoplay*'s circulation was 1,200,000. By 1980, it had dropped to a mere 300,000. The last issue appeared in May/June 1980, at which time the magazine was merged with *US*.

A British edition of *Photoplay* was first published in 1952; it became *Photoplay: Movies & Video* in April 1981 and continues to be published.

Information Sources

BIBLIOGRAPHY:
Gelman, Barbara, ed. *Photoplay Treasury*. New York: Crown, 1972.
Griffith, Richard, ed. *The Talkies: Articles and Illustrations from Photoplay Magazine, 1928–1940*. New York: Dover Publications, 1971.
Kreuger, Miles, ed. *The Movie Musical from Vitaphone to 42nd Street, as Reported in a Great Fan Magazine*. New York: Dover Publications, 1975.
Lowrie, Katharine. "Photoplay Suspends Publication." *Los Angeles Times*, March 29, 1980, Part II, p. 12.
Quirk, Lawrence, J. "Quirk of 'Photoplay.' " *Films in Review*, March 1955, pp. 97–107.
Scaramazza, Paul A., ed. *Ten Years in Paradise*. Arlington, Va.: The Pleasant Press, 1974.
Slide, Anthony. "FFM Interviews Ruth Waterbury." *Film Fan Monthly*, No. 141, March 1973, pp. 21–28.
———. "FFM Interviews Adele Whitely Fletcher." *Film Fan Monthly*, No. 152, February 1974, pp. 21–26.
INDEX SOURCES: None. [The Margaret Herrick Library of the Academy of Motion Picture Arts and Sciences has a card index to *Photoplay* from 1912 to 1980.]

REPRINT EDITIONS: University Microfilms. [For information on books reprinting articles from *Photoplay*, see "Bibliography."]
LOCATION SOURCES: Academy of Motion Picture Arts and Sciences; Cornell University; Library of Congress.

Publication History

MAGAZINE TITLE AND TITLE CHANGES: *Photoplay*.
VOLUME AND ISSUE DATA: Vol. I, No. 1–Vol. LIV, No. 12 (August 1911–December 1940), monthly except no issues published March–June 1913; as of January 1941 *Photoplay* adopted the volume and issue numbering system of *Movie Mirror*, which merged with it at that time; Vol. XVIII, No. 2–Vol. LXXXXIV, No. 3 (January 1941–May/June 1980), monthly except December/January issues combined from 1979 and final issue May/June 1980 a double issue.
PUBLISHER AND PLACE OF PUBLICATION: Photoplay Magazine Publishing Company, Suite 1208, 105 West Monroe Street, Chicago, Ill. (Vol. I, No. 1–Vol. II, No. 1); Photoplay Magazine Publishing Company, 600–630 Dearborn Street, Chicago, Ill. (Vol. II, No. 2–Vol. IV, No. 1); Photoplay Magazine Publishing Company, 608 South Dearborn Street, Chicago, Ill. (July 1913–October 1913, No volume and issue number given); Photoplay Publishing Company, 418 South Market Street, Chicago, Ill. (November 1913–February 1914); Photoplay Printing Company, 1100 Hartford Building, Chicago, Ill. (March 1914); Cloud Publishing Company, 1100 Hartford Building, Chicago, Ill. (April 1914–Vol. VII, No. 2); Photoplay Publishing Company, 8 South Dearborn Street, Chicago, Ill. (Vol. VII, No. 3–Vol. VII, No. 6); Photoplay Publishing Company, 350 North Clark Street, Chicago, Ill. (Vol. VIII, No. 1–Vol. XXIII, No. 6); Photoplay Publishing Company, 750 North Michigan Avenue, Chicago, Ill. (Vol. XXIV, No. 1–Vol. XXXVIII, No. 2); Photoplay Publishing Company, 919 North Michigan Avenue, Chicago, Ill. (Vol. XXXVIII, No. 3–Vol. XLVII, No. 1); Macfadden Publications, Inc. 333 North Michigan Avenue, Chicago, Ill. (Vol. XLVII, No. 2–Vol. LIV, No. 6); Macfadden Publications, Inc., 221 North LaSalle Street, Chicago, Ill. (Vol. LIV, No. 7–Vol. LIV, No. 12); Macfadden Publications, Inc., Washington and South Avenues, Dunellen, N.J. (Vol. XVIII, No. 2 [new numbering system]–Vol. XXVIII, No. 4); Macfadden Publications, Inc., 205 East Forty-second Street, New York 17, N.Y. (Vol. XXVIII, No. 5–Vol. LXI, No. 5); Macfadden-Bartell Corporation, 205 East Forty-second Street, New York 17, N.Y. (Vol. LXI, No. 6–Vol. LXXXVII, No. 6); The Macfadden Group, Inc., 205 East Forty-second Street, New York 17, N.Y. (Vol. LXXXVIII, No. 1–Vol. LXXXXIII, No. 3); The Macfadden Group, Inc., 215 Lexington Avenue, New York, N.Y. 10016 (Vol. LXXXXIII, No. 4–Vol. LXXXXIV, No. 3).
EDITOR: Neil Gladstone Caward (April 1912–February 1913); A. W. Thomas (October 1913–September 1914); Julian Johnson (May 1915–December 1919); James R. Quirk (January 1920–September 1932); Kathryn Dougherty (October 1932–January 1935); Ray Long (February 1935–May 1935); Kathryn Dougherty (June 1935–July 1935); Ruth Waterbury (August 1935–December 1940); Ernest V. Heyn (January 1941–May 1942); Helen Gilmore (June 1942–December 1947); Adele Whitely Fletcher (January 1948–August 1952); Tony Gray (September 1952–

January 1954); Ann Higginbotham (February 1954–July 1956); Isabel Moore (August 1956–March 1957); Evelyn Pain (April 1957–August 1961); Jack J. Podell (September 1961–September 1965); Mary Fiore (October 1965–August 1968); Patricia De Jager (September 1968–June 1971); Bernadette Carrozza (July 1971–June 1973); Lynne Dorsey (July 1973–May/June 1980).

Anthony Slide

PHOTOPLAYERS WEEKLY. See Appendix 2

PHOTOPLAY GUIDE TO BETTER PICTURES. See
FILMS IN REVIEW

PHOTO-PLAY JOURNAL. See Appendix 2
THE PHOTOPLAY MAGAZINE. See PHOTOPLAY

PHOTO-PLAY REVIEW. See Appendix 2

PHOTOPLAY VOGUE. See Appendix 2

PHOTO-PLAY WORLD. See Appendix 2

THE PHOTO PLAYWRIGHT

The *Photo Playwright* was a short-lived monthly of 1912 devoted to the interests of the beginning scenario writer struggling to sell material to the studios. Twenty-year-old owner and editor Monte M. Katterjohn, who later wrote *The Sheik* and film scripts for such Famous Players-Lasky stars as Gloria Swanson and Dorothy Dalton, established the Photoplay Enterprise Association in his hometown of Boonville, Indiana, to publish the journal and to assist budding talent with related services (typing, criticism, and marketing of submitted scenarios). With the help of studio connections he made from selling his own photoplays to Lubin, Vitagraph, IMP, and others, Katterjohn was able to provide hopeful novices with advice, information, and his own enthusiasm for the photoplay. In 1913 the publication ended when Katterjohn became editor of scenarios at Universal in New York.

The Photo Playwright contained material from five types of sources. Of most value to readers were articles written by studio scenario editors (for example,

"Ten Things I Would Tell a Beginner" by Mrs. Hartmann Breuil, editor of scripts at Vitagraph; "Scenario Procedure at the Studios" by Horace G. Plimpton, scenario editor for Thomas A. Edison, Inc.) and information reputedly obtained from the studios and incorporated into the monthly feature "The Photoplay Mart" which described each studio's changing needs, rules for submittal of material, and rate of pay.

Readers could also gain valuable information from reading synopses of scenarios published in the journal. In the monthly feature "Some Recent Photoplays," two or three scenarios were discussed and compared. In "Plots of the Plays" (a feature unfortunately only begun in the last issue), synopses of all scenarios produced in the preceding month were printed.

Of lesser value were the articles of advice and encouragement written by established writers and successful novices. Often the advice given was platitudinous and obvious. Much of the material written by established writers was extracted from other magazines, especially *The Moving Picture World*,* *The Motion Picture Story Magazine*, and *Motion Picture News*.*

Finally, Katterjohn's column "Brass Tack Talks" gave a potpourri of tips, gossip, news, and witticisms intended to give credibility to the journal, promote a fraternal feeling among scenario writers, and give the novice writer the feeling of being a part of this writing community.

The writing in the journal was on the whole undistinguished. The advice tended to be repetitive. Readers were constantly reminded to write about something new and unique, write for the actors, lead up to one climax, keep away from the triangle, keep trying, don't steal, keep reading *The Photo Playwright* and use its services. The analyses of the selected scenarios were elementary. In the first issue, Biograph's *The Mender of the Nets* was judged "immoral," presumably because the action depicted was both commonplace and unrealistic.

The Photo Playwright appeared on the scene at a time when schools for scenario writers and manuals for self-help in writing were common and for the most part flagrantly fraudulent. Robert Grau, writing in 1914, observed that of all the recent books written on scenario writing, "not over six of more than a hundred such volumes have been prepared by authors whose expression is due to actual achievement as photoplaywrights or from an association with the film studio's scenario departments."[1] In its connections with the industry and the dedication and enthusiasm it showed in the attempt made to promote the interest of the self-made writer, *The Photo Playwright* stands out as a legitimate and valuable publication of 1912, no doubt encouraging more than a few would-be writers of that year to make the step from idea to scenario, from dream to execution.

Notes

1. Robert Grau, *The Theatre of Science* (New York: Broadway Publishing Company, 1914), p. 306.

Information Sources

BIBLIOGRAPHY:
Katterjohn, Monte M. *The 1933 Motion Picture Almanac*. New York: Quigley Publishing
    Company, 1933, pp. 234–235.
INDEX SOURCES: None.
REPRINT EDITIONS: None.
LOCATION SOURCES: Library of Congress.

Publication History

MAGAZINE TITLE AND TITLE CHANGES: *The Photo Playwright*.
VOLUME AND ISSUE DATA: Vol. I, No. 1–Vol, I, No. 8 (April 1912–December
    1912), monthly.
PUBLISHER AND PLACE OF PUBLICATION: The Photoplay Enterprise Association,
    Studio Place, Boonville, Ind.
EDITOR: Monte M. Katterjohn.

Alan Gevinson

THE PICTUREGOER

The *Picturegoer* in its familiar weekly format endured for almost twenty-nine
years, from May 30, 1931, through April 23, 1960. Before that long run,
however, the magazine had had its predecessors. A weekly magazine titled
Pictures and the Picturegoer began life in 1911 and was edited—in its later days
at least—by Fred Dangerfield. It contained the normal fan magazine items: studio
gossip, articles on the stars, very slight reviews, stories of the films, and illustrations which, with time, have gained great historical interest. It continued
through the First World War, changed its name in 1920 to *Pictures for the
Picturegoer*, and gave way in 1921 to a far more imposing successor, *Picturegoer
Monthly*, published by Odhams Press, which had taken over the original weekly
in June 1920. The old weekly had cost two pence, rising to three pence in 1920;
the new monthly cost one shilling.

In style and format it challenged, not unsuccessfully, the American *Photoplay*,* and it signalled its ambitions from the start. For example, the first number
contained lengthy articles on D. W. Griffith and actress Alla Nazimova, and
although there was the usual short story version of a feature film, the film in
question was Mauritz Stiller's *Sir Arne's Treasure*—hardly standard fan magazine fodder. The next number contained a contribution by director Tod Browning, while critical standards were revealed by a warmly appreciative account of
Erich von Stroheim's *Blind Husbands*.

Title changes continued to haunt the paper. By 1922 the old *Pictures and the
Picturegoer* returned, though only on the inside pages, and in October 1925
there was one freak number whose cover legend ran *Picturegoer and Theatre*

Monthly. By now reviews tended to brevity, and little in the way of credits appeared. No. 125, May 1931, was the last number on the monthly, which had been edited by P. L. Mannock from 1927 to 1930 and Lionel Collier from 1930 to 1931.

When the return to weekly publication came, later that month, S. Rossiter Shepherd was announced as editor. Lionel Collier's name appeared above the still-slim reviews. The cost was two pence. In its first few months the new weekly made great efforts to improve its critical standards. By the end of June reviews were longer and cast lists provided. On November 28, 1931, full cast lists together with the director's name made their appearance, and this, together with sensible and blessedly unacademic reviewing, remained the paper's main strength, although screenplay, photographic, and other technical credits were largely ignored. All releases were included, and there was also, by the mid-thirties, a preview section with lengthy notices of films shown in London but not yet generally released (and this section also featured continental productions, never widely shown in those days). Shepherd's name as editor ceased to appear in April 1932, and thereafter *Picturegoer* never revealed its editor's name, although the introductory notes to the paper were signed by Malcolm D. Phillips, Guy Beacon, and others.

The general tone of the paper can perhaps best be caught by listing the main contents of one number chosen at random, that of January 25, 1936. The main article featured the distinguished scenarist Frances Marion. There was an article inveighing against Katharine Hepburn (then in much critical disfavor) and a biography of Claudette Colbert. There was a two-page spread from *Modern Times* and more stills from the Grace Moore vehicle, *On Wings of Song*. The preview section began with the French thriller, *Deuxième Bureau* (liked) and the French weepie, *Sans Famille* (disliked). The release section demonstrated the conscientiousness of the magazine's critics, although the reviewer thought little of Karl Freund's *Mad Love* and even less of *The Passing of the Third Floor Back* with Conrad Veidt.

Three weeks after the outbreak of the Second World War, *Film Weekly** was incorporated with *Picturegoer*, and the combined magazine was substantially the latter with very few of *Film Weekly*'s characteristics. In September 1941 a paper shortage, which had already caused a reduction in size, forced a change to biweekly publication, and *Film Weekly* was dropped from the masthead. Not until July 1941 could weekly publication recommence. The magazine survived, essentially unaltered through the fifties, and slowly its price moved upward, to three pence in 1940, three-and-a-half pence in 1951, four pence in 1956, and a final four-and-a-half pence in 1957.

But *Picturegoer*'s days were numbered. The flight of the mass film audience during the fifties took away many of those who enjoyed its popular features, while those who enjoyed serious film reviews could turn to other magazines such as *Films and Filming.** On January 30, 1960, the paper's cover ominously read

Picturegoer with Disc Date. On April 23, 1960, the truth was revealed, the magazine would be replaced by *Date*, "a sparkling new magazine for teens and twenties." There would be little welcome for Mr. Griffith there.

Information Sources

INDEX SOURCES: None.
REPRINT EDITIONS: None.
LOCATION SOURCES: University of Southern California (incomplete). [British Film
    Institute has a complete run.]

Publication History

MAGAZINE TITLE AND TITLE CHANGES: *Pictures and the Picturegoer* (1911–1920);
    Pictures for the Picturegoer (1920–1921); *Picturegoer Monthly* (1921–1931, ex-
    cept for October 1925 when *Picturegoer and Theatre Monthly*); *The Picturegoer*
    (1931–1960, incorporating *Film Weekly*, September 23, 1939–September 1941).
VOLUME AND ISSUE DATA: Vol. I, No. 1–Vol. XIX, No. 358 (1911–December
    1920), weekly; Vol. I, No. 1–Vol. XXI, No. 125 (January 1921–May 1931),
    monthly; Vol. I, No. 1–Vol. XXXIX, No. 1296 (May 1931–April 1960), weekly
    (except biweekly September 1941–July 1949).
PUBLISHER: The Pictures, Ltd., Adam Street, London, England (1911–1920); Odhams
    Press, Long Acre, London, England (June 1920–April 1960).
EDITOR: Fred Dangerfield (?–1920); P. L. Mannock (1927–1930); Lionel Collier (1930–
    1931); S. Rossiter Shepherd (1931–1932); no editor listed thereafter.

Jack Lodge

PICTUREGOER AND THEATRE MONTHLY. See THE
PICTUREGOER

PICTUREGOER MONTHLY. See THE PICTUREGOER

THE PICTURE NEWS, SCREEN, STAGE AND
VARIETY

In 1915, *The Picture News, Screen, Stage and Variety* began publication as *The Picture Palace News*, billed as "a weekly journal devoted to the Picture Theatre Industry and Public Alike." For a semifan publication, the articles were generally serious in tone, including pieces such as "The Cinema in Education," "The Technique of Film Acting," "Cinematography in War Time," and "D. W. Griffith on Film Acting." The magazine also featured short biographies and interviews with current film personalities, a fashion page, a children's corner, and short stories adapted from current film releases. This British magazine ceased publication in 1917.

Information Sources

INDEX SOURCES: None.
REPRINT EDITIONS: None.
LOCATION SOURCES: No information.

Publication History

MAGAZINE TITLE AND TITLE CHANGES: *The Picture Palace News* (November 8, 1915–September 2, 1916); *The Picture News, Screen, Stage and Variety* (September 9, 1916–January 27, 1917).
VOLUME AND ISSUE DATA: Vol. I, No. 1–Vol. III, No. 65 (November 8, 1915–January 27, 1917), weekly.
PUBLISHER AND PLACE OF PUBLICATION: No publisher listed, 453 West Street, London, England; later 62 Wardour Street, London, England.
EDITOR: A. E. Taylor.

Thomas A. Johnson

THE PICTURE PALACE NEWS. See THE PICTURE NEWS, SCREEN, STAGE AND VARIETY

PICTURE PLAY. See Appendix 2

PICTURES AND PICTUREGOER. See THE PICTUREGOER

PICTURES FOR THE PICTUREGOER. See THE PICTUREGOER

PICTURE SHOW

A popular British fan magazine which began publication in 1919, *Picture Show* remained almost unchanged for the first twenty years of its life. It featured film reviews with brief story outlines, stories adapted from current film releases, a fashion page, and answers to correspondents.

Picture Show was possibly the first magazine to offer loose photogravure portraits of film personalities every two weeks, through February 1920, and then a magnificent double-page art plate, forming the loose center section of the magazine. The day the first issue, bearing Charlie Chaplin's portrait on the blue-and-green cover, appeared on the newsstands was a great day for film enthusiasts. One had never seen such a lavishly produced magazine covering film.

In 1923 Elinor Glyn contributed a letter from Hollywood. Edith Nepean wrote a regular column of news items from the British studios which appeared from the twenties through the sixties. Louella Parsons was also a regular contributor. For twenty-four years, Edward Wood wrote for *Picture Show*, with his last article, "Lessons of the Past Point the Way to the Future," appearing on June 29, 1946. Maude Hughes was the best known of the magazine's reviewers, taking over that column in 1951.

Picture Show was the first periodical to publish hardcover annuals, which appeared from 1926 to 1943. There was a hiatus during the Second World War, but the annual reappeared from 1947 to 1961. In addition, lavish holiday and Christmas "extras" were published from 1934 to 1938.

During 1958 and 1959, television reviews began to appear, and it became increasingly apparent that the magazine was catering to the teenage reader only. The issue for September 10, 1960, announced that there was "Big News Inside." The "Big News" was that the magazine would have more pages, with photographs in color, but that the additional material was almost all nonfilm related. On December 31, 1960, *Picture Show* died without a whimper.

Information Sources

INDEX SOURCES: None.
REPRINT EDITIONS: None.
LOCATION SOURCES: No information.

Publication History

MAGAZINE TITLE AND TITLE CHANGES: *Picture Show* (at various times its title also incorporated *Film Periodical* and *T.V. Mirror*).
VOLUME AND ISSUE DATA: May 3, 1919–December 31, 1960, weekly, except every two weeks during August 30, 1941–July 3, 1949. [The first issue was numbered Vol. I, No. 1; but after Vol. LXXII, No. 1884, both volume and issue numbers were discarded.]
PUBLISHER AND PLACE OF PUBLICATION: Amalgamated Press, Fleetway House, Farringdon Street, London, England.
EDITOR: Unknown.

Thomas A. Johnson

PICTURE STORIES MONTHLY

A short-lived British fan magazine, very much in the fashion of the early *Photoplay*,* *Picture Stories Monthly* began life in 1913 as *Illustrated Films Monthly*. Its contents consisted mainly of stories adapted from current film releases, along with short biographies of the stars, gossip, and a series of magnificent portraits of the stars used as a frontispiece. After less than two years of publication, the magazine ceased to exist in early 1915.

Information Sources

INDEX SOURCES: None.
REPRINT EDITIONS: None.
LOCATION SOURCES: No information.

Publication History

MAGAZINE TITLE AND TITLE CHANGES: *Illustrated Films Monthly* (September 1913–August 1914); *Picture Stories Magazine* (September 1914–February 1915).
VOLUME AND ISSUE DATA: Vol. I, No. 1–Vol. III, No. 6 (September 1913–February 1915), monthly.
PUBLISHER AND PLACE OF PUBLICATION: F. F. W. Oldfield, Camberwell, London, England.
EDITOR: No editor listed.

Thomas A. Johnson

PICTURE WISE. See Appendix 2

POLISH FILM. See Appendix 4

POST SCRIPT

Post Script: Essays in Film and the Humanities is a scholarly journal devoted to exploring the interrelationships between film and the more traditional areas of the humanities. It grew out of a National Endowment for the Humanities seminar, "Character in Film and Fiction," which attracted participants from a variety of disciplines; subsequently, several of these scholars sought to create a forum for the sort of interdisciplinary study of film in which they had participated. Led by Gerald Duchovnay of Jacksonville University and Judy Riggin of Northern Virginia Community College, they put together an impressive editorial board, including such established scholars as Charles Affron, Leo Braudy, Bruce Kawin, and T. J. Ross, and obtained start-up funding from a combination of private donations and the Friends of the Fine Arts organization at Jacksonville University. With Jacksonville as its headquarters and Duchovnay serving as general editor, *Post Script* began its thrice-yearly publication schedule in Fall 1981.

While similar in general format and academic emphasis to journals like *Film Criticism** and *Film Heritage,* Post Script* has clearly established its interdisciplinary design, specifically inviting submissions which view film through the perspective afforded by other branches of the humanities. Of particular interest, the masthead announces, are studies on film and literature, film music, the influence of painting on film, the role of set design and costuming in filmmaking, and the response of film and the humanities to technology. The initial issue of the journal well illustrates this broad spectrum of concerns, as it includes essays on Morris Lapidus's movie-inspired architecture, the impact of new studies in brain lateralization on the problem of reading film subtitles, and the difficulties of translating film titles into other languages. Subsequent issues have continued in this vein, offering discussion of Lina Wertmuller's *Seven Beauties* from the perspective of Bruno Bettelheim's moral philosophy, and a psychoanalytic study of the relationship between film and dream.

At the same time, *Post Script* has published a number of more traditional studies of individual films, directors, and genres. These essays include analyses of such films as *Blow Out*, *The Last Laugh*, and *The Tramp*; discussions of the work of Preston Sturges, Howard Hawks, and Val Lewton; and treatments of the musical and horror genres. In addition, each issue of the journal so far has included a significant piece of primary source material for film scholarship. A two-part interview with Robert Altman appears in Vol. 1, Nos. 1 and 2, while later issues include interviews with animator Don Bluth (Vol. 1, No. 3) and director Louis Malle (Vol. 2, No. 1). Planned for a future number are a continuation of the Malle interview and an extensive bibliography of the year's work in film scholarship. More detailed treatment of single themes in film studies is also anticipated with the announcement of an upcoming issue on modernism and film to be edited by Robert P. Kolker.

Post Script has obviously sought to stake out an important territory for itself, one which has been partially covered in the past by a journal like *Literature/ Film Quarterly** but which has for the most part been neglected by publications which address a largely academic audience. In seeking to draw on writers from fields as various as the humanities themselves and to apply their singular perspectives to film, *Post Script* promises to provide a much more catholic context for film studies. Already it has published a number of highly interesting and rigorously researched essays which shed new light on film and suggest profitable avenues for future criticism. This interdisciplinary focus, combined with the highly readable nature of the articles previously printed, should ensure a place for *Post Script* in film studies and warrant a substantial increase over the journal's current (1984) list of more than two hundred subscribers.

Information Sources

INDEX SOURCES: FIAF International Index to Film Periodicals; Film Literature Index; MLA International Bibliography.
REPRINT EDITIONS: None.
LOCATION SOURCES: Cornell University; International Museum of Photography at George Eastman House; Library of Congress; New York Public Library; Stanford University; University of Arizona; University of Illinois; University of Iowa; University of Wisconsin at Madison.

Publication History

MAGAZINE TITLE AND TITLE CHANGES: *Post Script: Essays in Film and the Humanities*.
VOLUME AND ISSUE DATA: Vol. 1, No. 1 (Fall 1981) to present, three times a year.

PUBLISHER AND PLACE OF PUBLICATION: *Post Script*, Inc., Jacksonville University, Jacksonville, Fla. 32211.
EDITOR: Gerald Duchovnay.

J. P. Telotte

PRATFALL. See Appendix 1

PREMIERE. See AMERICAN PREMIERE

PREVUE. See Appendix 2

PRODUCERS GUILD OF AMERICA JOURNAL. See
JOURNAL OF THE PRODUCERS GUILD OF AMERICA

PROFILE. See FILM FAN MONTHLY

PROGRESS ADVANCE. See Appendix 3

PROJECTION ENGINEERING

With widespread implementation of sound within the motion picture industry during the late twenties and early thirties, theatre projectionists quickly gained new responsibilities inside the projection booth. Several publications appeared during the era, including *Projection Engineering*, dedicated to providing the projectionists with news of the latest advances in sound film technology and projection technique. *Projection Engineering* sought to cater to the gamut of industry personnel, from the "executives behind the industrial guns" to "the man in the booths who can make or brake a show."[1] To gain this wide appeal, the magazine resolutely limited its editorial content to the engineering aspects of projection, completely avoiding any partisanship with regard to equipment and, especially, avoiding involvement in the politics of the projectionists' labor organizations, traditionally among the most strident and vociferous within the International Alliance of Theatrical Stage Employees and Moving Picture Machine Operators (IATSE). The first issue of *Projection Engineering* appeared in September 1929, published by the same firm responsible for *Aviation Engineering* and *Radio Engineering*. In an introductory editorial, the editor clearly defined the magazine's goals, stating that the basic policy of *Projection Engineering* rests primarily on conservatism and constructiveness. Nothing is gained by the readers, or by ourselves, through the publication of engineering articles of a derogatory nature, even though the facts be true. If criticism cannot be constructive it is not worthy of publication. We feel much the same concerning articles on new devices or systems, worthy or unworthy, given unrightful importance through the gentle art of 'comparison.' Our principal objection to this class of material is that no actual information of value is offered. Being a technical publication, *Projection Engineering* is desirous of offering to its readers the facts and the facts only.[2]

For the next three-and-a-half years, true to its stated aim, *Projection Engineering* devoted its monthly issues to descriptions of the latest in motion picture projection and sound reproduction equipment, refraining from entering into any semblance of controversy involving the relative merits of manufacturers' equipment or labor issues concerning the projectionists. However, the policy embraced by *Projection Engineering* of remaining steadfastly impartial in order to appeal to a wide readership may have led to its demise; *Projection Engineering* published its final issue in March 1933. Rights to its publication were purchased by *International Projectionist*,* which officially absorbed the magazine with its April 1933 issue. Significantly, *International Projectionist* maintained an active voice in the labor welfare of the theatre projectionists and remained the only publication directed toward projectionists to survive through the Great Depression.

Today, *Projection Engineering* offers the historian a valuable source recounting the myriad technical advances in motion picture theatre sound and projection equipment during a particularly tumultuous period in the technical development of motion pictures.

Notes

1. "We Make Our Bow," *Projection Engineering*, September 1929, p. 4.
2. Ibid.

Information Sources

INDEX SOURCES: Engineering Index.
REPRINT EDITIONS: None.
LOCATION SOURCES: University of California at Los Angeles.

Publication History

MAGAZINE TITLE AND TITLE CHANGES: *Projection Engineering*.
VOLUME AND ISSUE DATA: Vol. I, No. 1–Vol. V, No. 3 (September 1929–March 1933), monthly.
PUBLISHER AND PLACE OF PUBLICATION: Bryan Davis Publishing Co., Inc., Albany, N.Y.

EDITOR: M. L. Muhleman (September 1929–February 1930); Donald McNicol (March 1930–March 1933).

William Lafferty

PROLETARSKOE KINO. See ISKUSSTVO KINO

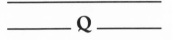

Q

QP HERALD. See MOTION PICTURE HERALD

QUARTERLY OF FILM, RADIO AND TELEVISION. See
FILM QUARTERLY

QUARTERLY REVIEW OF FILM STUDIES

A serious journal which issued its first number in 1976 and is written mostly by academics, *Quarterly Review of Film Studies* is sensitive to current trends in criticism. For example, a recent article discusses filmic image, starting with a quote from Stan Brakhage and continuing on to quote from Edmund Husserl and H. G. Gadamer, while another article on filmic narrativity draws on the theories of Boris Ezjenbaum, Christian Metz, and Roland Barthes. There is the expected treatment of films from the viewpoint of editing, camera angles, and imagery, as well as continuing interest in film history and the teaching of film.

At least one issue of each volume has been devoted to a single topic, and some of the more notable of these special issues have been "Application of Semiological and Structuralist Theory to Practical Criticism" edited by Marsha Kinder, "Feminist and Ideological Criticism" edited by Beverle Houston, "West German Film in the 1970s" edited by Eric Rentschler, and "Renoir's *The Rules of the Games*" edited by Nick Browne.

Roughly two-thirds of each issue is taken up with articles, with the remaining space given over to book reviews. Although not many books are reviewed, such coverage is lengthy, often running to five pages or more.

Michael Silverman edited the first two issues, and then Ronald Gottesman took over and has been editor to date, except for special issues. Gottesman is aided by a large editorial board, among whose members in 1982 were Dudley Andrew, Lewis Jacobs, Stanley Kauffmann, Jay Leyda, Gerald Mast, and Amos Vogel. Several persons from the board serve as the journal's executive committee.

Quarterly Review of Film Studies includes a few special columns, notably "Commentary," giving authors an opportunity to reply to reviews of their books; an infrequent "Archives" section, used mostly to report on conferences and articles in other periodicals dealing with film archives; and a "Conference" section, which summarizes talks of interest given at scholarly meetings.

Information Sources

INDEX SOURCES: FIAF International Index to Film Periodicals; Film Literature Index; Humanities Index.

REPRINT EDITIONS: University Microfilms.

LOCATION SOURCES: Academy of Motion Picture Arts and Sciences; Iowa State University; Swarthmore College; University of Arizona; University of California at Los Angeles; University of Illinois; University of Massachusetts; University of Oregon; University of Pennsylvania; University of Wisconsin at Madison.

Publication History

MAGAZINE TITLE AND TITLE CHANGES: *Quarterly Review of Film Studies*.

VOLUME AND ISSUE DATA: Vol. I, No. 1 (February 1976 to present), quarterly.

PUBLISHER AND PLACE OF PUBLICATION: Redgrave Publishing Company, 430 Manville Road, Pleasantville, N.Y. 10570 (Vol. I, No. 1–Vol. VI, No. 2); Redgrave Publishing Company, P.O. Box 67, South Salem, N.Y. 10590 (Vol. VI, No. 3, to present).

EDITOR: Michael Silverman (1976); Ronald Gottesman and Regina Fadiman (1978 to present).

Richard Heinzkill

QUIRK'S REVIEWS. See Appendix 2

R

RADIO AND TELEVISION MIRROR. See Appendix 2

RADIO ART. See Appendix 2

RADIO BROADCAST. See Appendix 2

RADIO DIGEST. See Appendix 2

RADIO FLASH. See Appendix 3

RADIO GUIDE. See Appendix 2

RADIO MIRROR. See Appendix 2

RADIO REVIEW AND TELEVISION NEWS. See
TELEVISION NEWS

REEL LIFE. See Appendix 3

LA REVUE DU CINEMA. See CAHIERS DU CINÉMA

RKO STUDIO CLUB NEWS. See Appendix 3

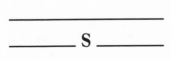

S

SBI: SHOW BUSINESS ILLUSTRATED. See SHOW
BUSINESS ILLUSTRATED

SCANNÁN

Scannán was the occasional publication of the Irish Film Society, Dublin, for
twenty-two years of the Society's forty-year existence. Its name was the Gaelic
for film and was pronounced "Scanawn."

In November 1945, Richard Delaney of the Portlaoise branch of the Society
recruited writers as distinguished as Richard Griffith, John Grierson, Paul Rotha,
and Dilys Powell, and from this small provincial town he launched the magazine.
Every aspect of cinema was covered by writers like Professor Felix Hackett,
Liam O'Laoire, Dr. Owen Sheehy Skeffington, T. J. M. Sheehy, Peter Sherry,
Colm O'Laoghaire, Geoffrey Dalton, and Alf MacLochlainn. The first nine issues
came from Portlaoise and placed due emphasis on film society and festival news
from home and abroad.

After a gap of ten years, the Cork branch of the Irish Film Society revived
the magazine under the title *Guth na Scannán* (The voice of the film) from 1956
to 1960, reverting to the original title in the latter year. Local and overseas film
information, coverage and criticism of the local Cork International Film Festival
films, articles like Alf MacLochlainn's interview with Alberto Cavalcanti (December 1958), and a special translation from the Russian of a dialogue between
Sergei Yutkevitch and Georges Sadoul (February 1960) reflected the policy of
the magazine.

Listed as Vol. 5, the magazine was now taken over by the Dublin branch of
the Irish Film Society, with whom it remained until its demise in 1968. Writers
like Geoffrey Dalton and John Manning provided perceptive articles, the former

specializing in witty poetic parodies of considerable originality. Dónal O Moráin of Gael-Linn discussed the new Ardmore Studios (December 1961). Alf MacLochlainn reappraised William Wellman's *Strange Incident* (February 1963) and Robert Flaherty's *Man of Aran* (November 1963), and wrote on the early Irish film by Walter MacNamara, *Ireland a Nation* (February 1966). George Fleeton contributed sophisticated studies of directors like Michelangelo Antonioni (February 1967). Issues of the magazine began to thin out after 1963, and only one issue appeared each year from 1966 to 1968, the last number appearing in March of the latter year. The Society itself bowed out in 1976 when the new Irish Film Theatre in Dublin took over its main function of presenting world cinema.

Information Sources

INDEX SOURCES: None.
REPRINT EDITIONS: None.
LOCATION SOURCES: No information. [Complete runs exist at the Irish Film Institute, Dublin, and the Liam O'Leary Film Archives, Dublin.]

Publication History

MAGAZINE TITLE AND TITLE CHANGES: *Scannán* (1945–1946); *Guth na Scannán* (1956–1960); *Scannán* (1960–1968).
VOLUME AND ISSUE DATA: Vol. I (1945–1946), six issues; Vol. II (1946), three issues; between November 1956 and March 1960 published as *Guth na Scannán* and *Scannán*, with the last four issues being listed as Vol. IV; Vol. V (1960–1961), four issues; Vol. VI (1961–1962), four issues; Vol. VII (1962–1963), three issues, Vol. VIII (1963–1964), two issues; single numbers appeared February 1966, February 1967, March 1968.
PUBLISHER AND PLACE OF PUBLICATION: Portlaoise branch of the Irish Film Society (1945–1946); Cork branch of the Irish Film Society (1956–1960); Dublin branch of the Irish Film Society, 5 North Earl Street, Dublin, Eire (1960–1968).
EDITOR: Richard Delaney (1945–1946); other later editors included Alf MacLochlainn.

Liam O'Leary

SCREEN

Screen and its sister journal *Screen Education*, which together became the repository of British film theory in the late sixties, developed from an altogether more modest source. In the fifties, the Society of Film Teachers initiated a bulletin, financed by the British Film Institute, to keep members informed of the society's meetings and discussions as well as to provide a wealth of information and tips about films in distribution, program notes, the successes and failures of experiments in the classroom, and future events. As an aid to schoolteachers, sometimes duplicated, sometimes printed, it provided a valuable source of ideas about teaching films to children and continued to perform this unique role for more than a decade.

In the sixties, the bulletin became the *Journal of the Society for Education in Films and Television*, and while its content changed toward a more discursive and analytic style, it retained its orientation toward teachers of young people. In this decade of youth culture, the journal opened up new areas of debate, treating seriously the realm of popular television, rock, and commercial cinema in looking at its effects on youth.

The rise of interest in the theories of Marshall McLuhan forced a change of direction, and the problem subtly altered. The issue became how to teach in a way that brought pupils to a realization of the artificiality and manipulation of the media. As film studies became a subject for higher education, being taught for the first time in universities and colleges, the readership and contributors to the journal also changed. The debates in the journal became more theoretical, more concerned with formulating the correct approach, and more removed from the everyday practices of teaching.

In 1968, Philip Crick was already asking, "Is Cinema a Language?" (No. 46), and a year later the journal became *Screen*, complete with a new philosophy. From the outset, *Screen* was the champion of structuralism. In a country that is unused to theoretical analysis, at first *Screen*'s emphasis on theory was challenging and dynamic; and regular contributors like Peter Wollen, Ben Brewster, Colin McCabe, Stephen Heath, and Laura Mulvey looked at film in stimulating new ways. Semiology, with its search for the structures and codes that inform modern cinema, offered in the pages of *Screen* a complete and very modern analysis of cinema.

Sometime in the mid-seventies, around the time that articles stopped any pretence of being about film teaching to concentrate on filmmaking, *Screen* moved from excitement toward sterility. Its writers became a closed group of intellectuals who wrote articles in a language that only other members of the sect could understand. And like any theory that is denied debate with other viewpoints, the result was stagnation.

In 1980 a welcomed change of format made the journal more accessible, and articles on "new" issues such as sexism and racism made the journal more alive. But it has never recovered its position as the dynamic center of debate in British film culture.

Information Sources

INDEX SOURCES: FIAF International Index to Film Periodicals; Film Literature Index; The New Film Index.
REPRINT EDITIONS: University Microfilms.
LOCATION SOURCES: Cornell University; Harvard University; Library of Congress; University of Chicago; University of Illinois; University of Iowa; University of Kansas; University of Wisconsin at Madison.

Publication History

MAGAZINE TITLE AND TITLE CHANGES: *Screen.*
VOLUME AND ISSUE DATA: Vol. XI, No. 1 (January/February 1969 to present),
    quarterly. [Old numbering system from *Journal of the Society for Education in
    Film and Television.*]
PUBLISHER AND PLACE OF PUBLICATION: Society for Education in Film and
    Television Ltd., 63 Old Compton Street, London W.1, England.
EDITOR: Kevin Gough-Yates and Terry Bolas (1969–1971); Sam Rohdie (1971–1974);
    Ben Brewster (1974–1977); Geoffrey Nowell-Smith (1977–1979); Mark Nash
    (1979–1980); Mandy Merck (1980 to present).

Sally Hibbin

SCREEN (U.S.). See Appendix 2

SCREEN ACTOR

In 1959 the Screen Actors Guild began publication of a new magazine, *Screen
Actor*, based on two earlier Guild publications, *The Screen Guild Magazine**
and *Screen Actor* (published from April 1938 through February 1947). The
magazine was intended to provide Guild members with news and opinions,
together with articles, book reviews, and news items of general interest. There
were occasional articles by performers, and of particular interest are a piece,
"Income Tax Reform," by Ronald Reagan (September 1959) and a series of
articles in 1960 by Nancy Davis Reagan's father, Loyal Davis.

By the late seventies, *Screen Actor* had virtually dropped all general articles
and replaced them with news items strictly relating to the Guild and to labor
matters. The last issue to appear, Summer 1982, featured Part One of an oral
history with character actor, Fritz Feld. If *Screen Actor* should resurface, it is
to be hoped that it will publish more pieces of a similar nature.

Information Sources

INDEX SOURCES: None.
REPRINT EDITIONS: None.
LOCATION SOURCES: Academy of Motion Picture Arts and Sciences; Library of
    Congress; New York Public Library; University of California at Los Angeles;
    University of Southern California.

Publication History

MAGAZINE TITLE AND TITLE CHANGES: *Screen Actor.*
VOLUME AND ISSUE DATA: Vol. I, No. 1–Vol. II, No. 3 (August 1959–March
    1960), monthly; Vol. II, No. 4–Vol. XIII, No. 3 (April-May 1960–May-June
    1971), bimonthly; Vol. XIII, No. 4–Vol. XXI, No. 4 (July 1971–Fall 1979),

quarterly [no issues between October 1973 and Winter 1974]; Vol. XXII, No. 1–
Vol. XXIV, No. 1 (Spring 1980–Summer 1982), three times a year.
PUBLISHER AND PLACE OF PUBLICATION: Screen Actors Guild, Inc., 7750 Sunset
Boulevard, Los Angeles, Calif. 90046.
EDITOR: Kenneth Thomson (August 1959–September-October 1964); Buck Harris (No-
vember-December 1964–October 1973); Paul Sargent Clark (Winter 1974–Winter
1975); Judith Rheiner (Spring 1975–January/February 1979); Kim Fellner (Spring
1979–Summer 1982).

Anthony Slide

SCREEN ALBUM. See Appendix 2

SCREEN BOOK. See Appendix 2

SCREEN EDUCATION

From 1959 to 1968, *Screen Education* served as the journal for the London-
based Society for Education in Film and Television (SEFT). Believing that film
and television were important new modes of communication, SEFT members
advocated expanding the traditional school curriculum to include instruction in
the appreciation, discrimination, and use of these media. *Screen Education* provided a forum to debate the philosophy and share the methodology of this
endeavor.

Addressing the fundamental premise for the study of film and television in
the classroom, A. W. Hodgkinson, a founding-member of SEFT, wrote:

The need for clear communication (which embraces both expression and
reception) has never been greater than today. The means of communication
have never been so powerful, so flexible. Teachers, of all people, need to
be versed in the arts of communication. In the field of screen communication—the language of the child and of the future—we who profess it
must meet its challenge.[1]

Other articles that dealt with the philosophy of screen education include: "Where
Do We Go from Here?" by Paddy Whannel (No. 7, March/April 1961), "The
Practical Question" by H. R. Wills (No. 26, September/October 1964), and A.
W. Hodgkinson's "Education Comes First" (No. 43, March/April 1968).

While the majority of SEFT members were secondary schoolteachers, the
journal addressed all levels of education—from primary to postsecondary—and
covered a wide array of topics. Nor did *Screen Education* confine itself to the
British school system. Many articles described screen study in other countries,

and particularly during the mid-sixties there were frequent contributions from U.S. sources. During this period *Screen Education* influenced a series of U.S. publications:

SEFTUS Newsletter, of which four issues were published between June 1964 and May 1965 by the Society for Education in Film and Television in the United States.

NSEC News, of which three issues were published between November 1965 and June 1966 by the National Screen Education Committee.

"Film Study Section" in *Film Society Review*, of which eighteen issues were published between September 1966 and May 1968 by the American Federation of Film Societies.

Screen Education News, of which ten issues were published between January 1968 and November/December 1969 by Film Board/National Screen Education Committee. Publication of *Screen Education News* was taken over in January/February 1970 by the New England Screen Education Association, and approximately eleven issues were published until Autumn 1972.

In September 1972, the New England Screen Education Association commenced publication of *Wide Angle*, and approximately fourteen issues were published until December 1975. (*Wide Angle* should not be confused with the critical journal of the same title.)

In addition to the writings of its members, the journal published a variety of articles by experts in the fields of education, film, and television. Examples of this diversity include: "The Cinema for Children" by Cesare Zavattini (No. 14, May/June 1962), Elsa Brita Marcussen on the role of UNESCO's International Centre of Films for Children, "The Job Ahead" (No. 22, January/February 1963), "The Cartoon Film in Advertising" by John Halas and Roger Manvell (No. 2, January 1960), and "Film Communication" by Sol Worth (No. 30, July/August 1965). The journal also dealt with the sociopolitical climate for screen education in Britain through opinion pieces and reports on major governmental studies of the mass media: *The Pilkington Report* (No. 8, May/June 1961; No. 16, September/October 1962) and *The Newsom Report* (No. 22, January/February 1964).

Within a single issue of *Screen Education*, one was likely to find articles on the philosophy and practice of teaching film and television, international news about screen study, interviews with media professionals, as well as critiques of current films, television programs, and books. Frequently, an entire issue would be devoted to a single topic, such as children's film and television, or international concerns. These special issues were: children's film and television (No. 17, January/February 1963); film club activities (No. 6, January 1961); film study (No. 20, July/August 1963); general studies (No. 36, September/October 1966); higher education (No. 13, March/April, 1962; No. 26, September/October 1964; No. 41, September/October 1967); international issues (No. 8, May/June 1961; No. 15, July/August 1962; No. 22, January/February 1964); primary school (No. 23, March/April 1964); school filmmaking (No. 4, June 1960; No. 9, July/

August 1961); school film societies (No. 10, September/October 1961; No. 25, July/August 1964); television (No. 2, January 1960; No. 11, November/December 1961; No. 16, September/October 1962; No. 27, January/February 1965); youth (No. 21, January/February 1962; No. 18, March/April 1963); young film-makers (No. 14, May/June 1962; No. 19, May/June 1963; No. 24, May/June 1964; No. 42, January/February 1968).

While *Screen Education* was the most widely circulated and enduring of the SEFT publications, it was only one journal in the Society's long and productive history. Its first publication, the *Society of Film Teachers' Bulletin*, began in December 1950 and was succeeded by three journals before *Screen Education* emerged in October 1959. By the time *Screen Education* became *Screen** in January 1969, the Society had also produced many handbooks, yearbooks, and occasional publications. The following is a general overview of those publications:

Edited by John Morris, five issues of *Society of Film Teachers' Bulletin* were published between December 1950 and March 1952. Edited by Derek J. Davies, six issues of *The Film Teacher* were published between Summer 1952 and Spring 1954. Edited by Jan Hoare, three issues of *Newsletter* were published between October 1954 and February 1955. Edited by Jan Hoare (April 1955–July 1956) and H. R. Wills (April 1956–May 1959), seventeen issues of *The Film Teacher* were published between April 1955 and May 1959. All of those publications were produced by the Society of Film Teachers, a London-based group, which became the Society for Education in Film and Television. In addition, the group published *Film Teacher's Handbook* (four issues between 1956/1957 and 1959/1960), which became *Screen Education Yearbook* (nine issues between 1960/1961 and 1969).

Other SEFT publications were *Film Making in Schools* by Sidney Rees and Don Waters (October 1960); *A Film Society Handbook* edited by R. C. Vannoey (1965); *A Handbook for Screen Education* compiled by Alex Richardson, R. C. Vannoey, and Don Waters (1963); *Information Sheets* (seven issues numbered 1–6B, April 1956–September 1958); *100 Films for Juniors; 40 Features and 60 Shorts for Primary Schools* compiled by S. G. P. Alexander (March 1964); *Running A School Film Society* by Jack Smith (1957); *TeenScreen* (January/February 1962 and May/June 1962); *T.V. Notes* (four issues published between June 1958 and February 1959); *Ten Films to Use* by R. C. Vannoey (1960); *Twenty Films to Use in Junior Film Societies* compiled by A. W. Hodgkinson (published jointly by the British Film Institute and the Society of Film Teachers); *Viewing Reports* (published occasionally between 1950 and 1959); *Young Film Makers*, a revised version of *Film Making in Schools*, by Sidney Rees and Don Waters (June 1963); and *Young Film Makers Symposium*, edited by H. R. Wills (1964).

A more detailed history of SEFT and its publications can be found in S. G. P. Alexander's articles: "Not So Much a Philosophy...More Like a Way of Life" (No. 27, January/February 1965); "Forming the Society of Film Teachers"

(No. 28, March/April 1965); "From SFT to SEFT" (No. 29, May/June 1965); and "We've Come a Long Way: The Story of the Society's Publications" (No. 31, September/October 1965).

Notes

1. "What Is Screen Education," No. 11, November/December 1961.

Information Sources

INDEX SOURCES: None.
REPRINT EDITIONS: None.
LOCATION SOURCES: Library of Congress (incomplete); University of California at Los Angeles (incomplete). [The British Film Institute Library has a complete run.]

Publication History

MAGAZINE TITLE AND TITLE CHANGES: *Screen Education*.
VOLUME AND ISSUE DATA: Nos. 1–5 (October 1959–September 1960), quarterly; Nos. 6–46 (January 1961–September/October 1968), bimonthly.
PUBLISHER AND PLACE OF PUBLICATION: Society for Education in Film and Television, London, England.
EDITOR: H. R. Wills.

Ron Polito

SCREEN FACTS

Screen Facts is best described as a nostalgia reference periodical which offered career articles with filmographies similar to those to be found in *Films in Review*.*
In addition, *Screen Facts* provided genre articles, such as "The Silent Serial" by William K. Everson (No. 1), "Oriental Detectives on the Screen" by Edward Connor (No. 8), and "Christ on the Screen" by Edward Connor (No. 16).

Founded in 1963 by film buff Alan G. Barbour,[1] *Screen Facts* was supposedly a bimonthly publication, but in reality no more than four issues were ever published in any one year through the magazine's demise with a double issue, No. 23/24, in 1972. Aside from the copyright year, no other date appeared on the magazine, which, with No. 21, changed its shape from 8 1/2" x 5 1/2" to legal size.

Among the more important articles to be found in *Screen Facts* are "The Films of D. W. Griffith" by William K. Everson (No. 3), "Deanna Durbin" by Gene Ringgold (No. 5), "Cornell Woolrich on the Screen" by Edward Connor (No. 5), "Lee Tracy" by Jack Jacobs (No. 6), "Karloff and Lugosi" by William K. Everson (No. 7), "Bette Davis" by Gene Ringgold (No. 9), "Geraldine Farrar" by DeWitt Bodeen (No. 10), "Hedy Lamarr" by Gene Ringgold (No. 11), "Shirley Temple" by Gene Ringgold (No. 12), "Maria Montez" by Jerry Vermilye (No. 13), "Ann Sheridan" by Ray Hagen (No. 14), "Pola Negri" by DeWitt Bodeen and Gene Ringgold (No. 15), "Raymond Walburn" by John

McCabe (No. 16), "Rudolph Valentino" by DeWitt Bodeen (No. 17), "Wini Shaw" by Ray Hagen (No. 17), "Donald O'Connor" by Alvin H. Marill (No. 18), "Viveca Lindfors" by Doug McClelland (No. 20), "Esther Williams" by William J. Pratt (No. 21), and "Bud Abbott and Lou Costello" by Alvin H. Marill (No. 22). The last issue, No. 23/24, featured "A Pictorial Salute to All-Time Favorite Universal Horror Films."

Notes

1. In addition to *Screen Facts*, Alan G. Barbour published a curious mixture of pieces, including reprints of the British magazine *Boys Cinema*; *Serial Quarterlies* (featuring synopses from serial pressbooks); *Screen Ads Monthly*; *Serial Pictorials* (containing full-page scenes from serials such as *Drums of Fu Manchu* and *Zorro's Fighting Legion*); as well as pamphlets with self-explanatory titles such as *Western Favorites*, *Lugosi*, *The Wonderful World of B Films*, and *Errol Flynn*.

Information Sources

INDEX SOURCES: None.
REPRINT SOURCES: None.
LOCATION SOURCES: Academy of Motion Picture Arts and Sciences; Cornell University; Library of Congress; New York Public Library; University of Southern California.

Publication History

MAGAZINE TITLE AND TITLE CHANGES: *Screen Facts*.
VOLUME AND ISSUE DATA: Nos. 1–5 (1963); Nos. 6–8 (1964); Nos. 9–12 (1965); Nos. 13 and 14 (1966); Nos. 15 and 16 (1967); Nos. 17–19 (1968); Nos. 20 and 21 (1969); No. 22 (1970); No. 23/24 (1972).
PUBLISHER AND PLACE OF PUBLICATION: Alan G. Barbour (copublisher Larry Edmunds Bookshop), P.O. Box 154, Kew Gardens, N.Y. 11415.
EDITOR: Alan G. Barbour.

Anthony Slide

SCREEN GREATS. See Appendix 2

SCREEN GUIDE. See Appendix 2

THE SCREEN GUILD MAGAZINE

In the spring of 1934, the Screen Actors' Guild commenced publication of a monthly magazine, *The Screen Player*, intended chiefly to bring news of interest to its members. Later in 1934 the Screen Actors' Guild was joined as publisher by the Screen Writers' Guild of the Authors' League of America. At that time, the title of the journal was changed to *The Screen Guilds' Magazine* and was later modified to *The Screen Guild Magazine* in 1936, the title used until the magazine's demise in 1938.

Although the emphasis of the periodical was heavily on the activities of the two Guilds and their negotiations for better contracts with management, the magazine did publish an extraordinary amount of interesting articles, such as "Why I Prefer the Stage to Pictures" by Mary Astor (Vol. 1, No. 3), "Cricket in California" by Boris Karloff (Vol. 1, No. 3), "Confessions of a Writer-Actor" by Robert Benchley (Vol. 1, No. 6), "An Actress' Working Day" by Genevieve Tobin (Vol. 1, No. 7), "Music and the Drama" by Upton Sinclair (Vol. 1, No. 8), "Sword Play in the Movies" by Fred Cavens (Vol. 1, No. 9), "A Camera Approach to Reality" by Joris Ivens (Vol. 3, No. 5), and "Television and the Movies" by Gilbert Seldes (Vol. 5, No. 1). John Paddy Carstairs contributed a regular column from London, and other writers included Eddie Cantor, Robert Montgomery, James Gleason, James Cagney, Dudley Nichols, Dorothy Parker, Fredric March, Leslie Howard, Michael Balcon, George Arliss, Richard Watts, Jr., Donald Ogden Stewart, and George Hurrell. Vol. 2, No. 5 (July 1935) was a special issue, "Color Comes to the Screen," with articles by Rouben Mamoulian, Kenneth Macgowan, and Robert Edmond Jones (all of whom were involved in the production of *Becky Sharp*).

Information Sources

INDEX SOURCES: None.
REPRINT EDITIONS: None.
LOCATION HOLDINGS: Academy of Motion Picture Arts and Sciences; Library of Congress, New York Public Library.

Publication History

MAGAZINE TITLE AND TITLE CHANGES: *The Screen Player* (March 15, 1934–June 15, 1934); *The Screen Guilds' Magazine* (August 1934–June 1936); *The Screen Guild Magazine* (July 1936–March 1938).
VOLUME AND ISSUE DATA: Vol. I, No. 1–Vol. V, No. 1 (March 15, 1934–March 1938), monthly.
PUBLISHER AND PLACE OF PUBLICATION: Screen Actors' Guild, 1655 North Cherokee Avenue, Hollywood, Calif. (Vol. I, No. 1–Vol. I, No. 4); The Screen Writers' Guild of the Authors' League and the Screen Actors' Guild, 1655 North Cherokee Avneue, Hollywood, Calif. (Vol. I, No. 5–Vol. V, No. 1).
EDITOR: No editor listed (March 15, 1934–June 15, 1934); Tristram Tupper (August 1934–December 1934); Robert Neville (January 1935–May 1935); Donald W. Lee (June 1935); Norman Rivkin (July 1935–June 1936); William Bledsoe (July 1936–October 1937); no editor listed (November 1937–March 1938).

Anthony Slide

THE SCREEN GUILDS' MAGAZINE. See THE SCREEN GUILD MAGAZINE

SCREEN INTERNATIONAL

Screen International: The Paper of the Entertainment Industry is the last major British entertainment industry "trade" paper. A continuation of *Daily Film Renter* (1934–1957), *The Cinema* (also known as *The Cinema News and Property Gazette*, 1913–1957), *The Daily Cinema* (1957–1968), *Today's Cinema* (1969–1971), *Cinema T.V. Today* (1971–1975), and *Kinematograph Weekly,* * *Screen International* has been published since its 1975 founding by British entrepreneur Peter King and edited by Peter Noble.[1] Like the American trade papers *Variety* * and *The Hollywood Reporter,* * *Screen International* reports on all major aspects of the entertainment industry but with a heavier emphasis on films and filmmaking than other topics. Being a British product, news in *Screen International* has less of an exclusively American scope than the other two, even though the paper now maintains an office in Los Angeles as well as London.

The titles of the columns and columnists have varied over the years. Only Peter Noble's column, "In Confidence," has remained the same. Like the columns of Hank Grant and Army Archerd in the American papers, Noble's column contains news items and extensive gossip about the entertainment industry. Other representative columns are "T.V. News" and "Hollywood Hotline." In recent years, television and the growing video industry have occupied considerable space within each of the weekly issues. Other features include film production charts, worldwide box-office reports, and the front-page "London Top Ten" report. Each issue is large, with some containing as many as one hundred pages.

For several years, beginning in 1977, *Screen International* published special daily issues during the Cannes Film Festival, but recently it has merely expanded its regular weekly issues to cover the festival. Other large editions of the paper are issued for various important film festivals and conventions throughout the world, with, yet again, a strong emphasis on television and video sales in the past few years.

Notes

1. A highly respected British film journalist, Peter Noble is the author of many books, including *Hollywood Scapegoat: The Biography of Erich von Stroheim* (1950), *Ivor Novello* (1951), and *The Negro in Films* (1948); from 1946 he has also edited the *British Film and Television Year Book*.

Information Sources

INDEX SOURCES: None.
REPRINT EDITIONS: World Microfilms.
LOCATION SOURCES: Academy of Motion Picture Arts and Sciences.

Publication History

MAGAZINE TITLE AND TITLE CHANGES: *Screen International and Cinema T.V. Today: The Paper of the Entertainment Industry* (September 6, 1975–January 17, 1976); *Screen International: The Paper of the Entertainment Industry* (January 24, 1976, to present).

VOLUME AND ISSUE DATA: Nos. 1–134 (September 6, 1975–April 15, 1978), weekly, published on a Saturday; No. 135 (April 22–28, 1978, to present), weekly, published on a Wednesday.
PUBLISHER AND PLACE OF PUBLICATION: Peter King (King Publications, Ltd.), 142 Wardour Street, London W1V 43R, England (Nos. 1–260); Peter King (King Publications, Ltd.), Kingston House, 6-7 Great Chapel Street, London W.1, England (No. 261 to present); American publication address (October 4–11, 1980, to present): 1542 North Genessee Avenue, Los Angeles, Calif. 90046.
EDITOR: Peter Noble.

Patricia King Hanson

SCREENLAND. See Appendix 2

SCREEN LEGENDS. See Appendix 2

SCREEN LIFE. See Appendix 2

SCREEN PICTORIAL. See Appendix 2

SCREEN PLAY. See Appendix 2

THE SCREEN PLAYER. See THE SCREEN GUILD MAGAZINE

SCREEN PLAY SECRETS. See Appendix 2

SCREEN PRODUCERS GUILD JOURNAL. See JOURNAL OF THE PRODUCERS GUILD OF AMERICA

SCREEN SECRETS. See Appendix 2

SCREEN STARS. See Appendix 2

SCREEN STORIES. See BOYS CINEMA

THE SCREEN WRITER

On June 11, 1945, the first issue of *The Screen Writer* was distributed free of charge to all the members of the Screen Writers' Guild, Inc. It was accompanied by a letter from the editorial committee which implored Guild members to participate in the magazine's "formative stage" and cautioned that maintaining a high-quality monthly publication would "demand enormous work and responsibility" on the part of "every single member of the Guild."[1] This responsibility included reacting to and shaping the magazine's contents, contributing articles, as well as securing paid subscriptions from nonmembers to cover the expense of publication

The first issue of *The Screen Writer* contained the customary editorial expressing the intent of the editor, Dalton Trumbo, and his staff: "We affirm as primary convictions that the motion picture is the most important of all international cultural mediums and that the screen writer is the primary creative force in the making of motion pictures." The editorial stated strongly that "the pages of *The Screen Writer* must be wide open to all shades of opinion."[2]

Although it promised to contain material of "lively interest not only to everyone in the motion picture industry, but to laymen as well," its primary purpose was to serve as "the actual voice" of the Screen Writers' Guild.[3] Union concerns remained the journal's major preoccupation throughout its run. The April 1948 issue commemorated the Guild's fifteenth anniversary and includes "A Brief History of the Guild" by screen writer Mary McCall, Jr.

Of particular historical interest are several of the journal's issues which follow the development of the proposed American Authors' Authority (AAA), a relatively radical idea put forth by conservative James M. Cain ("An American Authors' Authority," July 1946). The Authority was to represent various writers' groups, including screen writers, functioning in a manner similar to the American Society of Composers, Authors, and Publishers (ASCAP). The AAA would copyright an author's material and lease its use on a royalty basis. Both the Guild and *The Screen Writer* supported the movement, and the magazine eventually dedicated a special supplement to the subject (Vol. 11, No. 10). Eventually, Cain and the Guild withdrew support when the AAA became a politically "hot" issue and was nationally condemned as a pro-Communist concept.[4]

Although the vast majority of articles were concerned with the serious side of writing for the screen—how to maintain the integrity of the screenplay, the coming problem of television, or the battle for freedom of expression under Hollywood's censorship—there were occasional light pieces such as those written and illustrated by screenwriter/cartoonist Milt Gross or a poem by I. A. L. Diamond called "Hollywood Jabberwocky."

In addition to articles (mostly written by Guild members), *The Screen Writer* featured union news, current screen credits, editorials, letters, and book reviews. Frequent attention was given to American filmmaking abroad, including a series of reports from foreign correspondents in such European cities as Venice, London, and Paris.

Guild symposiums were reported on directors D. W. Griffith and Ernst Lubitsch and special sections were devoted to such topics as "Freedom on the Screen," "1% of the Gross—An Economic Primer of Screen Writing," and "What's Ahead for American Films."

In celebration of *The Screen Writer*'s third birthday (Vol. 4, No. 1), literary critic Frank Hursley evaluated the journal's first thirty-six issues. He found that the magazine was probably "the most consistent and successful attempt in literary history by a group of professional writers to evaluate their medium." "What distinguishes *The Screen Writer*," Hursley wrote, "is that it is written by the practitioners of a craft and directed to the attention and scrutiny of the other practitioners of the craft."[5]

Indeed, many of Hollywood's most important writers had contributed to the first three volumes. In addition to those on the editorial staff who wrote for the magazine (especially Dalton Trumbo and Philip Dunne), such names as Sidney Buchman, Alvah Bessie, Leonard Spigelgass, Budd Schulberg, Cyril Hume, Stephen Longstreet, and Oliver H. P. Garrett were among *The Screen Writer*'s contributors.

The Hollywood left wing was well represented. Five of the "Hollywood Ten" (Dalton Trumbo, John Howard Lawson, Albert Maltz, Adrian Scott, and Ring Lardner, Jr.) as well as two of the "Hollywood Nineteen" (Gordon Kahn and Howard Koch) were either on the editorial board or contributing authors.

According to Bruce Cook's biography of Dalton Trumbo:

> The fact that the preponderance of articles in *The Screen Writer* reflected liberal and radical views on all subjects was automatically attributed to Trumbo's influence. Yet he insisted, perhaps a little disingenuously, that his only standards were literary quality, general relevance, and respect for the Guild and its policies and objectives.[6]

Indeed, not all Guild members were in accordance with the magazine's perceived political bias, as is indicated by a letter from screenwriter Lewis R. Foster to Editor Trumbo, which was printed in the December 1945 issue:

> It is being said in the industry this morning that *The Screen Writer* has at last appeared in its true colors—red and yellow. The red part of it, of course, needs no explanation. The ideological leaning of yourself and other members of your staff are too well known to need enlightenment. The yellow tone [reflects]...the "bullying" tactics of staff writers to stick their chins out only when they feel the reassuring protection of a thousand odd screen writers at their back.[7]

Contributions were not restricted to screenwriters. Studio head Darryl F. Zanuck, cameraman James Wong Howe, directors such as William Wyler, Fred Zinnemann, and Sam Fuller, and even Production Code Administration president Eric Johnson represented other factions of the industry. Screenwriters who were also playwrights and novelists—F. Hugh Herbert, Louis Bromfield, and Raymond Chandler—concerned themselves with broader literary issues. James M. Cain's articles, in particular, appeared frequently.

Despite the staggered tenures of screenwriters Adele Buffington, Sonya Levien, Margaret Buell Wilder, and Isobel Lennart on the editorial board, few women contributed to the journal. Some prominent exceptions were Lillian Hellman, agent Audrey Wood, and screenwriter Mary C. McCall, Jr.

Beyond praising *The Screen Writer*'s evaluation of the writer's role in the filmmaking process, Frank Hursley's analysis found the most valuable articles to be those in which the writers "lay bare the economic structure of the movie industry" and examined money's influence over the final cinematic product. "Nobody knows better than the screen writer that the economics and aesthetics of moviedom are never very far apart," wrote Hursley.[8] He also noted a consistent plea for more "adult" entertainment and artistic integrity.

Perhaps Hursley's most interesting observation was identifying the journal's concern with issues of film "authorship," a subject that would not gain wide popularity in film criticism until the "auteur" movement of the sixties. "The most insistent demand, voiced time and time again in *The Screen Writer* and implicit in practically every article, is that the production of movies be somehow so managed that the centrality of the author...be preserved through to what appears on the screen."[9]

Joseph L. Mankiewicz's "Film Author! Film Author!" (May 1947) was particularly controversial and provoked responses the following month from Philip Dunne, Milton Krims, Allen Rivkin, Albert Lewin, Preston Sturges, Niven Busch, Norman Krasna, and Delmer Daves, grouped under the umbrella title, "Can Screen Writers Become Film Authors?"

Hursley was excited by what he read in the first three volumes of *The Screen Writer*. He felt things were "stirring" in Hollywood, calling for a kind of "revolution," and that the "blueprints for it are being drawn up, month after month, in *The Screen Writer*."[10] But the revolution would have to take place without the Guild mouthpiece. Only three issues after Hursley's glowing evaluation, *The Screen Writer* died the "unlamented death" predicted in the magazine's first editorial.

Apparently, this was not directly from a lack of funds, which is responsible for the end of many small journals. The September 1948 issue reported the results of the Guild's executive board decision that *The Screen Writer* be published on a voluntary basis. Since May of that year, under the editorship of John Larkin, the magazine was successfully published without a paid staff. Remarkably, the actual cost to the Guild for *The Screen Writer*'s publication of the July issue was only $419.95.

The *Screen Writer*'s original staff had warned against the possibility of the journal becoming "the personal organ of a small clique."[11] Despite the fact that during the last year of its publication many of the names associated with the extreme political left dropped from the editorial committee and were replaced by more moderate and conservative Guild members, the possibility of a politically related demise should not be excluded.

In a recent interview, Philip Dunne, a frequent contributor as well as a member of the editorial board, speculated that the magazine was, at least in part, "a casualty of the House Committee on Un-American Activities." Still, he defended the journal's original intent as essentially apolitical. "I believe the idea had been for a 'review' type magazine. It had nothing to do with internal politics or external politics, or anything at all—except the medium."[12]

However, it may have been as simple as a lack of manpower, both in terms of the voluntary staffing of the magazine and the number of contributions. Less than four years after its inception, *The Screen Writer*'s next-to-last issue echoed its original concern, a dependence on Guild support:

The real problem of *The Screen Writer* is to keep it a live and dynamic publication. . . . To do this, cogent material is essential. The editors have found that the members of the Guild are given to a great deal of promise, and considerably less performance. Unless this responsibility is felt keenly by every member of the Guild, *The Screen Writer* will either become a forum for the few or deteriorate.[13]

But there was no time for deterioration; the following issue proved to be the journal's last.

Notes

1. Letter from *The Screen Writer*'s Editorial Committee to Screen Writers' Guild members, June 11, 1945, Academy of Motion Picture Arts and Sciences.

2. "Editorial," *The Screen Writer*, Vol. 1, No. 1, June 1945, pp. 36–37.

3. Letter, June 11, 1945.

4. See Larry Ceplair and Steven Englund, *The Inquisition in Hollywood: Politics in the Film Community 1930–1960* (Garden City, New York: Anchor Press/Doubleday, 1980), pp. 251–252.

5. Frank Hursley, "An Evaluation of *The Screen Writer*," Vol. 4, No. 1, June/July 1948, p. 14.

6. Bruce Cook, *Dalton Trumbo* (New York: Charles Scribner's Sons, 1977), p. 169.

7. Letter from Lewis R. Foster to Dalton Trumbo, Editor, "Correspondence," *The Screen Writer*, Vol. 1, No. 7, December 1945, pp. 38–39.

8. Hursley, p. 15.

9. Hursley, pp. 15, 22.

10. Hursley, p. 22.

11. "Editorial," June 1945, p. 37.
12. Interview with Philip Dunne by author, August 31, 1983, Malibu, Calif.
13. "Editorial," *The Screen Writer*, Vol. 4, No. 3, September 1948.

Information Sources

BIBLIOGRAPHY:
Ceplair, Larry, and Englund, Steven. *The Inquisition in Hollywood: Politics in the Film Community 1930–1960* (Garden City, New York: Anchor Press/Doubleday, 1980).
Cook, Bruce. *Dalton Trumbo* (New York: Charles Scribner's Sons, 1977).
Dunne, Philip. *Take Two: A Life in Movies and Politics* (New York: McGraw-Hill Book Co., 1980).
Schwartz, Nancy Lynn. *The Hollywood Writers' Wars* (New York: Alfred A. Knopf, 1982).
INDEX SOURCES: The New Film Index.
REPRINT EDITIONS: None.
LOCATION SOURCES: Academy of Motion Picture Arts and Sciences; University of California at Los Angeles.

Publication History

MAGAZINE TITLE AND TITLE CHANGES: *The Screen Writer*.
VOLUME AND ISSUE DATA: Vol. I, No, 1–Vol. IV, No. 4 (June 1945–October 1948), monthly.
PUBLISHER AND PLACE OF PUBLICATION: The Screen Writers' Guild, Inc., 1655 North Cherokee, Hollywood 28, Calif.
EDITOR: Dalton Trumbo (June 1945–March 1946); Gordon Kahn (June 1947–December 1947); Richard English (January 1948–April 1948); John Larkin (May 1948–August 1948); Leonard Spigelgass (September 1948–October 1948).

Joanne L. Yeck

SEE. See WORLD FILM NEWS

SEFTUS NEWSLETTER. See SCREEN EDUCATION

THE SELIG POLYSCOPE COMPANY RELEASE HERALD. See Appendix 3

SELIG POLYSCOPE NEWS. See Appendix 3

SELZNICK STUDIO CLOSE-UP. See Appendix 3

SEQUENCE

From 1946 through 1951, *Sequence* was a lovely little magazine, created by a group of film sophisticates from Oxford University, the most notable of whom were Lindsay Anderson, Penelope Houston, and Gavin Lambert. The last two were to become editors of *Sight and Sound** and continue the *Sequence* approach to cinema in that publication, long after that approach was outdated. *Sequence* represented the avant-garde in British cinema, but apart from editorializing against much of contemporary popular British cinema, it limited its avant-gardism to fairly lightweight reviews of current films, a new approach to film history, finding new cinema heroes (notably John Ford), and selecting its film favorites (such as Barbara Bel Geddes). *Sequence* could be harsh in its comments, as with Lindsay Anderson's interview with Samuel Goldwyn in No. 13, but when it came to political theory, the magazine's attitude was confused. In the same issue, No. 5, as it editorialized against the House Un-American Activities Committee, it lauded as one of the ''people we like'' Ward Bond, a Hollywood archconservative.

Aside from its editors, *Sequence* boasted among its writers Catherine de la Roche (who contributed a major piece on the films of Mark Donskoi in No. 5), Lotte H. Eisner, Irish filmmaker George Morrison, Douglas Slocombe (who wrote on Gregg Toland in No. 8), Satyajit Ray (who wrote ''Renoir in Calcutta'' in No. 10), and John Huston (who wrote on Robert Flaherty in No. 14). It is also worth noting that the last issue was edited by Lindsay Anderson and Karel Reisz, both of whom are credited with the creation of the British ''Free Cinema'' movement of the late fifties.

Despite a rise in circulation from six hundred to four thousand, *Sequence* ran into major financial difficulties, which led to its demise with No. 14 (although that demise may also have been brought on by its editors' and writers' increasing interests in other areas of cinema). In its final issue, *Sequence* asked, ''Has anything been accomplished in these fourteen issues?'' and replied, ''Not much, beyond the satisfaction of having said a say, 'fired our ringing shot, and passed.' . . .Not surprising that we made few friends, and influenced fewer people. Our only excuse is that the sentiments were at least sincere: those films hurt us as much as our comments hurt their makers.''

Information Sources

INDEX SOURCES: The New Film Index.
REPRINT EDITIONS: World Microfilms.
LOCATION SOURCES: Academy of Motion Picture Arts and Sciences.

Publication History

MAGAZINE TITLE AND TITLE CHANGES: *Sequence*.
VOLUME AND ISSUE DATA: No. 1 (December 1946); No. 2 (Winter 1947); No. 3 (Spring 1948); No. 4 (Summer 1948); No. 5 (Autumn 1948); No. 6 (Winter 1948/

1949); No. 7 (Spring 1949); No. 8 (Summer 1949); No. 9 (Autumn 1949); No.
10 (New Year 1950); No. 11 (Summer 1950); No. 12 (New Year 1951); No. 13
(New Year 1952).
PUBLISHER AND PLACE OF PUBLICATION: The Oxford University Film Society
[no address listed] (Nos. 1–3); Sequence, 19 Hanover Terrace, Regent's Park,
London N.W.1, England (Nos. 3–11); London Film Club, 20/21 Tooks Court,
London E.C.4, England (Nos. 12–14).
EDITOR: Lindsay Anderson, Penelope Houston, and Peter Ericcson (Nos. 1–3); Peter
Ericcson and Gavin Lambert (No. 4); Lindsay Anderson, Peter Ericcson, and
Gavin Lambert (Nos. 5–9); Lindsay Anderson and Peter Ericcson (Nos. 10–11),
Lindsay Anderson (Nos. 12–13); Lindsay Anderson and Karel Reisz (No. 14).

Anthony Slide

SERIAL QUARTERLY. See Appendix 2

SERIAL WORLD. See Appendix 2

SHADOWLAND. See Appendix 2

SHADOWPLAY. See Appendix 2

THE SHERRY PUNCH. See Appendix 3

THE SHOOTING STAR. See Appendix 1

SHORT SUBJECT QUARTERLY. See THE FILM DAILY

SHOW (1961)

When *Show* was launched in Autumn 1961, *Life* was twenty cents (later to
go to thirty-five) and *Holiday* was sixty. *Show*, with approximately the same
number of pages as each of them, appeared on the newsstands at seventy-five
cents. Millionaire Huntington Hartford did not set out to publish just another
magazine; *Show* saw itself as the successor to *Vanity Fair*. It proclaimed in the
first issue it would be "the definitive magazine of the performing arts, and our
view of those arts will be broad." Six issues later, *Show*'s readers were informed

that "we are now convinced that the arts cannot be separated from the other vital pieces of our culture—painting, sculpture, architecture and design, and the wide world of literature." Between the beginning and the end, almost four years later, there was a succession of graphically stylish issues that never failed to entertain and inform, tried to be thought provoking, but never succeeded in fulfilling its amibition of being a trend setter.

With such a broad field of interest to cover in every issue, it was lucky if each of the arts was represented monthly by a feature article. Often the film was acknowledged by a personality feature on a female star, such as Monica Vitti, Doris Day, Susannah York, Natalie Wood, Jeanne Moreau, Sophia Loren, or Greta Garbo. In addition, Richard Schickel wrote about Fred Zinnemann, Carlos Fuentes about Luis Buñuel, and Stanley Price about David Lean. There was a report of a visitation to the filming location of *The Night of the Iguana*. Overall, the coverage of the Hollywood scene was scarcely in depth.

Television received some attention, again through its stars. Richard Boone, Ernie Kovacs, and Jackie Gleason were the subjects of feature stories, as were producers Bill Todman and Mark Goodson. There was a discussion of the portrayal of the Second World War on television but otherwise not much that could be labeled penetrating analysis. Television shows were regularly reviewed in a separate column conducted at various times by Brock Brower, Warren Miller, Dan Wakefield, Myra Magid, Carol Rinzler, and Martin Levin. For movie reviews, *Show* relied largely on Arthur Schlesinger, Jr., helped out once in a while by Stanley Kauffmann and Donald La Badie.

The content of *Show* varied widely. There were feature articles and reviews from the worlds of art, music, and theatre. Literature was represented by running selections from forthcoming books by William Golding, Jack Kerouac, Robert Lowell, Gunter Grass, Leonard Woolf, and Louis Auchincloss. Reports from London, Berlin, Warsaw, Paris, Laos, and Cuba gave the magazine an international flavor. Several special issues were put together: the arts in South America, the arts in Europe, murder, U.S. politics, William Shakespeare, international movies, and two on Japan.

Late in 1964, after sinking an estimated seven million dollars into *Show* and getting its circulation up to 200,000, Huntington Hartford sold the magazine to Gilman Kraft, publisher of *Playbill*. Hartford was scheduled to continue to participate in editorial decisions, but for the last three issues he was simply listed on the masthead as "founder."

Six years after the magazine's demise, Hartford resurrected his publication under the same title, *Show* (1970).*

Information Sources

BIBLIOGRAPHY:
Alpert, Hollis. "Exciting New Magazines for Show Business." *Saturday Review*, September 9, 1961, pp. 48–49.
"Enthusiasts." *Newsweek*, October 21, 1963, p. 109.

"Hybrid." *Newsweek*, August 20, 1962, p. 53.
"New Group Encourages Inter-American Cultural Exchange." *Publishers' Weekly*, December 17, 1962, pp. 17–18.
"New Magazines Seek Paydirt in Culture." *Business Week*, September 2, 1961, pp. 79–80.
"Show Business." *Time*, August 17, 1962, p. 42.
"Show Goes On." *Newsweek*, September 11, 1961, p. 94.
"Show Goes On." *Time*, June 12, 1964, p. 82.
"Show Sold." *Time*, November 13, 1964, p. 71.
"Show Stopper." *Newsweek*, May 10, 1965, p. 99.
"Two for the Show." *Newsweek*, March 20, 1961, p. 67.
"What's New?" *Time*, September 15, 1961, p. 67.
INDEX SOURCES: None.
REPRINT EDITIONS: None.
LOCATION SOURCES: Brown University; Columbia University; Library of Congress; New York Public Library; Pennsylvania State University Library; University of Arkansas; University of California at Los Angeles; University of Miami; University of Texas at Austin; Virginia State University Library.

Publication History

MAGAZINE TITLE AND TITLE CHANGES: *Show*.
VOLUME AND ISSUE DATA: Vol. I, No. 1 (October 1961); Vol. I, No. 2 (November 1961); Vol. I, No. 3 (December 1961); Vol. II–Vol. III (January 1962–December 1963), monthly; Vol. IV (January–December 1964), monthly except double issue July/August; Vol. V, No. 1 (January 1965); Vol. V, No. 2 (March 1965); Vol. V, No. 3 (April 1965); Vol. V, No. 4 (May 1965).
PUBLISHER AND PLACE OF PUBLICATION: Hartford Publications, Inc., 140 East Fifty-seventh Street, New York, N.Y. (Vol. I, No. 1–Vol. V, No. 1); MOTA Company, Inc., 640 Fifth Avenue, New York, N.Y. 10019 (Vol. V, No. 2–Vol. V, No. 4).
EDITOR: Robert M. Wool (October 1961–February 1963); Marvin Barrett (March 1963–June 1964); Huntington Hartford (July/August 1964–January 1965); George Christy and Walter Wager (March 1965); Ben M. Hall (April 1965); Brian O'Doherty (May 1965).

Richard Heinzkill

SHOW (1970)

Another attempt by Huntington Hartford to establish a leading entertainment magazine, this 1970–1977 incarnation of *Show* started publication with the subtitle "The Magazine of Films and the Arts" and ended with the subtitle "The Magazine of Entertainment and the Arts." A more accurate subtitle would have been "The Magazine about Show Business People." *Show* kept its attention focused on persons and not issues. An eager and curious public has always wanted to read about the stars and anyone involved in show business, and this publication aimed to satisfy that curiosity at a level above that of the usual fan magazine. The majority of the articles were fairly short, well illustrated, and not sensational.

Show was respectable but not staid. It had a healthy interest in sex. Well-illustrated articles on groupies, Russ Meyer, and censorship gave it ample opportunity to explore contemporary morality and to make the magazine more visually appealing to the male commuter looking on the newsstand for something to read. A feature titled "Showcase" utilized provocative pin-up-style photographs to introduce starlets with "new talent."

Overall, the movies received the most attention, with television, theatre, and rock music close behind. Occasionally a piece on opera and dance appeared. The editorial features were supplemented by a number of regular features, such as gossipy reports from the night club world and accounts of the latest in fashions, books, recordings, music, and theatre.

For a long time each issue contained at least one article on the filming of a recent feature, such as *Catch 22*, *The Devils*, or *Putney Swope*. Directors were not ignored, and there were interviews with Ingmar Bergman and Robert Altman, as well as features on Ken Russell, Paul Williams, and Joseph Losey. Occasionally there was a feature article with a nonpersonality slant, including pieces on the American Film Institute, blacks in film, and a look at the graphic art of titles.

Television received a fair amount of attention; stars such as Johnny Carson, Loretta Swit, and Sandy Duncan were regularly featured; Jean Stapleton talked about "All in the Family" and Lance Loud on "An American Family". There were also articles on sex and science fiction on television and the use of the teleprompter. The August 6, 1970, issue was devoted entirely to television.

As might be expected, *Show* included reviews of films and television shows, but as time went on these became shorter and shorter until, by the last issue, television shows were summarized in one or two sentences and the movie review section consisted of one lengthy review accompanied by a two-page spread filled with capsule reviews of eighteen recent releases.

Andrew Sarris, Budd Schulberg, Gene Youngblood, and Rex Reed were among those who contributed articles in the first years. Later the magazine was almost entirely staff-written.

Every attempt was made to give the reader that feeling of being an insider. A Show Magazine Club was established on New York's Fifty-second Street, where "celebrities drop in by the hour to have a drink, a snack or just mingle with the crowd." To promote this image, readers were invited to drop in also, on the first Tuesday of each month, which was Show Magazine Night, and meet "the faces inside and behind the magazine." A feature, "Show Club News," reported on those celebrities who had been seen at the club.

Show never quite found the right formula. The editorial content, the auxiliary enterprise, and publishing frequency never caught fire. Like his earlier attempt at such a magazine (*Show* [1961]*), *Show* again proved enough of a drain on even Huntington Hartford's pocketbook, and he stopped publication after forty-five issues.

Information Sources

INDEX SOURCES: None.
REPRINT EDITIONS: None.
LOCATION SOURCES: University of Oregon (incomplete).

Publication History

MAGAZINE TITLE AND TITLE CHANGES: *Show*.
VOLUME AND ISSUE DATA: Vol. I, Nos. 1–6 (January 1970–June 1970), monthly;
    Vol. I, Nos. 7–13 (June 25, 1970–September 17, 1970), biweekly; not published
    October 1970–February 1971; Vol. II, No. 1–Vol. IV, No. 9 (March 1971–
    December 1977), monthly. [Issues for Vols. III–IV are designated erroneously
    Vols. II–III.]
PUBLISHER AND PLACE OF PUBLICATION: Show Publications, Inc., 6618 Sunset
    Boulevard, Hollywood, Calif. 90028 (Vol. I); H & R Publications, Inc., 866
    United Nations Plaza, New York, N.Y. 10017 (Vol. II, No. 1–Vol. IV, No. 2);
    H & R Publications, Inc., 801 Second Avenue, New York, N.Y. 10017 (Vol.
    IV, No. 3–Vol. IV, No. 9).
EDITOR: Dick Adler (January 1970–June 1970); Digby Diehl (June 1970–September
    1970); Ann Guerin (1971–1972); William Deerfield (1973). [Throughout, Hun-
    tington Hartford was Editor-in-Chief.]

Richard Heinzkill

SHOW BUSINESS ILLUSTRATED

"With this first issue, you have purchased a seat on the aisle, front row, center, to the most exciting, colorful, provocative, entertaining, wonderful show in the world." Thus did Hugh Hefner welcome charter readers to his production of *Show Business Illustrated*. He promised to look at show business not only from out front but from behind the scenes, to allow readers to meet the stars "as real people." In reality, the contents were always interesting, even if they did not quite live up to the publisher's hype.

The personalities featured in that first issue (September 5, 1961) were Marlon Brando, visited on location in Tahiti by Arthur Knight, and Jackie Gleason, visited on location in Paris by Richard Gehman. In subsequent issues there were a photo essay on Carol Burnett, an article on Jack Parr, and interviews with Newton Minow, Rod Serling, and Federico Fellini. More substantial articles, now looking somewhat dated, were George Feldman's predictions for communication satellites and an article on censorship. Patrick Dennis's *Little Me* was serialized in the first seven issues, followed by a serialization of David Susskind's autobiography.

By its eighth issue, *Show Business Illustrated* was looking more conventional. That issue stared into the year ahead—1963—and back to 1961. It presented awards for the best and worst of the previous year and took a second look at the eight young ladies who had been the "SBI Beauties" of 1961. Also included was a satirical piece by Gene Fowler on the hazards of being a professional writer employed by a major studio in the thirties.

Four issues later, *Show Business Illustrated* announced it was combining with *Show* (1961)* to bring its readers "the verve of SBI and the beauty of *Show*." Thus Hugh Hefner's entertainment publication became submerged into Huntington Hartford's excursion into the field.

Information Sources

BIBLIOGRAPHY:

Alpert, Hollis. "Exciting New Magazines for Show Business." *Saturday Review*, September 9, 1961, pp. 48–49.

"New Magazine Gets a Shake-Up." *Business Week*, December 9, 1961, p. 130.

"New Magazines Seek Paydirt in Culture." *Business Week*, September 2, 1961, pp. 79–80.

"Newcomers." *Time*, August 25, 1961, p. 39.

"Playmate." *Newsweek*, May 8, 1961, p. 60.

"That's Show Biz." *Newsweek*, August 28, 1961, p. 72.

"Two for the Show." *Newsweek*, March 20, 1961, p. 67.

INDEX SOURCES: None.

REPRINT EDITIONS: None.

LOCATION SOURCES: Harvard University; Library of Congress; New York Public Library; Stanford University; University of California at Los Angeles; University of Illinois; University of Iowa.

Publication History

MAGAZINE TITLE AND TITLE CHANGES: *Show Business Illustrated* (September 5, 1961–November 1, 1961); *SBI: Show Business Illustrated* (November 14, 1961–April 1962).

VOLUME AND ISSUE DATA: Vol. I, No. 1–Vol. II, No. 1 (September 5, 1961–January 23, 1962), biweekly; Vol. II, No. 2–Vol. II, No. 4 (February 1962–April 1962), monthly.

PUBLISHER AND PLACE OF PUBLICATION: HMH Publishing Co., Playboy Building, 232 East Ohio Street, Chicago, Ill.

EDITOR: Hugh Hefner.

Richard Heinzkill

SHOW NEWS (RKO). See Appendix 3

SIGHT AND SOUND

On the editorial page of *Sight and Sound*, it is described as "an independent critical magazine sponsored and published by the British Film Institute. It is not an organ for the expression of official BFI policy: signed articles represent the views of their authors." The accusation that it was a mouthpiece of the Institute had on occasion been levelled against it: in fact, its first appearance antedated the formation of the BFI by over a year. The first number came out in Spring 1932, subtitled "A Quarterly Review of Modern Aids to Learning," and was published under the auspices of the British Institute of Adult Education. In 1933 the BFI took it over, reducing the price from 1 shilling (5 pence) to 6 pence (2 1/2 pence). It was presented with a new cover but was not otherwise greatly changed. Even during its pre-Institute days, it devoted an appreciable amount of space to feature entertainment films: the index to the first volume contained over a hundred such titles as against about forty educational. C. A. Lejeune's list of "films you ought to see" in the first issue contained *Westfront 1918*, *Kameradschaft*, *Congress Dances*, *Un Soir de Rafle*, *A Nous la Liberté*, *Tabu*, and *Round the World in 80 Minutes*. In No. 3 she considered *Grand Hotel* "probably the best value for money the commercial talkie has ever produced."

Other reviewers in those days included Paul Rotha and Alistair Cooke, and as time went on, more and more attention was paid to the film as an end in itself as well as an educational tool. Items by filmmakers appeared (including, in 1938, an interesting article by Méliès written just before his death), together with surveys on the cinema in countries throughout the world. At this time, sales were restricted to members of the BFI, and in 1938 the financial position showed a loss of 450 pounds sterling.

With the outbreak of war, the magazine narrowly escaped extinction. Proposals were made, first to suspend publication altogether, then to amalgamate it with *The Monthly Film Bulletin*.* However, *Sight and Sound* was finally reprieved and permitted to retain its identity. In 1941 it succumbed to wartime restrictions, shrinking to half its page size and losing its illustrations for the duration. The content policy remained much the same, except for the limitations of subject unavoidable in the circumstances. A new feature, "News from the Societies," was started in 1941.

After the war, in 1946, *Sight and Sound* returned to its original size in a worthy, but somewhat dull and forbidding, format. The turn of policy toward the art and entertainment film continued, accelerated probably by the Radcliffe Report, which radically altered the aims and objectives of the Institute in its recommendations, starting it off on a fresh footing and injecting new life into a somewhat tired and lethargic body. A "Film in Education Supplement" disappeared, and the name of the editor (hitherto omitted) appeared on the appropriate page—R. W. Dickinson.

In 1949 it again took on a new look and became more like the publication it is today. In addition it was issued monthly, retaining the price of 2 shillings and

6 pence (12 1/2 pence) from after the war. For the first time, it went out on public sale. The build-up took some years, but by 1959 the circulation figures reached fifteen thousand, and the whole look and tone of the magazine became a good deal livelier, under the editorship of Gavin Lambert. Contributors of articles and reviews included Lindsay Anderson, Wolf Mankowitz, and Kenneth Tynan; and solemnity and pontification were lightened by features such as "The Seventh Art," a highly amusing collection of quotations from some of the wilder flights of idiocy indulged in by writers on the cinema, which lasted for several years and would be welcomed back. A notable feature in these years was the wide coverage of books, magazines, and other publications both British and foreign. The book review section, in fact, greatly exceeded that of the present day, which seems overselective for a quarterly publication.

Another interesting series of the period was a monthly "Revaluation" of a well-known film of early years (*Mother*, *The Italian Straw Hat*, *Shooting Stars*, *Siegfried*, and so forth), contributed mainly by Roger Manvell.

A special number, "Films in 1951," was issued in that year to celebrate the Festival of Britain, containing interviews with a large number of British film-makers and a well-illustrated survey of the previous ten years. Thereafter, the magazine reverted to quarterly publication (the monthly experiment having proved unsuccessful) with an increase in size and a price of 3 shillings and 6 pence (17 1/2 pence), and in June 1952 it showed a profit for the first time. In the same year, following an international Brussels referendum, "The Ten Best Films," *Sight and Sound* asked eighty-five critics from ten countries to submit a similar list, and this has been continued every ten years since. The winner in 1952 was De Sica's *Bicycle Thieves*, and in all three following decades the winner has been *Citizen Kane*, leaving Orson Welles as top director with seventy-one votes and Jean Renoir as runner-up (for *La Règle du Jeu*) with fifty-one.

In 1956, Penelope Houston took over the editorship, a post she has held to the present day, achieving a consistently high standard. In 1965 *Sight and Sound* was awarded the Plaquette Leone di S. Marco at the Venice Film Book Exhibition run in connection with the Film Festival. Throughout the sixties and seventies, the table of contents has remained on much the same lines, though always fully sensitive to the changing scene, and the price rising steadily and inexorably to its present inflation-boosted £1.15 ($3.50). Sales reached thirty thousand for the first time in 1969.

From time to time in the past, complaints were levelled against *Sight and Sound*: that it was too esoteric; that the opinions of contributors tended to be identified, especially overseas, with those of the Institute—and even the British government; in particular that not enough space was given to British films. Whether or not this last point was true in the past, it can hardly be upheld today, in a periodical subtitled "International Film Quarterly." Recently, also, increasing coverage has been given to television and its development, with articles such as a study of the work of Dennis Potter, "A Scan of the Video Industry," and "High Definition T.V."

In the autumn of 1982, *Sight and Sound* produced a special fiftieth anniversary number; and at the same time a handsome volume of selected articles from through the years was published by Faber & Faber, including names (other than those mentioned above) such as Richard Winnington, James Agee, John Grierson, S. M. Eisenstein, Alfred Hitchcock, Satyajit Ray, and Louise Brooks. Both celebrations are justified by a magazine which, through the years, has maintained a reputation as one of the most influential and best-produced "serious" film periodicals in the world.

Information Sources

BIBLIOGRAPHY:
Butler, Ivan. *To Encourage the Art of the Film: The History of the British Film Institute.* London: Robert Hale, 1971.
Wilson, David, ed. *Sight and Sound* (London: Faber & Faber, 1982).
INDEX SOURCES: British Humanities Index; The Critical Index; FIAF International Index to Film Periodicals; Film Literature Index; Humanities Index; The New Film Index; Retrospective Index to Film Periodicals.
REPRINT EDITIONS: World Microfilms.
LOCATION SOURCES: Academy of Motion Picture Arts and Sciences; New York Public Library; University of Illinois; Yale University.

Publication History

MAGAZINE TITLE AND TITLE CHANGES: *Sight and Sound.*
VOLUME AND ISSUE DATA: Vol. I, No. 1–Vol. XIIX, No. 70 (Spring 1932–Autumn 1949), quarterly; Vol. XIX, No. 1–Vol, XX, No. 2 (January 1950–June 1951), monthly; Vol. XXI, No. 1 (August/September 1951 to present), quarterly. A special number, "Films in 1951," appeared in July 1951.
PUBLISHER AND PLACE OF PUBLICATION: British Institute of Adult Education, 39 Bedford Square, London W.C.1, England (Vol. I, No.1–Vol. II, No. 7); British Film Institute, 4 Great Russell Street, London W.C.1, England (Vol. II, No. 8–Vol. XVI, No. 64); British Film Institute, 164 Shaftesbury Avenue, London W.C.2, England (Vol. XVII, No. 65–Vol. XXIX, No. 2); British Film Institute, 81 Dean Street, London W1V 6AA, England (Vol. XXIX, No. 3–Vol. XLVI, No. 4); British Film Institute, 127 Charing Cross Road, London WC2 OEA, England (Vol. XLVII, No. 1, to present).
EDITOR: R. W. Dickinson (?–1948); Gavin Lambert (1949–1956); Penelope Houston (1956 to present).

Ivan Butler

SIGHTLINES

Sightlines, official publication of the Educational Film Library Association (EFLA), offered on the cover of its first issue a photograph of Buckminster Fuller's geodesic dome at the U.S. Pavilion of Canada's Expo '67, with a caption below reading "World of Film—Past, Present, Future." In that first issue (May-

June 1967), the past was represented by a profile of documentary master Robert J. Flaherty in an on-going series headed "Who's Who in Filmmaking." The "Film List," another regular feature, offered five pages of pertinent data (descriptive synopsis, running time, source, and so on) of current 16mm films. Predictions of future developments in the informational and educational film field were given in James L. Limbacher's "A Message from the EFLA President," foreseeing the "quick emergence of Super-8 films," and in an article entitled "EVR (Electronic Video Recording): The Wave of the Future?"

In later issues of that first year, *Sightlines* included a profile of John Grierson (father of the documentary film movement); an explanation of "computer cinema"; an article on "The Best Ten" (films with highest audience ratings in the collections of EFLA's member film libraries, such as *An Occurrence at Owl Creek Bridge, The Red Balloon, The Louvre, Night and Fog*); an article on EFLA's twenty-fifth anniversary (1943–1968), reviewing its activities as well as the growth of nontheatrical films and filmstrips during those years; and a listing of "Dance Films, Folk and Ethnic," issued as a service supplement for reference and programming purposes.

In the intervening years, *Sightlines* has maintained a reasonable balance between serving its members and other readers with useful information and helping raise the artistic levels of U.S. film collections versus promoting new technologies. The primary focus, like that of EFLA, has remained to offer practical information and guidance needed to run an audio-visual library, film collection, or media center in a school, university, public library, or other organization.

Over the years, *Sightlines* has reflected the major changes in the content of these libraries and centers. In 1970 the magazine published articles by or about black filmmakers William Greaves, Cliff Frazier, and Ossie Davis, as well as articles on film teaching in universities and filmmaking by students; filmographies on drug abuse, sex education, death and dying, and movies about movie making—subjects which were generally overlooked or taboo before then. Women filmmakers made an appearance as a movement, rather than as isolated individuals, in 1973 and 1974, in "Who's Who" articles on Martha Coolidge, Amalie Rothschild, and Cinda Firestone—followed in subsequent years by articles on Edie Lynch, Kathleen Laughlin, and Barbara Kopple.

Occasional "Who's Who in Video" columns, begun in the early seventies, reflected the growing involvement of schools and libraries in the U.S. with electronic images (though not with the CBS system that was described in *Sightlines'* first issue). A regular video column was begun in late 1978, and the Spring 1983 issue was devoted entirely to video.

In the early eighties, articles and film lists on Hispanic and other ethnic American groups, as well as Islamic and other Third World subjects, appeared with some frequency. Supplements to James L. Limbacher's *Feature Films on 8mm, 16mm, and Videotape* (R. R. Bowker) also appear in *Sightlines* on a regular basis.

Information Sources

INDEX SOURCES: Film Literature Index; Library Literature; Media Review Digest.
REPRINT EDITIONS: University Microfilms.
LOCATION SOURCES: Educational Film Library Association; Illinois State University;
    Library of Congress; University of California at Los Angeles; University of Illinois;
    University of Iowa; University of Kansas; Virginia State University Library; Wash-
    ington State University Library.

Publication History

MAGAZINE TITLE AND TITLE CHANGES: *Sightlines*.
VOLUME AND ISSUE DATA: Vol. I, No. 1–Vol. VI, No. 6 (May-June 1967–July/
    August 1973), bimonthly; Vol. VII, No. 1–Vol. VII, No. 5 (1973–1974), five
    times a year; Vol. VIII, No. 1 (Fall 1974 to present), quarterly.
PUBLISHER AND PLACE OF PUBLICATION: Educational Film Library Association,
    Inc., 17 West Sixtieth Street, New York, N.Y. 10023 (Vol. I, No. 1–Vol. IX,
    No. 3); Educational Film Library Association, Inc., 43 West Sixty-first Street,
    New York, N.Y. 10023 (Vol. IX, No. 4–Vol. XVI, Nos. 1/2); Educational Film
    Library Association, Inc., 45 John Street, New York, N.Y. 10038 (Vol. XVI,
    No. 3, to present).
EDITOR: Emily S. Jones (1966–1969); Esmé J. Dick (1969–1972); Nadine Covert (1972
    to present).

Cecile Starr

THE SILENT PICTURE

Among the areas least examined in film history has been the silent cinema,
and it was to fill that gap that Paul O'Dell and Anthony Slide began *The Silent
Picture* in 1968 in London. The first issue consisted of two historical articles
(on Kalem's serial queens and on John Bunny) and one critical/analytical article
(on the use of fate in D. W. Griffith's Biograph films). This ratio of historical
articles (and interviews) as opposed to articles concerned with aesthetics was
generally constant during the early years of the magazine. The historical bent
was most apparent in the special issues on George Pearson (No. 2) and D. W.
Griffith (No. 4) where there was only one article in the two issues devoted to
aesthetic questions (by Paul O'Dell on Griffith's techniques in the films up to
The Birth of a Nation).

Yet this emphasis on documentation as opposed to aesthetic studies was not
a weakness, since the magazine was not tied to any critical school or line of
argument and thereby avoided a narrowing viewpoint. At the same time, the
emphasis on historical documentation was not just a sterile exercise in thinly
disguised hagiography (which too often was the case with many articles on the
silent cinema in, say, *Films in Review**). There was a clear intent by the editors
to use the magazine to demonstrate that most histories of the silent era had only
caught the highlights and none of the depths of that period. The eclecticism of

The Silent Picture, then, was one of its main strengths, as it showed that the silent cinema was not bound to the history of a few actors, directors, and producers in America and Britain. The stars were covered (Lillian Gish in No. 6; Marion Davies in No. 7), of course, but there were also articles on Ivan Mosjoukine (No. 3 and No. 5), George B. Samuelson (No. 5), "Pimple" (No. 6), Caroline van Dommelen (No. 15), as well as a special issue devoted to German silent film (No. 8).

This aim of the magazine was not spelled out editorially, as there was almost no editorial comment in the early issues except through the "Edith Nepean Column" which began in issue No. 5 and was used by the editors to comment on anything of note related to the silents (such as Robert Harron's alleged suicide in No. 5; announcing a distributor of 8mm silent films in No. 7; an obituary for Lev Kuleshov in No. 8). However, attempts to restrict the access to silent films undoubtedly led to the abandonment of this policy in issue No. 10, which contained several articles dealing with the question of copyright of silent films and Raymond Rohauer. From this time on, editorials (though they may be more accurately called commentaries) were a regular feature of the magazine.

Beginning with issue No. 13, Anthony Slide edited *The Silent Picture* from the United States, though the business office was still in England. Aside from an increase in typographical errors, the move had little effect on the magazine except for an increase in interviews with Hollywood actors (Jane Novak in No. 14; Babe London and Carter De Haven in No. 15; George Walsh in No. 16; Mae Marsh in No. 17) and the dropping of the Edith Nepean column. Beginning with No. 17, *The Silent Picture* changed publishers. The new publisher's main innovations seem to have been a publisher's page (instead of an editorial) and a table of contents. After issue No. 19, *The Silent Picture* ceased publication, killed by the financial problems which seem to dog all small magazines.

It is unfortunate that *The Silent Picture* quit publishing, since it is now, more than ever, apparent that work on the silent era needs to be done immediately while people who worked then are still alive. At the same time as it interviewed survivors from the silents, the magazine also was able to present that period in its diversity and depth and suggested the information that was still waiting to be mined. Whether resurrecting the career of George Pearson or publishing the last (and one of the few) interviews with Mae Marsh, *The Silent Picture* sought to explore a period which too many film historians pass over with the same received opinions and facts. By opening up the silent era, the magazine did a service for all who are in film studies.

Information Sources

INDEX SOURCES: FIAF International Index to Film Periodicals; Film Literature Index; The New Film Index.
REPRINT EDITIONS: Arno Press; University Microfilms.
LOCATION SOURCES: Academy of Motion Picture Arts and Sciences; Library of Congress (incomplete); Northwestern University.

Publication History

MAGAZINE TITLE AND TITLE CHANGES: *The Silent Picture*.
VOLUME AND ISSUE DATA: Nos. 1–19 (Winter 1968-69–1974), quarterly.
PUBLISHER AND PLACE OF PUBLICATION: The Silent Picture, 140 Westbourne
  Terrace, London W.2., England (Nos. 1–7); The Silent Picture, 613 Harrow Road,
  London W.10, England (Nos. 8–13); The Silent Picture, 37 Campden Road, South
  Croydon, CR2 7ER, England (Nos. 14–16); First Media Press, 1121 Carney Street,
  Cincinnati, Ohio 45202 (Nos. 17–18); First Media Press, 6 East Thirty-ninth
  Street, New York, N.Y. 10016 (No. 19).
EDITOR: Paul O'Dell and Anthony Slide (Nos. 1–5); Anthony Slide (Nos. 6–19).

Val Almendarez

SILVER SCREEN. See Appendix 2

SMPTE JOURNAL

On January 24, 1916, ten young motion picture engineers and equipment
manufacturers met in a hotel in Washington, D.C., and signed into existence
the Society of Motion Picture Engineers (SMPE). Numbered among the ten were
film and television technology pioneer C. F. Jenkins; Donald J. Bell of the newly
formed camera company, Bell & Howell; and W. Burton Wescott, one of the
founding engineers of Technicolor. The technical society they formed, the SMPE,
was given a shape (who might join, their qualifications and responsibilities) and
a published outlet for the results of members' researches (the journal entitled
Transactions of the Society of Motion Picture Engineers). The Society was also
given a mission: "advancement in the theory and practice of motion picture
engineering and the allied arts and sciences, the standardization of the mechanisms and practices employed therein, and the maintenance of a high professional
standing among its members." (*Transactions*, No. 1). This Society has changed
substantially throughout the years, as its present name, The Society of Motion
Picture and Television Engineers (SMPTE), indicates; but the shape, the publication, and the mission of the Society have remained the same to the present.

The SMPE had as its most basic aim in 1916, as documented in the *SMPTE
Journal* (from 1916 through 1929 called the *Transactions*), the standardization
of motion picture technology. The film industry in 1916 had not yet been com-
plicated by commercially acceptable wide-screen films, synchronized sound films,
or color photography. But it was in a chaotic state of different film widths,
sprocket-hole sizes, inconsistent raw stock emulsions, wildly different camera
and projector speeds, and nonstandard laboratory technology and procedures.
The SMPE founders knew that the industry would never mature without
standardization.

The Society began its work in three ways. First, they held monthly meetings in Washington and in other chapters around the country as the Society rapidly grew, where members presented papers on new technologies, basic research and problem-solving techniques, or the results achieved by the various standardization committees that had been established. Second, the Society began to hold yearly technical conferences where papers were, and still are today, read on specific groups of technology, such as camera, film stocks, laboratory, and so forth. An activity ancillary to the conferences, which today remains a vital part of these events, is the equipment manufacturers' exhibits where new technology is unveiled. Last, and perhaps most important, the Society began to publish meritorious papers in its publication, a tradition beginning in 1916 and continuing without interruption to the present. That publication, now known as the *SMPTE Journal*, is unique; it is the only single, comprehensive, and complete record of the development of film and television technologies in any language.

The *SMPTE Journal* began publication in July 1916 as the *Transactions*, a quarterly review of the Society's small membership's researches and committee reports. Through the early twenties, it reflected the Society's concern with standardization. Issue No. 2 contains articles entitled "Precision, the Dominant Factor in Motion Picture Machines"; "Motion Picture Film Perforation"; and "Condensers, Their Contour, Size, Location and Support." Succeeding issues dealt with the standardization of cameras and frame-line spacing (No. 3); motion picutre nomenclature (No. 4); the projection booth (No. 5); standardization of exposure (No. 6); and sprocket teeth and film perforation (No. 7).

By the early twenties, much of the work in standardization had been accomplished. Most significant equipment and film manufacturers had joined the SMPE as sustaining members, and the heads and employees of these companies regularly staffed the various SMPE standardization committees—a self-regulating relationship. In addition, by this time major studios had developed which concentrated both production facilities and talent into a few exclusive areas. The era of the itinerant craftsman, with his own equipment (particularly cameras with any one of a variety of film sizes and speeds), ended when these studios opened their own camera departments, stages, laboratories, and outdoor locations. Standardization had arrived.

The *Transactions of the SMPE* reflected these changes. Less was heard of standardization (except for new technologies) and more of how these standardized tools might be creatively used. Such articles as "The Use of Artificial Illuminants in Motion Picture Studios" (No. 13), "Graininess in Motion Picture Negatives and Positives" (No. 14), and "A Method of Using Miniatures or Models for the Introduction of Extra Detail in Motion Pictures" (No. 15) all illustrate the flexing of creative muscle, the use of tools rather than the tools themselves. In addition to these kinds of articles and the standard fare consisting of articles on lens improvements, new chemical baths or lab machines, or projector and camera accessories were articles that detail the beginnings of several future motion picture revolutions.

No. 16 contains an article by Dr. Lee DeForest entitled "The Phonofilm," an optical sound-on-film technology developed by Theodore Case and E. I. Sponable. The same issue also features "Radio Photographs, Radio Movies, and Radio Vision" by C. F. Jenkins, writing on television; "The Cine Kodak and Kodascope" by C. E. K. Mees, Kodak's head of research, writing about the introduction of the 16mm film/camera/projector system. All appeared in 1923. Subsequent issues feature articles such as "Stereoscopic Pictures" (No. 17), "Panoramic Motion Pictures" (No. 18), "A New Camera for Screen News Cinematographers" (No. 23), "Some Developments in the Production of Animated Drawings" (No. 25), and "Something More about Progress in Subtractive Process Color Photography" (No. 30).

The period between 1926 and 1932 was one of great change for the film industry, one spurred on by major developments in film technology. Sound motion pictures—"talkies"—became a commercial viability. The first engineering note on this new technology was P. M. Rainey's article in issue No. 30 entitled "Some Technical Aspects of Vitaphone." Western Electric, an SMPE sustaining member, had developed electrical phonograph recording in 1924, under J. P. Maxwell, and then applied it to sound movies. In 1926 they introduced the Vitaphone, a 33 1/3 rpm disc synchronized with a camera for recording and a projector for exhibition. They sold it to Warner Bros. Studios, which then introduced the era of sound movies.

But technology proceeded on several fronts simultaneously. Issue No. 31 quickly followed with E. I. Sponable's "Some Technical Aspects of the Movietone," a sound-on-film system he developed with Theodore Case and sold to Fox Studios.

During the following two years, sound as a technology and as a creative tool dominated the pages of the *Transactions*. By 1930, the SMPE Standards and Nomenclature Committee had established and published in the *Transactions* standards for sound recording speed, locations and design of soundtracks and recording apparatus, the sizes of various disc and optical recording media, all of which covered every aspect of the new sound technology. By 1930 the sound revolution, at least technologically, was over. Then, in January 1930, the *Transactions* changed its name to the *Journal of the Society of Motion Picture Engineers* and went monthly.

Motion picture technology was growing increasingly more and more sophisticated, as was technology in America in general. Taking advantage of greatly improved research facilities at industrial and university levels, the rise of the electronics industry, and the establishment of research facilities in particular at General Electric, RCA, and AT&T, the film industry grew with three more major technological revolutions: color film in the forties, and wide screen and stereophonic sound in the early fifties.

The *Journal*, during the late thirties and early forties, is filled with articles on mono, bipack, and tripack color film stocks and modified cameras to handle such films; the problems of sound-on-film on color film stocks; new laboratory chemicals and procedures (particularly for Kodachrome film); color projection and screens; color process photography; color theory; and lighting for color.

During this time, the *Journal* also reflected the American Second World War effort. Numerous articles detailed new advances in 16mm films and lightweight cameras, new air reconnaissance technology when permitted, conservation methods at all the major film studios, the major Hollywood effort in producing huge quantities of educational and instructional films for all the armed forces, and the training programs in film production for servicemen.

The end of the war released an enormous quantity of both domestic and foreign optical and electronic technology, and the film industry was quick to pick up on it. Television broadcasting began commercially in 1947 at the Columbia Broadcasting System (CBS), taking the country by storm with its novelty. In partial response, the industry introduced both wide-screen films in a wide variety of nonstandardized formats and magnetic stereo sound recording and playback. The *Journal* during this period is filled with articles introducing each screen format and discussing its specific technology, and other articles dealing with the aesthetics of wide-screen sizes in general and how binaural (stereo) sound should be properly used. Fully documented in the *Journal* are the development and eventual fates of VistaVision (Paramount); CinemaScope (20th Century-Fox, under E. I. Sponable, head of their research and development); Cinerama, utilizing three cameras/projectors; Todd AO; Techniscope and Technirama; and all the systems and formats developed during the fifties.

Stereo magnetic recording received a tremendous boost after World War II after the discovery of very sophisticated recording devices developed in Germany during the thirties (a time when there was no exporting of advanced technology) and "captured" at the war's end. In the *Journal* from 1951 through 1955 there were thirteen major standards and research articles on magnetic sound, including those on head wear, noise suppression, mag sound-on-film, playback equipment, and speakers. During the heyday of stereo magnetic sound recording and playback in theatres, 1956 to 1960, the *Journal* featured thirty-five standards and articles on the topic, major articles such as "American, Four Magnetic Sound Records on 35mm Film," June 1958; "CinemaScope Magnetic Reproduce Heads," December 1956, the wide screen system that with or without mag tracks has become the standard today; and "Magnetic Recording Media Considerations for Improving Masters and Dubs," October 1958.

The fifties brought, however, the beginnings of a technological revolution far greater than CinemaScope and stereo sound. It was television. The *Journal* had covered the development of T.V. from its first issue, particularly due to the interests of C. F. Jenkins. It got its first big boost in 1927/1928 with the invention of the Iconoscope, perfected by Dr. Vladimir Zworykin working first for Westinghouse and then RCA. *Journal* and Society interest continued to build until the "President's Message" in the January 1950 issue of the *Journal*:

To me it seems that we are approaching another turning point in the art just as we did some twenty years ago when sound became a commercial reality. The imminence of this coming change is due in part at least to the rapid growth of a new method of presenting scenes and people in action, capable of bringing motion pictures directly into the home, as well as directly into the theatre. I refer of course to television, with its important additional sense of immediacy.

That month the name of the Society and the name of the *Journal* was expanded to include the word *television*. This change was made, no doubt, with some resistance. But the change was made, and the basis of the future strength of both the Society and its journal was then secure.

While the *Journal* in the fifties, sixties, and seventies faithfully records all standards and articles on new and re-newed motion picture technologies and processes, the *Journal* from 1950 on is in truth a record of the developing technologies of television. During these three decades, television has come to dominate the *Journal*—it has not replaced motion pictures in its pages, but it does overshadow it. The 1956–1960 index is the first with a separate videotape heading. Video recording was perfected in 1956 at Ampex, an event that began the end of film use at television stations. That invention is fully documented in the *Journal*, in 1956, written by the head of the Ampex research team. The same index lists headings for television: cameras, pick-up equipment, lenses; closed-circuit; color; educational; film and film recording; international; lighting; military; picture quality; screens; and studio production—over three hundred articles during that five year period. The SMPTE had arrived.

The *Journal* documents the introduction of rapidly introduced new generations of video cameras; computer-assisted editing and special effects equipment; the use of video technology in space (a significant subheading) in addition to film; and most important, standards. This SMPTE activity to the video industry was, and still is, as critical to economic and technological success as it was to the early motion picture industry. With far more numerous and complex electronic components and designs than seen in motion picture technology, the need for international standardization, and publication of those standards in the *Journal*, was critical. The SMPTE standards, recommended by committees made up of SMPTE members employed by the industries developing these technologies, cover every aspect imaginable. Included during the past thirty years are: standards for 8mm, 1/2″, 3/4″, 1″, and 2″ tape and the machines and metal reels made to handle such tape; the parameters of various recording formats, both U.S. and foreign standards; Time Code (SMPTE), now the international standard; camera and monitor record and playback controls such as black-as-white levels, color, and ancillary transmission signals. Further standards cover telecine machines, including all video signals and how they may be transmitted—the signal from one machine to another, the signal broadcast over the air, and how that signal may be received in the home. Newer standards work covers signals to and from satellites; certain cable technology; home satellite receiving equipment; electronic newsgathering equipment, especially micro and minicam camera units; and mobile recording and transmission technology.

Now this industry is in the midst of an even newer revolution—digital technology. The composite analog video signal is now reduced to sophisticated digital codes, transmitted as a series of simple number codes and then recomposed at the destination into picture and sound, with little if any quality loss. The *Journal*, which is making these standards available internationally to the industry, is now even more the single most important record and reference for the developers and users of this newest generation of technology.

During the *Journal*'s sixty-seven-year history an enormous amount of theory and technology has been introduced, used, and then discarded. The *Journal* has faithfully recorded this process as it applies to the motion picture and television industries. No other record documenting the failures and successes of these activities, no other record of the ideas behind these industries exists anywhere. It is the single, documented resource written by the participants, the one that shows what film and television were, are, and perhaps will be.

Information Sources

INDEX SOURCES: Applied Science and Technology Index; Engineering Index; Film Literature Index; Photographic Abstracts. [The Society has published indices, all with author and subject headings, as follows: July 1916–June 1930; January 1930–December 1935; January 1936–December 1945; January 1946–December 1950; with the December 1950 issue the Journal began publication of yearly indices; in addition, there are five-year indices for January 1951–December 1955; January 1956–December 1960; January 1961–December 1965; January 1966–December 1970; January 1971–December 1975; January 1976–December 1980.]

REPRINT EDITIONS: University Microfilms.

LOCATION SOURCES: Academy of Motion Picture Arts and Sciences; Library of Congress; New York Public Library.

Publication History

MAGAZINE TITLE AND TITLE CHANGES: *Transactions of the Society of Motion Picture Engineers* (July 1916–December 1929); *Journal of the Society of Motion Picture Engineers* (January 1930–December 1949); *Journal of the Society of Motion Picture and Television Engineers* (January 1950–December 1953); *Journal, SMPTE* (January 1954–December 1954); *SMPTE Journal* (January 1955–December 1955); *Journal of the SMPTE* (January 1956–December 1975); *SMPTE Journal* (January 1976 to present).

VOLUME AND ISSUE DATA: No. 1 (1916); No. 2 (October 1916); No. 3 (April 1917); No. 4 (July 1917); No. 5 (October 1917); No. 6 (April 1918); No. 7 (November 1918); No. 8 (April 1919); No. 9 (October 1919); Nos. 10–18 (May 1920–May 1924), each May and October; Nos. 19-20–27-28 (May 1925–October 1926), double issues each May and October; Nos. 29-30–35-36 (April 1927–September 1928), double issues each April and September; No. 37-38 (May 1929); Vol.

XIV, No. 1 (January 1930 to present), monthly. [Volume numbers first appeared with Vol. X, No. 27-28.]

PUBLISHER AND PLACE OF PUBLICATION: The Society of Motion Picture and Television Engineers, 862 Scarsdale Avenue, Scarsdale, N.Y. 10583.

EDITOR: No editor listed (1916–1929); Lloyd A. Jones, pro tem (1930); Sylvan Harris (1931–1943); Harry Smith, Jr. (1943–1947); Helen M. Stote (1948–1949); Victor H. Allen (1950–1975); Tom King (1975–1979); David Howell (1979–1980); Jack Christiansen (1980–1982); Jeff Friedman (1982 to present).

Stephen C. Chamberlain

SOCIETY FOR FILM TEACHERS' BULLETIN. See SCREEN EDUCATION

SOUND WAVES

"Believing that the day of science in pictures is here and that the first step of the motion picture of the future is being taken," editorialized Cedric E. Hart in the first issue, "I have made the decision, accordingly, to publish *Sound Waves* as a medium of expression, for the industry in these matters." *Sound Waves*, founded in 1928, was promoted as the magazine of the talking picture (or talker). In reality, the majority of its short pieces on stars, directors, writers, and technicians seemed to feature decidedly unimportant, if not totally unknown, individuals.

Typical of the curious articles to be found in *Sound Waves* is one on George Simons, "Youthful He-Man" (Vol. 1, No. 3), who had arrived in Hollywood to train for prospective movie and talkie work. The magazine offered space not only to unknowns but also to "has-beens" such as Sheldon Lewis who wrote "Proper Use of the Voice" (Vol. 1, No. 6) and appears to have been featured in almost every issue.

Celebrities pontificated on the sound motion picture. William S. Hart declared, "Speech...is artificial" (Vol. 1, No. 3), while D. W. Griffith announced, "I am sure the legitimate stage and the silent picture will be things of the past within five years" (Vol. 2, No. 5). *Sound Waves* did include a useful "Sound Shooting Schedule," first published in Vol. 1, No. 7, which gave information on sound directors, sound engineers, and sound systems, as well as more commonplace information. It also began publishing reviews, by Joseph Berne, with Vol. 2, No. 1 (January 15, 1929). *Sound Waves* survived, however, only until 1931.

Information Sources

INDEX SOURCES: None.

REPRINT EDITIONS: None.

LOCATION SOURCES: Academy of Motion Picture Arts and Sciences (incomplete); New York Public Library (incomplete).

Publication History

MAGAZINE TITLE AND TITLE CHANGES: *Sound Waves*.
VOLUME AND ISSUE DATA: Vol. I, No. 1–Vol. V, No. 3 (August 15, 1928–June 1931), biweekly. [Date of last issue unconfirmed.]
PUBLISHER AND PLACE OF PUBLICATION: Sound Waves Publishing Company, 1711 Winona Boulevard, Hollywood, Calif.
EDITOR: Cedric E. Hart.

Anthony Slide

SOVETSKII EKRAN. See ISKUSSTVO KINO

SOVETSKOE KINO. See ISKUSSTVO KINO

SOVIET FILM. See Appendix 4

SOVIET FILMS. See Appendix 4

STAR LAND. See Appendix 2

STARLOG. See Appendix 2

STILLS

Started in October 1980 by a group of students at Oxford University, *Stills'* initial aim was to tie film and theatre into a single critical perspective. It soon shed its theatre coverage and its student connections, however, and, two years later, after a publication gap of nearly ten months, the magazine was effectively relaunched from a London base and with the profile it has maintained ever since: as an independent critical journal dealing with film and television, aimed more at people working in the film and television industries than at the general public but without the drab chunks of scarcely digested press releases that tend to characterize trade papers.

Early issues concentrated on the "accepted" areas of art cinema, with a long article by James Monaco on French cinema (No. 1), extended pieces on German expressionism (Mark Mazowa, No. 2), and on Tarkovsky (Mark Ward, No. 2),

Robert Bresson (Jonathan Hourigan, No. 3), Satyajit Ray (Wendy Allen and Roger Spikes, No. 3), and King Vidor's *The Crowd* (Wendy Allen, No. 4). As early as the second issue (Spring 1981), however, *Stills* began to carry some of the articles that were to become its real stock-in-trade: on film distribution in Britain (Archie Tait), the future of British television (James Saynor), and video (Jean Young).

Since its move to London, *Stills* has maintained a balance between industry and art and between film and television (including the latter's offshoots—video, cable, and satellite). A series of articles has charted the changing face of British television, with regular columns on developments in America from Brian Winston. There have also been feature-length articles on areas of television which are very much part of the British cultural scene but which tend to be ignored by the other "film" magazines: directors Philip Saville (by Bill Cormack, No. 7) and Jim Goddard (by Martyn Auty, No. 9) and producer Kennith Trodd (Julian Petley, No. 9). There have also been numerous articles, long and short, on the implications of Britain's fourth television channel, its feature film program (by Chris Auty, No. 8), various aspects of current affairs and feature programming, and the awarding of Britain's first cable franchises (by Jerome Swann, Graham Wade, and Bill Grantham, No. 10).

The film section has largely abandoned its historical perspectives for articles with a stronger "news" content—pieces on the "battle of the Bonds" in 1983 (by Sheila Johnston, No. 7), the Australian and Dutch film industries (William Routt, No. 8, and Nick Roddick, No. 9), and areas of film financing in Britain (No. 7) and the United States (No. 9) by economic journalist Alan Stanbrook. Special dossiers have examined the state of the British film industry and the American independent production context. *Stills* has carried interviews with major international filmmakers—including Francis Ford Coppola, Richard Attenborough, Rainer Werner Fassbinder, Alain Tanner, Wim Wenders, Carlos Saura, and Claude Lelouch—as well as long articles, with career profiles, on filmmakers who are *not* directors: cinematographers, production designers, screenwriters, producers, and editors.

There is a regular film reviews section geared to British releases, and reports from film and television festivals, conferences, and markets from around the world, from Cannes to Havana, Manila to Miami, and Berlin to Bombay. A more recent development has been the introduction of corporate profiles of production companies and production facilities, together with regular location reports from films in production.

What sets *Stills* apart from other British film magazines like *Sight and Sound** is its commitment to the solid, critical coverage of television and to the notion that cinema needs to be viewed as much as an industry as an art form. It is, perhaps, the first British media magazine to have bridged the gap between those who make films and those who watch and write about them.

Information Sources

INDEX SOURCES: None.
REPRINT EDITIONS: None.
LOCATION SOURCES: No information. [British Film Institute Library has a complete
     run.]

Publication History

MAGAZINE TITLE AND TITLE CHANGES: *Stills.*
VOLUME AND ISSUE DATA: Vol. I, No. 1 (October 1980 to present), bimonthly with
     some irregularity.
PUBLISHER AND PLACE OF PUBLICATION: Stills Publishing Company Limited, 6
     Denmark Street, London W.C.2, England.
EDITOR: Nicholas Kent (Film Editor: Wendy Allen [Nos. 1–5], Nick Roddick [No. 6
     to present]; Television Editor: James Saynor [No. 3 to present]).

Nick Roddick

THE STUDIO SKELETON. See Appendix 3

SUPER-8 FILMAKER

Super-8 Filmaker commenced publication in the winter of 1972/1973, at a
time when Super 8mm filmmaking was increasing in popularity as its predecessor,
Standard 8mm, was phased out by Kodak. The magazine published news items
and articles on all aspects of filmmaking on the Super 8mm substandard gauge
and announced that it was intended for the beginning and serious amateur filmmaker, as well as the professional. As interest in Super 8mm began to wane,
with the introduction of videotape, *Super-8 Filmaker* tried to change; it took a
new name, *Moving Image*, and devoted equal time to both video and Super
8mm. As *Moving Image* it lasted a mere seven issues.

For an overview of the history of Super 8mm, there is no better source than
Super-8 Filmaker. It was the preeminent magazine on the subject, with an
announced circulation—at the height of its popularity—of fifty thousand copies.
In addition, *Super-8 Filmaker* published the occasional article of more general
interest, such as "The Life and Times of the Two-Reel Comedy" by Leonard
Maltin (Vol. 2, No. 2), "An Interview with Irvin Kershner" (Vol. 8, No. 5),
and a series of articles by Anthony Slide on films available for collecting in
Super 8mm, during 1974 and 1975.

Information Sources

INDEX SOURCES: Film Literature Index.
REPRINT EDITIONS: None.
LOCATION SOURCES: Academy of Motion Picture Arts and Sciences; New York Public
     Library; University of Illinois; University of Pittsburgh; University of Vermont.

Publication History

MAGAZINE TITLE AND TITLE CHANGES: *Super-8 Filmaker* (Winter 1972/1973–July/August 1981); *Moving Image* (September/October 1981–June 1982).

VOLUME AND ISSUE DATA: Vol. I, No. 1–Vol. I, No. 4 (Winter 1972/1973–Fall 1973), quarterly; Vol. I, No. 5–Vol. IV, No. 4 (November/December 1973–July/August 1976), bimonthly; Vol. IV, No. 5–Vol. IX, No. 5 (September/October 1976–July/August 1981), eight times a year; as *Moving Image*, Nos. 1–7 (September/October 1981–June 1982), eight times a year.

PUBLISHER AND PLACE OF PUBLICATION: PMS Publishing Company, Inc., 342 Madison Avenue, New York, N.Y. 10017 (Vol. I, No. 1–Vol. I, No. 4); PMS Publishing Company, Inc., 145 East Forty-ninth Street, New York, N.Y. 10017 (Vol. I, No. 5–Vol. III, No. 5); PMS Publishing Company, Inc., 3161 Fillmore Street, San Francisco, Calif. 94123 (Vol. III, No. 6–Vol. VII, No. 2); PMS Publishing Company, Inc., 609 Mission Street, San Francisco, Calif. 94105 (Vol. VII, No. 3– Vol. IX, No. 5); as *Moving Image*, PMS Publishing Company, Inc., 609 Mission Street, San Francisco, Calif. 94105 (Nos. 1–7).

EDITOR: Joyce Newman (Winter 1972/1973–November/December 1974); Tiiu Lukk (September/October 1975–March/April 1977); Bruce F. W. Anderson (May 1977–September/October 1979); Richard J. Jantz (November 1979–July/August 1981); as *Moving Image*, Richard J. Jantz (September/October 1981–June 1982).

Anthony Slide

SWEDISH FILMS NEWS BULLETIN. See Appendix 4

SWORD. See Appendix 1

T

TAKE ONE

Take One, first published September/October 1966, was a lively magazine geared to a youthful and enthusiastic audience. Its features ranged from serious and informative to silly, with its opinions sometimes wild and outrageous. Always an inexpensive magazine, it was published at various times with the assistance of the Canada Council, the Ontario Arts Council, and the Canadian Film Development Corporation. Plagued with financial difficulties, it was not published during 1975 but resumed the following year. The pop-art quality of its style and content were toned down in an effort, perhaps, to secure wider readership, and while it continued to feature articles that were candid and outspoken, the fresh comic-book quality had essentially disappeared.

Take One had a shifting number of regular columns and a fluctuating stable of correspondents in North America, Europe, and Asia. Some of its more recurring columns were "Reflections on the Current Scene" (later titled "Coffee, Brandy and Cigars") by Herman G. Weinberg; "Women in Film" by variously, Kay Armatage, Barbara Martineau, and Sandra Lowell; "Hollywood Is Our Beat" by Hal Aigner, Jon Carroll, and Michael Goodwin; and "Overlooked and Underrated," a forum for opinions on movies considered to be just that. In addition, other departments included a booker's guide to 16mm, classified advertisements, lists of film festivals and competitions, letters to the editor, and a news page filled with both personal and professional gossip.

The editorial content reflected a sometimes schizophrenic mixture of quality and junk, which always took itself seriously. Typical of the articles to be found in *Take One* are "Requiem for a Dragon Departed" by Phil Ochs, on the late Bruce Lee (Vol. 4, No. 3); "Kennedy Death Films" by Mitch Tuchman, on a home movie purporting to prove a conspiracy in the president's death (Vol. 6, No. 6); "Just a Dancer Gone Wrong: The Complication of James Cagney" by

Patrick McGilligan, on the actor's early attempts to gain control of his films
(Vol. 4, No. 5); "Cancelled" by Alanna Nash, the story of blacklisted actress
Jean Muir (Vol. 7, No. 10). Mitch Tuchman wrote "Pauline Kael, The Desperate
Critic" (Vol. 15, No. 12), an article in which he asked the question "has Pauline
Kael lost her maverick quality?" Director Henry Hathaway discussed his films
with Scott Eyman in a straightforward and earthy interview entitled "I Made
Movies" (Vol. 5, No. 1).

There were some issues devoted to single topics, usually extensive, informative, and highly readable. Vol. 5, No. 2, was devoted to Alfred Hitchcock;
billed as "A Friendly Salute," it contained a "major assessment" of the director's career by John Russell Taylor, a critical guide to his films and interviews
with some of his actors, including Ingrid Bergman, Cary Grant, and James
Stewart. "Women in Film" (Vol. 3, No. 2) included an interview with Shirley
Clarke, views of women on film in film, and "Canadian Women Directors: A
Filmography" compiled by Alison Reid. "Hollywood New Wave" was reviewed
and discussed in Vol. 2, No. 12, with primary coverage given to Roger Corman,
Laszlo Kovacs, and New World Pictures.

Among the writers who have contributed to *Take One* are Gideon Bachmann,
Jan Dawson, Stuart Kaminsky, James Monaco, John H. Dorr, Annette Insdorf,
François Truffaut, Richard Dreyfuss, Kit Carson, Jay Cocks, Joan Mellen, Peter
Bogdanovich, Mordecai Richler, Gordon Hitchens, and John Simon.

In December 1976 a *Take One Filmletter* was initiated. A four-page newsletter,
it was available to paid-up subscribers of the magazine and contained "late
breaking" news and minor articles. The *Take One Filmletter* was sent out between issues of the magazine and ceased publication in August 1978.

Information Sources

INDEX SOURCES: Canadian Periodical Index; FIAF International Index to Film Periodicals; Film Literature Index; Multi-Media Reviews Index.
REPRINT EDITIONS: University Microfilms.
LOCATION SOURCES: Academy of Motion Picture Arts and Sciences (incomplete); Harvard University; Library of Congress; Stanford University; University of California at Los Angeles; University of Chicago; University of Colorado; Yale University.

Publication History

MAGAZINE TITLE AND TITLE CHANGES: *Take One*
VOLUME AND ISSUE DATA: Vol. I, No. 1–Vol. V, No. 4 (September/October 1966–October 1976), bimonthly; Vol. V, No. 5–Vol. VII, No. 9 (December 1976–November 1979), monthly. [There was some irregularity in publication and no issues published during 1975.]
PUBLISHER AND PLACE OF PUBLICATION: Unicorn Publishing Corporation, P.O.

Box 1778, Station B, Montreal, Quebec, Canada H3B 3L3.
EDITOR: Peter Lebensold (September/October 1966–February 1979); Phyllis Platt (March 1979–November 1979).

Kristine Kreuger

TAYLOR TOPICS. See Appendix 1

TELEVISION

Billed as ''The World's First Television Journal,'' *Television* first appeared in March 1928 under the auspices of the Television Society of the United Kingdom. Alfred Dinsdale, renowned British television engineer and author of an early, important book on television technology (*First Principles of Television*, 1932), edited the first numbers of *Television*. In an editorial in its first issue, the journal pronounced its mission as being a disseminator of technical information on this nascent medium:

Of all scientific subjects, perhaps, the one which is creating the most interest in the public mind at the present time is television. It is, however, a subject upon which almost no literature or authentic information has been available, either to the interested amateur or to the scientist.

It is the object of this, the first journal of its kind in the world, to fill this want, and to supply an organ the sole object of which will be to keep interested members of the public supplied with up-to-date and authentic information upon this new branch of science, which bids fair in time to rival wireless broadcasting in importance and popularity.[1]

Television oriented itself particularly toward the amateur television experimenter, publishing, along with articles describing technical advances worldwide in the medium, ''constructional'' articles on making simple television receivers. In that first issue *Television* offered its readers, by special arrangement with the Baird Television Development Company, free licenses to use J. L. Baird's patents in the construction of television equipment. Indeed, throughout the thirties *Television*, as well as The Television Society, fully supported Baird's activities, motivated in large part by patriotism. In a note appended to an article concerning the television activities of General Electric in the United States, Dinsdale stated:

The article indicates the immense interest and activity shown in television by the great American corporations, who have been spending vast sums of money upon research into the subject. It will be doubly encouraging to the British reader to know that in the field of television British enterprise and inventive genius was first, and still maintains an indisputable lead.[2]

As a supporter of Baird and "British enterprise," *Television* remained wary of American progress in the medium. In the eighth issue Sydney A. Moseley, noted British journalist and pioneer radio commentator, exhorted his countrymen to support British television, believing it "the duty of every Britisher to give encouragement and help to the British side of the invention."[3] Particularly after Baird sold rights to his patents to an American syndicate in 1928, *Television* became especially wary of American competition in the field, and with reason. The first years of the journal saw the international motion picture industry become dominated either directly or indirectly by American sound film equipment manufacturers, a condition not overlooked by those in the British television industry or the editors of *Television*. By October 1929 the journal published a rallying article provokingly titled "Selling America to the World! Can the U.S. 'Corner' World Entertainment?"[4] Shaw Desmond, the article's author, maintained that AT&T and RCA were locked in a "gargantuan struggle" for control of entertainment in the States, the British Empire, and, ultimately, the entire world, with the weapon being television. Desmond's prognostication, for a wide variety of reasons, never fully materialized, but his warning to the British industry indicated the editorial tenor of *Televison*'s early days. The publication's patriotic fervor revolved about an explicit support for the Scotsman Baird's television devices; this support reached its apogee when Sydney Moseley, a tireless promoter of Baird and future Baird Television Corporation director and Baird biographer, replaced Dinsdale as editor of *Television* with the February 1930 issue. *Television* maintained its support for Baird and British television in general throughout the early thirties, a support which implied as well a support of mechanical scanning systems. Whereas *Television*'s American counterpart, *Television News*,* devoted considerable attention to cathode-ray tube developments, *Television* remained skeptical of such American and Continental developments, staying steadfast to the spirit of a February 1929 editorial in which the magazine's editors stated unequivocally that Baird's mechanical system was the only practical method of scanning and synchronization available.[5]

However, by 1932 *Television* underwent a swift editorial transition with its sale by The Television Press to Benn Brothers Ltd., the highly respected publishers of several major British technical journals. In an editorial appearing in the June 1932 issue, the new publishers stressed that they had published Baird's first technical article in 1925 in their *The Electrician* and claimed that they would "continue to give the strongest support to the British system of television that has now been adopted by the broadcasting authorities,"[6] a reference to the BBC's experimental transmissions using Baird equipment. The new publishers cautioned, though, that "the progress of television as a whole will be our aim, and every system, whatever its origin or nationality, will receive impartial treatment in these columns.''[7]

For the next eighteen months *Television*, under the auspices of Benn Brothers Ltd., continued to review technical developments in television, but the emphasis upon the Baird system diminished appreciably. In January 1934 the ownership of *Television* again changed hands, with Bernard Jones Publications Ltd., publishers of *Amateur Wireless*, assuming control. With this ownership change, *Television* lost completely the aura of advocacy it once held for British and Baird television devices, becoming very much a monthly devoted to the concerns of the amateur experimenter, emphasizing current news in television technology and receiver construction. By February 1935, reflecting its change in direction, *Television* became *Television and Short-Wave World*; the publishers claimed that the name change reflected their conviction that the future of television lay in the short-wave spectrum of the broadcast band, but the change reflected more their desire to broaden the magazine's readership and advertising base, a situation in which *Television News* had found itself the previous year.[8] For the remainder of the decade, *Television and Short-Wave World* covered technical advances and news of interest to the amateur, especially the radio amateur. In October 1939, reflecting yet another change in technology and reader interest, the magazine became *Electronics and Television and Short-Wave World* and endures as *Electronic Engineering* today.

Besides the coverage it gave to the nascent technology of television over half a century ago, *Televison*'s interest for today's broadcast historians revolves about its partisan coverage of the work of J. L. Baird and how the journal rallied to support his work and British enterprise in general during the early days of the commercial exploitation of television.

Notes

1. "Editorial," *Television*, March 1928, p. 7.

2. Dr. E. F. W. Alexanderson, "The General Electric Company's Recent Television Experiments in America," *Television*, April 1928, pp. 9–12.

3. Sydney A. Moseley, "Sydney A. Moseley Airs His Views on Television," *Television*, October 1928, pp. 13–14.

4. Shaw Desmond, "Selling America to the World!" *Television*, October 1929, pp. 405–406, 408.

5. "Editorial," *Television*, February 1929, p. 4.

6. "Editorial," *Television*, June 1932, p. 125.

7. *Ibid.*

8. "Comment of the Month, Our Larger Scope," *Television and Short-Wave World*, February 1935, p. 51.

Information Sources

INDEX SOURCES: *Engineering Index.*
REPRINT EDITIONS: None.
LOCATION SOURCES: Cleveland Public Library.

Publication History

MAGAZINE TITLE AND TITLE CHANGES: *Television* (March 1928–January 1935); *Television and Short-Wave World* (February 1935–September 1939); *Electronics and Television and Short-Wave World* (October 1939–May 1941); *Electronic Engineering* (June 1941 to present).
VOLUME AND ISSUE DATA: Vol. I, No. 1 (March 1928 to present), monthly.
PUBLISHER AND PLACE OF PUBLICATION: The Television Press, Ltd., London, England (Vol. I, No. 1–Vol. V, No. 51); Benn Brothers Ltd., London, England (Vol. V, No. 52–Vol. VII, No. 70); Bernard Jones Publications Ltd., London, England (Vol. VII, No. 71–Vol. VIII, No. 83).
EDITOR: Alfred Dinsdale (March 1928–January 1930); Sydney Moseley (February 1930–May 1932). No editor listed for later issues.

William Lafferty

TELEVISION AGE. See TELEVISION/RADIO AGE

TELEVISION AND SHORT-WAVE WORLD. See
TELEVISION

TELEVISION NEWS

Television News debuted in March 1931, founded by prolific writer and inventor Hugo Gernsback. Gernsback, himself a pioneer television experimenter, published the bimonthly magazine through his Popular Book Corporation as one of his many publishing endeavors and remained the magazine's editor throughout its brief existence.

In the first issue of *Television News*, Gernsback set the editorial tone for the new periodical when he decried the lack of commercial exploitation of the fledgling television medium and stated his belief that individual amateur radio experimenters, if aware of progress being made in the medium, could substantially hasten technical improvement and commercial implementation of television. Gernsback summarized the purpose of his new magazine in light of this belief:

Up to the present time, there has been no regular periodical in this country to describe accurately from month to month the advances in television from each and every angle and to show the reader what work has been done, not only in this country, but the world over. And I sincerely believe that the time is ripe to launch a magazine on television at the present time. The next two years may possibly prove to be the most important in the life of the new art; and, the more experimenters and the more television fans who become interested in the art, the quicker it will advance and the sooner it will be put on the stable basis which it deserves.[1]

For the next two years *Television News* pursued the mission Gernsback saw for it, keeping the experimenter and "fan" abreast of current developments in television technology. The magazine's format generally included four sections. In his lead editorials in every issue, Gernsback made pronouncements upon the latest technical advances and their practical potential, and he offered his personal views on pertinent subjects, ranging from the relative merits of American versus European television technology of the era to the rights of experimenters to have access to the broadcast band for transmission tests. A feature section included the technical news Gernsback deemed so important to the experimenter, with articles often authored by well-known engineers and gleaned from international technical journals; these articles ran the gamut of contemporary television technology of the time, ranging from the somewhat esoteric such as single-side band television transmission to an ongoing presentation of the latest in both mechanical and electronic scanning techniques. The impartiality of *Television News* within the scanning controversy set the American journal apart from its British counterpart, *Television*,* which, because of its editorial and patriotic biases toward J. L. Baird's mechanical scanning system, treated the cathode ray tube as a technological step-child during the early thirties. Each issue also included a "how-to" section primarily devoted to aspects of television receiver construction for amateur experimenters. A "miscellaneous" section included diverse subjects, ranging from the latest statements of the Radio Manufacturers Association regarding television to the construction of induction brakes for Nipkow discs, answers to readers' technical queries, and a patent digest.

Television News, true to Gernsback's stated aim for the magazine, succeeded in presenting the early developments in television technology which formed the foundation for full-scale implementation of commercial television production and broadcasting in the United States and Europe after the Second World War. The importance today of the short-lived journal resides in the comprehensive treatment it gave to that technical progress during the "pre-history" of television, an era which has now come under the close scrutiny of broadcast historians. For example, recently the British journal *The Historical Journal of Film, Radio & Television** published a reprint of six pages of an early issue of *Television News* describing early television studio production, evidently because of the piece's historical significance.[2] However, the halting and sporadic development of that television technology during the Great Depression indirectly led to the demise of *Television News*. Gernsback claimed that television-related advertising could not sustain the magazine, and that a broader readership and advertising base had to be found within the legions of radio manufacturers and hobbyists. With the appearance of its eleventh issue, for November/December 1932, therefore, the magazine became *Radio Review and Television News*, Gernsback merging the resurrected title of a radio journal he briefly published in the mid-1920s. In an editorial announcing a new direction in the magazine's orientation, Gernsback lamented the then-current state of the television industry, claiming that those in the business had "identified themselves so much with selling worthless stock to the public that they did not have much time to turn out merchandise."[3] Gernsback promised that both international radio and television developments would figure prominently in the pages of the retitled magazine, but after two more issues *Radio Review and Television News* ceased publication.

Notes

1. Hugo Gernsback, "The Television Art," *Television News*, March-April 1931, p. 7.

2. W. J. Toneski, "How We Staged the World's First Television Plays," *Historical Journal of Film, Radio and Television*, Vol. 2, No. 2, 1982, pp. 158–163 (reprinted from *Television News*, September-October 1931, pp. 260–263, 315).

3. Hugo Gernsback, "Two Magazines in One," *Television News*, November-December 1932, p. 215.

Information Sources

INDEX SOURCES: None.
REPRINT EDITIONS: None.
LOCATION SOURCES: Carnegie Public Library, Pittsburgh.

Publication History

MAGAZINE TITLE AND TITLE CHANGES: *Television News* (March-April 1931–September-October 1932); *Radio Review and Television News* (November-December 1932–January-February 1933).
VOLUME AND ISSUE DATA: Vol. I, No. 1–Vol. II, No. 6, bimonthly.
PUBLISHER AND PLACE OF PUBLICATION: Popular Book Corporation, New York, N.Y.
EDITOR: Hugo Gernsback.

William Lafferty

TELEVISION QUARTERLY

When Federal Communications Commissioner Newton Minow declared in 1961 that television was "a vast wasteland," there were a number of reactions. A new president, John F. Kennedy, agreed, as did the head of the National Association of Broadcasters, Leroy Collins. Several other media-related organizations listened carefully to this criticism.

One of the groups especially interested in these remarks was the National Academy of Television Arts and Sciences (NATAS). One year later, in February 1962, the Academy began publication of its official journal, *Television Quarterly*. Until this time, the NATAS had been known as a nonprofit association dedicated "to the advancement of television." It had also started the Emmy Awards. Amid Minow's call in 1962 for Federal Communications Commission hearings to discuss direct governmental regulation of the networks, the time had come for a more formal and organized response from the industry. It took several forms, one of which was *Television Quarterly*.

The first editor, William Bluem, and his editorial board established five general categories for coverage in the *Quarterly*.[1] Television, they felt, was an educational, informational, social force. They also took the view that it had to be seen in terms of its relationship with the government. At the same time, however, it was important to view this medium in the context of industrial, artistic, and scientific activities. The Board also believed that the purpose of the journal was to be critical and independent and to generate new ideas about television.

It would be accurate to portray the first five years of the *Quarterly* as emphasizing television primarily as a source of amusement and only secondarily as a teaching medium.[2] The relationship of government to broadcasting was also discussed, usually stressing government's power over the medium. Thus in the midst of critical articles on programs such as "Route 66," "Amos and Andy," "Mr. Novak," "The Fugitive," and "Peyton Place," there were also contributions such as "ETV—Education Is Not Enough" (Vol. 1, No. 2) and "The Students Are Watching" (Vol. 4, No. 2). In the area of governmental aspects, the very first issue concerned government's role in the American system of broadcasting. There were other topics, such as broadcasting and racial issues, the craft of interviewing (by Mike Wallace and Hugh Downs), church and television, and design in television, but these were exceptions to the main themes. Commentary on foreign television was also published and included countries such as France, Germany, the U.S.S.R, Saudi Arabia, and India.

When David Manning White took over the editing duties in 1968, there was a dominant shift, emphasizing television as a socioeducational force. Among the articles published were "Mass Media as an Educational Institution" (Vol. 6, No. 2), "Public Television—A Search for Identity" (Vol. 7, No. 1), "Television and Violence" by Nicholas Johnson (Vol. 8, No. 1), and Whitney Young's "The Social Responsibilities of Broadcasters" (Vol. 8, No. 2). A trickle of articles on news broadcasting by Walter Cronkite and Edward Jay Epstein and others also began to appear. The relationship of the broadcasting industry to the government was also discussed from a variety of viewpoints. There were articles such as "Press or Government—Who's Telling the Truth?" by Bill Moyers, (Vol. 7, No. 3), "Fairness, Balance, Equal Time" (Vol. 9, No. 4), and Robert Sarnoff's "Must We Accept Government Intimidation?" (Vol. 10, No. 4). There were also occasional articles on specific programs, although that area was greatly reduced.

Economic problems beset *Television Quarterly* in the fall of 1970. Publication was suspended until the fall of 1972, when Harriet Van Horne became the editor. The emphasis articulated by Professor White while he was editor was to continue. There was a greater concern with issues relating to television news, the impact of television on the viewer, and religious and censorship issues. The *Quarterly* followed the practice of reflecting the changing activities and issues currently facing the television industry, something that was to continue under Richard Pack, the editor who followed Van Horne in 1981. There were, for example, articles like Gabe Pressman's "Happy News—No!" (Vol. 14, Nos. 2/3), "T.V. News—The Way It Looks in the Boondocks" (Vol. 15, No. 1),"What Network News Should Be" (Vol. 16, No. 3),"Broadcast Journalism—Isn't It Time to Do Better?" (Vol. 16, No. 3), and "News vs. Entertainment—Do Local Directors Care?" (Vol. 16, No. 4). As religious programming grew, so too did its coverage in *Television Quarterly*. "Religion on the Tube" (Vol. 16, No. 2), "Religion on Television, A Change of Values" (Vol. 16, No. 3), and "Old Time Religion on T.V.—Bane or Blessing?" (Vol. 17, No. 3) were among the articles presented. Closely related to religion was the issue of censorship, perhaps best discussed in Harriet Van Horne's "The Moral Majority and Us" (Vol. 18, No. 1). The more serious subject matter of this period stands in contrast to some of the earlier issues of the journal.

Subject matter on the question of government regulation, an issue in the early sixties, was still being discussed ten years later. Articles on politics as well as fairness abounded. Among the key citations in this area are "Is 'Perfect Fairness' Possible?" (Vol. 12, No. 1), "Updating Federal Regulation at Last" (Vol. 14, No. 1), "Why Limit Broadcasters' Rights?" (Vol. 16, No. 4), and "Broadcast Unregulation in the 1980's" (Vol. 19, No. 1).

The *Quarterly* also pursued other topics in the seventies and early eighties. In addition to periodic discussion of foreign television activities and coverage of television programs (such as "Star Trek" and "The Addams Family"), there were articles on public broadcasting, television and higher education, sex roles in television, television and human behavior, and the family hour. Also discussed were questions dealing with gay life in television, sports (especially football), women in television news, and cameras in the courtroom.

The authors who have written for *Television Quarterly* have been just as diverse as the topics which the journal has approached. A listing of prominent names who have been associated with specific articles would be too lengthy to present here, but certain names do stand out. Among them are Walter Cronkite, Gabe Pressman, Steve Allen, William Paley, Robert Sarnoff, Nicholas Johnson, Marshall McLuhan, Marlene Sanders, Frank Stanton, Jeff Greenfield, and Reuven Frank.

Television Quarterly should be considered the major journal on issues related to the televison industry. In addition to timely book reviews and national and international coverage of television issues, it has also served as a forum for debate and thought-provoking writing.

Notes

1. Susan T. Ginsberg and David Manning White, "A Brief History of the *Television Quarterly*," *Television Quarterly*, Vol. 9, No. 1, 1969, p. 62.

2. Ginsberg and White, p. 64.

Information Sources

BIBLIOGRAPHY:
Ginsberg, Susan T., and White, David Manning. "A Brief History of the *Television Quarterly.*" *Television Quarterly*, Vol. 9, No. 1, 1969, pp. 60–68.
INDEX SOURCES: FIAF International Index to Television Periodicals.
REPRINT EDITIONS: University Microfilms.
LOCATION SOURCES: Harvard University; Library of Congress; New York Public Library; Oklahoma State University; Pennsylvania State University; University of California at Los Angeles; University of Southern California; University of Utah; University of Vermont; University of Wisconsin at Madison.

Publication History

MAGAZINE TITLE AND TITLE CHANGES: *Television Quarterly.*
VOLUME AND ISSUE DATA: Vols. I–IX (February 1962–Fall 1970); Vol. X, No. 1 (Fall 1972 to present), quarterly.
PUBLISHER AND PLACE OF PUBLICATION: National Academy of Television Arts and Sciences, 110 West Fifty-seventh Street, New York, N.Y. 10019.
EDITOR: A. William Bluem (1962–1968); David Manning White (1968–1970); Harriet Van Horne (1972–1981); Richard Pack (1981 to present).

Kim Fisher

TELEVISION/RADIO AGE

Television Age began publication as a monthly in 1953 while the Federal Communications Commission wrestled with such thorny issues as the development of an industry-wide color system, the solvency of ultra-high frequency (UHF) stations, and the predictable avalanche of license filings following the 1952 lifting of the four-year television-station license freeze. The magazine's objectives, according to editor and publisher Sol J. Paul, were to publish "a quality publication that would, in effect, be a transmission belt between the industry on the one hand and the advertising agencies and advertisers on the other."[1]

From its inception, *Television Age* devoted itself primarily to the financial aspects of the young visual medium. Coverage of television's technological, sociological, legal, cultural, journalistic, and educational issues were also included, with particular attention paid to either the implicit or explicit impact of each development on industry economics.

The graphics and layout of *Television Age* have always tended toward a literally bold and busy look, while the editorial mix has been one of businesslike and reportorial coverage of developments tempered with a gingerly, even boosterish, treatment of issues facing the media employing most or all of the publication's subscribers.

Articles in early issues, aimed at readers recruited to the fledgling medium from various other industries, had a decidedly "how-to" tone ("How Ratings

Work," "How to Buy Film Packages"). The subject of color, "the next frontier of this burgeoning business,"[2] dominated many issues during the magazine's first few years.

In 1956, *Television Age* became a biweekly, which it remains today, published "every other Monday" by the Television Editorial Corporation.

Growing international interest in television led to the Corporation's publishing of a semiannual international report, begun in 1961 as a portion of the regular issue. In 1962 the Corporation purchased the *World Radio-Television Handbook* (WRTH), a compendium of broadcast information published in Copenhagen. Although WRTH was sold four years later, the connection helped to broaden the scope of *Television Age*. Similarly, Television Editorial Corporation acquired *The Magazine of Wall Street* in 1966. And although editor-publisher Paul sold the financial magazine five years later, the tie brought *Television Age* even closer to the heart and soul of its coverage—finances in the money capital of the world.

Television Age added to its coverage as of 1970, changing its title to *Television/Radio Age* and offering regular features and articles aimed at industry personnel involved in the buying, selling, and managing of radio time.

In the early eighties, regular departments in *Television/Radio Age* included "Radio Report," "Business Barometer," "Programming," "Production," "Commercials," "Spot Report," "Media Professionals," "Wall Street Report," and "Inside the FCC." Feature articles and reports have addressed topics such as children's T.V. programming, black radio stations, T.V. news and public affairs, sports coverage, and the rapidly changing cable T.V. industry.

In 1976, an international edition of *Television/Radio Age* was inaugurated as a separate publication but printed as a quarterly supplement.

The tone and viewpoint of *Television/Radio Age* at present is one of nervous anticipation about the cataclysmic changes in store for the mass media, especially television, in the near future: a mixture of optimistic excitement that the pioneerlike exhilaration of the early fifties will return along with a pessimistic fear that the gold mine that has been commercial T.V. will soon be tarnished.

Notes

1. Sol J. Paul, "The First Twenty-Five Years," *Television/Radio Age*, Twenty-fifth Anniversary Issue, August 28, 1978.

2. Ibid.

Information Sources

BIBLIOGRAPHY:
Paul, Sol. J. "The First Twenty-Five Years." *Television/Radio Age*, Twenty-fifth Anniversary Issue, August 28, 1978, pp. 6–8.
INDEX SOURCES: FIAF International Index to Television Periodicals.
REPRINT EDITIONS: University Microfilms.
LOCATION SOURCES: Library of Congress; New York Public Library; University of South Dakota.

Publication History

MAGAZINE TITLE AND TITLE CHANGES: *Television Age* (1953–1970); *Television/ Radio Age* (1970 to present).
VOLUME AND ISSUE DATA: Vol. I, No. 1–Vol. IV, No. 1 (August 1953–August 1956), monthly; Vol. IV, No. 2 (September 10, 1956, to present), biweekly.
PUBLISHER AND PLACE OF PUBLICATION: Sol. J. Paul, 1270 Avenue of the Americas, New York, N.Y. 10020.
EDITOR: Sol J. Paul.

Bill Wine

THE THESPIAN. See Appendix 1

TODAY'S CINEMA. See SCREEN INTERNATIONAL

TRANSACTIONS OF THE SOCIETY OF MOTION PICTURE ENGINEERS. See SMPTE JOURNAL

TRANS-ATLANTIC REVIEW. See Appendix 3

THE TRIANGLE. See Appendix 3

T.V. GUIDE

Triangle Publications publisher (and eventual ambassador to the court of St. James) Walter Annenberg created *T.V. Guide* in 1953 by buying and merging three independent local television magazines (Philadelphia's *T.V. Digest*, Chicago's *T.V. Forecast*, New York's *T.V. Guide*) and unprecedentedly binding each market's local listings inside a standard national color section. Twenty-five years later, the weekly pocket-sized television consumer's viewing guide had amassed the largest circulation (over 20 million) and highest advertising income of any magazine in publishing history.

Although the regional listings have undoubtedly been the main attraction to *T.V. Guide*'s readership—and they have become increasingly detailed over the years—the fact that daily newspapers have long carried daily television listings, however sketchy they might be, indicates that the nonlistings components of *T.V. Guide* represent more than mere wrapping paper for the magazine's loyal customers.

The editorial stance of the magazine has remained essentially the same over *T.V. Guide*'s three decades. From the beginning, it has been—not surprisingly— that of a booster of the television medium, that is, enthusiastic about all of T.V.'s potential and theory, and much but not all of its practice. And while the early fan-magazine tone has evolved into a more sober, straightforward reportorial one, the editors of *T.V. Guide* seem to have assiduously avoided the crusading mantle throughout the magazine's history. Occasionally, however, the magazine has opened its editorial doors to spokespersons and allowed them to contribute essays on television-oriented controversies (senators and Federal Communications commissioners, for example, on issues such as violence in programming, the Fairness Doctrine, and journalistic ethics).

The mix of editorial features in a typical issue has remained remarkably consistent. There are usually a half-dozen or so feature articles, perhaps two on television actors or personalities (one high profile, one lesser known), one on a successful program or some aspect of programming, one centered on the medium's technology, one on a timely controversy, and one on a light, anecdotal slice of T.V. life. Where a mid-fifties edition might offer articles on Red Skelton, Edward R. Murrow, "Kraft T.V. Theater," the quiz show scandals, Arthur Godfrey's feud with the press, and the antics of chimp J. Fred Muggs, a mid-eighties lineup might include profiles of Bob Hope and Veronica Hamel, a look at children's animated programming, a report on the latest technological developments in T.V.-set design, a piece on hard-hitting editorials by local stations, and a backstage peek at the Miss America Pageant. In addition to the featured articles (rarely of a length to tax legitimately the television viewer's attention span), there has always been a package of supplementary columns and viewing-recommendation "closeups."

Standard columns have included program previews, series reviews (critic Cleveland Amory from 1963 on, replaced by Robert MacKenzie in 1977), movie reviews (longtime contributor Judith Crist), editorials, T.V.-news-blurb updates, and letters to the editors. The closeups, integrated into the listings, are programs the editors consider unique or particularly worthwhile.

Being based in Radnor, Pennsylvania—far removed from television centers on both coasts—has lent *T.V. Guide* a helpful journalistic distance from the industry it covers but has placed it somewhat off the beaten video track, a disadvantage somewhat obscured by the aggressive advertising the publication does on television itself.

The key hurdle for *T.V. Guide* in the next few years is the manner of its adaptation to the changing face and structure of American television. As cable technology nudges American T.V. from a broadcasting to a narrowcasting medium, the publication will have to accommodate the virtual rearrangement of the television landscape. Even as recently as 1978, the existence of cable systems could barely be detected in *T.V. Guide*'s pages. Since that year—during which the magazine's circulation peaked at slightly over 20 million—the publication's circulation has, like that of the commercial networks whose offerings dominate its pages, decreased slowly but steadily, season after season, to the present level of approximately 17 million. And with the proliferation of cable systems and program sources has come the inevitable proliferation of television-listings publications.

How—or whether—*T.V. Guide* should try to be, and list, all things for all viewers will remain the key question its editors and publishers must address as the American television medium continues its virtual transmogrification into that of a wired nation.

Information Sources

BIBLIOGRAPHY:
"Big Little Book." *Philadelphia Magazine*, December 1967, pp. 115–118.
Harris, Jay S., ed. *T.V. Guide: The First 25 Years*. New York: Simon and Schuster, 1978.
T.V. Guide Roundup. New York: Holt, Rinehart and Winston, 1960.
"Why Cable T.V. Is Unraveling T.V. Guide." *Philadelphia Magazine*, July 1981, pp. 108–153.
INDEX SOURCES: Access; The Magazine Index.
REPRINT EDITIONS: Microfilm Department at *T.V. Guide*.
LOCATION SOURCES: Library of Congress; Los Angeles Public Library (incomplete); Minnesota Historical Society; Stanford University.

Publication History

MAGAZINE TITLE AND TITLE CHANGES: *T.V. Guide*.
VOLUME AND ISSUE DATA: Vol. I, No. 1 (April 3, 1953, to present), weekly.
PUBLISHER AND PLACE OF PUBLICATION: Triangle Publications, Box 400, Radnor, Pa. 19088.
EDITOR: Walter H. Annenberg (1953–1956); Merrill Panitt (1956–1981); Roger Youman and David Sendler (1981 to present).

Bill Wine

T.V. RADIO MIRROR. See Appendix 2

T.V. TIME. See Appendix 2

U

UNIFRANCE FILM. See Appendix 4

UNIJAPAN QUARTERLY. See Appendix 4

UNITALIA FILM. See Appendix 4

UNIVERSAL CITY NEWS. See Appendix 3

(THE) UNIVERSAL WEEKLY. See Appendix 3

UNIVERSITY FILM PRODUCERS ASSOCIATION JOURNAL. See THE JOURNAL OF THE UNIVERSITY FILM AND VIDEO ASSOCIATION

UNIVERSITY FILM PRODUCERS COUNCIL (NOTES). See THE JOURNAL OF THE UNIVERSITY FILM AND VIDEO ASSOCIATION

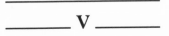

VARIETY

For almost eighty years *Variety* has been the leading show business trade paper—as it is so often described, the Bible of Show Business. Its importance to the film industry cannot be overestimated, and its research value to anyone studying the industry is limitless. Its honesty and integrity has never been questioned. As Douglas Gilbert wrote in *American Vaudeville*, "It hit Broadway like a thousand of brick: an honest publication whose summaries of acts and plays were fearless and uncompromising, one that flayed an act with a left-hook critique, often printed in the same issue containing the act's paid advertisement."[1]

Variety began life, on December 16, 1905, as a trade paper chiefly covering the vaudeville scene (along with circuses, parks, burlesque, minstrels, and fairs), soon embraced the legitimate stage and film, and now covers every aspect of the entertainment industry, although its coverage of the music field is generally considered to be inferior to that of *Billboard*. (Interestingly, in the early years, *Variety*'s biggest competitor was *Billboard*, which offered extensive film coverage in the teens and was not then regarded as a music-oriented trade paper.)

Variety was founded by Sime Silverman (May 19, 1872–September 22, 1933), who had previously worked on the New York *Morning Telegraph*. *Variety* is his lasting memorial, but Silverman had also acquired the New York *Clipper* in 1923 and that same year began publication of *Times Square Daily*, which he once described as "the worst newspaper in the world."[2] *Variety* is presently run by Sime's grandson Syd, whose son Mark (another *Variety* employee) likened the paper to "a family grocery store." *Variety* has occupied the same offices, on New York's West Forty-sixth Street, since 1920 (when Silverman purchased the building from a theatrical costumier named Madame Frances).

In its first issue, *Variety* announced,

We want you to read it. It will be interesting for no other reason than that it will be conducted on original lines for a theatrical newspaper. The first, foremost and extraordinary feature of it will be FAIRNESS. Whatever there is to be printed of interest to the professional world WILL BE PRINTED WITHOUT REGARD TO WHOSE NAME IS MENTIONED OR THE ADVERTISING COLUMNS. "ALL THE NEWS ALL THE TIME" and "ABSOLUTELY FAIR" are the watchwords.

One of the "original lines" adopted by *Variety* and continued through the present is having its writers (whom Sime Silverman dubbed "muggs") use abbreviations of their names with which to sign pieces. Among the best known of such abbreviations are Sime for Sime Silverman, Chic for Epes W. Sargent (who was with Silverman when *Variety* was founded), Abel for the paper's best-known editor Abel Green, Jolo for Joshua Lowe, Robe for Robert Landry (who joined the paper in 1926), Hawk for Robert F. Hawkins (*Variety*'s international editor), Mosk for Gene Moskowitz (the late head of the Paris office), and Murf for Art Murphy.

Another eccentricity unique to *Variety* is its creation of a language all its own. This language extends from turning nouns into verbs to the invention of new words. Torso-tosser, for example, translates into strip-tease artist, hoofology means dancing, a megger is a director, talker (*never* talkie) means a sound film, to lay an egg is to fail, and so forth. Equally extraordinary (and now legendary) have been *Variety*'s unique headlines, including "Wall Street Lays an Egg" (which appeared on the front page of the issue for October 30, 1929, announcing the Wall Street crash) and "Stix Nix Hix Pix" (meaning that the Middle West is opposed to films of rural drama).[3] In 1938, George Bernard Shaw told Bennett Cerf, "I thought I knew the English language until one day I saw *Variety* in a friend's home. Upon my soul, I didn't understand a word of it."[4] In all fairness, it should be pointed out that in recent years *Variety* has toned down considerably its use of slang expressions, and most articles and reviews are written today in concise and acceptable terms.

By the summer of 1906 *Variety* had established itself, doubling its number of pages to as many as thirty-two an issue. It published its first anniversary issue—of sixty-four pages—on December 15, 1906, and began a tradition which continues through the present. However, anniversary issues now appear, traditionally, each January and run to almost three hundred pages in length. Each anniversary issue includes listings entitled "Big Rental Films of the Year" and "All-Time Film Rental Champs" (of the U.S.-Canada Market), an index to books reviewed during the year, an index to film reviews, and a necrology for the year.

In addition to its special anniversary issues, *Variety* has also published special issues for Cannes, MIFED (Milan International Film, TV Film and Documentary Market), the American Film Market, NATPE (National Association of Television Program Executives), as well as television annuals and home video annuals. The last two continue a tradition begun in 1937/1938 when *Variety* produced a separate *Radio Annual*, modeled after *International Motion Picture Almanac*, which continued through 1958, by which time it was known as *Variety Radio Annual and Television Year Book*.

The first mention of films to be found in *Variety* is in the issue for December 23, 1905, and is a reference to films on the vaudeville bills at Hurtig and Seamon's and Tony Pastor's theatres. Reviewing the film program at the former, *Variety* commented, "The pictures show how fatal it is to flirt with a traveling artist. The heroine is driven from home three times and in between is evicted and has her sewing machine taken by the installment collector. She is a much persecuted lady."

The first news items concerning film appeared in the issue of September 6, 1906: "There is on its way to this country through the agency of Pitrot and Girard a talking moving picture, the 'talking' being arrived at through a phonograph attachment. The pictures are colored and the effect is said to be very realistic. It will arrive shortly and will first be seen at 'Dreamland,' Coney Island."[5]

As early as April 1906, advertisements for moving picture projectors appeared in *Variety*, and by November of the same year, the paper was also publishing occasional advertisements of films for rental and sale.

Film reviews per se did not appear until January 19, 1907, and then only as "new acts" in the vaudeville section of the paper. A year later *Variety* began publication of a one-page section titled "Moving Picture News and Reviews." The first film to be reviewed in *Variety* was *The Life of a Cowboy*. The paper discontinued reviewing films in March 1911 and did not reintroduce a review section until January 1913; apparently a number of companies (Kleine, Essanay, and Selig) convinced *Variety* that it was wasting space in reviewing films (particularly when such reviews might be critical of the productions of those companies).

Player credits along with reviews were introduced in 1914, and, as far as can be ascertained, Famous Players-Lasky and World were the first studios to make such credits available to *Variety*. Lengthier credits began appearing in April 1922, with running times first being given in March 1923. On January 15, 1930, *Variety* introduced capsule reviews which appeared alongside the full-length reviews. *Variety*'s reviews have always been scrupulously unbiased, and the paper continues to examine films from the viewpoint of box-office potential.[6]

Whereas vaudeville and the legitimate stage took up a major portion of *Variety*'s pages in its early years, from the twenties onward the motion picture has comprised almost half of the space in each issue, moving from the back of the paper to the front as the film industry began to rise in importance. From its beginnings through the teens, the front cover of *Variety* always featured a photograph of a stage or screen personality, but in the twenties major news stories were featured on the front page, a policy which has continued through the present.

From the twenties through the forties a substantial portion of the middle pages of *Variety* was given over to radio. The paper reported not only news relating to the medium but also published reviews of all the major radio broadcasts. In 1946 *Variety*'s managing editor, Robert Landry, published *This Fascinating Radio Business* (Bobbs-Merrill).

Regular features in *Variety* include news items, feature articles, film reviews, obituaries, a listing of the fifty top-grossing films of the week, reports on film grosses city by city, amusement stock quotations from the New York Stock Exchange, minor news items grouped under the headings of "New York Soundtrack" or "Hollywood Soundtrack" (a fairly recent innovation), and reports on travel (New York-Los Angeles; Los Angeles-New York; Europe-U.S.; U.S.-Europe). Non-American film news of lesser interest appears in the international section of the paper, which also includes an international soundtrack feature, from London, Paris, Berlin, Copenhagen, Sydney, Rio de Janeiro, and so on. Nonfilm related items (except those of exceptional importance which make it to the front page or inside the front cover) are relegated to the back half of the paper and include homevideo, radio-television, music-records, personal appearances, auditorium-arena, legitimate, and literati.

Notes

1. Douglas Gilbert, *American Vaudeville* (New York: Whittlesey House, 1940), p. 373.

2. For more information on Sime Silverman, see Dayton Stoddard, *Lord Broadway* (New York: Wilfred Funk, 1941).

3. Further examples of *Variety*'s "slanguage" may be found in Bernard Sobel, ed., *The Theatre Handbook* (New York: Crown, 1940).

4. Quoted in Ibid.

5. September 9, 1906, p. 8.

6. In 1983, Garland Publishing commenced publication of an anthology, *Variety Film Reviews*, 1907–1980, in fifteen volumes. In 1982, Scarecrow Press published *Index to Motion Pictures Reviewed by Variety, 1907–1980* by Max Joseph Alvarez. Garland Publishing is also responsible for a number of *Variety*- sponsored volumes, all edited by Mike Kaplan: *Variety International Show Business Reference Guide* (1981), *Variety Major Showbusiness Awards* (1982), and *Variety International Motion Picture Marketplace, 1982–1983* (1982).

Information Sources

BIBLIOGRAPHY:

Alvarez, Max Joseph. *Index to Motion Picture Reviews by Variety, 1907–1980*. Metuchen, N.J.: Scarecrow Press, 1982.

Brownell, Richard B. "There's No Green like Abel Green."*Good Housekeeping*, October 1954, pp. 67, 197–201.

Colton, Helen. "Show-Biz Bible." *Pageant*, April 1945, pp. 70–74.

Landry, Robert J. "Variety's Four-Letter Signatures the Dog-Tags of Its Critics." *Variety*, January 9, 1974, p. 26.

McWilliams, Michael. "10 Things You Always Wanted to Know about 'Variety.' " *The Movies*, Vol. I, No. 3, September 1983, pp. 32–34.

Perry, Jeb H. *Variety Obits: An Index to Obituaries in Variety, 1905–1978* (Metuchen, N.J.: Scarecrow Press, 1980).

Rose, Frank. "Biz Rag Boffo Say Buffs." *Esquire*, May 1981, pp. 55–64.

Silverman, Syd. "Variety at 75." *Variety*, January 14, 1981, p. 6.

"Sime Silverman, 1872–1933." *Daily Variety*, September 23, 1933, p. 1.

Wiesberg, Frank. "A Critic Confesses." *Variety*, December 24, 1915, pp. 16–17.

INDEX SOURCES: FIAF International Index to Film Periodicals (selective and recent issues only); FIAF International Index to Television Periodicals (T.V. program reviews only); The Music Index (selective).

REPRINT EDITIONS: Brookhaven Press; Kraus-Thomson; New York Public Library Photoduplication Department.

LOCATION SOURCES: Academy of Motion Picture Arts and Sciences; Library of Congress; New York Public Library; University of Illinois; University of Southern California.

Publication History

MAGAZINE TITLE AND TITLE CHANGES: *Variety.*

VOLUME AND ISSUE DATA: Vol. I, No. 1 (December 16, 1905, to present), weekly.

PUBLISHER AND PLACE OF PUBLICATION: The Variety Publishing Company, 1402 Broadway, New York, N.Y. (Vol. I, No. 1, December 16, 1905–Vol. XIII, No. 11, February 20, 1909); The Variety Publishing Company/Variety, Inc., 1536 Broadway, New York, N.Y. (Vol. XIII, No. 12, February 27, 1909–Vol. LVII, No. 10, January 31, 1920); Variety, Inc., 154 West Forty-sixth Street, New York, N.Y. 10036 (Vol. LVII, No. 11, February 6, 1920, to present).

EDITOR: Sime Silverman (1905–1933); Abel Green (1933–1973); Syd Silverman (1973 to present).

Anthony Slide

VARIETY (DAILY). See DAILY VARIETY

VARIETY RADIO DIRECTORY

It is curious that *Variety*, a publication most closely identified with film, should never have compiled a motion picture annual and yet, for four years (1937/1938–1940/1941), produced a unique radio annual, *Variety Radio Directory*, unquestionably the most important reference source on radio not only for the years covered but also, because of the substantial amount of historical data included, for the life of the medium up to the Second World War.

Each issue of *Variety Radio Directory* contains more than one thousand pages. Among the detailed information to be found in those pages are listings on network programs, guest artists on such programs, twelve thousand names of program series, federal regulations relating to broadcasting, studio signs, production terms, lists of network personnel, and listings of stations by state. In addition, *Variety Radio Directory* contains two hundred pages of biographies on radio personalities and staff.

Information Sources

INDEX SOURCES: None.
REPRINT EDITIONS: None.
LOCATION SOURCES: Academy of Motion Picture Arts and Sciences; Library of Congress.

Publication History

MAGAZINE TITLE AND TITLE CHANGES: *Variety Radio Directory.*
VOLUME AND ISSUE DATA: Vol. I (1937–1938); Vol. II (1938–1939); Vol. III (1939–1940); Vol. IV (1940–1941).
PUBLISHER AND PLACE OF PUBLICATION: Variety, Inc., 154 West Forty-sixth Street, New York, N.Y.
EDITOR: Edgar A. Grunwald.

Anthony Slide

THE VELVET LIGHT TRAP

The Velvet Light Trap describes itself as a journal of film history and criticism. It was started in 1971 by its first editor, Russell Campbell, as a vehicle for writers involved in the Madison, Wisconsin, film scene, which has included as many as twenty active film societies at one time. It was published fairly regularly from June 1971 to Spring 1978, with eighteen issues appearing during that time, each issue devoted to a single topic. After a four-year hiatus between 1978 and 1982, *The Velvet Light Trap* resumed publication, and two further issues have appeared up to the time of this writing.

The Hollywood feature film has been the primary focus of the publication, with issues devoted to John Ford (No. 2), politics and the American cinema (No. 4), the western (No. 12), and MGM (No. 18). Although the periodical gained support from the National Endowment for the Arts and has been distributed nationally, it has continued to be published in Wisconsin and to concentrate upon Wisconsin writers (many of them students or faculty at the University of Wisconsin).

The quality of the writing suggests that the contributors are dedicated and disciplined enthusiasts. Both pedantry and adulation are generally avoided. Because the United Artists Collection is housed at the Wisconsin Center for Film and Theatre Research, in Madison, and includes the Warner Bros. films and papers and prints of all the RKO features, *The Velvet Light Trap* has relied heavily upon these resources. No. 1 was devoted to Warner Bros., as was No. 15, while RKO was the topic of No. 10.

Information Sources

INDEX SOURCES: FIAF International Index to Film Periodicals; Film Literature Index.
REPRINT EDITIONS: University Microfilms.
LOCATION SOURCES: Academy of Motion Picture Arts and Sciences; Library of Congress; University of Illinois; University of Wisconsin at Madison.

Publication History

MAGAZINE TITLE AND TITLE CHANGES: *The Velvet Light Trap*.
VOLUME AND ISSUE DATA: No. 1 (June 1971); No. 2 (August 1971); No. 3 (Winter 1971/1972); No. 4 (Spring 1972); No. 5 (Summer 1972); No. 6 (Fall 1972); No. 7 (Winter 1972/1973); No. 8 (1973); No. 9 (Summer 1973); No. 10 (Fall 1973); No. 11 (Winter 1974); No. 12 (Spring 1974); No. 13 (Fall 1974); No. 14 (Winter 1975); No. 15 (Fall 1975); No. 16 (Fall 1976); No. 17 (Winter 1977); No. 18 (Spring 1978); No. 19 (1982); No. 20 (Summer 1983).
PUBLISHER AND PLACE OF PUBLICATION: Arizona Jim Co-op, c/o The 602 Club, 602 University Avenue, Madison, Wis. 53703 (Nos. 1–2); Arizona Jim Co-op, 522 State Street, Apt. B, Madison, Wis. 53703 (Nos. 3–8); Arizona Jim Co-op, Old Hope Schoolhouse, Cottage Grove, Wis. 53527 (Nos. 9–11; no publisher listed, Old Hope Schoolhouse, Cottage Grove, Wis. 53527 (Nos. 12–17); no publisher listed, P.O. Box 3355, Madison, Wis. 53704 (No. 18); John Davis, P.O. Box 9240, Madison, Wis. 53715 (Nos. 19–20).
EDITOR: Russell Campbell (Nos. 1–8); John Davis and Susan Dalton (Nos. 9–13); John Davis (Nos. 14–18); Leslie Midkiff DeBauche, Darryl Fox, Mary Beth Haralovich, Donald Kirihara, and Cathy Root Klaprat (No. 19); Matthew H. Bernstein, Brad Chisholm, Kevin Hagopian, Donald Kirihara, and Cathy Root Klaprat (No. 20).

Timothy Johnson

VERSATILITY. See Appendix 1

VIDEOGRAPHY

Beginning publication in the spring of 1976, *Videography* covers all aspects of video and is particularly oriented to those working professionally in the field. It is a major source of information for changes in the technology affecting the television industry and has covered subjects as varied as video in schools and public access to cable television. Each issue includes evaluations of video programs and video equipment, news items, articles, and interviews. Of major historical importance was *Videography*'s interview with Vladimir Zworykin, "the father of television" (Vol. I, No. 9).

The magazine provides an annual guide to video equipment and through the years has published guides to UCRs and cameras; video studios, state by state and city by city; film-to-tape transfer facilities; along with a survey of post-production facilities, a Who's Who in local cable programming, and a corporate T.V. report.

Information Sources

INDEX SOURCES: Film Literature Index.
REPRINT EDITIONS: University Microfilms.
LOCATION SOURCES: Duke University; Library of Congress; University of Arizona; University of Southern California.

Publication History

MAGAZINE TITLE AND TITLE CHANGES: *Videography*.
VOLUME AND ISSUE DATA: Vol. I, No. 1 (April 1976 to present), monthly.
PUBLISHER AND PLACE OF PUBLICATION: United Business Publications, Inc., 750 Third Avenue, New York, N.Y. 10017 (Vol. I, No. 1–Vol. III, No. 4); United Business Publications, Inc., 475 Park Avenue South, New York, N.Y. 10016 (Vol. III, No. 5, to present).
EDITOR: Barry Ancona (April 1976–August 1977); Peter Carnicas (September 1977–June 1980); Marjorie Costello (July 1980 to present).

Anthony Slide

VIETNAM'S SCREEN. See Appendix 4

VIEWS AND FILM INDEX. See THE FILM INDEX

VISION. See FILM COMMENT

VITAGRAPH BULLETIN. See Appendix 3

THE VITAGRAPH EXHIBITOR. See Appendix 3

VITAGRAPH LIFE PORTRAYALS. See Appendix 3

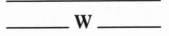

W

WARNER CLUB NEWS. See Appendix 3

WEEKLY MOVIE RECORD. See Appendix 2

THE WESTERN FILM NEWSLETTER. See Appendix 2.

WIDE ANGLE

Wide Angle, "a film quarterly of theory, criticism and practice," began in Spring 1976 when Giulio Scalinger asked Peter Lehman to edit a series of essays dealing with that year's Athens (Ohio) International Film Festival. The result was Vol. 1, No. 1, entitled "The Rise of the American Cinema," of *Wide Angle*. Scalinger became executive editor, overseeing the project and guiding it through the first three volumes. Lehman, who was teaching at Ohio University in Athens after studying film at the University of Wisconsin, has continued to serve as editor. Following the format of the first number, *Wide Angle* became the only American film journal organized thematically. Each issue focusses on a special topic—a director, a genre, a national cinema, a particular critical approach—supplemented by "added attractions" such as interviews, festival reports, and book reviews.

From the outset, *Wide Angle* has been generously supported by the Ohio University Department of Film, the Athens International Film Festival, and by grants from the National Endowment for the Arts and the Ohio Arts Council. One result is the journal's pleasing format with perfect binding, clear photographic illustrations and frame enlargements, and appealing cover designs (the cover for Vol. 3, No. 1, on silent film, a sepia-toned still from *Intolerance*, is nearly as spectacular in its detail as the film itself). Perhaps the graphics and layout for the earlier issues were a bit cluttered and incongruous with the academic writing style, but these distractions have become less evident in recent numbers.

In soliciting manuscripts, *Wide Angle* announced its intention "to encourage the publication of diverse methodologies and viewpoints." Aside from this statement, Lehman has avoided committing the journal to any particular critical perspective in his editorials at the beginning of each issue; instead these serve primarily to introduce and provide synopses for the articles that follow. Nevertheless, it is possible to discern certain major concerns in the eighteen issues of *Wide Angle* that have so far appeared: semiotics, involving close study of editing and mise-en-scene with the aid of the analyzing projector; Lacanian psychoanalytical readings of classical Hollywood texts, revealing their inherent ideological practice; revisionist models of film history, highlighting the economic context of the industry and its products. In general, *Wide Angle* has been especially receptive to contemporary film theory, while apparently evolving from the auteur and genre orientation associated with *Cahiers du Cinéma** (early issues on Godard, Hawks, Ford, comedy, silent, and independent film) to the theoretical polemics currently identified with *Screen** (see, especially, the *Wide Angle* Hitchcock number and the readings of his films in the issue on sexual difference, where the director is not so much an artist as a spokesman for the ideology of Hollywood).

Throughout this evolution, *Wide Angle* has borne the imprint of its editor, Peter Lehman, and his academic connections with Madison and Athens. One can read a great deal about Blake Edwards, for example, who became the subject of a book co-authored (with William Luhr) by Lehman: the longest article in the inaugural issue is devoted to Edwards's *Gunn*; two other lengthy articles on Edwards by Lehman and Luhr appear in subsequent numbers (Vol. 1, No. 4; Vol. 3, No. 2) along with an interview with the director (Vol. 3, No. 3); yet another essay on Edwards's *Victor/Victoria* is promised for the forthcoming issue, "The New Hollywood" (Vol. 5, No. 4). The topic of the editor's dissertation, John Ford, became the subject of an early issue (Vol. 2, No. 4), and Lehman has conducted most of the interviews appearing in every number. In addition, many of the articles in *Wide Angle* have come from graduate students and faculty members of the University of Wisconsin and Ohio University. The influence of two editorial board members, Joseph Anderson and Dudley Andrew, can also be felt in various ways. Anderson contributed the introductory essay to the number on Japanese cinema (Vol. 1, No. 4) and may have encouraged the subsequent articles and translations—most of them quite valuable—dealing with Japanese film, particularly the work on Nagisa Oshima (Vol. 2, No. 1; Vol. 2, No. 4; Vol. 4, No.2) and by Tadao Sato (Vol. 1, No. 4; Vol. 3, No. 2). Andrew published an important piece, "The Neglected Tradition of Phenomenology in

Film Theory'' (Vol. 2, No. 2) and seems to have had a hand in subsequent theoretical articles emanating from the University of Iowa.

For all the solid backing *Wide Angle* has received, the journal has run into problems establishing both its identity and continuity. Much of the magazine's difficulty can be traced to its policy of thematic organization and its tendency so far to remain something of an in-house publication. Selecting special topics in advance (often coinciding with the theme of the annual Ohio University Conference on Film) naturally limits the pool of manuscripts the editors can expect. And although the editorial board rejects many more unsolicited articles than it publishes, quality control has sometimes seemed lacking at *Wide Angle*. As a result, magazines far less slick if also more narrowly polemical, like *Cineaste** and *Jump Cut,** have generally provided more stimulating—and readable—film criticism. The Hitchcock issue (Vol. 4, No. 1) seems symptomatic: three of the major articles are jargon-laden psychoanalytical readings by graduate students uncovering the sexual ideology inscribed in specific films, all following Vittorio Giacci's essay, "Allegory of Ambiguous Sexuality in Hitchock's Films." Whatever happened to the "diverse methodologies and viewpoints" *Wide Angle* invites from its contributors or the "pluralism" Lehman advocated in one of his editorials? More than likely, the editors were left here with little else from which to choose. For perhaps the same reason, the Howard Hawks issue (Vol. 1, No. 2) appears padded (espcially the interview with the director) and the number on political cinema (Vol. 3, No. 3) lacking in consideration of major films, historical contexts, or Third World representatives. And while the younger writers for *Wide Angle* have mastered the currently fashionable jargon of "Frenchspeak" transmitted in English across the Atlantic by *Screen*, they have yet to exert the originality and impact of such *Screen* writers as Stephen Heath (who contributed an essay on Oshima to *Wide Angle*), Laura Mulvey, and, of course, Christian Metz.

The journal has also been plagued by difficulties maintaining regular publication. At present, *Wide Angle* is two years behind schedule. In addition, the price per number has jumped from $2.00 (Vol. 2, No. 4) to $4.50 (Vol. 5, No. 3) over the past ten issues. Johns Hopkins University Press recently took over as *Wide Angle*'s distributor, a move which should improve both the journal's continuity and its intellectual authority as well as increasing its circulation among libraries and bookstores.

Wide Angle remains a potentially valid concept within a handsome package. With better management, broader input, and a little luck, it may yet become as good as it looks and in the process rival the preeminence of *Film Quarterly** among American academic journals.

Information Sources

INDEX SOURCES: Arts & Humanities Citation Index; FIAF International Index to Film Periodicals; Film Literature Index; Media Review Digest.
REPRINT SOURCES: University Microfilms.

LOCATION SOURCES: Cornell University; Emory University; Indiana University; Library of Congress; University of Arkansas; University of Chicago; University of Colorado at Boulder; University of Illinois; University of Minnesota; University of Southern California.

Publication History

MAGAZINE TITLE AND TITLE CHANGES: *Wide Angle*.
VOLUME AND ISSUE DATA: Vol. 1, No. 1 (Spring 1976 to present), quarterly.
PUBLISHER AND PLACE OF PUBLICATION: Ohio University Department of Film of the College of Fine Arts and the Athens Center for Film and Video, Box 388, Athens, Ohio 45701.
EDITOR: Peter Lehman.

Lloyd Michaels

WIDE ANGLE (New England Screen Education Association). See SCREEN EDUCATION

WID'S DAILY. See THE FILM DAILY

WID'S FILMS AND FILM FOLKS. See THE FILM DAILY

WOMEN & FILM

Existing from 1972 to 1975, *Women & Film* was a cheaply produced but useful and serious attempt to provide an organ for the dissemination of knowledge on women in film from a left-wing viewpoint. The articles were concerned with both women as filmmakers and the depiction of women in films. Among the more important articles published by *Women & Film* were ''The Image of Women in Film'' by Sharon Smith (No. 1) and ''Early Suffrage Films'' by Gretchen Bataille (No. 3 & 4). Interviews also proved a valuable part of *Women & Film*, and among those covered by the journal were Nelly Kaplan (No. 2), Lina Wertmüller (No. 5-6), Agnes Varda (No. 5-6), and Eleanor Perry (No. 7).

Information Sources

INDEX SOURCES: FIAF International Index to Film Periodicals; Film Literature Index.
REPRINT EDITIONS: University Microfilms.
LOCATION SOURCES: Northwestern University; Smith College; Stanford University; University of Arizona; University of Illinois; University of Kansas; University of Minnesota; University of Pittsburgh; University of Southern California; University of Vermont.

Publication History

MAGAZINE TITLE AND TITLE CHANGES: *Women & Film.*
VOLUME AND ISSUE DATA: No. 1 (1972); No. 2 (1972); No. 3 & 4 (1973); No. 5-
6 (1974); No. 7 (Summer 1975).
PUBLISHER AND PLACE OF PUBLICATION: Women & Film, 2802 Arizona Avenue,
Santa Monica, Calif. 90404 (Nos. 1-5-6); Women & Film, P.O. Box 4501,
Berkeley, Calif. 94704 (No. 7).
EDITOR: Siew-Hwa Beh and Saunie Salyer.

Anthony Slide

WORKERS THEATRE. See NEW THEATRE AND FILM

WORLD FILM NEWS AND TELEVISION PROGRESS

In its first issue (April 1936), the "controllers" (as they called themselves)
of *World Film News and Television Progress*—John Grierson, Alberto Cavalcanti, Forsyth Hardy, G. D. Robinson, Norman Wilson, and Basil Wright—
explained the periodical's origin and purpose:

> *World Film News* is the *Cinema Quarterly*[*] in new dress. *Cinema Quart-
> erly* was founded by two young Edinburgh men, Norman Wilson and
> Forsyth Hardy. Over the past three years they have devotedly built a service
> of intelligent film criticism. . . . Some months ago, associates of the paper
> decided to improve its news service. Most of us were directly involved in
> professional film production and in the development of new uses for the
> film in educational and other fields. In a hundred places creative work of
> one sort or another was being done. We needed a digest of news which
> would keep us informed of cinema's growing points. *Cinema Quarterly*
> had, of necessity, to rely on theory. [*World Film News*] has more infor-
> mation, and less theory.[1]

During its two-and-a-half years of existence, *World Film News* presented news
items and articles on film and the fledgling television industry, both British and
international, which were impeccably written by the likes of Alistair Cooke,
Lotte H. Eisner, Otis Ferguson, Robert Flaherty, Ezra Goodman, John Grierson,
Humphrey Jennings, C. A Lejeune, Paul Rotha, Gilbert Seldes, Marie Seton,
and Basil Wright. As an example of the quality of the magazine's contributors,
the issue for November 1936 contained an article by J. B. Priestley, "English
Films and English People," *plus* George Bernard Shaw's "The Art of Talking
for the Talkies."
Each issue would contain reprints of reviews from British and American
periodicals, articles on film societies and amateur filmmaking (by Andrew Buch-

anan), and, from July 1936, a series on British cameramen. In the last months of *World Film News'* existence, it also featured record reviews by Stan Patchett. The majority of issues contained one or more interviews, and among those covered were Charles Laughton (April 1936), John Logie Baird (May 1936), Hedda Hopper (August 1936), Oliver Messel (August 1936), Edward Everett Horton (October 1936), Will Hay (November 1936), Hugh Walpole (May 1937), Pudovkin (October 1937), Emlyn Williams (November 1937), Edgar Kennedy (July 1938), Clifford Odets (August 1938), and Will Fyffe (October 1938).

For reasons unexplained in the periodical, as of September 1938, the title appeared to change to *See*, although *World Film News* still appeared in a prominent position on the front cover. Equally unexplained was its demise in 1938, which can only be regretted by all who care about dignity in film reporting.

Notes

1. "WFN Policy," Vol. I, No. 1, April 1936, p. 15.

Information Sources

INDEX SOURCES: None.
REPRINT EDITIONS: World Microfilms ("Little Magazines" series).
LOCATION SOURCES: Academy of Motion Picture Arts and Sciences; New York Public Library; Princeton University.

Publication History

MAGAZINE TITLE AND TITLE CHANGES: *World Film News and Television Progress* (April 1936–August 1938); *See: World Film News* (September 1938–November 1938).
VOLUME AND ISSUE DATA: Vol. I, No. 1–Vol. III, No. 7 (April 1936–November 1938), monthly except double issue May-June 1938.
PUBLISHER AND PLACE OF PUBLICATION: Cinema Contact Ltd., Oxford House, 9-15 Oxford Street, London W.1, England (Vol. I, No. 1–Vol. II, No. 7); Cinema Contact Ltd., 34 Soho Square, London W.1, England (Vol. II, No. 8–Vol. III, No. 7).
EDITOR: H. N. Feld (April 1936–June 1936); Marion A. Grierson (July 1936–August 1936); no editor listed but assumed to be Marion A. Grierson (September 1936–November 1938).

Anthony Slide

WRANGLER'S ROOST. See Appendix 2

—— **Y** ——

YUGOSLAV FILM. See Appendix 4

Fan Club Journals

Fan clubs are not quite as old as the cinema itself, but they do date back at least to the twenties, with two of the oldest being the Rudolph Valentino Memorial Guild and the Ramon Novarro Fan Club, both of which are located in London. The latter publishes a very occasional mimeographed newsletter aimed not so much at telling its members about the late Ramon Novarro but more about the activities of the members.

Documenting fan clubs is difficult, simply because they are generally organized by individuals on a part-time basis and their addresses change as their elected presidents change. The major source for information on fan clubs is the National Association of Fan Clubs (whose president is Mrs. Blanche Trinajstick, 2730 Baltimore Avenue, Pueblo, Colo. 81003). In addition, Chaw Mank writes a regular column on fan clubs in *Classic Film/Video Images.**

One of the earliest of fan club organizations was the International Fan Club League, established in 1940. Another group was the Universal Fan Club Service, which claimed—in the mid-fifties—to represent 350 fan clubs worldwide. Beginning in 1957 it published a newsletter to keep its member clubs closer in touch.

Just as it is hard to document the existence of a specific fan club, it is even more difficult to document journals published by such clubs, none of which appear to be listed in the Library of Congress *Union List of Serials*. Fan club journals are generally mimeographed and contain a letter from the star honored by the club, answers to fans' questions, and news of the star's current activities. They are generally of minimal research value.

The best of the fan club journals is unquestionably *Barbra*, honoring Barbra Streisand, of which ten issues appeared between January 1979 and Spring 1983. *Barbra* was a glossy quarterly, unusual for a fan club journal in that it was to all extents and purposes a professional publication (with a $4.95 cover price), edited from No. 5 (Summer 1981) by writer/biographer James Spada. Karen Swenson's in-depth studies of the making of the various Streisand features, and critical reaction thereto, which appeared in each issue give the magazine lasting research value.

Jeanette MacDonald and Nelson Eddy are two stars with major cult followings. From 1935 until fairly recently, the Nelson Eddy Music Club published the mimeographed *The*

Shooting Star. Similarly, the Jeanette MacDonald International Fan Club (1185 Woodward Avenue, Topeka, Kans. 66604) continues to publish a mimeographed magazine titled *The Golden Comet*. There is also *Mac/Eddy Today*, published by the Jeanette Macdonald/ Nelson Eddy Friendship Club (P.O. Box 1915, Burbank, Calif. 91507), a glossy quarterly which first appeared in November 1977 featuring a plethora of photographs, many in color, as well as reprints of magazine and newspaper articles on the stars.

Two of the earliest fan clubs to publish magazines were the Billie Dove Fan Club of Chicago, Ill., which produced *Dove Tails* in 1931, and the John Stuart Fan Club of England, which published (in the early thirties) a journal titled *Film*. In October and December 1936, a periodical titled *Charles Ray's Hollywood Digest* appeared. It was not really a fan club journal, being more a popular magazine utilizing the name of the former silent star (who by this time had fallen upon hard times). It did contain a number of interesting articles, notably "Is Winchell a Heel?" by Charles Ray (No. 1), "The Theatre Could Die" by Melvyn Douglas (No. 1), "Color" by Darryl F. Zanuck (No. 2), and "Opera on the Screen" by Bing Crosby (No. 2).

In the late thirties and early forties, a British fan club with the marvelous name of Deanna Durbin Devotees published *Deanna's Diary*, of which at least one issue was professionally printed. Two issues of the *Beulah Bondi Bulletin* appeared—on August 16, 1940, and November 30, 1940—but were probably intended as promotional press material for the character actress rather than gossip journals for the fans.

At least two publications have appeared from the Laurel and Hardy fan clubs, which are organized as "tents" named after the comedians' various films. The Sons of the Desert Tent published a mimeographed newsletter titled *The Finishing Touch*, the first issue of which appeared in 1977. The Way Out West Tent first published a fairly professionally produced journal, *Pratfall*, in 1969.

There are two journals devoted to Al Jolson: *Jolie* (published at 2981 Westmoor Drive, Columbus, Ohio 43204) and *The Jolson Journal*, published by the International Al Jolson Society (Box 399, Brownsburg, Quebec, Canada). *Sword* is the title of the journal of the International Errol Flynn Society, based in England, the first issue of which appeared in 1978. *Taylor Topics*, the first issue of which appeared in Spring 1982, is the newsletter of the International Elizabeth Taylor Fan Club (2125 Lockport Street, Niagara Falls, N.Y. 14305).

A number of lesser stars have had their own fan club journals. From the mid-sixties through the mid-seventies, the Agnes Moorehead Fan Club published a variety of newsletters under various titles, including *The Call Board, Moorehead Memos*, and *Versatility*. In 1959, and possibly later, the Carolyn Jones Fan Club produced a bulletin which was later titled *Intimate Carolyn Jones*. A mimeographed quarterly titled *The Thespian*, first published in Spring 1954, was offered by the Official Cameron Mitchell Fan Club of Hollywood. The Max Steiner Music Society, "aiming to perpetuate the music of Max Steiner," has published a variety of journals: *The Max Steiner Journal* (first published 1977), *The Max Steiner Music Society Newsletter* (first published mid-sixties), and *The Max Steiner Annual* (first published 1967). *Limelight on Liza* was a printed journal devoted to Liza Minnelli, published from Fall 1977 to Spring 1980. In the seventies, the Chad Everett Fan Club of Los Angeles produced a mimeographed journal titled *Chad's Quarterly*. *The Freedonia Gazette* (Darien 28, New Hope, Pa. 18938) is a twenty-page, semiprofessional journal which first appeared in 1979 and is billed as "*The* Magazine devoted to the Marx Brothers." For Mark Hamill fans there is *On the Mark* (P.O. Box 5276, Orange, Calif. 92667), an offset-printed quarterly, the first issue of which (dated Winter

1982) features a report on what Mark did in 1981—exactly the sort of thing one would expect to read in a fan club journal.

For those interested in the work of various stuntmen, from Yakima Canutt to Jock Mahoney, there is *Falling for Stars*. An irregular publication which first appeared July/August 1974, *Falling for Stars* is edited by John G. Hagner and published by the Hollywood Stuntmen's Hall of Fame.

Fan club journals do not limit their devotions exclusively to stars. Since June 1979, the *G.W.T.W. Collectors Club Newsletter* (8373 Discovery Boulevard, Walkersville, Md. 21793) has appeared for all those keenly interested in anything to do with the 1939 feature, *Gone with the Wind*. Similarly, collectors of material relating to Walt Disney productions are served by *The Disneyana Collector* (Grolier Enterprises, Sherman Turnpike, Danbury, Conn. 06816), a professional newsletter-style quarterly, first published Summer 1982.

The two most popular films of recent years both have their own fan clubs and fan club journals. *Bantha Tracks*, first published in 1978, is the professional newsletter of the Official Star Wars Fan Club (P.O. Box 2202, San Rafael, Calif. 94912). *E. T. Communicator*, first published in 1982, is the newsletter of the E. T. Fan Club (P.O. Box E. T., Mt. Morris, Ill. 61054).

Fans of Jim Henson's Muppets cannot be without *The Muppet Magazine* (Telepictures Publications, 475 Park Avenue, New York, N.Y. 10016), an amusing glossy journal first published January 1983. Finally, Elvis Presley enthusiasts should subscribe to *Graceland News* (P.O. Box 61431, Memphis, Tenn. 38116), a newspaper-style quarterly first published Spring 1982 and named after the entertainer's home. (There is also an English Elvis Presley fan club journal, titled *Elvishly Yours Magazine*.)

Fan Magazines

It would be easy to dismiss all fan magazines as worthless. Yet they offer valuable documentation for both the film scholar and the sociologist. Throughout the silent era, and certainly through the thirties, most fan magazines provided not only honest (and many times well-written) film reviews but also articles and interviews which, read with a certain amount of intelligence and a discerning eye, can give the researcher a wealth of unique information. From a sociological viewpoint, Carl F. Cotter summed up fan magazines when he wrote in *The Coast*, "These fans, who spent from five cents (for *Hollywood*) to a quarter (for *Photoplay*[*]) on their cinematic scriptures, literally govern their lives by them. Not only do they pattern their hair styles, their clothes, their cookery, and their behavior after those of their favorite actors and actresses as interpreted by the sob-sisters; most of them also base their most profound thinking on the words of the same authorities."[1]

Fan magazines created their own brand of writers, notably Adela Rogers St. Johns, Ruth Waterbury, Adele Whiteley Fletcher, James Frederick Smith, Hazel Simpson Naylor, and Ruth Hall. The majority of such writers were women, just as the majority of the fan magazine readers were comprised of women. Many fan magazine writers contributed pieces under multiple names. In the silent era, for example, Lillian May also wrote as Lillian Montanye, Roberta Courtlandt as Pearl Gaddis, and Edwin M. La Roche as Peter Wade. In addition, writers would supplement their incomes by acting as press representatives for the very stars and directors about whom they wrote. During the silent era, apparently, fan magazine editors could see nothing wrong in publishing an article on or an interview with a star, written by that personality's personal representative.

Of all fan magazines, *Photoplay* is the best known and most important. During the silent era its closest rival, and an equally intelligent journal, was *Motion Picture Magazine* (which remained in existence until recently) and on which critic/historian Edward Wagenknecht provides the following comments:

The Motion Picture Story Magazine, as it was called until March 1914 when it dropped the word *Story*, was the first film magazine published for the general reader, and it must have played a very large role in developing a film-conscious generation. Its first number was dated February 1911, and until March 1912 it devoted itself exclusively to the exploitation of General Film product. The first number was small and largely reprinted in March. Until July 1911 it experimented with various formats, but from then until September 1912, it used a cover comprised of an elaborately designed and framed logo in the upper half and a scene from a current film below. After March 1912 the cover might be an all-over scene from a film, a portrait of a player, or almost anything else; in 1914 there were even some covers reproducing paintings that had nothing to do with films.

Each issue opened with a section of portraits of players, well printed on heavy, coated paper, but the bulk of the space was devoted to fictionalized and well-illustrated stories taken from current films. There were even some brief articles, mostly on film subjects, and very bad verses were used mainly as "fillers." From almost the very beginning there were two departments: the editorial-like "Musings of the Photoplay Philosopher" and "Answers to Inquiries," afterward known as "The Answer Man." This last proved very popular and came to occupy considerable space. The first "Chats with the Players" appeared in December 1911. Florence Lawrence and Jack Halliday were the subjects, and the department then occupied only two pages. "Greenroom Jottings," consisting of news of the movie world, was added in 1912, and letters, verses, and so forth from readers were published. There were player popularity contests and even contests in which readers might participate: one called for filling in the blanks in a story with players' names. Until 1914, however, the publication was essentially a fiction and picture magazine.

From the middle of 1914 the stories were fewer and no longer listed under a separate heading, and more space began to be given to what went on behind the screen rather than on it. Already in the January 1914 "Edison Number" there had been an interview with the inventor; in February appeared the first installment of an elaborate debate on censorship. Star publicity was stepped up, at first in departments, then, increasingly, in articles devoted to individual players. All the nonfiction material was very genteel, and some of it even dealt with technical matters.

By 1916 capsule reviews of films were appearing in the front advertising sections. All the covers were now devoted to colorful portraits of the stars, excellently printed on dull paper. Interiorly, however, the publication was less handsome than it had been in the earlier days, and by 1917 there was not much left of the old format except that each number still opened with a gallery of players, now being printed in rotogravure. Except that as time passed reviews of films became increasingly more important, the tendencies that have been sketched here persisted substantially to the end of the silent period, except that in March 1918 a larger size page was adopted.

Of the literally dozens of fan magazines which began publication in the teens and twenties the following are the more important:

Filmplay Journal, first published in 1921, was promoted as "The Screen's Distinctive Magazine" and boasted a number of well-written articles. Of particular interest is a series by Janet Flanner, published during March, April, and May 1922, on film going in Greece, Turkey, and Paris.

Motion Picture Classic (September 1915–August 1931) appeared under a variety of names, including *Motion Picture Supplement* and *Classic*. With its sister magazine, *Motion Picture*, it was one of the most influential fan magazines of the era, published by the colorful Eugene V. Brewster, who, from all accounts, ran a veritable writers' factory at the Brooklyn brownstone which was for many years the magazine's home.

Movie Weekly (February 4, 1921–September 26, 1925) probably holds more interest for the sociologist than the film scholar since it was the nearest equivalent to contemporary fan magazines, the bulk of which are published by Macfadden Publications, whose founder, Bernarr Macfadden established *Movie Weekly*. The magazine features the 1921 equivalent of today's gossip articles, such as "My First Love in the Paris Latin Quarter" by Betty Blythe, "Why I Wrote *Three Weeks*" by Elinor Glyn, and "The Joy of the Ready-to-Wear" by Constance Binney. There is even a centerfold!

Moving Picture Stories was published on a weekly basis from January 3, 1913, through the thirties. Each issue consisted basically of player credits and adaptations—at least for the teen years—of half a dozen or so short fiction films, the staple of early cinema. At the back of each issue, a couple of articles would deal, in a very gossipy fashion, with a director or star. The fact that virtually all of the articles had first appeared in *The Universal Weekly* [see Appendix 3], under different bylines, and that virtually all of the films covered were released by Universal, leads one to assume that *Moving Picture Stories* was, in fact, published by Universal. The magazine provides a fascinating glimpse of the almost moribund idea that film goers would not only want to see the films but also read the stories, adapted from the screen, in a far more detailed form than the cinema itself could provide. A ten-minute film could take a full twenty minutes to read as presented in fictionalized form in *Moving Picture Stories*.

Edited by Delbert Essex Davenport (who also wrote as Bert Essex), *Photo-Play Journal* (May 1916–February 1921) boasted an advice column titled "For You and for Me" contributed by actress/personality Madame Olga Petrova.

Screenland (1921–1927) might well be described as a typical fan magazine, were it not for articles such as "Mr. Mencken and the Movies" (June 1922), in which critic H. L. Mencken has decidedly negative things to say about the current crop of films, and a defensive piece, "The Arbuckle Case," by Gouverneur Morris (November 1921).

Madame Petrova also contributed—in this case interviews—to *Shadowland* (September 1919–October 1923), a gorgeous journal published by Eugene V. Brewster and promoted as "The Magazine of Magazines." *Shadowland* featured serious articles on stage and screen, well-written but anonymous film and theatre reviews, and frankly pin-up-style photographs of seminude showgirls and film personalities.

Other fan magazines which began publication during the silent era are: *Movie Digest* (1925), which should not be confused with the later *Movie Digest*, edited by David Ragan, which began publication in January 1972 in a style similar to *Photoplay* but with the articles perhaps of a slightly more intelligent quality; *Movie Pictorial* (1913–1916); *Pantomime* (1921–1922); *The Photo Drama Magazine* (first published 1921); *Photo-Play Review* (1915); *Photo-Play World* (1917–1920); *Photoplay Vogue* (first published 1915); *Photoplayers Weekly* (1914–1917); *Picture Play* (1915–1941), which eventually became *Charm*; and *Weekly Movie Record* (first published 1915).

There was no decrease in the number of fan magazines after the coming of sound. There was a decrease, however, in the serious quality of much of the writing. In 1935 the Catholic Church urged a boycott of fan magazines as unsuitable reading for family audiences, complaining that such magazines specialized in "nudes" and "leg art."[2] The Church's objections had little influence on the fan magazine audience, and the publications continued in importance through the forties. Indeed, so important were fan magazines in the thirties that in the early years of the decade *The Hollywood Reporter** ran a series titled "Reviewing the Fan Mags" which reported on the contents of a specific magazine. For example, on August 18, 1933, *The Hollywood Reporter* discussed *Movie Mirror*, revealing that it featured Claudette Colbert on the cover, consisted of ninety-six pages and contained advertising broken down as follows: M-G-M, 1263 square inches; Paramount, 906 square inches; RKO Radio, 382 square inches; Fox, 363 square inches; Warner Bros., 284 square inches; United Artists, 140 square inches.

The Second World War marked a reduction in the number of comic books and other fan magazines, but there was no shortage of film fan journals. Writing in *Atlantic Monthly*, Gordon Kahn reported on a 1947 visit to a typical Hollywood newsstand, where he found copies for sale of *Modern Screen, Photoplay, Silver Screen, Movie Show, Movie Story, Movie Play, Movie Fan, Movieland, Movie Life, Movie Stars Parade, Movies, Motion Picture, Screen, Screen Album, Screen Guide, Screen Stars, Screenland, Picture Wise, Star Land*, and *New Stars*, along with the French-language *Cinemonde* and the Spanish-language *Cine Mundial*.[3]

Film boasted the largest number of fan magazines, but there was also a reasonable number of radio fan journals available. The earliest were *Radio Art* (1923–1939) and *Radio Broadcast* (1922–1930), which merged with *Radio Digest* (1922–1939). The best-known radio fan magazine was *Radio Guide* (1931–1940), which was to become *Movie and Radio Guide* (1940–1943), a change in title which indicates radio's falling popularity. Similar title changes are to be found in film magazines during the fifties, when television shares cobilling in the titles. Another radio fan magazine was *Radio Mirror* (1933–1954), which was later known as *Radio and Television Mirror* and *T.V. Radio Mirror*.

A British monthly, *Screen Pictorial* started life in 1931 as a general magazine titled *The New Royal Magazine*. It featured excellent articles by the likes of James Agate and Beverly Nichols and included a regular column by critic C. A. Lejeune. *Screen Pictorial* took on its new title in January 1935 and ceased publication in September 1939, a victim of the Second World War. All other major British fan magazines are discussed in the body of the book, but one other journal deserves passing reference, and that is *ABC Film Review*, first published in 1950, and somewhat unique in that it was available for sale only at theatres belonging to Britain's ABC Cinema Chain.

The major American fan magazines from the "Golden Age" of the cinema are: *Modern Screen* (first published 1930); *Movie Action Magazine* (1935–1936); *Movie Classic*, which superseded *Motion Picture Classic; Movie Life* (first published 1937) and billed as "Hollywood's Only All-Picture Magazine"; *Movie Mirror* (1931–1940); *Movies Stars* (1940–1958) and also known as *Movie Stars Parade; Movie Story Magazine*, which presented new films in story form; *Movieland and T.V. Time* (1943–1958), which continued publication through the sixties as *T.V. Time* and also published annuals in the late fifties; *Movies* (1939–1941); *The New Movie* (1929–1935); *Screen Album; Screen Book* (1928–1940), which later became *Screen Life; Screen Guide* (first published 1936); *Screen Play* (1925–1928), which became *Screen Secrets* (1928–1930), then became *Screen Play Secrets* (1930–1931), and eventually merged with *Screen Book; Screen Stars* (first published 1943); *Shadowplay* (first published 1933); and *Silver Screen* (1930–1954).

In 1944, Liberty acquired control of *Screenland, Silver Screen*, and *Movie Show*. Most of the fan magazines, however, were controlled by Macfadden, Dell, or Fawcett Publications.

On May 31, 1957, *The Wall Street Journal* published a story on fan magazines with the headline, "More Fan Magazines Battle for Readers, Using Come-On Covers but Hollow Stories." It was a headline which more than adequately described fan magazines of the sixties onward. Typical of the stories promised on the covers of more recent fan magazines are: "Why Shirley Jones's Sex Opinions Broke Up Her Marriage" (*Movie Life*, May 1972); "Liz Will Adopt a Negro Baby!" (*Movie Mirror*, April 1967); "Debbie:

Lend Me Your Husband, Liz...After All, I Gave You Mine!'' (*Modern Screen*, January 1966); and "Cops Seize Onassis's Dirty Picture Collection" (*Motion Picture*, February 1971).

New fan magazines continued to appear. *Movies Illustrated* (1963–1966) presented film plots told in photographs, with feature articles, many of which were historically oriented. *Famous Monsters of Filmland*, which began publication in 1958, has become something of a cult journal to horror film enthusiasts. In 1971, NATO (the National Organization of Theatre Owners) began publication of *Movies Now*, to be distributed to theatre patrons. Two years later, *Fighting Stars*, a magazine devoted to celebrities who practice the art of self-defense, began publication. For adult film enthusiasts, *Continental Film Review*, first published in England in November 1952, provides a happy mix of titillating photographs and intelligent articles; it became *Continental Film and Video Review* in August 1980.

There are at least two magazines oriented to serial enthusiasts. *Serial World* was first published in Winter 1974. *Serial Quarterly*, first published January/March 1966, was edited and published by Alan J. Barbour (who was also responsible for *Screen Facts**).

Bijou (1977) was a noble attempt at producing an intelligent *and* popular film periodical. It featured interviews with Anita Loos and Sophia Loren (No. 2) and Ellen Burstyn and Elliott Gould (No. 3). Leonard Maltin wrote on studio trademarks (No. 2), and Joseph McBride reported on Katharine Hepburn's working methods (No. 3). Contributors included Foster Hirsch, Jeanine Basinger, Ronald Bowers, and Jeff Rovin.

Prevue (218 North Sixth Street, P.O.Box 974, Reading, Pa. 19603-0974) began publication in 1981 and is a curious mix. The book reviews are fairly intelligent, as are the celebrity interviews and features on the latest film releases (all heavily illustrated), but interspersed are advertisements for books of nude photographs and volumes with titles such as *Amateur Bondage*.

Starlog Press (475 Park Avenue, New York, N.Y. 10016) produces a variety of fan magazines. *Starlog*, first published in 1977, is the best known. Another journal is *Fangoria*, described as "The magazine of motion picture thrills, chills and horror, for all you brave souls with a taste for terror!" Starlog Press is also responsible for "Official Movie Magazines" and "Poster Magazines" providing the complete stories of the films, biographies of the stars, and so forth for such titles as *Staying Alive, Octopussy, Star Trek III, Annie, Superman III, Fame*, and *High Road to China*.

Beginning in the mid-sixties, a number of fan magazines were published which featured only one or two personalities in each issue. *Film and T.V. Careers* (first published Fall 1963) devoted each number to an individual star and included intelligent filmographies; No. 1 featured Elizabeth Taylor, No. 2 Judy Garland, and No. 3 Bette Davis. *Screen Legends* (first published May 1965) also included filmographies and took a look at two stars in each issue. James Dean and Carroll Baker were featured in No. 1, followed by Paul Newman and Marilyn Monroe in No. 2. *Screen Greats* (first published 1970) was similar to *Screen Legends* but offered quizzes on the stars, instead of the obviously more useful filmographies. Among the personalities featured in *Screen Greats* were Clark Gable (No. 3) and Greta Garbo (No. 8). The latest incarnation of this type of magazine is *One Woman* (36 East Twelfth Street, New York, N.Y. 10003), which promises to devote each issue to a single female personality. The magazine "seeks to bring out the reality of one beautiful woman's inner life, along with photographic pieces of the dream—the fleeting faces and moods of the fantasy that she embodies." The first issue of *One Woman* (Fall 1983) was devoted to Morgan Fairchild and included a lengthy interview.

Lowbrow Cinema (Cinema Graffiti, c/o Brian Camp, 831 Havemeyer Avenue, Bronx, N.Y. 10473) began publication in the summer of 1982 as a newsletter devoted to the "B" picture. The first issue featured the Three Stooges and the late black actor Clarence Muse. *Wrangler's Roost* (1970–1971) was a similar mimeographed British newsletter devoted to the "B" western. In the United States there is *The Western Film Newsletter*, published by Grady Franklin (1943 Jasmine, Indianapolis, Ind. 46219).

Filmex Flash, first published March/April 1975, features news items and articles of interest to the film buffs who support the Los Angeles International Film Exposition (Filmex). Published every two months since January/February 1982, *Hi News* is the newsletter-style magazine of Hollywood International, Inc. (2078 Hawthorne Place, Nashville, Tenn. 37212), "an organization which fully recognizes the fascination we all have with the film and television industry." Lawrence J. Quirk, the nephew of *Photoplay*'s James R. Quirk, edits a mimeographed periodical titled *Quirk's Reviews* (74 Charles Street, New York, N.Y. 10014), which began publication in 1972 and features film-buff-oriented articles and reviews billed as "penetrating, independent and spirited."

The current major fan magazine for film buffs is *Hollywood Studio Magazine* (3960 Laurel Canyon Boulevard, Studio City, Calif. 91604), a monthly, glossy periodical which began publication in May 1966. *Hollywood Studio Magazine* features news items and articles (virtually all of which are historically oriented) written strictly for the film buff rather than the scholar. There is a large classified advertisement section, and the "Collectors Corner" department can provide useful documentation on the current value of movie memorabilia.

Notes

1. Carl F. Cotter, "The Forty Hacks of the Fan Mags," *The Coast*, February 1939, p. 1.

2. "Boycott on Fan Mags," *Daily Variety*, Vol.7, No. 1, March 6, 1935, pp. 1, 5.

3. Gordon Kahn, "The Gospel According to Hollywood," *Atlantic Monthly*, Vol. 179, No. 5, May 1947, p. 98.

In-House Journals

From the beginning of this century through the present, film producers have published journals to promote their films to exhibitors. Such journals range in format from a simple newsletter to a lavishly produced magazine, such as MGM's *The Lion's Roar*, which would put *Vanity Fair* to shame. These periodicals are designated "in-house journals," for want of a better phrase, because they are published purely to sell an in-house product—motion pictures—and consist entirely of information on that product and the personalities involved therewith. Some of the earlier journals provide nothing more than credits and synopses, while others offer promotional stories for exhibitors to use in "selling" the films. Whatever their contents, in-house journals are important research tools, and it is unfortunate that they are so inadequately documented and that runs of any substance are limited almost exclusively to two libraries: the New York Public Library at Lincoln Center and the Margaret Herrick Library of the Academy of Motion Picture Arts and Sciences.

Some of the earliest house organs include *The Bison Magazine, The Eclair Bulletin* (circa 1910–1914), *Kalem Kalendar* (circa 1911–1914), and *Mack Sennett Weekly* (circa 1917–1919). From 1902 through 1912, the American Biograph Company published single-sheet *Biograph Bulletins*, each providing a frame enlargement photograph and a one-paragraph synopsis for individual films. From September 1914 through October 1915, the Biograph Company also published a weekly magazine, titled *The Biograph*, offering a little more detailed information, but unfortunately *The Biograph* appeared after the company's best known director, D. W. Griffith, had moved elsewhere.

The Edison Company published *The Edison Kinetogram* in both an American and a British edition from August 1909 through January 1916. *The Edison Kinetogram* included both synopses and detailed player credits, along with suggestions for musical accompaniment and short biographies of the company's leading personalities. The Chicago-based Essanay Company published *Essanay News* as early as 1910 and simultaneously issued *The Essanay Guide*. That same year, a New York company, Carlton Motion Picture Laboratories (in association with the New York Motion Picture Company), published *Film Fancies*.

Reel Life was an impressive film magazine from the Mutual Film Corporation, published from 1912 to 1917. Another distributor, Triangle (which released the productions of the

Fine Arts Company, Thomas H. Ince, and Mack Sennett), published a quality journal titled *The Triangle* from 1915 to 1917. The Brooklyn-based Vitagraph Company of America published at least three house organs: *Vitagraph Bulletin* (first issued in 1910), *Vitagraph Life Portrayals* (first published July 1, 1911, and still published as late as 1915), and *The Vitagraph Exhibitor* (first published May 1, 1917). Out of Chicago, the Selig Polyscope Company published *Selig Polyscope News* (first issued in 1910) and *The Selig Polyscope Company Release Herald* (first issued in 1914). In addition, Selig published a newsletter strictly for use in the journalistic field and titled *Paste-Pot and Shears*. Pathé published *Pathéplays*, which was later superseded by *Pathé Messenger*. In 1917, the William Fox Company first published *Exhibitors' Bulletin*.

One of the most elegant of the early house organs was *Paramount Progress*, first published December 3, 1914, under the editorship of J. S. Johnson. *Motion Picture News** (December 12, 1914) commented, "*Paramount Progress* is most attractively printed on a superior quality paper and bears every mark of refinement." In July 1915 the journal became *Paramount Magazine*, and when the company began utilizing the name Artcraft, it became *Paramount-Artcraft Progress Advance*. Later Paramount periodicals include *Paramount Service* (published in Britain during the twenties and thirties), *Paramount around the World* (1928–1932), and which later became *Paramount International News* (1933–1938), *Paramount Parade* (1936–1960), and *Paramount World* (published in the fifties and sixties). The current Paramount studio publication is *Paramount Pictures Corporation News* (first published May/June 1982).

The best known of early house organs is *The Universal Weekly*, published from 1912 to 1936, which was known as *The Moving Picture Weekly* from 1915 to 1922. Much of the same information as can be found in *The Universal Weekly* is also in *Moving Picture Stories* (first published January 3, 1913), which would seem to imply that the latter was surreptitiously published by Universal. Prior to publication of *The Universal Weekly*, Universal's founder, Carl Laemmle, had published *The Implet* (issued, as far as can be ascertained, from January 20, 1912 to June 8, 1912). In Great Britain, Universal productions were released under the brand name of Trans-Atlantic, and thus the British Universal periodical was titled *Trans-Atlantic Review* (published from November 1, 1913 to April 14, 1917).

Other early house organs include *Film Follies* (published by the Christie Film Company circa 1919), *The Sherry Punch* (first issued in 1916 by the William L. Sherry Feature Film Company), *The Studio Skeleton* (first published in 1919 by Samuel Goldwyn), *The Lubin Bulletin* (published by the Philadelphia-based Lubin Company), and *Motion Picture Times* (published by the Selznick Company). *The Dotted Line* was a weekly journal from Producers Distributing Corporation from 1922 through at least 1926.

Because there were fewer film companies during the sound era, hence there were fewer house organs. *Columbia Mirror*, a monthly published by Columbia Pictures from 1934 through at least 1941, featured one film per issue. A similar publication was *Close-Up* from the Selznick Studios (and published in the forties). A typical issue of *Close-Up* includes a feature article on *Mr. Blandings Builds His Dream House*, along with articles on the stars—Cary Grant, Myrna Loy, and Melvyn Douglas—as well as general articles such as "Should You Build in '48?" "New Way to Cut Building Costs," and "Mr. Blandings Tells You How, Hints from Popular Mechanics."

The most sumptuous of sound house organs is M-G-M's *The Lion's Roar*, published bimonthly from 1941 through at least 1946 and boasting a full-color cover and extensive interior color advertising. An English edition was also published. Other MGM publications include *The Distributor* (a weekly issued from 1925 through at least 1941), *MGM Studio News* (published bimonthly from 1935 through at least 1940), *MGM Studio Club News* (published bimonthly from 1936 through at least 1947), and the current *MGM/UA Exclusive Story* (published bimonthly from February 1983).

Some publications, such as *MGM Studio Club News*, were issued as staff newsletters. Similar magazines include Warner Bros.' *Warner Club News* and *Action*, published by the 20th Century-Fox Studio Club from 1940 through at least the mid-fifties.

RKO's staff publication was *RKO Studio Club News*, published from October 1935 to December 1956. RKO's best-known publication was *Radio Flash*, first published, as a weekly, in 1930, which later became *New RKO Radio Flash* and was revived by the studio in July/September 1977 as *The Flash*. RKO also produced the annual *Show News* from the late twenties through the fifties.

Current studio house organs include *Focus on Fox* (published by 20th Century-Fox on a monthly basis since 1975), *Disney Times* (published bimonthly by Walt Disney Studios from October 1979), and *Entertainer* (published since March 21, 1981, by Avco Embassy Pictures). MCA/Universal has two in-house journals: *Universal City News* (first published 1979) and *MCA Ink* (a monthly for its employees, first published October 1, 1982).

National Film Journals

National film journals, promoting the films of specific countries, are generally sponsored by a government agency or by a consortium of film producers. They are published simultaneously in a variety of languages and contain news items, synopses, and credits for current productions. For this type of information they can be invaluable, particularly when published by a country for which little English-language film documentation is available. Such journals are usually issued in nothing more than mimeographed format, despite which they generally always contain photographs. Material to be found in these publications can often be reprinted elsewhere at no cost.

It is perhaps interesting to note that the United States, which must be considered the world's largest film producer (at least as far as prestige and box-office importance are concerned), does not publish a national film journal, although it does have the Motion Picture Association of America to promote American films around the world. The Eastern European bloc is perhaps the largest publisher of such materials.

As these journals are intended primarily for public relations purposes within the film community, few libraries carry them, and few are listed in the Library of Congress *Union List of Serials*. The following summary is, of necessity, incomplete, and it has not always been possible to verify dates of first or last issues for many of the periodicals.

Sovexport, on behalf of the Soviet film industry, publishes the monthly magazine *Soviet Film*, which is a surprisingly colorful periodical, available in Russian, English, French, German, Spanish, and Arabic versions; and, unlike any other national film journal, it is to be found for sale on newsstands in the United States. *Soviet Film* is a successor to *Soviet Films*, published since the thirties.

Bulgarian Film News was first published in October 1957 and was succeeded in 1960 by *Bulgarian Films*, published eight times a year by the Bulgarian Cinematography State Corporation in English, French, Spanish, and Russian editions. More a magazine than a newsletter, *Bulgarian Films* includes articles and interviews; a recent issue (Vol. 24, No. 3, 1983) features articles such as "The Bulgarian Cinematheque in 1982" and "Trends in the Treatment of Contemporary Themes" as well as an interview with actor Kiril Variishi and pieces on new releases.

The Czechoslovak Film, which began life after the Second World War as *Bulletin of the Czechoslovak Nationalized Film*, is published monthly in English, Russian, French, German, and Spanish. *Hungarofilm Bulletin*, which is very spartan in appearance, began life as *Bulletin of Hungarian Cinematography* and has been published since 1965. *Yugoslav Film* has appeared since the sixties, as has *Film Polski*, which, as far as can be ascertained, was first published in 1963 and changed its name in January 1969 to *Polish Film*.

German Film Export, the monthly West German national film journal of the fifties, was more like a German fan magazine than a trade promotion. Finland has published two national journals, *Facts about Finland*, the bulletin of the Finnish Film Foundation published from 1971 to 1977, and *Film in Finland*, with text in English, French, and German, published since 1970. In 1978, *Facts about Finland* merged with a third publication, *Finland Filmland*, to become *Facts about Film in Finland*. Finland's neighbor Sweden has published *Film in Sweden* three times a year from 1965 to 1972, as well as *Swedish Films News Bulletin*, which appeared from 1974 to 1979. *Unitalia Film*, representing the interests of the Italian film industry, appeared from 1950 to 1973. It began as a printed magazine and ended its days as a mimeographed newsletter, containing general articles on Italian cinema and even pieces by Italian filmmakers.

China's Screen, a profusely illustrated color magazine, appears to have commenced publication in the late seventies; it is published by the China Film Export and Import Corporation of Beijing, China. In the sixties and seventies, Vietnam produced *Vietnam's Screen*. *Unijapan Quarterly* was first published in July 1958. A handsomely produced periodical, providing nothing more than credits and synopses for features of the quarter—shorts and documentaries are also covered briefly—this Japanese publication is the most sumptuous of all national film journals and can be faulted only for its curious use (or misuse) of the English language. In addition to the *Quarterly*, the Association for the Diffusion of Japanese Films Abroad has also published a Japanese film year book. As the New Zealand film industry blossomed in recent years, it gave rise to a publication, *New Zealand Film* (first published in the late seventies), prepared by the New Zealand Film Commission.

Unifrance Film is known worldwide for its expert promotion of French cinema. Since 1950 it has published *Unifrance Film*. In May 1976, Unifrance commenced publication of a monthly magazine, *Cinéma Français*, a glossy periodical featuring articles on French films and filmmakers. In 1981 *Cinéma Français* was replaced by *Unifrance Film Bulletin*, a stark, newsletter-style publication.

Journals by Country

Australia

THE AUSTRALIAN JOURNAL OF
  SCREEN THEORY
CANTRILLS FILMNOTES
CINEMA PAPERS

Bulgaria

KINOIZKUSTVO
See also Appendix 4

Canada

CINEMA CANADA
TAKE ONE

China

See Appendix 4

Czechoslovkia

FILM A DOBA
See also Appendix 4

Denmark

KOSMORAMA

Eire

FILM DIRECTIONS
THE IRISH LIMELIGHT
SCANNÁN

Finland

See Appendix 4

France

ANTHOLOGIE DU CINÉMA
ART ET ESSAI
L'AVANT-SCÈNE DU CINÉMA
CAHIERS DU CINÉMA
See also Appendix 4

Germany

FILMFAUST
FILMKRITIK
See also Appendix 4

Hungary

MAGYAR FILM
See also Appendix 4

Italy

BIANCO E NERO
See also Appendix 4

Japan

MOVIE/T.V. MARKETING
See also Appendix 4

New Zealand

See Appendix 4

Poland

KINO
See also Appendix 4

Romania
CINEMA

Sweden
CHAPLIN
See also Appendix 4

Switzerland
CLOSE UP (later U.K.)

United Kingdom
AFTERIMAGE
THE BIOSCOPE
BOYS CINEMA
THE BUSINESS OF FILM
THE CINEGOER
CINEMA
CINEMA CHAT
CINEMA QUARTERLY
CINEMA STUDIES
CINEMA WORLD ILLUSTRATED
EYEPIECE
FILM
FILM ART
FILM DOPE
FILM FLASHES
FILM PICTORIAL
FILMS AND FILMING
FILM WEEKLY
FOCUS ON FILM
FRAMEWORK
GIRLS CINEMA
THE HISTORICAL JOURNAL OF
   FILM, RADIO & TELEVISION
KINEMATOGRAPH WEEKLY
MONOGRAM
THE MONTHLY FILM BULLETIN
MOVIE
THE MOVIE
PENGUIN FILM REVIEW
THE PICTUREGOER
THE PICTURE NEWS, SCREEN,
   STAGE AND VARIETY
PICTURE SHOW
PICTURE STORIES MONTHLY
SCREEN
SCREEN EDUCATION
SCREEN INTERNATIONAL

SEQUENCE
SIGHT AND SOUND
THE SILENT PICTURE (later U.S.)
STILLS
TELEVISION
WORLD FILM NEWS
See also Appendixes 2 and 3

U.S.A.
ACADEMY LEADER
ACTION
AFAA BULLETIN
AMERICAN CINEMATOGRAPHER
AMERICAN CLASSIC SCREEN
AMERICAN FILM
AMERICAN PREMIERE
BRIGHT LIGHTS
BROADCASTING
CAHIERS DU CINÉMA IN ENGLISH
CAMERA OBSCURA
CHANNELS
CINEASTE
CINEFANTASTIQUE
CINEFEX
CINEMA (1930)
CINEMA (1947)
CINEMA (1962–1976)
CINEMA ARTS
CINEMA DIGEST
CINEMAGES
CINEMA HALL-MARKS
CINEMA JOURNAL
CINEMA PROGRESS
CLASSIC FILM/VIDEO IMAGES
COMMENTATOR
COMMUNICATION BOOKNOTES
CTVD
DAILY VARIETY
DIALOGUE ON FILM
EMMY
ENTERTAINMENT LAW REPORTER
ENTERTAINMENT WORLD
EXHIBITOR'S TRADE REVIEW
EXPERIMENTAL CINEMA
FANTASCENE
FILM & HISTORY
FILM AND T.V. MUSIC
FILM COMMENT

FILM CRITIC
FILM CRITICISM
FILM CULTURE
THE FILM DAILY
FILMFACTS
FILM FAN MONTHLY
FILMFRONT
FILM HERITAGE
THE FILM INDEX
THE FILM JOURNAL
FILM LIBRARY QUARTERLY
FILMMAKERS NEWS & VIDEO
  MONTHLY
THE FILM MERCURY
FILMMUSIC NOTEBOOK
FILM NEWS
FILMOGRAPH
FILM QUARTERLY
FILM READER
FILM REPORTS
FILM REVIEW DIGEST
FILMS
FILMS IN REVIEW
FILMWISE
FOCUS!
FUNNYWORLD
GRAND ILLUSIONS
THE HOLLYWOOD REPORTER
HOLLYWOOD VAGABOND
IMAGE
INTERNATIONAL FILM REVIEW
THE INTERNATIONAL
  PHOTOGRAPHER
INTERNATIONAL PROJECTIONIST
THE JOURNAL OF POPULAR FILM
  AND TELEVISION
JOURNAL OF THE PRODUCERS
  GUILD OF AMERICA
THE JOURNAL OF THE UNIVERSITY
  FILM AND VIDEO ASSOCIATION
JUMP CUT
KALEIDOSCOPE
LIMELIGHT
LITERATURE/FILM QUARTERLY
THE MAGAZINE
MARQUEE
MILLENNIUM
THE MOTION PICTURE DIRECTOR

MOTION PICTURE HERALD
MOTION PICTURE NEWS
THE MOTION PICTURE
  PROJECTIONIST
MOTOGRAPHY
MOVIEGOER
THE MOVIES
MOVIETONE NEWS
THE MOVING PICTURE WORLD
NEWSREEL
NEW THEATRE AND FILM
ON FILM
ON LOCATION
PANORAMA
PHOTOPLAY
THE PHOTO PLAYWRIGHT
POST SCRIPT
PROJECTION ENGINEERING
QUARTERLY REVIEW OF FILM
  STUDIES
SCREEN ACTOR
SCREEN FACTS
THE SCREEN GUILD MAGAZINE
THE SCREEN WRITER
SHOW (1961)
SHOW (1970)
SHOW BUSINESS ILLUSTRATED
SIGHTLINES
THE SILENT PICTURE
SMPTE JOURNAL
SOUND WAVES
SUPER-8 FILMAKER
TELEVISION NEWS
TELEVISION QUARTERLY
TELEVISION/RADIO AGE
T.V. GUIDE
VARIETY
VARIETY RADIO DIRECTORY
THE VELVET LIGHT TRAP
VIDEOGRAPHY
WIDE ANGLE
WOMEN & FILM
See also Appendixes 1, 2, and 3

U.S.S.R.

ISKUSSTVO KINO
See also Appendix 4

Vietnam

See Appendix 4

Yugoslavia

EKRAN
See also Appendix 4

Journals by Type and Subject Matter

Academic
CINEMA JOURNAL
FILM & HISTORY
FILM CRITICISM
FILM HERITAGE
FILM QUARTERLY
FILM READER
THE HISTORICAL JOURNAL OF
   FILM, RADIO & TELEVISION
THE JOURNAL OF POPULAR FILM
   AND TELEVISION
THE JOURNAL OF THE UNIVERSITY
   FILM AND VIDEO ASSOCIATION
LITERATURE/FILM QUARTERLY
POST SCRIPT
QUARTERLY REVIEW OF FILM
   STUDIES
WIDE ANGLE

Academy of Motion Picture Arts and Sciences
ACADEMY LEADER

Adult Films
AFAA BULLETIN
See also Appendix 2

American Film Institute
AMERICAN FILM
DIALOGUE ON FILM

American Society of Cinematographers
AMERICAN CINEMATOGRAPHER

Animation
FUNNYWORLD

Autographs
NEWSREEL

Cinematography
AMERICAN CINEMATOGRAPHER
EYEPIECE
THE INTERNATIONAL
   PHOTOGRAPHER

Direction
ACTION
THE MOTION PICTURE DIRECTOR

Directors Guild of America
ACTION

Educational
CINEMA PAPERS
FILM LIBRARY QUARTERLY
FILM NEWS
SCREEN EDUCATION
SIGHTLINES

Fan Oriented

BOYS CINEMA
THE CINEGOER
CINEMA CHAT
CINEMA WORLD ILLUSTRATED
FILM FLASHES
FILM PICTORIAL
FILM WEEKLY
GIRLS CINEMA
PHOTOPLAY
THE PICTUREGOER
THE PICTURE NEWS, SCREEN,
  STAGE AND VARIETY
PICTURE SHOW
See also Appendixes 1 and 2

Fantasy/Science Fiction/Horror

CINEFANTASTIQUE
CINEFEX
FANTASCENE
See also Appendixes 1 and 2

Feminist Cinema

CAMERA OBSCURA
WOMEN & FILM

Film

ACADEMY LEADER
ACTION
AFAA BULLETIN
AFTERIMAGE
AMERICAN CINEMATOGRAPHER
AMERICAN CLASSIC SCREEN
AMERICAN FILM
AMERICAN PREMIERE
ANTHOLOGIE DU CINÉMA
THE AUSTRALIAN JOURNAL OF
  SCREEN THEORY
L'AVANT-SCÈNE DU CINÉMA
BIANCO E NERO
THE BIOSCOPE
BOYS CINEMA
BRIGHT LIGHTS
THE BUSINESS OF FILM
CAHIERS DU CINÉMA
CAHIERS DU CINÉMA IN ENGLISH
CAMERA OBSCURA
CANTRILLS FILMNOTES

CHAPLIN
CINEASTE
CINEFANTASTIQUE
CINEFEX
THE CINEGOER
CINEMA (1930)
CINEMA (1947)
CINEMA (1962–1976)
CINEMA (Romania)
CINEMA (United Kingdom)
CINEMA ARTS
CINEMA CANADA
CINEMA CHAT
CINEMA DIGEST
CINEMAGES
CINEMA HALL-MARKS
CINEMA JOURNAL
CINEMA PAPERS
CINEMA PROGRESS
CINEMA QUARTERLY
CINEMA STUDIES
CINEMA WORLD ILLUSTRATED
CLASSIC FILM/VIDEO IMAGES
CLOSE UP
COMMENTATOR
COMMUNICATION BOOKNOTES
CTVD
DAILY VARIETY
DIALOGUE ON FILM
EKRAN
ENTERTAINMENT LAW REPORTER
ENTERTAINMENT WORLD
EXHIBITOR'S TRADE REVIEW
EXPERIMENTAL CINEMA
EYEPIECE
FANTASCENE
FILM
FILM A DOBA
FILM & HISTORY
FILM AND T.V. MUSIC
FILM ART
FILM COMMENT
FILM CRITIC
FILM CRITICISM
FILM CULTURE
THE FILM DAILY
FILM DIRECTIONS
FILM DOPE

FILMFACTS
FILM FAN MONTHLY
FILMFAUST
FILM FLASHES
FILMFRONT
FILM HERITAGE
THE FILM INDEX
THE FILM JOURNAL
FILMKRITIK
FILM LIBRARY QUARTERLY
FILMMAKERS FILM & VIDEO
   MONTHLY
THE FILM MERCURY
FILMMUSIC NOTEBOOK
FILM NEWS
FILMOGRAPH
FILM PICTORIAL
FILM QUARTERLY
FILM READER
FILM REPORTS
FILM REVIEW DIGEST
FILMS
FILMS AND FILMING
FILMS IN REVIEW
FILM WEEKLY
FILMWISE
FOCUS!
FOCUS ON FILM
FRAMEWORK
FUNNYWORLD
GIRLS CINEMA
GRAND ILLUSION
THE HISTORICAL JOURNAL OF
   FILM, RADIO & TELEVISION
THE HOLLYWOOD REPORTER
HOLLYWOOD VAGABOND
IMAGE
INTERNATIONAL FILM REVIEW
THE INTERNATIONAL
   PHOTOGRAPHER
INTERNATIONAL PROJECTIONIST
THE IRISH LIMELIGHT
ISKUSSTVO KINO
THE JOURNAL OF POPULAR FILM
   AND TELEVISION
JOURNAL OF THE PRODUCERS
   GUILD OF AMERICA

THE JOURNAL OF THE UNIVERSITY
   FILM AND VIDEO ASSOCIATION
JUMP CUT
KALEIDOSCOPE
KINEMATOGRAPH WEEKLY
KINO
KINOIZKUSTVO
KOSMORAMA
LIMELIGHT
LITERATURE/FILM QUARTERLY
THE MAGAZINE
MAGYAR FILM
MARQUEE
MILLENNIUM
MONOGRAM
THE MONTHLY FILM BULLETIN
THE MOTION PICTURE DIRECTOR
MOTION PICTURE HERALD
MOTION PICTURE NEWS
THE MOTION PICTURE
   PROJECTIONIST
MOTOGRAPHY
MOVIE
THE MOVIE
MOVIEGOER
THE MOVIES
MOVIETONE NEWS
MOVIE/T.V. MARKETING
THE MOVING PICTURE WORLD
NEWSREEL
NEW THEATRE AND FILM
ON FILM
ON LOCATION
PENGUIN FILM REVIEW
PHOTOPLAY
THE PHOTO PLAYWRIGHT
THE PICTUREGOER
THE PICTURE NEWS, STAGE,
   SCREEN AND VARIETY
THE PICTURE SHOW
PICTURE STORIES MONTHLY
POST SCRIPT
PROJECTION ENGINEERING
QUARTERLY REVIEW OF FILM
   STUDIES
SCANNÁN
SCREEN
SCREEN ACTOR

SCREEN EDUCATION
SCREEN FACTS
THE SCREEN GUILD MAGAZINE
SCREEN INTERNATIONAL
THE SCREEN WRITER
SEQUENCE
SHOW (1961)
SHOW (1970)
SHOW BUSINESS ILLUSTRATED
SIGHT AND SOUND
SIGHTLINES
THE SILENT PICTURE
SMPTE JOURNAL
SOUND WAVES
STILLS
SUPER-8 FILMAKER
TAKE ONE
VARIETY
WIDE ANGLE
WOMEN & FILM
WORLD FILM NEWS
See also Appendixes 1, 2, 3, and 4

Film Collecting
CLASSIC FILM/VIDEO IMAGES

Film Societies
FILM
FILM CRITIC
SCANNÁN

Independent/Experimental Films
AFTERIMAGE
CANTRILLS FILMNOTES
CINEASTE
FILM CULTURE
FILMWISE
MILLENNIUM

Juvenile
BOYS CINEMA
GIRLS CINEMA
See also Appendixes 1 and 2

Legal Matters
ENTERTAINMENT LAW REPORTER

Music
FILM AND T.V. MUSIC
FILMMUSIC NOTEBOOK
See also Appendix 1

National Film and Photo League
FILMFRONT

National Film Society
AMERICAN CLASSIC SCREEN

Political
CINEASTE
EXPERIMENTAL CINEMA
FILMFRONT
JUMP CUT
NEW THEATRE AND FILM

Popular
AMERICAN FILM
FILMS AND FILMING
THE MOVIES
ON FILM
SHOW
SHOW BUSINESS ILLUSTRATED
T.V. GUIDE
See also Appendix 2

Projection
INTERNATIONAL PROJECTIONIST
THE MOTION PICTURE
  PROJECTIONIST
PROJECTION ENGINEERING

Radio
BROADCASTING
COMMUNICATION BOOKNOTES
DAILY VARIETY
ENTERTAINMENT LAW REPORTER
FILM QUARTERLY
THE HISTORICAL JOURNAL OF
  FILM, RADIO & TELEVISION
THE HOLLYWOOD REPORTER
TELEVISION/RADIO AGE
VARIETY
VARIETY RADIO DIRECTORY
See also Appendix 2

Screen Actors Guild

SCREEN ACTOR
THE SCREEN GUILD MAGAZINE

Screenwriting

THE PHOTO PLAYWRIGHT
THE SCREEN WRITER

Scripts

L'AVANT SCÈNE DU CINÉMA

Technical

AMERICAN CINEMATOGRAPHER
CINEFEX
EYEPIECE
PROJECTION ENGINEERING
SMPTE JOURNAL
SUPER-8 FILMAKER
TELEVISION
TELEVISION NEWS
VIDEOGRAPHY

Television

AMERICAN CINEMATOGRAPHER
AMERICAN FILM
BROADCASTING
CHANNELS
COMMUNICATION BOOKNOTES
CTVD
DAILY VARIETY
EMMY
ENTERTAINMENT LAW REPORTER
ENTERTAINMENT WORLD
FILM AND T.V. MUSIC
FILM QUARTERLY
THE HISTORICAL JOURNAL OF
    FILM, RADIO & TELEVISION
THE HOLLYWOOD REPORTER
THE JOURNAL OF POPULAR FILM
    AND TELEVISION
THE MAGAZINE
MOVIE/T.V. MARKETING
ON LOCATION
PANORAMA
SCREEN EDUCATION
SCREEN INTERNATIONAL

SHOW (1961)
SHOW (1970)
SIGHT AND SOUND
SMPTE JOURNAL
STILLS
TELEVISION
TELEVISION NEWS
TELEVISION QUARTERLY
TELEVISION/RADIO AGE
T.V. GUIDE
VARIETY
VIDEOGRAPHY
See also Appendix 2

Theatres

MARQUEE

Trade

ART ET ESSAI
THE BIOSCOPE
BROADCASTING
THE BUSINESS OF FILM
CINEMA CANADA
CINEMA PAPERS
DAILY VARIETY
ENTERTAINMENT WORLD
EXHIBITOR'S TRADE REVIEW
THE FILM INDEX
FILM REPORTS
THE HOLLYWOOD REPORTER
INTERNATIONAL FILM REVIEW
THE IRISH LIMELIGHT
KINEMATOGRAPH WEEKLY
LIMELIGHT
MAGYAR FILM
MOTION PICTURE HERALD
MOTION PICTURE NEWS
MOTOGRAPHY
MOVIE/T.V. MARKETING
THE MOVING PICTURE WORLD
ON LOCATION
SCREEN INTERNATIONAL
VARIETY
VARIETY RADIO DIRECTORY
See also Appendix 3

General Bibliography

For magazine articles and books relating to specific periodicals included in this book, check the "Bibliography" section of the entry for that periodical.

Bell, Arthur. "Oh, Those Movie Magazines." *Cosmopolitan*, February 1975, pp. 169–172, 210.

Carroll, Jon. "Hot Topix." *Village Voice*, April 27, 1982, p. 42.

Cotter, Carl F. "The Forty Hacks of the Fan Mags." *The Coast*, February 1939, pp. 18–21.

Cowie, Peter, ed. "Magazines" sections in *International Film Guide*. London: Tantivy Press, 1964 to present.

Fishbein, Ed. "They Found It at the Movies." *Los Angeles Herald-Examiner*, December 21, 1980, Section E, pp. 1, 7.

Gilbert, Basil. "Film Periodicals—A Historical Survey, Part 1: The United States." *Cinema Papers*, No. 14, October 1977, pp. 142–143, 187.

————. "Film Periodicals—A Historical Survey, Part 2: Great Britain." *Cinema Papers*, No. 15, January 1978, pp. 238–239, 279, 283.

————. "Film Periodicals—A Historical Survey, Part 3: Europe." *Cinema Papers*, No. 16, April/June 1978, pp. 330–331.

Grover, Stephen. "Winds of Change Blow in Editorial Suites of Movie Magazines." *The Wall Street Journal*, March 6, 1974, pp. 1, 14.

Henry, William A., III. "Trades Blow No Ill Winds." *Time*, September 27, 1982, p. 50.

Hobson, Dick. "Handout Journalism: Flacks Pack Slack Hacks." *New West*, July 19, 1976, pp. 45–53.

Ingram, Joan, ed. *Film and Television Periodical Holdings*. London: British Film Institute, 1983.

Kahn, Gordon. "The Gospel According to Hollywood." *Atlantic Monthly*, Vol. CLXXIX, No. 5, May 1947, pp. 98–102.

MacDougall, A. Kent. "More Fan Magazines Battle for Readers, Using Come-On Covers But Hollow Stories." *The Wall Street Journal*, May 31, 1967, p. 20.

McHenry, Murphy. "Dishing That Fan Mag Guff." *Daily Variety*, September 24, 1936, p. 51.

Magliozzi, Ron. "Film Publications." In *The Whole Film Sourcebook*, edited by Leonard Maltin. New York: Universe Books/New American Library, 1983, pp. 339–388.

Nemcek, Paul L. *Screen Romances: The Golden Years (1929–1945); A Collector's Guide.* n.p.: Paul L. Nemcek, 1968.

Ramsaye, Terry. "A Greater Paper for a Greater Industry." *Motion Picture Herald*, January 3, 1931, pp. 31, 109.

Slide, Anthony. *"Motion Picture Classic."* Library of Congress Photoduplication Service flyer, July 1975.

———. *"Movie Weekly."* Library of Congress Photoduplication Service flyer, November, 1975.

———. *"Moving Picture Stories."* Library of Congress Photoduplication Service flyer, November 1975.

———. "Early Film Magazines: An Overview." In *Aspects of American Film History prior to 1920*. Metuchen, N.J.: Scarecrow Press, 1978, pp. 98–104.

———. "The Story of the Film Magazine." In *Film Review*, edited by F. Maurice Speed. London: W. H. Allen, 1979, pp. 91–102.

Spiegel, Irwin O. "Public Celebrity v. Scandal Magazine—The Celebrity's Right to Privacy." *Southern California Law Review*, Vol. XXX, No. 3, April 1957, pp. 280–312.

Warfield, Nancy. "A Film Student's Index to the National Board of Review Magazine, 1926–1948." *The Little Film Gazette of N.D.W.*, Vol. V, No. 2, December 1974.

Wilkie, Jane. *Confessions of an Ex-Fan Magazine Writer*. New York: Doubleday, 1981.

Index

Contributors

NANCY ALLEN is Communications Librarian at the University of Illinois at Urbana.

VAL ALMENDAREZ is Coordinator of the National Film Information Service of the Academy of Motion Picture Arts and Sciences.

JOHN BELTON is Assistant Professor of Film at Columbia University and the author of *Robert Mitchum* (1976) and *Cinema Stylists* (1983).

ANIKO BODROGHKOZY is presently a student at Columbia University.

DEIRDRE BOYLE has written on film and video for *American Film, Televisions*, and *Sightlines* and is currently a Guggenheim Fellow writing a history of documentary video.

DENNIS R. BRUNNING has been a commercial filmmaker and holds degrees in communications, history, and sociology.

SAMUEL S. BRYLAWSKI is a Reference Librarian in the Recorded Sound Reference Center of the Motion Picture, Broadcasting, and Recorded Sound Division of the Library of Congress.

IVAN BUTLER is the author of *The Horror Film* (1967), *Religion in the Cinema* (1969), *The Cinema of Roman Polanski* (1970), and a history of the British Film Institute, *To Encourage the Art of the Film* (1971).

STEPHEN C. CHAMBERLAIN is Chairman of the Archival Papers and Historical Committee of the Society of Motion Picture and Television Engineers.

PAT COWARD was on the staff of the British Film Institute from 1964 to 1979 and is presently a London-based indexer and researcher.

DANIEL EINSTEIN is on the staff of the ATAS/UCLA Television Archives.

KIM FISHER is the Humanities Librarian at Oklahoma State University; in his ten-year career, he has also held academic library positions at Virginia Commonwealth University in Richmond.

JOHN A. GALLAGHER is a filmmaker and writer, and author of *Tay Garnett* (1985).

ALAN GEVINSON studied filmmaking at New York University and worked in documentary film production; he is currently on the staff of the American Film Institute Catalog.

BARBARA HALL is on the staff of the Margaret Herrick Library of the Academy of Motion Picture Arts and Sciences.

PATRICIA KING HANSON is presently Editor of the *American Film Institute Catalog: Feature Films 1911–1920*; she was formerly Associate Editor of the *Magill's Survey of Cinema* series.

STEPHEN L. HANSON is a Reference Librarian at the University of Southern California and a former Associate Editor of the *Magill's Survey of Cinema* series.

LAWRENCE HAVERHILL is a screenwriter, an off-Broadway actor, and a contributor to *The Whole Film Sourcebook* (1983).

DAVID HEAD is a Lecturer in German at the University of Bath (England); his main research interest is the role of adaptation in the German cinema.

RICHARD HEINZKILL is a Reference Librarian at the University of Oregon and compiler of *Film Criticism: An Index to Critics' Anthologies* (1975).

SALLY HIBBIN is a London-based writer and researcher.

CECILE B. HOROWITZ is a researcher and cataloger at the Motion Picture, Broadcasting, and Recorded Sound Division of the Library of Congress.

THOMAS A. JOHNSON is a professional pianist and composer who worked as an accompanist to silent films and has a large collection of early film memorabilia.

TIMOTHY JOHNSON holds a Ph.D. in Cinema from the University of Southern California and has contributed to the *Magill's Survey of Cinema* series.

ANNE KAIL is on the staff of the Margaret Herrick Library of the Academy of Motion Picture Arts and Sciences.

KRISTINE KREUGER is on the staff of the Margaret Herrick Library of the Academy of Motion Picture Arts and Sciences.

WILLIAM LAFFERTY holds a Ph.D. in Radio-Television-Film from Northwestern University; he is an Assistant Professor in the Department of Theatre Arts at Wright State University, with a special interest in the history of film and broadcast technology.

ROHAMA LEE, an Overseas Press Club journalist and feature/documentary screenwriter, was editor/publisher of *Film News* for thirty-four years.

RICHARD J. LESKOSKY teaches Cinema Studies courses and is Assistant Director of the Unit for Cinema Studies of the University of Illinois at Urbana-Champaign.

JACK LODGE taught Classics at London's Westminster Abbey Choir School until his retirement; he has written for *The Movie*.

JANET E. LORENZ is a freelance writer and critic who reviews films for SelecTV and has contributed to a number of film reference books.

GREGORY MARTINO is presently a student at Columbia University.

MICHELE McCAULEY is on the staff of the Margaret Herrick Library of the Academy of Motion Picture Arts and Sciences.

LLOYD MICHAELS is editor of *Film Criticism*.

JAN MILLSAPPS is an independent filmmaker who also teaches film production and theory at the University of South Carolina.

IB MONTY is Director of Det Danske Filmmuseum.

LISA MOSHER is Serials Librarian of the Margaret Herrick Library of the Academy of Motion Picture Arts and Sciences.

JOHN E. O'CONNOR is co-editor of *Film & History* and is on the faculty of the New Jersey Institute of Technology.

LIAM O'LEARY is the founder/curator of Ireland's only film archives and is author of *Invitation to the Film* (1946), *The Silent Cinema* (1965), and *Rex Ingram* (1980).

RON POLITO, a founding member of the Society for Education in Film and Television in the U.S. and the New England Screen Education Association, is currently Chairman of the Art Department of the University of Massachusetts at Boston.

NICK RODDICK is Film Editor of *Stills*.

HARI S. RORLICH is a graduate of the University of Bucharest and holds a Ph.D. in Slavic Folklore from the University of Wisconsin at Madison and a Master of Library Science from the University of Southern California (USC); he is a librarian at the J. Paul Getty Center for the History of Art and Humanities.

KAY SALZ is the Manager of the CBS News Documentary Film Archives; she was formerly the Coordinator of the American Film Festival and is Editor of *Film Service Profiles*.

LILLIAN SCHIFF is a freelance writer with special interest in film and children's literature.

MICHAEL SEVASTAKIS is a member of the Roman Catholic Congregation of Teaching Brothers, the Brothers of the Christian Schools; he holds a Ph.D. in Cinema Studies from New York University and is Chairman of the Communication Arts Department of the College of Mount Saint Vincent and Manhattan College in Riverdale, New York.

RICHARD SHALE is Assistant Professor of English at Youngstown State University, Ohio, and the author of *Academy Awards: An Ungar Reference Index* and *Donald Duck Joins Up: The Walt Disney Studio during World War II*.

EDWARD S. SMALL is Director of Film Studies at the University of Missouri at Columbia and is Executive Vice-President of the University Film and Video Association.

CECILE STARR is a freelance writer, teacher, lecturer, and filmmaker.

J. P. TELOTTE teaches film and literature at the Georgia Institute of Technology and has written for *Film Criticism, Journal of Popular Film and Television, Literature/Film Quarterly*, and *Post Script*.

EDWARD WAGENKNECHT is a distinguished critic and scholar whose film-related books include *The Movies in the Age of Innocence* (1962), *Marilyn Monroe* (1967), and *The Films of D. W. Griffith* (1975).

MALVIN WALD is the writer and/or producer of some three hundred features and television documentaries, including *The Naked City, Al Capone, Hollywood: The Golden Years*, and *Grizzly Adams*.

JAMES M. WELSH is Editor of *Literature/Film Quarterly* and co-author of *His Majesty the American* (1977) and *Abel Gance* (1978).

BILL WINE, who teaches Communications at La Salle College, has written on the media for *The Village Voice, Philadelphia Daily News, Philadelphia Inquirer*, and *New Jersey Monthly Magazine*.

JOANNE L. YECH has a Ph.D. in Cinema Studies from the University of Southern California and is presently teaching in Los Angeles while she completes a history of Hollywood women's film.

About the Editor

ANTHONY SLIDE has held executive positions with both the American Film Institute and the Academy of Motion Picture Arts and Sciences. He is the editor of the seven-volume *Selected Film Criticism* series and the ''Filmmakers'' series, both published by the Scarecrow Press. He has lectured at Columbia University, the Library of Congress, the Museum of Modern Art, and the Pacific Film Archive in Berkeley; produced a documentary short, *Portrait of Blanche Sweet*; served as a consultant for the ABC/20th Century-Fox television series, *That's Hollywood*; and been involved in a number of programs for American, West German, and Ulster television. Anthony Slide was editor and co-founder of *The Silent Picture*. For five years he wrote a monthly column for *Films in Review*, and his articles have appeared in many publications, including *American Film, Cineaste, Emmy, Focus on Film*, and the *Los Angeles Times*. Among his more than one dozen books on the history of popular entertainment are *Early American Cinema* (1970), *The Films of D. W. Griffith*, with Edward Wagenknecht (1975), *The Big V: A History of the Vitagraph Company* (1976), *Early Women Directors* (1977), *The Vaudevillians* (1981), *Great Radio Personalities* (1982), and *Fifty Classic British Films, 1932–1982* (1985).